AN INTRODUCTION TO GRO

from Grove Music and Oxfor

Written by leading international scholars, Grove Music Guides provide authoritative information on key areas of music scholarship. Each Grove Music Guide offers a curated set of articles selected by volume editors from the larger *Grove* dictionary available online, and provides in-depth yet accessible content for anyone interested in the study of music. With musical examples and illustrations to support the articles, Grove Music Guides serve not only as exceptional foundation texts but also as access points to further study in the full dictionary and other resources available at Oxford Music Online.

About Grove Music

Grove Music Online is the world's premier online music encyclopedia, offering comprehensive coverage of music, musicians, music-making, and music scholarship.

Updated monthly, *Grove Music Online* is an essential tool for anyone interested in researching, teaching, or just learning more about music. Written and edited by nearly 9,000 subject experts, *Grove*'s 51,000 articles offer clear overviews of topics from a scholarly perspective and include extensive bibliographies, which are curated to guide users through existing scholarship. *Grove*'s 33,000 biographical articles provide life information and detailed works lists for composers, performers, and other important musical figures. *Grove Music Online* also features more than 5,000 images, musical examples, and links to audio and video examples. It is the perfect starting point for scholarly research, but with a clear and engaging writing style, *Grove* is easily accessible to amateur music lovers as well.

While *Grove Music Online* was first launched in 2001, it originated as a print dictionary that has been in continuous publication since 1878. The online edition includes updated versions of previous *Grove* publications as well as thousands of articles commissioned specifically for the online edition.

We invite you to explore all Oxford Music Online has to offer with one month of free access. Please write to our editorial team at: grovemusic-editor@oup.com.

The Grove Music Guide to American Film Music

. . .

The Grove Music Guide to American Film Music

Edited by

DANIEL GOLDMARK

WITH PETER GRAFF, CONTRIBUTING EDITOR

OXFORD
UNIVERSITY PRESS

OXFORD
UNIVERSITY PRESS

Oxford University Press is a department of the University of Oxford. It furthers the University's objective of excellence in research, scholarship, and education by publishing worldwide. Oxford is a registered trade mark of Oxford University Press in the UK and certain other countries.

Published in the United States of America by Oxford University Press
198 Madison Avenue, New York, NY 10016, United States of America.

Library of Congress Cataloging-in-Publication Data
Names: Goldmark, Daniel, editor.
Title: The Grove Music guide to American film music / editor in chief, Daniel Goldmark.
Description: New York, NY : Oxford University Press, [2019] | Includes bibliographical references and index.
Identifiers: LCCN 2018055564 | ISBN 9780190636265 (pbk.)
Subjects: LCSH: Motion picture music–United States–Bio-bibliography–Dictionaries. | Television music–United States–Bio-bibliography–Dictionaries. | Film composers–Biography–Dictionaries.
Classification: LCC ML102.M68 G76 2019 | DDC 781.5/420973–dc23
LC record available at https://lccn.loc.gov/2018055564

Cover Illustration:
The opening of the film *Vertigo* is accompanied by the New York Philharmonic at Avery Fisher Hall in New York.
BRIAN HARKIN/The New York Times/© The New York Times

1 3 5 7 9 8 6 4 2
Printed by Marquis, Canada

Contents

Acknowledgements

The editor would like to thank James Aldridge, Charles Hiroshi Garrett, Scott Gleason, Peter Graff, Jarryn Ha, Neil Lerner, Marty Marks, Jeannie Pool, Anna-Lise Santella, and Warren Sherk for their assistance and feedback throughout the genesis of this book, along with the countless artists, writers, historians, and archivists who created the music that is the subject of this book and/or helped preserve the stories of its creation and influence for future generations.

About the Editor

Daniel Goldmark is Professor of Music and Director of the Center for Popular Music Studies at Case Western Reserve University in Cleveland. He works on American popular music, film and cartoon music, and the history of the music industry. Goldmark is the author or editor of several books, including *The Cartoon Music Book* (A Cappella, 2001), *Tunes for 'Toons: Music and the Hollywood Cartoon* (Univ. California, 2005) and *Beyond the Soundtrack: Representing Music in Cinema* (Univ. California, 2007).

Goldmark also spent several years working in the animation and music industries. He was an archivist at Spümcø Animation in Hollywood, where he also worked as the music coordinator on the short cartoons "Boo-Boo Runs Wild" and "A Day in the Life of Ranger Smith." For five years Goldmark was research editor at Rhino Entertainment in Los Angeles, where he also produced or co-produced several collections and anthologies, including a two-CD set of the music of Tom & Jerry composer Scott Bradley, and a two-CD anthology entitled *Courage: the Complete Atlantic Recordings of Rufus Harley.*

Contributors

David Ades, The Robert Farnon Society
Mike Alleyne, Middle Tennessee State University
Dan Blim, Denison University
Geoffrey Block, University of Puget Sound
Durrell Bowman, Independent scholar
Janet B. Bradford, Brigham Young University
Mark Brill, University of Texas, San Antonio
Philip Brophy, Royal Melbourne Institute of Technology
Jon Burlingame, University of Southern California, Thornton School of Music
Ross Care, Independent Scholar
Brendan G. Carroll, International Korngold Society
Karen Collins, University of Waterloo
David Cooper, University of Leeds
Timothy M. Crain, University of Massachusetts Lowell
Kate Daubney, University of Leeds
James Deaville, Carleton University
Bill Dobbins, Eastman School of Music
Paul C. Echols, Mannes School of Music
Tristian Evans, Bangor University
William A. Everett, University of Missouri-Kansas City
George J. Ferencz, University of Wisconsin Whitewater
Thomas L. Gayda, Independent Scholar
Jessica Getman, University of Michigan
Steven E. Gilbert, California State University, Fresno
Daniel Goldmark, Case Western Reserve University
Peter Graff, Case Western Reserve University
Thomas S. Hischak, SUNY Cortland
Julie Hubbert, University of South Carolina
Preston Neal Jones, Independent author
David Kershaw, University of York
Randall D. Larson, Independent author
Neil Lerner, Davidson College
Mary Jo Lodge, Lafayette College
Barry Long, Bucknell University
Richard C. Lynch, Franklin and Marshall College
Martin Marks, Massachusetts Institute of Technology
Jennifer Matthews, University of Notre Dame
Clifford McCarty
Michael Meckna, Texas Christian University
Steve Metcalf, University of Hartford
Sergio Miceli, Universidade de São Paulo
Giordano Montecchi, Conservatorio di Musica Arrigo Boito di Parma
David Neumeyer, University of Texas at Austin, *emeritus*
Louis Niebur, University of Nevada, Reno
Christopher Palmer
Jon Pareles, *The New York Times*
Nathan Platte, The University of Iowa
Howard Pollack, University of Houston
Jeannie Gayle Pool, Independent scholar

John Richardson, University of Turku
Ronald W. Rodman, Carleton College
William Rosar, Independent scholar
Daniel Sheridan, McMaster University and Carleton University
Warren M. Sherk, Margaret Herrick Library
John Snelson, Royal Opera House
Lee Snook, University of Exeter
Fred Steiner
Edward Strickland, Independent author
Richard Swift, University of California, Davis
Matthew Alan Thomas, University of Southern California
Steven D. Wescott, Independent scholar
James Wierzbicki, The University of Sydney
Kenneth Winters, Independent musician, editor, and author
Mary A. Wischusen, Wayne State University

A Note on the Use of this Book

1. ALPHABETIZATION. Entries are ordered alphabetically within each section according to their headings, which are treated as if continuous, ignoring spaces, hyphens, ampersands, apostrophes, accents, modifications, and diacritical marks. These rules apply up to the first mark of punctuation, then again thereafter if that mark is a comma. Parenthesized letters and words, and square-bracketed matter, are ignored in alphabetization.

2. USAGES. In the editing of this dictionary every effort has been made to achieve consistency in presentation. Orthography and terminology follow American practices. Some of the particular editorial usages in the dictionary are explained below:

Dates. Dates are given according to the Gregorian calendar. Methods of citing dates that are approximate or conjectural are outlined in §4 below.

Pitch notation. The system used is a modified version of Helmholtz's: middle C is *c'*, with octaves above as *c''*, *c'''*, etc., and octaves below as *c*, *C*, *C'*, *C''*, etc. Italic type is use for specific pitches; pitch-classes are given in roman capital letters.

Place names. In article texts names of states (United States) and provinces (Canada) are given if there is a risk of confusion between two places with the same name; for places outside the United States and Canada country names are given where this may be helpful. Where a city's name has changed in the course of history, an attempt has been made to call it by the name current at the time under discussion. Occasionally, common sense demands a little flexibility in the application of this rule.

Titles. In article texts, titles of works are italicized unless they are descriptive or generic (e.g., Nocturne, Symphony no. 1); album titles and film titles are italicized (e.g. *Saturday Night Fever*); song titles are printed in roman type in quotation marks (e.g., "As Time Goes By"); excerpts from larger works, when discussed as such, are printed in roman type in quotation marks (e.g., "Maria" from *West Side Story*).

3. AUTHORS. The names of authors appear at the ends of the articles to which they apply. Where authorship is joint or multiple, this is indicated, and the contribution of each author is shown by reference to the numbered sections of the article. Where two or more names appear, separated only by a comma, the entire authorship is joint or the contributions are fused to a degree where it would be impractical to show how responsibility was divided. A signature of the form

DELORES KIRK/CARLOS JONES
indicates that an article originally by Delores Kirk (an article originally published in *The New Grove Dictionary of American Music* or *Grove Music Online*) has been revised and updated by Carlos Jones;

DELORES KIRK/R
signifies editorial revision and updating of an article by Delores Kirk. A signature of the form

DELORES KIRK (with CARLOS JONES)
means that Delores Kirk is the principal author and that Carlos Jones contributed material that deserved acknowledgment.

4. ARTICLE HEADINGS. Articles on persons begin with their name and place and date of birth and death:
Marcus, Lucille (*b* Cleveland, 1 Jan 1800; *d* Seattle, 31 Dec 1870)

Parentheses and brackets in name headings have special meanings:

Marcus, Lucille (Corinne) – full name "Lucille Corinne Marcus"; "Corinne" not normally used

Marcus, Lucille C(orinne) – full name "Lucille Corinne Marcus"; normally used as "Lucille C. Marcus"

Marcus [Marcuse], **Lucille** – the name "Marcus" sometimes takes the form "Marcuse"; or "Marcuse" is an earlier family spelling of the name "Marcus"

Marcus, Lucille [Angel] – Lucille Marcus is sometimes known as "Angel"

Marcus, Lucille [Hughes, Scarlett] – "Lucille Marcus" is the pseudonym or stage name under which Scarlett Hughes is generally known; or Lucille Marcus used the pseudonym or stage name "Scarlett Hughes" (this is made clear in the text of the entry)

Marcus, Lucille [Scarlett Jo] – "Lucille Marcus" is the name under which Scarlett Jo Marcus is generally known

Marcus [née Hughes], **Lucille** – "Marcus" is Lucille Hughes's married name, under which she is generally known

Marcus [Hughes], **Lucille** – Lucille Marcus has the married name or pseudonym "Hughes"; or Lucille Hughes is generally known under the name "Marcus" (this is made clear in the text of the entry)

Marcus, Mrs. [Lucille] – Lucille Marcus was known professionally as "Mrs. Marcus."

Figures known by a sobriquet that cannot be interpreted as consisting of a surrogate forename and surname are under the last element of their name (e.g., "Waters, Muddy," "Mahal, Taj").

Places and dates of birth and death are given where they are known; where nothing is known, nothing is stated. For places in the United States, states names are given, in abbreviated form, and for places in Canada provinces are given, in abbreviated form. For places outside the United States and Canada, country names are given. Where dates of baptism and burial are given, dates of birth and death are unknown. If the year but not the month or day of birth is known, that is indicated in the form

(*b* Cleveland, 1800; *d* Seattle, 31 Dec 1870)

In certain cases, the date of birth may given with less precision: for example, "1800–05" (at some time between those years), "*c*1800" (around that year), or "?1800" (to signify conjecture). Where a birthdate cannot be conjectured, *fl* (*floruit*: "she or he flourished") dates may be given, e.g., "*fl* 1825," "*fl* 1820–35," etc.

5. ARTICLE DEFINITIONS. All articles begin with a statement defining the subject. Articles on people begin with a statement of nationality, if other than American, and a description. Reference to a person's immigration, taking of citizenship, or naturalization is normally made in the text. The word or words of description outline the subject's musical significance—essentially the reason for her or his being entered in the dictionary. Supplementary activities may be referred to in the text. Articles on genres, terms, etc. normally begin with a definition of the subject and may continue with a statement of the terms of reference of the article, in which attention is drawn to its specifically American film music subject matter.

6. ARTICLE STRUCTURE. The longer texts in the dictionary are normally divided into sections for ease of reference. The most usual division is into sections numbered with Arabic numerals and having headings in large and small capitals (e.g. 1. LIFE, 2. WORKS). Sections of this kind may be subdivided into smaller ones, numbered with parenthesized lower-case roman numerals and having headings in italics.

7. CROSS-REFERENCES. Cross-references in the dictionary are distinguished by the use of small capitals, for example:
see COPLAND, AARON.

If the reference is in running prose it takes the form
she was a pupil of AARON COPLAND.

All cross-references give the title of the article referred to in exactly the wording in which it appears, in bold type (but excluding parenthesized matter), at the head of the entry.

For cross-references that take place within articles, some are placed at the ends of short articles, or at the ends of sections, directing the reader to another entry where further information relevant to the subject may be found; these may, as appropriate, embody such formulae as "*see also*" or "for a fuller discussion *see*." Many cross-references are found in running text; cross-references are typically not included for entries that would be expected to be appear in this dictionary unless there is particular material to which special attention needs to be drawn.

8. WORK-LISTS. Work-lists are designed to show a composer's output and to serve as a starting-point for its study. Many work-lists are complete; other work-lists offer a representative selection of works. Withdrawn works and juvenilia are not normally cited except in lists for major composers. An attempt has been made to include basic publication information, including a composer's principal publishers, and, in the case of manuscript material, locations.

Longer work-lists are normally categorized by genre, function, or medium, and items listed chronologically within categories. Shorter work-lists are normally organized chronologically. Numbers from established listings are normally given. A statement of the genre may be given in certain cases. Titles may be given in short form; alternative titles are parenthesized. For dramatic works, a parenthesized arabic numeral following the title denotes the number of acts. Names in parentheses are those of text authors (or sources), librettists, book authors, or lyricists for vocal works, of choreographers for dance music. Where a key is named, it precedes the details of instrumentation; capital letters denote major keys, lower-case minor. Alternative instrumentation is denoted by a slash. Instrumental doubling is denoted by a plus sign. For voices, abbreviations separated by commas denote soloists, and those printed continuously represent a choral group; thus "S, A, Bar, SATB" stands for "soprano, alto, and baritone soloists with a chorus of soprano, alto, tenor, and bass." Unless they are parenthesized (when they constitute information on publication), places and dates following dates of composition are those of first performance.

Editions that include a substantial number of works are cited at the heads of work-lists. Smaller editions, and editions of individual works or groups of works in modern anthologies or collections, are cited alongside particular entries. Any abbreviation found in a work-list and not in the abbreviations list at the beginning of this book is explained at the head of the list (or section of the list) concerned.

9. BIBLIOGRAPHIES. Many articles in the dictionary are followed by bibliographies, which in general have been supplied by authors. They normally include studies on which authors have drawn as well as recommended reading. Bibliographies are not normally intended to represent complete lists of the literature on the topic.

Bibliographies are chronologically arranged; items are listed in order of first publication (chronologically within categories for a bibliography that is categorized as some longer ones are). Items published in the same year are listed alphabetically by author, or, for the same author, by title. At the head, certain standard works of reference may be listed in abbreviated form, in alphabetical order of abbreviation. Bibliographical abbreviations are listed on p. xxv.

For books that have appeared in several editions, only the first and most recent are cited, unless there is particular reason to note intermediate editions—for example, because one was revised or translated, or one has been photographically reprinted (which is denoted by *R*). Thus, while "1950, 4/1958" is a common form of citation, "1950, 2/1951/*R1978*, rev. 3/1955, 4/1958" is also possible, to signify that the second edition was reprinted and the third substantially revised. Places of publication are normally given only for first publication. Title-page breaks and punctuation (other than commas) may be represented by a colon. Every effort has been made to find terminal page numbers where they were previously missing or unknown. Reference to a single page number normally indicates the initial page, unless designated as a single-page article (e.g., "5 only"). For periodicals not through-paginated by volume, the fascicle number within the volume is indicated after a slash (e.g. "xiv/3"). Unpublished works are dated, where possible, and provided with an abbreviation identifying the library where they may be found.

Electronic resources are cited where applicable, including online databases, and selected websites that are hosted by or partnered with major educational, research, or government institutions, that are authoritative, and that contain peer-reviewed scholarship. Readers are directed to Internet search engines to locate other online resources, such as personal websites maintained by subjects entered in the dictionary.

General Abbreviations

ABC American Broadcasting Company
AFM American Federation of Musicians
ASCAP American Society of Composers, Authors, and Publishers
A&R Artists and repertoire

BA Bachelor of Arts
BAFTA British Academy of Film and Television Arts
BBC British Broadcasting Corporation
BM Bachelor of Music
BMI Broadcast Music, Inc.

CBC Canadian Broadcasting Corporation
CBS Columbia Broadcasting System
Col(s). Column(s)

DMP Dynamic Music Partners

EA Electronic Arts

HBO Home Box Office

ISCM International Society for Contemporary Music

MCA Music Corporation of America
MGM Metro-Goldwyn Mayer (movie studio)
MIDI Musical Instrument Digital Interface
MM Master of Music
MTV Music Television (cable TV channel)
MUTEL Music for Television

NBC National Broadcasting Company
NDSU North Dakota State University
NES Nintendo Entertainment System
NYU New York University

PBS Public Broadcasting Service
PC Personal Computer
PO Philharmonic Orchestra
PRC Producers Releasing Corp.

RCM The Royal Conservatory of Music
RKO (Pictures) Radio-Keith-Orpheum
ROTC Reserve Officers' Training Corps

SCEI Sony Computer Entertainment Inc.
SO Symphony Orchestra
SOCAN Society of Composers, Authors and Music Publishers of Canada

TNT Turner Network Television

UA United Artists (of Metro-Goldwyn Mayer)
UCLA The University of California, Los Angeles
UFA Universum-Film Aktiengesellschaft
UPA United Productions of America
USC University of Southern California

WB Warner Bros.

Bibliographical Abbreviations

AcM	*Acta musicologica*
ACAB	*American Composers Alliance Bulletin*
AM	Associates in Music
ARL	Association of Research Libraries
b	born
c.	circa [about]
CBY	*Current Biography Yearbook* (1955–)
Cptr(s)	computer(s)
d	died
DAB	*Dictionary of American Biography* (New York, 1928–37, suppls., 1944–)
DB	*Down Beat*
diss.	dissertation
ed.	editor, edited by
edn.	edition
eds.	editors
EwenD	D. Ewen: *American Composers: a Biographical Dictionary*
ff	following (pages)
GroveA	*The New Grove Dictionary of American Music*
IAWM	International Alliance for Women in Music
JM	*Journal of Musicology*
JT	*Jazz Times*
JSAM	*Journal of the Society for American Music*
KdG	*Komponisten der Gegenwart*, ed. H.-W. Heister and W.-W. Sparrer
MEJ	*Music Educators Journal*
ML	*Music & Letters*
MM	*Modern Music*
MusAm	*Musical America*
MQ	*Musical Quarterly*
no(s).	number(s)
op(s)	Opera(s)
op.	Opus
PNM	*Perspectives of New Music*
R	Revised
repr.	Reprinted
SchullerEJ	G. Schuller: *Early Jazz* (New York, 1968/R)
SchullerSE	G. Schuller: *The Swing Era* (New York, 1989)
vol(s)	volume(s)

Library Abbreviations

US-DLC	Library of Congress
US-LAuc	Los Angeles, University of California at Los Angeles, William Andrews Clark Memorial Library
US-LAum	Los Angeles, University of California at Los Angeles, Music Library
US-LAusc	Los Angeles, University of Southern California, School of Music Library
US-NHoh	New Haven (CT), Yale University, Oral History Archive
US-NYp	New York, Public Library at Lincoln Center, Music Division
US-PRV	Provo (UT), Brigham Young University
US-SY	Syracuse (NY), University Music Library
US-Wc	Washington, DC, Library of Congress, Music Division

Works List Abbreviations

A Alto (voice)
a Alto (instrument)
ACA American Composers Alliance
addl additional
arr arranged

B Bass (voice)
b Bass (instrument)
Bar Baritone (voice)
BN Blue Note
Bn Bassoon

cant(s). Cantata(s)
cel Celesta
chbr Chamber
chor Chorus
cl Clarinet
clav Clavier
collab. Collaborator, collaborated (with)
Conc. Concerto

dir(s). Director(s)
db Double bass

ens Ensemble

fl Flute

gui Guitar

hn Horn
hp Harpsichord

incl. Includes, including
inst(s) Instrument(s)

mar Marimba
Mez Mezzo-soprano
MSS Manuscript(s)
musl. Musical
mvt(s) Movement(s)

nar(s) Narrator(s)

ob Oboe
Orat Oratorio
orch Orchestra
orchd Orchestrated
org Organ
ov(s). Overture(s)

perc Percussion
perf(s). Performance(s), performed (by)
pf Piano(forte)
posth. Posthumous(ly)

qt(s) Quartet(s)
qnt(s) Quintet(s)

rev. Revision(s); revised (by/for)

S Soprano (voice)
s Soprano (instrument)
spkr(s) Speaker(s)
str(s) String(s)
sym(s). Symphony (symphonies), symphonic

T	Tenor (voice)
timp	Timpani
tpt	Trumpet
trans.	Translation, translated by
trbn	Trombone
Tr	Treble (voice)
va	Viola
vc	Cello
vn	Violin
v, vv	Voice, voices
v., vv.	Verse, verses
ww	woodwind

Introduction

"Interest in film music as a topic for serious study has increased since 1960, and the literature has grown in quantity and quality."

This statement appeared in the original *New Grove Dictionary of American Music* in 1984. Roy Prendergast's *A Neglected Art: A Critical Study of Music in Films* had just recently appeared (in 1977); John Williams had only been nominated for twenty-one Academy Awards related to his work as a film composer and/or songwriter (as of this writing, he's up to fifty-one nominations and five wins); the first Nintendo Entertainment System was about to begin its ascent as a game changer for home entertainment; and the video for Michael Jackson's "Thriller" had recently appeared to great acclaim on MTV. More than thirty years have since passed, and few among us could have predicted how much the interest in—and available scholarship on—music and visual media would expand.

The Grove Music Guide to American Film Music documents the lives and works of many of the individuals responsible for writing music for some of the most popular and well-known films, television shows, video games, and music videos ever created. The contents of this volume come from the second edition of *The Grove Dictionary of American Music* (2013), for which I served as one of the senior editors. Many of the articles have been updated to include new films (for those composers still working), new bibliographic references, and a few corrections. A handful of new biographical articles were also commissioned, and several images that were not in the *Grove Dictionary* have been added as well.

After the publication of the *New Grove Dictionary of Music and Musicians* in 1980, someone had the bright idea of excerpting, as it were, the entire twenty-volume set into a series of infinitely shorter, easier to find, and more affordable paperback books, featuring a variety of key composers or themes, such as the *New Grove Mozart*, the *New Grove Bach Family*, the *New Grove Second Viennese School*, the *New Grove North European Baroque Masters*, and so on. This book is, in no small way, indebted to that series. Also arriving hot on the heels of the *New Grove* was the *New Grove Dictionary of American Music* (aka the *AmeriGrove*), edited by H. Wiley Hitchcock and Stanley Sadie (the latter having been the editor of the *New Grove*), which appeared in 1984. In the thirty years since the appearance of these two monumental collections, our knowledge of—and interest in—topics related to American music in particular has expanded considerably, demonstrated no more clearly than the expansion of the *AmeriGrove* from four volumes in 1984 to eight in 2013.

The coverage of film music in the revised *AmeriGrove* moved far beyond the first edition, which, besides a few key topics, focused on the most recognizable film composers; more than 100 articles about composers were added. This expansion also meant that key figures who had been omitted previously could have their stories told, including arrangers and orchestrators (Paul Marquardt); composers who seldom achieved lead credits on big budget films but whose music appeared in dozens if not hundreds of more low-budget fare (William Lava, David Buttolph); music directors who played key roles in the administration of Hollywood film studio music departments (Leo Forbstein, Joseph Gershenson); and composers of generalized mood music for use in wide and varied situations, who almost never received on-screen credits, but whose music became emblematic of the most fundamental themes in film scores (John Zamecnik, Karl Hajos). Conversely, we chose to include figures whose work, through a combination of productivity, time in the field, and influence, has become integral to our understanding of music in popular media. Famous composers who only dabbled in media have thus not been included because this work is not representative of their larger output. (Leonard Bernstein is probably the most obvious example: he wrote a single original film score, albeit a notable one, *On the Waterfront* [1954].)

Perhaps the most dramatic change in the scope of film music coverage is the move far, far beyond film. Television music had already begun to receive some critical attention by the late 1970s, but the continued growth of the medium has exponentially amplified the topic for discussion. While television was once seen as a less than respectable—and lower-visibility—option for composers, nowadays the barriers have largely fallen away, and many in the industry, such as Michael Giacchino and Christophe Beck, can be found working in both media, often simultaneously. The same can be said for video games. While largely a novelty in the 1970s when the original *New Grove Dictionary* was being assembled, no one can argue that video games have not become as normal a part of daily modern life as reading or television—which, given the ability nowadays to read, watch TV, and play games on your phone or other digital device, further blurs the lines between the media considered in this book. And once again, composers like Giacchino and Beck show us that success in one format does not preclude success in another.

This volume could have been solely an assemblage of biographical articles, but we felt strongly that we should include some context for the stylistic, technological, and even cultural changes that effect the way we understand and shape the discourse of music and media. We've thus included articles—drawn once again from the second edition of the *AmeriGrove*—on film music, television music, the television musical, production music, music videos, video game music, and musical films. In addition to providing excellent overviews of each subject area, the articles also include bibliographies for those interested in further reading.

More than simply a biographical directory, however, each entry provides a brief bibliography of existing scholarship on the person or topic. In some cases, almost no secondary literature exists. A lack of primary materials is often the culprit in this case; many composers never received on-screen credits for their work, keeping casual fans in the dark about who scored their favorite film or video game. Production studios have largely been reticent if not downright secretive about the workings of their various internal departments, and getting written documentation can seem like trying to retread Indiana Jones' treacherous path, with bureaucratic booby traps, pitfalls, and dead ends lying in wait to disable or kill one's search for information. Families and/or heirs who possess papers, hold the rights to documentation, or simply know stories may not appreciate, understand, or care about maintaining the historical legacies of composers; similarly, the work involved with keeping up someone's profile may be too time-consuming and costly. Whatever the reason, the fact remains that far too many of the composers included here—to say nothing of those not in this collection—remain under-documented or simply anonymous to the world. Hopefully some readers of this book will be inspired or frustrated (or both) by the lacuna of scholarly material and be moved to conduct new research, particularly beyond the realms of Hollywood, on which this collection focuses. Similarly, it might have been true at one time that the film composing world was a white men's club; fortunately far more women and people of color have, since the original *AmeriGrove*, made their careers writing music for television, film, and video, several of whom are included herein. But there is still more research needed in this area. We hope to expand the scope of the biographies in *Grove Music Online* as scholarship catches up with current practice.

This book is intended first and foremost as a musical primer for the student of American film, television, and video, whether you're a casual fan, a longtime listener, or wanting to gain a deeper understanding of those who have shaped the modern media soundtrack. While some entries overflow with sources, particularly those that have been popular subjects for historians, others are quite brief. For those interested in delving further yet into the lives detailed within this book, an exhaustive bibliographic guide to literature on film and television music can be found in Warren M. Sherk, *Film and Television Music: A Guide to Books, Articles, and Composer Interviews* (Latham, MD: 2011)—although given the ongoing outpouring of work in music and media, ever more can be found via various online search engines. Likewise with the work lists: some composers' work in media has been limited but influential, while others' has been extraordinarily prolific. Works lists are curated to emphasize key works in film, television and video game music. In some cases we have included abbreviated lists in other genres, for those who have extensive work outside film or other media, in order to provide a clear sense of each person's larger musical output. *The Grove Music Guide to American Film Music* is also intended to work in tandem with *Grove Music Online* (www.oxfordmusiconline.com/grovemusic), creating a rich, interactive experience for readers interested in American film music within a larger musical context.

Daniel Goldmark, *Editor*

I. Concepts

Film music

Film music has encompassed an increasingly wider set of musical practices since its introduction in the late nineteenth century; it can refer to music in live or recorded form, created to accompany the exhibition of motion pictures, whether those pictures are recorded on film, videotape, optical disc, or streamed online.

1. Introduction.

Film music is an international phenomenon, but the United States has been one of the main centers of film production and achievement since the beginning of the twentieth century, and its film music has generally remained independent, developing its own distinctive techniques and aesthetic principles. The history of music for sound films in the United States differs in several respects from that of its European counterparts. First, the evolution of US film music was connected both artistically and economically with the semi-industrialized Hollywood studio system. Demands for a large and continuous production of music encouraged departmentalized concepts and procedures, with emphasis and reliance on teamwork: many early film scores were collaborations in which several composers, working with mutually accepted themes, strove to write music in a uniform, conventional, and therefore anonymous style. Second, many of the most influential composers and music directors in Hollywood during the heyday of the studio system were immigrants, mainly from Central Europe and the USSR. The conservative musical traditions which most brought with them—their principal models were composers of the late Romantic period—were largely responsible for the quasi-symphonic style of much US film music from the 1930s to the mid-1950s. Finally, whereas European film makers commissioned scores from concert composers as a matter of course, Hollywood (except for a few attempts in the 1930s) made little effort to do so. As a result, US concert composers have mainly contributed music for documentary, animated, and experimental films, and Hollywood composers constitute a largely separate group. Most of them have worked exclusively in the film-music medium—into the latter twentieth century many did so under contract to a single studio; only a few (notably Bernard Herrmann, Leonard Rosenman, Miklós Rózsa, John Williams, and Howard Shore) have found success as composers and conductors of concert music as well.

In the following discussion of US film music two points should be borne in mind: its history is comprehensible only within the context of the history of the cinema itself, and there is—whether in terms of style, production, or genre—more than one sort of film music.

2. Film music before synchronized sound.

Public exhibitions of motion pictures in the United States date from the mid-1890s, and evidence suggests a wide variety of practices regarding music and accompaniment. Thomas A. Edison and others sought for years to invent machines capable of combining camera images and phonographic sounds, but could not solve the many problems of amplification and synchronization. Edison's Kinetophone—essentially a Kinetoscope, a peephole-equipped machine that played a very brief loop of film—added sound to film by way of a phonograph, which could be heard through a set of earphones. The machine was only marginally successful, and few other attempts to link music with film in this period are known.

Silent motion pictures were often accompanied by live music, at first typically provided by a pianist or reed-organ player and later by larger ensembles or theater organists. At first the choice as to what music should be played was left largely to the individual performer, who relied mostly on his or her improvisatory skills and theatrical experience for guidance. Before movie theaters existed in large numbers, films were shown in various arenas, including vaudeville houses, fairground booths, and legitimate theaters—places where musicians were used to accompany a large variety of acts. But increasingly between 1903 and 1915, as the length of film narratives and the number of specialized motion-picture theaters grew, the need was felt by film producers and exhibitors for more specialized music and a more systematic control of its performance. This need was met by music publishers, who brought out codified collections of incidental pieces and mood music, arranged from preexisting or newly composed material, as well as catalogues of such collections. Film producers also looked to publishers, composers, and arrangers to create suggestions for music for individual films. Music publishers, often in association with film studios, generated lists of compositions to be used with a film, frequently (although not consistently) called "cue sheets": these named appropriate compositions (or types of music) for a whole film, segment by segment, typically with reference to collections available from the publishers. Cue sheets flourished throughout the 1920s until the demise of the silent film.

The written film score became prominent after 1915—the year that saw the distribution of D.W. Griffith's epochal epic *The Birth of a Nation,* which had a score composed, compiled, and arranged primarily by Joseph Carl Breil. Special orchestras toured with the film. From this date full scores were compiled, published, and distributed with dozens (perhaps hundreds) of major Hollywood films. Every large US city had grand theaters, each with a spectacular organ and resident orchestra to perform such scores, and also to give stage shows and concerts. The music directors of New York's principal movie theaters amassed large libraries to help them to produce full film scores for national distribution: William Axt and David Mendoza at the Capitol, for example, created a complete score for *The Big Parade* (1925), and Hugo Riesenfeld at the Rialto and Rivoli produced one for *Beau Geste* (1926). Such scores were rarely completely original (although Mortimer Wilson composed a fine one for *The Thief of Bagdad* in 1924). Partly compiled and partly composed scores were highly skilful pastiches, as evidenced by the work of Breil and Walter Cleveland Simon; such scores had the additional value (as it was perceived at the time) of introducing US audiences to edited versions of many concert works. A number of landmark scores for silent films have been reconstructed by contemporary scholars, including Gillian Anderson and Martin Marks.

A screening of *Sherlock, Jr.* (1924) with a live ensemble.
Metro Pictures Corporation/Photofest ©Metro Pictures Corporation

Thematic Music Cue Sheet

BUSTER KEATON
in
THE CAMERAMAN
with
Marceline Day
A Buster Keaton Production
Directed by Edward Sedgwick
Story by Clyde Bruckman and Lew Lipton
Continuity by Richard Schayer
Compiled by Ernst Luz

METRO-GOLDWYN-MAYER PICTURES

A METRO-GOLDWYN-MAYER PICTURE
Length of film 8 reels (6930 feet) Maximum projection time 1 hour, 20 minutes

1 AT SCREENING .... You're A Real Sweetheart (Friend) (WHITE) .... 1¼ Min.
Copyr. 1928 Leo Feist
NOTE: Play introduction and chorus.
2 (Action) PLAY ONCE AND SEGUE .... Battle Effects by Drummer .... 1¼ Min.
3 (Title) AND THERE ARE OTHERS .... A Busy Thoroughfare (Baron) (YELLOW) .... 2½ Min.
Copyr. 1927 Irving Berlin
4 (Action) KEATON AND GIRL ALONE ON SCREEN .... You're A Real Sweetheart (Friend) (WHITE) (Chorus) ..... 1¼ Min.
Copyr. 1928 Leo Feist
5 (Action) KEATON LOOKING AT BOARD .... The Kewpies' Rendezvous (Kempinski) .... 1½ Min.
Copyr. 1919 Photo Play M. Co
6 (Action) KEATON TAKES OFF CAP .... You're A Real Sweetheart (Friend) (WHITE) .... 1½ Min.
Copyr. 1928 Leo Feist
NOTE: Play verse and chorus.
7 (Action) KEATON SITS DOWN BY RADIATOR .... Sweet Lavender (Wheeler) .... 3 Min.
Copyr. 1922 Sonnemann Mus. Co

A cue sheet for *The Cameraman* (1928).
MGM/Photofest ©MGM

3. The 1930s: the advent of sound.

Music for motion pictures was only at the beginning of its artistic development when the silent era came to an abrupt end. Although many European and a few American composers had written original scores of more than passing interest during the 1920s, artistic growth had been constrained by technical difficulties, and continuing calls for greater use of specially composed film scores went largely unanswered. Motion pictures with synchronized sound (using various processes) began to appear, and the success of *The Jazz Singer* (1927) and other films in the late 1920s prompted a rapid conversion to sound-film production. It was only the exact synchronization of music and image, made possible by the perfection of sound-on-film techniques, that finally freed composers to explore the full dramatic and expressive potential of film music. While the scores for early sound films continued to take the form of pastiches, the music, like the other sound elements—speech and sound effects—became an integral part of the film. As a new genre, music for sound films reached the peak of its development in the United States during the first decade of its existence; by the end of 1939 its fundamental artistic and technical principles were firmly established and, not accounting for the considerable technological changes in film making and composing, are still valid and applicable.

Except for the small ensembles that were sometimes employed to play mood music during filming as encouragement for the actors, film makers in the silent

Poster for the film *The Jazz Singer*, 1927.
RA/Lebrecht Music and Arts

Crowds clamoring outside the Warners' Theatre during the run of *The Jazz Singer* (1927). Pictures/Photofest ©Warner Bros. Pictures

era rarely concerned themselves with music until a film was completed and ready for distribution. With the arrival of sound, however, music became an essential ingredient of film production, and studios began to establish music departments with staff orchestras. The first studio music directors were recruited mainly from the orchestra pits of silent-movie theaters. Men such as William Axt, Nathaniel Finston, David Mendoza, Erno Rapee, and Hugo Riesenfeld were experienced in the compilation of film scores and familiar with mood-music libraries; this made them particularly valuable during the transition to sound films, when synchronized scores and sound effects (and sometimes even dialogue) were hastily added to newly completed silent films awaiting distribution. When Hollywood began to produce musical films, the studios turned to musicians from the Broadway musical theater. Conductors and arrangers such as Victor Baravalle, Arthur Lange, Alfred Newman, Max Steiner, and Herbert Stothart became film-studio music executives; successful songwriters such as Irving Berlin, Sam Coslow, Buddy DeSylva, Arthur Freed, and Richard A. Whiting were offered lucrative composing contracts, and some also became producers.

Film music in the earliest days of sound consisted almost exclusively of songs. There was little demand for composition in the general sense, for Hollywood's music departments were devoted primarily to the production of material for musicals and operetta-like films (*see* MUSICAL FILM), and to furnishing the theme or "title" songs that were interpolated in many nonmusical films. Despite the thirty-year tradition of musical accompaniment for silent pictures, many film directors and musicians questioned how to use music in the new sound medium, and were sometimes uncertain whether it should be used at all. Scoring practices changed from month to month; musical policies varied from studio to studio. Some film makers feared that audiences would be confused by hearing an invisible orchestra, and, partly because of the limitations of early recording technology, there was much initial resistance to the presence of music under dialogue. The scores for all but a few early sound dramas and comedies consequently consist only of music to accompany main and end titles (i.e. the credits at the beginning and end of the film) and of "source" or realistic music for scenes set in ballrooms, restaurants, nightclubs, and the like. The few examples of underscoring (the term used by most screen composers to denote mood music as opposed to source music) are mainly of two types: "characteristic" or pantomimic pieces in silent-film style (often selected from mood-music libraries), used for set pieces such as rides in the park, street scenes, and comedy chases; and fanfares or brief pieces of entrance-and-exit music to accompany royal personages in period and costume dramas. Love scenes in contemporary romances were occasionally accompanied by a "love theme," almost invariably cast in the mold of a ballad from a Broadway musical; its use was often justified by the presence in the scene of a radio or phonograph.

By the middle of the 1930s, however, music was generally accepted by film makers and the public as an equal partner with speech and sound effects. Much credit for the increasing use of original composition is due to Steiner, whose music for *Cimarron* (1931) drew favorable comments from the press and the film industry. His score for *Symphony of Six Million* (1932), a mixture of original music and adaptations of Jewish melodies, is notable as one of the first in Hollywood to include substantial amounts of music under dialogue. During the same year Steiner composed a number of lengthy scores that were essentially original: *Bird of Paradise*, *The Most Dangerous Game*, *A Bill of Divorcement*, and *King Kong* (completed in January 1933). His music for *The Informer* (1935) embodies many characteristics typical of the Hollywood symphonic score of the 1930s, including its use of identifying themes, musical illustration, and a "heavenly choir" finale. Steiner scored several important adventure romances and biographical films for Warner Bros., including *The Charge of the Light Brigade* (1936), *The Life of Emile Zola* (1937), and *Jezebel* (1938), while for David Selznick he oversaw a team of composers and arrangers in creating one of the longest and most famous of all film scores, *Gone with the Wind* (1939).

Three other eminent pioneers of the 1930s were Stothart, Newman, and Erich Korngold. Stothart began his Hollywood career with MGM in 1929 as a music director for film operettas and musicals; he furnished scores for some of MGM's most outstanding productions, including *Queen Christina* (1934), *Mutiny on the Bounty* (1935), and *Romeo and Juliet* (1936). Many of his scores of the 1930s borrow melodies from concert and operatic works.

Like Steiner and Stothart, Newman was recruited from the Broadway musical theater. He became music director at United Artists and attracted attention in 1931 with his Gershwinian, symphonic jazz composed to accompany the main titles of *Street Scene* (an arrangement for piano solo, published in 1933, appears to have been the first non-vocal film music issued in the United States as sheet music for sale to the public). Newman's dramatic flair was revealed in the music for *The Dark Angel* (1934), which makes use of impressionistic, polytonal tone-painting in the film's "mental vision" sequences. His first large score in symphonic style, *Beloved Enemy* (1936), employs multiple themes and leitmotivic development, and shows a keen sense of musical characterization; his multithematic technique reached a peak of complexity and sophistication in *Beau Geste*, *The Hunchback of Notre Dame*, and *Wuthering Heights* (all 1939).

Korngold came to Hollywood from Vienna late in 1934, when the studios were reviving the costume adventure dramas that had been popular in the 1920s. This genre, in which large-scale scores in grand symphonic style were appropriate, was one for which Korngold's flamboyant, operatic mode of expression was admirably suited. He composed his first original score for Warner Bros., *Captain Blood*, in 1935, and thereafter worked almost exclusively for that studio, writing the music for some of its most highly regarded films: *Anthony Adverse* (1936), *The Prince and the Pauper* (1937), *Juarez* (1939), and *The Private Lives of Elizabeth and Essex* (1939). He eventually signed a contract with Warner Bros. and thus became the first and, until Miklós Rózsa, the only composer of international reputation to work in the studios on a contractual basis. The comparatively small number of Korngold's original film scores (eighteen in thirteen years) belies his importance in the development of American film music, for the grandeur, exuberance, and brilliant orchestration of his music influenced the work of many composers. His *The Adventures of Robin Hood* (1938) exemplifies, perhaps more than any other score from the first decade of sound, the Hollywood Romantic symphonic style at its finest.

Among the dozens of other composers who worked in Hollywood during the 1930s, the most prominent were George Antheil, William Axt, Robert Russell Bennett, David Buttolph, Adolph Deutsch, Hugo Friedhofer, Richard Hageman, Leigh Harline, W. Franke Harling, Werner Heymann, Frederick Hollander, Werner Janssen, Arthur Lange, Cyril Mockridge, David Raksin, Hugo Riesenfeld, Heinz Roemheld, Frank Skinner, Dimitri Tiomkin, Ernst Toch, Franz Waxman, Roy Webb, and Victor Young.

Many films of the 1930s and early 1940s—especially low-budget productions such as "B" pictures, Westerns, and serials—were partly or entirely scored by means of "tracking," that is, the reuse of music tracks from other films. The musicians' union succeeded in prohibiting this in 1944, thus rendering worthless millions of dollars' worth of soundtrack owned by the studios.

4. 1940–60.

By 1940 the sound-film score was recognized as a new and legitimate musical form. Newspapers and magazines printed articles on scoring and interviews with screen composers; critiques of the latest film scores and polemical writings about the functions and aesthetics of film music appeared in journals such as *Pacific Coast Musician* and *Modern Music*; *Film Music Notes*, the organ of the National Film Music Council, began publication in 1941 with brief commentaries, usually written by the composers themselves, on recent film scores. Film-studio music departments were thriving: each had an orchestra and a salaried staff of composers, arrangers, orchestrators, copyists, librarians, vocal coaches, and music editors. The day-to-day experience of studio work created a group of versatile composers capable of writing in a variety of styles for every sort of film. Several pioneer composers were working under contract at major studios: Steiner and Korngold at Warner Bros., Stothart at MGM, Young at Paramount, and Webb at RKO. Newman held the music directorship of Twentieth Century-Fox from 1939 until 1960 and was one of the most powerful and influential musicians in Hollywood. By his death in 1970 he had completed over two hundred scores and received nine Academy Awards and forty-five nominations. (The Newman family has remained prominent in Hollywood to this day: Lionel Newman was Alfred's brother, David and Thomas Newman are his sons, and Randy Newman his nephew.) Most of the composers who attained major stature in the 1940s—Friedhofer, Harline, Raksin, Rózsa, Skinner, Tiomkin, and Waxman—already had experience in the studio system. Of those who first joined the ranks of film composers during this decade, some, including Daniele Amfitheatrof, Bernard Herrmann, Bronislaw Kaper, Sol Kaplan, Hans J. Salter, and Paul Sawtell, achieved wide recognition within a few years; others, such as George Duning, Herschel B. Gilbert, Ernest Gold, Walter Scharf, and Marlin Skiles, did not do so until the 1950s.

During the 1940s a few composers attempted to break away from the prevailing late nineteenth-century style of film music, which was criticized in some quarters as anachronistic and unsuitable for some types of plot. Foremost among these composers was Aaron Copland, whose brief involvement with Hollywood yielded some of the finest film music composed in the United States; the folklike melodies, austere harmonies, and light-textured orchestrations of *Of Mice and Men* (1939) and *Our Town* (1940) made a profound impression on many of his colleagues. Another who sought newer and simpler modes of expression was Friedhofer. Although his highly acclaimed score for *The Best Years of our Lives* (1946) is symphonic in scope and employs leitmotivic procedures, much of its musical language is rooted in the simple, modal tunes of the American folk heritage. An earlier and somewhat different example is Raksin's score for the detective melodrama *Laura* (1944), which is almost entirely monothematic and is imbued with post-impressionistic harmonies and modern, almost pop-style orchestral colors; it achieves a remarkable synthesis of the serious and popular aspects of film music. Herrmann evolved an original, easily identifiable style that was neo-Romantic in tone but rarely founded on the leitmotif method; much of his music consists of varied repetition and development of melodic cells constructed from brief, often rhythmically distinctive germ motifs. He excelled in imaginative use of orchestral color and, in many of his later scores, wrote for unorthodox groupings of brass, winds, and percussion. Among his most admired scores are those for *Citizen Kane* (1941), *Vertigo* (1958), and *Psycho* (1960).

The most noticeable changes in usage and style took place in the 1950s, however, in the wake of some significant shifts in the thematic content of Hollywood films. Postwar disillusionment and cynicism in the United States prompted questioning of once-accepted moral and spiritual values, resulting in the making of a number of films concerning social problems, neurotic crime melodramas, and maverick detective stories. The new emphasis on realism led to an increased "realistic" use of music, usually in the form of jazz or swing, emanating from a visible source such as a jukebox, radio, record player, or nightclub band. In many cases, however, the music was not merely incidental, but had a subtle psychological connection with the scene it accompanied. Some composers also began to experiment with elements of blues and jazz in underscoring (though their use was not altogether new—isolated examples occur in music for main titles, montages, and city traffic scenes in films as far back as the 1930s). Alex North successfully combined the sonorities and rhythms of modern jazz with symphonic scoring in *A Streetcar Named Desire* (1951). Bop and progressive jazz of the late 1940s provided the inspiration for another landmark score, Leith Stevens's *The Wild One* (1953), which featured Shorty Rogers and his band. Other notable jazz-oriented scores include Elmer Bernstein's *The Man with the Golden Arm* (1955), Johnny Mandel's *I Want to Live!* (1958), and Duke Ellington's *Anatomy of a Murder* (1959). Leonard Rosenman made a sensational début as a film composer in 1955 with his partly atonal music for *East of Eden*.

Electronic instruments were used with increasing frequency after World War II, particularly in films with such themes as the supernatural, horror, mental disturbance, and science fiction. Waxman made effective use of an electric violin in *Suspicion* (1941), and Herrmann's unconventional ensemble for *The Day the Earth Stood Still* (1951) included theremins and amplified violin, guitar, and double bass. The theremin was also used by Rózsa in the psychological drama *Spellbound* and a realistic tragedy dealing with alcoholism, *The Lost Weekend* (both 1945), and by Webb for the thriller *The Spiral Staircase* (also 1945). A remarkable experiment of the 1950s was the totally electronic music (described in the credits as "Electronic Tonalities") created by Louis and Bebe Barron for *Forbidden Planet* (1956).

Bernard Herrmann, left, and director Alfred Hitchcock during the production of *Vertigo* (1958).
Paramount Pictures/Photofest ©Paramount Pictures

Walt Disney experimented with multitrack recording (three of music and a control track) in *Fantasia* (1940), but because of wartime restrictions and the studios' lack of interest, stereophonic sound did not appear in films until the development of Cinerama in 1952. The first picture in general release to have true stereo music was *The Robe* (1953); its score, by Newman, was recorded in three discrete channels (with microphones left, center, and right), to be played back on three independent loudspeakers spaced behind the screen. The most significant technological advance in film music of the post-war period was the change from "optical soundtrack" to magnetic tape for recording. Thirty-five-mm magnetic-coated film stock, adopted by almost all studios in Hollywood by the end of 1952, permitted music to be recorded more quickly and easily than ever before; music tracks had greater fidelity and less background noise, and could be cut and edited with unprecedented ease and precision.

5. The 1960s and 70s.

During the late 1940s and the 1950s the incursion of television, antitrust actions by the government, and rising production costs brought about a sharp decline in the output of films from the major studios. Faced with rising competition from independent and foreign makers, they were forced to reduce their budgets: in the aftermath of a musicians' strike in 1958 staff orchestras were eliminated; many of the most powerful music directors retired or were discharged, and those who took their places were little more than office managers; most staff composers, arrangers, and orchestrators were dismissed; and the studio music department as a training ground for film composers became a thing of the past. The few eminent composers from the first two decades of the sound film who remained active at the beginning of the 1970s found their services less in demand, and a new generation of film composers working in the symphonic style emerged: Elmer Bernstein, Gerald Fried, Ernest Gold, Jerry Goldsmith, Leonard Rosenman, and John Williams. A growing number of films were also being scored by composers of popular music, including Les Baxter, Jerry Fielding, Quincy Jones, Henry Mancini, Johnny Mandel, Nelson Riddle, and Lalo Schifrin, some of whom had served apprenticeships in television. More pop and jazz musicians worked in film music during the 1970s; the best-known are Ralph Burns, John Cacavas, Bill Conti, Dominic Frontiere, David Grusin, J.J. Johnson, Gil Melle, and Patrick Williams.

Composers continued to write symphonic scores, particularly for historical epics and spectaculars, such as *El Cid* (Rózsa, 1961), *Taras Bulba* (Waxman, 1962), *How the West was Won* (Newman, 1962), *Cleopatra* (North, 1963), and *The Fall of the Roman Empire* (Tiomkin, 1964); disaster epics, such as *The Towering Inferno* (Williams, 1974) and *Jaws* (Williams, 1975); and space adventures, such as the cycle initiated by *Star Wars* (Williams, 1977). Others wrote scores notable for their economy of instrumentation and restraint of expression, including Bernstein (*To Kill a Mockingbird*, 1963), Goldsmith (*A Patch of Blue*, 1965), North (*Who's Afraid of Virginia Woolf?*, 1966), Schifrin (*Cool Hand Luke*, 1967), and Raksin (*Will Penny*, 1968); Herrmann's music for the macabre thriller *Psycho* (1960) is remarkable in being scored for a large string orchestra, usually associated with sentiment and romance.

A significant increase in the use of popular music for scoring nonmusical films took place during the 1960s. Much of it was attributable to the growing importance of the youth market (by 1968 almost half the film audience was between sixteen and twenty-four years of age). Almost as influential, however, was the changing nature of American cinema. The social disenchantment and cynicism of the 1950s exploded, during the 1960s, into open rebellion against traditional moral and societal tenets, and this stimulated the production of anti-establishment films in contemporary, sometimes harshly realistic settings; further, the demise of the Production Code of the Motion Picture Producers Association in 1968 brought new freedom to the screen. There was little room in this new, unglamorous cinema for the earlier Romantic music. Moreover, for many of the new generation of young, independent film makers, music meant songs. The use of jazz or rock scores by producers hoping for a hit song or gold record was carried at times to such extremes that some mainstream composers, such as Bernstein and Mancini, who had made use of pop and jazz elements in some of their scores, publicly expressed dismay: though acknowledging that such music was appropriate for some contemporary stories, for example *The Graduate* (1967) or *Midnight Cowboy* (1969), they criticized its indiscriminate use in dramatic films that would have been better served by formal scoring.

A more controversial development was the use by some film makers of commercial recordings for underscoring. Though few could argue against the relevance and effectiveness of pop records in youth-oriented pictures such as *Easy Rider* (1969) and *American Graffiti* (1973), criticism was leveled against some directors who resorted to recordings of classical music as substitutes for or adjuncts to original scores. During production most films are given temporary scores, assembled from commercial recordings and studio library tracks, for demonstration purposes. Many producers and directors become accustomed to these "temp tracks" and find it difficult to accept a new score. Perhaps the best-known example of the use of commercial recordings as underscoring for a film is the science-fiction spectacular, *2001: A Space Odyssey* (1968), which Stanley Kubrick, after rejecting North's music, scored with commercial recordings of Richard Strauss, the younger Johann Strauss, Aram Khachaturian, and György Ligeti that had been used for the "temp track." Another controversial case was that of producer and director William Friedkin, who rejected the music Lalo Schifrin had written for *The Exorcist* (1973) and instead used music by George Crumb, Hans Werner Henze, Krzysztof Penderecki, and Anton Webern.

The advances that took place in the 1970s in the technology of electronic sound generation, and the proliferation of sonic resources brought about by experiments with ethnic and invented instruments and noise makers, offered film composers new sounds and colors with which to work. By the 1980s a film score that did not use a synthesizer, electronic organ, or ethnic instruments was a rarity. But although scores using avant-garde techniques became more acceptable in Hollywood, they remain limited, for the most part, to science-fiction films and those with bizarre or fantastic themes. Serialism, electronic sounds, and *Klangfarben* are important elements in Rosenman's score for *Fantastic Voyage* (1966). Goldsmith used a variety of ethnic and newly devised percussion instruments, prepared piano, and unconventional orchestral techniques in *Planet of the Apes* (1968). Schifrin composed a score that incorporates serial and aleatory procedures, Moog synthesizer sounds, electronic effects, and many novel percussion sonorities for the feature-length documentary on the insect world *The Hellstrom Chronicle* (1971). Williams's score for the psychological drama *Images* (1972) includes aleatory sequences written for the Japanese percussionist Stomu Yamash'ta, who performs on taiko drums as well as on metal and glass sculptures made by Bernard and François Baschet.

6. Into the 21st century.

The orchestral score remained popular into the twenty-first century, led not only by the many successful scores for blockbusters by John Williams and his cohort, but also by a new generation of composers who successfully adapted the orchestral style to contemporary trends, and incorporated popular styles more than ever before. Some of the most influential of today's composers have backgrounds in film (James Horner, Thomas Newman) while many got started by performing in pop or rock bands (Danny Elfman, Hans Zimmer, James Newton Howard, Howard Shore). As science fiction and fantasy themes became especially popular at the turn of the millennium, more and more orchestral scores in the vein of late 1930s Hollywood appeared, culminating in Howard Shore's theme-laden music for the trio of successful films (2001–3) based on Tolkien's *Lord of the Rings* trilogy.

Likewise, many musicians coming out of popular music have maintained a scoring style consistent with their backgrounds, and have been responsible for numerous successful and influential film scores. Mark Mothersbaugh, a founding member of the new wave band Devo, took a facility for synthesizers and electronic music and created unique themes and scores for numerous television series and films, including "Rugrats," "Pee-Wee's Playhouse," and the first four features directed by Wes Anderson. More recent cross-overs include RZA, a hip-hop artist affiliated with Wu-Tang Clan, who scored Tarantino's *Kill Bill Vol. 1* (2003), and Jonny Greenwood, who provided music for Paul Thomas Anderson's period drama *There Will be Blood* (2007) while maintaining his work as the guitarist and keyboardist with the band Radiohead.

The use of popular song in film scores has become increasingly significant in recent decades. In the wake of the massive success of the soundtrack for *Saturday Night Fever* (1979), studios have continued to search for individual songs or to produce soundtracks that could be sold in the form of a compilation album for added revenue. The rise of MTV in the 1980s meant that youth audiences further linked popular music with video imagery. Film studios immediately tried to emulate MTV with rapid editing techniques and by prominent placement of songs throughout a film. The success of this practice—producing popular soundtrack albums for films like *Top Gun* (1986), *Forrest Gump* (1994), and *William Shakespeare's Romeo + Juliet* (1996)—shows that the relationship between the film and music industries has become closer than ever. The film score created largely—or entirely—through the use of popular songs, in which original music has no functional role in the film, became commonplace by the late 1990s. As a result the role of the music supervisor, once a largely administrative one, became far more important as the potential economic benefits of soundtrack albums continued to grow. Amongst the more influential music supervisors during the 1980s and 90s were Kathy Nelson, Becky Shargo, Randall Poster, and Karyn Rachtman.

The advent of digital recording technology, and particularly the remarkably inexpensive and ever-improving fidelity of synthesized instruments, has meant that electronic sounds have become a regular element of film scores. A vogue for scores produced entirely or largely with synthesized music occurred in the late 1970s into the 1980s; notable scores include *Chariots of Fire* (1981) and *Blade Runner* (1982), both by Vangelis; and *Witness* (1985) by Schifrin. As studios no longer employ staff composers, most scores are now created in a "mock" or basic version in a home studio, which can nonetheless mimic the sounds of an infinitely large and varied ensemble. Final scores for films often represent an enhanced version of the computer-generated audio files with some "live" tracks added to provide depth and warmth.

7. Animated films.

Walt Disney's cartoons of the late 1920s and early 1930s, such as *Steamboat Willie* and the "Silly Symphony" series, were an important early means of demonstrating the potential for creative use of sound. In the 1930s many other studios followed Disney's lead, and animated films attracted a highly specialized and innovative group of composers, including Carl Stalling, Scott Bradley, and Leigh Harline. The medium calls for precise timing of every bar and note of music down to a twenty-fourth of a second (the shortest possible length of a single frame of film). Timings are established before the music is composed, and the music also has to follow the action in continually varying rhythms. Mainly for economic reasons, orchestras for animated films are usually smaller than those used for feature films. For this reason—and also because of the frequently satiric or comic nature of the material—composers have tended to avoid the Romantic idiom of dramatic films. The crucial differences between the two genres, however, are the compression, unyielding continuity, and constant mimicry of the action in the music for cartoons, the latter of which was dubbed "mickey mousing" not long after Mickey Mouse became popular. This approach is often castigated when applied to films made by live actors (except in comedy and slapstick sequences), but it was employed by the composers of animated-film music with great skill: they followed the visual material with a succession of tiny musical fragments and yet, despite the many changes in tempo, the music holds together smoothly. In the early 1950s some of the most impressive scores for animated films were composed at the UPA studio, notably Kubik's for *Gerald McBoing Boing* (1950) and Raksin's for *The Unicorn in the Garden* (1953). By the 1960s, however, most studio animation was being done for television, where the craft became even more standardized and specialized than before. (Television also spawned two new mini-genres using animated film music: commercials and program titles.)

While in general cartoon music has remained apart from the Hollywood mainstream, the boundaries became blurred in feature-length animated films, again

Recording the vocals for Walt Disney's *Three Little Pigs* (1933), from left: Walt Disney, Dorothy Compton (second pig), Pinto Colvig (Practical Pig/Big Bad Wolf), Mary Moder (first pig), and composer Frank Churchill.
(AP Photo)

led by Disney. Frank Churchill's songs for *Snow White and the Seven Dwarfs* (1938) effectively made it into a musical, and in the background score for the same film, as well as in others, such as *Pinocchio* (1940), Harline carefully blended dramatic idioms into the more typical comic sections. More recent examples of full-length dramatic scores composed by leading figures in Hollywood are Michael Giacchino's for *The Incredibles* (2004) and Hans Zimmer's for *Kung Fu Panda* (2008).

8. Documentary films.

Some of the earliest examples of films that were not to be understood as fictions, but were instead created to be realistic and informational, and thus ancestors to the documentary film, were early newsreels, which were given specialized musical accompaniments by the 1910s. Volume two of J.S. Zamecnik's *Sam Fox Moving Picture Music Catalogue* (1913) includes an entire section devoted to "Weekly—Pathé, Gaumont, etc." and contains movements with titles like "European Army Maneuvers," "Paris Fashions," and "Aeroplane or Regatta Races." Early manuals explaining how to accompany films with music instructed musical directors to bring greater decorum and dignity to newsreels than to fictional features. Musical accompaniments to later documentaries would continue with this level of seriousness and an infrequency of irony. The Museum of Modern Art has preserved a cue sheet that accompanied screenings of Robert Flaherty's 1922 film *Nanook of the North* (described on the title card as "A story of life and love in the actual

Arctic"), a film often pointed to as the originator of the genre of documentary film, even though *actualitiés* from the earliest days of film's history, wherein film makers captured motion photography of unstaged quotidian activities, were also documentary in nature.

Documentary films made in the United States offered composers more artistic freedom. The composer Gail Kubik, who scored music for several documentaries and served as the director of music for the domestic branch of the Office of War Information's Film Bureau during World War II, explained in *Modern Music* that "the Industry's insistence on employing the synthetic musical style that makes an MGM score sound just like one from Warners, Twentieth Century, or Paramount, has had the effect not only of divorcing the country's serious composers from the film factories, but also of throwing them into the arms of the documentarians." Aaron Copland was able to convince Hollywood producers of his music's viability for use in commercial film only after composing the score for the documentary *The City* (1939). It demonstrated his music's accessibility for the industry decision makers who feared a modernist approach, and his subsequent Hollywood scoring garnered him tremendous popular and critical attention. The production of expository documentary films offered radically increased opportunities for composers to offer their input about the editing of a film; in the factory line of Hollywood's commercial film industry, composers rarely got to offer input about a film's editing. Virgil Thomson's critically successful collaborations with the US government film maker Pare Lorentz, first in the Resettlement Administration's *The Plow That Broke the Plains* (1936) and then in the Farm Security Administration's *The River* (1937), provided Thomson with the opportunity, for example, to write fugues, a technique whose more complex textures were generally regarded as too distracting in Hollywood feature films. Numerous other concert hall composers have made brief forays into composing for documentary film, among them: Marc Blitzstein, William Schuman, Alex North, Mel Powell, Daniel Pinkham, Lukas Foss, Henry Brant, Paul Chihara, David Diamond, Paul Bowles, Roy Harris, and Philip Glass.

The film theorist Bill Nichols observes that the conventions of expository documentaries—such as addressing the viewer directly with voice-of-authority narration, the recounting of a history, and the advancing of an argument—continue to appear with regularity in television news, reality television, and the kinds of documentaries one encounters on PBS. For some types of documentary film making, such as *cinema vérité* or direct cinema, the addition of a composed soundtrack, added after the actual filming, signaled an effort to control the representation in ways that were considered undesirable and artificially mediating. The introduction of portable synchronous sound recording technologies in the early 1960s led to a greater number of documentary films that lacked background scores, although observational documentaries about musicians, where the music could originate from a visible source on the screen, flourished in the

1960s, as can be heard in examples such as *Don't Look Back* (D.A. Pennebaker, 1965), about Bob Dylan, and *Gimme Shelter* (Al and David Maysles, 1970), about the Rolling Stones. The *vérité* approach to film making influenced Hollywood films in the 1970s, as films like *Mean Streets* (Martin Scorsese, 1973), *American Graffiti* (George Lucas, 1973), and *Dog Day Afternoon* (Sidney Lumet, 1975) eschewed newly-composed symphonic music in favor of music ostensibly originating from an on-screen source. Examples such as these point to the challenges of untangling the musical practices in documentary and fictional films.

9. Scholarship on film music.

Interest in film music as a topic for serious study saw an increase in the 1960s, and the literature has grown in quantity and quality, with a substantial rise since the 1990s (see Sherk 2011). Scholarly attention to film music has long been fraught by the hybrid nature of the discourse, particularly prior to the 1980s: neither those in musicology nor in cinema studies seemed especially willing to engage the critical methods of the other discipline. Most early musicological studies tended toward examination of scores without accounting for decisions regarding factors such as cinematography and editing. Discussions from the film perspective dealt primarily with music in historical or social terms rather than from analytical or theoretical points of view. Literature on film music through Hollywood's golden age largely emanated from the practitioners themselves. The first doctoral dissertation on the topic came from a film composer, Fred Steiner, whose work for television and films did not prevent him from completing a study of Alfred Newman's early film music at USC in 1981.

The discourse changed profoundly with the publication of Claudia Gorbman's *Unheard Melodies* (1987), the first true fusion of musicological and film studies approaches, supported by grounding in narrative theory. Perhaps most influential was Gorbman's use of Gérard Genette's theories of narration, from which she appropriated the terms diegetic, for "music that (apparently) issues from a source within the narrative," nondiegetic (transforming Genette's term "extradiegetic") for music with "lack of a narrative source," and metadiegetic, which occupies the theoretical or conceptual space between the other two terms (Gorbman 1987, 22–3). Other early influential studies by Kalinak (1992) and Flinn (1992) continued on the path forged by Gorbman but called into question what some perceived as an unnecessary transference of one descriptive dichotomy (source vs. underscore) for another (diegetic vs. nondiegetic). Chion's *Audio-Vision* (1994; from the 1990 French), translated by Gorbman, provided an additional variety of tools for those wishing to dismantle the soundtrack, in large part by further subdividing and problematizing notions of where sound comes from, both within the narrative and beyond it. Many others have continued to discuss the diegetic/metadiegetic divide, with special attention going toward the liminal space that the terms cannot address (Gorbman's meta-diegetic).

In the last two decades interest in film musicology has skyrocketed. Whereas scholarly articles had once appeared very sporadically in many disparate periodicals, several academic journals dedicated to the topic have since appeared, all of which have slightly different ideological and discursive slants; these include *Music and the Moving Image*, *Music, Sound and the Moving Image*, *The Journal of Film Music*, and *The Soundtrack*. The number of books published that deal with the general theme of music and media has likewise surged, including monographs, edited collections of essays, anthologies of historically significant documents, and focused critiques of single film scores. Conferences dedicated to exploring not only film music but also the much wider field of sound studies in relation to visual media have also grown in number, just as panels exploring varied topics of music, sound, and media regularly populate the annual conferences of musicology and cinema studies organizations.

See also MUSICAL FILM; TELEVISION MUSIC.

Bibliography

E. Lang and G. West: *Musical Accompaniment of Moving Pictures* (Boston, 1920/*R*)
G.W. Beynon: *Musical Presentation of Motion Pictures* (New York, 1921)
H.A. Potamkin: "Music and the Movies," *MQ*, xv (1929), 281–96
G. Antheil: "On the Hollywood Front," *MM*, xiv–xvi (1936–9)
A. Copland: "Music in the Films," *Our New Music* (New York, 1941), 260–75
Film Music Notes (1941–58)
L. Morton: "On the Hollywood Front," *MM*, xxi–xxiii (1944–6)
A. Deutsch: "*Three Strangers*," *Hollywood Quarterly*, xi (1946), 214
H. Eisler (with T. Adorno): *Composing for the Films* (New York, 1947)
F.W. Sternfeld: "Music and the Feature Films," *MQ*, xxxiii (1947), 517–32
P.S. Carpenter: "Hollywood Carousel," *Music: an Art and a Business* (Norman, OK, 1950), 40
F. Skinner: *Underscore* (Los Angeles, 1950/*R*)
L. Morton: "Composing, Orchestrating, and Criticizing," *Hollywood Quarterly*, vi/2 (1951), 191–206
C. McCarty: *Film Composers in America: a Checklist of their Work* (Los Angeles, 1953/*R*)
R. Manvell and J. Huntley: *The Technique of Film Music* (New York, 1957, 2/1975)
F. Lewin: "The Soundtrack in Nontheatrical Motion Pictures," *Journal of the Society of Motion Picture and Television Engineers*, lxviii (1959), 113, 407, 482
L. Rosenman: "Notes from a Sub-culture," *PNM*, vii/1 (1968), 122–35
W. Johnson: "Face the Music," *Film Quarterly*, xxii/4 (1969), 3–19
C. Hofmann: *Sounds for Silents* (New York, 1970)
E. Hagen: *Scoring for Films: a Complete Text* (New York, 1971)
T. Thomas: *Music for the Movies* (South Brunswick, NJ, and New York, 1973)
E. Barnouw: *Documentary: a History of the Nonfiction Film* (New York, 1974, 2/1983)
J.L. Limbacher: *Film Music: from Violins to Video* (Metuchen, NJ, 1974)
Film Music Notebook (1974–8)
I. Bazelon: *Knowing the Score: Notes on Film Music* (New York, 1975)

C.M. Berg: *An Investigation of the Motives for and Realization of Music to Accompany the American Silent Film, 1896–1927* (New York, 1976)

A. Ulrich: *The Art of Film Music: a Tribute to California's Film Composers* (Oakland, CA, 1976)

D. Meeker: *Jazz in the Movies: a Guide to Jazz Musicians, 1917–1977* (London, 1977)

R.M. Prendergast: *A Neglected Art: a Critical Study of Music in Films* (New York, 1977)

J. Newsom: "David Raksin: a Composer in Hollywood," *Quarterly Journal of the Library of Congress*, xxxv (1978), 142–72

W. Sharples: "A Selected and Annotated Bibliography of Books and Articles on Music in the Cinema," *Cinema Journal*, xvii (1978), 36–67

M. Marks: "Film Music: the Material, Literature, and Present State of Research," *Notes*, xxxvi (1979–80), 282–325; rev. in *Journal of the University Film and Video Association*, xxxiv/1 (1982), 3–40

T. Thomas: *Film Score: the View from the Podium* (South Brunswick, NJ, and New York, 1979)

C. Gorbman: "Bibliography on Sound in Film," *Yale French Studies*, no.60 (1980), 269–86

J. Newsom: "A Sound Idea: Music for Animated Films," *Quarterly Journal of the Library of Congress*, xxxvii (1980), 279–309

J.L. Limbacher: *Keeping Score: Film Music, 1972–1979* (Metuchen, NJ, 1981)

F. Steiner: *The Making of an American Film Composer: a Study of Alfred Newman's Music in the First Decade of the Sound Era* (diss., U. of Southern California, Los Angeles, 1981)

M. Rózsa: *Double Life: the Autobiography of Miklós Rózsa* (New York, 1982)

I.K. Atkins: *Source Music in Motion Pictures* (Rutherford, NJ, 1983)

R. Faulkner: *Music on Demand: Composers and Careers in the Hollywood Film Industry* (New Brunswick, NJ, 1983)

R. Larson: *Musique fantastique: a Survey of Film Music in the Fantastic Cinema* (Metuchen, NJ, 1985)

I.B. Newsom, ed.: *Wonderful Inventions: Motion Pictures, Broadcasting, and Recorded Sound at the Library of Congress* (Washington, DC, 1985)

C. Gorbman: *Unheard Melodies: Narrative Film Music* (Bloomington, IN, and London, 1987)

G. Anderson: *Music for Silent Films 1894–1929* (Washington, DC, 1988)

C. McCarty, ed.: *Film Music 1* (New York and London, 1989)

M. Chion: *L'audio-vision* (Paris, 1990; Eng. trans., 1994, as *Audio-Vision: Sound on Screen*)

F. Karlin and R. Wright: *On the Track: a Guide to Contemporary Film Scoring* (New York and London, 1990)

C. Widgery: *The Kinetic and Temporal Interaction of Music and Film: Three Documentaries of 1930s America* (diss., U. of Maryland, 1990)

S.C. Smith: *A Heart at Fire's Center: the Life and Music of Bernard Herrmann* (Berkeley, 1991)

D. Stubblebine: *Cinema Sheet Music: a Comprehensive Listing of Published Film Music From "Squaw Man" (1914) to "Batman" (1989)* (Jefferson, NC, 1991)

C. Flinn: *Strains of Utopia: Gender, Nostalgia, and Hollywood Film Music* (Princeton, NJ, 1992)

K. Kalinak: *Settling the Score: Music and the Classical Hollywood Film* (Madison, WI, 1992)

M. Marks: *Music and the Silent Film: Contexts and Case Studies, 1895–1924* (New York, 1993)

R.S. Brown: *Overtones and Undertones: Reading Film Music* (Berkeley and Los Angeles, 1994)

F. Karlin: *Listening to Movies: the Film Lover's Guide to Film Music* (New York, 1994)

K. Gabbard: *Jammin' at the Margins: Jazz and the American Cinema* (Chicago and London, 1996)

N. Lerner: *The Classical Documentary Score in American Films of Persuasion: Contexts and Case Studies, 1936–1945* (diss., Duke U., 1997)

R. Stilwell: "'I just put a drone under him . . .': Collage and Subversion in the Score of Die Hard," *ML*, lxxviii (1997), 551–80

J. Smith: *The Sounds of Commerce: Marketing Popular Film Music* (New York, 1998)

J. Buhler, C. Flinn, and D. Neumeyer, eds.: *Music and Cinema* (Hanover and London, 2000)

A. Kassabian: *Hearing Film: Tracking Identifications in Contemporary Hollywood Film Music* (New York, 2001)

P. Robertson Wojcik and A. Knight, eds.: *Soundtrack Available: Essays on Film and Popular Music* (New York, 2001)

R. Stilwell: "Music in Films: a Critical Review of Literature, 1980–1996," *Journal of Film Music*, i/1 (2002), 19–61

R. Altman: *Silent Film Sound* (New York, 2005)

D. Goldmark: *Tunes for 'Toons: Music and the Hollywood Cartoon* (Berkeley and Los Angeles, 2005)

D. Goldmark, L. Kramer, and R. Leppert, eds.: *Beyond the Sound Track: Representing Music in Cinema* (Berkeley and Los Angeles, 2007)

J. Wierzbicki: *Film Music: a History* (New York, 2008)

N. Lerner, ed.: *Music in the Horror Film: Listening to Fear* (New York, 2010)

P. Franklin: *Seeing Through Music: Gender and Modernism in Classic Hollywood Film Scores* (Oxford, 2011)

M. Holbrook: *Music, Movies, Meanings, and Markets: Cinemajazzmatazz* (New York, 2011)

M. Kerins: *Beyond Dolby (Stereo): Cinema in the Digital Sound Age* (Bloomington, IN, 2011)

J. Richardson: *An Eye for Music: Popular Music and the Audiovisual Surreal* (Oxford, 2011)

W. Sherk: *Film and Television Music: a Guide to Books, Articles, and Composer Interviews* (Lanham, MD, 2011)

J. Brown and A. Davison: *The Sounds of the Silents in Britain* (Oxford, 2012)

R. Dyer: *In the Space of a Song: the Use of Song in Film* (New York, 2012)

K. Kalinak, ed.: *Music in the Western: Notes from the Frontier* (New York, 2012)

J. Wierzbicki, ed.: *Music, Sound and Filmmakers: Sonic Style in Cinema* (New York, 2012)

A. Ashby: *Popular Music and the New Auteur: Visionary Filmmakers after MTV* (Oxford, 2013)

K. Bartig: *Composing for the Red Screen: Prokofiev and Soviet Film* (Oxford, 2013)

J. Haines: *Music in Films on the Middle Ages: Authenticity vs. Fantasy* (New York, 2013)

D. Neumeyer, ed.: *The Oxford Handbook of Film Music Studies* (Oxford, 2013)

J. Richardson, C. Gorbman, and C. Vernallis, eds.: *The Oxford Handbook of New Audiovisual Aesthetics* (Oxford, 2013)

K. Spring: *Saying it with Songs: Popular Music and the Coming of Sound to Hollywood Cinema* (Oxford, 2013)

C. Vernallis, A. Herzog, and J. Richardson, eds.: *The Oxford Handbook of Sound and Image in Digital Media* (Oxford, 2013)

K.J. Donnelly: *Occult Aesthetics: Synchronization in Sound Film* (Oxford, 2014)
J. Fleeger: *Mismatched Women: the Siren's Song through the Machine* (Oxford, 2014)
J. Fleeger: *Sounding American: Hollywood, Opera, and Jazz* (Oxford, 2014)
L. Jacobs: *Film Rhythm after Sound: Technology, Music, and Performance* (Oakland, CA, 2014)
S. Meyer: *Epic Sound: Music in Postwar Hollywood Biblical Films* (Bloomington, IN, 2014)
S. Pelkey and A. Bushard, eds.: *Anxiety Muted: American Film Music in a Suburban Age* (Oxford, 2014)
M. Slowik: *After the Silents: Hollywood Film Music in the Early Sound Era, 1926–1934* (New York, 2014)
C. Tieber and A. Windisch, eds.: *The Sounds of Silent Films: New Perspectives on History, Theory and Practice* (London, 2014)
B. Winters: *Music, Performance, and the Realities of Film: Shared Concert Experiences in Screen Fiction* (New York, 2014)
M. Dwyer: *Back to the Fifties: Nostalgia, Hollywood Film, and Popular Music of the Seventies and Eighties* (Oxford, 2015)
A. Howell: *Popular Film Music and Masculinity in Action: a Different Tune* (New York, 2015)
D. Kulezić-Wilson: *The Musicality of Narrative Film* (New York, 2015)
D. Neumeyer: *Meaning and Interpretation of Music in Cinema* (Bloomington, IN, 2015)
H. Rogers, ed.: *Music and Sound in Documentary Film* (New York, 2015)
M. Cooke and F. Ford, eds.: *The Cambridge Companion to Film Music* (Cambridge, 2016)
K. Leonard: *Music for Silent Film: a Guide to North American Resources* (Middleton, WI, 2016)
R. Hickman: *Reel Music: Exploring 100 Years of Film Music* (New York, 2017)
K. LaFave: *Experiencing Film Music: a Listener's Companion* (Lanham, MD, 2017)
M. Mera, R. Sadoff, and B. Winters, eds.: *The Routledge Companion to Screen Music and Sound* (New York, 2017)
S. Meyer, ed.: *Music in Epic Film: Listening to Spectacle* (New York, 2017)
N. Platte: *Making Music in Selznick's Hollywood* (New York, 2018)

FRED STEINER, MARTIN MARKS/DANIEL GOLDMARK (1–5, 7)
DANIEL GOLDMARK (6, 9) NEIL LERNER (8)/R

Musical film

By strict definition, a musical film, or movie musical, is a film that utilizes songs sung by characters rather than a movie that just includes singing or music on the soundtrack. There are exceptions to this definition, such as movies about classical composers that feature only instrumental music, or films that are comprised of dance and have no singing, but the true screen musical involves story, characters, songs, and usually dance. Since the very first talkies included songs, the history of the film musical begins with the advent of cinematic sound. Eventually most movies employed a musical soundtrack, much as stage melodramas had relied on an orchestral underscoring. It was the singing (and usually dancing as well) that made movie musicals distinctive. The genre has evolved over the decades and audiences' expectations for a film musical have changed greatly. Yet movie musicals have always conjured up a somewhat fantastic and highly romanticized kind of reality that still makes them unique.

1. Beginnings.

The technology for sound movies was in place long before there was a demand for talkies. As early as 1913 Thomas Edison had developed a method of synchronizing sound with images, calling it the Kinetophone. But the movie studios were not interested. More and more moviegoers flocked to see silent films each year and none felt deprived because the actors could not be heard. By the mid-1920s the technology had improved and short, experimental talkies were made. It was not until 1926 that the minor-league studio Warner Brothers, in financial trouble and seeking any novelty to save them, presented the feature *Don Juan*, which contained no spoken dialogue but had a synchronized musical soundtrack and sound effects. The movie was given a lot of publicity and interest was great enough that Warners gambled on a film that would change the course of American cinema.

The Jazz Singer (1927) has gone down in history as the first talkie but in reality it was a silent film with a handful of songs. The star Al Jolson and the other actors were silent until they broke into song. The only dialogue heard consisted of Jolson's ad-libs between numbers and a halting monologue delivered to his mother while he played the piano. Moviegoers liked what they saw and heard and *The Jazz Singer* was a major hit. Warners followed with the very saccharine *The Singing Fool* (1928), another Jolson silent with songs, and other studios scrambled to get in on the act. In fact it was MGM, not Warners, that offered the first all-talking movie musical, *The Broadway Melody* (1929). This primitive but effective film was a backstage musical, soon to become the most-copied formula for screen musicals, and also boasted an original musical score and even a scene in early two-color Technicolor. RKO had a hit with its screen version of the Broadway operetta *Rio Rita* (1929), Fox joined in with *Sunny Side Up* (1929), Paramount with *The Love Parade* (1929), and Universal with *King of Jazz* (1930). The race was on and it looked like talkies, particularly musicals, were here to stay.

As audiences rushed to see the early musicals, the studios were frantically trying to learn just how the new genre worked. Should screen musicals be filmed versions of stage musicals? Must a musical number be presented from the viewpoint of a theatergoer in a playhouse? Should characters break into song for no reason? Or must all musical numbers be part of a nightclub act or Broadway show? Then there were the many problems regarding the filming of musicals. The sound cameras were large and practically stationary. The effectiveness of microphones was uneven. Full orchestras had to assemble on the set and play while the actors sang and danced until it was discovered that a pre-recorded soundtrack to which the performers lip-synched was more effective. It was also necessary for the studios to create new departments for writing songs, recording music, and rehearsing songs and dance. A new kind of movie performer was needed and the studios eagerly put Broadway stars under contract without even knowing how they might come across on the screen. The early years of the movie musical were not so much a period of deliberate trial and error as one of furious activity without direction or methodology. The public demanded musicals and the demand was met with some superb results but mostly misconceived and tiresome formula musicals.

Such a rampant growth of musicals in Hollywood soon backfired. By 1931 there were too many musicals on the market, the novelty of the new genre wore off, and audiences started to avoid movie musicals. The studios began to panic, canceling contracts, aborting musicals in production, and cutting songs from finished products and releasing them as nonmusical talkies. By 1933 it looked like the new genre was dead, a passing fad that had run its course. Talkies were certainly here to stay but they wouldn't be singing or dancing.

2. Rebirth.

Historians point to two 1933 movie musicals that saved the genre and started a tradition for quality and popular musicals that would last over two decades. Warners' *42nd Street* and RKO's *Flying Down to Rio* were not only hits at a time when most musicals failed but both opened up fresh possibilities for the genre and showed the ways in which a screen musical could do things no Broadway production could. *42nd Street* was another backstager but it was both gritty, in the typical Warner style, and spectacular. The production numbers, imaginatively choreographed and filmed by Busby Berkeley, offered musical entertainment on a scale impossible in any playhouse. *Flying Down to Rio* also had spectacle, most memorably the title number with chorus girls tied to airplanes in flight, but it also had a slick kind of romanticism not seen before. Fred Astaire and Ginger Rogers played secondary roles in the plot but when they took to the dance floor a certain kind of movie magic was born. Warners would continue with a series of popular backstagers, such as *Footlight Parade* (1933), *Gold Diggers of 1933*, and its sequels, and RKO starred Astaire and Rogers in a series of beloved musicals that utilized their considerable acting, singing, and dancing talents.

The 1930s and the Depression saw a rise in movie attendance as audiences looked for an escape from reality and no genre was more escapist than the film musical. Each studio took its individual approach to Depression-era musicals. Warner Brothers, because they had a head start in the new genre and had developed the technology for talkies, dominated movie musicals for much of the 1930s. Their movies confronted the Depression issue and depicted hard times in its backstage musicals, as with *Dames* (1934), *Wonder Bar* (1934), *Go Into Your Dance* (1935), and *Varsity Show* (1937). MGM took a more romantic approach, offering highly polished musicals with lavish production values, such as *Dancing Lady* (1933), *Going Hollywood* (1933), *The Merry Widow* (1934), *Naughty Marietta* (1935) and the other Jeanette MacDonald-Nelson Eddy operettas, *Broadway Melody of 1936* (1935) and its sequels, *The Great Ziegfeld* (1936), *Born to Dance* (1936), *Rosalie* (1937), *The Great Waltz* (1938), and *The Wizard of Oz* (1939). RKO offered sleek art-deco musicals with Astaire and Rogers, including *The Gay Divorcee* (1934), *Roberta* (1935), *Top Hat* (1935), *Follow the Fleet* (1936), *Swing Time* (1936), *Shall We Dance* (1937), and *Carefree* (1938). Columbia, Paramount, United Artists, Universal, and Fox (later Twentieth Century-Fox) did not cultivate distinctive styles but built their musicals around their stars. Fox had Shirley Temple who was featured in such Depression-chasers as *Baby Take a Bow* (1934), *Curly Top* (1935), *Poor Little Rich Girl* (1936), and *Rebecca of Sunnybrook Farm* (1938). Paramount offered Bing Crosby, Mae West, and other stars in such 1930s films as *She Done Him Wrong* (1933), *The Big Broadcast of 1936* (1935) and its sequels, *High, Wide and Handsome* (1937), and *Sing You Sinners* (1938). United Artists boasted a series of hits with Eddie Cantor, including *Roman Scandals* (1933), *Kid Millions* (1934), and *Strike Me Pink* (1936), Universal offered such notable movies as *Show Boat* (1936) and *One Hundred Men and a Girl* (1937), and by the end of the decade even Walt Disney moved into feature musicals with the animated *Snow White and the Seven Dwarfs* (1937). The Depression may have devastated the country but it was a time of rebirth and strength for the American movie musical.

3. A golden age.

The 1940s and first half of the 1950s are often considered the golden age of the movie musical. Rarely did they have the social impact of Depression-era musicals but the entertainment values and the craftsmanship were very high. MGM led the other studios in quality because of its huge resources of money, materials, and talent. The Freed Unit, a group within MGM headed by producer Arthur Freed, created many of the best musicals of this era. The Mickey Rooney-Judy Garland "let's put on a show" musical *Babes in Arms* (1939) was the first Freed production, followed by such memorable films as *Strike Up the Band* (1940), *Babes on Broadway* (1941), *For Me and My Gal* (1942), *Cabin in the Sky* (1943), *Meet Me in St. Louis* (1944), *The Harvey Girls* (1946), *Till the Clouds Roll By* (1947), *Good News* (1947), *Easter Parade* (1948), *Words and Music* (1948), *On the Town* (1949), *Annie Get Your Gun* (1950), *Show Boat* (1951), *An American in Paris* (1951), *Singin' in the Rain* (1952), *The Band Wagon* (1953), *Silk Stockings* (1957), and *Gigi* (1958). Warner Brothers did not dominate the musical genre as it had in the 1930s yet it still came up with such treasured movies as *Yankee Doodle Dandy* (1942), *Thank Your Lucky Stars* (1943), *Rhapsody in Blue* (1944), and *A Star Is Born* (1954). Paramount offered Bing Crosby and Bob Hope in *Road to Singapore* (1940) followed by six more "road" musicals, as well as *Birth of the Blues* (1941), *Star Spangled Rhythm* (1942), *The Fleet's In* (1942), *Holiday Inn* (1942), *Going My Way* (1944), *Blue Skies* (1946), *White Christmas* (1954), and *Funny Face* (1957). Fox built many of its musicals around its two top 1940s stars, Alice Faye and Betty Grable, coming up with such films as *Down Argentine Way* (1940), *Sun Valley Serenade* (1941), *The Gang's All Here* (1943), and *Mother Wore Tights* (1947), as well as *State Fair* (1945), *There's No Business Like Show Business* (1954), *The King and I* (1956), and *South Pacific* (1958). Columbia's top attraction was Rita Hayworth who starred in such hits as *You'll Never Get Rich* (1941), *You Were Never Lovelier* (1942), and *Cover Girl* (1944), and the studio also offered such musicals as *The Jolson Story* (1946), *Jolson Sings Again* (1949), *Pal Joey* (1957), and *Porgy and Bess* (1959). The other studios played a smaller role in the golden age but even their infrequent contributions resulted in such favored musicals as *One Night in the Tropics* (1940), *Up in Arms* (1944), *Can't Help Singing* (1944), *Hans Christian Andersen* (1952), *The Glenn Miller Story* (1954), and Disney animated musicals such as *Pinocchio* (1940), *Cinderella* (1949), and *Lady and the Tramp* (1955).

4. Decline.

The advent of television and the breakdown of the old studio system are among the factors that led to the decline in movie attendance in the late 1950s, and no genre suffered more than the movie musical. Often the most expensive to produce, musicals cost even more when the studios tried to woo audiences with widescreen, lengthy, spectacular musicals with intermissions and limited showings.

In the 1960s going to a film musical typically resembled going to see an expensive Broadway show. In fact, most of the musicals of this era were adaptations of stage musicals and not original film creations. Sometimes the result was a financial success, such as *West Side Story* (1961), *The Music Man* (1962), *Bye Bye Birdie* (1963), *My Fair Lady* (1964), *The Sound of Music* (1965), *Funny Girl* (1968), and *Oliver!* (1968); other times the film was a financial embarrassment, as with *Camelot* (1967), *Finian's Rainbow* (1968), *Paint Your Wagon* (1969), and *Hello, Dolly!* (1969). Among the original movie musicals of the decade were *Robin and the 7 Hoods* (1964), *Mary Poppins* (1964), *Thoroughly Modern Millie* (1967), *Doctor Dolittle* (1967), *Star!* (1968), *Chitty Chitty Bang Bang* (1968), *Goodbye, Mr. Chips* (1969), and *Darling Lili* (1969); they were a mixed bag in terms of quality and box office acceptance.

By the 1970s the studios, what was left of them, gave up on the big-budget musical and smaller, shorter, and often more challenging musicals appeared. These works did not resemble the lavish Freed Units products of the past but often came closer to the gritty Warner Brothers musicals. There was an edge to such films as *Cabaret* (1972), *Lady Sings the Blues* (1972), *Nashville* (1975), *New York, New York* (1977), *Saturday Night Fever* (1977), *The Buddy Holly Story* (1978), *The Rose* (1979), *All That Jazz* (1979), *Fame* (1980), *La Bamba* (1987), *Bird* (1988), *For the Boys* (1991), *Evita* (1996), and even *Moulin Rouge* (2001). Some of these barely qualified as musicals according to the strict definition. Others, such as *Flashdance* (1983), *Footloose* (1984), and *Dirty Dancing* (1987), were dance melodramas in which none of the characters sang, the pulsating score only needed to serve as background for the dance and romance.

There were still traditional musicals and the expected adaptations of stage hits during this three-decade decline. *Song of Norway* (1970), *Fiddler on the Roof* (1971), *1776* (1972), *Mame* (1974), *Grease* (1978), *The Wiz* (1978), *Hair* (1979), *Annie* (1982), *A Chorus Line* (1985), and *Little Shop of Horrors* (1986) were among the stage transfers and very few of them found favor with audiences. If the Broadway-style musical was still alive on the screen, it was in animated films. The Disney studio enjoyed a renaissance with its feature-length animated movies beginning with *The Little Mermaid* (1989). Such subsequent movies as *Beauty and the Beast* (1991), *Aladdin* (1992), *The Lion King* (1994), *Pocahontas* (1995), *The Hunchback of Notre Dame* (1996), *Hercules* (1997), *Mulan* (1998), and *Tarzan* (1999) were not only finely crafted and often highly appealing; they were also full-fledged musicals. Just as the genre seemed to be waning, these lively animated films defied the decline and celebrated the musical panache of the past.

5. Movie musicals today.

Film musicals in the twenty-first century are a mixed bag with no particular pattern, trend, or guarantee of success. The Broadway adaptations continue as in

Anika Noni Ross, Beyoncé Knowles, and Sharon Leal in *Dreamgirls*, 2008.
(DreamWorks SKG/Photofest)

the past but, as in previous decades, the hits—such as *Chicago* (2002), *Dreamgirls* (2006), *Hairspray* (2007), *Sweeney Todd* (2008)—were equaled by disappointments: *Phantom of the Opera* (2004), *Rent* (2005), *The Producers* (2005), and *Nine* (2009). Original musicals varied, from the biographies *De-Lovely* (2004), *Ray* (2004), and *Walk the Line* (2005), to the youth-oriented musicals *Camp* (2003), *High School Musical 3* (2008), and *Fame* (2009), to the occasional effort at something more challenging, such as *Hedwig and the Angry Inch* (2001) and *Across the Universe* (2007). The contemporary film musical flounders about with no clear direction. In many ways the current situation is not unlike those days in the late 1920s when the studios were trying to figure out just what a film musical was and how to deal with the new genre.

Bibliography

D. McVay: *The Musical Film* (London, 1967)
J. Burton: *The Blue Book of Hollywood Musicals* (Watkins Glen, NY, 1975)
H. Fordin: *The World of Entertainment: Hollywood's Greatest Musicals* (New York, 1975)
S. Green: *Encyclopedia of Musical Film* (New York, 1981)
J. Feuer: *The Hollywood Musical* (Bloomington, IN, 1982)
E. Mordden: *The Hollywood Musical* (New York, 1982)
T. Sennett: *Hollywood Musicals* (New York, 1982)
C. Hirschhorn: *The Hollywood Musical* (New York, 2/1983)
R. Altman: *The American Film Musical* (Bloomington, IN, 1987)
J. Springer: *They Sang, They Danced, They Romanced* (New York, 1991)
J. Parish and M. Pitts: *The Great Hollywood Musicals* (Metuchen, NJ, 1992)
R. Fehr and F. Vogel: *Lullabies of Hollywood: Movie Music and the Movie Musical*, 1915–1992 (Jefferson, NC, 1993)
E. Bradley: *The First Hollywood Musicals* (Jefferson, NC, 1996)

S. Green: *Hollywood Musicals Year by Year* (Milwaukee, 2/1999)
T. Hischak: *Film It With Music: an Encyclopedic Guide to the American Movie Musical* (Westport, CT, 2001)
R. Knapp: *The American Musical and the Performance of Personal Identity* (Princeton, NJ, 2006)
T. Hischak: *The Oxford Companion to the American Musical: Theatre, Film and Television* (New York, 2008)
R. Barrios: *A Song in the Dark: the Birth of the Musical Film* (New York, 2/2010)
R. Knapp, M. Morris, and S. Ellen, eds.: *The Oxford Handbook of the American Musical* (New York, 2011)
B. Grant: *The Hollywood Film Musical* (Malden, MA, 2012)
R. Barrios: *Dangerous Rhythm: Why Movie Musicals Matter* (Oxford, 2014)
D. Garcia: *The Migration of Musical Film: From Ethnic Margins to American Mainstream* (New Brunswick, NJ, 2014)
C. Flinn: "The Music of Screen Musicals," *The Cambridge Companion to Film Music* (Cambridge, 2016), 231–46
E. Mordden: *When Broadway Went to Hollywood* (New York, 2016)
P. Doyle: "Reverb, Acousmata, and the Backstage Musical," *The Routledge Companion to Screen Music and Sound* (New York, 2017), 577–89
W. Everett and P. Laird, eds.: *The Cambridge Companion to the Musical* (Cambridge, 3/2017)

THOMAS S. HISCHAK/R

Music in Video Games

Video game music is distinct from music in most other media forms in that when composed well (according to the standards of the game community), the music is dynamic; that is, responsive to game events and player actions. This can mean, for instance, that various parameters of the music (such as tempo, key, and instrumentation), or sequences or sections of music, are altered based in real time on what is happening in the game. For example, a player-generated change in music occurs in Koji Kondo's music for *Super Mario World* (Nintendo, 1992); when the player's character Mario jumps on a character (the dinosaur, Yoshi), a layer of percussion is added to the music. When the player jumps off, the percussion track is removed. In addition to player-generated changes, run-time game parameters such as player health, number of enemies, time of day, or location in the game can alter what music is being played.

In some cases, game music is composed in non-linear sections or "audio chunks" that can be sequenced in real time for multiple variations of playback, and therefore is reliant on a software program to control the timing and sequence of musical events. This dynamic composition developed in part as a response to the repetitive nature of game-play, as well as out of a conscious effort to make games feel more immersive and responsive to the player. Due to this degree of real-time responsiveness, in addition to serving all of the functions of music found in film, music in games serves the additional functions of drawing a player's attention to particular situations in the game (such as an enemy in the area, or the run-time parameters mentioned above) with the goal of warning or signaling to the player to take action.

The history of music in video games can be divided into roughly three significant periods that represent major changes in the dominant technology coupled with subsequent approaches in composition: the analogue era (up to the early 1980s), the sound chip era (up to about the early 1990s), and the compressed raw audio era (from the early 1990s onwards). These eras overlap to some degree; for instance, synthesized music from sound chips (usually MIDI-based) is still used in some games, and smaller handhelds use chips as well as even some analogue equipment.

1. Analog era.

Video games in the earliest days grew from out of the arcade coin-operated industry that had previously relied on electromechanical games and pinball. While these games initially depended on simple bells, chimes, solenoids, and other mechanically controlled means to provide sounds, by the late 1970s electronic sound components were incorporated into the machines. Some electromechanical arcade games had 4-track and later 8-track tape-player units incorporated into the consoles to play music and sound effects. Hybrid electromechanical/solid-state games also existed, combining 8-track tapes with analogue or digital sound, for instance, in Atari's *Triple Hunt* (1977). Many early video games—typically made by the same companies that had made pinball, slot machines, and other electromechanical games—therefore shared similar uses of sound, primarily designed to attract the passersby to the machine and generate excitement.

Sound in electronic video games before the mid-1980s commonly used one of two technologies: piezoelectric beepers or programmable sound generators. Although early games used analogue circuitry, beeper sound was typically controlled and manipulated digitally, and was nearly always some form of pulse wave that created a simple "beep" whose frequency could be adjusted. Electromagnetic PC internal speakers were also referred to as beepers, since they, too, often emitted no more than a simple beep. In the analogue days of electromagnetic and piezoelectric sound technology, the sounds that were available to the composers and sound designers of the games were dependent on the hardware circuitry. As such, music was rare beyond a short title theme and winning and losing songs.

2. Sound chip era.

Programmable sound generator sound chips were also used in the late 1970s and early 1980s, and typically had three separate tone generators and a noise generator. This meant that (where memory and processor speed allowed) four simultaneous sounds (three tonal) could be heard. The sound created, however, was typically limited to pulse waves (square waves usually, sounding rough and obviously synthesized), and most sounds were reserved for sound effects. Most of the sound effects were employed for feedback given to the player based on the player's actions: for instance, the player has been injured or died, the player is under attack, the player has taken an action (fired a gun, jumped, bumped into a wall), the player has earned points, or there is a change in gamestate (for instance, a new level is begun). Music was often limited to title themes, since processors had a difficult time simultaneously processing player action, graphics, and sound. As processor speeds and memory increased, short loops of music were included in games. Notable is Shigeru Miyamoto's *Donkey Kong* (Nintendo, 1981), in which a bassline borrowed from John Lennon's *Ballad of John and Yoko* permeates the game-play. The same year *Frogger* introduced on-going dynamic background music with a series of songs that changed as the player either died or guided a frog into a safe house.

Games in the mid-1980s were typically created by individuals or small teams, and music was usually an afterthought, integrated into the game when all other components were programmed. Many of the early composers were programmers who borrowed music from popular songs and the public domain. Moreover, many game companies (particularly in the United States) preferred for the composers to remain uncredited, and while fan communities have sprung up to begin to attribute the music to particular people (one notable example is Brad Fuller, audio director for Atari), much of the music remains anonymous.

More advanced sound chips developed throughout the 1980s, using FM synthesis and then wavetable synthesis, replacing the characteristic pulse-wave sound with a wider variety of possible instrument sounds, although aesthetically the music remained quite similar, with a bassline, two treble lines that would provide melody and accompaniment, and a percussion track often provided by shaped bursts of white noise. Integrating music remained cumbersome and often the task of a programmer, although as the decade progressed game composition increasingly became more of a dedicated task. As soundcards developed for home PCs, and MIDI advanced composer's abilities to provide programmers with data rather than sheet music or cassette recordings, game music took on more advanced compositional traits. Instead of straight loops, sections could be transposed, re-sequenced on the fly, and even algorithmically generated. Notable American composers from the era include Brian Schmidt (*NARC*, Williams, 1988), Chris Grigg (*Maniac Mansion*, LucasFilm Games, 1987), Clint Bajakian (*Monkey Island 2*, LucasFilm Games, 1991), and Michael Land (*The Secret of Monkey Island*, LucasFilm Games, 1990).

3. Compressed raw audio era.

With the rise of CD-ROM technology in the early 1990s, dynamic game music became less common in favor of pre-recorded music in relatively short one-or two-minute loops. The downside of pre-recorded music was that it could not remain as interactive and responsive as chipset music, although it opened up a much wider range of instrumentation for composers. Games released on the PlayStation One, for instance, exploited the chance to use pre-recorded and licensed music in games, and the rise of game music soundtracks began. Some composers still used the console's chipset, however, notably Nobuo Uematsu's soundtrack for *Final Fantasy VII* (Squaresoft, 1997). Notable American composers from the era include those mentioned above as well as George "The Fat Man" Sanger (*7th Guest*, Virgin, 1993), Robyn Miller (*Myst*, Brøderbund, 1993), and Tommy Tallarico (*Prince of Persia*, Brøderbund, 1989).

In the early 2010s game music has found a balance between the technology and the demands for a dynamic, responsive score. Top titles are commonly recorded with full orchestras, although the majority of games rely on sampled sound. Composers can test out their transitions and interactivity using popular middleware engines (software packages that provide an interface between the music and the game engine). Smaller titles and shorter low-budget games known as casual games (including social networking and mobile games) may still use MIDI and rely on sound chips from time to time, although increasingly they, too, rely on pre-recorded samples. Composers still grapple with memory allotment that limits the number of simultaneous channels that may be used for music, and with other constraints of composing for video games, including the indefinable length of game-play. Generally speaking, however, looping has been abandoned in larger console titles in favor of simple fade-outs when the player has been stuck on one level for a length of time. Notable American composers today include Marty O'Donnell (*Halo*, Bungie 2001), Jack Wall (*Mass Effect*, Bioware, 2007), Michael Giacchino (*Medal of Honor*, EA, 1999), Tom Salta (*Tom Clancy's Ghost Recon Advanced Warfighter*, Ubisoft, 2006), Garry Schyman (*Bioshock*, Irrational Games, 2007), and Guy Whitmore (*The Operative: No One Lives Forever*, Monolith, 2000).

Today some game franchises (such as the *Madden* and *Grand Theft Auto* series) have become known for breaking new bands to audiences, increasing the success of Good Charlotte, Franz Ferdinand, Arctic Monkeys, and the Streets, among others. Many game companies have formed associations with record labels, such as Electronic Arts's EA Trax, Next Level Music, and EA Recordings, and songs may now be released simultaneously as part of the artist's album and the game soundtrack.

4. Music-based games.

Music-based games, also known as rhythm-action games, are video games in which the player must respond in some way to the rhythm or melody being presented, typically through repeating the same melody or rhythm (by pressing buttons, swinging controllers, or the like) or timing a bodily reaction to the rhythm (dancing, pushing buttons, etc.) with custom-designed controllers.

Atari was perhaps the first company to release an electronic rhythm-action game, with their *Touch Me*, produced as both a coin-operated arcade machine in 1974 and handheld device in 1978. *Touch Me* played a sequence of lights and sounds from four buttons and four tones, and asked the player to repeat the pattern. The game was redesigned by Milton Bradley in 1977 as the more famous *Simon*, which became an instant hit, but the phenomenon disappeared from games for a time, perhaps because of the limitations of the early game technology. By the mid-1980s rhythm-action games saw a resurgence as game companies sought increasing novelty in the face of fierce competition. Nintendo introduced a "Power Pad" to the Nintendo Entertainment System (NES) in 1988, which consisted of a floor mat with control buttons built in for the feet, whereupon dancing games like *Dance Aerobics* (Bandai, 1989) would become forerunners to today's popular dance rhythm-action games like *Dance Dance Revolution* (Konami, 1999).

PaRappa the Rapper (SCEI, 1996), released on PlayStation, incorporated ideas from rhythm-action games into a storyline: PaRappa was trying to win the love of a girl, Sunny, and had to practice rapping to the beat of various drummers to improve his skill. A button was to be hit in the correct order with correct timing to keep the beat, significantly relying on memorization, much like *Simon*, and a popular idea that has persisted through to today's rhythm-action games. Other more narrative-style games have incorporated elements of rhythm-action into them (such as in *The Legend of Zelda's Oracle of Ages*, Nintendo, 2001, in which the player must dance in time to the rhythm), or *Toejam and Earl: Panic on Funkotron* (Sega, 1992), in which the player can play along with the percussion in a funk-based soundtrack in a *Simon*-type memory game.

Although many of these earlier types of rhythm-action games used the regular game controllers, there are often special add-on controllers for contemporary rhythm-action games. *Donkey Konga* (Nintendo, 2003) included "DK Bongo" drums, *Guitar Hero* (RedOctane, 2005) a guitar-shaped controller, and *DJ Hero* (Activision, 2009) includes a DJ turntable. Dancing games, such as *Pump It Up*

High school students playing *Guitar Hero*, 2005.
(AP Photo/John Smock)

(Andamiro, 1998), *In The Groove* (Roxor Games, 2004, since bought out by Konami), and of course *Dance Dance Revolution* (Konami, 1999), experienced a period of particular popularity in the early to mid-2000s, spawning considerable fan communities around the world, and to some extent reviving a dying coin-op business. Other music-based games, including remixing games such as *FreQuency* (Harmonix, 2001) and singing games like *SingStar* (Sony, 2004), have also more recently put the player in a performer role. Handheld consoles also spawned their share of rhythm-action hits, including *Elite Beat Agents* (for the Nintendo DS, 2006), *Phase* (Harmonix 2007, for iPod), and *Electroplankton* (Nintendo, 2006) in which elements must be tapped or spun with the stylus.

The current most popular rhythm-action games are undoubtedly the *Guitar Hero* franchise and its followers and related series, *Rock Band* (Harmonix, 2007), spun off from the original creators of *Guitar Hero* and adding bass, vocals, and drums. New game releases like *PowerGig: Rise of the SixString* (Seven45Studios, 2010) offer the potential to play real (conventional) electric guitars modified with buttons. Entire games have been devoted to specific popular recording artists (such as *The Beatles* and the *Green Day Rock Band* editions), and the games have helped to revive careers of a variety of pop stars whose older hit songs have been included. More recently these games have become viewed by the music industry as a new way to market and promote music to gamers, and most major record labels have exclusive deals signed with game companies. Indeed, the popularity of *Guitar Hero* led to ASCAP seeking fees from arcade owners for the first time, in 2009. Moreover, communities exist online in which fans create and share note maps for other music for the games, expanding the games with alternative or bootleg versions.

Bibliography

D. Bessell: “What’s That Funny Noise? An Examination of the Role of Music in *Cool Boarders 2, Alien Trilogy* and *Medievil 2*,” *ScreenPlay: Cinema/videogames/interfaces*, ed. G. King and T. Krzywinska (London, 2002), 136–44

A. Kassabian: “The Sound of a New Film Form,” *Popular Music and Film*, ed. I. Inglis (London, 2003), 91–101

G. Sanger: *The Fat Man on Game Audio: Tasty Morsels of Sonic Goodness* (Berkeley, CA, 2003)

T.M. Fay, S. Selfon, and T.J. Fay: *DirectX 9 Audio Exposed: Interactive Audio Development* (Plano, TX, 2004)

J. Demers: “Dancing Machines: Dance Dance Revolution: Cybernetic Dance, and Musical Taste,” *Popular Music*, xxv (2006), 401–14

K. Collins: *Game Sound: an Introduction to the History, Theory and Practice of Video Game Music and Sound Design* (Cambridge, MA, 2008)

P. Shultz: “Music Theory in Music Games,” *From Pac-Man to Pop Music: Interactive Audio in Games and New Media*, ed. K. Collins (Aldershot, 2008), 177–89

W. Gibbons: “Blip, Bloop, Bach? Some Uses of Classical Music on the Nintendo Entertainment System,” *Music and the Moving Image*, ii/1 (2009), 40–52

K. Miller: *Playing Along: Digital Games, YouTube, and Virtual Performance* (Oxford, 2012)

K. Collins: *Playing with Sound: a Theory of Interacting with Sound and Music in Video Games* (Cambridge, MA, 2013)

W. Cheng: *Sound Play: Video Games and the Musical Imagination* (Oxford, 2014)

K.J. Donnelly, W. Gibbons, and N Lerner, eds.: *Music in Video Games: Studying Play* (New York, 2014)

W. Phillips: *A Composer's Guide to Game Music* (Cambridge, MA, 2014)

M. Austin: *Music Video Games: Performance, Politics, and Play* (New York, 2016)

M. Kamp, T. Summers, and M. Sweeney, eds.: *Ludomusicology: Approaches to Video Game Music* (Sheffield, 2016)

T. Summers and J. Hannigan: *Understanding Video Game Music* (Cambridge, 2016)

K. Miller: *Playable Bodies: Dance Games and Intimate Media* (New York, 2017)

W. Gibbons: *Unlimited Replays: Video Games and Classical Music* (New York, 2018)

KAREN COLLINS/R

Production music

It typically comprises recorded music of a broad range of styles and genres, which is produced and owned by production music libraries and licensed for use in commercial media, such as theme music or background music in film, television, radio, and other media.

Music for productions has existed since the silent film era, early on supplied in the form of cue sheets and anthologies used by pianists, small orchestras, and other ensembles to be performed in real time with a film. Over time, recorded media has replaced printed materials as the main way to distribute music. Many large production music companies have compiled extensive sound and audio libraries for commercial distribution, including Boosey & Hawkes, Sony BMG, and many others. Since these libraries generally own the rights to the music, they license it directly to a client without the need to gain permission from composers or writers.

Revenue from production music is created through several models. The first is a licensing fee with the production music library, paid in advance for authorization to synchronize music from a particular library to a piece of film or video. A second practice is through performance royalties, generated when music is publicly performed. These fees are collected by performing rights societies established to monitor usage and administer royalties on behalf of its member composers, artists, and publishers. Most countries have their own performance rights organizations, such as ASCAP, BMI, or other organizations such as the Production Music Association. Another method of revenue creation combines the comprehensive licensing of music already contained in the catalogue of a production music library along with original music, created by a contracted composer to meet the artistic demands of a specific project. In this situation, the composer of the newly created music typically retains the rights to the music for a negotiated period of time; eventually the music is subsumed into the catalogue of the music production company, at which time the library can license the new music as its property and recover its original production costs. Finally, the royalty free model offers for an upfront fee a way to purchase or license a compact disc of music (or to download the same music), which can then be used as many times as needed without any further payments or fees by the original purchaser. If the music is broadcast in any fashion, however, the broadcaster is responsible for performance royalties, hence the somewhat misleading nature of the practice.

Bibliography

R. Sauer: "Photoplay Music: a Reusable Repertory for Silent Film Scoring, 1914–1929," *American Music Research Center Journal* (1998), 55–76

R. Fink: "Orchestral Corporate," *ECHO* ii/1 (2000)

P. Mandell: "Production Music in Television's Golden Age: an Overview," *Performing Arts: Broadcasting*, ed. I. Newsome (Washington, DC, 2002), 148–69

D. Hollander: "Library Music: Mood Music," *Wax Poetics*, xxxviii (2009), 48–56

J. Fitzgerald: "Make 'em Laugh, Make 'em Cry: the Use of Production Music in Australian Reality Television Series *Nerds FC*," *Perfect Beat*, x/1 (2009), 15–37

P. Graff: "Re-evaluating the Silent-Film Music Holdings at the Library of Congress," *Notes*, xxviii/1 (2016), 33–76

TIMOTHY M. CRAIN/R

Television music

A term for all music that is broadcast on television. It has functioned in several different ways, reflecting the array of genres and modes of broadcasting. In American television, music has been heard as entertainment through the performances of songs and instrumental works by classical, jazz, country, pop, rock, and other performers, in other words, music presented as music. It has also been heard as "production music," to underscore dramatic programs, enhance mood and narrative structure and meaning (similar to music's function in films), and as a way to mark transitions within a television program and between programs. Music has functioned in these ways in both programs and in commercials. During the early years of television, these modes of television music were discrete, but from the 1980s the distinctions in the form that music takes have been blurred.

The functions of television music listed above may be generalized in three categories, using terminology for narrative agency. First, it can be "extradiegetic" – used to navigate and transition through the many programs and advertisements of a broadcasting schedule, often called the "flow" of television: from program to station break and vice versa, and between station breaks, public service announcements, program promotions, and commercials. Second, television music can be "intradiegetic," used as background or mood music within narrative programs, such as situation comedies, dramas, and documentaries. Intradiegetic music is usually "acousmatic," meaning the source of the music is not seen on the screen. Finally, television music can be "diegetic," that is, music whose source appears on screen and is heard as part of the action or the mise-en-scène of a program. Diegetic music is often performed by musicians shown on the screen in genres such as musical variety shows, late-night talk shows, and music videos, but may also be featured in a narrative program.

A historical periodization of musical practice in television is tied to developments in the broadcasting practices and technology of the medium itself. However, musical practice periods in TV differ somewhat from many media theorists' periodization of television in general. As in any periodization, there are significant overlaps where traits of a certain period can be found earlier and continue on into the next period. With these caveats, the history of television music in television can be viewed as progressing through four overlapping stages: a "pre-broadcasting" period (*c*1925–48), an experimental era during which television and television programs served as exhibitions and curiosities for demonstrations private and public; a "radiophonic" period (*c*1948–55), in which television music borrowed heavily from vaudeville, live theater, and radio (its immediate electronic media predecessor), while also experimenting with new modes of presentation; a cinematic period (*c*1955–80) marked by improved production and broadcasting practices of diegetic and extradiegetic music, but also by the involvement and influence of film studios in television production, when music followed the conventions of Hollywood film scoring; and a "televideo" period (from 1981) characterized by a proliferation of musical styles and a breakdown of intertextual boundaries that has been marked by the importing of popular music into TV episodes, but also the export of music from TV episodes to CDs, Internet websites, and podcasts.

Music has been an integral part of American television from its earliest days and has served as a reflection of the musical tastes of the American public through the years. This reflection can be found in the historic shift from light classical and popular standard musical styles used between the 1940s and 1970s to the rock and pop music that was adopted in the 1980s. Moreover, the dual function of television music as artistic text and commodity text has reflected perceptions of television as a whole and is perhaps a uniquely American way of utilizing artistic texts such as music for commercial ends. Much of what has been seen and heard on television has been of high artistic quality, but it has also had to be popular with a significant portion of the viewing audience in order to attract and maintain sponsorship from private corporations.

Early experimental broadcasts in the 1920s, such as those of the television pioneer Charles Jenkins, often featured musicians as subjects. The era of broadcast television can be said to have begun on 21 July 1931 when the CBS network went on the air with the "Television Inaugural Broadcast," airing on W2XAB, an experimental station in New York. The broadcast featured Kate Smith and other singers, as well as George Gershwin, who was interviewed and who played some of his piano pieces. NBC began experimental broadcasts from New York's Empire State Building in 1932, but did not begin public broadcasting until 1939, when its "First Night" program featured the musician Fred Waring and his Pennsylvanians.

World War II delayed the widespread development of television, but after the war television stations began public broadcasting on a national scale. The first post-war musical variety show was "Hour Glass," which first aired on 9 May 1946 and featured Dennis Day and Peggy Lee as regulars on the show. The show retained a vaudeville concept from radio and theater, featuring comedy sketches, ballroom dancing, and musical numbers accompanied by a live orchestra. Uncertain of the role of music on television, James Petrillo, the president of the AFM, sought to ban live music on TV until a remuneration schedule could be worked out. The ban was lifted on 20 March 1948 when the major networks (NBC, CBS, ABC, and DuMont) worked out an agreement with the union, and musical variety shows flourished. While continuing the "vaudeo" (vaudeville on video) format of "Hour Glass," "Texaco Star Theater" (starring Milton Berle) set a musical standard by hiring an orchestra and the singer Pearl Bailey to feature as regulars on the show.

From 1948 music developed in the three modes of broadcasting. The remainder of this article will cover each in turn, along with historical coverage of music in animated cartoons and television advertising.

1. Extradiegetic music.

Extradiegetic music is a musical category unique to broadcast media like television and radio, where many texts are temporally juxtaposed against each other in broadcasting time in a phenomenon called "flow." Extradiegetic music, or music outside of a "diegesis" (story), often serves as a transition between these texts. Some examples of extradiegetic television music are theme music, music for station breaks, network logos, and "bumpers."

Studio logos are brief musical mottos that help to identify the network on which a program is being viewed or the studio that produced a particular program. Although these musical texts are brief, they have significant histories and have been written by composers who work for particular studios. Perhaps the most famous of these is the three-note motif (G–E–C) that has been used to identify the NBC television network. Employing the motif reportedly took three years to implement, and it was finally played on a glockenspiel in 1926 for NBC radio. It was later transferred to television. The other networks also employed such musical logos: CBS used compositions by Jerry Goldsmith and Bill Conti, and ABC employed logos by Dominic Frontiere and Harry Geller. Musical logos identifying production studios have also been used at the end of TV programs, with notable examples by Stanley Wilson, Walter Greene, Quincy Jones, and Pete Rugolo (all for MCA/Universal), and William Lava, George Duning, and Frank Comstock (all Warner Bros.).

Perhaps the most popular musical aspect of television is theme music. Musical themes carry both extradiegetic and intradiegetic traits, transitioning broadcasting away from the flow of television and into the diegetic world of a particular TV show. Themes to TV shows have several functions: extradiegetically, they announce that a particular show is about to air and entice the viewer to come and watch, a mechanism that Tagg (2000) calls an "appellative" function. Intradiegetically, a theme provides a narrative frame to a show, serving as opening and closing, while also identifying the genre or overall mood of the program. Composers of TV theme music seek to create music that is unique to the particular program, while also providing musical style traits, or "topics," that are familiar to the audience. Certain style topics of music have been associated with certain TV genres, usually based on pre-existing patterns with which the audience is familiar. For example, a situation comedy may feature light, upbeat music, while dramas feature more somber, serious-sounding music. Television themes are perhaps the greatest source of television discourse, as the themes repeated week after week are retained in the audience's memory. Some themes have reached such popularity that they have been disseminated through commercial recordings, the sale of sheet music, and performances by professional and school groups. Notable themes in this regard have been those to "Peter Gunn" (Henry Mancini), "Bonanza" (David Rose), "Hawaii Five-O" (Morton Stevens), and "The Rockford Files" and "Hill Street Blues" (both Mike Post).

Many early television programs used fragments of pre-existing music as themes. Some early effective examples of this practice are: "Sergeant Preston of the Yukon," which used Reznicek's overture to *Donna Diana*; "The Lone Ranger," which employed part of Rossini's overture to *Guillaume Tell*; and "Alfred Hitchcock Presents," which drew on Gounod's *Funeral March of a Marionette*. Other programs relied on libraries from small B-movie studios for their theme music. Early filmed TV Westerns, such as "Hopalong Cassidy" and "The Cisco Kid" are among these programs.

Theme music in television has developed through two generic categories: instrumental themes and theme songs (with lyrics). Of the notable theme songs in American TV history, several have persisted in American cultural memory, beginning with "The Ballad of Davy Crockett" by Tom Blackburn and George Bruns, and continuing with, among others, "The Ballad of Jed Clampett" (from "The Beverly Hillbillies") by Lester Flatt and Earl Scruggs (music) and Paul Henning (lyrics), "The Brady Bunch Theme" by Frank De Vol, "Three's Company" by Don Nicholl and Joe Raposo, and "I'll be there for you" ("Friends") by David Crane, Marta Kauffman, Michael Skloff, Allee Willis, Phil Sōlem, and Danny Wilde. Perhaps not coincidentally, many theme songs have correlated with situation comedies, Westerns, or children's programming, while instrumental themes tend to correlate with dramas, news, and documentary programs.

Although themes have been used to denote particular television programs, the musical style in which these themes have been composed has often served to connote the genre of the program. Musical style in this sense can be understood in relationship to commonly disseminated labels that have been popular with mass audiences, particularly the stylistic categories that have been adopted from format radio. Stylistic labels such as classical, jazz, rock, and country have been useful as signifying devices that correlate with television shows. For example, situation comedies of the 1950s usually featured music that could be described as light classical, and detective and private investigator programs of the 1960s often used jazz. The history of network television programs may be seen as a shift from light classical and the cinematic Hollywood symphonic style to a plethora of musical styles that includes rock and pop music.

Along with theme music, other extradiegetic musical devices are notable for TV: the "bumper" is a brief segment (three to five seconds) of music derived from the theme accompanying the logo of the show that is broadcast during commercial breaks. The bumper's function is to remind viewers that the show will return after commercials. "Act-ins' and "act-outs" are transition segments of music that transition from show to commercial or commercial to show. Musical act-ins have usually been accompanied by an establishing shot of the narrative setting, while act-outs have been accompanied by "stage waits" where the actors freeze a pose, usually in reaction to a suspenseful event. Both types of cues are heard as intradiegetic music (during the action of the show), but serve to transition to or from a commercial break.

2. Intradiegetic music.

Music also plays a role in narrative television by furnishing background, or "underscore," music for narrative programs, similar to the role of music in narrative films. Like film music, intradiegetic television music often uses themes as leitmotifs to signify characters and settings in a TV narrative. Music also creates moods in the story, recalls past events or predicts future events, builds action or suspense, reveals the inner thoughts of characters, and transitions from scene to scene. In the early years dramatic music on TV functioned much like its counterpart in film, often anchoring the audience to the image and sounds of a program and adding another dimension of sound and meaning to the show.

During the radiophonic era dramatic genres such as anthology dramas and soap operas were acted live on stage, and live music accompanied the action. In these programs a pianist, organist, or small orchestra would play as live action took place in an adjacent studio, with the conductor or solo performer watching a monitor. Because such production practice was expensive, many producers soon opted to use recorded music, where a music editor would "needle drop" musical cues from a vinyl LP record. This practice led to the AFM banning recorded music from its members until a deal for a system for paying royalties was negotiated in 1950 (even though no such system existed for the film industry).

As TV emerged in the late 1940s, film studios regarded it as a rival medium and either ignored it or sought to limit its influence. At the same time small, independent film companies sprang up to make films for television. Frederick Ziv, who developed a radio–television syndicate, became one of the most famous of these independent producers and began his career with the daytime children's Western series "The Cisco Kid," with music by Albert Glasser. Glasser set the trend in early TV scoring by recording a set of cues in France to circumvent the expense of hiring union musicians and to avoid the AFM ban. These cues were recycled in the show and even sold to other shows, creating a library like those used in B movies.

Glasser's work compiling his small library of cues for specific TV series led to imitators. The MUTEL ("Music for Television") Music Service was created by David Chudnow, a former music editor for Republic and Monogram film studios, in 1951. Many of the cues in MUTEL probably originated in stock tracking libraries that Chudnow had assembled for B movies in film studios where he was a music supervisor. Chudnow created MUTEL in part because of the AFM's ban on recording cues for TV tracking and partly as a way to market his pre-existing stock cue library. The MUTEL scoring service provided both custom themes for such early TV series as "The Adventures of Superman" and a library of cues for tracking episodes of many shows. Among the other TV series that made much use of MUTEL were "Racket Squad," "Captain Midnight," "Broken Arrow," "Annie Oakley," "Sky King," and "Ramar of the Jungle." Other TV music packaging services followed, including Omar Music, Gordon Music, Guild Production Aids, Structural Music, and the Capitol "Q"-Series Library (*see* PRODUCTION MUSIC).

The major film studios ended the boycott of network television in 1955, when Warner Bros. produced three programs, "Cheyenne," "King's Row," and "Casablanca," based on their earlier studio films. Of the three, only "Cheyenne," a Western starring Clint Walker, was successful. Music for the series was scored by the B-movie composers William Lava and Leith Stevens; the other two programs contained music by David Buttolph. As other film studios followed, many film music composers tried their hand at composing for the new medium. Bernard Herrmann, who had scored *Citizen Kane* and many of the Alfred Hitchcock films of the 1950s, composed the original theme music for "The Twilight Zone" and "Have Gun – Will Travel" and provided music for several episodes of these programs as well as cues for "Gunsmoke" and "The Alfred Hitchcock Hour." Leonard Rosenman, who composed scores for such films as *The Cobweb* and *East of Eden*, scored several episodes of "Combat!," "Marcus Welby, M.D.," and "The Virginian," among other TV shows. Herschel Burke Gilbert who composed several Academy Award–calibre film scores (*The Moon is Blue, Carmen Jones*), composed music for such TV Westerns as "The Rifleman" and "Gunsmoke" and for popular shows like "Perry Mason" and "Burke's Law." As television gained viewership, a symbiotic relationship between film and TV scoring became apparent, with many film composers working in television, but also newly minted television composers moving to film. Jerry Goldsmith worked primarily in television in the 1950s, scoring programs like "Climax!," "Dr. Kildare," and "The Man from U.N.C.L.E.," before breaking into film in the 1960s with scores for *Lonely are the Brave, Seven Days in May*, and *Von Ryan's Express*. John Williams, who began his career as a TV music copyist, scored programs like "Kraft Suspense Theater" and Irwin Allen's sci-fi series "The Time Tunnel" and "Lost in Space," before composing for blockbuster movies including the *Star Wars* and *Indiana Jones* films.

Much music in this cinematic period of TV was composed in the post-Romantic symphonic style of much Hollywood film music, but other musical styles began to creep into television music. Henry Mancini's "Peter Gunn" score and other programs of the late 1950s and early 1960s used jazz. The police drama "M Squad" featured a theme composed by Count Basie and a score by Shorty Rogers. Other shows that followed Basie's and Mancini's lead were "77 Sunset Strip" and "Hawaiian Eye," with words and music by Mack David and Jerry Livingston, respectively. Bluegrass and country music were included in pastoral programs like "The Beverly Hillbillies" and, later, "The Dukes of Hazard," the latter featuring music performed by Waylon Jennings.

Rock and pop music slowly made its way into intradiegetic television music, just as it had with diegetic television music. The first show to treat rock music intradiegetically was "The Monkees" in 1966. Taking advantage of the popularity of the Beatles' films *A Hard Day's Night* and *Help!*, the producers Bert Schneider and Bob Rafelson sought to create a made-for-TV group based on the Beatles that could be exploited for record sales. The program featured four charismatic actor-musicians shown performing songs composed by the Hollywood insiders Tommy Boyce and Bobby Hart in an unconventional weekly situation comedy format. Songs performed during the show blended diegetic and intradiegetic music that accompanied rapidly paced visual montages of the actors on screen. The commercial success of "The Monkees" led to at least one imitator, "The Partridge Family" (1970–74, with the teen-idol singer David Cassidy). The show also set a precedent for featuring pop music within a story line and was followed by programs like "Fame" (1982–7), a television adaptation of the film musical, and "Cop Rock" (1990), a bizarre and unsuccessful hybridization of police drama and film musical.

Other TV shows in the 1960s featured music that pointed to an increased influence of rock. "Hawaii Five-O," a police drama that had its début in 1968, featured a theme song composed by the CBS music director Morton Stevens with a big band sound and a rock beat played by Polynesian-sounding drums. "Ironside" (music by Quincy Jones) and "The Mod Squad" (music by Earle Hagen) also featured rock-influenced theme music as did Mike Post's scoring for "The Rockford Files."

Although these composers paved the way for greater musical stylistic diversity on television, authentic rock music truly came to narrative television with the program "Miami Vice." By 1984 music videos had become influential as purveyors of popular music in the United States, and the editing techniques of quick cuts and montage, and the surrealistic images of music video became compelling for television as well. The NBC president Brandon Tartikoff appointed Michael Mann to produce an "MTV cops" concept show, and Mann chose the Czech keyboard player Jan Hammer, who had played with the jazz-fusion group the Mahavishnu Orchestra in the 1970s, to compose music for the series. Hammer's theme suggests truly progressive rock of the 1980s, utilizing synthesizer, distorted guitar, and Latin-style percussion.

Hammer's music to "Miami Vice" marked the beginning of a postmodern "televideo" era for TV music in which the use of music on TV expanded, as did the multiplicity of musical styles on TV. Programs like "Northern Exposure" featured a wide array of intradiegetic music ranging from opera to blues, rock, and pop. The soundtrack of the show is permeated with music, and the distinction between diegetic and intradiegetic music is blurred. Post continued his work with scores that could be called easy listening or smooth jazz in "Hill Street Blues," and rock and world music in "NYPD Blue." Also, the proclivity demonstrated in "Miami Vice" to feature pop tunes in its narrative was copied by shows like "Beverly Hills, 90210," "The O.C.," "Buffy the Vampire Slayer," "Dawson's Creek," and "Grey's Anatomy." In turn, from the 1980s music exhibited postmodern traits of self-reflexive parody and pastiche in programs like "Chicago Hope," "Pee-wee's Playhouse," and "The Simpsons." Rap music, or at least a version of it, appeared with "The Fresh Prince of Bel-Air."

Despite the plethora of music styles featured in TV programs of the 1980s and 90s, the overall trend in narrative shows was to include less music. Shows like "Frasier" and "Seinfeld" had attenuated theme music at the beginning in order to get viewers into the show more quickly and to provide more time for advertising.

With the advent of cable television in the 1980s, and its specialty channels such as Home Box Office (HBO) and MTV, a strategy of narrowcasting was developed which involved programs being marketed to specific demographic audiences. Programs would also feature popular music that was often compiled on CD or MP3 downloads, and websites would be developed based on the show. Popular music that would appeal to this demographic was featured in episodes of the show, and music from these episodes in turn would be marketed through the sale of CDs and MP3 downloads and broadcast from Internet websites generated by the production studio and from fans. The result of such intertextual and intermedia proliferation of music has demonstrated the importance of multiple modes of presentation and highlighted the dominance of large corporate conglomerates that own both TV network and recording companies. Programs in the 1990s and 2000s like "Buffy the Vampire Slayer," "Dawson's Creek," "Beverly Hills, 90210," and "The X Files" generated many websites and music CD sales, all of which generated more interest in the TV show.

3. Diegetic television music.

The broadcasting of diegetic music—musicians performing on the screen—on early television was prevalent for two reasons: music performance was a continuation of the broadcast practices on radio and audiences were used to broadcast music; and music acts were inexpensive for fledgling TV stations to program.

As a novelty, early television broadcast a wide range of programs, from sporting events to current news events, as well as live artistic performances. Classical music broadcasts, in particular, were prevalent on American networks in the late 1940s and early 1950s, in part because television was considered an elite medium in its early years. Television sets were expensive, and owned only by a wealthier demographic, so programming was designed to cater to this audience.

NBC, in particular, continued many of its musical programs from its radio broadcasts of the 1940s, such as ten televised concerts of the NBC Symphony Orchestra between 1948 and 1954, when Arturo Toscanini retired as its conductor. These concerts were simulcast on NBC radio and television stations, a practice unique at the time. The NBC Opera Company produced forty-three different broadcasts from 1949 to 1964, beginning with Gian Carlo Menotti's *The Old Maid and the Thief* on 16 March 1949. The one-act opera was commissioned for NBC radio in 1939. NBC's first made-for-TV opera was Menotti's *Amahl and the Night Visitors*, first broadcast on 24 December 1951. Other television operas commissioned by the NBC Opera Unit included *The Marriage* by Bohuslav Martinů (1953), *Griffelkin* by Lukas Foss (1955), and *La grande Bretèche* by Stanley Hollingsworth (1957). CBS countered with television operas by Norman Dello Joio, Carlisle Floyd, Ezra Laderman, and Igor Stravinsky (*The Flood*, 1962), but perhaps became more famous for the broadcast of Leonard Bernstein's "Young People's Concerts," broadcast from Carnegie Hall from 1958 to 1972. NBC broadcast its last opera, Menotti's *The Labyrinth*, on 3 March 1963, while CBS halted opera broadcasts with Benjamin Lees's *Medea in Corinth* on 26 May 1974. ABC, while not specifically commissioning operas for television, periodically broadcast performances from the New York Metropolitan Opera in the early years of the network.

As TV sets became less expensive, more viewers from a wider demographic were able to buy them, and thus a plurality of musical styles was broadcast to appeal to the mass viewing market. Eventually, the special broadcasts and commissions for new classical works died out as other TV genres such as dramas, situation comedies, sporting events, and news and current events programs gained popularity. Almost all classical music broadcast, both of opera and from the concert hall, was taken over by such public television networks as PBS, which began in 1961.

The influence of Broadway on television was evident in the NBC broadcast of the Broadway musical *Peter Pan* starring Mary Martin in the title role. The musical was broadcast in color on 7 March 1955, as a special live presentation on the program "Producer's Showcase," a ninety-minute weekly anthology series. The musical was so popular, it was presented again in 1956 and 1960, with nearly the same cast for each broadcast. CBS responded later, by broadcasting *Once upon a Mattress*, a popular 1959 Broadway musical starring Carol Burnett, on 3 June 1964. Her appearance on this show catapulted her career with the network, leading to her presenting her own comedy–variety show (1967–78).

Also in this early period, variety shows were developed to feature musicians who adapted to the medium and were popular with audiences. One of the earliest musical stars was Perry Como, a popular crooner from radio whose smooth, satiny voice adapted well to television audio. Other popular musicians followed, notably, the singer Dean Martin (who co-hosted "The Colgate Comedy Hour" with Jerry Lewis), Arthur Godfrey, and Frank Sinatra, all of whom hosted their own TV shows. Some big-band personalities also made the transition to television: Tommy and Jimmy Dorsey hosted the program "Stage Show" (1954), the bandleader Fred Waring hosted "The Fred Waring Show" (from 1949), and Paul Whiteman hosted "Paul Whiteman's Goodyear Revue" (1949–52) and "On the Boardwalk with Paul Whiteman" (1954). The most successful was the bandleader Lawrence Welk, who hosted "The Lawrence Welk Show" for more than twenty-five years from 1955.

During the 1950s and 60s diegetic music on television developed primarily in two areas: the musical variety show that abandoned the vaudeville format and sought greater sophistication through jazz and Broadway music; and the late-night talk show. In the variety format, stars like Sinatra and Como continued hosting programs in which they and guest stars sang jazz standards and Broadway show tunes. Nat "King" Cole, a talented jazz pianist and vocalist, sought to break the colour barrier on television with "The Nat King Cole Show" in 1956. Seeking to host his own show after scoring many hit records in the 1950s, Cole sang, played piano, and featured dozens of renowned jazz artists. Although NBC was supportive of the show, a sponsor could never be found, and Cole cancelled the show after a one-year run. Dinah Shore proved that women musicians could host their own programs, starring in "The Dinah Shore Chevy Show" that began in 1956 and ran through 1963. The popular film and Broadway star Judy Garland also hosted her own show for a season (1963). Other shows followed, hosted by the musicians Sammy Davis, Jr., Steve Allen, Leslie Uggams, Danny Kaye, Steve Lawrence, and Dean Martin. Perhaps the most popular and successful of all variety shows was "The Andy Williams Show," which ran off and on from 1962 to 1971. As rock music became more popular, shows by the Smothers Brothers and Sonny and Cher were featured as experiments as to how the new musical form would adapt to the old format of the variety show. While these programs sought to cater to a new generation of TV watchers, they mostly rehashed the old formulas of standard variety shows.

Despite the popularity of musicians hosting their own programs, the program perhaps most responsible for broadcasting the widest variety of musical styles on television was "The Ed Sullivan Show," hosted by Ed Sullivan, a former newspaper columnist and critic. Sullivan had a talent for identifying performers, especially musicians, who would attract viewers to the program. His show was one of the longest running in television history, beginning in June 1948 and running until CBS cancelled it in 1971. Along with comedy, dance, and acrobatic acts every week, Sullivan featured music performances of classical, jazz, Broadway, opera, folk, rock, and soul. The show was especially noted for widely introducing Elvis Presley (1956) and the Beatles (1964) onto the American music scene. In addition, Sullivan brought to the show such rock bands as the Rolling Stones, the Four Seasons, the Animals, Gladys Knight and the Pips, and the Who; such jazz greats as Cole, the Duke Ellington Orchestra, the Mills Brothers, and Louis Armstrong; and classical and pop-classical artists like Sergio Franchi, Jan Peerce, Liberace, Roberta Peters, and Itzhak Perlman. Sullivan's show exemplified the musical eclecticism of network TV that was prevalent in its formative years but which had waned by the 1980s.

Music also played a significant role on late-night talk shows. One of the earliest experiments in late-night television was "Tonight!," which premiered in 1953 and starred Steve Allen, a notable comedian, jazz pianist, and writer of more than eight thousand songs. The show featured plenty of jazz played by Allen himself and the NBC Orchestra, which at the time was a jazz big band directed by Skitch Henderson. Allen also hosted jazz musicians on the show, blazing a televisual trail for African American jazz artists including Earl Hines, Billie Holiday, Lionel Hampton, Sarah Vaughan, Dizzy Gillespie, and Miles Davis. After "Tonight!" Allen went on to host other late-night and prime-time shows including "The Steve Allen Show," featuring the Donn Trenner Orchestra, which included such virtuoso musicians as the guitarist Herb Ellis and the trombonist Frank Rosolino. Later incarnations of "Tonight!" included the same high standards in music. Jack Paar's show featured his orchestra director José Melis. Skitch Henderson returned in 1962 with "The Tonight Show starring Johnny Carson," but left in 1966 and was replaced first by Milton DeLugg, who was in turn replaced by Henderson's lead trumpeter, Carol "Doc" Severinsen, who headed the NBC Orchestra until Carson's retirement in 1992. After Carson, "The Tonight Show with Jay Leno" featured the jazz saxophonist Branford Marsalis as bandleader from 1992 to 1995; Marsalis was replaced by Kevin Eubanks, a Berklee-trained musician who was the band's guitarist. After Allen's show, music was used mostly for "play-ons" and "play-offs," that is, music to bring guests onto and off the stage. However, talk shows frequently had the orchestras play to the audience during commercial breaks and often featured the band alone or with guest performers.

Jazz and swing artists dominated both variety show and late-night talk genres in the 1960s and 70s. Big bands were led by such swing artists as David Rose ("The Red Skelton Show"), Les Brown ("The Bob Hope Show," "The Steve Allen Show," "The Dean Martin Show," "The Hollywood Palace"), Sammy Spear ("The Jackie Gleason Show"), Skitch Henderson ("Tonight!"), Severinson ("The Tonight Show starring Johnny Carson"), Mitch Miller ("Startime," "The Mitch Miller Show," "Sing along with Mitch"), Johnny Mann ("The Joey Bishop Show"), and Mort Lindsey ("The Merv Griffin Show"), among others. The jazz pianist Billy Taylor became the first African American to become the music director of a talk show, performing on "The David Frost Show" from 1969 to 1972. By the 1990s and 2000s successful imitations of Carson's talk show included "The Late Show with David Letterman," featuring Paul Shaeffer, a keyboard player who started his career on "Saturday Night Live"; "The Arsenio Hall Show" with bandleader Michael Wolff; and "Late Night with Conan O'Brien," featuring the Max Weinberg Seven, whose leader was also the drummer for Bruce Springsteen's E Street Band.

Despite the hegemony of jazz, Broadway, and Tin Pan Alley standards, rock gradually made headway in American television, beginning with Elvis Presley's appearance on "Stage Show" on 4 February 1956. That same year, he also performed for "The Milton Berle Show," "The Steve Allen Show," and "The Ed Sullivan Show." After Presley's success on his show, Sullivan, in particular, began to feature rock-and-roll artists, which culminated in his hosting of the Beatles on 7 February 1964, another landmark event.

Although shows like Sullivan's helped to bring rock music into the TV mainstream, rock and pop music was popular on locally produced shows that aired to local youth audiences. One such show was "American Bandstand" which made the jump from a local TV music show in Philadelphia to a nationally syndicated series on 5 August 1957. The show began as a local music show in 1952, hosted by two Philadelphia DJs. When Dick Clark took over the nationally syndicated version in 1957, he brought in top pop acts daily until 1963, then weekly until 1987. The show featured ordinary (but auditioned) teenagers dancing to recorded music and guest artists including, among others, Danny & the Juniors, Fats Domino, Jerry Lee Lewis, Connie Francis, Fabian, and Patsy Cline (in the 1950s); Smokey Robinson, Marvin Gaye, and Cass Eliot (1960s); Stevie Wonder, Billy Preston, Tony Orlando, Marilyn McCoo, and Michael Jackson (1970s); and Billy Ocean, Gary U.S. Bonds, and Huey Lewis and the News (1980s).

The success of "American Bandstand" marked a shift in musical style on television, as appearances of jazz and Tin Pan Alley musicians began to decline, while appearances by rock stars became more frequent. Clark produced a spin-off show called "Where the Action Is" (1965–74), in which many top American and British

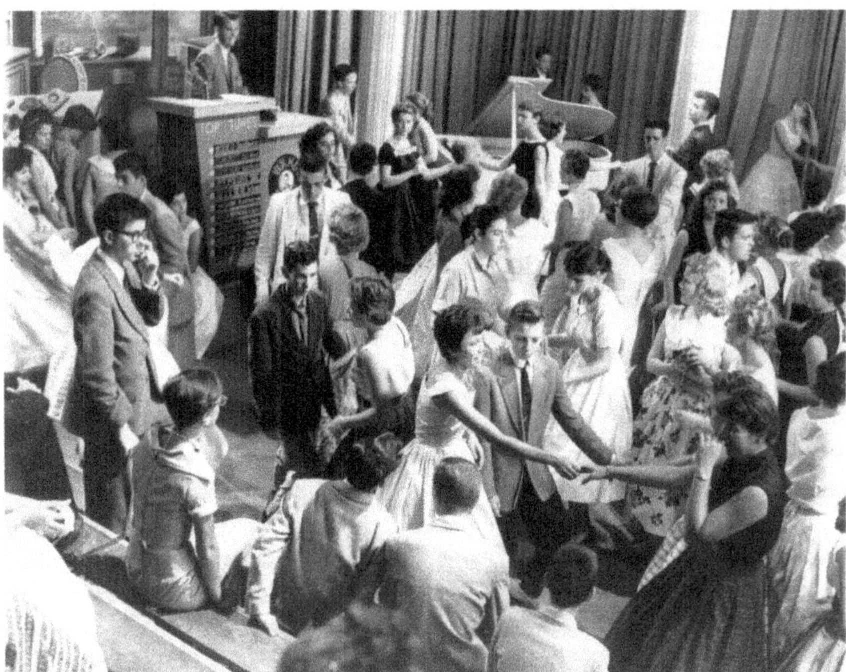

Dick Clark, at podium at upper left, and a roomful of young music fans at a recording of "American Bandstand" in 1958.
(AP Photo)

acts starred, including Otis Redding, the Four Seasons, the Association, the Zombies, Peter and Gordon, and the Everly Brothers. Regulars on almost every show were the made-for-TV pop group Paul Revere and the Raiders. Shorter-lived, youth-oriented variety shows were "Shindig" (1964–6, on ABC), which was hosted by the DJ Jimmy O'Neil and featured its house band, the Shindogs, and a female vocal quartet, the Blossoms; and "Hullabaloo," a more buttoned-down show on NBC. Other rock variety shows that aired on American television through these years included "The Lloyd Thaxton Show," "Solid Gold," "Soul Train," "Don Kirshner's Rock Concert," and "The Midnight Special." Of these, "Soul Train," an African American version of "American Bandstand" hosted by Don Cornelius, was still in syndication in the early 2010s after beginning in 1971.

Country music also had a few outlets in national television, notably "Ozark Mountain Jubilee," (ABC, 1955–61), "The Tennessee Ernie Ford Show" (NBC, ABC 1955–65), and "The Johnny Cash Show" (1969–71). "Hee Haw," a comedy–variety show starring the country musicians Buck Owens and Roy Clark, was also popular, and "Austin City Limits" (from 1975) has featured blues, rock, folk, bluegrass, and related styles broadcast from the public television station KLRU (formerly KLRN) at the University of Texas, Austin. Finally, the folk music movement was represented in its heyday by ABC's "Hootenanny," which had its début in 1963, but lasted only one season due to a controversy created when Pete Seeger and the Weavers refused to sign government loyalty oaths to appear on the show.

Perhaps the shift toward pop and rock reached its greatest outlet on television with "Saturday Night Live," an innovative comedy–variety show that aired during the late-night talk show slot on Saturday on NBC. The program began its run in 1975 and was still being broadcast in the 2010s. Besides featuring its own house band, the show presented a weekly guest musical group, usually a popular rock band or solo artist. By the beginning of the twenty-first century, the show had employed a variety of music directors.

Yet another diegetic music genre is the talent show, in which non-celebrities perform on television. An early version was "The Original Amateur Hour," which was an adaptation of a radio favorite, "Major Bowes Amateur Hour." A few other programs followed, including a comic spin on the genre with "The Gong Show," and in the 2000s shows like "America's Got Talent" appeared. The genre reached its most elegant and popular form with "American Idol," in which amateur singers compete for a major recording contract.

With the advent of cable television, audiences became more fragmented, as new networks sprang up trying to appeal to target audiences. As the three primary networks lost influence and audiences, others changed the face of music in television. The greatest of these new musical cable networks was MTV, which began broadcasting music videos in 1981. Imitations of MTV were developed for other niche demographic markets during the 1980s and 90s, notably VH1 (for older rockers), Black Entertainment Television, Country Music Television, and the Nashville Network, not to mention music specials on premium cable channels such as HBO and Showtime. The popularity of music videos soon became apparent as another medium by which to broadcast music and to bolster record sales.

4. Cartoon music.

Children's cartoon shows provided the same types of music as that found in adult programming. Although many early cartoons on television were transplants from earlier film shorts (MGM's *Tom and Jerry,* Warner Bros.' *Merrie Melodies,* and Fleischer Studios' *Popeye the Sailor*), made-for-TV cartoons developed by the late 1950s and flourished by the 1960s. To appeal to the new baby-boomer generation, a spate of cartoon shows were produced by William Hanna and Joseph Barbera ("The Ruff and Reddy Show," "The Huckleberry Hound Show," "The Yogi Bear Show," "The Flintstones," and "The Jetsons"), whose scores and theme songs were composed by Hoyt Curtin; these continued through the 1990s with programs like "Smurfs" (which included collage scores containing classical pieces), "Scooby-Doo," and "Jonny Quest." Walt Disney adapted its cartoons to television along with its entire production stable, and by the 1990s the studio had its own network on cable television. Another notable cartoon series was "Rugrats," produced in 1991 for the Nickelodeon children's cable network with music by Mark and Bob Mothersbaugh; the former was a founder of the band Devo and composed music for other shows like "Clifford the Big Red Dog," and "Pee-wee's Playhouse." Subsequently animated shows such as "The Simpsons" (theme music by Danny Elfman, music by Alf Clausen), "Family Guy" (music by Walter Murphy and Ron Jones), and "King of the Hill" (theme music by the Refreshments, music by Roger Neill and Greg Edmonson) have followed the format of "The Flintstones" as adult cartoons and have employed music imaginatively, using musical style and specific pieces to conjure up parody, metaphor, and irony in their narratives. These programs have also revealed a different kind of labor separation in the TV music business, as numerous composers, orchestrators, conductors, and arrangers have been involved in their production.

5. Advertising music.

Music in TV advertising reflects many of the trends for television music in general. As in television programming, music in commercials may also be considered to operate extradiegetically, intradiegetically, and diegetically. In its early form it tended to be in a light classical style (although several popular songs were also appropriated with new lyrics extolling the product), with some experiments with jazz, while rock and pop styles were developed from the 1970s to the 2000s. The primary form of musical advertising in the early years of television was the "jingle," usually defined as a brief, catchy tune with lyrics that included the name of the product being advertised. Like TV themes, jingles have persisted in the memory of many American TV watchers. Such jingles as "You can trust your car to the man who wears the star" (Texaco), "Snap! Crackle! Pop!" (Kellogg's Rice Krispies), "When you've said Budweiser, you've said it all" (Budweiser), and "Winston tastes good, like a cigarette should" (R.J. Reynolds Tobacco Co.) were common during the heyday of the televisual jingle. Like television music itself, commercials evolved to use pop and rock music, begun perhaps by the cola wars of advertising between Coca-Cola and Pepsi. In 1969 the Coca-Cola Co. bought into an advertising campaign in which hundreds of youths from around the world were pictured with bottles of Coke singing a pop-style song, "I'd like to teach the world to sing." Pepsi followed suit with their own advertising campaigns, eventually using celebrities in their commercials: from 1984 Michael Jackson sang new lyrics to his pop songs (for example, "You're a whole new generation" to the tune of his hit Billy Jean) and allowed the use of his songs as underscore (Bad); and from 1991 Ray Charles sang the jingle "You've got the right one, baby." Another notable campaign was the "Like a Rock" campaign for Chevrolet (General Motors) trucks in the 1990s, which used the song by the American rock singer Bob Seger. After the 1990s, jingles as an advertising strategy were used less and less by advertising agencies, causing several jingle composers to bemoan the loss.

Besides jingles, music in commercials has often served to underscore dramatic action on the screen. In this regard TV commercials can be segmented into several types, such as mini-narratives ("slice of life") and testimonials, all of which flourished side by side on network television. Regardless of form, both advertising professionals and music scholars have commented that music functions in specific ways in successful campaigns, notably by creating moods and feelings, and can unify aspects of an advertisement by being entertaining and able to wed the visuals to the message, highlight the action, embellish the optical effects, and give an inexpensively and locally produced spot the feeling of being a Hollywood production. It has been said that music should arrest the viewer's attention and provide a structural continuity to the ad.

Much early thinking about music in advertising centered on the philosophies of Rosser Reeves, who believed music should contain a strong advertising message and appeal to the widest possible demographic. As television evolved, however, music followed the narrowcasting strategy of targeting specific market demographics by using rock and pop for young audiences, country music for rural audiences, and so on. Most theorists on advertising music agree that, above all, music in commercials should be entertaining, with a lyrical language that simultaneously establishes authority or advocacy for a product, while producing an artistic surface message that sugar-coats the appeal to buy a commodity with an aesthetic dimension of music.

See also FILM MUSIC AND TELEVISION MUSICAL.

Bibliography

R. Bowman: "Music for Films in Television," *Film Music Notes*, viii/5 (1949), 20

J.F. Cooke: "The New World of Television: a Conference with Paul Whiteman," *Etude*, no.67 (1949), 341–2

H. Sosnik: "Scoring for Television," *Variety* (5 Jan 1949), 95

B.B. Nalle: "Music for Television Drama," *Music Journal*, xx/1 (1962), 120–21

H. Castleman and W.J. Podrazik: *Watching TV: Four Decades of American Television* (New York, 1982)

W. Woodward: *An Insider's Guide to Advertising Music* (New York, 1982)

R. Faulkner: *Music on Demand: Composers and Careers in the Hollywood Film Industry* (New Brunswick, 1983)

S. Westcott: *A Comprehensive Bibliography of Music for Film and TV* (Detroit, 1985)

W. Hawes: *American Television Drama: the Experimental Years* (Birmingham, AL, 1986)

J. Fiske: *Television Culture* (London, 1987)

E.A. Kaplan: *Rocking around the Clock: Music Television, Postmodernism, and Consumer Culture* (New York, 1987)

D. Huron: "Music in Advertising: an Analytic Paradigm," *MQ*, lxxiii (1989), 557–74

S. Karmen: *Through the Jingle Jungle* (New York, 1989)

W. Boddy: *Fifties Television: the Industry and its Critics* (Urbana, IL, 1990)

L.M. Scott: "Understanding Jingles and Needledrop: a Rhetorical Approach to Music in Advertising," *Journal of Consumer Research*, xvii (1990), 223–36

R. Williams: *Television: Technology and Cultural Form* (Middletown, CT, 1992)

J. Burlingame: *TV's Biggest Hits: the Story of Television Themes from "Dragnet" to "Friends"* (New York, 1996)

N. Cook: *Analyzing Musical Multimedia* (New York, 1998)

J. Mundy: *Popular Music on Screen* (Manchester, 1999)

P. Tagg: *Kojak, Fifty Seconds of Television Music: toward the Analysis of Affect in Popular Music* (New York, 2000)

M. Weingarten: *Station to Station: the History of Rock 'n' Roll on Television* (New York, 2000)

P. Mandell: "Production Music in Television's Golden Age: an Overview," *Performing Arts: Broadcasting*, ed. I. Newsome (Washington, DC, 2002), 148–69

J. Barnes: *Television Opera: the Fall of Opera Commissioned for Television* (Woodbridge, UK, 2003)

T. McCourt and N. Zuberi: "Music on Television," *Encyclopedia of Television* (Chicago, 2004), 1569–77

K.J. Donnelly: *The Spectre of Sound: Music in Film and Television* (London, 2005)

G. Edgerton: *The Columbia History of American Television* (New York, 2007)

R. Rodman: *Tuning In: American Narrative Television Music* (New York, 2009)

J. Deaville, ed.: *Music in Television: Channels of Listening* (New York and London, 2011)

D. Railton and P. Weston: *Music Video and the Politics of Representation* (Edinburgh, 2011)

K.J. Donnelly and P. Hayward: *Music in Science Fiction Television: Tuned to the Future* (New York, 2013)

N. Graakjær: *Analyzing Music in Advertising: Television Commercials and Consumer Choice* (New York and London, 2015)

J. Halfyard: *Sounds of Fear and Wonder: Music in Cult TV* (London, 2016)

L. Giuffre and P. Hayward: *Music in Comedy Television: Notes on Laughs* (New York, 2017)

RONALD W. RODMAN/R

Television musical

A type of musical created expressly for the television format with live actors. It developed in much the same way as its stage counterpart: it first appeared as a variety or spectacular format, then as song- and dance-driven revue shows, next as stand-alone revues or book-driven works, and, in a development unique to the medium of television, as an entirely musical series, often uniting elements of the book musical and the revue in a hybrid format.

Although regular broadcast television did not emerge in the United States until 1948, the first made-for-television musical was aired in 1944: *The Boys from Boise*, with music by Sam Medoff. Early television musicals included either musical theater numbers that were generally unrelated to a central theme or they featured occasional musical numbers (sometimes dances) typically interspersed with nonmusical acts, much like vaudeville. In one famous example from 1954, the major networks of the time all broadcast "A General Foods Tribute to Rodgers and Hammerstein," with an all-star cast. Notable examples of the variety format include "The Texaco Star Theater" with Milton Berle, which migrated from radio in 1948 and ran until 1956, and "The Ed Sullivan Show" (1948–71). Later shows featured song or dance more prominently in what might be loosely defined as a revue but which often featured music and dance styles atypical for the musical theater stage of the time, since they were heavily influenced by popular music. Some examples of this format include the influential "American Bandstand" (1952–89), which featured performances by pop stars and teens dancing to contemporary pop music, and later talent-contest–driven shows such as "Star Search" (1983–95, 2002–4) and "American Idol" (from 2002). Beginning in 2006, with the British hit "How do you Solve a Problem like Maria?," a talent competition focused on casting a major role in a West End revival of *The Sound of Music*, a new subgenre of such contests emerged focused specifically on the casting of stage musicals, including *Joseph and the Amazing Technicolor Dreamcoat* and *Oliver!* in London and *Grease* and *Legally Blonde* on Broadway.

In the category of stand-alone musicals on television, two distinct types exist. The first includes pieces written specifically for television, with characters unique to these one-time events and featuring original scores, some by creative teams drawn from the Broadway stage; they are usually libretto-driven. While the first opera written for television, *Amahl and the Night Visitors* (1951), by Gian Carlo Menotti, set the precedent for this type of show, Richard Rodgers and Oscar Hammerstein's *Cinderella* (1957) and Stephen Sondheim's *Evening Primrose* (1966) stand as the most famous and acclaimed of the early examples. Disney has found great success with made-for-television stand-alone book musicals such as *High School Musical* (2006) and *Camp Rock* (2008), both of which spawned numerous sequels and theatrical adaptations. The second type consists of single musical episodes of a normally nonmusical television series. These have appeared on many series, the first being the 1956 "operetta" episode of "I Love Lucy," and they most often are in revue formats, as they were on "The Drew Carey Show," "7th Heaven," and "Ally McBeal" and on numerous animated series, most prominently "The Simpsons" and "Family Guy," Sometimes such episodes have emerged as sophisticated, libretto-driven pieces. The series "Buffy the Vampire Slayer" (1997–2003) famously produced an acclaimed musical episode, *Once More, with Feeling* (2001); other examples occurred in a 2007 "Scrubs" episode and in two "Xena: Warrior Princess" episodes in 1998 and 1999.

The third type of television musical is unique to the medium – an entirely musical series. This approach, though popular on British television, found only limited success with American audiences until 2009. The earliest example of the form is the 1968 American series "That's Life" on ABC, which attempted to blend a one-hour situation comedy format with an original book musical. It lasted only eight episodes. Dennis Potter's British miniseries "Pennies from Heaven" (1978), "The Singing Detective" (1986), and "Lipstick on your Collar" (1993) pioneered the form in the United Kingdom. All employed the unusual convention of singers' lip-synching to pre-recorded tracks, typically of well-known British pop songs. Later British miniseries hits "Blackpool" (2004) and its sequel "Viva Blackpool" (2005) also employed the Potter lip-synching convention, which may have contributed to the flop of their American counterpart, "Viva Laughlin" (2007), canceled after two episodes. Other American flops include a musical series based on the film *Seven Brides for Seven Brothers* (1982–3) which ran for twenty-two episodes, and "Cop Rock" (1990), which melded the police drama with the musical but lasted only eleven episodes. With the advent of the smash hit "Glee" in 2009, the musical television series finally found success with American audiences; the Emmy award winning series ran for six seasons. "Glee" melded elements of the British formula for television musical success with new American ones. It mainly uses previously released music, nearly all of it in a pop idiom, but departs from the Potter precedent by having the actors themselves perform the songs. Post "Glee," several other American musical series have emerged, to varying degrees of success. Many have functioned as backstage

A scene from the "Glee" pilot episode, 2009. From left: Jenna Ushkowitz, Chris Colfer, Kevin McHale, Amber Riley, Lea Michele.
Fox Broadcasting/Photofest ©Fox Broadcasting

musicals, taking viewers behind the scenes of a Broadway musical in "Smash" (2012–13), the country music scene in "Nashville" (2012–16), and a hip hop music studio in "Empire" (from 2015). Other recent American musical series, including "Crazy Ex-Girlfriend" (from 2015) and "Galavant" (2015–16), have dispensed with the realistic behind-the-scenes framework, and have instead allowed their characters to burst into song much as their stage counterparts might.

Bibliography

W.T. Leonard: *Theatre: Stage to Screen to Television* (Metuchen, NJ, 1981)

G.W. Woolery: *Animated TV Specials: the Complete Directory to the First Twenty-Five Years, 1962–1987* (Metuchen, NJ, 1989)

R.C. Lynch: *TV and Studio Cast Musicals on Record: Discography of Television Musicals and Studio Recordings of Stage and Film Music* (Westport, CT, 1990)

A. McNeil: *Total Television: a Comprehensive Guide to Programming from 1948 to the Present* (New York, 3/1991)

V. Terrace: *Television Specials: 3,201 Entertainment Spectaculars, 1939–1993* (Jefferson, NC, 1995)

J. Baxter: *Television Musicals: Plots, Critiques, Casts and Credits for 222 Shows, 1944–1996* (Jefferson, NC, 1997)

M. Weingarten: *Station to Station: the History of Rock and Roll on Television* (New York, 2000)

J.K. Muir: *Singing a New Tune* (New York, 2005)

R. Knapp: *The American Musical and the Performance of Personal Identity* (Princeton, NJ, 2006)

M.J. Lodge: "Beyond 'Jumping the Shark': the New Television Musical," *Studies in Musical Theatre*, i (2008), 293–305

S. Horburn: "Unifying the Audience: an Overview of Television Musicals," *Sound and Music in Film and Visual Media* (New York, 2009) 261–83

R. Stillwell: "The Television Musical," *The Oxford Handbook of the American Musical* (New York, 2011), 152–66

K. Kessler: "Broadway in the Box: Television's Infancy and the Cultural Cachet of the Great White Way," *Journal of Popular Music Studies*, xxv/3 (2013), 349–70

J. Sternfeld: "'Everything's Coming Up Kurt': the Broadway Song in *Glee*," *Gestures of Music Theater: the Performativity of Song and Dance* (New York, 2014) 128–45

M. Lodge: "Big Dreams on the Small Screen: the Television Musical," *The Cambridge Companion to the Musical* (Cambridge, 2017), 423–37

MARY JO LODGE

Video [music video]

In their relationship to music, the terms "video" and "music video" are used primarily to refer to a form of short film, whose soundtrack exclusively or predominantly consists of a popular song, its origins intended for television presentation with the purpose of promoting a recording of the song. Since the early 1980s, especially with the advent of MTV in 1981, music videos have been integral to the marketing procedures of popular music. In the early twenty-first century they spread to new media, including computers and portable smart phones. Despite their name, music videos, or video clips, were initially produced using traditional celluloid film technology and transformed to electronic media in the post-production process. In the 2000s the production process moved toward digital filming technology, and the use of CGI (computer-generated imagery) in post-production became increasingly prevalent. More than simply marketing devices, music videos in the early 2000s became commercial products and aesthetic objects in their own right: they were viewed in the form of DVD collections, television shows, and such websites as YouTube, in much the same way as sound recordings.

1. History.

The predecessors of music video in its early twenty-first-century form can be traced back to the experiments to synchronize film with recorded sound that began in the earliest days of film. These experiments also included forms governed by the primary determinant distinguishing music video from narrative film music: the use of the film medium for visual illustration of songs as opposed to the film music practice of providing music to accompany visual narration. Thus in the 1910s and 1920s silent "song-plug" films were produced that were presented with live performances of the songs that they illustrated. An additional significant precursor of music videos starting in the late 1920s are the song numbers of film musicals, which resemble music videos inasmuch as many of the most popular videos have been song and dance numbers set to popular music, and because an element of fantasy is found in both forms. The synchronization of action to pre-recorded music soundtracks in animated films is a further important precursor. Such films were produced by the German filmmaker Oskar von Fischinger from 1921, and this technique was popularized in Disney's series of *Silly Symphonies* short films (from 1929) and the full-length animation *Fantasia* (1940). During the 1930s and 1940s a great number of musical short films were produced, each featuring one or two songs by a popular artist and intended as preludes to the main feature film in cinemas. In the 1940s "visual jukebox" films under the designation Panoram Soundies were produced in the United States, followed in the 1960s by the French color film jukebox Scopitone. Other predecessors of and possible influences on music video include such experimental films as Fernand Léger's *Ballet mécanique* (1924), with music by Georges Antheil, and Dziga Vertov's *Man with a Movie Camera* (1929), whose highly rhythmic editing style closely resembles many a music video. Following on from the tradition of the film musical, the images and sounds of "youth films" starting in the 1950s certainly influenced the audiovisual style of some music videos. The techniques of dramatizing popular songs on television, notably on the 1950s American show "Your Hit Parade," were an additional influence. Avant-garde video art starting in the 1960s is thought by several commentators to have influenced the aesthetic style of music videos, as well as stylistic incorporations from such earlier artistic movements as surrealism.

The expanding pop culture of the 1960s furthered the development of new conventions concerning the visualization of rock music, not least through the influence of the Beatles films directed by Richard Lester, *A Hard Day's Night* (1964) and *Help!* (1965). The Beatles, as well as other British groups, also produced early examples of "promo films" promoting particular songs (e.g., "Penny Lane" and "Strawberry Fields Forever") intended for television presentation and featuring many of the formal characteristics typical of later videos; these, however, did not attract any wider attention or achieve tangible commercial effects. The impact of Elvis Presley's film musicals in the United States was comparable, although this was more in terms of the image of the star performer than the way the visuals were edited to music. The first video alleged to have had a substantial influence on sales of a song was the clip produced by Jon Roseman and Bruce Gowers for Queen's "Bohemian Rhapsody" in 1975; for that reason, as well as for its then innovative use of visual special effects, it is often cited as the first music video. Following this example, during the second half of the 1970s an increasing number of video clips were produced, notably by artists with a marked emphasis on visual image elements, such as David Bowie in the United Kingdom and Devo in the United States. Frank Zappa produced a number of film shorts, including *Inca Roads* (1974) and *City of Tiny Lites* (1979), which employed the avant-garde technique of stop animation. Something similar is found in Peter Gabriel's acclaimed "Sledgehammer" video, produced in 1986 by Stephen Johnson in collaboration with Nick Park of Aardman Animations and the Brothers Quay. The animation technique known as rotoscoping, which involves tracing outlines from filmed images, is found in several early videos, notably the Norwegian group A-Ha's "Take on me" (dir. S. Barron, 1985).

Music video proper emerged in the early 1980s as a routine marketing technique for popular music. Its development as a form was closely connected to corresponding technological and demographic changes. Satellite and cable technology had enabled the establishment of specialized commercial television channels aimed at particular segments of the audience, known as narrowcasting. This technology was used for the dissemination of music video to a pop and rock audience whose relationship with the medium of television had grown less antagonistic than it had been in the earlier days of rock history. MTV, the first twenty-four-hour music video cable channel, was launched in the United States on 1 August 1981. Its impact as a promotional tool was allegedly demonstrated by such phenomena as the success of British "new wave," "new romantic," and "synth pop" styles in the United States. Music video was rapidly established as a regular element in the marketing of popular music. Production budgets and aesthetic ambitions soon increased, an illustrative example being the extravagant thirteen-minute video produced for Michael Jackson's "Thriller" (dir. J. Landis, Epic Records, 1982). MTV was followed by other cable and satellite video services, such as VH-1 (1985) in the United States and Music Box (1984), MTV Europe (1987), the Power Station (1990), and the Voice (2004) in various European countries.

The technological shift since the late 1990s toward distribution via the internet and high-speed wireless communication has led to some noticeable transformations in the patterns of production and consumption associated with music videos. Such social networking sites as YouTube have become a primary channel for distributing the promotional material of popular artists, including music videos. This direction has accelerated as a result of record industry involvement in this mode of distribution. The same is true of Apple's iTunes, which in the early 2010s was selling music videos for consumption on a variety of media, from personal computers to cell phones. Other platforms and operating systems were offering similar availability. Despite the primary mode of music video distribution shifting to the internet, MTV, the cable channel that instigated the music video boom of the 1980s, has itself moved toward more lucrative forms of programming, notably reality television. Robbie Williams' album *Reality killed the video star* (Virgin, 2009) comments on this turn toward reality television in much the same way as the Buggles' song "Video killed the radio star" (dir. R. Malcahy, Island, 1979)—the video of which was the first to be shown on MTV—announced the birth of the era of music videos. It is worth noting that during the early twenty-first century music video aesthetics were permeating other audiovisual forms, including the editing style of feature films, video games, live performances, and such online forms as fan videos and mash-ups.

A small number of performing artists have made a significant cultural impact on the development of music videos. Most of these have extended the song and dance tradition of film musicals. Numerous mainstream pop artists in North America belong to this group, including Madonna, Prince, and Michael Jackson in the 1980s; Britney Spears, Jennifer Lopez, Pink, and Justin Timberlake in the 1990s; and Katy Perry, Rihanna, Beyoncé Knowles, and Lady Gaga in the 2000s. Aside from mainstream pop, visually orientated performers, including Björk, Peter Gabriel, and Gorillaz (fronted by Blur's Damon Albarn), collaborating with recognized visual artists, have had a significant impact on music video aesthetics. Music videos have also been an important distribution and marketing device to artists working in such genres as rap, alternative rock, electronic dance music, metal, and punk.

2. Aesthetics.

Since the visual dimension of music video is created with the purpose of visualizing a popular song, its formal disposition tends bear a close relation to the structural aspects of song form. Most of the musicological research on music videos supports the contention that they take as their starting point the structures of the pre-existing songs. Videos are built around the verses, choruses, and bridges, lower-level phrase structures, and in many cases individual beats of songs. Images respond to the rhythms of the music but are never fully determined by them. Typically the relationship is more flexible and dynamic. Rhythm is not the only relevant factor, however. Visual images may also be shaped in more indeterminate ways by the melodic lines, timbres, harmonic textures, and the general affective tone of the music, as well as by the linguistic imagery and semantic content of song lyrics. The centrality of the image of the star performer is a further factor that should not be overlooked. The star often becomes an idée fixe in the visual palette employed by the director. Often the entire focus of a video will be the director's representations of a performer's star identity. So prevalent is this modus operandi that the effects of challenging it—for example, in videos by Gorillaz, Aphex Twin, and George Michael—are striking.

Visual narration is sometimes based on narrative elements in the words of the song, but generally narration in a video tends to be radically condensed and is rather fragmentary. A second important category of visual content is the one constituted by the imagery of musical performance, which is often set in surroundings simulating the conventions of stage performance of rock and pop music. In addition to visual narrative and performance images, many videos feature a rapidly shifting montage of more or less coherent images not immediately relatable to the words of the song; this type of visual material ("dreamlike visuals") has come to be regarded as typical and bears a conspicuous similarity to the techniques of surrealist visual artists working several decades earlier. Animation and technical special effects are often used to create striking and unusual images. Visual thematics are often strongly influenced by conventional genre norms in different popular genres, such as the gothic horror imagery common in heavy metal videos or the use of "realistic" street images in videos featuring artists who aspire to established notions of rock authenticity. In addition, visual quotations from various areas of popular culture—film, television, advertising—as well as from high art, are common.

3. Theory.

Research on music videos in the 1980s was largely instigated by E. Ann Kaplan's pathbreaking work. Several aspects of her writing are worthy of mention. First, she theorizes music videos in relation to then popular psychoanalytical theories of spectatorship in the field of film studies. Her understanding of the visual dimension of music videos allows her to pay close attention to theories of media flow, the analysis of visual style, and matters of mise-en-scène. Kaplan's writing pays close attention to gender representation, which she theorizes by means of a conceptual apparatus drawing on Laura Mulvey's writing on the "scopophilic" gaze (implying voyeurism) and Lacanian psychoanalytical theory. Especially impressive is her analysis of Madonna: she describes her as a new type of gutsy female performer whose ambiguous representation in videos both affirms and subverts conventional gender positions. Kaplan's writing on gender representation in music videos set a benchmark for numerous subsequent studies. She is, furthermore, the first scholar to posit a relationship between avant-garde forms and those found in commercial videos. She theorizes this relationship as arising from a postmodernist sensibility, which collapses the boundaries between high and low cultural forms. Most controversial about Kaplan's writing is her belief that videos are intrinsically postmodern. In comparison to other visual media forms, she argues, videos broke established codes of linear visual narration and thematized these codes in a self-reflexive way. In her view, this produces a free-play of blank signifiers (implying pastiche more than parody) that is understood to be symptomatic of the fragmented postmodern condition while offering an implicit critique of conventional audiovisual forms. Writing in the early 1990s, Andrew Goodwin contested this view, while also taking issue, justifiably, with Kaplan's relative neglect of sound. To concentrate solely on these deficiencies, however, is to overlook her contribution in the other areas mentioned above. It is true that she categorizes all videos on one level as postmodern, but she also classes them according to a more nuanced taxonomy as belonging to the categories romantic, socially conscious, nihilist, classical and postmodernist. Postmodernism in this theorization is a style among others.

Goodwin's own writing claims to offer a musicology of the image, but in fact he does not go as far as later writers in addressing the role of sound in shaping our perception of visual images and vice versa. This is due to the survey-like approach of his writing, which rarely allows him to comment on music video in any more than a few rows of text. Nevertheless, he does shift the emphasis toward a bimodal understanding of the form that is rooted in contextualized discussions of cultural forms. What is more, he complicates existing theorizations of visual incorporation in music videos by adding to postmodern pastiche the categories social criticism, self-reflexive parody, parody, promotion, and homage. Goodwin's attention to the attempts of directors and musicians alike to visualize music added an important dimension to the writing on the subject. The appropriateness of his use of the term "synaesthesia" as the means by which such visualization is realized, however, has been debated.

Since 2000 a certain trend in the research on music videos belies their oft-reported diminishing status as a cultural form. A unifying feature of this writing is a concentration on close readings of individual music videos as a means of accounting for how they achieve their expressive effects. Most of this work does not assume videos to be autonomous aesthetic objects, however, but rather views them instead as operating as a node within a complex field of intertextual and cultural relations. This research typically pays closer attention to how individual viewers and listeners experience videos.

Nicholas Cook discusses music videos as part of a broader theorization of audiovisual culture that attends to complex construction of meanings in videos and the different meanings they produce in different audience groups. A key concept in his theoretical apparatus is what he calls emergent meanings: those arising from moment-to-moment combinations of sound and visuals in specific audiovisual configurations. Primarily, however, Cook seeks to extend Goodwin's call for a musicology of the image by arguing that musical meanings are primary, and that these are essentially embellished in song texts and visual imagery. He takes as his example Madonna's "Material Girl," a video Kaplan discusses, and provides an alternative reading that is formally rigorous in its attention to musical detail. The musicological rigor of Cook's analysis is conspicuous, although his assumption of musical primacy to some extent determines the outcome of his analyses. He nevertheless offers a credible example of what a musicology of the image might look like.

Stan Hawkins' theoretical models of audiovisual analysis are critically distanced from Kaplan's work on spectatorship, while the visual positioning and posturing of artists before the camera receives more detailed analysis than that found in Cook's work. Hawkins goes further than Kaplan when addressing musical signification by showing how the visual text correlates with concomitant musical gestures and meanings. Close attention to rhythm, timbre, texture, melody, and harmony informs Hawkins' analytic studies, as well as a discursive approach to cultural identity, especially with respect to gender and ethnicity. The cultural construction of gender identities and issues of audiovisual masquerade are among the main themes explored in his analytical work. In contrast to such musicologists as Cook, who concentrate on musical continuities and occasional discrepancies within them, Hawkins' writing concentrates more on significant details and their intertextual points of reference. A further difference is how Hawkins balances his attention equally between visual performances, song texts, musical sound, and cultural context. No single element is assumed to be primary.

Carol Vernallis' writing is less musicological than that of Hawkins. Instead, it pays close attention to the editing techniques of video producers and how these shape our understanding of musical sounds. A central claim of her work is that the various elements of music videos—music, lyrics, visual montage, and showcasing of the star—vie for prominence, leaving audiences at a loss to predict how these should be weighted. This element of competition ensures that an aspect of indeterminacy is always present in our interpretations of videos. In this way, they are true to the semantic ambiguity of the songs on which they are based, whose lyrics rarely spell out clearly identifiable narrative propositions. Thus, all of the elements might be said to function similarly to the music, which carries the primary responsibility as a bearer of emotional content. The impression of open-endedness in videos can be understood as emancipatory to the extent that this transgresses media norms and highlights more fluid experiences.

An aspect that has come to the fore in the later interpretations of music videos is the extent to which intertextual exchange between different media is an unavoidable characteristic of the form. This includes the incorporation of imagery from other media forms in music videos, but conversely also concerns the myriad ways in which music video aesthetics are shaping other media forms. In this sense such a video as Britney Spears' "Toxic" becomes a point of convergence for audiovisual conventions originating in gaming, science fiction cinema, physical comedy, and pornography. As Hawkins and John Richardson theorize, intertextuality is a useful route into readings of agency alongside musical subjectivity in "Toxic." Notably, this video has been parodied by numerous other artists and users on such social networking sites as YouTube. In the 2010s this mobility between different media forms seemed typical of the state of the art by which videos were an object of exchange more than a fixed artistic work.

Bibliography

M. Shore: *The Rolling Stone Book of Rock Video* (London, 1984)

E.A. Kaplan: *Rocking around the Clock: Music Television, Postmodernism* and *Consumer Culture* (New York, 1987)

A. Goodwin: *Dancing in the Distraction Factory: Music Television and Popular Culture* (Minneapolis, 1992)

S. Frith, A. Goodwin, and L. Grossberg, eds.: *Sound and Vision: the Music Video Reader* (New York, 1993)

A. Björnberg: "Structural Relationships of Music and Images in Music Video," *Popular Music*, xiii/1 (1994), 51–74

N. Cook: *Analysing Musical Multimedia* (Oxford, 1998)

S. Hawkins: *Settling the Pop Score: Pop Texts and Identity Politics* (Aldershot, 2002)

C. Vernallis: *Experiencing Music Videos: Aesthetics and Cultural Context* (New York, 2004)

R. Beebe and J. Middleton, eds.: *Medium Cool: Music Videos from Soundies to Cellphones* (Durham, 2007)

S. Hawkins and J. Richardson: "Remodeling Britney Spears: Matters of Intoxication and Mediation," *Popular Music and Society*, xxx (2007), 605–29

J. Sexton: *Music, Sound and Multimedia* (Edinburgh, 2007)

H. Keazor and T. Wübbena, eds.: *Rewind, Play, Fast Forward: the Past, Present and Future of the Music Video* (Bielefeld, 2010)

J. Richardson: "Plasticine Music: Surrealism in Peter Gabriel's 'Sledgehammer'," *Peter Gabriel: from Genesis to Growing Up*, ed. M. Drewett, S. Hill, and K. Kärki (Aldershot, 2010), 195–210

J. Richardson: *An Eye for Music: Popular Music and the Audiovisual Surreal* (Oxford, 2011)

K. Miller: *Playing Along: Digital Games, YouTube, and Virtual Performance* (Oxford, 2012)

J. Richardson, C. Gorbman, and C. Vernallis, eds.: *The Oxford Handbook of New Audiovisual Aesthetics* (New York, 2013)

H. Rogers: *Sounding the Gallery: Video and the Rise of Art-Music* (Oxford, 2013)

C. Vernallis: *Unruly Media: YouTube, Music Video, and the New Digital Cinema* (Oxford, 2013)

B. Kinskey: *We Used to Wait: Music Videos and Creative Literacy* (Cambridge, 2014)

M. Dwyer: *Back to the Fifties: Nostalgia, Hollywood Film, and Popular Music of the Seventies and Eighties* (New York, 2015)

M. Ables: "Wild Side: Self-Styling and the Aesthetics of Metal in the Music Videos of Mötley Crüe," *Heavy Metal, Gender and Sexuality: Interdisciplinary Approaches* (Abingdon, 2016), 99–108

F. Dhaenens: "Reading Gay Music Videos: an Inquiry into the Representation of Sexual Diversity in Contemporary Music Videos," *Popular Music and Society* xxxix/5 (2016), 532–46

J. McCombe: "Authenticity, Artifice, Ideology: Heavy Metal Video and MTV's 'Second Launch', 1983–1985," *Metal Music Studies* ii/3 (2016), 405–11

S. Shaviro: *Digital Music Videos* (New Brunswick, NJ, 2017)

S. Johansson, A. Werner, and G. Goldenzwaig, eds.: *Streaming Music: Practices, Media, Cultures* (Abingdon, 2018)

JOHN RICHARDSON/R

II. Biographies

Amfitheatrof [Amfitheatrov; Amfiteatrov], Daniele (Alexandrovich)

(*b* St Petersburg, Russia, 16/29 Oct 1901; *d* Rome, Italy, 7 June 1983). Italian composer and conductor of Russian origin. A grandson of the composer Nikolay Sokolov and a brother of the cellist Massimo Amfitheatrof, he studied with Vītols in St. Petersburg and Křička in Prague, but the greater part of his training was undertaken in Rome, where he studied composition with Respighi at the Conservatorio di S Cecilia (diploma 1924) and the organ at the Pontifical Academy of Sacred Music. He was engaged as a pianist, organist, and chorus assistant at the Augusteo (1924–9), also conducting the orchestra under Molinari's supervision. Thereafter he was artistic director of the Genoa and Trieste radio stations and conductor and manager for Italian radio in Turin; he also conducted elsewhere in Europe. In 1937 he went to the United States as associate conductor of the Minneapolis SO, and in 1939 he settled in Hollywood as a film composer, becoming an American citizen in 1944. He moved to New York in the 1950s and then to Venice.

Most of Amfitheatrof's works are in a Respighi-like Romantic-Impressionist style marked by vivid orchestral coloring. His more than seventy film scores are occasionally experimental in their instrumentation, and, though lacking in personality, reveal considerable versatility. Amfitheatrof worked with such directors as Max Ophüls, Fritz Lang, Henry Hathaway, Anthony Mann, Sidney Lumet, George Cukor, and Sam Peckinpah, gaining Academy Award nominations for *Guest Wife* (1945) and *Song of the South* (1946). He did not, however, adjust to the profound linguistic changes in film music of the 1970s, and this led to his prematurely cutting short his work.

Works

(*selective list*)

Film scores

La signora di tutti (M. Ophüls), 1934
Lassie Come Home (F.M. Wilcox), 1943
Days of Glory (J. Tourneur), 1944

Guest Wife (S. Wood), 1945
I'll be Seeing You (W. Dieterle), 1945
Song of the South (H. Foster and W. Jackson), 1946
The Beginning or the End (N. Taurog), 1947
The Lost Moment (M. Gabel), 1947
Another Part of the Forest (M. Gordon), 1948
Letter from an Unknown Woman (M. Ophüls), 1948
Rogue's Regiment (R. Florey), 1948
The Fan (O. Preminger), 1949
House of Strangers (J.L. Mankiewicz), 1949
The Damned Don't Cry (V. Sherman), 1950
The Desert Fox (H. Hathaway), 1951
Devil's Canyon (A. Werker), 1953
Salome (W. Dieterle), 1953
Human Desire (F. Lang), 1954
The Naked Jungle (B. Haskin), 1954
The Mountain (E. Dmytryk), 1956
Trial (M. Robson), 1956
The Unholy Wife (J. Farrow), 1957
From Hell to Texas (H. Hathaway), 1958
Heller in Pink Tights (G. Cukor), 1960
That Kind of Woman (S. Lumet), 1960
Major Dundee (S. Peckinpah), 1965

Principal publisher: Ricordi

Opera

The Staring Match (J. McNeely), 1965

Orchestral

Poema del mare, 1925
Il miracolo delle rose, 1927
Italia, 1929
Panorama americano, 1933
Pf Conc., 1937–46

Choral

De profundis, 1944
Requiem, perf. 1962

Chamber

Sonata, vc, pf, 1930
Pf Trio, 1932

Bibliography

M. Tibaldi Chiesa: "Daniel Amfitheatrof," *L'Ambrosiano* (27 May 1933), 3

D. Amfitheatrof: "La musica per film negli Stati Uniti d'America," *La musica nel film*, ed. E. Masetti (Rome, 1950), 118–28

C. McCarty: *Film Composers in America: a Checklist of their Works* (Glendale, CA, 1953/*R*)

M. Evans: *Soundtrack: the Music of the Movies* (New York, 1975)

G. Tintori, *Duecento anni di Teatro alla Scala. Cronologia opere-balletti-concerti 1778–1977*, (Bergamo, 1979)

S. Miceli, *Musica per film. Storia, Estetica-Analisi, Tipologie* (Milan–Lucca, 2009)

CHRISTOPHER PALMER/SERGIO MICELI

Applebaum, Louis

(*b* Toronto, ON, 3 April 1918; *d* Toronto, ON, 20 April 2000). Canadian composer and arts administrator. He studied the piano with Boris Berlin, and theory and composition with Healey Willan, Ernest MacMillan, and Leonard B. Smith, before continuing composition studies with Roy Harris and Bernard Wagenaar in New York (1940–41). For the next eight years, Applebaum worked for the National Film Board of Canada, producing some 250 film scores. During this period he became increasingly concerned with improving the position of professional musicians in Canada. His combined interests in creative and socioeconomic development led to a career that influenced every aspect of Canadian music. During the 1960s he served as consultant for CBC television and chair of the planning committee for the National Arts Centre, Ottawa. His 1965 *Proposal for the Musical Development of the Capital Region* led to the formation of the National Arts Centre Orchestra and the University of Ottawa music department. Throughout the 1970s he served as executive director of the Ontario Arts Council and in 1980 became co-chair of the Federal Cultural Review Committee.

Applebaum composed incidental music for more than fifty productions of the Stratford (Ontario) Shakespearean Festival (1953–90) and wrote fanfares to announce performances at the Festival Theatre. In 1955, partly to supplement the work of theater musicians, he founded the music wing of the festival, which consists of concerts, opera workshops, and conferences. In addition to a steady stream of theater music (including four ballets) as well as film and television scores, he wrote many instrumental and vocal works. His numerous honors include the Canadian Centennial Medal (1967) and appointment to the Order of Canada (1995). In 1998, in celebration of his eightieth birthday, a concert of his works was performed in Toronto.

Works

(selective list)

Film scores

(as composer or music director)
Call for Volunteers (dir. F.R. Crawley), 1941
The Story of G.I. Joe (dir. W.A. Wellman), 1945
Farewell to Yesterday (dir. J. Kenas), 1950
Operation A-Bomb (dir. B. Benjamin), 1952
Oedipus Rex (dir. T. Guthrie and A. Polonsky (uncredited)), 1957
Paddle to the Sea (dir. B. Mason (as W. Mason)), 1966
Karsh: The Searching Eye (dir. H. Rasky), 1986

Vocal

City of the Prophet (Bible: *Jeremiah*), Bar, pf, 1952
A Folio of Shakespearean Songs, medium v, pf, 1954–87
Cherry Tree Carol (trad.), SATB, 1958
King Herod, SATB, 1958
Algoma Central "In the Tracks of the Black Bear," S, fl, hp, 1976
Inunit, 1v, orch, 1977
Of Love and High Times, S, SATB, opt. fl, opt. hn, opt. perc, 1979
The Last Words of David, cantor, SATB, 1980
Ode to a Birthday City: 1834/Toronto/1984 (L. Sinclair), spkr, solo vv, SATB, orch, 1984
2 Nostalgic Yiddish Folk Songs (trad.), SATB, 1987
Play On, solo vv, SATB, vn, cl, 2 pf, orch, 1987

Orchestral

Suite of Miniature Dances, 1953
Action Stations, 1962
Revival Meeting and Finale from "Barbara Allen," 1964
Suite of Miniature Dances, band, 1964
Concertante, 1967
Fanfare and Anthem, 1969
Homage, 1969
Place Setting, 1973
Dialogue with Footnotes, jazz band, orch, 1984
Celebration York, band, 1985
High Spirits, ov., band, 1986
Passacaglia & Toccata, band, 1986
Balletic Ov., 1987

Chamber and solo instrumental

3 Stratford Fanfares, brass, perc, 1953
Essay, fl, 1971
2 Ceremonial Fanfares, 5–6 tpt, *c*1984
4 Dances in a 19th-Century Style, brass qnt, opt. perc, 1987
The Harper of Stones (ghost story, R. Davies), nar, chbr ens, 1987

Bibliography

W. Pitman: *Louis Applebaum: a Passion for Culture* (Toronto, 2002)

KENNETH WINTERS/R

Arnold, David

(*b* Luton, 23 Jan 1962). British film, television, video game, and popular music composer and producer. Best known for his scores for James Bond films of the late 1990s and the 2000s, Arnold began his career scoring the student films of the director Danny Cannon, leading to their professional collaboration on *The Young Americans* (1993). For this film, Arnold co-wrote the song "Play Dead" with the Icelandic singer Björk. This project brought Arnold to the attention of the producer Roland Emmerich, who hired him to compose the music for *Stargate* (1994). He worked with Emmerich again on two more films (*Independence Day* (1996) and *Godzilla* (1998)), composing large, brass-heavy orchestral scores that matched the over-the-top quality of these blockbusters. During the 2000s, Arnold also developed a professional relationship with the director John Singleton, scoring four of his films, beginning with *Shaft* (2000), incorporating more popular music and in general a more electronic sound palate for these films. After producing *Shaken and Stirred: the David Arnold James Bond Project*, a collection of James Bond theme songs covered by a variety of popular artists, Arnold came to the attention of John Barry, the longtime Bond composer who recommended Arnold for *Tomorrow Never Dies*. In addition to a 1997 James Bond video game, he also scored the next four Bond films. Arnold also scored a music library for the British television series, "Little Britain," returning for subsequent seasons and specials to contribute additional cues. In 2001 Arnold arranged the theme for the long-running British television program "Doctor Who" for use in CD-only audio adventures from Big Finish Productions. In addition to his film and television composing, he continues to produce recordings for many popular artists.

Works

Film scores

The Young Americans (dir. D. Cannon), 1993
Stargate (dir. R. Emmerich), 1994
Last of the Dogmen (dir. T. Murphy), 1995
Independence Day (dir. Emmerich), 1996
A Life Less Ordinary (dir. D. Boyle), 1997
Tomorrow Never Dies (dir. R. Spottiswoode), 1997
Godzilla (dir. Emmerich), 1998

The World is Not Enough (dir. M. Apted), 1999
Shaft (dir. J. Singleton), 2000
Baby Boy (dir. Singleton), 2001
The Musketeer (dir. P. Hyams), 2001
Zoolander (dir. B. Stiller), 2001
Changing Lanes (dir. R. Michell), 2002
Die Another Day (dir. L. Tamahori), 2002
Enough (dir. M. Apted), 2002
2 Fast 2 Furious (dir. Singleton), 2003
The Stepford Wives (dir. F. Oz), 2004
Four Brothers (dir. Singleton), 2005
Stoned (dir. S. Woolley), 2005
Amazing Grace (dir. Apted), 2006
Casino Royale (dir. M. Campbell), 2006
Hot Fuzz (dir. E. Wright), 2007
Agent Crush (dir. S. Robinson), 2008
How to Lose Friends and Alienate People (dir. R.B. Weide), 2008
Quantum of Solace (dir. M. Forster), 2008
The Chronicles of Narnia: the Voyage of the Dawn Treader (dir. Apted), 2010
Made in Dagenham (dir. N. Cole), 2010
Morning Glory (dir. Michell), 2010
Paul (dir. G. Mottela), 2011
Unwatchable (short, dir. M. Hawker), 2011
Eddie (short, dir. C. Kristensen), 2013
Wright vs. Wrong (short, dir. L. Ashton (as L. Baker) and A. Maxey), 2013
The Inbetweeners 2 (dir. D. Beesley and I. Morris), 2014
The Bathroom (short, dir. S.P. Jackson), 2015

Television music

UC: Undercover, 2001
Little Britain, 2003–6
Crooked House, 2008
Little Britain USA, 2008
Free Agents, 2009
Stiller & Meara, 2010–11
Sherlock, 2010–17
The Matt Lucas Awards, 2012
Mr. Stink, 2012
Gangsta Granny, 2013
The Trectate Middoth, 2013
Jekyll & Hyde, 2015
Good Omens, 2018–19

Video-game music

Guinness World Records 2005, 2004
GoldenEye 007, 2010

Bibliography

J. Burlingame: *The Music of James Bond* (New York, 2012)

LOUIS NIEBUR/R

Axt, William L.

(*b* New York, 19 April 1888; *d* Ukiah, CA, 13 Feb 1959). American composer and conductor. After private music study in Berlin, he conducted for Oscar Hammerstein's Manhattan Opera Company, which closed in 1910, and then for productions on Broadway. By 1921 he had become an assistant conductor at the Capitol Theater, where silent films were presented with full orchestral accompaniment; in 1923, in partnership with David Mendoza, he replaced Erno Rapee as principal conductor. In addition to conducting, he composed incidental film music for the Capitol as needed, including fifty-seven pieces published in the *Capitol Photoplay Series* (New York, 1923–7). From 1925 to 1929 he collaborated with Mendoza in New York on compilation scores for at least twenty MGM films, beginning with *The Big Parade*. Their collaboration continued with the music for *Don Juan* (1926), the first feature film score to be presented using the Vitaphone process, which mechanically synchronized the playback of music recorded on wax discs with the projection of the film. In 1929 or 1930 he moved to Hollywood, where he played a key role in the MGM music department. He continued to work for MGM, providing music for numerous films, until his retirement in the early 1940s.

Neither in the collaborations with Mendoza, nor in the MGM films is a distinctive Axt style easily discernible; his works of the 1920s, however, serve as excellent examples of the compilation score. In the music for *The Big Parade*, principal themes exhibit clear expressive content and undergo simple, skillful transformations; new music is interwoven with arrangements of pre-existent pieces to create a smooth pastiche. The scores of the 1930s are often sparse, consisting mainly of modest mood pieces and source music. Many of these are polished examples of MGM's star-centered style, in which the craftsmanship of the composer was subordinated to the effect of the whole. Axt's contributions to *Grand Hotel* (1932), however, were singled out by contemporary critics as an early and effective demonstration of orchestral music's dramatic potency in sound film.

Works

(*selective list*)

Film scores

(*collab. D. Mendoza*)
Ben-Hur (dir. F Niblo and others), 1925
The Big Parade (dir. K. Vidor), 1925

La Bohème (dir. Vidor), 1926
Don Juan (dir. A. Crosland), 1926
Our Dancing Daughters (dir. H. Beaumont), 1928
White Shadows in the South Seas (dir. W.S. Van Dyke), 1928
A Woman of Affairs (dir. C. Brown), 1928
The Kiss (dir. J. Feyder), 1929
The Single Standard (dir. J.S. Robertson), 1929

Film scores

(*without Mendoza*)
Smilin' Through (dir. S. Franklin), 1932
Broadway to Hollywood (dir. W. Mack and J. White (uncredited)), 1933
Dinner at Eight (dir. G. Cukor), 1933
The Thin Man (dir. W.S. Van Dyke), 1934
Pursuit (dir. E.L. Marin), 1935
Libeled Lady (dir. J. Conway), 1936
The Last of Mrs Cheney (dir. R. Boleslawski), 1937

Bibliography

GroveA (M. Marks) [incl. further bibliography]
Musical Courier (27 Dec 1923)
E.J. Lewis: "The Archive Collection of Film Music at the University of Wyoming," *Cue Sheet*, vi (1989), no.3, pp.89–99; no.4, pp.143–60
D. James: "Performing with Silent Films," *Film Music I*, ed. C. McCarty (1989), 61–79

MARTIN MARKS/R

Barber, Lesley

(*b* Guelph, ON, 23 June 1962). Canadian film and television composer, orchestrator, conductor, pianist, and producer. Barber began composing at the age of ten and was an award winner in Canada's SOCAN National Competition for Young Composers. She studied music at the University of Western Ontario (BM 1985) and composition at the University of Toronto (MA 1988), where she worked with the composers Gustav Ciamaga and Lothar Klein. She has composed music for various CBC radio dramas, made her film début with her score for Patricia Rozema's award-winning film *When Night is Falling* (1995), and has written scores for Miramax, New Line, Focus Features, Nickelodeon, Warner Bros. and Home Box Office.

Barber has also composed music for the more than twenty theater productions of Canadian plays, including *Unidentified Human Remains* and *The True Nature of Love* (Brad Fraser), *Love and Anger* (George F. Walker), *Nothing Sacred* (George F. Walker), *The Warriors* (Michel Garneau), and *Escape from Happiness*

(George F. Walker). The latter two of these received Canadian Dora Awards for Outstanding Original Score. As a composer of new music for the concert hall her commissions include works for the Canadian Electronic Ensemble, Hemispheres, the harpist Erica Goodman, the percussionist Beverly Johnston, and the pianist Eve Egoyan.

Works

Film scores

What's his Face (dir. S. Beveridge), 1995
When Night is Falling (dir. P. Rozema), 1995
Turning April (dir. G. Bennett), 1996
Bach Cello Suite no.6: Six Gestures (dir. Rozema), 1997
Los Locos (dir. J.-M. Vallée), 1997
Luminous Motion (dir. B. Gordon), 1998
A Price above Rubies (dir. B. Yakin), 1998
Mansfield Park (dir. Rozema), 1999
This Might be Good (dir. Rozema), 2000
You Can Count on Me (dir. K. Lonergan), 2000
The Little Bear Movie (dir. R. Jafelice), 2001
Marion Bridge (dir. W. von Carolsfeld), 2002
Uptown Girls (dir. Yakin), 2003
Comeback Season (dir. B. McCulloch), 2006
A Thousand Years of Good Prayers (dir. W. Wang), 2007
Death in Love (dir. Yakin), 2008
Victoria Day (dir. D. Bezmozgis), 2009
Girls on Top (dir. C. Nicolaou), 2010
The Moth Diaries (dir. M. Harron), 2011
The Pool Date (short, dir. P. Sisam), 2012
The Scan (short, dir. E. Spalding), 2012
How to Change the World (dir. J. Rothwell), 2015
The Apology (dir. T. Hsiung), 2016
Manchester by the Sea (dir. Lonergan), 2016
A Better Man (dir. L. Jackman and A. Khan), 2017
Bird (short, dir. M. Parker), 2017
Irreplaceable You (dir. S. Laing), 2018

Television music

Maurice Sendak's Little Bear, 1995
Yo-Yo Ma Inspired by Bach (series), 1997
Seven Little Monsters (series), 2000–2003
Hysterical Blindness, 2002
The Real Jane Austen, 2002
A Child's Garden Party, 2011

Pete's Christmas, 2013
Beaches, 2017

Concert works

Shapes of Light, Shapes of Thunder, 1989
5 Pieces, vn, cl, bn, pf, 1991
Rhythmic Voodoo, perc, elecs, 1992
Long White Line, orch, 1993
Marshland, str qt, 1996
Music for a Lonely Zamboni, pf trio, 2001

Bibliography

"Lesley Barber," Canadian Music Center website: http://www.musiccentre.ca
E. Lumley: "Barber, Lesley," *Canadian Who's Who 2003* (Toronto, 2003)

JEANNIE GAYLE POOL/R

Barry, John [Prendergast, John Barry]

(*b* York, England, 3 Nov 1933; *d* Oyster Bay, NY, 30 Jan 2011). English composer. As a boy he worked at his father's theater chain in the north of England and listened to such established Hollywood composers as Steiner, Korngold, and Waxman. He contemplated a career as a film composer and left school to study music with Francis Jackson, then the Master of Music at York Minster. During his national service (1952–5) he studied jazz arranging and orchestration by mail with Stan Kenton's famous arranger William Russo.

In 1957 he formed the John Barry Seven, a jazz-rock group, and was music director for the singer Adam Faith on several hit songs, including "What do you Want" (1959, Parlophone). The Seven's recording "Hit and Miss" (1960, EMI) was adopted as the theme for the BBC's popular television show "Juke Box Jury." Around this time Barry wrote, performed, and recorded pop music, appearing with his group on such influential shows as "Six-Five Special" and "Drumbeat." He later worked as a music director for EMI and Ember Records.

Following his first film score, for *Beat Girl* (1960, with Faith), Barry gained fame for his fusion of jazz, pop, and orchestral sounds in the James Bond films, beginning with his arrangement of Monty Norman's *James Bond Theme* for *Dr. No* (1962) and concluding with his music for *The Living Daylights* (1987). His soundtrack for the 007 film *Goldfinger* (1964) displaced the Beatles at the top of the American charts; his title songs for *Thunderball* (1965), *You Only Live Twice* (1967), *Octopussy* (1983), and *A View to a Kill* (1985) also charted.

While the Bond films attracted most of the attention, Barry also scored a wide variety of other British films including *Zulu* (1964); six Bryan Forbes films including *King Rat* (1965), *The Whisperers* (1967), and *Deadfall* (1968), in which Barry appears conducting the London PO performing his single-movement guitar concerto; the cimbalom-flavored *The Ipcress File* and the hip *The Knack . . . and how to get it* (both 1965); and the African lion adventure *Born Free* (1966), which won Oscars for his score and title song. He added choir to his lavish orchestral scores for the period films *The Lion in Winter* (1968, another Oscar winner), *The Last Valley* (1971), and *Mary, Queen of Scots* (1971).

Barry gradually developed a more lush, romantic style that suited such movies as the romantic fantasy *Somewhere in Time* (1980), *Out of Africa* (1985), and the Western *Dances with Wolves* (1990), the last two of which won him further Academy Awards. He revisited his earlier, jazzy style in the concept album *Americans* (1976) and in his scores for *Body Heat* (1981), *The Cotton Club* (1984), and *Playing by Heart* (1998).

Barry achieved sporadic success with stage musicals. He had West End hits with *Passion Flower Hotel* (1965) and *Billy* (1974, starring Michael Crawford) and Broadway failures with *Lolita, My Love* (1971, with lyrics by Alan Jay Lerner) and *The Little Prince and the Aviator* (1981), both of which closed during previews. *Brighton Rock* (2004, based on the Graham Greene novel) played briefly in

John Barry
© Mary Robert/Lebrecht

London. For *Billy*, *The Little Prince*, and *Brighton Rock*, Barry collaborated with the lyricist Don Black, with whom he had worked on songs from the mid-1960s.

Barry's television themes also proved popular, notably those for "The Persuaders!" (1971), "The Adventurer" (1972), and "Orson Welles' Great Mysteries" (1973). He was profiled on American television in "Great Performances" (1993) and on the British program "Omnibus" (2000). He moved to America in 1975 and, late in his career, turned his attention to such reflective orchestral concept albums as *The Beyondness of Things* and *Eternal Echoes*. He was named an Officer of the British Empire in 1999, received an honorary doctorate from the University of York in 2001, and became the first composer to receive the British Academy of Film and Television Arts Fellowship in 2008.

Works

Film scores

Beat Girl (dir. E.T. Gréville), 1960
Never Let Go (dir. J. Guillermin), 1960
The Amorous Prawn (dir. A. Kimmins), 1962
Mix me a Person (dir. L. Norman), 1962
From Russia with Love (dir. T. Young), 1963
Goldfinger (dir. G. Hamilton), 1964
Man in the Middle (dir. G. Hamilton), 1964
Séance on a Wet Afternoon (dir. B. Forbes), 1964
They all Died Laughing (dir. D. Chaffey), 1964
Zulu (dir. C. Endfield), 1964
Four in the Morning (dir. A. Simmons), 1965
The Ipcress File (dir. S.J. Furie), 1965
King Rat (dir. B. Forbes), 1965
The Knack. . . and how to get it (dir. R. Lester), 1965
Mister Moses (dir. R. Neame), 1965
The Party's Over (dir. G. Hamilton), 1965
Thunderball (dir. T. Young), 1965
Born Free (dir. J. Hill and T. McGowan), 1966
The Chase (dir. A. Penn), 1966
The Quiller Memorandum (dir. M. Anderson), 1966
The Wrong Box (dir. B. Forbes), 1966
Dutchman (dir. A. Harvey), 1967
The Whisperers (dir. B. Forbes), 1967
You Only Live Twice (dir. L. Gilbert), 1967
Boom! (dir. J. Losey), 1968
Deadfall (dir. B. Forbes), 1968
The Lion in Winter (dir. A. Harvey), 1968
Petulia (dir. R. Lester), 1968
The Appointment (dir. S. Lumet), 1969
Midnight Cowboy (dir. J. Schlesinger), 1969

On her Majesty's Secret Service (dir. P.R. Hunt), 1969
Monte Walsh (dir. W. A. Fraker), 1970
Diamonds are Forever (dir. G. Hamilton), 1971
The Last Valley (dir. J. Clavell), 1971
Mary, Queen of Scots (dir. C. Jarrott), 1971
Murphy's War (dir. P. Yates), 1971
They might be Giants (dir. A. Harvey), 1971
Walkabout (dir. N. Roeg), 1971
Alice's Adventures in Wonderland (dir. W. Sterling), 1972
Follow me! (dir. C. Reed), 1972
A Doll's House (dir. P. Garland), 1973
The Dove (dir. Charles Jarrott), 1974
The Man with the Golden Gun (dir. G. Hamilton), 1974
The Tamarind Seed (dir. B. Edwards), 1974
The Day of the Locust (dir. J. Schlesinger), 1975
King Kong (dir. J. Guillermin), 1976
Robin and Marian (dir. R. Lester), 1976
The Deep (dir. P. Yates), 1977
First Love (dir. J. Darling), 1977
The White Buffalo (dir. J.L. Thompson), 1977
The Betsy (dir. D. Petrie), 1978
Game of Death (dir. R. Clouse and B. Lee), 1978
The Black Hole (dir. G. Nelson), 1979
Hanover Street (dir. P. Hyams), 1979
Moonraker (dir. L. Gilbert), 1979
Starcrash (dir. L. Cozzi), 1979
Inside Moves (dir. R. Donner), 1980
Night Games (dir. R. Vadim), 1980
Raise the Titanic! (dir. J. Jameson), 1980
Somewhere in Time (dir. J. Szwarc), 1980
Touched by Love (dir. G. Trikonis), 1980
Body Heat (dir. L. Kasdan), 1981
The Legend of the Lone Ranger (dir. W.A. Fraker), 1981
Frances (dir. G. Clifford), 1982
Hammett (dir. W. Wenders), 1982
Murder by Phone (dir. M. Anderson), 1982
The Golden Seal (dir. F. Zuniga), 1983
High Road to China (dir. B.G. Hutton), 1983
Octopussy (dir. J. Glen), 1983
The Cotton Club (dir. F.F. Coppola), 1984
Mike's Murder (dir. J. Bridges), 1984
Until September (dir. R. Marquand), 1984
Jagged Edge (dir. R. Marquand), 1985
Out of Africa (dir. S. Pollack), 1985
A View to a Kill (dir. J. Glen), 1985
The Golden Child (dir. M. Ritchie), 1986

Howard the Duck (dir. W. Huyck), 1986
A Killing Affair (dir. D. Saperstein), 1986
Peggy Sue got Married (dir. F.F. Coppola), 1986
Hearts of Fire (dir. R. Marquand), 1987
The Living Daylights (dir. J. Glen), 1987
Masquerade (dir. B. Swaim), 1988
Dances with Wolves (dir. K. Costner), 1990
Chaplin (dir. R. Attenborough), 1992
Indecent Proposal (dir. A. Lyne), 1993
My Life (dir. B.J. Rubin), 1993
Ruby Cairo (dir. G. Clifford), 1993
The Specialist (dir. L. Llosa), 1994
Across the Sea of Time (dir. S. Low), 1995
Cry the Beloved Country (dir. D. Roodt), 1995
The Scarlet Letter (dir. R. Joffé), 1995
Swept from the Sea (dir. B. Kidron), 1997
Mercury Rising (dir. H. Becker), 1998
Playing by Heart (dir. W. Carroll), 1998
Enigma (dir. M. Apted), 2001

Television music

(*selective list*)
Elizabeth Taylor in London, 1963
Sophia Loren in Rome, 1964
The Glass Menagerie, 1973
Love among the Ruins, 1975
Eleanor and Franklin, 1976
Eleanor and Franklin: the White House Years, 1977
The Gathering, 1977
The War between the Tates, 1977
Young Joe: the Forgotten Kennedy, 1977
The Corn is Green, 1979
Willa, 1979
Svengali, 1983

Orchestral

Americans, 1976
The Beyondness of Things, 1999
Eternal Echoes, 2001

Bibliography

R.S. Brown: *Overtones and Undertones: Reading Film Music* (Los Angeles, 1994)
E. Fiegel: *John Barry: a Sixties Theme, from James Bond to Midnight Cowboy* (London, 1998)

B. Stanley: "Some Like it Cool: a Tale of Sex, Spies, Success and Cimbalons," *Mojo* (2001), Dec, 67–74
G. Leonard, P. Walker, and G. Bramley: *John Barry: the Man with the Midas Touch* (Bristol, 2008)
J. Burlingame: "Billion Dollar Composer: John Barry," *Daily Variety* (3 Nov 2008)
B. Handy: "The Man who Knew the Score," *Vanity Fair* <http://www.vanityfair.com/culture/features/2009/02/john-barry200902> (2009)
J. Burlingame: *The Music of James Bond* (Oxford, 2012)

JON BURLINGAME/R

Bassman, George

(*b* New York, 7 Feb 1914; *d* Los Angeles, 26 June 1997). American composer, arranger, and songwriter. The son of Russian-Jewish immigrants, Bassman studied at the Boston Conservatory of Music. From 1931 to 1934 he arranged for big bands, including those led by Duke Ellington and Benny Goodman. During this period he composed (with lyricist Ned Washington) the Tommy Dorsey theme "I'm Getting Sentimental Over You." From 1934 to 1936 he was key arranger for conductor Andre Kostelanetz's radio show. In 1936 he moved to Hollywood, where he joined MGM as arranger, composer, and general music/vocal director. He worked on many of the studio's early classic and lesser-known musicals, including *The Wizard of Oz* (1939), for which he composed some of the cyclone music, *Honolulu* (1939), *As Thousands Cheer* (1943), and *Cabin in the Sky* (1943). He also composed dramatic underscores for *The Clock* (1945) and *The Postman Always Rings Twice* (1946).

In 1947 Bassman was a victim of the HUAC blacklistings. Returning to New York he worked in television and on Broadway, where he orchestrated Frank Loesser's *Guys and Dolls*. He later returned to scoring small features such as *The Joe Louis Story* (1953) and the sleeper hit *Marty* (1955). Bassman returned to MGM for Sam Peckinpah's *Ride the High Country* (1962), creating an epic yet intimate Americana sound that exemplified the scaled-down shift in Hollywood scoring that had occurred in the 1950s. He later adapted this music for his last film, *Mail Order Bride* (1964). When his scores for later films (including *Bonnie and Clyde*, 1967) were rejected Bassman retired from Hollywood and died, reportedly in obscurity, in Los Angeles in 1997.

Works

Film scores

Suzy (dir. G. Fitzmaurice), 1936
Conquest (dir. C. Brown), 1937
A Damsel in Distress (dir. G. Stevens), 1937

The Last Gangster (dir. E. Ludwig), 1937
Bulldog Drummond's Peril (dir. J. Hogan), 1938
A Day at the Beach (dir. F. Freleng), 1938
Everybody Sing (dir. E. Marin), 1938
Marie Antoinette (dir. W. Van Dyke), 1938
Sweethearts (dir. Van Dyke), 1938
At the Circus (dir. E. Buzzell), 1939
Babes in Arms (dir. B. Berkeley), 1939
Broadway Serenade (dir. R. Leonard), 1939
Gulliver's Travels (dir. D. Fleischer and W. Bowsky), 1939
Honolulu (dir. Buzzell), 1939
The Ice Follies of 1939 (dir. R. Schünzel), 1939
Lady of the Tropics (dir. J. Conway), 1939
The Wizard of Oz (dir. V. Fleming), 1939
Broadway Melody of 1940 (dir. N. Taurog), 1940
Go West (dir. Buzzell), 1940
I Take This Woman (dir. Van Dyke), 1940
Little Nellie Kelly (dir. Taurog), 1940
Babes on Broadway (dir. Berkeley), 1941
Lady Be Good (dir. N. McLeod), 1941
Ziegfeld Girl (dir. Leonard and Berkeley), 1941
Cairo (dir. Van Dyke), 1942
For Me and My Gal (dir. Berkeley), 1942
Lover (dir. G. Cukor Her Cardboard), 1942
Panama Hattie (dir. McLeod), 1942
Ship Ahoy (dir. Buzzell), 1942
Tortilla Flat (dir. Fleming), 1942
As Thousands Cheer (dir. G. Sidney), 1943
Best Foot Forward (dir. Buzzell), 1943
Cabin in the Sky (dir. V. Minnelli), 1943
Du Barry Was a Lady (dir. R. Ruth), 1943
Girl Crazy (dir. Taurog and Berkeley), 1943
Presenting Lily Mars (dir. Taurog), 1943
Bud Abbott and Lou Costello in Hollywood (dir. S. Simon), 1945
The Clock (dir. Minnelli), 1945
The Postman Always Rings Twice (dir. T. Garnett), 1946
Two Smart People (dir. J. Dassin), 1946
The Romance of Rosy Ridge (dir. R. Rowland), 1947
Big Leaguer (dir. R. Aldrich), 1953
The Joe Louis Story (dir. R. Gordon), 1953
A Slight Case of Larceny (dir. D. Weis), 1953
Marty (dir. D. Mann), 1955
Mayerling TV (dir. A. Litvak), 1957
The Great Chase (dir. H. Cort), 1962
Ride the High Country (dir. S. Peckinpah), 1962
Mail Order Bride (dir. B. Kennedy), 1964

Bibliography

A. Harmetz: *The Making of The Wizard of Oz* (New York, 1977), 92–5, 98

C. Goldman: "George Bassman: Rhapsody In Black," *Film Score Monthly*, ix/6 (2004), 14–16, 44

ROSS CARE

Beck, Christophe [Chris]

(*b* Montreal, 9 Jan 1969). Canadian composer of television and film scores. After taking private music lessons and playing with rock bands, he attended Yale University (BA 1992) where he studied music composition and wrote two musicals and an opera. He then studied at the University of Southern California's film scoring program (1992–3) where his teachers included JERRY GOLDSMITH. After getting his first television scoring assignment with the Canadian series "White Fang," Beck went on to score multiple episodes of the critically acclaimed cult television series "Buffy the Vampire Slayer." As a series regular for most of seasons two, three, and four, Beck introduced a number of recurring and continually developing melodic motifs that enhanced the narrative and dramatic power of the ironic show. His work on "Buffy" earned him an Emmy award in 1998 for best music composition in a series; after leaving regular composition duties for the series after season five, he made notable returns for the episodes *The Gift* (the episode marking the end of "Buffy's" run on the WB network), and *Once More, with Feeling* (a musical episode of the series for which Beck arranged and orchestrated songs written by series creator Joss Whedon). Beck's "Buffy" scores employed heavily processed electronic sounds and samples of orchestral instruments, creating virtual orchestras that he occasionally augmented with a small number of live performers.

Since 1999 he has composed mainly for feature films, where his deft ability to write in a number of musical styles—from experimental timbres and throbbing techno to delicate orchestral and piano passages—has made him a sought-after composer associated with many big budget and high-grossing films from the first two decades of the twenty-first century, including, most notably, Disney's animated *Frozen* in 2013.

Works

Film scores

Past Perfect (dir. J. Heap), 1996
Guinevere (dir. A. Wells), 1999
Let the Devil Wear Black (dir. S. Title), 1999
Bring it On (dir. P. Reed), 2000
Stealing Harvard (dir. B. McCulloch), 2002
The Tuxedo (dir. K. Donovan), 2002

Cheaper by the Dozen (dir. S. Levy), 2003
Confidence (dir. J. Foley), 2003
The Event (dir. T. Fitzgerald), 2003
Just Married (dir. Levy), 2003
Under the Tuscan Sun (dir. Wells), 2003
A Cinderella Story (dir. M. Rosman), 2004
Garfield: the Movie (dir. P. Hewitt), 2004
Saved! (dir. B. Dannelly), 2004
Without a Paddle (dir. S. Brill), 2004
Elektra (dir. R. Bowman), 2005
The Pink Panther (dir. Levy), 2006
We are Marshall (dir. McG), 2006
Drillbit Taylor (dir. Brill), 2008
The Hangover (dir. T. Phillips), 2009
Burlesque (dir. S. Antin), 2010
Death at a Funeral (dir. N. LaBute), 2010
Hot Tub Time Machine (dir. S. Pink), 2010
Red (dir. R. Schwentke), 2010
Waiting for "Superman" (dir. D. Guggenheim), 2010
Cedar Rapids (dir. M. Arteta), 2011
Crazy, Stupid, Love. (dir. G. Ficarra and J. Requa), 2011
The Hangover Part II (dir. Phillips), 2011
The Muppets (dir. J. Bobin), 2011
Tower Heist (dir. B. Ratner), 2011
The Guilt Trip (dir. A. Fletcher), 2012
Paperman (short, dir. J. Kahrs), 2012
Pitch Perfect (dir. J. Moore), 2012
The Road We've Traveled (short, dir. Guggenheim), 2012
This Means War (dir. McG), 2012
The Watch (dir. A. Schaffer), 2012
Charlie Countryman (dir. F. Bond), 2013
Frozen (dir. C. Buck and J. Lee), 2013
The Hangover Part III (dir. Phillips), 2013
The Internship (dir. Levy), 2013
R.I.P.D. (dir. Schwentke), 2013
Runner Runner (dir. B. Furman), 2013
Alexander and the Terrible, Horrible, No Good, Very Bad Day (dir. M. Arteta), 2014
Cake (dir. D. Barnz), 2014
Edge of Tomorrow (dir. D. Liman), 2014
Endless Love (dir. S. Feste), 2014
Good Kill (dir. A. Niccol), 2014
Let's be Cops (dir. L. Greenfield), 2014
Muppets Most Wanted (dir. Bobin), 2014
Red Army (dir. G. Polsky), 2014
Ant Man (dir. P. Reed), 2015
Frozen Fever (short, dir. Buck and Lee), 2015
Get Hard (dir. E. Cohen), 2015

Hot Pursuit (dir. A. Fletcher), 2015
Hot Tub Time Machine 2 (dir. Pink), 2015
The Peanuts Movie (dir. S. Martino), 2015
Sisters (dir. Moore), 2015
Trolls (dir. M. Mitchell and W. Dohrn), 2016
American Made (dir. D. Liman), 2017
LOU (dir. D. Mullins), 2017
An Ordinary Man (dir. B. Silberling), 2017
The 12th Man (dir. H. Zwart), 2017
Anon (dir. Niccol), 2018
Ant-Man and the Wasp (dir. Reed), 2018
Gringo (dir. N. Edgerton), 2018

Television music

White Fang, 1993
Buffy the Vampire Slayer, 1997–2001
Angel, 1999–2000
The Practice, 1999–2000
The Cat in the Hat Knows a Lot About That!, 2012
Little Brother, 2012
Rogue, 2012
30 for 30: Soccer Stories, 2014

Bibliography

N. Holder with J. Mariotte and M. Hart: *Buffy the Vampire Slayer: The Watcher's Guide*, 2 (New York, 2000), 433–7

J. Bond: "Elektra-fied (Christophe Beck scores *Elektra*)," *Film Score Monthly*, ix (2004), 20–21

A. Cox and R. Fülöp: "'What Rhymes with Lungs?': When Music Speaks Louder than Words," *Music, Sound and Silence in "Buffy the Vampire Slayer"*, ed. P. Attinello, J.K. Halfyard, and V. Knights (Surrey, England, 2010), 61–78

R. Haskins: "Variations on Themes for Geeks and Heroes: Leitmotif, Style and the Musico-dramatic Moment," *Music, Sound and Silence in "Buffy the Vampire Slayer"*, ed. P Attinello, J.K. Halfyard, and V. Knights (Surrey, England, 2010), 45–60

NEIL LERNER/R

Bernstein, Elmer

(*b* New York, 4 April 1922; *d* Ojai, CA, 18 Aug 2004). American composer and conductor. He was trained as a pianist but also studied composition with Israel Citkowitz, Roger Sessions, Ivan Langstroth, and Stefan Wolpe. He attended New York University, then enlisted in the Army Air Corps (1942); he arranged and composed music for some eighty programs for the Armed Forces Radio Service and was a concert pianist for three years after his discharge. Norman Corwin then engaged him to score radio drama, which led to composition for films; Bernstein's third film, *Sudden Fear* (1952), attracted favorable attention. In 1955, despite suffering career difficulties due to McCarthyism, he rose to sudden prominence with his score for *The Man with the Golden Arm*. In this, as in several scores that followed (e.g. *Walk on the Wild Side*, 1962), he effectively blended jazz into a modern symphonic idiom to suit gritty stories and contemporary settings. He subsequently became known for his rousing scores for Westerns and action films (notably *The Magnificent Seven*, 1960, and *The Great Escape*, 1963), and in the 1970s and 80s he showed a flair both for youth-market comedies such as *National Lampoon's Animal House* (1978) and for intimate adult dramas, including several Irish films.

Throughout a career of over two hundred film and television scores, Bernstein crafted memorable themes, such as that for *To Kill a Mockingbird* (1963), and showed a fondness for thematic metamorphosis, lively rhythmic ostinatos, and clean-cut, economical instrumental textures. In later years, he again blended jazz into his scores for period pieces such as *Devil in a Blue Dress* (1995), and from the 1980s made a point of using the ondes martenot. In the 1990s he worked with Martin Scorsese on a series of films, including a remake of *Cape Fear* (1991), for which he adapted Bernard Herrmann's score from the 1962 film. With his last film score, *Far From Heaven* (2002), Bernstein received his fourteenth Academy Award nomination. Bernstein also led efforts to secure screen composers' incomes and copyrights and promoted the appreciation of film music through his writing. He founded the Film Music Collection (1974–8), which published *Film Music Notebook* and released recordings, mostly by other eminent film composers and conducted by Bernstein.

Works

(*selective list*)

Film scores

Saturday's Hero (dir. D. Miller), 1951
Sudden Fear (dir. Miller), 1952
The Man with the Golden Arm (dir. O. Preminger), 1955
The View from Pompey's Head (dir. P. Dunne), 1955
The Ten Commandments (dir. C.B. de Mille), 1956
Fear Strikes Out (dir. R. Mulligan), 1957
Sweet Smell of Success (dir. A. Mackendrick), 1957
Desire under the Elms (dir. D. Mann), 1958
God's Little Acre (dir. Mann), 1958
Kings Go Forth (dir. D. Daves), 1958
Some Came Running (dir. V. Minnelli), 1958
The Story on Page One (dir. C. Odets), 1959
From the Terrace (dir. M. Robson), 1960

The Magnificent Seven (dir. J. Sturges), 1960
Summer and Smoke (dir. P. Glenville), 1961
Birdman of Alcatraz (dir. J. Frankenheimer), 1962
Walk on the Wild Side (dir. E. Dmytryk), 1962
The Great Escape (dir. Sturges), 1963
To Kill a Mockingbird (dir. Mulligan), 1963
Love with the Proper Stranger (dir. Mulligan), 1963
Baby the Rain Must Fall (dir. Mulligan), 1964
The World of Henry Orient (dir. G.R. Hill), 1964
The Hallelujah Trail (dir. Sturges), 1965
The Sons of Katie Elder (dir. H. Hathaway), 1965
Hawaii (dir. Hill), 1966
Return of the Seven (dir. B. Kennedy), 1966
Thoroughly Modern Millie (dir. Hill), 1967
The Bridge at Remagen (dir. J. Guillermin), 1969
True Grit (dir. Hathaway), 1969
The Liberation of L.B. Jones (dir. W. Wyler), 1970
Big Jake (dir. G. Sherman), 1971
See No Evil (dir. R. Fleischer), 1971
The Trial of Billy Jack (dir. F. Laughlin), 1974
From Noon Till Three (dir. F.D. Gilroy), 1976
The Shootist (dir, D. Siegel), 1976
Slap Shot (dir. Hill), 1977
National Lampoon's Animal House (dir. J. Landis), 1978
The Great Santini (dir. L.J. Carlino), 1979
Airplane! (dir. J. Abrahams, D. Zucker, and J. Zucker), 1980
An American Werewolf in London (dir. Landis), 1981
Heavy Metal (dir. G. Potterton), 1981
Stripes (dir. I. Reitman), 1981
The Chosen (dir. J.P. Kagan), 1982
Trading Places (dir. Landis), 1983
Ghostbusters (dir. Reitman), 1984
The Black Cauldron (dir. T. Berman), 1985
Spies Like Us (dir. Landis), 1985
Da (dir. M. Clark), 1988
My Left Foot (dir. J. Sheridan), 1989
The Field (dir. Sheridan), 1990
The Grifters (dir. S. Frears), 1990
Cape Fear (dir. M. Scorsese), 1991, arr. of music by B. Herrmann
A Rage in Harlem (dir. B. Duke), 1991
Rambling Rose (dir. M. Coolidge), 1991
The Babe (dir. A. Hiller), 1992
The Age of Innocence (dir. Scorsese), 1993
Mad Dog and Glory (dir. J. McNaughton), 1993
Devil in a Blue Dress (dir. C. Franklin), 1995
Frankie Starlight (dir. M. Lindsay Hogg), 1995
Hoodlum (dir. Duke), 1997

John Grisham's "The Rainmaker" (dir. F. Coppola), 1997
Twilight (dir. R. Benton), 1998
Bringing Out the Dead (dir. Scorsese), 1999
Wild Wild West (dir. B. Sonnenfeld), 1999
Far From Heaven (dir. T. Haynes), 2002

Other works

How Now, Dow Jones (musical, C. Leigh; M. Shulman), New York, 7 Dec 1967
Conc., gui, orch, 1999
3 suites, orch
2 song cycles
works for pf, va, and pf

Bibliography

T. Thomas: *Music for the Movies* (South Brunswick, NJ, and New York, 1973), 185–94
I. Bazelon: Interview, *Knowing the Score: Notes on Film Music* (New York, 1975), 170–80
E. Bernstein: "Film composers vs. the Studios," *Film Music Notebook*, ii/1 (1976), 31–9
T. Thomas: "Elmer Bernstein," *Film Score: the View from the Podium* (South Brunswick, NJ, and New York, 1979, rev. 2/1991 as *Film Score: the Art and Craft of Movie Music*), 238–49
J. Macmillan: "A Filmography/Discography of Elmer Bernstein," *Soundtrack!* (Mechelen, Belgium), xiv/54 (1995), 23–41
G. Marmorstein: *Hollywood Rhapsody: Movie Music and its Makers* (New York, 1997), 136–41
Obituary, *New York Times* (20 Aug 2004)
M. Morris: "The Order of Sanctity: Sound, Sight, and Suasion in *The Ten Commandments*," *Oxford Handbook of Film Music Studies*, ed. D. Neumeyer (Oxford, 2014), 424–44
M. Whitmer: "Musically Recreating the Fifties in *Far from Heaven* (2002)," *Anxiety Muted: American Film Music in a Suburban Age*, ed. A. Bushard and S. Pelkey (New York, 2015), 239–59
M. Whitmer: *Elmer Bernstein's The Magnificent Seven: a Film Score Guide* (Lanham, MD, 2017)

CHRISTOPHER PALMER/CLIFFORD MCCARTY/MARTIN MARKS/NATHAN PLATTE/R

Blanchard, Terence (Oliver)

(*b* New Orleans, 13 March 1962). American trumpeter and film composer. He began piano lessons at the age of five and switched to the trumpet in 1970. While enrolled at the New Orleans Center for Creative Arts (from 1978), he met the saxophonist Donald Harrison. In 1980 he won a music scholarship to Rutgers

University and toured with Lionel Hampton's Orchestra. Two years later he and Harrison replaced Wynton and Branford Marsalis in Art Blakey's Jazz Messengers. Following the success of their joint album *New York Second Line* (1984, Concord), they left the group in 1986. Blanchard began collaborating with the filmmaker Spike Lee when he was invited to play on the soundtrack of *School Daze* in 1988, and he subsequently performed on *Do the Right Thing* in 1989. That year Blanchard curtailed his recording and performing in order to develop a new embouchure. After composing the score for Lee's *Jungle Fever* (1991), he has provided the soundtracks for most of the director's films. His scores are rooted in African American popular traditions and combine influences from world music and electronica as well as jazz. In 1992 Blanchard composed a score for Lee's film *Malcolm X* that received critical acclaim and subsequently arranged the music into a suite for his quintet. *When the Levees Broke* (2006) is an outstanding example among Blanchard's documentary film scores. His album based on this score, entitled *Tale of God's Will (A Requiem for Katrina)* (2007, BN), won a Grammy for Best Large Jazz Ensemble Album. Among his other albums, *Bounce* (2003, BN) merges hard bop with afro-pop and *Flow* (2005, BN) verges towards electronic fusion. *Choices* (2009, Concord) is inspired by the empowerment of African Americans in post-Katrina New Orleans and includes quotations from an interview with the civil rights activist Cornel West. Blanchard has maintained a strong commitment to jazz education and mentorship, and was appointed the artistic director of the Thelonious Monk Institute of Jazz in 2000. Motivated by his commitment to the revitalization of his hometown, in 2007 the Monk Institute moved from Los Angeles to New Orleans, where it was hosted at Loyola University until 2012.

Works

Film scores

Jungle Fever (dir. S. Lee), 1991
Malcolm X (dir. Lee), 1992
Sugar Hill (dir. L. Ichaso), 1993
Crooklyn (dir. Lee), 1994
The Inkwell (dir. M. Rich), 1994
Trial by Jury (dir. H. Gould), 1994
Clockers (dir. Lee), 1995
Get on the Bus (dir. Lee), 1996
4 Little Girls (dir. Lee), 1997
Eve's Bayou (dir. K. Lemmons), 1997
'Til There Was You (dir. S. Winant), 1997
Summer of Sam (dir. Lee), 1999
Bamboozled (dir. Lee), 2000
Love & Basketball (dir. G. Prince-Bythewood), 2000
Next Friday (dir. S. Carr), 2000

The Caveman's Valentine (dir. Lemmons), 2001
Glitter (dir. V. Curtis-Hall (as Curtis Hall)), 2001
Original Sin (dir. M. Cristofer), 2001
25th Hour (dir. Lee), 2002
Barbershop (dir. T. Story), 2002
Dark Blue (dir. R. Shelton), 2002
People I Know (dir. D. Algrant), 2002
Negroes with Guns: Rob Williams and Black Power (dir. S. Dickson and C. Roberts), 2004
She Hate Me (dir. Lee), 2004
Jesus Children of America (dir. Lee), 2005
Flow: Living in the Stream of Music (dir. J. Gabour), 2006
Inside Man (dir. Lee), 2006
Waist Deep (dir. Curtis-Hall), 2006
Who the #$&% is Jackson Pollock? (dir. H.M. Moses (as H. Moses)), 2006
Steep (dir. M. Obenhaus), 2007
Talk to Me (dir. Lemmons), 2007
Cadillac Records (dir. D. Martin), 2008
Miracle at St. Anna (dir. Lee), 2008
Bunraku (dir. G. Moshe), 2010
The Key Man (dir. P. Himmelstein), 2011
Red Tails (dir. A. Hemingway), 2012
Black or White (dir. M. Binder), 2014
Chi-Raq (dir. Lee), 2015
The Comedian (dir. T. Hackford), 2016
Great Performers: L.A. Noir (dir. A. Canaan Mann, G. Prince-Bythewood, and A. Kirwin), 2016
BlacKkKlansman (dir. Lee), 2018

Television music

Assault at West Point: the Court-Martial of Johnston Whittaker, 1994
The Promised Land, 1995
The Color of Courage, 1998
Free of Eden, 1998
Gia, 1998
The Tempest, 1998
Having Our Say: the Delany Sisters' First 100 Years, 1999
The Wonderful World of Disney, 1999
Navigating the Heart, 2000
The Truth About Jane, 2000
Bojangles, 2001
A Girl Thing, 2001
Jim Brown: All American, 2002
Redemption: the Stan Tookie Williams Story, 2004
Suckers Free City, 2004

Heartless, 2005
Their Eyes Were Watching God, 2005
Independent Lens, 2006
When the Levees Broke: a Requiem in Four Acts, 2006
If God is Willing and da Creek Don't Rise, 2010
Gun Hill, 2011
Abducted: the Carlina White Story, 2012
Katrina 10 Years after the Storm with Robin Roberts, 2015

Bibliography

K. Gabbard: "Signifyin(g) the Phallus: Representations of the Jazz Trumpet," *Jammin' at the Margins: Jazz and the American Cinema* (Chicago, 1996), 138–59
M. Schelle: *The Score: Interviews with Film Composers* (Los Angeles, 1999)
A. Margo: *Contemporary Cat: Terence Blanchard with Special Guests* (Lanham, MD, 2002)
M. Thomas: *Jazz in Documentary Film, Dynamic Canons* (diss., U. of Southern California, 2011)

MATTHEW ALAN THOMAS/R

Bradford, James [Jimmy] C(harles)

(*b* Rochester, NY, 13 June 1885; *d* New York, 11 May 1941). American composer and conductor. Born into a musical family, Bradford studied scoring and conducting with Tali Esen Moran at the Great Auditorium in Ocean Grove, New Jersey. He earned a reputation as a skilled orchestra conductor, directing various ensembles, including the Ogden Crane School of American Opera (*c*1905–7), the Mando Operatic Company (1913), and Bradford's Banjo Orchestra (1914). Bradford entered the film industry in 1914 as music director at New York's Broadway Theater, where he remained until December 1920. Bradford's greatest contribution to the early film industry was his pioneering work on the thematic cue sheet. Starting in 1915, Paramount enlisted Bradford to create musical settings that they printed in their weekly magazine. By 1917, his musical suggestions appeared in *Moving Picture Weekly* and, a year later, *Moving Picture World.* Along with Hugo Riesenfeld, Erno Rapee, and Joseph Carl Breil, Bradford joined the newly formed Synchronized Scenario Music in 1921 to produce piano-conductor scores that were distributed to theaters across the country. Shortly thereafter in 1922, Bradford left the company along with its president, M.J. Mintz, to form the Cameo Music Publishing Co. At Cameo, Bradford compiled over four hundred of their iconic Thematic Music Cue Sheets, which distinctly featured musical incipits for each cue. In addition to cue sheets, Bradford arranged film scores throughout the 1920s and 30s, and in 1931, he formed the James C. Bradford Corporation, which prepared synchronized film scores with music, dubbed dialogue, and sound effects.

Works

(selective list)

Cue sheets

American Pluck
Beau Geste
Cabiria
Captain Swagger
The Cat and the Canary
The Crown of Lies
Drums of the Desert
East is West
Firemen, Save My Child
The Fleet's In
The Gay Defender
Get Your Man
The Great Mail Robbery
His Tiger Lady
Honeymoon Abroad
Hula
Intolerance
The Jazz Age
King Cowboy
Ladies of the Mob
The Legion of the Condemned
The Michigan Kid
Miss Bluebeard
Nanook of the North
The Nth Commandment
The Private Life of Helen of Troy
Red Hair
Seven Footprints of Satan
Show Folks
Silk Stockings
The Song and Dance Man
Stocks and Blondes
Subway Sadie
Ten Modern Commandments
Two Can Play
Wagon Master
What Price Glory
The Wizard of Oz
Wonderful Chance

Film scores

The Fall of the Romanoffs (dir. H. Brenon), 1917
Sporting Life (dir. M. Tourneur), 1918
The Heart of Humanity (dir. A. Holubar), 1919
Roped (dir. J. Ford), 1919
Isobel or The Trail's End (dir. E. Carewe), 1920
So Long Letty (dir. A. Christie), 1920
The Stealers (dir. C. Cabanne), 1920
The Sheik (dir. G. Melford), 1921 (1938 sound reissue)
Richard the Lion-Hearted (dir. C. Withey), 1923
Captain Blood (dir. D. Smith and A.E. Smith), 1924
No More Women (dir. L. Ingraham), 1924
Triumph (dir. C.B. DeMille), 1924
Western Yesterdays (dir. F. Ford), 1924
Tumbleweeds (dir. K. Baggot and W.S. Hart), 1925 (1939 sound reissue, collab. A. Guttmann)
Moana (documentary, dir. F.H. Flaherty and R.J. Flaherty), 1926
The Son of the Sheik (dir. G. Fitzmaurice), 1926
Black Butterflies (dir. J.W. Horne), 1928
Mamba (dir. A.S. Rogell), 1930
Isle of Paradise (documentary, dir. C.T. Trego), 1932
Savage Gold (documentary, dir. G. Dyott), 1933
Juarez and Maximillian (dir. M.C. Torres and R.J. Sevilla), 1934
Schlitz on Mount Washington (short, dir. C. Young), 1935

Bibliography

"J.C. Bradford Dies; a Film Music Aide," *New York Times* (13 May 1941)
"James C. Bradford Dies; Was Film Music Pioneer," *Film Daily*, lxxix/93 (1941), 3
Obituary, *Variety*, cxlii/10 (1941), 54
G. Anderson: *Music for Silent Films 1894–1929: a Guide* (Washington, DC, 1988)
C. McCarty: *Film Composers in America: a Filmography 1911–1970* (New York, 2000), 45
R. Altman: *Silent Film Sound* (New York, 2004)

PETER GRAFF

Bradley, Scott

(*b* Russellville, AK, 26 Nov 1891; *d* Chatsworth, CA, 27 April 1977). American composer and conductor. He studied organ and harmony with Horton Corbett. After working as a theater musician in Houston, Texas, he moved to Los Angeles in 1926 and played in theater and radio orchestras, including those affiliated with KHJ and KTM. He first became known in the early 1930s as a composer of tone poems and works for orchestra and chorus, including an oratorio, *Thanatopsis* (1934), which premèred the same year he married local professional singer Myrtle Aber.

Bradley was hired by animators Rudy Ising and Hugh Harman, formerly of the Warner Bros. animation studio, to provide music for a short sequence of animation in Paramount's 1933 feature adaptation of *Alice in Wonderland*. When the duo began producing animated shorts for MGM, Bradley was hired to score the cartoons, beginning with *The Discontented Canary* (1934). He stayed with the animation unit when they moved to the MGM lot in 1937. During the 1940s he studied with composer Mario Castelnuovo-Tedesco, who served as a teacher/mentor for many film composers in Hollywood at that time. Bradley maintained an active public profile as a composer, giving lectures and writing articles on film and cartoon music through the 1940s and 50s; he was also a member of numerous groups that supported new music, including the California Society of Composers. Bradley scored practically all MGM cartoons until the division was shuttered in 1957. He then retired from film composing, although his concert works—in particular *Cartoonia* (1938), inspired by cartoon scores—were performed in southern California and elsewhere in the United States through the 1960s.

Bradley's scores were unique among other cartoon composers of the time, and they stand out as some of the more experimental music created for mainstream Hollywood cinema, demonstrating his fondness for Hindemith and Schoenberg; his experiments with twleve-tone rows can be heard in cartoon scores beginning in the early 1940s. His papers are held at the Cinema-Television Library at the University of Southern California.

Works

(*selective list*)

Feature film scores

(*all partial contributions*)
Courage of Lassie (dir. F.M. Wilcox), 1946
The Kissing Bandit (dir. L. Benedek), 1948
The Yellow Cab Man (dir. J. Donohue), 1950
Dangerous When Wet (dir. C. Walters), 1952
Blackboard Jungle (dir. R. Brooks), 1955

Short films

The Discontented Canary (dir. R. Ising), 1934
A Tale of the Vienna Woods (dir. R. Ising), 1934
Honeyland (dir. R. Ising), 1935
Bottles (dir. H. Harman), 1936
Little Cheeser (dir. R. Ising), 1936

Swing Wedding (dir. H. Harman), 1937
Art Gallery (dir. H. Harman), 1939
The Bear That Couldn't Sleep (dir. R. Ising), 1939
The Blue Danube (dir. H. Harman), 1939
The Mad Maestro (dir. F. Freleng and H. Harman), 1939
Peace on Earth (dir. H. Harman), 1939
The Fishing Bear (dir. R. Ising), 1940
Puss Gets the Boot (dir. J. Barbera, W. Hanna, and R. Ising), 1940
Romeo in Rhythm (dir. R. Ising), 1940
Tom Turkey and His Harmonica Humdingers (dir. H. Harman), 1940
Abdul the Bulbul Ameer (dir. R. Allen and H. Harman), 1941
Dance of the Weed (dir. R. Ising and J. Brewer), 1941
The Midnight Snack (dir. J. Barbera, W. Hanna, and R. Ising), 1941
The Night Before Christmas (dir. J. Barbera, W. Hanna and R. Ising), 1941
The Prospecting Bear (dir. R. Ising), 1941
Rookie Bear (dir. R. Ising), 1941
Barney Bear's Victory (dir. R. Ising), 1942
The Blitz Wolf (dir. T. Avery), 1942
The Bowling Alley Cat (dir. J. Barbera and W. Hanna), 1942
Dog Trouble (dir. J. Barbera, W. Hanna and M. Lah), 1942
The Early Bird Dood It (dir. T. Avery), 1942
Fine Feathered Friend (dir. J. Barbera and W. Hanna), 1942
Fraidy Cat (dir. J. Barbera, W. Hanna and R. Ising), 1942
Puss N' Toots (dir. J. Barbera, W. Hanna and M. Lah), 1942
Baby Puss (dir. J. Barbera and W. Hanna), 1943
Dumb Hounded (dir. T. Avery), 1943
The Lonesome Mouse (dir. J. Barbera and W. Hanna), 1943
One Ham's Family (dir. T. Avery), 1943
Red Hot Riding Hood (dir. T. Avery), 1943
Sufferin' Cats! (dir. J. Barbera and W. Hanna), 1943
War Dogs (dir. J. Barbera and W. Hanna), 1943
What's Buzzin' Buzzard (dir. T. Avery), 1943
Who Killed Who? (dir. T. Avery), 1943
Yankee Doodle Mouse (dir. J. Barbera and W. Hanna), 1943
Barney Bear's Polar Pest (dir. G. Gordon), 1944
Batty Baseball (dir. T. Avery), 1944
Bear Raid Warden (dir. G. Gordon), 1944
Big Heel Watha (dir. T. Avery), 1944
The Bodyguard (dir. Barbera and Hanna), 1944
Happy Go Nutty (dir. Avery), 1944
Million Dollar Cat (dir. Barbera and Hanna), 1944
Mouse Trouble (dir. Barbera and Hanna), 1944
Puttin' On the Dog (dir. J. Barbera and W. Hanna), 1944
Screwball Squirrel (dir. Avery), 1944
Zoot Cat (dir. Barbera and Hanna), 1944
Flirty Birdy (dir. J. Barbera and W. Hanna), 1945
Jerky Turkey (dir. T. Avery), 1945

The Mouse Comes to Dinner (dir. J. Barbera and W. Hanna), 1945
Mouse in Manhattan (dir. J. Barbera and W. Hanna), 1945
Quiet Please (dir. J. Barbera and W. Hanna), 1945
Screwy Truant (dir. T. Avery), 1945
Shooting of Dan McGoo (dir. T. Avery), 1945
Swing Shift Cinderella (dir. T. Avery), 1945
Tee for Two (dir. J. Barbera and W. Hanna), 1945
Wild and Woolfy (dir. T. Avery), 1945
Henpecked Hoboes (dir. T. Avery), 1946
The Hick Chick (dir. T. Avery), 1946
Lonesome Lenny (dir. T. Avery), 1946
The Milky Waif (dir. J. Barbera and W. Hanna), 1946
Northwest Hounded Police (dir. T. Avery), 1946
Solid Serenade (dir. J. Barbera and W. Hanna), 1946
Springtime for Thomas (dir. J. Barbera and W. Hanna), 1946
Trap Happy (dir. J. Barbera and W. Hanna), 1946
The Cat Concerto (dir. J. Barbera and W. Hanna), 1947
Cat Fishin' (dir. J. Barbera and W. Hanna), 1947
Dr. Jekyll and Mr. Mouse (dir. J. Barbera and W. Hanna), 1947
Hound Hunters (dir. T. Avery), 1947
The Invisible Mouse (dir. J. Barbera and W. Hanna), 1947
King-Size Canary (dir. T. Avery), 1947
A Mouse in the House (dir. J. Barbera and W. Hanna), 1947
Part Time Pal (dir. J. Barbera and W. Hanna), 1947
Red Hot Rangers (dir. T. Avery), 1947
Salt Water Tabby (dir. J. Barbera and W. Hanna), 1947
Slap Happy Lion (dir. T. Avery), 1947
Uncle Tom's Cabana (dir. T. Avery), 1947
The Cat That Hated People (dir. T. Avery), 1948
Half-Pint Pygmy (dir. T. Avery), 1948
Little 'Tinker (dir. T. Avery), 1948
Lucky Ducky (dir. T. Avery), 1948
Mouse Cleaning (dir. J. Barbera and W. Hanna), 1948
Old Rockin' Chair (dir. J. Barbera and W. Hanna), 1948
Professor Tom (dir. J. Barbera and W. Hanna), 1948
What Price Fleadom (dir. T. Avery), 1948
Bad Luck Blackie (dir. T. Avery), 1949
Cat and Mermouse (dir. J. Barbera and W. Hanna), 1949
Doggone Tired (dir. T. Avery), 1949
Goggle Fishing Bear (dir. P. Blair and M. Lah), 1949
Hatch Up Your Troubles (dir. J. Barbera and W. Hanna), 1949
Heavenly Puss (dir. J. Barbera and W. Hanna), 1949
House of Tomorrow (dir. T. Avery), 1949
Jerry's Diary (dir. J. Barbera and W. Hanna), 1949
The Little Orphan (dir. J. Barbera and W. Hanna), 1949
Out-Foxed (dir. T. Avery), 1949
Tennis Chumps (dir. J. Barbera and W. Hanna), 1949

Jerry and the Lion (dir. J. Barbera and W. Hanna), 1950
Little Quacker (dir. J. Barbera and W. Hanna), 1950
Saturday Evening Puss (dir. J. Barbera and W. Hanna), 1950
Texas Tom (dir. J. Barbera and W. Hanna), 1950
Tom and Jerry in the Hollywood Bowl (dir. J. Barbera and W. Hanna), 1950
Ventriloquist Cat (dir. T. Avery), 1950
Car of Tomorrow (dir. T. Avery), 1951
Casanova Cat (dir. J. Barbera and W. Hanna), 1951
Daredevil Droopy (dir. T. Avery), 1951
Droopy's Double Trouble (dir. T. Avery), 1951
His Mouse Friday (dir. J. Barbera and W. Hanna), 1951
Jerry and the Goldfish (dir. J. Barbera and W. Hanna), 1951
Jerry's Cousin (dir. J. Barbera and W. Hanna), 1951
Symphony in Slang (dir. T. Avery), 1951
Caballero Droopy (dir. D. Lundy), 1952
Flying Cat (dir. J. Barbera and W. Hanna), 1952
Magical Maestro (dir. T. Avery), 1952
One Cab's Family (dir. T. Avery), 1952
Rock-a-Bye Bear (dir. T. Avery), 1952
Two Mouseketeers (dir. J. Barbera and W. Hanna), 1952
Barney's Hungry Cousin (dir. D. Lundy), 1953
Jerry and Jumbo (dir. J. Barbera and W. Hanna), 1953
Johann Mouse (dir. J. Barbera and W. Hanna), 1953
Little Johnny Jet (dir. T. Avery), 1953
That's My Pup (dir. J. Barbera and W. Hanna), 1953
Three Little Pups (dir. T. Avery), 1953
T.V. of Tomorrow (dir. T. Avery), 1953
Billy Boy (dir. T. Avery), 1954
Dixieland Droopy (dir. T. Avery), 1954
Farm of Tomorrow (dir. T. Avery), 1954
Hic-Cup Pup (dir. J. Barbera and W. Hanna), 1954
Homesteader Droopy (dir. T. Avery), 1954
Mice Follies (dir. J. Barbera and W. Hanna), 1954
Neopolitan Mouse (dir. J. Barbera and W. Hanna), 1954
Posse Cat (dir. J. Barbera and W. Hanna), 1954
Touché Pussy Cat! (dir. J. Barbera and W. Hanna), 1954
Cellbound (dir. T. Avery and M. Lah), 1955
Deputy Droopy (dir. T. Avery and M. Lah), 1955
Field and Scream (dir. T. Avery), 1955
The First Bad Man (dir. T. Avery), 1955
Pecos Pest (dir. J. Barbera and W. Hanna), 1955
Pup on a Picnic (dir. J. Barbera and W. Hanna), 1955
Barbecue Brawl (dir. J. Barbera and W. Hanna), 1956
Blue Cat Blues (dir. J. Barbera and W. Hanna), 1956
Busy Buddies (dir. J. Barbera and W. Hanna), 1956
Downbeat Bear (dir. J. Barbera and W. Hanna), 1956
Millionaire Droopy (dir. T. Avery), 1956

Muscle Beach Tom (dir. J. Barbera and W. Hanna), 1956
Give and Tyke (dir. J. Barbera and W. Hanna), 1957
One Droopy Knight (dir. M. Lah), 1957
Droopy Leprechaun (dir. Lah, Barbera and Hanna), 1958
Happy Go Ducky (dir. J. Barbera and W. Hanna), 1958
Robin Hoodwinked (dir. Barbera and Hanna), 1958
Sheep Wrecked (dir. M. Lah), 1958
Tot Watchers (dir. J. Barbera and W. Hanna), 1958

Orchestral

The Valley of the White Poppies (1931)
The Headless Horseman (1932)
Thanatopsis (including soloists and choir) (1934)
Cartoonia (1938)

Writings

"Cartoon Music of the Future," *Pacific Coast Musician* (21 June 1941)
"'Music in Cartoons,' Excerpts from a talk given at The Music Forum, 28 Oct 1944," *Film Music Notes*, iv/3 (1944)
"Personality on the Sound Track," *MEJ*, xxxiii/3 (1947), 28–30

Bibliography

I. Dahl: "Notes on Cartoon Music," *Film Music Notes*, viii/5 (1949), 3–13
D. Goldmark: *Tunes for 'Toons: Music and the Hollywood Cartoon* (Berkeley, CA, 2005)

DANIEL GOLDMARK

Breil, Joseph Carl

(*b* Pittsburgh, 29 June 1870; *d* Los Angeles, 23 Jan 1926). American singer, composer, and conductor. He began to study piano and violin at the age of eleven, and singing at sixteen. He attended St. Fidelis College, Butler, Pennsylvania, and Curry University, Pittsburgh, before going to Leipzig to study law. While in Leipzig he decided to pursue a career in music and took courses at the Conservatory and studied singing with Ewald. He also had singing lessons in Milan and Philadelphia (with Giuseppe del Puente) and sang as principal tenor of the Emma Juch Opera Company (1891–2). Then he settled in Pittsburgh, where he taught singing and was choir director of St. Paul's Cathedral (1892–7); for six years thereafter he worked for a variety of theater companies, and from 1903 to 1910 as an editor.

Breil first gained recognition as a composer with his incidental music to *The Climax* in 1909; three years later he wrote and conducted one of the first scores composed expressly for a film (*Queen Elizabeth*). Breil's association with

D.W. Griffith resulted in several film scores, including *The Birth of a Nation* (1915) and *Intolerance* (1916). The former included selections from the symphonic repertory and popular songs from the Civil War as well as much original music by Breil. His one-act opera *The Legend* was produced at the Metropolitan Opera in 1919.

Works

(selective list)

Film scores

Queen Elizabeth (dir. H. Desfontaines and L. Mercanton), 1912
The Prisoner of Zenda (dir. H. Ford, E.S. Porter), 1913
Cabiria (dir. G. Pastrone), 1914
The Birth of a Nation (dir. D.W. Griffith), 1915
Double Trouble (dir. C. Cabanne), 1915
The Lily and the Rose (dir. P. Powell), 1915
The Martyrs of the Alamo (dir. C. Cabanne), 1915
The Penitentes (dir. J. Conway), 1915
Intolerance (dir. D.W. Griffith), 1916
The Wood Nymph (dir. P. Powell), 1916
The Lost Battalion (dir. B.L. King), 1919
The Green Goddess (dir. S. Olcott), 1923
The White Rose (dir. D.W. Griffith), 1923
The White Sister (dir. H. King), 1923
America (dir. D.W. Griffith), 1924, collab. A. Finck

Stage

The Climax (incid music, E. Locke), 1909
Love Laughs at Locksmiths (comic op, Breil), 1910
The Seventh Chord (incid music, A. Miller), 1913
The Sky Pilot (incid music, F. Mandel and G.H. Brennan), 1917
The Legend (op, J. Byrne), 1919
Der Asra (op, Breil, after H. Heine), 1925

Vocal

sacred works, incl. 2 masses, solo vv, SATB
3 partsongs

MSS in *US-DLC*

Principal publishers: Berge, Chappell

Bibliography

D.J. Teall: “Mr. Breil’s ‘Legend’ Embodies his Theories of Practical Democracy,” *MusAm*, xxviii/22 (1918), 5
B.D. Ussher: “Joseph Carl Breil,” *MusAm*, xliii/15 (1926), 39 [obituary]

E.E. Hipsher: "Joseph Carl Breil," *American Opera and its Composers* (Philadelphia, 1927), 87

M. Marks: *Music and the Silent Film: Contexts and Case Studies, 1895–1924* (New York, 1997)

A. Clyde: "Joseph Carl Breil and the Score for *The Birth of a Nation*," *Cue Sheet*, xvi/1 (2000), 5–31

J. Gaines and N. Lerner: "The Orchestration of Affect: the Motif of Barbarism in Breil's *The Birth of a Nation* Score," *The Sounds of Early Cinema*, ed. R. Altman and R. Abel (Bloomington, 2001), 252–70

R. Altman: *Silent Film Sound* (New York, 2004)

M. Cooke: *A History of Film Music* (Cambridge, 2008)

WARREN M. SHERK

Broughton, Bruce

(*b* Los Angeles, 8 March 1945). American composer, primarily for film and television. The son and grandson of Salvation Army musicians, he began studying the piano and trumpet by the age of seven and travelled across the western United States throughout his youth, gaining practical experience as a performer in brass bands. He graduated *cum laude* from the University of Southern California with a composition degree in 1967 and worked at CBS Television through the mid-1970s, first as a music supervisor and then as a composer for series including "Gunsmoke" and "Hawaii Five-0." He became one of television's leading composers, earning a record ten Emmy Awards from 1981 to 2005 (for such diverse fare as the drama series "Dallas" and the animated "Tiny Toon Adventures"; period miniseries like "The First Olympics, Athens 1896"; and television films including the Willa Cather adaptation *O Pioneers!* and the light-hearted *Eloise at the Plaza*).

Broughton's ease with Americana subjects—including the 1982 Civil War miniseries "The Blue and the Gray"—led to his first major feature, the Western *Silverado*, which earned a 1985 Oscar nomination. He quickly became a sought-after composer, especially for films that demanded symphonic treatment, among them *Young Sherlock Holmes, The Boy Who Could Fly, Harry and the Hendersons, The Rescuers Down Under, Honey I Blew Up the Kid, Tombstone*, and *Homeward Bound: the Incredible Journey*. He also composed the first orchestral score for a video game, *Heart of Darkness* (1999), a series of Roger Rabbit cartoon shorts, and a number of scores for Disney theme-park rides.

At the same time, Broughton became a leader in the Hollywood music community, serving as the president of the Society of Composers and Lyricists, a governor of both the Academy of Television Arts & Sciences and the Academy of Motion Picture Arts & Sciences, and eventually a member of the board of directors of American Society of Composers, Authors, and Publishers. In the late 1990s and early 2000s, Broughton turned more of his attention to concert work, composing dozens of new pieces for orchestra, band, and chamber ensemble.

Works

Film and television scores

Feature films

The Prodigal (dir. J.F. Collier), 1983
The Ice Pirates (dir. S. Raffill), 1984
Silverado (dir. L. Kasdan), 1985
Young Sherlock Holmes (dir. B. Levinson), 1985
The Boy Who Could Fly (dir. N. Castle), 1986
Sweet Liberty (dir. A. Alda), 1986
Big Shots (dir. R. Mandel), 1987
Cross My Heart (dir. A. Bernstein), 1987
Harry and the Hendersons (dir. W. Dear), 1987
The Monster Squad (dir. F. Dekker), 1987
Square Dance (dir. D. Petrie and M. Nesmith), 1987
Last Rites (dir. D.P. Bellisario), 1988
Moonwalker (dir. J. Kramer, W. Vinton, J. Blashfield, and C. Chilvers), 1988
The Presidio (dir. P. Hyams), 1988
The Rescue (dir. F. Fairfax), 1988
Jacknife (dir. D. Jones), 1989
Betsy's Wedding (dir. Alda), 1990
Narrow Margin (dir. Hyams), 1990
The Rescuers Down Under (dir. H. Butoy and M. Gabriel), 1990
All I Want for Christmas (dir. R. Lieberman), 1991
Honey I Blew Up the Kid (dir. R. Kleiser), 1992
Stay Tuned (dir. Hyams), 1992
For Love or Money (dir. B. Sonnenfeld), 1993
Homeward Bound: The Incredible Journey (dir. D. Dunham), 1993
So I Married an Axe Murderer (dir. T. Schlamme), 1993
Tombstone (dir. G.P. Cosmatos), 1993
Baby's Day Out (dir. P. Read Johnson), 1994
Holy Matrimony (dir. L. Nimoy), 1994
Miracle on 34th Street (dir. L. Mayfield), 1994
Carried Away (dir. B. Barreto), 1996
Homeward Bound 2: Lost in San Francisco (dir. D.R. Ellis), 1996
House Arrest (dir. H. Winer), 1996
Infinity (dir. M. Broderick), 1996
Shadow Conspiracy (dir. Cosmatos), 1997
A Simple Wish (dir. M. Ritchie), 1997
Krippendorf's Tribe (dir. T. Holland), 1998
Lost in Space (dir. S. Hopkins), 1998

One Tough Cop (dir. Barreto), 1998
Last Flight Out (dir. J. Jameson), 2004
Bambi II (dir. B. Pimental), 2006
The Pledge, (dir. J.W. Myers) 2011
Alone Yet Not Alone (dir. R. Bengston and G.D. Escobar), 2013
A Christmas Tree Miracle (dir. J.W. Myers), 2013
Well Played (dir. J. Kagan), 2013
Soarin' Around the World (dir. T. Fitzgerald), 2016
Shot (dir. Kagan), 2017

Television series

(*selective list*)

Gunsmoke, 1973
Hawaii Five-0, 1973
Quincy, M.E., 1977
Dallas, 1979
How the West was Won, 1979
Buck Rogers in the 25th Century, 1981
Two Marriages, 1983
Amazing Stories, 1985
Tiny Toon Adventures, 1990
Dinosaurs, 1991
Tales from the Crypt, 1991
Capitol Critters, 1992
JAG, 1995
First Monday, 2002

Television movies and miniseries

(*selective list*)
Desperate Voyage, 1980
Killjoy, 1981
The Blue and the Gray, 1982
One Shoe Makes It Murder, 1982
Cowboy, 1983
This Girl for Hire, 1983
The First Olympics: Athens 1896, 1984
The Master of Ballantrae, 1984
Passions, 1984
Stormin' Home, 1985
George Washington II: the Forging of a Nation, 1986
The Thanksgiving Promise, 1986
Sorry, Wrong Number, 1989
The Old Man and the Sea, 1990
O Pioneers!, 1991
True Women, 1997

Glory & Honor, 1998
Jeremiah, 1998
Night Ride Home, 1999
The Ballad of Lucy Whipple, 2001
Bobbie's Girl, 2002
Damaged Care, 2002
The Locket, 2002
Roughing It, 2002
Eloise at Christmastime, 2003
Eloise at the Plaza, 2003
Lucy, 2003
The Dive from Clausen's Pier, 2005
Warm Springs, 2005
Safe Harbor, 2009
Hollywood in Vienna, 2011
Texas Rising, 2015
The Orville, 2017

Concert music

Orchestral

Conc., tuba, orch, 1979
Conc., picc, chbr orch, 1992
English Music, hn, str, 1995
Modular Music I, II, 2003
And on the Sixth Day, ob, orch, 2004
Mixed Elements, orch, 2006
Saloon Music, tpt, pit orch, 2006
A Tiny Sym. for Str, 2007
Fanfares: Mosaic for Orch, 2008
Triptych: Three Incongruities, vn, chbr orch, 2008

Symphonic band

Excursions, tpt, band, 1999
American Hero, 2001
New Era, 2008
Oliver's Birthday, tpt, band, 2008
In the World of Spirits, 2011

Brass band or brass ensemble

A Frontier Overture, brass band, 1982
Harlequin, brass band, 1984
California Legend, brass band, 1985
Concert Piece, 8 tpt, 1999
Euphonies, 8 hn, 1999

Masters of Space and Time, brass band, 2001
Fanfares, Marches, Hymns and Finale, brass, perc, 2004
Variations on a Sonata, double brass quartet, tuba, 2006
Hornworks, 5 hn, tuba, 2010

Chamber

General William Booth Enters into Heaven, Bar, pf, 1967
Sonata, tuba, 1979
Sparrows, 4 fl, 1984
Toccata, 2 hp, mallet perc, 1986
Bipartition, vc, tuba, 1989
Ballad, trbn, pf, 1998
Tyvek Wood, hp, va, fl, 2001
Fingerprints of Childhood, fl, vn, va, 2002
Bounce, bn, 2 str qt, db, 2003
Sonata, hn, pf, 2004
A Primer for Malachi,fl, cl, pf, vc, 2005
Short Stories, mar, pf, 2005
Gold Rush Songs, vn, pf, 2006
Hudson River Valley, woodwind octet, 2006
Remembrance, a sax, pf, 2006
Three American Portraits, brass qnt, 2006
Conversations, cl, str qt, 2007
Sonata, vn, 2007
5 pieces, pf, 2009
when a body meets a body, brass qnt, 2009
Sonatina, vn, 2010

Bibliography

T. Thomas: *Music for the Movies* (Beverly Hills, CA, 2/1997)
M. Schelle: *The Score: Interviews With Film Composers* (Los Angeles, 1999)
C. DesJardins: *Inside Film Music: Composers Speak* (Los Angeles, 2007)
J. Burlingame: "Bruce Broughton at 65," *Film Music Society* (2010), http://www.filmmusicsociety.org/news_events/features/2010/030810.html
T. Hoover: "Keeping Score with Bruce Broughton," *Keeping Score: Interviews with Today's Top Film, Television, and Game Music Composers*, ed. T. Hoover (Boston, 2010), 97–103

JON BURLINGAME/R

Bruns, George

(*b* Sandy, OR, 3 July 1914; *d* Portland, OR, 23 May 1983). American arranger and composer. A veteran of the big-band era, Bruns is today primarily known as the composer of music for Walt Disney films, and especially for "The Ballad of Davy Crockett," the song that helped to launch one of the major pop culture fads of the 1950s.

Bruns played piano at age six and tuba and brass in high school. He attended Oregon State Agricultural College, where he participated in the ROTC band. While obtaining experience with various big bands, he served as arranger and musical director on Portland radio. After moving to Los Angeles, he organized his own small instrumental group and was active in recording.

In 1953 he joined the animation studio UPA (United Productions of America) and scored a few shorts. Bruns moved to Disney that same year, working on the studio's first television ventures, including "The Mickey Mouse Club." In 1954 he composed (with lyrics by Tom Blackburn) "The Ballad of Davy Crockett" for an episode of the weekly "Disneyland" television series. The folklike tune, also featured in the 1955 theatrical film, became a number-one hit and led to Bruns's rise in Disney music from the 1950s through the 1970s. He also wrote "Yo Ho (A Pirate's Life for Me)" for the Disneyland park attraction *Pirates of the Caribbean.*

Although Bruns's grounding was primarily in jazz, he proved a versatile arranger and music director as well as a moderately gifted composer. He adapted the symphonic Tchaikovsky ballet score for Disney's animation epic *Sleeping Beauty* (1959) and updated Victor Herbert's classic music for the studio's first live-action musical, *Babes in Toyland* (1961). He mainly provided underscoring but occasionally also songs for many animated and live-action features, and drew on his jazz roots for films such as *101 Dalmatians* (1961), *The Jungle Book* (1967), and *The Aristocats* (1970). He received four Academy Award nominations for his Disney feature work and retired in 1976.

Works

Film scores

Short films

Christopher Crumpet (dir. R. Cannon), 1953
Little Boy with a Big Horn (dir. R. Cannon), 1953
Magoo's Masterpiece (dir. P. Burness), 1953
A Cowboy Needs a Horse (dir. B. Justice), 1956
In the Bag (dir. J. Hannah), 1956
Jack and Old Mac (dir. B. Justice), 1956
Paul Bunyan (dir. L. Clark), 1958
Noah's Ark (dir. B. Justice), 1959
The Saga of Windwagon Smith (dir. C.A. Nichols), 1961
Freewayphobia (dir. L. Clark), 1965
Freewayphobia #2: Goofy's Freeway Trouble (dir. L. Clark), 1965

It's Tough to Be a Bird (dir. W. Kimball), 1969
I'm No Fool with Electricity (dir. L. Clark), 1970

Feature films

Davy Crockett, King of the Wild Frontier (dir. N. Foster), 1955
Westward Ho the Wagons! (dir. W. Beaudine), 1955
Davy Crockett and the River Pirates (dir. N. Foster), 1956
Johnny Tremain (dir. R. Stevenson), 1957
Old Yeller (dir. R. Stevenson), 1957
Perri: a True-Life Fantasy (dir. P. Kenworthy and R. Wright), 1957
The Light in the Forest (dir. H. Daugherty), 1958
Tonka (dir. L.R. Foster), 1958
Sleeping Beauty (dir. C. Geronimi), 1959
The Absent-Minded Professor (dir. R. Stevenson), 1961
Babes in Toyland (dir. J. Donohue), 1961
101 Dalmatians (dir. C. Geronimi, H. Luske and W. Reitherman), 1961
Son of Flubber (dir. R. Stevenson), 1963
The Sword in the Stone (dir. W. Reitherman), 1963
The Fighting Prince of Donegal (dir. M. O'Herlihy), 1966
Follow Me, Boys! (dir. N. Tokar), 1966
The Ugly Dachshund (dir. N. Tokar), 1966
The Adventures of Bullwhip Griffin (dir. J. Neilson), 1967
The Jungle Book (dir. W. Reitherman), 1967
The Horse in the Gray Flannel Suit (dir. N. Tokar), 1968
The Love Bug (dir. R. Stevenson), 1968
The Aristocats (dir. W. Reitherman), 1970
Robin Hood (dir. W. Reitherman), 1973
Herbie Rides Again (dir. R. Stevenson), 1974

Television music

Disneyland/Walt Disney's Wonderful World of Color, 1954–70
Mickey Mouse Club, 1955–9
Zorro, 1957–9
Beetle Bailey, 1963
Cowboy in Africa, 1967

Bibliography

The Illustrated Disney Song Book (New York, 1979), 42–3 [with introd. by D. E. Tietyen]
R. Care: "George Bruns," *The Cue Sheet*, xviii/3–4, (2002) 35–7
R. Care: "Make Walt's Music: Music for Disney Animation, 1928–1967," *The Cartoon Music Book*, ed. D. Goldmark and Y. Taylor (Chicago, 2002), 34–5

ROSS CARE

Burwell, Carter

(*b* New York, 18 Nov 1954). American composer. Although he enjoyed music and studied the piano in his youth, he did not immediately or actively pursue music as a profession. In 1977 he graduated from Harvard University, where he had studied mathematics and computer science and was interested in drawing and animation. After college he designed computer software for a biology laboratory and worked as an animator at the New York Institute of Technology. He also continued to develop his interest in electronic and computer music, an interest that began at Harvard, where he was a graduate assistant for Ivan Tcherepnin at the Harvard Electronic Music Studio. Burwell played in a number of art-minded New York-based rock bands in the late 1970s and early 80s including the Same, Thick Pigeon, and Radiante. He contributed vocals for these groups, but it was his unique and creative percussive effects and sound designs that attracted attention.

In 1984 Burwell was asked by the emerging film directors Joel and Ethan Coen to score their first film, *Blood Simple.* The success of the film and its quirky score propelled Burwell into a career in film composing. Burwell collaborated with the Coen brothers on all but one of the eighteen feature films that they made during the period 1984 to 2018 and has scored films for other distinguished directors including David Mamet, Spike Jonze, Sidney Lumet, Julian Schnabel, and David O. Russell.

Burwell's success as a film composer stems from his unusually broad and eclectic style and the independent function he sees for music in film. "My interest," he once observed in an interview, is "in having music contribute something that's not already present in the picture, as opposed to supporting what's already present" (Rona, p.119). As a result, Burwell's scores are often just as much sound design as they are melodic composition. His compositional choices are made in consideration of the film's sound and in close collaboration with sound mixers, designers, and effects supervisors.

The breadth of his scoring style is also reflected in the instrumentation choices he makes. They range from yodeling, banjos, and folk instruments of various Western and non-Western cultures to synthesizers and electronic sound designs to large orchestras. Burwell's approach to traditional thematic or melodic composition is equally distinctive. In writing themes, he notes, "I like to work through something that's very simple and then explore it, but I don't like complexity for complexity's sake. I'm fascinated with what they call the science of complexity, but I believe that happens naturally . . . and my creations I prefer to be simple, to distinguish themselves from the natural world" (Burwell, p.208).

The range and flexibility of his film scoring style have made Burwell a favorite of prestigious auteur filmmakers and blockbuster Hollywood directors alike. As well as being one of the most sought-after composers working in Hollywood, Burwell has also written a number of non-film music works, primarily for dance and theatre productions.

Works

(selective list)

Film and television scores

(Film scores unless otherwise noted)

Blood Simple (dir. J. Coen and E. Coen (uncredited)), 1984
Psycho III (dir. A. Perkins), 1986
Raising Arizona (dir. J. Coen and E. Coen (uncredited)), 1987
Miller's Crossing (dir. J. Coen and E. Coen (uncredited)), 1990
Barton Fink (dir. J. Coen and E. Coen (uncredited)), 1991
Doc Hollywood (dir. M. Caton-Jones), 1991
Storyville (dir. M. Frost), 1992
Wasteland (dir. D. Hefner and D.L. Hefner (as D. Hefner)), 1992
And the Band Played On (dir. R. Spottiswoode), 1993
Kalifornia (dir. D. Sena), 1993
The Hudsucker Proxy (dir. J. Coen and E. Coen (uncredited)), 1994
Rob Roy (dir. Caton-Jones), 1995
Fargo (dir. J. Coen and E. Coen (uncredited)), 1996
Conspiracy Theory (dir. R. Donner), 1997
The Jackal (dir. Caton-Jones), 1997
The Spanish Prisoner (dir. D. Mamet), 1997
The Big Lebowski (dir. J. Coen and E. Coen (uncredited)), 1998
Gods and Monsters (dir. B. Condon), 1998
Velvet Goldmine (dir. T. Haynes), 1998
Being John Malkovich (dir. S. Jonze), 1999
The General's Daughter (dir. S. West), 1999
The Hi-Lo Country (dir. S. Frears), 1999
Mystery, Alaska (dir. J. Roach), 1999
Three Kings (dir. D.O. Russell), 1999
Before Night Falls (dir. J. Schnabel), 2000
Hamlet (dir. M. Almereyda), 2000
A Knight's Tale (dir. B. Helgeland), 2001
The Man Who wasn't There (dir. J Coen and E. Coen (uncredited)), 2001
Adaptation (dir. Jonze), 2002
The Rookie (dir. J.L. Hancock), 2002
Simone (dir. A. Niccol), 2002
Intolerable Cruelty (dir. J. Coen and E. Coen (uncredited)), 2003
The Alamo (dir. Hancock), 2004
Kinsey (dir. Condon), 2004
The Ladykillers (dir. J. Coen and E. Coen (uncredited)), 2004
Fur (dir. S. Shainberg), 2006
The Hoax (dir. L. Hallstöm), 2006
Before the Devil Knows You're Dead (dir. S. Lumet), 2007
No Country for Old Men (dir. E. and J. Coen), 2007
Burn after Reading (dir. E. and J. Coen), 2008

In Bruges (dir. M. McDonagh), 2008
Twilight (dir. C. Hardwicke), 2008
The Blind Side (dir. Hancock), 2009
A Serious Man (dir. E. and J. Coen), 2009
Where the Wild Things Are (dir. Jonze), 2009
Howl (dir. R. Epstein and J. Friedman), 2010
The Kids are All Right (dir. L. Cholodenko), 2010
True Grit (dir. E. and J. Coen), 2010
Mildred Pierce (TV miniseries), 2011
Moving Gracefully Toward the Exit (dir. P. Regnier and J.B. Andro), 2011
The Twilight Saga: Breaking Dawn Part 1 (dir. B. Condon), 2011
Seven Psychopaths (dir. McDonagh), 2012
The Twilight Saga: Breaking Dawn Part 2 (dir. Condon), 2012
The Fifth Estate (dir. Condon), 2013
Olive Kitteridge (TV miniseries), 2014
Anomalisa (dir. D. Johnson and C. Kaufman), 2015
Carol (dir. Haynes), 2015
The Family Fang (dir. J. Bateman), 2015
Legend (dir. Helgeland), 2015
Mr. Holmes (dir. Condon), 2015
The Finest Hours (dir. C. Gillespie), 2016
The Founder (dir. Hancock), 2016
Hail, Caesar! (dir. E. and J. Coen), 2016
Goodbye Christopher Robin (dir. S. Curtis), 2017
Three Billboards outside Ebbing, Missouri (dir. McDonagh), 2017
Wonderstruck (dir. Haynes), 2017
The Ballad of Buster Scruggs (dir. E. and J. Coen), 2018

Theater

Three Confessions, 1984
Pantomime, 1985
The "Sometimes" Bishop of Polynesia, 1987
Widows, 1988
The Myth Project, 1989
The Celestial Alphabet Event, 1991
Mother, 1994
The 14th Ward, 1996
Cara Lucia, 2003
Anomalisa, 2005
Hope Leaves the Theater, 2005
Sawbones, 2005

Dance

RAB, 1984
The Return of Lot's Wife, 2003

Bibliography

J. Rona: "Raising Carter Burwell," *Keyboard Magazine*, xxvi (2000), no.8, pp.118–19; no.9 p.134 only

P. Verna: "Composer Spotlight," *Mix Magazine*, xxv/10 (2001), 225, 234–6, 238

C. Burwell: "Composing for the Coen Brothers," *Soundscape: the School of Sound Lectures, 1998–2001*, ed. L. Sider, D. Freeman, and J. Sider (New York, 2003), 195–208

M. Chion: "The Man Who was Indeed There (Carter Burwell and the Cohen Brothers' Films)," *The Soundtrack*, i/3 (2008), 175–81

C. Burwell: "No Country for Old Music," *The Oxford Handbook of New Audiovisual Aesthetics*, ed. J. Richardson, C. Gorbman, and C. Vernallis (New York, 2013), 168–70

T. Cochrane: "Composing the Expressive Qualities of Music: Interviews with Jean-Claude Risset, Brian Ferneyhough, and Carter Burwell," *The Emotional Power of Music: Multidisciplinary Perspectives on Musical Arousal, Expression, and Social Control*, ed. T. Cochrane, B. Fantini, and K. Scherer (New York, 2013), 23–40

JULIE HUBBERT/R

Buttolph, David

(*b* New York, 3 Aug 1902; *d* San Diego, 1 Jan 1983). American composer, arranger, conductor, music director, and pianist. He was musically trained by, and performed with, the Grace Church Choir School in New York from age eight. Deciding on a music career as a teenager, he attended what is now the Juilliard School, where he was a student of pianist Helena Augustin and studied music with Percy Goetschius and A. Madley Richardson. After receiving a diploma in 1921, he enrolled in the postgraduate piano program for two years before furthering his music studies with conductor Clemens Heinrich Krauss in Austria, and with conductor Hugo Rühr and composer Walter Courvoisier in Germany. He supported himself in Europe by playing piano in small jazz combos in nightclubs and coaching opera singers. Returning to New York in 1927, he found work writing, arranging, performing, and conducting music for the National Broadcasting Company. As an NBC radio artist, he was associated with the Cities Service Concerts and served as a vocal coach and arranger for the Cavaliers quartet. For two years in the early 1930s he was a radio station musical director in Schenectady, New York. A brief job at Fox Music Publishing in New York led to his relocating to Hollywood in 1933, where he became a composer and arranger for film, notably for Westerns. Admired for his speed and stylistic diversity, his music reflects his early love of opera but can be lacking in complexity. Employed by Fox Film Corp., and its successor, Twentieth Century-Fox, he collaborated on films scored by Alfred Newman in the 1940s, developing thematic material and fitting music to film alongside Cyril Mockridge and Edward Powell. After accepting Leo Forbstein's job offer at Warner Bros. in 1948, he worked primarily there before retiring in 1963. He also composed for television, including a memorable theme song for "Maverick." He lived in Europe from 1964 to 1973.

Works

(selective list)

Film scores

This is the Life (dir. M. Neilan), 1935
Stanley and Livingstone (dir. H. King and O. Brower), 1939
The Mark of Zorro (dir. R. Mamoulian), 1940
The Return of Frank James (dir. F. Lang), 1940
Tobacco Road (dir. J. Ford), 1941
Western Union (dir. F. Lang), 1941
Thunder Birds (dir. W.A. Wellman), 1942
Guadalcanal Diary (dir. L. Seiler), 1943
Buffalo Bill (dir. W.A. Wellman), 1944
Till We Meet Again (dir. F. Borzage), 1944
The House on 92nd Street (dir. H. Hathaway), 1945
Margie (dir. H. King), 1946
Somewhere in the Night (dir. J.L. Mankiewicz), 1946
Boomerang! (dir. E. Kazan), 1947
Kiss of Death (dir. H. Hathaway), 1947
13 Rue Madeleine (dir. H. Hathaway), 1947
Give My Regards to Broadway (dir. L. Bacon), 1948
Rope (dir. A. Hitchcock), 1948, uncredited
Colorado Territory (dir. R. Walsh), 1949
Three Secrets (dir. R. Wise), 1950
Along the Great Divide (dir. R. Walsh), 1951
Carson City (dir. A. De Toth), 1952
My Man and I (dir. W.A. Wellman), 1952
House of Wax (dir. A. De Toth), 1953
I Died a Thousand Times (dir. S. Heisler), 1955
The Horse Soldiers (dir. J. Ford), 1959

Film songs

A Cry in the Night, 1956 [title song]

Television music

Warner Bros. Presents (ABC), 1955–7
Conflict (ABC), 1956–7
The Virginian (NBC), 1963–4

Orchestral

A Free Fantasy after *St. James Infirmary* for Cities Service Concerts, NBC radio, 1930

MSS in Brigham Young University, Harold B. Lee Library, Special Collections

Bibliography

J. Rodriguez, ed.: *Music and Dance in California* (Hollywood, CA, 1940)

H. Hoffmann, comp.: *"A" Western Filmmakers: a Biographical Dictionary of Writers, Directors, Cinematographers, Composers, Actors and Actresses* (Jefferson, NC, 2000)

F. Steiner: "A Conversation with David Buttolph," *The Cue Sheet* xviii/1–2 (2002), 3–20

WARREN M. SHERK

Chihara, Paul (Seiko)

(*b* Seattle, WA, 9 July 1938). American composer. He studied composition with Robert Palmer at Cornell University (MA in English literature 1961, DMA 1965), and continued his studies with Nadia Boulanger in Paris (1962–3), Ernst Pepping in Berlin (1965–6), and Gunther Schuller at the Berkshire Music Center (1966). He joined the faculty of UCLA in 1966 and was associate professor of music until 1976; during those years he founded and directed the Twice Ensemble, conducted the collegium musicum, and was composer-in-residence for the Los Angeles Chamber Orchestra (1971–4). He was Andrew Mellon Professor at the California Institute of Technology in 1975 and taught at the California Institute of the Arts (1976). In 1980 he became composer-in-residence for the San Francisco Ballet. He re-joined the UCLA faculty in 1996 and was Visiting Professor in 1999. He has written over fifteen film scores and has worked as a consultant and arranger for stage musicals, including Duke Ellington's *Sophisticated Ladies* (1981). He has received commissions from the Boston SO (Saxophone Concerto, 1981), Los Angeles PO (Symphony no.2, 1981), the Cleveland Orchestra (Viola Concerto, 1989), and the Chamber Music Society of Lincoln Centre (*Minidoka*, 1996) among others.

Chihara's works reflect his interest in oriental music through their emphasis on shifts in timbral coloring and limited pitch movement. *Logs* for double bass (1966) explores a group of brief phrases that may be repeated and combined in different orderings, or altered by the use of vibrato, accent, microtones, or unusual performance techniques. The resultant sonorities may be modified electronically. His later music develops these techniques, emphasizing the patternings of pitch and timbral units. Chihara also employs borrowed materials, as in the *Missa Carminum* which makes use of liturgical chant and traditional folksongs.

Works

(*selective list*)

Film and television music

Death Race 2000 (dir. P. Bartel), 1975

I Never Promised You a Rose Garden (dir. A. Page), 1977

Prince of the City (dir. S. Lumet), 1981
China Beach, 1986–90
Crossing Delancey (dir. J.M. Silver), 1988

Stage

Shinju (Lovers' Suicide) (ballet, 1, after Chikamatsu), 1975
Mistletoe Bride, 1978
The Infernal Machine (musical, 1, J. Larson, after J. Cocteau), 1978–80, rev. as Oedipus Rag
The Tempest (ballet, after W. Shakespeare), 1980
Shogun the Musical (musical, J. Clavell), 1990

Orchestral

Forest Music, 1970
Windsong, vc, orch, 1971
Grass, db, orch, 1972
Ceremony III, fl, orch, 1973
Ceremony IV, 1973
Gui Conc., 1975
Sym. no.1 "Sym. in Celebration" (Ceremony V), 1975
Conc., str qt, orch, 1980
Sax Conc., 1981
Sym. no.2 "Birds of Sorrow," 1981
Double Conc., vn, cl, orch, 1999

Chamber and solo instrumental

Logs, db, 1966
Driftwood, str qt, 1967
Branches, 2 bn, perc, 1968
Willow Willow, fl, tuba, perc, 1968
Redwood, va, perc, 1971
Ceremony I, ob, 2 vc, db, perc, 1972
Ceremony II, amp fl, 2 amp vc, perc, 1974
Elegy, pf trio, 1974
Pf Trio, 1974
The Beauty of the Rose is in its Passing, bn, 2 hn, hp, perc, 1976
Str Qt (Primavera), 1977
Sinfonia concertante, 9 insts, 1980
Sequoia, str qt, tape, 1984
Forever Escher, sax qt, str qt, 1995
Minidoka (Reminiscences of . . .), ens, tape, 1996
Sonata, va, pf, 1997
Sonata, va, pf, 1998

Choral

Magnificat, 6 female vv, 1965
Ave Maria—Scarborough Fair (Lat., trad.), 6 male vv, 1971

Missa Carminum (Lat., trad.), 8vv, 1975
Arrs. for musicals, incl. Ellington: Sophisticated Ladies, 1981

Principal publishers: C.F. Peters, G. Schirmer

Bibliography

EwenD
M. Schelle: *The Score: Interviews with Film Composers* (Los Angeles, 1999), 129–54
R. Carl: "Chihara: 'Ain't No Sunshine'; Piano Quintet, 'La Foce'; 'Minidoka'; 'An Afternoon on the Perfume River,'" *Fanfare*, xxxii/4 (2009), 118–19

RICHARD SWIFT/STEVE METCALF/R

Churchill, Frank

(*b* Rumford, ME, 20 Oct 1901; *d* Castaic, CA, 14 May 1942). American composer, songwriter, and pianist. He studied for a time at UCLA, but dropped out to pursue a musical career. He was not an academically trained musician but possessed particular, intuitive talents for playing piano and improvisation. He began his career as a dance band and theater pianist; in Hollywood he worked in radio and played inspirational "mood" music on the sets of silent films. In 1930 Walt Disney discovered Churchill at the RKO studios. Disney originally engaged him to score Mickey Mouse and Silly Symphonies shorts. "Who's Afraid of the Big Bad Wolf" (lyrics by Ann Ronell), from *The Three Little Pigs* (1933), was the studio's first hit song and swept depression-era America. Its popular success led to Churchill's writing the songs for Disney's first animated feature, *Snow White and the Seven Dwarfs* (1937). "Whistle While You Work" and "Some Day My Prince Will Come," with lyrics by Disney story man Larry Morey, were two of the most popular songs from the score that became a best-selling 78 rpm album at the film's release. Several of his last songs were included in *Dumbo* (1941), co-written with Oliver Wallace. Churchill's song "Baby Mine" became another popular standard. *Dumbo* won the Academy Award for Best Music: Scoring of a Musical Picture. A creator of child-like, sometimes hauntingly beautiful melodies, the troubled Churchill was afflicted by alcoholism. Churchill died by his own hand before the release of *Bambi* (1942). But his songs (lyrics again by Morey) and poignant melodies were developed into a highly sophisticated orchestral and choral score by a musical staff headed by arranger Edward Plumb (who also composed some of the background score). The *Bambi* score was also nominated for "Best Song" and "Best Score." After his death Churchill melodies appeared in *Ichabod and Mister Toad* (1949), the song "Merrily On Our Way," and *Peter Pan* (1952), the instrumental crocodile theme.

Works

Short film scores

The Castaway (dir. W. Jackson), 1931
The China Plate (dir. W. Jackson), 1931
The Clock Store (dir. W. Jackson), 1931
Egyptian Melodies (dir. W. Jackson), 1931
Bugs in Love (dir. B. Gillett), 1932
Touchdown Mickey (dir. W. Jackson), 1932
The Whoopee Party (dir. W. Jackson), 1932
Lullaby Land (dir. W. Jackson), collab. L. Harline, 1933
Mickey's Gala Premier (dir. B. Gillett), 1933
Old King Cole (dir. D. Hand), 1933
The Steeplechase (dir. B. Gillett), 1933
The Three Little Pigs (dir. B. Gillett), 1933
Ye Olden Days (dir. B. Gillett), 1933
Camping Out (dir. D. Hand), 1934
The Dognapper (dir. D. Hand), 1934
The Flying Mouse (dir. D. Hand), 1934
Funny Little Bunnies (dir. W. Jackson), collab. L. Harline, 1934
Gulliver Mickey (dir. B. Gillett), 1934
Orphan's Benefit (dir. B. Gillett), 1934
Playful Pluto (dir. B. Gillett), 1934
Shanghaied (dir. B. Gillett), 1934
The Golden Touch (dir. W. Disney), 1935
Mickey's Man Friday (dir. D. Hand), 1935
On Ice (dir. B. Sharpsteen), collab. L. Harline and B. Lewis, 1935
Pluto's Judgment Day (dir. D. Hand), collab. L. Harline, 1935
The Robber Kitten (dir. D. Hand), 1935
Three Orphan Kittens (dir. D. Hand), 1935
The Tortoise and the Hare (dir. W. Jackson), 1935
More Kittens (dir. D. Hand and W. Jackson), 1936
Thru the Mirror (dir. D. Hand), 1936
Toby Tortoise Returns (dir. W. Jackson), collab. L. Harline, 1936
Donald and Pluto (dir. B. Sharpsteen), 1937

Feature film scores

Snow White and the Seven Dwarfs (dir. D. Hand), collab. L. Harline, P. Smith, 1937
Dumbo (dir. B. Sharpsteen), collab. O. Wallace, 1940
Bambi (dir. D. Hand), collab. E. Plumb and P. Smith, 1941
The Reluctant Dragon (dir. A. Werker and H. Luske), 1941

Bibliography

R. Care: "Make Walt's Music: Music for Disney Animation, 1928–1967," *The Cartoon Music Book*, ed. D. Goldmark and Y. Taylor (Chicago, 2002), 21–36

R. Care,: "Symphonists for the Sillies: The Composers for the Disney Shorts," *Funnyworld*, no.18 (1978), 38–48

R. Care: "Threads of Melody: Walt Disney's Bambi, The Evolution of a Major American Film Score," *Wonderful Inventions: Motion Pictures, Broadcasting, and Recorded Sound at the Library of Congress*, ed. I. Newsom (Washington, DC, 1998), 80–115

L. Danley: "Frank Churchill," *The Cue Sheet*, xviii/34 (2002), 9–15

ROSS CARE

Clausen, Alf Heiberg

(*b* Minneapolis, 28 March, 1941). American composer for television, conductor, arranger, and orchestrator. Clausen grew up in Jamestown, ND, where he took up French horn and piano, as well as singing in school choirs. He attended North Dakota State University studying mechanical engineering before a summer in New York City being exposed to first-run Broadway musicals and other professional musical settings convinced him he should pursue music instead. He took up string bass and baritone sax and graduated with a degree in music in 1963, followed by a masters degree at Berklee College of Music.

After moving to southern California, his first high-profile professional gig was as an arranger for the second season of "The Donny and Marie Show," and eventually conductor and music director for the show's third season. He moved away from variety and into scripted drama with his work on "Moonlighting"; during this time he also scored the comedy series "ALF," along with intermittent work on many other series and made-for-TV movies, as well working as an orchestrator on numerous films. He began working on "The Simpsons" during the series' second season, and remained with the show until 2017. Clausen's unusually long run on a single show, totaling twenty-seven years, allowed him to help define the sound for scripted animated television comedies, a genre that exploded in popularity in light of the acclaim and longevity of "The Simpsons." He has been nominated thirty times for Emmy Awards; twenty-three of those were for his work on "The Simpsons"; he won twice.

Television music

(*selective list*)
Moonlighting, 1985–9
Alf, 1986–1990
The Simpsons, 1990–2017
The Critic, 1994–2001
Bette, 2000–2001

Bibliography

D. Adams: "*The Simpsons*' Secret Weapon: Alf Clausen," *Film Score Monthly* ii/2 (1997), 24–33

"Alf Clausen: Primetime Tunes," *Masters of Music: Conversations with Berklee Greats*, ed. M. Small, A. Taylor, and J. Feist (Boston, 1999), 214–25
D. Goldmark: "An Interview with Alf Clausen," *The Cartoon Music Book*, ed. D. Goldmark and Y. Taylor (Chicago, 2002), 239–52
T. Swift: "D'oh!-re-mi: North Dakotan Alf Clausen Makes Music for 'The Simpsons.'" NDSU Magazine iii/2 (Spring 2003), 20–29

DANIEL GOLDMARK

Conti, Bill

(*b* Providence, RI, 13 April 1942). American composer and musical director. He majored in the piano and composition at Louisiana State University and received the master's degree from Juilliard. After seven years studying and composing in Italy he received his first movie break when Paul Mazursky was shooting *Blume in Love* (1973) in Venice. Conti was hired to supervise music for that film and subsequently to provide music for the same director's *Harry and Tonto* (1974) and *An Unmarried Woman* (1978). Conti's biggest commercial break came when he scored Sylvester Stallone's *Rocky* (1976) and three of the successful film's ensuing sequels. The original Rocky theme,"Gonna Fly Now (Theme from Rocky)," reached number one on the *Billboard* Pop Singles Chart in July of 1977, and received a Best Song Oscar nomination for Conti and his lyricists. Conti is one of a decreasing number of composers to create successful original hits specifically for Hollywood films. He also scored ensuing Stallone productions including *Paradise Alley* (1978) and *F.I.S.T.* (1978).

Conti had a second major hit with another title song, sung by Sheena Easton in the James Bond film *For Your Eyes Only* (1981). In 1983 the composer won an Oscar for his Americana-flavoured score for Philip Kaufman's *The Right Stuff*, and continued his epic style with a lengthy score for the Civil War television miniseries, "North and South," in 1986. The prolific Conti is also active in television, both as composer and conductor. He has composed themes and scores for many television shows and miniseries, including "Heaven and Hell: North and South Book III," and "Falcon Crest." He served as the musical director for many Academy Awards shows, including the eightieth annual show in 2008, and remains active in musical supervision. In 1995 Conti was awarded ASCAP's Golden Soundtrack Award for lifetime achievement.

Works

(*selective list*)

Film scores

Microscopic Liquid Subway to Oblivion (dir. J.W. Shadow), 1970
Blume in Love (dir. P. Mazursky), 1973

Harry and Tonto (dir. Mazursky), 1974
Next Stop, Greenwich Village (dir. Mazursky), 1976
Rocky (dir. J.G. Avildsen), 1976
Handle with Care (dir. A. Rafkin), 1977
The Big Fix (dir. J. Kagan (as J.P. Kagan)), 1978
F.I.S.T. (dir. N. Jewison), 1978
Paradise Alley (dir. S. Stallone), 1978
Slow Dancing in the Big City (dir. Avildsen), 1978
Uncle Joe Shannon (dir. J.C. Hanwright), 1978
An Unmarried Woman (dir. Mazursky), 1978
A Man, a Woman and a Bank (dir. N. Black), 1979
Rocky II (dir. Stallone), 1979
Gloria (dir. J. Cassavetes), 1980
Private Benjamin (dir. H. Zieff), 1980
Carbon Copy (dir. M. Schultz), 1981
For Your Eyes Only (dir. J. Glen), 1981
Neighbors (dir. Avildsen), 1981
Victory (dir. J. Huston), 1981
I, the Jury (dir. R.T. Heffron), 1982
Rocky III (dir. Stallone), 1982
That Championship Season (dir. J. Miller), 1982
Bad Boys (dir. R. Rosenthal), 1983
The Right Stuff (dir. P. Kaufman), 1983
The Bear (dir. R.C. Sarafian), 1984
Grand Canyon: the Hidden Secrets (dir. K. Merrill), 1984
The Karate Kid (dir. Avildsen), 1984
Mass Appeal (dir. G. Jordan), 1984
Unfaithfully Yours (dir. Zieff), 1984
Gotcha! (dir. J. Kanew), 1985
The Karate Kid, Part II (dir. Avildsen), 1986
Baby Boom (dir. C. Shyer), 1987
Broadcast News (dir. J.L. Brooks), 1987
Masters of the Universe (dir. G. Goddard), 1987
Cohen and Tate (dir. E. Red), 1988
The Karate Kid, Part III (dir. Avildsen), 1989
Lean on Me (dir. Avildsen), 1989
Rocky V (dir. Avildsen), 1990
The Adventures of Huck Finn (dir. S. Sommers), 1993
Rookie of the Year (dir. D. Stern), 1993
The Next Karate Kid (dir. C. Cain), 1994
The Scout (dir. M. Ritchie), 1994
Spy Hard (dir. R. Friedberg), 1996
The Real Macaw (dir. M. Andreacchio), 1998
Wrongfully Accused (dir. P. Proft), 1998
The Thomas Crown Affair (dir. J. McTiernan), 1999
Rocky Balboa (dir. Stallone), 2006
The Perfect Game (dir. W. Dear), 2009
6 Foot Rule (dir. A.J. Mangano), 2012

Television music

The Pirate, 1978
Murder Ink, 1980
Cagney & Lacey, 1982
North and South, 1985
Bionic Showdown: the Six Million Dollar Man and the Bionic Woman, 1989
American Gladiators, 1989–93
The 62nd Annual Academy Awards, 1990
Heaven & Hell: North & South, Book III, 1994
The 75th Annual Academy Awards, 2003
The 78th Annual Academy Awards, 2006
The 80th Annual Academy Awards, 2008
Dynasty, 2017–18

Video-game music

The Godfather, 2006
The Godfather II, 2009

Bibliography

J. Murrells: *Million Selling Records from the 1900s to the 1980s* (New York, 1984), 101 only
S. Simak: "Bill Conti," *Film Music around the World*, ed. R. Larson (San Bernadino, CA, 1987), 67–70
J. Burlingame: *Sound and Vision: 60 Years of Motion Picture Soundtracks* (New York, 2000), 51–3

ROSS CARE/R

Copland, Aaron

(*b* Brooklyn, NY, 14 Nov 1900; *d* North Tarrytown, NY, 2 Dec 1990). American composer for screen, stage, and concert hall. Before Aaron Copland became interested in writing music for film in the late 1930s, he was already recognized as one of his generation's leading composers. Notable early works like his Piano Concerto (1926) or his *Piano Variations* (1930) were regarded as modernist for their use of jazz elements and extended dissonances, but by the mid-1930s Copland's output was becoming more accessible to wider audiences, with pieces like *El Salón México* (1936) and *Billy the Kid* (1938). His interest in film music occurred, then, as part of his broader efforts to cultivate and reach a larger audience, a shift to a more accessible musical style that has been connected with Copland's own phrase, "imposed simplicity." At the time Copland pondered the writing of film music—he travelled to Hollywood in June of 1937 in search of film work and met with several executives, though he left empty handed—the industry practices of composing and recording music for sound film were hardly a decade old and had been dominated by the musical styles of European post-romanticism and by European émigré composers like Max Steiner and Erich Wolfgang Korngold.

Following the lead of Virgil Thomson—whose influential scores for Pare Lorentz's US government films *The Plow That Broke the Plains* (1936) and *The River* (1937) were met with critical praise and larger audiences than those for autonomous new music concerts—Copland turned to writing music for a documentary film, *The City*, which was shown to great acclaim at the 1939 New York World's Fair. Copland was soon offered a contract by Lewis Milestone to compose a score for an adaptation of John Steinbeck's *Of Mice and Men*. Copland flew to Hollywood in October 1939 and had six weeks to generate his score, which was longer than most composers were given for a single film; his score was notable for its relatively sparse instrumentation and avoidance of the more conventional post-romantic harmonic language.

Copland began lecturing and writing about his Hollywood experience for both specialized and broad audiences (in the pages of *Modern Music* and the *New York Times*, respectively) in which he articulated a theory of film music's function as well as offered some critiques of industry practices (such as the significant ability of a sound engineer to make drastic decisions in terms of volume levels). Copland also looked askance at the frequent use of post-romantic style and the practices of leitmotivic scoring and Mickey-Mousing. Dividing his time between East and West Coasts, Copland continued to score Hollywood films throughout the 1940s. He was third on playwright Thornton Wilder's list of composers for an adaption of the play *Our Town*, ranking below Virgil Thomson and George Antheil, though his non-sentimental score (with orchestration by Jerome Moross) was well received by critics. *The North Star*, which valorized Soviet peasants during a Nazi attack and had an impressive cast and crew, would become a problem for Copland and others involved with it during the rise of McCarthyism after World War II. After *The North Star*, Copland focused on concert hall projects like his Third Symphony, devoting only a few weeks to a short documentary film for the Office of War Information in 1945 (*The Cummington Story*), but by 1948 he returned to score his final two Hollywood films: *The Heiress* and *The Red Pony*, the latter another adaptation of the work of John Steinbeck. A re-release of *The North Star*, titled *Armored Attack*, had several scenes edited out and the addition of a voice-over narration and some footage from the 1956 Hungarian uprising.

Copland had resisted some of the requests for him to incorporate source music into his score for *The Heiress*, and he complained after receiving the Best Score Oscar about the title music not even being his. Despite the Academy of Motion Picture Arts and Sciences's high regard for Copland's work (Copland's five Hollywood scores between 1939 and 1949 were recognized with six nominations and one Oscar for Best Score (for *The Heiress*) from the Academy), and owing perhaps to some combination of his outspoken criticism of Hollywood, his investigation by McCarthy, and his rising fees, Copland ceased to write film music in the 1950s. He would only compose one more film score in his career: *Something Wild*, a low-budget independent film directed by Jack Garfein; the film drew relatively little attention from audiences and critics, and Copland created a concert suite from it called *Music for a Great City*.

Despite having only a small number of film scores, his style quickly and persistently became a stylistic convention within Hollywood's musical vocabulary. Hugo Friedhofer's score for *The Best Years of Our Lives* has been identified as early evidence of Copland's influence, and Copland's style (as heard in film scores like *The Red Pony* but even more so in ballet scores like *Billy the Kid* and *Rodeo*) has been particularly vital in the genre of the Western and for images of frontiers. In particular, Copland's fondness for wide open spaces (both melodically and harmonically), together with his sparse orchestration that favored winds and brass over strings, his preferences for static or slow-moving, diatonic harmonies, and his repetition of rhythmic and melodic motives, have been continually utilized in later scores for film and television; this pastoral idiom has been deployed across the political spectrum for various arguments about the United States's national character and values.

Works

Film scores

The City (dir. R. Steiner and W. Van Dyke), 1939
Of Mice and Men (dir. L. Milestone), 1939
Our Town (dir. S. Wood), 1940
The North Star (dir. L. Milestone), 1943
The Cummington Story (dir. H. Grayson and L. Madison), 1945
The Heiress (dir. W. Wyler), 1949
The Red Pony (dir. L. Milestone), 1949
Something Wild (dir. J. Garfein), 1961

Writings

(*selective list*)
"Tip to Moviegoers: Take Off Those Ear-Muffs," *New York Times Magazine* (6 Nov 1949), 28–32
"The Aims of Music for Films," *New York Times* (10 March 1940)
"Second Thoughts on Hollywood," *Modern Music*, xvii/3 (1940), 141–7

Bibliography

F.W. Sternfeld: "Copland as a Film Composer," *MQ*, xxxvii/2 (1951), 161–75
H. Pollack: *Aaron Copland: the Life and Work of an Uncommon Man* (New York, 1999)
K. Gabbard: "Race and Appropriation: Spike Lee Meets Aaron Copland," *American Music*, xxxviii/4 (2000), 370–90
N. Lerner: "Copland's Music of Wide Open Spaces: Surveying the Pastoral Trope in Hollywood," *MQ*, lxxxv/3 (2001), 477–515

S. Bick: "*Of Mice and Men*: Copland, Hollywood, and American Musical Modernism," *AM*, xxiii/4 (2005), 426–72

N. Lerner: "Aaron Copland, Norman Rockwell, and the 'Four Freedoms': the Office of War Information's Vision and Sound in *The Cummington Story* (1945)," *Aaron Copland and His World*, ed. C. Oja and J. Tick (Princeton, NJ, 2005), 351–77

B. Levy: "The Great Crossing: Nostalgia and Manifest Destiny in Aaron Copland's *The Red Pony*," *Journal of Film Music* ii/2–4 (2009), 201–24

M. Whitmer: "Reinventing the Western Film Score: Jerome Moross and *The Big Country*," *Music in the Western: Notes from the Frontier*, ed. K. Kalinak (New York, 2012), 51–76

A. Bushard: "The Very Essence of Tragic Reality: Aaron Copland and Thomas Newman's Suburban Scoring," *Anxiety Muted: American Film Music in a Suburban Age*, ed. S. Pelkey and A. Bushard (New York, 2015), 260–85

NEIL LERNER

Courage, Alexander [Sandy] (Mair Jr.)

(*b* Philadelphia, 10 Dec 1919; *d* Pacific Palisades, CA, 15 May 2008). American composer, arranger, and orchestrator for television and film. After playing the piano, cornet, and French horn as a child, he graduated from the Eastman School of Music (BM, theory, 1941). He then served on the West Coast as a bandleader for the US military during World War II. After the war he became a staff composer and conductor with CBS Radio in Los Angeles, and worked on series such as "The Camay Hour," "Sam Spade," and "Screen Guild Players," and the crime drama "Broadway is My Beat." In 1948 he began working with the MGM studio and started building a reputation as one of the top arrangers in the industry through his work on a number of well-known film musicals, including *My Fair Lady, Show Boat, Funny Face, The Unsinkable Molly Brown*, and *Fiddler on the Roof*. While he sometimes composed original music for feature films, much of his work in Hollywood came in scoring for the relatively new medium of television. In addition to writing music for episodes of series like "Peyton Place," "Voyage to the Bottom of the Sea," "Wagon Train," "National Velvet," and "Daniel Boone," Courage gained his greatest fame for the title music to Gene Roddenberry's science fiction series, "Star Trek." Roddenberry selected Courage from a list of composers that included Jerry Goldsmith, Elmer Bernstein, Franz Waxman, Hugo Friedhofer, and John Williams. In January 1965, Courage wrote and recorded the music for the pilot episode of "Star Trek," titled *The Cage*, and while NBC turned down that first effort, the company took the unusual step of inviting a second pilot, for which Courage also wrote the music. Claiming inspiration from the W. Franke Harling song *Beyond the Blue Horizon*, whose driving accompaniment underneath a disjunct melody prefigures important features of the "Star Trek" theme, Courage followed Roddenberry's instructions not to write something with electronics; his title music unexpectedly joined together woodwinds, electric organ, a wordless soprano voice, and bongos with a beguine rhythm. Courage's theme for "Star Trek" was incorporated into the subsequent themes of most of the theatrical feature films and spin-off series. Courage continued to compose for several other television series, most notably for "The Waltons," and he became a frequent orchestrator for John Williams and Jerry Goldsmith.

Works

(selective list; film scores unless otherwise noted)

Film and television music

Handle with Care (dir. D. Friedkin), 1958
The Left Handed Gun (dir. A. Penn), 1958
Day of the Outlaw (dir. A. De Toth), 1959
National Velvet (TV series), 1961
The Untouchables (TV series), 1963
Voyage to the Bottom of the Sea (TV series), 1964–8
Daniel Boone (TV series), 1964–70
Lost in Space (TV series), 1966–8
Star Trek (TV series), 1966–9
Judd for the Defense (TV series), 1967
Medical Center (TV series), 1970–72
The Waltons (TV series), 1972–81
Apple's Way (TV series), 1974
Eight is Enough (TV series), 1977
Falcon Crest (TV series), 1981–2
Superman IV: the Quest for Peace (dir. S.J. Furie), 1987

Orchestrations and arrangements

Guys and Dolls (dir. J.L. Mankiewicz), 1955
The Vintage (dir. J. Hayden), 1957
The Big Country (dir. W. Wyler), 1958
My Fair Lady (dir. G. Cukor), 1964
The Unsinkable Molly Brown (dir. C. Walters), 1964
The Agony and the Ecstasy (dir. C. Reed), 1965
Doctor Dolittle (dir. R. Fleischer), 1967
Hello, Dolly! (dir. G. Kelly), 1969
Fiddler on the Roof (dir. N. Jewison), 1971
The Island of Dr. Moreau (dir. D. Taylor), 1977
Star Trek: the Motion Picture (dir. R. Wise), 1979
Heart Like a Wheel (dir. J. Kaplan), 1983
Baby: Secret of the Lost Legend (dir. B. Norton (as B.W.L. Norton)), 1985
Legend (dir. R. Scott), 1985
Extreme Prejudice (dir. W. Hill), 1987
Indiana Jones and the Last Crusade (dir. S. Spielberg), 1989
Hook (dir. S. Spielberg), 1991

Basic Instinct (dir. P. Verhoeven), 1992
Dennis the Menace (dir. N. Castle), 1993
Jurassic Park (dir. Spielberg), 1993
Rudy (dir. D. Anspaugh), 1993
Congo (dir. F. Marshall), 1995
First Knight (dir. J. Zucker), 1995
Star Trek: First Contact (dir. J. Frakes), 1996
Air Force One (dir. W. Petersen), 1997
Small Soldiers (dir. J. Dante), 1998
The Mummy (dir. S. Sommers), 1999
Hollow Man (dir. P. Verhoeven), 2000

Bibliography

F. Steiner: "Keeping Score of the Scores: Music for Star Trek," *Quarterly Journal of the Library of Congress*, xl/1 (1983), 4–16

J. Burlingame: *TV's Biggest Hits: the Story of Television Themes from "Dragnet" to "Friends"* (New York, 1996)

M. Heuger and C. Reuter: "Zukunftsmusik? Science Fiction-Soundtracks und die Vorstellungen vom zukünftigen Musiklevel: Das Beispiel Star Trek," *Musik im virtuellen Raum: Osnabrück 1997*, 207–25

J. Bond: *The Music of Star Trek: Profiles in Style* (Los Angeles, 1999)

R. Rodman: "'Coperettas,' 'Detecterns,' and Space Operas: Music and Genre Hybridization in American Television," *Music in Television: Channels of Listening*, ed. J. Deaville (New York and London, 2011), 35–56

N. Lerner: "Hearing the Boldly Goings: Tracking the Title Themes of the Star Trek Television Franchise, 1966–2005," *Music in Science Fiction Television: Tuned to the Future*, ed. K. Donnelly and P. Hayward (New York, 2013), 52–71

NEIL LERNER/R

Cutler, Miriam

(*b* Long Island, NY, 1952). American performer, songwriter, composer, and producer. She began her career as a singer/horn player in various bands that toured the West Coast, including the Mystic Knights of the Oingo Boingo. She learned music arranging by writing charts for her own bands, Miss Alice Stone Ladies Society Orchestra and Miriam Cutler & Swingstreet. She opened her own recording studio and moved from live performance into composing, writing songs for feature films including *Bachelor Party*, *Grandview USA*, and *Slaves to the Underground*, as well as special songs for the children's educational show "Square One" (PBS). In the 1980s she wrote scores for several dozen low-budget horror films for Vista Street productions, including the cult favorite *Witchcraft* series, which gave her an opportunity to learn the technology and gain experience as a film composer. Since 1988 she has scored numerous feature films, television

Miriam Cutler, 2012
(Photo by Katy Winn/Invision/AP)

specials, and corporate videos, and in recent years has focussed on independent documentaries. She also has co-produced live jazz albums on Polygram/Verve for Joe Williams, Nina Simone, Marlena Shaw, and Shirley Horn. Cutler has served as composer-in-residence for Circus Flora, has been featured at Charleston's Spoleto Festival and the Kennedy Center, and has served on documentary film festival juries for the Sundance Film Festival, American Film Institute, the Independent Spirit Awards, and the International Documentary Association.

Works

Film scores

Witchcraft II: the Temptress (dir. M. Woods), 1989
Getting Lucky (dir. M.P. Girard), 1990

Time Barbarians (dir. J.J. Barmettler), 1990
Under Crystal Lake (dir. K. Kertenian), 1990
Cause of Death (dir. P.J. Jones), 1991
Pushed to the Limit (dir. M. Mileham), 1992
Witchcraft IV: the Virgin Heart (dir. J. Merendino), 1992
Beyond Fear (dir. R.F. Lyons), 1993
Divorce Law (dir. Girard), 1993
Married People, Single Sex (dir. M. Sedan), 1993
Witchcraft V: Dance with the Devil (dir. T. Hsu), 1993
Body Parts (dir. Girard), 1994
Eyes of the Serpent (dir. R.J. Gale), 1994
Streets of Rage (dir. R. Elfman (as A. Sumatra)), 1994
Witchcraft VI: the Devil's Mistress (dir. J. Davis), 1994
Witchcraft VIII: Salem's Ghost (dir. Barmettler), 1996
Girl Crazy (dir. R. Dutcher), 1997
Silent Scream (dir. J. Chean), 1999
God's Army (dir. R. Dutcher), 2000
Amy's Orgasm (dir. Davis), 2001
Bloodline (dir. B. Burgess), 2008

Documentaries

(*selective list*)
Licensed to Kill (dir. A. Dong), 1997
Scouts Honor (dir. T. Shepard), 2001
Lost in Mancha (dir. K. Fulton and L. Pepe), 2002
China Blue (dir. M.X. Peled), 2005
Absolute Wilson (dir. K. Otto-Bernstein), 2006
Thin (dir. L. Greenfield), 2006
Ghosts of Abu Ghraib (dir. R. Kennedy), 2007
One Bad Cat: the Reverend Albert Wagner Story (dir. T.G. Miller), 2008
A Powerful Noise (dir. T. Cappello), 2008
Shouting Fire: Stories from the Edge of Free Speech (dir. L. Garbus), 2009
Straightlaced: How Gender's Got us All Tied Up (dir. D. Chasnoff), 2009
The Desert of Forbidden Art (dir. T. Georgiev and A. Pope), 2010
Family Affair (dir. C. Colvard), 2010
The Fence (dir. R. Kennedy), 2010
God Willing (dir. E. Griego), 2010
One Lucky Elephant (dir. L. Leeman), 2010
Poster Girl (dir. S. Nesson), 2010
Awaken the Dragon (dir. L. Oakley), 2011
Paul Goodman Changed My Life (dir. J. Lee), 2011
Vito (dir. J. Schwarz), 2011
Band of Sisters (dir. M. Fishman), 2012
Ethel (dir. R. Kennedy), 2012
Kings Point (dir. S. Gilman), 2012

American Promises (dir. J. Brewster and M. Stephenson), 2013
One Last Hug: Three Days at Grief Camp (dir. I.T. Brodsky), 2014
The Hunting Ground (dir. K. Dick), 2015
Mind/Game: the Unquiet Journey of Chamique Holdsclaw (dir. R. Goldsmith), 2015
Finding Kukan (dir. R. Lung), 2016
A Plastic Ocean (dir. C. Leeson), 2016
Dark Money (dir. K. Reed), 2018
Love Gilda (dir. L. Dapolito (as L. D'Apolito)), 2018
RBG (dir. J. Cohen, B. West), 2018

Television music

Pandemic: Facing Aids, 2003

Bibliography

E. Albrecht: *The Contemporary Circus: Art of the Spectacular* (Lanham, MD, 2006)
G. Jolliffe and A. Zinne: "The Music Composer: Miriam Cutler," *The Documentary Filmmakers Handbook: a Guerilla Guide* (New York, 2006), 296–301
C. Chrisafulli: "Writing Music for Nonfiction Films," *Hollywood Reporter* (10 April 2008)

JEANNIE GAYLE POOL/R

Danna, Jeff

(*b* Burlington, ON, 9 Oct, 1964). Canadian composer and guitarist, brother of MYCHAEL DANNA. He initially began writing film scores in the period from 1989 to 1991, in collaboration with his brother for three independent Canadian films. He later composed music for the Canadian television series "Sweating Bullets" (1991–3), for Canadian director Stuart Gillard, and for multiple scores for Canadian-born Roger Spottiswoode. Danna moved from Burlington to Los Angeles in 1991, settling in Pasadena, and since then has mainly composed scores for various American and international directors, including Richard Attenborough, Nanette Burstein and Brett Morgen, Troy Duffy, Tim Blake Nelson, and Alexander Witt. Most of Danna's scores employ conventional orchestral instruments in a heavily orchestrated style.

In addition, Danna has composed many scores for American television, including made-for-television movies, theme songs, and various episodes of ongoing series. He collaborated with his brother on numerous scores, including *The Matthew Shepard Story* (2002), *Tideland* (2005), *Fracture* (2007), *Lakeview Terrace* (2008), *The Imaginarium of Doctor Parnassus* (2009), *The Good Dragon* (2015), *Billy Lynn's Long Halftime Walk* (2016), *Storks* (2016), and *The Breadwinner* (2017).

Mychael Danna, left, and Jeff Danna, 2015
(Photo by Vince Bucci/Invision for the Television Academy/AP Images)

Works

Film scores

Kung Fu: the Legend Continues (TV movie, dir. J. Taylor), 1992
At Sachem Farm (Higher Love) (dir. J. Huddles), 1998
My Own Country (TV movie, dir. M. Nair), 1998, with A. Rollins
The Boondock Saints (dir. T. Duffy), 1999
New Blood (dir. M. Hurst), 1999
Green Dragon (dir. T. Linh Bui), 2001, with M. Danna
O (dir. T. Blake Nelson), 2001
Easter (dir. R. Caliban), 2002
The Kid Stays in the Picture (dir. N. Burstein and B. Morgen), 2002
The Matthew Shepard Story (TV movie, dir. R. Spottiswoode), 2002, with M. Danna

Ice Bound (TV movie dir. Spottiswoode), 2003
Kart Racer (dir. S. Gillard), 2003
Spinning Boris (dir. Spottiswoode), 2003
The Visual Bible: the Gospel of John (dir. P. Saville), 2003
Resident Evil: Apocalypse (dir. A. Witt), 2004
Ripley under Ground (dir. Spottiswoode), 2005
Tideland (dir. T. Gilliam), 2005, with M. Danna
Silent Hill (dir. C. Gans), 2006
Chicago 10 (dir. Morgen), 2007
Closing the Ring (dir. R. Attenborough), 2007
Fracture (dir. G. Hoblit), 2007, with M. Danna
Lakeview Terrace (dir. N. LaBute), 2008, with M. Danna
The Boondock Saints II: All Saints Day (dir. Duffy), 2009
Cry of the Owl (dir. J. Thraves), 2009
Formosa Betrayed (dir. A. Kane), 2009
The Imaginarium of Doctor Parnassus (dir. Gillam), 2009, with M. Danna
Leaves of Grass (dir. Blake Nelson), 2009
The Last Rites of Ransom Pride (dir. T. Russell), 2010
Repeaters (dir. C. Bessai), 2010
Sophie & Sheba (dir. L. Bristow), 2010
Thin Ice (dir. J. Sprecher), 2011
Erased (dir. P. Stölzl), 2012
Silent Hill: Revelation 3D (dir. M.J. Bassett), 2012, with A. Yamaoka
The Colony (dir. J. Renfroe), 2013
Bad Country (dir. C. Brinker), 2014, with J. Fee
Shock Value (dir. D. Rath), 2014
Anesthesia (dir. Blake Nelson), 2015
The Good Dinosaur (dir. P. Sohn), 2015, with M. Danna
Billy Lynn's Long Halftime Walk (dir. A. Lee), 2016, with M. Danna
Storks (dir. N. Stoller), 2016, with M. Danna
The Breadwinner (dir. N. Twomey), 2017, with M. Danna

Television music

Sweating Bullets, various episodes, 1991–3
Beverly Hills 90210, various episodes, 1997–8
Kid Notorious, series theme, 2003
Miss Spider's Sunny Patch Friends, various episodes, 2004–6
The Zula Patrol, various episodes, 2005–7
Camelot, 2010
Babar and the Adventure of Badou, 2010–11
Continuum, 2012–4
Tyrant, 2014–6
Alias Grace, 2017, with M. Danna

Bibliography

B. Borzykowski: "Holly Brood," *Words & Music*, xiv (Fall 2007), 12–14

DURRELL BOWMAN/R

Danna, Mychael

(*b* Winnepeg, 20 Sept 1958). Canadian composer and keyboardist, brother of JEFF DANNA. Raised in Burlington, Ontario, Danna studied composition at the University of Toronto, where he won the 1985 Glenn Gould Composition Scholarship. His first significant score was for Canadian director Atom Egoyan's début feature-length film *Family Viewing* (1987). The two have collaborated on eleven films. Danna also worked from 1987 to 1992 as the composer-in-residence of Toronto's McLaughlin Planetarium.

Danna's work with Egoyan is notable for having introduced the use of electronic music (including synthesizers) and elements of minimalism and multicultural/world music into what Danna calls "romantic minimalism" ("Spoiled by Images," 1996). This approach led to collaborations with various other directors and several dance companies. He has worked with other Canadian directors including John Greyson, Julia Kwan, and Deepa Mehta as well as with Vancouver-based American director Charles Martin Smith. Danna has scored films for acclaimed directors such as Mira Nair, Billy Ray, Terry Gilliam, James Magnold, Ang Lee, and István Szabó, among many others. In addition, Danna has composed scores for television series, made-for-television films, short films, and theatre. He collaborated with his brother on the scores for Timothy Linh Bui's *Green Dragon*, Gregory Hoblit's *Fracture*, Neil LaBute's *Lakeview Terrace*, Terry Gilliam's *The Imaginarium of Doctor Parnassus*, and Peter Sohn's *The Good Dinosaur*. Danna's dance compositions include *Dead Souls* (1996) and *Gita Govinda* (2001). In 2013 he won an academy award for his original score to Ang Lee's *Life of Pi*.

Works

Film scores

Family Viewing (dir. A. Egoyan), 1987
Speaking Parts (dir. Egoyan), 1989
The Adjuster (dir. Egoyan), 1991
Exotica (dir. Egoyan), 1994
Dance me Outside (dir. B. McDonald), 1995
Kama Sutra: a Tale of Love (dir. M. Nair), 1996
Lilies (dir. J. Greyson), 1996
The Ice Storm (dir. A. Lee), 1997
The Sweet Hereafter (dir. Egoyan), 1997

Felicia's Journey (dir. Egoyan), 1999
Girl, Interrupted (dir. J. Mangold), 1999
Green Dragon (dir. T. Linh Bui), 2001, with J. Danna
Hearts in Atlantis (dir. S. Hicks), 2001
Monsoon Wedding (dir. Nair), 2001
Ararat (dir. Egoyan), 2002
The Snow Walker (dir. C. Martin Smith), 2003
Being Julia (dir. I. Szabó), 2004
Vanity Fair (dir. Nair), 2004
Capote (dir. B. Miller), 2005
Eve and the Fire Horse (dir. J. Kwan), 2005
Tideland (dir. T. Gilliam), 2005, with J. Danna
Water (dir. D. Mehta), 2005
Little Miss Sunshine (dir. J. Dayton and V. Faris), 2006
The Nativity Story (dir. C. Hardwicke), 2006
Where the Truth Lies (dir. Egoyan), 2006
Breach (dir. B. Ray), 2007
Fracture (dir. G. Hoblit), 2007, with J. Danna
Surf's Up (dir. A. Brannon and C. Buck), 2007
Adoration (dir. Egoyan), 2008
Heaven on Earth (dir. Mehta), 2008
Lakeview Terrace (dir. N. LaBute), 2008, with J. Danna
Management (dir. S. Belber), 2008
Stone of Destiny (dir. M. Smith), 2008
(500) Days of Summer (dir. M. Webb), 2009
Chloe (dir. Egoyan), 2009
The Imaginarium of Doctor Parnassus (dir. T. Gilliam), 2009, with J. Danna
The Time Traveler's Wife (dir. R. Schwentke), 2009
Going the Distance (dir. N. Burstein), 2010
The Whistelblower (dir. L. Kondracki), 2010
Moneyball (dir. Miller), 2011
Life of Pi (dir. A. Lee), 2012
Devil's Knot (dir. Egoyan), 2013
The Captive (dir. Egoyan), 2014
Transcendence (dir. W. Pfister), 2014
The Good Dinosaur (dir. P. Sohn), 2015, with J. Danna
Remember (dir. Egoyan), 2015
Sanjay's Super Team (dir. S. Patel), 2015 (short)
Billy Lynn's Long Halftime Walk (dir. Lee), 2016, with J. Danna
Storks (dir. N. Stoller), 2016, with J. Danna
The Breadwinner (dir. N. Twomey), 2017, with J. Danna
The Man Who Invented Christmas (dir. B. Nalluri) 2017

Television music

New Amsterdam, 2009
Dollhouse, 2009–10
Camelot, 2011

World without End (miniseries), 2012
Tyrant, 2014–16
The Last Tycoon, 2016
Alias Grace, 2017, with J. Danna

Dance

Dead Souls, 1996
Gita Govinda, 2001

Writings

"Spoiled by Images," *Words & Music*, iii (March 1996), 8 only

Bibliography

D. Adams: "An Interview with Mychael Danna," *Film Score Monthly* (Jan 1998), 34–40

D. Morgan: "Playing with Paradoxes: Mychael Danna on *The Sweet Hereafter*," *Knowing the Score: Film Composers Talk About the Art, Craft, Blood, Sweat, and Tears of Writing Music for Cinema*, ed. D. Morgan (New York, 2000), 244–57

B. Borzykowski: "Holly Brood," *Words & Music*, xiv (Fall 2007), 12–14

M. Mera: *Mychael Danna's "The Ice Storm": a Film Score Guide* (Lanham, MD, 2007)

L. Whitesell: "Musical Eclecticism and Ambiguity in *The Sweet Hereafter*," *American Music* xxix/2 (2011), 229–63

DURRELL BOWMAN/R

Darby, Ken

(*b* Hebron, NE, 13 May 1909; *d* Sherman Oaks, CA, 24 Jan 1992). American vocal director, arranger, lyricist, and performer. After his family moved to California, Darby studied harmony, counterpoint, and composition at Santa Monica Junior College and played organ for silent films. At the dawn of the sound era he formed a vocal group, The King's Men Quartet, with three of his college classmates. Their audition at Paramount led to an appearance in the film *Sweetie* (1929) and much ensuing film work. They appear disguised as the Marx Brothers in MGM's *Honolulu* (1939).

In the 1930s and early 1940s Darby and The King's Men also worked with the bandleader Paul Whiteman, made their own recordings, and backed up Bing Crosby's Decca records. At MGM, Darby was vocal director on *The Wizard of Oz* (1939) and his technical expertise helped create the whimsical voices of the Munchkins. At Disney he worked on *Make Mine Music* (1946) and *Melody Time* (1948), and arranged and directed the important choral sections for *Song of the South* (1946).

His prolific Hollywood work, for which he won three Academy Awards, peaked at Twentieth Century-Fox, where he was Alfred Newman's associate and vocal director. His work included vocal direction and arrangements for *Carousel* (1956), *South Pacific* (1958), and other big films based on Broadway musicals. During the CinemaScope era of the mid-fifties Darby also created choral effects, uniquely using his choir as an integral section of the orchestra, for scores such as *The Robe* (1953) and *The Egyptian* (1954) by Alfred Newman, and *River of No Return* (1954) by Leigh Harline. Darby again worked with Newman on *How the West Was Won* (1962) and the religious epic *The Greatest Story Ever Told* (1965). He served as a vocal coach for stars ranging from Elvis Presley and Fabian to Joanne Woodward and Marilyn Monroe. He sometimes also supplied song lyrics, often uncredited, for various productions.

Works

Film scores

Sweetie (dir. F. Tuttle), 1929
We're Not Dressing (dir. N. Taurog), 1934
The Girl of the Golden West (dir. R.Z. Leonard), 1938
Honolulu (dir. E. Buzzell), 1939
Dumbo (dir. S. Armstrong, N. Ferguson, W. Jackson, J. Kinney, B. Roberts, B. Sharpsteen and J. Elliotte), 1940
Higher and Higher (dir. T. Whelan), 1943
Step Lively (dir. T. Whelan), 1944
Make Mine Music (dir. R. Cormack, C. Geronimi, J. Kinney, H. Luske and J. Meador), 1946
Song of the South (dir. W. Jackson and H. Foster), 1946
Melody Time (dir. C. Geronimi, W. Jackson, J. Kinney and H. Luske), 1948
So Dear to My Heart (dir. H.D. Schuster and H. Luske), 1948
The Adventures of Ichabod and Mr. Toad (dir. J. Algar, C. Geronimi and J. Kinney), 1949
The Beautiful Blonde from Bashful Bend (dir. P. Sturges), 1949
Dancing in the Dark (dir. I. Reis), 1949
Oh, You Beautiful Doll (dir. J.M. Stahl), 1949
My Blue Heaven (dir. H. Koster), 1950
Bird of Paradise (dir. D. Daves), 1951
David and Bathsheba (dir. H. King), 1951
Meet Me After the Show (dir. R. Sale), 1951
Rancho Notorious (dir. F. Lang), 1952
With a Song in My Heart (dir. W. Lang), 1952
Call Me Madam (dir. W. Lang), 1953
The Girl Next Door (dir. R. Sale), 1953
The Robe (dir. H. Koster), 1953
Tonight We Sing (dir. M. Leisen), 1953
Demetrius and the Gladiators (dir. D. Daves), 1954
The Egyptian (dir. M. Curtiz), 1954
How to Marry a Millionaire (dir. J. Negulesco), 1954

Prince Valiant (dir. H. Hathaway), 1954
River of No Return (dir. O. Preminger and J. Negulesco), 1954
There's No Business Like Show Business (dir. W. Lang), 1954
Three Coins in the Fountain (dir. J. Negulesco), 1954
Daddy Long Legs (dir. J. Negulesco), 1955
The Girl in the Red Velvet Swing (dir. R. Fleischer), 1955
A Man Called Peter (dir. H. Koster), 1955
Seven Cities of Gold (dir. R.D. Webb), 1955
Bus Stop (dir. J. Logan), 1956
The Girl Can't Help It (dir. F. Tashlin), 1956
The King and I (dir. W. Lang), 1956
Love Me Tender (dir. R.D. Webb), 1956
An Affair to Remember (dir. L. McCarey), 1957
The Three Faces of Eve (dir. N. Johnson), 1957
Will Success Spoil Rock Hunter? (dir. F. Tashlin), 1957
The Best of Everything (dir. J. Negulesco), 1959
Hound Dog Man (dir. D. Siegel), 1959
Journey to the Center of the Earth (dir. H. Levin), 1959
Porgy and Bess (dir. O. Preminger and R. Mamoulian), 1959
Elmer Gantry (dir. R. Brooks), 1960
Flower Drum Song (dir. H. Koster), 1961
How the West Was Won (dir. J. Ford, H. Hathaway, G. Marshall, and R. Thorpe), 1962
State Fair (dir. J. Ferrer), 1962
The Greatest Story Ever Told (dir. G. Stevens, D. Lean, and J. Negulesco), 1965
Camelot (dir. J. Logan), 1967
Finian's Rainbow (dir. F.F. Coppola), 1968

Writings

Hollywood Holyland: the Filming and Scoring of The Greatest Story Ever Told (Metuchen, NJ, 1992)

Bibliography

P. Cook: "Ken Darby: Has Specialized in the Cinematic Use of the Singing Human Voice," *Films in Review*, xx/6 (1969), 335–56

A. Harmetz: *The Making of The Wizard of Oz* (New York, 1977), 90, 92, 97–8, 197

ROSS CARE

David, Mack

(*b* New York, 5 July 1912; *d* Rancho Mirage, CA, 30 Dec 1993). American lyricist and composer. He attended Cornell University for two years, then left to study law briefly at St. John's University, soon giving up these pursuits to follow his love for songwriting. He started writing lyrics for popular songs in the early 1930s, achieving his first major successes (1939–40) in partnership with André Kostelanetz. He subsequently wrote over a thousand songs, including many for film and television, receiving eight Academy Award nominations, the first in 1950 for his song "Bibbidi, Bobbidi, Boo" from the Walt Disney animated film of *Cinderella*. In the early 1950s he wrote songs with Jerry Livingston for three musicals for Dean Martin and Jerry Lewis; other collaborators have included Ellington, Bacharach, Basie, Gold, and Mancini. His composing style was flexible enough to produce hits for The Shirelles, Ella Fitzgerald, and the Judds as well as theme music for *Casper the Friendly Ghost*. He also wrote the English lyrics for "La vie en rose"; when it was translated into French, Edith Piaf made the song into a worldwide sensation.

He contributed the title songs to many films, including *Walk on the Wild Side* (1962), *Hud* (1963), *It's a Mad, Mad, Mad, Mad World* (1963), and *The Dirty Dozen* (1967), and also wrote the score for *Cat Ballou* (1965). His work on Broadway ranged from contributions to the revues *Bright Lights of 1944* and *Sophisticated Ladies* (1981) to the musical *Molly* (1973). In 1975 he was granted a patent for an "electronic composer," a system for composing a variety of different songs from fragmentary recordings. His brother Hal David has also been a successful lyricist, most notably in his collaborations with Bacharach.

Bibliography

Obituary, "Mack David, 81, a Composer and Lyricist," *New York Times* (1 Jan 1994)

RICHARD C. LYNCH/R

Davis, Don

(*b* Anaheim, CA, 4 Feb 1957). American composer and orchestrator for television and film. Having played the trumpet and piano as a youth, Don Davis earned the BA in Music Theory from UCLA in 1979. After studying composition with Henri Lazarof and orchestration with Albert Harris, Davis began to work with Joe Harnell as an orchestrator for the television series "The Incredible Hulk." Continuing as an orchestrator for Mark Snow in the series "Hart to Hart," Davis had the opportunity to compose four episodes on his own. His work on "Beauty and the Beast," remarkably diverse and melodramatic for a weekly prime-time drama, was recognized with an Emmy award and led to even more work as a television composer and film orchestrator. Bearing the influences of earlier timbral innovators like Bernard Herrmann and Jerry Goldsmith, Davis became an orchestrator for film composers such as James Horner and Randy Newman, among others. He first worked with filmmakers Larry and Andy Wachowski in their neo-noir thriller *Bound* before writing the score for *The Matrix* and its sequels. Davis's score for *The Matrix* received critical acclaim for its use of atonality and unusual timbres, including several cues requiring prepared piano and string writing using pitch clusters. Canonic writing appears throughout the score, providing a musical analog to the visual and thematic emphasis on mirrors and reflections. Davis playfully created titles for his cues from anagrams of phrases like "Wachowski Brothers" (i.e. "Bow Whisk Orchestra") and "The Matrix" (i.e. "Threat Mix" and "Mix the Art"). Along with the experimental, avant-garde cues, the score also turns to more traditional musical codes, such as the use of a wordless choir to suggest something celestial or an allusion to Richard Strauss's famous opening of *Also sprach Zarathustra* as Neo defeats the Agent at the end of *The Matrix*. In addition to writing concert-hall music based on his film scores (e.g. *Illicit Felicity*, based on his score for *Bound*), Davis has continued to compose new music for the concert hall and stage, staging an opera première (*Río de Sangre*) in 2010.

Works

Film scores

(*selective list*)

Aliens (dir. J. Cameron), 1986
Flowers in the Attic (dir. J. Bloom), 1987
Robin Hood: Prince of Thieves (dir. K. Reynolds), 1991
Maverick (dir. R. Donner), 1994
The Pagemaster (dir. P. Hunt (as M. Hunt) and J. Johnston), 1994
Apollo 13 (dir. R. Howard), 1995
Toy Story (dir. J. Lasseter), 1995
Bound (dir. L. and L. Wachowski (as The Wachowski Brothers)), 1996
James and the Giant Peach (dir. H. Selick), 1996
Michael (dir. N. Ephron), 1996
Titanic (dir. Cameron), 1997
Warriors of Virtue (dir. R. Yu), 1997
A Bug's Life (dir. J. Lasseter and A. Stanton), 1998
The Lesser Evil (dir. D. Mackay), 1998
Pleasantville (dir. G. Ross), 1998
House on Haunted Hill (dir. W. Malone), 1999
The Matrix (dir. L. and L. Wachowski (as The Wachowski Brothers)), 1999
Universal Soldier: the Return (dir. M. Rodgers), 1999
Meet the Parents (dir. J. Roach), 2000
Antitrust (dir. P. Howitt), 2001
Behind Enemy Lines (dir. J. Moore), 2001
Jurassic Park III (dir. J. Johnston), 2001
The Matrix Reloaded (dir. L. and L. Wachowski (as The Wachowski Brothers)), 2003
The Matrix Revolutions (dir. L. and L. Wachowski (as The Wachowski Brothers)), 2003
The Marine (dir. J. Bonito), 2006
The Good Life (dir. S. Berra), 2007, with J. Peterson

Ten Inch Hero (dir. D. Mackay), 2007
Toy Story 3 (dir. L. Unkrich), 2010
Cars 3 (dir. B. Fee), 2017
Tokyo Ghoul (dir. K. Hagiwara), 2017, as D. Deivisu
Beyond the Sky (dir. F. Sestito), 2018

Television music

The Incredible Hulk, 1978
Hart to Hart, 1983–4
Beauty and the Beast, 1987–90
Tiny Toon Adventures, 1990–3
Star Trek: The Next Generation, 1993
SeaQuest 2032, 1994–5
The Task, 2017

Concert works

(*selective list*)
Chamber Symphony, 1981
Bleeding Particles, str, 1983
Afterimages, vn, pf, 1994
Of the Illuminated (orat), 1995
No Exit, fl, hp, 1996
Illicit Felicity, pf, 1999
Río de Sangre (op), 2010

Bibliography

D. Adams: "The Matrix Conclusions," *Film Score Monthly* viii–ix (Oct–Nov 2003), 16–20
C. DesJardins: "Don Davis," *Inside Film Music: Composers Speak* (Los Angeles, 2006), 61–9

NEIL LERNER/R

Debney, John

(*b* Glendale, CA, 18 Aug 1956). American film composer. Son of Disney producer Louis Debney, John Debney attended the California Institute of the Arts (BA in composition, 1979) and apprenticed with television composers MIKE POST and Hoyt Curtin. Debney at first scored several short, TV, and independent films, but primarily composed TV scores (such as for Disney), winning Emmys for "The Young Riders" (1989), "SeaQuest DSV" (1993–4, main title), and "The Cape" (1996). He is adept at a variety of music and film genres, prefers the emotional resonances made possible by traditional orchestral scoring, and conducts his own recording sessions.

John C. Debney, 2015
Photo/Josef Vostarek (CTK via AP Images)

Debney was nominated for a 2005 Academy Award for his voice-, choir-, and woodwind-oriented score for *The Passion of the Christ* (2004). The film's soundtrack album was also very successful (peaking at number nineteen on *Billboard*'s US album chart), and he reworked his score into a symphony for large orchestra and choir, which he conducted at its 2005 première in Rome. He has also conducted a number of classic film scores in new recordings for the Varèse Sarabande label. In 2005 he received ASCAP's Henry Mancini Lifetime Achievement Award.

Works

Film and television scores

(*Film scores unless otherwise noted*)
Deer in the Works (short film, dir. R. Underwood), 1980
The Wonderful World of Disney (TV), 1982
Donald Duck's 50th Birthday (dir. A. Solt and P. Savenick), 1984, with P.J. Smith
Dragon's Lair (TV), 1984
Sport Goofy in Soccermania (dir. M. O'Callaghan), 1987
The Wild Pair (dir. B. Bridges), 1987, with M. Colombier
Not Since Casanova (dir. B. Thompson), 1988
Police Academy (TV), 1988
A Pup Named Scooby-Doo (TV), 1988–91
Trenchcoat in Paradise (dir. M. Coolidge), 1989
The Young Riders (TV), 1989
Dink, the Little Dinosaur (TV), 1989–91

Jetsons: the Movie (dir. J. Barbera and W. Hanna), 1990
Hocus Pocus (dir. K. Ortega), 1993
Star Trek: Deep Space Nine (TV), 1993
SeaQuest DSV (TV), 1993–4
Star Trek: the Next Generation (TV), 1994
Cutthroat Island (dir. R. Harlin), 1995
In Pursuit of Honor (TV), 1995
The Cape (TV), 1996
Doctor Who (TV), 1996
I Know What You Did Last Summer (dir. J. Gillespie), 1997
Liar Liar (dir. T. Shadyac), 1997
The Relic (dir. P. Hyams), 1997
Dick (dir. A. Fleming), 1999
End of Days (dir. Hyams), 1999
Inspector Gadget (dir. D. Kellogg), 1999
My Favorite Martian (dir. D. Petrie), 1999
Jimmy Neutron: Boy Genius (dir. J.A. Davis), 2001, with B. Causey
The Princess Diaries (dir. G. Marshall), 2001
Spy Kids (dir. R. Rodriguez), 2001, with others
The Scorpion King (dir. C. Russell), 2002
Spy Kids 2: the Island of Lost Dreams (dir. R. Rodriguez), 2002, with R. Rodriguez
Bruce Almighty (dir. T. Shadyac), 2003
Elf (dir. J. Favreau), 2003
The Passion of the Christ (dir. M. Gibson), 2004
Chicken Little (dir. M. Dindal), 2005
Sin City (dir. F. Miller, R. Rodriguez, and Q. Tarantino), 2005, with others
Idlewild (dir. B. Barber), 2006
Evan Almighty (dir. Shadyac), 2007
Meet Dave (dir. B. Robbins), 2008
My Best Friend's Girl (dir. H. Deutch), 2008
Aliens in the Attic (dir. J. Schultz), 2009
Hannah Montana: the Movie (dir. P. Chelsom), 2009
Hotel for Dogs (dir. T. Freudenthal), 2009
Old Dogs (dir. W. Becker), 2009
The Stoning of Soraya M. (dir. C. Nowrasteh), 2009
Iron Man 2 (dir. J. Favreau), 2010
Predators (dir. N. Antal), 2010
Snowmen (dir. R. Kirbyson), 2010
Valentine's Day (dir. Marshall), 2010
Yogi Bear (dir. E. Brevig), 2010
The Change-Up (dir. D. Dobkin), 2011
The Double (dir. M. Brandt), 2011
Dream House (dir. J. Sheridan), 2011
New Year's Eve (dir. Marshall), 2011
No Strings Attached (dir. I. Reitman), 2011
The Sims Medieval (video game), 2011
Alex Cross (dir. R. Cohen), 2012

Hatfields & McCoys (TV), 2012
A Thousand Words (dir. B. Robbins), 2012
The Three Stooges (dir. B. and P. Farrelly), 2012
Bonnie & Clyde (TV), 2013
The Call (dir. B. Anderson), 2013
Jobs (dir. J.M. Stern), 2013
The After (TV), 2014
The Cobbler (dir. T. McCarthy), 2014, with N. Urata
Draft Day (dir. I. Reitman), 2014
Forever (TV), 2014
Houdini (TV), 2014
Stonehearst Asylum (dir. Anderson), 2014
Walk of Shame (dir. S. Brill), 2014
American Odyssey (TV), 2015
Broken Horses (dir. V.V. Chopra), 2015
Point of Honor (TV), 2015
The SpongeBob Movie: Sponge Out of Water (dir. P. Tibbitt and M. Mitchell), 2015
Texas Rising (TV), 2015
Wolves and Dogs: Howl for Full Moon (dir. C. Cameron), 2015
Game of Silence (TV), 2016
Ice Age: Collision Course (dir. M. Thurmeier and G.T. Chu), 2016
League of Gods (dir. K. Hui), 2016
Mother's Day (dir. Marshall), 2016
Scrat: Spaced Out (dir. G.T. Chu and M. Thurmeier), 2016
The Young Messiah (dir. C. Nowrasteh), 2016
Flint (TV), 2017
The Greatest Showman (dir. M. Gracey), 2017, with J. Trapanese
Home Again (dir. H. Meyers-Shyer), 2017
Linda from HR (TV), 2017
The Orville (TV), 2017
Santa Clarita Diet (TV), 2017
Beirut (dir. Anderson), 2018
Madden NFL 19 (video game), 2018

Concert music

The Passion of the Christ Sym., chorus, orch, 2005

DURRELL BOWMAN/R

De Packh, Maurice

(*b* New York, 21 Nov 1896; *d* Beverly Hills, CA, 24 May 1960). American composer, arranger, orchestrator, and conductor. He studied the piano with Maurice Gould and Jeanne Franco and composition and orchestration with Frank Saddler. During the 1920s he worked as an arranger for Broadway musicals, including

The Girlfriend, Manhattan Mary, and the *Ziegfeld Follies* of 1920 and 1921. He also wrote songs for the 1922 musical *Glory*. He established the De Packh Ensemble, which he conducted between 1928 and 1931, then in 1933 he went to Hollywood as an arranger and orchestrator. He worked first for MGM and smaller studios on films such as *The Dancing Lady* (1933) and *Rip Tide* (1934). He was also one of the team of five principal orchestrators who assisted composer Max Steiner with *Gone with the Wind* (1939), a score that exemplifies the richness of orchestral timbre and complexity of arrangement that were hallmarks of film music of the time. In the early 1940s he moved to Twentieth Century-Fox, where he worked on a number of Betty Grable musicals, including *Four Jills in a Jeep* (1944), *The Dolly Sisters* (1945), and *Mother Wore Tights* (1947), for which Alfred Newman's musical direction won an Academy Award.

Works

(*selective list*)

Film scores

(*as orchestrator and arranger*)
The Dancing Lady (dir. R.Z. Leonard), 1933
Riptide (dir. E. Goulding), 1934
The Dancing Masters (dir. M. St. Clair), 1943
Four Jills in a Jeep (dir. W.A. Seiter), 1944
Irish Eyes Are Smiling (dir. G. Ratoff), 1944
The Bullfighters (dir. M. St. Clair and S. Laurel), 1945
The Dolly Sisters (dir. I. Cummings), 1945
I Wonder Who's Kissing Her Now (dir. L. Bacon), 1947
Mother Wore Tights (dir. W. Lang), 1947
When My Baby Smiles at Me (dir. W. Lang), 1948
Letter to Three Wives (dir. J.L. Mankiewicz), 1949
American Guerrilla in the Philippines (dir. F. Lang), 1950
Viva Zapata (dir. E. Kazan), 1952
Daddy Long Legs (dir. J. Negulesco), 1955
Anastasia (dir. A. Litvak), 1956

Bibliography

W. Sherk: "Films Orchestrated by Maurice de Packh," *The Cue Sheet* viii/3 (1991),
W. Sherk: "Music from the Films: The Lawrence Morton-Maurice de Packh Interview," *The Cue Sheet* viii/3 (1991)

KATE DAUBNEY/R

Deutsch, Adolph

(*b* London, UK, 20 Oct 1897; *d* Palm Desert, CA, 1 Jan 1980). American conductor, arranger, and composer of English birth. Best known today as musical director for MGM musicals such as *Annie Get Your Gun* (1950) and *The Band Wagon* (1953), Deutsch was born in London where he enrolled in the Royal Academy of Music at the age of eight. In 1910 he emigrated to the USA and became fascinated by American popular music and jazz. By the 1920s he was arranging for dance bands and spent three years as composer-arranger and associate music director for Paul Whiteman. On Broadway in the early 1930s he orchestrated and conducted the musicals of Rodgers and Hart, Gershwin, and Berlin. In the late 1930s Deutsch came to Hollywood, where he was under contract to Warner Bros. from 1937 to 1945. He was part of Warner's "second string" musical unit, and composed for B-pictures and such noir classics as *The Maltese Falcon* (1941) and *High Sierra* (1941). After a brief period of freelancing, Deutsch signed with MGM as arranger/conductor. For the studio's celebrated musicals unit he conducted classics such as *The Band Wagon* (1953) as well as lesser-known works such as the Romberg bio, *Deep In My Heart* (1954), and Cole Porter's *Les Girls* (1957). He also worked on *Funny Face* (1957), essentially an MGM musical produced at Paramount. At MGM he also composed background scores for such non-musical films as *Intruder in the Dust* (1949), *Little Women* (1949), for which he adapted Max Steiner's original 1937 score, and *Tea and Sympathy* (1956). Later Deutsch scored two of Billy Wilder's comedies for United Artists, *Some Like It Hot* (1959) and *The Apartment* (1960). He won several Academy Awards for his musical direction and was a founder and president of the Screen Composers Association. There is now an extensive Deutsch archive in the American Heritage Center at the University of Wyoming.

Works

Film scores

They Won't Forget (dir. M. LeRoy), 1937
Cowboy from Brooklyn (dir. L. Bacon), 1938
The Oklahoma Kid (dir. L. Bacon) 1939
The Fighting 69th (dir. W. Keighley), 1940
They Drive by Night (dir. R. Walsh), 1940
Torrid Zone (dir. W. Keighley), 1940
The Maltese Falcon (dir. J. Huston), 1941
Across the Pacific (dir. J. Huston), 1942
All Through the Night (dir. V. Sherman), 1942
George Washington Slept Here (dir. W. Keighley), 1942
Lucky Jordan (dir. F. Tuttle), 1942
Action in the North Atlantic (dir. L. Bacon), 1943
Northern Pursuit (dir. R. Walsh), 1943

The Mask of Dimitrios (dir. J. Negulesco), 1944
Uncertain Glory (dir. R. Walsh), 1944
Danger Signal (dir. R. Florey), 1945
Escape in the Desert (dir. E. Blatt), 1945
Nobody Lives Forever (dir. J. Negulesco), 1946
Three Strangers (dir. J. Negulesco), 1946
Blaze of Noon (dir. J. Farrow), 1947
Ramrod (dir. A. De Toth), 1947
Luxury Liner (dir. R. Whorf), 1948
The Barkleys of Broadway (dir. C. Walters), 1949
Intruder in the Dust (dir. C. Brown), 1949
Little Women (dir. M. LeRoy), 1949
Take Me Out to the Ball Game (dir. B. Berkeley), 1949
Whispering Smith (dir. L. Fenton), 1949
Annie Get Your Gun (dir. G. Sidney and B. Berkeley), 1950
The Big Hangover (dir. N. Krasna), 1950
Father of the Bride (dir. V. Minnelli), 1950
Pagan Love Song (dir. R. Alton), 1950
Stars in My Crown (dir. J. Tourneur), 1950
Show Boat (dir. G. Sidney), 1951
The Belle of New York (dir. C. Walters), 1952
Million Dollar Mermaid (dir. M. LeRoy), 1952
The Band Wagon (dir. V. Minnelli), 1953
The Long, Long Trailer (dir. V. Minnelli), 1953
Torch Song (dir. C. Walters), 1953
Deep in My Heart (dir. S. Donen), 1954
Seven Brides for Seven Brothers (dir. S. Donen), 1954
Interrupted Melody (dir. C. Bernhardt), 1955
Oklahoma (dir. F. Zinnemann), 1955
The Rack (dir. A. Laven), 1956
Tea and Sympathy (dir. V. Minnelli), 1956
Funny Face (dir. S. Donen), 1957
Les Girls (dir. G. Cukor), 1957
The Matchmaker (dir. J. Anthony), 1958
Some Like It Hot (dir. B. Wilder), 1959
The Apartment (dir. B. Wilder), 1960
Go Naked in the World (dir. R. MacDougall), 1961

Bibliography

R. Behlmer: disc notes, *"The Maltese Falcon" and Other Classic Film Scores by Adolph Deutsch*, Marco Polo CD 8 225169 (2000)

J. Burlingame: *Sound and Vision: 60 Years of Motion Picture Soundtracks* (New York, 2000), 60–61

ROSS CARE

De Vol, Frank

(*b* Moundsville, WV, 20 Sept 1911; *d* Lafayette, CA, 27 Oct 1999). American composer and arranger. Growing up in the family of a bandleader in Canton, Ohio, he taught himself saxophone and played piano and violin in a theater. De Vol provided arrangements for Horace Heidt and His Musical Knights in the 1930s before joining Alvino Rey's band. Beginning in the 1940s, De Vol provided arrangements for songs recorded by many popular singers, including Nat King Cole, Ella Fitzgerald, Tony Bennett, and Doris Day. In the 1950s, De Vol began composing for Hollywood films, notably collaborating with director Robert Aldrich on several of his films. During his career as a film composer, De Vol was nominated for four Academy Awards for his scores for *Pillow Talk* (1959), *Hush . . . Hush, Sweet Charlotte* (1964), *Cat Ballou* (1965), and *Guess Who's Coming to Dinner* (1967). De Vol also composed for several television programs, notably the theme music for *My Three Sons, Family Affair*, and *The Brady Bunch*. De Vol also performed as an actor, notably portraying bandleader Happy Kyne on the talk-show parodies *Fernwood 2 Night* and *America 2-Night*.

Works

Film scores

The Big Knife (dir. R. Aldrich), 1955
Kiss Me Deadly (dir. R. Aldrich), 1955
Attack (dir. R. Aldrich), 1956
Pardners (dir. N. Taurog), 1956
The Ride Back (dir. A.H. Miner and O. Rudolph), 1957
Pillow Talk (dir. M. Gordon), 1959
Murder, Inc. (dir. B. Balaban and S. Rosenberg), 1960
Lover Come Back (dir. D. Mann), 1961
Boys' Night Out (dir. M. Gordon), 1962
What Ever Happened to Baby Jane? (dir. R. Aldrich), 1962
McLintock! (dir. A.V. McLaglen), 1963
The Thrill of It All (dir. N. Jewison), 1963
Under the Yum Yum Tree (dir. D. Swift), 1963
The Wheeler Dealers (dir. A. Hiller), 1963
Hush . . . Hush, Sweet Charlotte (dir. R. Aldrich), 1964
Send Me No Flowers (dir. N. Jewison), 1964
Cat Ballou (dir. E. Silverstein), 1965
The Flight of the Phoenix (dir. R. Aldrich), 1965
The Glass Bottom Boat (dir. F. Tashlin), 1966
Caprice (dir. F. Tashlin), 1967
The Dirty Dozen (dir. R. Aldrich), 1967
Guess Who's Coming to Dinner (dir. S. Kramer), 1967
Ulzana's Raid (dir. R. Aldrich), 1972

Emperor of the North (dir. R. Aldrich), 1973
The Longest Yard (dir. R. Aldrich), 1974
Doc Savage: the Man of Bronze (dir. M. Anderson), 1975
Hustle (dir. R. Aldrich), 1975
The Choirboys (dir. R. Aldrich), 1977
Herbie Goes to Monte Carlo (dir. V. McEveety), 1977
The Frisco Kid (dir. R. Aldrich), 1979
Herbie Goes Bananas (dir. V. McEveety), 1980

Television movies

The Reluctant Heroes, 1971
Female Artillery, 1973
Key West, 1973
Hey, I'm Alive, 1975
Panache, 1976
The Millionaire, 1978
The Ghosts of Buxley Hall, 1980
The Wild Women of Chastity Gulch, 1982

Television series

Wagon Train, 1959
Dr. Kildare, 1963
My Three Sons, 1965
The Virginian, 1968
Family Affair, 1969–71
The Brady Bunch, 1969–74
Dusty's Trail, 1973–4
McCloud, 1973–5
Fernwood 2 Night, 1977
America 2-Night, 1978
The Love Boat, 1978
Disneyland, 1980–82
The Brady Brides, 1981
Hotel, 1983

Bibliography

R.R. Faulkner: *Music on Demand: Composers and Careers in the Hollywood Film Industry* (New Brunswick, NJ, 1983)

K. Schoemer: "The Lives They Lived: Frank DeVol, b. 1911," *New York Times Magazine* (2 Jan 2000)

P. Green and F. Price: *A History of Television's "The Virginian," 1962–1971* (Jefferson, NC, 2006)

S. Greaves: "The Many Sides of Frank DeVol," *Score*, xxiv/1 (2009), 5–7

DANIEL SHERIDAN

Dolan, Robert Emmett

(*b* Hartford, CT, 3 Aug 1906; *d* Los Angeles, 26 Sept 1972). American conductor, composer, arranger, and film producer. He attended Loyola College, later studying with Joseph Schillinger and Ernst Toch. Beginning in 1927, he conducted Broadway musicals by several of its leading songwriters, including Schwartz (*Flying Colors*, 1932), Romberg (*May Wine*, 1935), Arlen (*Hooray for What?*, 1937), Porter (*Leave it to Me*, 1938), Kern (*Very Warm for May*, 1939), and Berlin (*Louisiana Purchase*, 1940). He also appeared frequently as a network radio conductor during the 1930s. He joined Paramount in 1941 and worked on several dozen films, variously as composer, arranger, conductor, or musical director, including *Holiday Inn* (1942), *Lady in the Dark* (1944), and *Blue Skies* (1946). He also served as producer for the lavish Paramount musicals *White Christmas* (1954) and *Anything Goes* (1956), an opportunity rarely afforded Hollywood's music executives. With lyricist Johnny Mercer, Dolan wrote a few film songs as well as the musical comedies *Texas, L'il Darlin'* (1949) and *Foxy* (1964). In New York he taught at the Juilliard School in the 1960s and was engaged to conduct *Juno* (Blitzstein, 1959) and *Coco* (Previn, 1969) on Broadway. His *Music in Modern Media* (New York, 1967) is a valuable document of soundtrack recording practice in the United States just before multiple magnetic tracks came into common usage. His manuscripts are held at the University of Wyoming.

GEORGE J. FERENCZ

Elfman, Danny [Daniel Robert]

(*b* Los Angeles, 29 May 1953). American composer, rock singer, arranger, and guitarist. With his brother Richard he formed the theater company the Mystic Knights of the Oingo Boingo in the 1970s, which in 1979 became Oingo Boingo, an eight-piece, new wave band led by Elfman as vocalist and songwriter. During the 1980s the band developed a distinctive synthesizer and horn-based sound; occasionally its songs were featured in youth-market films, such as for the title song of *Weird Science* (1985), but its ten or so albums had limited commercial success and it formally broke up in 1995.

Beginning in 1985 Elfman also began scoring films, becoming especially well known for his association with the director Tim Burton; after *Batman* (1989), he became one of Hollywood's most sought-after younger composers. He has worked on nearly all of Burton's films, creating colorful, rhythmically driving, and knowingly referential scores, well matched to Burton's surreal style. Elfman has also written the theme music for many television shows, notably "The Simpsons." Objecting to the overbearing use of sound effects in such action-driven films as *Batman* and *Batman Returns* (1992), he has sought out projects that give greater prominence to music. His lyrical gifts are evident in *Edward*

Danny Elfman, right, with Tim Burton, 1993
Photo © DILTZ/Bridgeman Images

Scissorhands (1990; one of many scores in which he included a wordless choir) and *Black Beauty* (1994). Other films, especially *Dolores Claiborne* (1995), *Good Will Hunting* (1997), *Big Fish* (2003), and *Milk* (2008), show great subtlety and inventiveness, particularly in blending synthesized timbres with both standard and exotic instruments.

Elfman has acknowledged the influence of such film composers as Rota, Herrmann, and Korngold, as well as of classical works such as Stravinsky's *Histoire du soldat* (to which he wittily alluded in *Beetlejuice,* 1988). In 2005, Elfman made his first foray into concert music with the orchestral suite, *Serenada Schizophrana,* which had its première at Carnegie Hall. The following year his *Overeager Overture* received its première at the Hollywood Bowl. He has defended himself, somewhat abrasively, against criticism for his lack of formal training and seeming dependency on orchestrators and conductors, particularly Steve Bartek (a member of Oingo Boingo) and Shirley Walker: such claims have been well refuted.

Works

(*selective list*)

Film scores

Pee-wee's Big Adventure (dir. T. Burton), 1985
Back to School (dir. A. Metter), 1986
Beetlejuice (dir. T. Burton), 1988
Midnight Run (dir. M. Brest), 1988

Scrooged (dir. R. Donner), 1988
Batman (dir. T. Burton), 1989
Darkman (dir. S. Raimi), 1990
Dick Tracy (dir. W. Beatty), 1990
Edward Scissorhands (dir. T. Burton), 1990
Batman Returns (dir. T. Burton), 1992
The Nightmare Before Christmas (dir. H. Selick), 1993
Sommersby (dir. J. Amiel), 1993
Black Beauty (dir. C. Thompson), 1994
Dead Presidents (dir. A. Hughes and A. Hughes), 1995
Dolores Claiborne (dir. T. Hackford), 1995
To Die For (dir. G. Van Sant), 1995
The Frighteners (dir. P. Jackson), 1996
Mars Attacks (dir. T. Burton), 1996
Mission: Impossible (dir. B. De Palma), 1996, incorporates theme by Schifrin
Flubber (dir. L. Mayfield), 1997
Good Will Hunting (dir. G. Van Sant), 1997
Men in Black (dir. B. Sonnenfeld), 1997
A Civil Action (dir. S. Zaillian), 1998
Psycho (dir. G. Van Sant), 1998, adapted from score by Herrmann
A Simple Plan (dir. S. Raimi), 1998
Anywhere But Here (dir. W. Wang), 1999
Instinct (dir. J. Turteltaub), 1999
Sleepy Hollow (dir. T. Burton), 1999
The Family Man (dir. B. Ratner), 2000
Proof of Life (dir. T. Hackford), 2000
Planet of the Apes (dir. T. Burton), 2001
Spy Kids (dir. R. Rodriguez), 2001
Chicago (dir. R. Marshall), 2002
Men in Black II (dir. B. Sonnenfeld), 2002
Spider-Man (dir. S. Raimi), 2002
Hulk (dir. A. Lee), 2003
Spider-Man II (dir. S. Raimi), 2004
Charlie and the Chocolate Factory (dir. T. Burton), 2005
Corpse Bride (dir. T. Burton and M. Johnson), 2005
Charlotte's Web (dir. G. Winick), 2006
Nacho Libre (dir. J. Hess), 2006
The Kingdom (dir. P. Berg), 2007
Meet the Robinsons (dir. S.J. Anderson), 2007
Hellboy II: The Golden Army (dir. G. del Toro), 2008
Milk (dir. G. Van Sant), 2008
Wanted (dir. T. Bekmambetov), 2008
Notorious (dir. G. Tillman Jr.), 2009
Taking Woodstock (dir. A. Lee), 2009
Terminator Salvation (dir. McG), 2009
Alice in Wonderland (dir. T. Burton), 2010

The Next Three Days (dir. P. Haggis), 2010
The Wolfman (dir. J. Johnston), 2010
Real Steel (dir. S. Levy), 2011
Restless (dir. G. Van Sant), 2011
Dark Shadows (dir. T. Burton), 2012
Frankenweenie (dir. T. Burton), 2012
Hitchcock (dir. S. Gervasi), 2012
Men in Black 3 (dir. B. Sonnenfeld), 2012
Promised Land (dir. G. Van Sant), 2012
Silver Linings Playbook (dir. D.O. Russell), 2012
American Hustle (dir. D.O. Russell), 2013
Epic (dir. C. Wedge), 2013
Oz the Great and Powerful (dir. S. Raimi), 2013
The Unknown Known (dir. E. Morris), 2013
Big Eyes (dir. T. Burton), 2014
Mr. Peabody & Sherman (dir. R. Minkoff), 2014
Avengers: Age of Ultron (dir. J. Whedon), 2015
The End of the Tour (dir. J. Ponsoldt), 2015
Fifty Shades of Grey (dir. S. Taylor-Johnson), 2015
Goosebumps (dir. R. Letterman), 2015
Alice Through the Looking Glass (dir. J. Bobin), 2016
Before I Wake (dir. M. Flanagan), 2016
The Girl on the Train (dir. T. Taylor), 2016
The Circle (dir. J. Ponsoldt), 2017
Fifty Shades Darker (dir. J. Foley), 2017
A Glory Sewn (dir. T.J. Dixon), 2017
Justice League (dir. Z. Snyder), 2017
Tau (dir. F. D'Alessandro), 2017
Tulip Fever (dir. J. Chadwick), 2017
Don't Worry, He Won't Get Far on Foot (dir. G. Van Sant), 2018
Fifty Shades Freed (dir. J. Foley), 2018

Television music

Amazing Stories, 1985
The Simpsons, 1989, theme
When We Rise, 2017
other animated series

Publishers: Hal Leonard, Warner Bros.

Bibliography

R. Doerschuk and J. Burger: "Danny Elfman: Plotting More High-Tech Mischief with Oingo Boingo," *Keyboard*, xiii/19 (1987), 30ff

R. Doerschuk: "Danny Elfman: the Agony and the Ecstasy of Scoring *Batman,*" *Keyboard*, xv/10 (1989), 80ff

"An Open Letter from Danny Elfman," *Keyboard*, xvi/3 (1990), 47, 62–3
D. Schweiger: "Danny Elfman Returns," *Soundtrack!*, xi/43 (1992), 17–20
D. Adams: "Tales from the Black Side: an Interview with Danny Elfman," *Film Score Monthly* (Los Angeles), ii/4 (1997), 20–26
D. Adams: "The Evolution of Elfman," *Film Score Monthly* (Los Angeles), iv/1 (1999), 20–23, 46
M. Russell: *Film Music* (Boston, 2000), 146–59
J. Halfyard: *Danny Elfman's "Batman": a Film Score Guide* (Lanham, MD, 2004)
P. Hayward: "Inter-Planetary Soundclash: Music, Technology and Territorialisation in *Mars Attacks!*," *Off the Planet*, ed. P. Hayward (Eastleigh, UK, 2004), 176–87
D. Adams: "Mortality Plays: Danny Elfman," *Film Score Monthly* x/4 (2005), 32–9
H.S. Wright: "The Film Music of Danny Elfman: a Selective Discography," *Notes* lxii/4 (2006), 1030–42
N. Lerner: "Danny Elfman: 'Funny Circus Mirrors'," *Sound and Music in Film and Visual Media*, ed. G. Harper, R. Doughty, and J. Eisentraut (New York, 2009), 524–32
R. Larson: "Danny Elfman: From Boingo to *Batman* (1990)," *Celluloid Symphonies: Texts and Contexts in Film Music History*, ed. J. Hubbert (Berkeley, CA, 2011), 443–51

MARTIN MARKS/R

Farnon, Robert

(*b* Toronto, ON, 24 July 1917; *d* Guernsey, 23 April 2005). Canadian arranger, composer, and conductor. He began his career as a trumpet player in dance bands and later worked for Percy Faith's CBC Orchestra. By 1942 he had composed two symphonies, and in 1944 he came to Britain as conductor of the Canadian Band of the Allied Expeditionary Force, alongside Glenn Miller and George Melachrino fronting the US and British bands. He took his army discharge in Britain, where Decca contracted him to work with their leading singers such as Vera Lynn and Gracie Fields; the BBC granted him a radio series with his own orchestra. He began composing for the cinema, and early successes out of some forty scores included *Spring in Park Lane*, *Maytime in Mayfair*, and *Captain Horatio Hornblower R.N.* The emergence of LPs provided orchestra leaders such as Farnon the opportunity to develop their arranging and composing talents more fully, and his Decca albums from the 1950s have become highly prized by admirers, especially fellow musicians in the United States. Many have acknowledged his influence, including John Williams, Henry Mancini, Quincy Jones, and Johnny Mandel. Farnon's light orchestral cameos are among the finest to have been written since World War II, notably *Journey into Melody* (1946), *State Occasion* (1946), *Jumping Bean* (1947), *Portrait of a Flirt* (1947), *A Star Is Born* (1947), *Peanut Polka* (1950), *The Westminster Waltz* (1955), and the *Colditz March* (1972). His tone poems *Lake of the Woods* (1951) and *À la claire fontaine* (1955) have been compared favorably to the orchestral works of Claude Debussy and Maurice Ravel. Farnon's orchestral style was influenced by the exciting North American rhythms of his youth, yet respects the traditions of light music he encountered in Britain. His scores are remarkable for the delicate, decorative touches he introduces for so many instruments in support of the main melodies.

In 1945 Farnon conducted his Canadian Army band for a sequence in the film *I Live in Grosvenor Square*. Thus began a working relationship with producer Herbert Wilcox, with whom he worked on *Spring in Park Lane*, one of British cinema's most successful films at the time. Warner Bros. also employed Farnon for their UK productions *Captain Horatio Hornblower R.N.* and *Where's Charley?*—both of which demanded substantial scores (albeit markedly different in terms of musical style due to production specifications).

Farnon wrote hundreds of works for the London publisher Chappell, many of which are familiar worldwide as signature tunes. The BBC commissioned his Rhapsody for violin and orchestra in 1958, but his later career concentrated on arranging and conducting for international stars such as Tony Bennett, Bing Crosby, Lena Horne, George Shearing, Eileen Farrell, Joe Williams, and Sarah Vaughan. His skill as an arranger was recognized with a Grammy Award in 1996 for a track on an album with trombonist J.J. Johnson; in Britain he received four Ivor Novello Awards, including one for outstanding services to British music (1991). In 1998 he was awarded the Order of Canada. (*EMC2*, M. Miller)

Towards the end of his life he completed two major works: Symphony no.3 (the "Edinburgh"), which was given its première by conductor Iain Sutherland in Edinburgh three weeks after his death, and a jazz bassoon concerto, *Romancing the Phoenix* (based on *Saxophone Tripartite*, 1971), given its premièred by bassoonist Daniel Smith on 13 September 2009 in Malvern, England.

Works

(*selective list*)

Film scores

I Know Where I'm Going (dir. M. Powell and E. Pressburger), partial scoring, un-credited, 1945
Just William's Luck (dir. V. Guest), 1947
Maytime in Mayfair (dir. H. Wilcox), 1948
Spring in Park Lane (dir. H. Wilcox), 1948
William Comes to Town (dir. V. Guest), 1948
Elizabeth of Ladymead (dir. H. Wilcox), 1949
Circle of Danger (dir. J. Tourneur), 1950
The Dancing Years (dir. H. French), 1950
Captain Horatio Hornblower R.N. (dir. R. Walsh), 1951
Where's Charley? (dir. D. Butler), 1952
His Majesty O'Keefe (dir. B. Haskin and B. Lancaster), 1954
Lilacs in the Spring (dir. H. Wilcox), 1954

All for Mary (dir. W. Toye), 1955
Gentlemen Marry Brunettes (dir. R. Sale), 1955
It's a Wonderful World (dir. V. Guest), 1956
King's Rhapsody (dir. H. Wilcox), 1956
True As a Turtle (dir. W. Toye), 1956
The Little Hut (dir. M. Robson), 1957
The Sheriff of Fractured Jaw (dir. R. Walsh), 1958
Expresso Bongo (dir. V. Guest), 1960
The Road to Hong Kong (dir. N. Panama), 1962
The Truth about Spring (dir. R. Thorpe), 1965
Shalako (dir. E. Dmytryk), 1968
Bear Island (dir. D. Sharp), 1979

Television themes

Colditz, 1972
The Secret Army, 1977
A Man Called Intrepid, 1980
Kessler, 1981
The Cabbage Patch, 1983

Orchestral

Sym. no.1, 1940
Sym. no.2 "Ottawa", 1942
The Princess and the Ugly Frog, 1943
Canadian Caravan, 1945
Journey into Melody, 1946
Ottawa Heights, 1946
State Occasion, 1946
Willie the Whistler, 1946
How Beautiful is Night, 1947 [addl. lyrics, M. Raskin, 1963]
In a Calm, 1947
Jumping Bean, 1947
Pictures in the Fire, 1947
Portrait of a Flirt, 1947
A Star is Born, 1947
All Sports March, 1948
Gateway to the West, 1948
Grandstand, 1948
Manhattan Playboy, 1948
Goodwood Galop, 1950
Huckle Buckle, 1950
Melody Fair, 1950
Peanut Polka, 1950
Proud Canvas, 1950
Sophistication Waltz, 1950

Lake of the Woods, 1951
Alcan Highway, 1952
Playtime, 1952
Almost a Lullaby (Prairie Sunset), 1953
Mid Ocean, 1953
Poodle Parade, 1953
World Series, 1953
En route, 1954
Malaga, 1954
A Promise of Spring, 1954
Scherzando for Tpt, 1954
Swing Hoe, 1954
À la claire fontaine, 1955
Derby Day, 1955
Int for Hp, 1955
The Westminster Waltz, 1955
Boom Town, 1956
La casita mia, 1956
The Frontiersmen, 1956
Lazy Day, 1956
Moomin, 1956
Blue Moment, 1957
Open Skies, 1957
City Streets, 1958
Dominion Day, 1958
Mr. Punch, 1958
Rhapsody for Vn and Orch, 1958
The First Waltz, 1959
Headland Country, 1959
Holiday Flight, 1959
Little Miss Molly, 1959
Hymn to the Commonwealth, 1960
On the Seashore, 1960
Travel Topic, 1962
Pleasure Drive, 1964
Westbound Passage, 1964
Prelude and Dance for Harmonica and Orch, 1966
Horn-a-Plenty, 1969
Power and Glory, 1969
Shepherd's Delight, 1969
Sounds of History, 1969
Flute Fantasy, 1973
The Snow Goose, 1973
A Violin Miniature, 1973
In a Dream World, 1974
Concorde March, 1975

Canadian Rhapsody, 1983
The Wide World, 1983
Lake Louise, 1984
The Magic Island, 1984
Swallow Flight, 1984
Nautical Trilogy, 1993
Royal Walkabout, 1993
For Eileen, 1995
Cascades to the Sea, conc., pf, orch, 1998
Cruise World, 1998
Hollywood Stars, 1999
Scenic Wonders, 1999
Sym. no.3 "The Edinburgh", 2004

Brass band

Here Comes the Band, 1966
Une vie de matelot, 1975
Morning Cloud, 1977
Crown Ceremonial, 1978

Jazz works

Portrait of Lorraine, 1964
The Pleasure of your Company, 1969 [for Oscar Peterson]
Saxophone Tripartite, 1971
Travellin' Jazz, 1973
Trumpet Talk, 1973
Two's Company, 1973

Songs

Country Girl, 1966
The Last Enemy (C.A. Arlington), 1990

DAVID ADES

Fielding, Jerry

(*b* Pittsburgh, PA, 17 June 1922; *d* Toronto, ON, 17 Feb 1980). American composer. He played clarinet as a child and briefly attended the Carnegie Institute (now Carnegie Mellon School of Music) before studying arranging with Max Adkins, music director at Pittsburgh's Stanley Theatre. At age seventeen he toured with Alvino Rey's big band; he later arranged for the bands of Tommy Dorsey, Claude Thornhill, Jimmie Lunceford, and Charlie Barnet.

In Los Angeles from 1942 Fielding was writing vocal arrangements for the Town Criers, who in turn were signed to Kay Kyser's band; soon Fielding was arranging regularly for Kyser's radio quiz show the "Kollege of Musical Knowledge." By 1947 Fielding was conducting for Jack Paar's radio show. More radio music engagements followed, including "The Life of Riley," Mickey Rooney's "The Hardy Family," and Groucho Marx's "You Bet Your Life." Fielding made the transition to television with Marx's popular quiz show in 1950; later he conducted Hoagy Carmichael's "Saturday Night Revue" and, in 1952, he hosted his own half-hour jazz show on a Los Angeles television station.

Fielding's leftist political sensibilities were deemed suspicious by the House Un-American Activities Committee. He was blacklisted by the networks and studios after he took the Fifth Amendment in an appearance before a HUAC subcommittee in December 1953. As such, he took a band on the road before spending much of the rest of the decade in Las Vegas arranging for celebrity entertainers such as Frank Sinatra, Mitzi Gaynor, Debbie Reynolds, and Betty Hutton. It was Hutton who broke the blacklist by insisting—when she got her own television show in 1959—that Fielding be her musical director.

Fielding pursued further studies with Ernst Toch and Mario Castelnuovo-Tedesco and began writing dramatic scores for television and films. *Advise and Consent* featured his first major film score in 1962. In 1966 he met director Sam Peckinpah on a television project ("Noon Wine"). They enjoyed a fruitful and sometimes volatile relationship over the course of six film projects. Their collaborations led to Fielding's composition of Oscar-nominated scores for *The Wild Bunch* and *Straw Dogs* and one that was written but rejected (by the producers) for *The Getaway*.

Fielding also scored six films for director Michael Winner (including expansive Americana in *Lawman* and a serial score for *The Mechanic*) and four for Clint Eastwood (including an Oscar-nominated Western score for *The Outlaw Josey Wales* and a jazz score for *The Gauntlet*). Throughout the 1960s and 70s Fielding also worked regularly in television, for which he composed the familiar "Hogan's Heroes" march and music for the lighthearted Rock Hudson detective drama "McMillan and Wife"; he won a posthumous Emmy for the TV-movie *High Midnight*. Fielding died of congestive heart failure while working in Canada.

Works

Film scores

Advise and Consent (dir. O. Preminger), 1962
The Nun and the Sergeant (dir. F. Adreon), 1962
For Those Who Think Young (dir. L.H. Martinson), 1964

McHale's Navy (dir. E. Montagne), 1964
McHale's Navy Joins the Air Force (dir. E. Montagne), 1965
The Crazy World of Laurel and Hardy (dir. B. Scott), 1967
The Wild Bunch (dir. S. Peckinpah), 1969
Suppose They Gave a War and Nobody Came? (dir. H. Averback), 1970
Johnny Got His Gun (dir. D. Trumbo), 1971
Lawman (dir. M. Winner), 1971
The Nightcomers (dir. M. Winner), 1971
Straw Dogs (dir. S. Peckinpah), 1971
Chato's Land (dir. M. Winner), 1972
The Getaway (dir. S. Peckinpah), unused, 1972
Junior Bonner (dir. S. Peckinpah), 1972
The Outfit (dir. J. Flynn), 1973
Scorpio (dir. M. Winner), 1973
Bring Me the Head of Alfredo Garcia (dir. S. Peckinpah), 1974
The Gambler (dir. K. Reisz), 1974
The Super Cops (dir. G. Parks), 1974
The Black Bird (dir. D. Giler), 1975
The Killer Elite (dir. S. Peckinpah), 1975
The Bad News Bears (dir. M. Ritchie), 1976
The Enforcer (dir. J. Fargo), 1976
The Outlaw Josey Wales (dir. C. Eastwood), 1976
Demon Seed (dir. D. Cammell), 1977
Semi-Tough (dir. M. Ritchie), 1977
The Big Sleep (dir. M. Winner), 1978
Gray Lady Down (dir. D. Greene), 1978
Beyond the Poseidon Adventure (dir. I. Allen), 1979
Escape from Alcatraz (dir. D. Siegel), 1979
Below the Belt (dir. R. Fowler), 1980
Funeral Home (dir. W. Fruet), 1980

Television series music

(*selective list*)
The Betty Hutton Show, 1959
The Tom Ewell Show, 1961
Broadside, 1964
Hogan's Heroes, 1965
Run Buddy Run, 1966
He & She, 1967
The Good Guys, 1968
The Queen and I, 1969
The Chicago Teddy Bears, 1971
Bridget Loves Bernie, 1972
The Little People (The Brian Keith Show), 1972
The Snoop Sisters, 1972

Diana, 1973
Faraday and Company, 1973
The Cop and the Kid, 1975
On the Rocks, 1975
The Bionic Woman, 1976
The Andros Targets, 1977
W.E.B., 1978

Television film music

Hunters Are for Killing, 1970
Ellery Queen: Don't Look Behind You, 1971
Once Upon a Dead Man, 1971
A War of Children, 1972
Shirts/Skins, 1973
Honky Tonk, 1974
Unwed Father, 1974
Hustling, 1975
Matt Helm, 1975
Little Ladies of the Night, 1977
Lovey: A Circle of Children, Part II, 1978
High Midnight, 1979
Mr. Horn, 1979

Bibliography

L. Feather: "From Pen to Screen: Jerry Fielding," *International Musician* (Nov 1969)
L. Tomkins: "Jerry Fielding," *Crescendo International*, Sept and Nov 1974, May 1975
J.A. Quantrill: "Jerry Fielding: a Biographical Sketch," *Film Music Notebook*, iii/3 (1977)
P. Seydor: "Jerry Fielding: The Composer as Collaborator," *Film Music Notebook*, iii/3 (1977)
N. Redman: "Jerry Fielding," *Dictionary of American Biography*, Supplement no.10 (1976–80), 1995

JON BURLINGAME

Finston, Nat W.

(*b* New York, 24 Feb 1890; *d* Los Angeles, 19 Dec 1979). American executive, music director, conductor, and violinist. He began music lessons at age seven after his grandfather gave him a violin. Studies include violin with Solomon Elin, piano and harmony with E.J. Falk, and, later, composition with Pietro Floridia. From 1907 to 1917 he performed with the Volpe SO, Sam Franko Quartette, Russian SO, Boston Opera Orchestra, New York City SO, and New York PO.

Embarking on a career as a music director and conductor in motion picture theaters, he was in New York at the Rialto for three years and the Capitol for one. In 1921 he relocated to Chicago where he served as the general music director for the Balaban & Katz theater chain, conducting at the Tivoli, Chicago, and Uptown. When Balaban & Katz theaters merged with those owned by Paramount in 1925, Finston returned to New York to become general music director for the newly formed Publix Theaters. He wrote *Valse Silhouette* and collaborated on a handful of other compositions which were used to accompany silent films. After a brief stint at the Rivoli, he opened the flagship Paramount Theater, conducting there through 1928. At the same time, he supervised scoring for the first Paramount Movietone sound films for Victor Talking Machine in New Jersey. This led to his assignment to found the music department at Paramount's studio in Hollywood. Serving as general music director from 1928 to 1934, his responsibilities included conducting, hiring composers and orchestrators, and supervising scoring, music research, and clearance. From 1935 to 1944 he headed the music department at Metro-Goldwyn-Mayer where he brought musicians from Jose Iturbi to Albert Coates to the screen. Finston's brother-in-law, Nathaniel Shilkret, came to work at the studio. After leaving MGM, Finston headed the music division at the Selznick-Saphier Agency, established Finston Music Service for independent producers, and founded Symphony Films where he coproduced *Song of My Heart* (1948).

Works

(selective list)

Film scores

(music director or supervisor)
Innocents of Paris (dir. R. Wallace), 1929, score by J. Leipold
Paramount on Parade (dir. D. Arzner), 1930, score by H. Jackson
Love Me Tonight (dir. R. Mamoulian), 1932, score by Leipold
Alice in Wonderland (dir. N.Z. McLeod), 1933, score by D. Tiomkin
Design for Living (dir. E. Lubitsch), 1933, score by Leipold
The Sign of the Cross (dir. C.B. DeMille), 1933, score by R. Kopp
The Song of Songs (dir. Mamoulian), 1933, score by K. Hajos
Cleopatra (dir. DeMille), 1934, score by R. Kopp
The Big Broadcast of 1936 (dir. N. Taurog), 1935, score by Leipold
Mutiny on the Bounty (dir. F. Lloyd), 1935, score by H. Stothart
Paris in Spring (dir. L. Milestone), 1935, score by F. Hollander
The Wizard of Oz (dir. V. Fleming, and others), 1939, score by Stothart
Blonde Inspiration (dir. B. Berkeley), 1941, score by B. Kaper
Bataan (dir. T. Garnett), 1943, score by Kaper
Gaslight (dir. G. Cukor), 1944, score by Kaper
Song of My Heart (dir. B. Glazer), 1948

Compositions

(for silent film accompaniment)
composer, with others, all circa 1925
If You Should Die
Little Coquette
Satin Fan
Sleepy Eyes
Valse Silhouette

Writings

"The Screen's Influence in Music," *Music and Dance in California*, ed. J. Rodriguez (Hollywood, CA, 1940)

Bibliography

T. Thackrey: "Conductor Brought Melody to Silent Films," *Los Angeles Times* (24 Dec 1979) [obituary]

WARREN M. SHERK

Forbes, Lou

(*b* St. Louis, MO, 12 Aug 1902; *d* Los Angeles, 17 June 1981). American music director, conductor, composer, and violinist. In Kansas City he played violin for the symphony orchestra and in the pit orchestras at the New Royal and Newman theaters. As a teenager he conducted at the New Royal. He took Lou Forbes as his professional name in the mid-1920s, perhaps to avoid confusion with his older brother, Leo F. Forbstein, who pursued a similar career path. For Paramount Publix, Forbes organized and directed theater orchestras and stage bands, for the Palace in Dallas in 1928, the Metropolitan in Houston in 1929, and the Paramount in Atlanta in 1930. His career as a musical director in Hollywood began at Universal Pictures in 1936. After two years he moved to Selznick International Pictures where he was active through 1944. For producer David O. Selznick, Forbes oversaw the production of music for *Gone With the Wind* (1939), *Intermezzo* (1939), and *Rebecca* (1940). During these years he also conducted the Lou Forbes Orchestra for radio. Hired in the music department at Samuel Goldwyn Productions in 1943 he served as music director from 1944 to 1946, notably for *The Kid from Brooklyn* (1946). Having scored two previous films and having studied privately with Max Steiner and Edward Kilenyi Sr. (1884–1968), Forbes transitioned to composing in 1947 and wrote music for more than two-dozen films in the ensuing fourteen years. These include three for the Protestant Film Commission; nine produced by RKO, where he often shared scoring duties with Howard Jackson; and nearly a dozen independent productions directed by Allan Dwan.

Works

(*selective list*)

Film scores

(*as music director or supervisor*)
Mysterious Crossing (dir. A. Lubin), 1936
The Adventures of Tom Sawyer (dir. N. Taurog), 1938, score by M. Steiner
Gone with the Wind (dir. V. Fleming, G. Cukor, and S. Wood), 1939, score by M. Steiner
Intermezzo, A Love Story (dir. G. Ratoff), 1939, score by M. Steiner
Made for Each Other (dir. J. Cromwell), 1939, score by H. Friedhofer
Rebecca (dir. A. Hitchcock), 1940, score by F. Waxman
Up in Arms (dir. E. Nugent), 1944, score by M.
Brewster's Millions (dir. A. Dwan), 1945, score by H. Friedhofer
Wonder Man (dir. H.B. Humberstone), 1945, score by H. Roemheld
The Kid from Brooklyn (dir. N.Z. McCleod), 1946, score by C. Dragon

Film scores

(*as composer*)
Pitfall (dir. A. de Toth), 1948
The Crooked Way (dir. R. Florey), 1949
Johnny One-Eye (dir. Florey), 1950
Appointment in Honduras (dir. J. Tourneur), 1953
Count the Hours (dir. D. Siegel), 1953
Cattle Queen of Montana (dir. Dwan), 1954
City Story (dir. Beaudine), 1954
Silver Lode (dir. Dwan), 1954

Film and theme songs

Since You Went Away, 1944 [title song]
Montana, 1954 [from Cattle Queen of Montana]
Passion Tango, 1954 [from Passion]
Heart of Gold, 1955 [from Tennessee's Partner]
The River's Edge, 1957 [title song]
The Bat Theme, 1959 [from The Bat]

WARREN M. SHERK

Forbstein, Leo

(*b* St. Louis, MO, 16 Oct 1892; *d* Los Angeles, 16 March 1948). American music director, conductor, and violinist. Musically educated by his mother and at the St. Louis Conservatory of Music, he was a violinist in theater orchestras when he came to the attention of owner Frank L. Newman. Forbstein was appointed music director for Newman's Theatre Royal in Kansas City as early as 1915. When the Newman Theater opened in that city in 1919, Forbstein became the director of the Newman Concert Orchestra. He arrived in Los Angeles in 1925 to lead Newman's Metropolitan Theater. Moving to Sid Grauman's Egyptian Theater in 1926 he compiled and conducted scores for *Sparrows* and *The Black Pirate.* Later that year he became the pit conductor at Grauman's Million Dollar Theater. His long association with Warner Bros. began in 1928 when he conducted at their namesake downtown theater when the company was acquiring First National. This led to his appointment in 1929 as music director for First National Pictures and his conducting the Vitaphone Symphony Orchestra. At Warner Bros.–First National he pioneered the recording and synchronizing of music in sound films and supervised hundreds of motion pictures, with music by Max Steiner, Erich Wolfgang Korngold, and others. He served as the head of Warner Bros. music department until his death in 1948.

Works

(*selective list*)

Film scores

(*as music director*)

Footlights and Fools (dir. W.A. Seiter), 1929, score by A. Reiser
Captain Blood (dir. M. Curtiz), 1935, score by E.W. Korngold
Anthony Adverse (dir. M. LeRoy, Curtiz (uncredited)), 1936, score by Korngold
The Charge of the Light Brigade (dir. Curtiz), 1936, score by M. Steiner
Gold Diggers of 1937 (dir. L. Bacon), 1936, score by H. Roemheld
The Life of Emile Zola (dir. W. Dieterle), 1937, score by Steiner
The Adventures of Robin Hood (dir. Curtiz, W. Keighly), 1938, score by Korngold
Jezebel (dir. W. Wyler), 1938, score by Steiner
Dark Victory (dir. E. Goulding), 1939, score by Steiner
The Private Lives of Elizabeth and Essex (dir. Curtiz), 1939, score by Korngold
The Letter (dir. Wyler), 1940, score by Steiner
The Sea Hawk (dir. Curtiz), score by Korngold
Casablanca (dir. Curtiz), 1942, score by Steiner
Yankee Doodle Dandy (dir. Curtiz), 1942, score by R. Heindorf, H. Roemheld
This Is the Army (dir. Curtiz), 1943, score by Heindorf
To Have and Have Not (dir. H. Hawks), 1944, score by F. Waxman
Mildred Pierce (dir Curtiz), 1945, score by Steiner
Rhapsody in Blue (dir. I. Rapper), 1945, score by Steiner

Saratoga Trunk (dir. S. Wood), 1945, score by Steiner
Deception (dir. Rapper), 1946, score by Korngold
Devotion (dir. C. Bernhardt), 1946, score by Korngold
Humoresque (dir. J. Negulesco), 1946, score by Waxman
Johnny Belinda (dir. Negulesco), 1948, score by Steiner
The Treasure of the Sierra Madre (dir. J. Huston), 1948, score by Steiner

WARREN M. SHERK

Friedhofer, Hugo (William)

(*b* San Francisco, 3 May ?1902; *d* Los Angeles, 17 May 1981). American orchestrator and composer. He gave up early study towards an artistic career in favor of musical training, first as a cellist, and then as an arranger and orchestrator. During the 1920s he studied with Domenico Brescia and worked as an arranger for theater and cinema orchestras, before joining Fox Studios in 1929 as an arranger for early sound film scores. These collaborative projects prepared him for his move to Warner Bros. in 1934 where he worked as principal orchestrator for Erich Wolfgang Korngold and Max Steiner. He orchestrated sixteen of Korngold's seventeen original film scores, including *The Adventures of Robin Hood* (1938) and *The Sea Hawk* (1940), and fifty-four of Steiner's seventy-seven scores for Warner Bros. between 1936 and 1947, notably including *Now, Voyager,* which won the Academy Award in 1942, and *Mildred Pierce* (1945). In 1943 he was offered a contract to compose for Twentieth Century-Fox, and he scored sixty-nine films as principal composer and two hundred as cocomposer. His first original film score was in 1938 for *The Adventures of Marco Polo,* and he went on to compose for a variety of films including *Broken Arrow, Vera Cruz,* and *An Affair to Remember*. He won the 1946 Academy Award for *The Best Years of our Lives*. Despite the modernist techniques of teachers such as Nadia Boulanger, Ernst Toch, and Ernest Kanitz, with whom Friedhofer studied in the late 1930s and early 40s, and the influence of jazz on the film scoring of consequent decades, his style is most clearly understood as a fusion of the thematic approach of Steiner and the atmospheric emphasis of Korngold, blended with more economic orchestration than he used for either composer. A large collection of Friedhofer's original scores is held in the Arts and Communications Archive, Brigham Young University, Utah.

Works

(selective list; all film scores)

(as principal composer)
The Adventures of Marco Polo (dir. A. Mayo and J. Cromwell), 1938
The Lodger (dir. J. Brahm), 1944

The Bandit of Sherwood Forest (dir. H. Levin and G. Sherman), 1946
The Best Years of our Lives (dir. W. Wyler), 1946
The Bishop's Wife (dir. H. Koster), 1947
Enchantment (dir. I. Reis), 1948
Joan of Arc (dir. V. Fleming), 1948
Broken Arrow (dir. D. Daves), 1950
Edge of Doom (dir. M. Robson), 1950
Ace in the Hole (dir. B. Wilder), 1951
Above and Beyond (dir. M. Frank and N. Panama), 1952
Vera Cruz (dir. R. Aldrich), 1954
The Rains of Ranchipur (dir. J. Negulesco), 1955
Violent Saturday (dir. R. Fleischer), 1955
Between Heaven and Hell (dir. R. Fleischer), 1956
An Affair to Remember (dir. L. McCarey), 1957
Boy on a Dolphin (dir. J. Negulesco), 1957
The Sun also Rises (dir. H. King), 1957
The Barbarian and the Geisha (dir. J. Huston), 1958
The Young Lions (dir. E. Dmytryk), 1958
One-Eyed Jacks (dir. M. Brando), 1960
Geronimo (dir. A. Laven), 1962
The Secret Invasion (dir. R. Corman), 1964
Von Richtofen and Brown (dir. R. Corman), 1971
Private Parts (dir. P. Bartel), 1973

(as orchestrator)
Captain Blood (dir. M. Curtiz), 1935
The Charge of the Light Brigade (dir. M. Curtiz), 1936
The Adventures of Robin Hood (dir. M. Curtiz and W. Keighley), 1938
Jezebel (dir. W. Wyler), 1938
Dark Victory (dir. E. Goulding), 1939
Juarez (dir. W. Dieterle), 1939
The Private Lives of Elizabeth and Essex (dir. M. Curtiz), 1939
Santa Fe Trail (dir. M. Curtiz), 1940
The Sea Hawk (dir. M. Curtiz), 1940
The Great Lie (dir. E. Goulding), 1941
King's Row (dir. S. Wood), 1942
Now, Voyager (dir. I. Rapper), 1942
Casablanca (dir. M. Curtiz), 1943
Devotion (comp. E.W. Korngold, dir. C. Bernhardt), 1943 (film released 1946)
Mildred Pierce (comp. M. Steiner, dir. M. Curtiz), 1945

Bibliography

F.W. Sternfeld: "Music and Feature Films," *MQ*, xxxii (1947), 517–32
L. Morton: "Film Music Profile: Hugo Friedhofer," *Film Music Notes*, x/1 (1950), 4–5

I.K. Atkins: *Hugo Friedhofer* (Los Angeles, 1974) [incl. complete list of films]
M. Skiles: *Music Scoring for TV and Motion Pictures* (Blue Ridge Summit, PA, 1976)
T. Thomas: *Film Score: the View from the Podium* (South Brunswick, NJ, and New York, 1979)
W. Darby and J. Du Bois: *American Film Music: Major Composers, Techniques, Trends, 1915–1990* (Jefferson, NC, 1991) [incl. complete list of films as principal composer, and complete list of orchestrations for Korngold and Steiner]
G. Burt: *The Art of Film Music: Special Emphasis on Hugo Friedhofer, Alex North, David Raksin, Leonard Rosenman* (Boston, 1994)
K.S. Daubney: *The View from the Piano: the Film Scores of Max Steiner, 1939–1945* (diss., U. of Leeds, 1996)
J. Duchen: *Erich Wolfgang Korngold* (London, 1996)
L. Danley, ed.: *Hugo Friedhofer: the Best Years of his Life* (Lanham, MD, 1999)
G. Lees: *Friends along the Way: a Journey through Jazz* (New Haven, CT, 2003)

KATE DAUBNEY

Gershenson, Joseph

(*b* Chişinău [Kishinev], Russia, 12 Jan 1904; *d* Los Angeles, 18 Jan 1988). American music director, conductor, and violinist of Russian birth. He was raised on Army posts in New York by his bandleader father, who left Russia for Germany, and arrived in the United States in 1906. A half-size violin given by a family friend led to his playing in a school orchestra. He later studied privately with violinist and composer Edward Kilenyi Sr. (1884–1968). He abandoned night classes in law and accounting to play the violin for vaudeville. Through conducting at RKO theaters the Colony (1924–5) and the Coliseum (1926–8), he met RKO circuit music director Milton Schwarzwald, and served as his assistant from 1928 to 1933. From 1933 to 1939, he produced one- and two-reel musical shorts directed by Schwarzwald for their company, Mentone Productions, which were distributed by Columbia and RKO. When RKO theater executive Nate Blumberg was named president of Universal in 1938, the pair followed him to Hollywood. For Universal, Gershenson produced musical shorts, notably singing Westerns, then features, as executive producer, for which he temporarily adopted Joseph G. Sanford as his name. He left when the studio merged with International Pictures in 1946. Lacking work, he returned to Universal-International in 1949 as assistant to music department head Schwarzwald. Upon Schwarzwald's death in 1950, Gershenson was appointed general music director, supervising all scoring until his retirement in 1969. He oversaw the work of composers Henry Mancini, Hans Salter, Frank Skinner, and others. When MCA bought the studio in 1959, Gershenson signed a non-exclusive contract and formed his own company, Major Music Enterprises, to supply music for film and television.

Works

(*selective list*)

Film scores

(*as musical director/supervisor and/or conductor*)
Creature from the Black Lagoon (dir. J. Arnold), 1954
The Glenn Miller Story (dir. A. Mann), 1954
Magnificent Obsession (dir. D. Sirk), 1954
The Far Country (dir. Mann), 1955
Man Without a Star (dir. K. Vidor), 1955
The Benny Goodman Story (dir. V. Davies), 1956
The Incredible Shrinking Man (dir. Arnold), 1957
Slaughter on Tenth Avenue (dir. A. Laven), 1957
Written on the Wind (dir. Sirk), 1957
Touch of Evil (dir. O. Welles), 1958
Imitation of Life (dir. Sirk), 1959
Pillow Talk (dir. M. Gordon), 1959
Spartacus (dir. S. Kubrick), 1960
Freud (dir. J. Huston), 1962
Lonely Are the Brave (dir. D. Miller), 1962
Lover Come Back (dir. D. Mann), 1962
The War Lord (dir. F. Schaffner), 1965
Thoroughly Modern Millie (dir. G.R. Hill), 1967
Sweet Charity (dir. B. Fosse), 1969

Film scores

(*as producer of musical shorts*)
All At Sea, 1933
With Best Dishes, 1939

Bibliography

I. Atkins: *The Reminiscences of Joseph Gershenson* (American Film Institute oral history, 1976)
R. Musiker and N. Musiker: *Conductors and Composers of Popular Orchestral Music: a Biographical and Discographical Sourcebook* (Westport, CT, 1998)

WARREN M. SHERK

Giacchino, Michael

(*b* Riverside, NJ, 10 Oct 1967). American film, television, and video game composer. Giacchino initially began his formal studies in film production at New York's School of Visual Arts. Upon graduating in 1990, he worked for Universal Studios' publicity department and later with Disney, which encouraged his musical training at the Juilliard School and the University of California, Los Angeles. While working as an assistant producer at Disney Interactive, Giacchino began submitting compositions for the video games being produced by the Disney subdivision. His subsequent work in video games includes two successful franchises, *Medal of Honor* (1999, 2002, 2007) and *Call of Duty* (2003, 2004, 2008), as well as two *Jurassic Park* games (1997, 1999)—a title he would revisit in 2015 for *Jurassic World*. The score to DreamWorks' *The Lost World: Jurassic Park* (1997) was revolutionary in the video game industry for its use of live orchestral recordings instead of synthesizers, which had been the custom. His video game music eventually captured the attention of J.J. Abrams, who offered him work on "Alias" (2001–6) and later television series including "Lost" (2004–10)—a show for which Giacchino gained significant attention and accolades—and "Fringe" (2008–13). As with many of his video game projects, Giacchino's scores for Abrams were recorded with a live studio orchestra, which was also notable for the early 2000s television industry. This partnership led to Giacchino's involvement on later Abrams projects including *Super 8* (2011) and two blockbuster franchises: *Star Trek* (2009, 2013, 2016) and *Mission: Impossible* (2006, 2011). In addition to working with Abrams, Giacchino is a frequent collaborator with Disney and Pixar; beginning with *The Incredibles* (2004), he has written for *Ratatouille* (2007), *Up* (2009), *Cars 2* (2011), *Inside Out* (2015), Disney's *Zootopia* (2016), *Coco* (2017), and *Incredibles 2* (2018). Giacchino's work in film and television has received critical acclaim in the form of an Oscar and a Golden Globe Award for Best Original Score (both for *Up*), multiple Grammys, an Emmy for his work on the television series "Lost," and dozens of other awards and nominations.

Works

(*selective list*)

Film scores

Legal Deceit (dir. M. Harris), 1997
My Brother the Pig (dir. E. Fleming), 1999
The Trouble with Lou (dir. G. Joackim), 2001
Redemption of the Ghost (dir. R. Friedman), 2002
Sin (dir. M. Stevens), 2003
The Incredibles (dir. B. Bird), 2004
The Family Stone (dir. T. Bezucha), 2005
Looking for Comedy in the Muslim World (dir. A. Brooks), 2005
Sky High (dir. M. Mitchell), 2005
Mission: Impossible III (dir. J.J. Abrams), 2006
Ratatouille (dir. B. Bird and J. Pinkava), 2007
Speed Racer (dir. L. Wachowski and L. Wachowski), 2008
Earth Days (dir. R. Stone), 2009
Land of the Lost (dir. B. Silberling), 2009
Star Trek (dir. J.J. Abrams), 2009

Up (dir. P. Docter and B. Peterson), 2009
Let Me In (dir. M. Reeves), 2010
50/50 (dir. J. Levine), 2011
Cars 2 (dir. J. Lasseter and B. Lewis), 2011
Mission: Impossible—Ghost Protocol (dir. B. Bird), 2011
Super 8 (dir. J.J. Abrams), 2011
John Carter (dir. A. Stanton), 2012
Star Trek: Into Darkness (dir. J.J. Abrams), 2013
Dawn of the Planet of the Apes (dir. M. Reeves), 2014
This is Where I Leave You (dir. S. Levy), 2014
Inside Out (dir. P. Docter and R. Del Carmen), 2015
Jupiter Ascending (dir. L. Wachowski and L. Wachowski), 2015
Jurassic World (dir. C. Trevorrow), 2015
Tomorrowland (dir. B. Bird), 2015
Dr. Strange (dir. S. Derrickson), 2016
Rogue One: A Star Wars Story (dir. G. Edwards), 2016
Star Trek Beyond (dir. J. Lin), 2016
Zootopia (dir. B. Howard, R. Moore, and J. Bush), 2016
The Book of Henry (dir. C. Trevorrow), 2017
Coco (dirs. L. Unkrich, A. Molina), 2017
Spider-Man: Homecoming (dir. J. Watts), 2017
War for the Planet of the Apes (dir. M. Reeves), 2017
Bad Times at the El Kingdome (dir. J.A. Bayona), 2018

Short films

No Salida, 1998
Los gringos, 1999
String of the Kite, 2003
The Karate Guard, 2005
One Man Band, 2005
Vowellet: An Essay by Sarah Vowell, 2005
Lifted, 2006
Checkmate, 2009
Doug's Special Mission, 2009
George & A.J., 2009
Glock, 2009
Partly Cloudy, 2009
Day & Night, 2010
Finding Louis, 2010
The Ballad of Nessie, 2011
La Luna, 2011
Dress, 2013
Riley's First Date?, 2015

Television music

Semper Fi, 2001
Alias, 2001–6

Phenomenon II, 2003
Lost, 2004–10
The Muppets' Wizard of Oz, 2005
What About Brian, 2006 (4 episodes)
Six Degrees 2006–7
Fringe, 2008–13
Alcatraz, 2012

Video-game music

Gargoyles, 1995
Maui Mallard in Cold Shadow, 1995
The Lost World: Jurassic Park, 1997
Small Soldiers, 1998
Small Soldiers: Squad Commander, 1998
Medal of Honor, 1999
T'ai Fu: Wrath of the Tiger, 1999
Warpath: Jurassic Park, 1999
Muppet Monster Adventure, 2000
Medal of Honor: Allied Assault, 2002
Medal of Honor: Frontline, 2002
Call of Duty, 2003
Secret Weapons Over Normandy, 2003
Alias, 2004
Call of Duty: Finest Hour, 2004
Call of Duty: United Offensive, 2004
The Incredibles, 2004
Black, 2006 (collab. C. Tilton)
Medal of Honor: Airborn, 2007
Fracture, 2008
Turning Point: Fall of Liberty, 2008
Star Trek: D-A-C, 2009
Up, 2009
LEGO: The Incredibles, 2018

Bibliography

J. Krogh: "Behind the Scenes of ABC's Alias," *Keyboard*, xxviii/7 (2002), 32–44

E. Philbrook: "Michael Giacchino – Man on a Mission," *ASCAP* (1 Oct 2005) <http://www.ascap.com/playback/2005/fall/features/giacchino.aspx>

K. Lindvig: "Ideology and Zeitgeist in the Music of Lost," *Studia musicological norvegica*, xxxii (2006), 105–25

A. Ross: "The Spooky Fill," *New Yorker*, lxxxvi/13 (2010): 60–67

J. Burlingame: "Oscar-Winning Composer Michael Giacchino Has Three Movies Opening This Summer," *Variety* cccxxvii/3 (2015), 71

PETER GRAFF

Glass, Philip

(*b* Baltimore, MD, 31 Jan 1937). American composer. Philip Glass is considered one of the founding figures of minimalist music. After studying at the University of Chicago (1952–6) and the Juilliard School (1957–62) he received a Fulbright scholarship that supported him to develop his craft with Nadia Boulanger in Paris (1964–6). During this period, he served as Ravi Shankar's music assistant for the film *Chappaqua*, which depicts the life of its director and protagonist, Conrad Rooks, and his struggles with drug addiction. On returning to the United States, Glass collaborated with the Chicago-based Kartemquin Film company on *Inquiring Nuns* and *Marco* (see Eaton, 2013). This period of soundtrack production was short-lived, however, as he later concentrated on concert music and opera, producing such key works as *Music in Twelve Parts* (1971–4) and *Einstein on the Beach* (1975–6).

He subsequently increased his output in film music commencing with *North Star* in 1977. Documenting the life and works of sculptor Mark di Suvero, Glass wrote for electronic instruments and vocals, commenting that "it wasn't really a film score but it was a wonderful compilation of image and music" (Russell and Young, 2000, 121). Later documentary soundtracks included the Errol Morris collaborations *The Thin Blue Line*, *A Brief History of Time*, *The Fog of War*, and *They Were There*, and Martin Scorsese's *Kundun*, based on the life of the Dalai Lama. Basil Gelpke and Ray McCormak's documentary on the international oil crisis, *A Crude Awakening*, combines interviews, archival footage, and time-lapse sequences. Similarly, the soundtrack is a potpourri of quotations from Glass's pre-existing concert works—e.g. *Mad Rush* (1979), *Glassworks* (1981), and String Quartet No. 2 (1984)—and earlier film soundtracks (*Mindwalk* and *A Brief History of Time*).

Often associated with sinister subject matters and conflict, or evocative of apocalyptic themes, his filmography is mostly absent of comedy. He began composing for horror films in the early 1990s, initially with a score for Bernard Rose's *Candyman*, and following its sequel he continued writing for psycho-thrillers including *Secret Window* and *Taking Lives*. He reworked Tod Browning's cult horror film *Dracula* (1931) with music performed by keyboards and string quartet against the backdrop of the film. Glass, alongside the Kronos Quartet and the musical director of the Philip Glass Ensemble, Michael Riesman, toured internationally with performances of *Dracula* in sellout concerts. On similar lines, he collaborated with Godfrey Reggio on the *Qatsi* trilogy, comprising *Koyaanisqatsi*, *Powaqqatsi*, and *Naqoyqatsi*, in which the music (performed by the Philip Glass Ensemble) is pitted against powerful visual montages. With the exception of sung prophetic sayings from the Hopi language, these films eschew any spoken dialogue, thereby reinforcing the symbiotic relationship between music and image.

His musical style is characterized by uses of chromaticism, major/minor tonal changes, and additive/reductive patterns, which are often regarded as elements well suited to films that depict complex personalities or solemn events. His idiosyncratic approach to tonality and his repetitive patterns often amplify a film's emotional content. Audience reviews of the music in *The Thin Blue Line* (based on the wrongful imprisonment of Randall Adams in Dallas for the murder of a police officer in 1976) are interspersed with such adjectives as "bleak," "moody," and "menacing" (see Evans, 2015). In Peter Weir's satirical *The Truman Show,* Glass introduced new listeners to his musical style via a Hollywood blockbuster while concurrently recycling some of his pre-existing film music including *Mishima, Powaqqatsi,* and *Anima Mundi.* Later, he composed for the adaptation of Michael Cunningham's novel *The Hours* (with excerpts from the opera *Satyagraha*; see McClary, 2007; Evans, 2015).

Despite once claiming to be "not interested in films," and claiming that he does not "particularly like the medium" or "know anything about it" (Morgan, 2000, 142), Glass's prolific scoring for cinema has brought recognition (and numerous awards) by audiences, critics, and film practitioners alike. The soundtrack to *The Truman Show* led to a Golden Globe award; *Kundun, Notes on a Scandal,* and *The Hours* received Oscar nominations for Best Music, while the latter received a BAFTA and a Classical Brit Award.

Works

(*selective list*)

Film scores

Chappaqua (dir. C. Rooks), 1966, collab. R. Shankar
Inquiring Nuns (dirs. G. Quinn and G. Temaner), 1968
Marco (dirs. Quinn and Temaner), 1970
North Star (dirs. F. de Menil and B. Rose), 1977
Koyaanisqatsi: Life out of Balance (dir. G. Reggio), 1982
Mishima: A Life in Four Chapters (dir. P. Schrader), 1984
Hamburger Hill (dir. J. Irvin), 1987
Powaqqatsi: Life in Transformation (dir. Reggio), 1987
The Thin Blue Line (dir. E. Morris), 1988
Mindwalk (dir. B.A. Capra), 1990
A Brief History of Time (dir. Morris), 1991
Merci la Vie (dir. B. Blier), 1991
Anima mundi (dir. Reggio), 1992
Candyman (dir. Rose), 1992
Compassion in Exile (dir. M. Lemle), 1992
Candyman II: Farewell to the Flesh (dir. B. Condon), 1995
Jenipapo (dir. M. Gardenberg), 1995
The Secret Agent (dir. C. Hampton), 1995
Bent (dir. S. Mathias), 1997
Kundun (dir. M. Scorsese), 1997
The Truman Show (dir. P. Weir), 1998
Dracula (dir. T. Browning), 1999

Short Films (dirs. M. Rovner, S. Neshat, P. Greenaway, and A. Egoyan), 2001
The Baroness and the Pig (dir. M. Mackenzie), 2002
The Hours (dir. S. Daldry), 2002
Naqoyqatsi: Life as War (dir. Reggio), 2002
The Fog of War (dir. Morris), 2003
Going Upriver: The Long War of John Kerry (dir. G. Butler), 2004
Secret Window (dir. D. Koepp), 2004
Taking Lives (dir. D.J. Caruso), 2004
Undertow (dir. D.G. Green), 2004
Neverwas (dir. J.M. Stern), 2005
A Crude Awakening: The Oil Crash (dirs. B. Gelpke and R. McCormack), 2006
The Illusionist (dir. N. Burger), 2006
Notes on a Scandal (dir. R. Eyre), 2006
Roving Mars (dir. Butler), 2006
Taiji: Chaotic Harmony (dir. S. Ch. Hon), 2006
Les Animaux Amoureux (dir. L. Charbonnier), 2007
Cassandra's Dream (dir. W. Allen), 2007
No Reservations (dir. S. Hicks), 2007
Les Regrets (dir. C. Kahn), 2009
Transcendent Man (dir. B. Ptolemy), 2009
Mr. Nice (dir. Rose), 2010
Nosso Lar (dir. W. de Assis), 2010
O Apostolo (dir. D. Simon), 2010
When the Dragon Swallowed the Sun (dir. Simon), 2010
Rebirth (dir. J. Whitaker), 2011
They Were There (dir. Morris), 2011
Visitors (dir. Reggio), 2013
Fantastic Four (dir. J. Trank), 2015, collab. M. Beltrami

Writings

ed. R.T. Jones: *Music by Philip Glass* (New York, 1987)
Opera on the Beach (London, 1988)
Words Without Music: a Memoir (New York, 2015)

Bibliography

W. Duckworth: *Talking Music: Conversations with John Cage, Philip Glass, Laurie Anderson, and Five Generations of American Experimental Composers* (New York, 1995)
C.M. Berg: "Philip Glass on Composing for Film and Other Forms: the Case of *Koyaanisqatsi* (1990)," *Writings on Glass*, ed. R. Kostelanetz (New York, 1997), 131–51
E. Grimes: "Interview: Education (1989)," *Writings on Glass*, ed. R. Kostelanetz (New York, 1997), 12–36
D. Morgan: *Knowing the Score: Film Composers Talk about the Art, Craft, Blood, Sweat, and Tears of Writing for Cinema* (New York, 2000)
K. Potter: *Four Musical Minimalists* (Cambridge, 2000)
M. Russell and J. Young: *Film Music Screencraft* (Boston, 2000)

J. Joe: "The Cinematic Body in the Operatic Theater: Philip Glass's *La Belle et la Bête*," *Between Opera and Cinema*, ed. J. Joe and R. Theresa (New York, 2002), 59–73
R. Leydon: "Toward a Typology of Minimalist Tropes," *Music Theory Online*, viii/4 (2002), http://www.mtosmt.org/issues/mto.02.8.4/mto.02.8.4.leydon.html
R. Maycock: *Glass: A Portrait* (London, 2002)
D. Schweiger: "Man of *The Hours*," *Film Score Monthly*, vii/10 (2002), 14–17, 48
M. Savlov: "The Ambience of Existential Dread: Philip Glass on the *Fog of War* Score," *The Austin Chronicle* (20 Feb 2004)
R. Fink: *Repeating Ourselves: American Minimal Music as Cultural Practice* (Berkeley, 2005)
C. DesJardins: *Inside Film Music: Composers Speak* (Los Angeles, 2006)
D. Goldwasser: "Interview: Philip Glass; Notes on a Scandal," *Soundtrack.Net* (11 Dec 2006), http://www.soundtrack.net/features/article/?id=216
M. LeBlanc: "Melancholic Arrangements: Music, Queer Melodrama, and the Seeds of Transformation in *The Hours*," *Camera Obscura*, xxi/1 (2006), 105–45
S. McClary: "Minima Romantica,"*Beyond the Soundtrack: Representing Music in Cinema*, ed. D. Goldmark, L. Kramer, and R. Leppert (Berkeley, 2007), 48–65
D. Jiang: "Composer Philip Glass Discusses Music for the Big Screen," *The Dartmouth* (20 Jan 2009), http://thedartmouth.com/2009/01/20/composer-philip-glass-discusses-music-for-the-big-screen
B. Lessard: "Cultural Recycling, Performance, and Immediacy in Philip Glass's Film Music for Godfrey Reggio's *Qatsi* Trilogy," *Sound and Music in Film and Visual Media*, ed. G. Harper, R. Doughty, and J. Eisentraut (New York, 2009), 493–504
P. ap Siôn and T. Evans: "Parallel Symmetries? Exploring Relationships between Minimalist Music and Multimedia Forms," *Sound and Music in Film and Visual Media*, ed. G. Harper, R. Doughty, and J. Eisentraut (New York, 2009), 671–91
J. Deaville: "The Beauty of Horror: Kilar, Coppola, and Dracula," *Music in the Horror Film: Listening to Fear*, ed. N. Lerner (New York, 2010), 187–205
J. Richardson: *An Eye for Music* (Oxford, 2012)
R.M.D. Eaton: "Minimalist and Postminimalist Music in Multimedia: from the Avant-Garde to the Blockbuster Film," *The Ashgate Research Companion to Minimalist and Postminimalist Music*, ed. K. Potter, K. Gann, and P. ap Siôn (Farnham, 2013)
R.M.D. Eaton: "Marking Minimalism: Minimal Music as a Sign of Machines and Mathematics in Multimedia," *Music and the Moving Image*, vii/1 (2014), 3–23
T. Evans: *Shared Meanings in the Film Music of Philip Glass: Music, Multimedia and Postminimalism* (London and New York, 2015)

TRISTIAN EVANS

Gold, Ernest

(*b* Vienna, Austria, 13 July 1921; *d* Santa Monica, CA, 17 March 1999). American composer of Austrian birth. He studied piano with his grandfather and violin with his father, later enrolling in the Vienna Music Academy. He emigrated with his family to the United States in 1938, where he studied harmony and orchestration with Otto Cesana and conducting with Leon Barzin at the National Orchestra

Association, New York. Earning a living as an accompanist and song writer, his early hit "Practice Makes Perfect" (1940) was followed by "Accidentally on Purpose" and "They Started Something." After settling in Hollywood in 1945 to work as an arranger, conductor, and composer in the film industry, he studied with George Antheil (1946–8) and conducted the Santa Barbara Civic Opera (1958–60). In 1964 he founded the Senior Citizens Orchestra, Los Angeles. He was the first film composer to have his name engraved on Hollywood's "Walk of Fame."

Works

(selective list)

Film scores

The Girl of the Limberlost (dir. M. Ferrer), 1945
The Falcon's Alibi (dir. R. McCarey), 1946
G.I. War Brides (dir. G. Blair), 1946
Smooth as Silk (dir. C. Barton), 1946
Exposed (dir. G. Blair), 1947
Jennifer (dir. J. Newton), 1953
The Defiant Ones (dir. S. Kramer), 1958
On the Beach (dir. S. Kramer), 1959
The Young Philadelphians (dir. V. Sherman), 1959
Exodus (dir. O. Preminger), 1960
Inherit the Wind (dir. S. Kramer), 1960
A Fever in the Blood (dir. V. Sherman), 1961
Judgement at Nuremberg (dir. S. Kramer), 1961
The Last Sunset (dir. R. Aldrich), 1961
A Child is Waiting (dir. J. Cassavetes), 1962
Pressure Point (dir. H. Cornfield and S. Kramer), 1962
It's a Mad, Mad, Mad, Mad World (dir. S. Kramer), 1963
Ship of Fools (dir. S. Kramer), 1965
The Secret of Santa Vittoria (dir. S. Kramer), 1969
The Wild McCullochs (dir. M. Baer Jr.), 1975
Cross of Iron (dir. S. Peckinpah), 1977

Stage

Song of the Bells (pageant), 1956
Too Warm for Furs (musl, E. Penney), *c*1956
Maria (pageant), 1957
I'm Solomon (musl, A. Croswell), New York, 1968

Orchestral

Pan American Sym., 1941
Pf Conc., 1943
Ballad, 1944
Sym. Preludes, 1944

Allegorical Ov., 1947
Sym. no.2, 1947
Audubon Ov., *c*1949
Band in Hand (B. Smith), nar, vv, band, 1966
Boston Pops March, 1966
other band works

Chamber and solo instrumental

Str Qt, *c*1948
Trio, vn, bn, pf, *c*1950, rev. as Sym., bn, pf, str, *c*1952
Sonatina, fl, pf, *c*1952
Pf Sonata, 1954
3 Miniatures, pf, 1968
15 other pf works
Many songs and choral works, incl. Songs of Love and Parting, *c*1963

Principal publishers: Chappell, Crystal, Marks, Piedmont, Simrock, Society for the Publication of American Music

Bibliography

F. Stadler and P. Weibel: *The Cultural Exodus from Austria* (Vienna and New York, 1995)
T. Thomas: *Film Score* (Munich, 1995)

THOMAS L. GAYDA

Goldenthal, Elliot

(*b* Brooklyn, NY, 2 May 1954). American composer. He learned piano as a child and in his teens also played trumpet and sang in a touring blues band. In the 1970s he studied at the Manhattan School with John Corigliano and later informally with Aaron Copland. His first important works were for classical chamber ensembles. The largest and best known of his concert works is *Vietnam Oratorio*, first performed in April 1995 to mark the twentieth anniversary of the end of the Vietnam War. Its texts are in Vietnamese, Latin, and English and include poems by Yusef Komunyakaa. Its style is decidedly modern, and the eclectic vocal and instrumental writing includes a prominent solo cello part written for Yo-Yo Ma.

Since the late 1980s Goldenthal has also composed stage and film scores. Of particular interest are his collaborations with the theater director Julie Taymor, his longtime personal companion; these include popular productions of plays by Gozzi for the American Repertory Theater in Cambridge, Massachusetts, and a critically acclaimed revival of the oratorio-like *Juan Darien* (Lincoln Center, 1996). The film scores, technically polished and subtle, embrace a remarkable range of past and present idioms, including Wagnerian passage-work, atonality, minimalism, dynamic counterpoint, synthesized timbres, and modal choral writing. They include several Hollywood blockbusters in the science fiction, action, and horror genres (*Alien*^{3}, two Batman sequels, *Demolition Man, Heat,* and *Sphere*), whose scores often outshine the films they have been written for. In working with the idiosyncratic Neil Jordan, Goldenthal found an independent director with a creativity and originality to match his own. Their association began with *Interview with the Vampire* (1994) and continued through scores for *Michael Collins* (1996) and *The Butcher Boy* (1997) which are as diverse, unsettling, and fascinating as the films themselves.

Works

(selective list)

Stage

The Transposed Heads (musl, after T. Mann), New York, 1987
Juan Darien, a Carnival Mass (after L. Quiroga and Requiem Mass), New York, 1988, rev. 1996
A Midsummer Night's Dream (incid music), 1994
The Taming of the Shrew (incid music), 1994
The Tempest (incid music), 1994
Titus Andronicus (incid music), 1994
The Green Bird (incid music), 1996
The King's Stag (incid music), 1996
The Serpent Women (incid music), 1996
Othello (ballet, 1997)
Recordare (incid music), 2005
Grendel (op, Beowulf and J. Gardner), 2006
Liberty's Taken (musl), 2007
Grounded (incid music), 2015
M. Butterfly (2017)

Film scores

Drugstore Cowboy (G. Van Sant), 1989
Pet Sematary (M. Lambert), 1989
Grand Isle (TV movie, Lambert), 1991
Alien^3 (D. Fincher), 1992
Fool's Fire (TV movie, J. Taymor), 1992
Demolition Man (M. Brambilla, 1993)
Cobb (R. Shelton), 1994
Golden Gate (J. Madden), 1994
Interview with the Vampire (N. Jordan), 1994
Roswell (TV movie, J. Kagan), 1994
Batman Forever (J. Schumacher), 1995
Heat (M. Mann), 1995

Michael Collins (Jordan), 1996
A Time to Kill (Schumacher), 1996
Batman & Robin (Schumacher), 1997
The Butcher Boy (Jordan), 1997
Sphere (B. Levinson), 1998
In Dreams (Jordan), 1999
Titus (Taymor), 1999
Final Fantasy: the Spirits Within (Hironobu Sakaguchi), 2001
Frida (Taymor), 2002
The Good Thief (Jordan), 2002
S.W.A.T. (C. Johnson), 2003
Across the Universe (Taymor), 2007
Public Enemies (Mann), 2009
The Tempest (Taymor), 2010
A Midsummer Night's Dream (Taymor), 2014
Our Souls at Night (2017)

Instrumental

Sonata for Str Bass, 1977
Brass Qt no.1, 1980
Brass Qt no.2 (1983)
Pastime Variations, chbr orch (1988)
Shadow Play Scherzo (1988)
Conc., tpt, pf (?1996)
Adagietto Doloroso, str qt (2013)
Othello Symphony (2013)
Str Qt no. 1 "The Stone Cutters" (2013)
Symph, g♯ (2014)
Lyric Suite, str qt, pf, str orch (2015)
For Trumpet and Strings (2017)

Vocal

Los Heraldos Negros (C. Vallejo), song cycle, 1977
Jabberwocky (L. Carroll), B-Bar, 4 ww (1981)
Fire Water Paper: a Vietnam Orat, S, Bar, solo vc, children's vv, vv (1995)

Principal publisher: Warner Bros.

Bibliography

R. Brown: "Film Musings," *Fanfare*, xviii (1994–5), no.4, pp. 403–4; no.5, pp. 372–3
D. Adams: "Elliot Goldenthal: Interview with the Composer," *Film Score Monthly*, no.61 (1995), 12–15
D. Adams: "Obligatory Batman Dept.: Elliot Goldenthal," *Film Score Monthly*, ii/5 (1997), 13–15 [interview]
R. Hershon: "Film Composers in the Sonic Wars," *Cinéaste*, xxii/4 (1997), 10–13

R. Davis: *Complete Guide to Film Scoring* (Boston, 1999, 2/2010), 299–304
D. Morgan: *Knowing the Score* (New York, 2000), 195–201, 267–76
R. Lee: "The Goldenthal Touch," *Opera News*, lxx/11 (2006), 8
S. Murphy: "The Tritone Within: Interpreting Harmony in Elliot Goldenthal's Score for *Final Fantasy: The Spirits Within*," *The Music of Fantasy Cinema*, ed. J. Halfyard (London, 2012), 148–74

MARTIN MARKS/R

Goldsmith, Jerry [Jerrald]

(*b* Los Angeles, 10 Feb 1929; *d* Beverly Hills, CA, 21 July 2004). American composer and conductor. In the 1940s he studied the piano with Jakob Gimpel and theory and composition with Castelnuovo-Tedesco; he also attended Los Angeles City College, as well as Rózsa's classes at the University of Southern California. In the 1950s he worked primarily for CBS, composing and conducting music first for radio, then for television. His television credits include numerous scores for such live dramatic programs as "Climax!" and "Playhouse 90," as well as for episodes of long-running series such as "Gunsmoke" and "The Twilight Zone." Although he continued to write for television with some frequency during the 1960s and 70s, after 1962 he mostly scored feature films. Over four decades he completed scores for more than 160 films and collaborated repeatedly with directors including Schaffner, Ridley Scott, Dante, Verhoeven and Schepisi. He worked closely with two outstanding orchestrators, Arthur Morton and Alexander Courage.

Goldsmith's dramatic imagination was fertile and eclectic: *A Patch of Blue* (1965) is scored in chamber-music fashion, with a prominent solo harmonica and a touching waltz theme for the piano; *Planet of the Apes* (1968) is scored for a large orchestra augmented by unusual instruments (including ram's horn and mixing bowls) and features serial techniques; in addition to an ensemble that includes four pianos and four harps, *Chinatown* (1974) uses solo trumpet and strings, its main theme being a moody, nostalgic jazz tune. Goldsmith always displayed a strong commitment to modernist and avant-garde styles, particularly for horror, fantasy, or science fiction films, genres for which he became well known. He used aleatory techniques (*Mephisto Waltz*, 1971), and borrowed stylistically from such leading composers as Stravinsky and Orff (*The Omen*, 1976), Bartók (*Freud*, 1962, and *Coma*, 1978), and Berg at his most expressionistic (*Poltergeist*, 1982). While avoiding purely electronic scores, Goldsmith often blended synthesized timbres into symphonic or chamber textures (Darter). Several scores contain more traditional melodies, richly harmonized and developed, notably those for *Star Trek: the Motion Picture* (1979) and its sequels and *First Knight* (1995). His stylistic range also covers a wide variety of pop and jazz styles such as disco (*Gremlins*, 1984) and big-band jazz (*L.A. Confidential*, 1997). Adulated by soundtrack collectors, recordings of Goldsmith's scores are abundant and highly prized. During the 1990s he produced and conducted new recordings of major film scores by Alex North, including the latter's rejected score for *2001*. In the early 2000s Goldsmith continued to work on new projects, even as his health declined. His last assignment, *Looney Tunes: Back in Action* (2003), reunited him with director Joe Dante and afforded another opportunity to display the extraordinary stylistic versatility he had developed over his career.

Works

(*selective list*)

Film scores

Studs Lonigan (dir. I. Lerner), 1960
Freud (dir. J. Huston), 1962
Lonely Are the Brave (dir. D. Miller), 1962
Lilies of the Field (dir. R. Nelson), 1963
Seven Days in May (dir. J. Frankenheimer), 1963
Rio Conchos (dir. G. Douglas), 1964
The Satan Bug (dir. J. Sturges), 1964
A Patch of Blue (dir. G. Green), 1965
Von Ryan's Express (dir. M. Robson), 1965
The Blue Max (dir. J. Guillermin), 1966
The Sand Pebbles (dir. R. Wise), 1966
In Like Flint (dir. Douglas), 1967
Sebastian (dir. D. Greene), 1967
The Detective (dir. Douglas), 1968
Planet of the Apes (dir. F. Schaffner), 1968
Justine (dir. G. Cukor), 1969
The Ballad of Cable Hogue (dir. S. Peckinpah), 1970
Patton (dir. Schaffner), 1970
The Mephisto Waltz (dir. P. Wendkos), 1971
The Wild Rovers (dir. B. Edwards), 1971
The Other (dir. R. Mulligan), 1972
Papillon (dir. Schaffner), 1973
Chinatown (dir. R. Polanski), 1974
The Wind and the Lion (dir. J. Milius), 1975
Logan's Run (dir. M. Anderson), 1976
The Omen (dir. R. Donner), 1976
Islands in the Stream (dir. Schaffner), 1977
Twilight's Last Gleaming (dir. R. Aldrich), 1977
Capricorn One (dir. P. Hyams), 1978
Coma (dir. M. Crichton), 1978
Alien (dir. R. Scott), 1979
The Great Train Robbery (dir. Crichton), 1979
Star Trek, the Motion Picture (dir. Wise), 1979

Outland (dir. Hyams), 1981
First Blood (dir. T. Kotcheff), 1982
Poltergeist (dir. T. Hooper), 1982
Psycho II (dir. R. Franklin), 1983
Twilight Zone: the Movie (dir. J. Landis and others), 1983
Under Fire (dir. R. Spottiswoode), 1983
Gremlins (dir. J. Dante), 1984
Legend (dir. Scott), 1985, European version
Rambo: First Blood Part II (dir. G.P. Cosmatos), 1985
Hoosiers (dir. D. Anspaugh), 1986
Innerspace (dir. Dante), 1987
Lionheart (dir. Schaffner), 1987
Star Trek V: the Final Frontier (dir. W. Shatner), 1989
Gremlins 2: the New Batch (dir. Dante), 1990
The Russia House (dir. F. Schepisi), 1990
Total Recall (dir. P. Verhoeven), 1990
Love Field (dir. J. Kaplan), 1991
Basic Instinct (dir. Verhoeven), 1992
Medicine Man (dir. J. McTiernan), 1992
Rudy (dir. Anspaugh), 1993
Angie (dir. M. Coolidge), 1994
I.Q. (dir. Schepisi), 1994
City Hall (dir. H. Becker), 1995
First Knight (dir. J. Zucker), 1995
The Ghost and the Darkness (dir. S. Hopkins), 1996
Star Trek: First Contact (dir. J. Frakes), 1996
The Edge (dir. L. Tamahori), 1997
L.A. Confidential (dir. C. Hanson), 1997
Mulan (dir. B. Cook, T. Bancroft), 1998
Star Trek: Insurrection (dir. Frakes), 1998
The Haunting (dir. J. De Bont), 1999
The Mummy (dir. S. Sommers), 1999
Hollow Man (dir. P. Verhoeven), 2000
Star Trek: Nemesis (dir. S. Baird), 2002
The Sum of All Fears (dir. P. Robinson), 2002
Looney Tunes: Back in Action (dir. J. Dante), 2003

Television music

Series themes and episodes

(dates are for complete series)
Studio One, 1948–8
Hallmark Hall of Fame, 1951–8
General Electric Theater, 1953–62
Climax!, 1954–8
Gunsmoke, 1955–75

Playhouse 90, 1956–60
Wagon Train, 1957–65
Have Gun Will Travel, 1957–66
The Twilight Zone, 1959–64
Thriller, 1960–62
Dr. Kildare, 1961–6 [theme]
The Man from U.N.C.L.E., 1964–8 [theme]
The Waltons, 1972–81 [theme]
Barnaby Jones, 1973–80 [theme]
Star Trek: Voyager, 1995–2001 [theme]

Mini-series and television films

The Red Pony, 1973
QB VII, 1974
A Tree Grows in Brooklyn, 1974
Babe, 1975
Contract on Cherry Street, 1977
Masada, 1981

Other works

Christus Apollo (R. Bradbury), cant., nar, C, chorus, orch, 1969
Othello, ballet, 1971
Music for Orch, 1972

Bibliography

E. Bernstein: "A Conversation with Jerry Goldsmith," *Film Music Notebook* (Los Angeles), iii/2 (1977), 18–31

T. Thomas: "Jerry Goldsmith," *Film Score: the View from the Podium* (South Brunswick, NJ, and New York, 1979, 2/1991 as *Film Score: the Art and Craft of Movie Music*), 285–97

J. McBride, ed.: "The Composer: Jerry Goldsmith," *Filmmakers on Filmmaking: the American Film Institute Seminars on Motion Pictures and Television* (Los Angeles, 1983), 133–46

T. Darter: "Jerry Goldsmith," *Keyboard*, xi (1985), no.2, pp.19–20, 22–6; no.4, pp.44ff

R. Bohn and others: "A Filmography/Discography of Jerry Goldsmith: Updated," *Soundtrack!*, xii/47 (1993), 22–42

S.M. Fry: "Jerry Goldsmith: a Selective Annotated Bibliography," *The Cue Sheet*, x/3–4 (1993–4), 28–39

"A Tribute to Jerry Goldsmith," *Soundtrack!*, xviii/69 (1999), 22–51

D. Morgan: *Knowing the score* (New York, 2000)

Obituary, *New York Times* (23 July 2004)

M. Heintzelman: "The Dante/Goldsmith Project: Nine Films, Nine Scores, One Sensibility," *Film Score Monthly*, x/6 (Nov–Dec 2005)

C.J. Miller: "Seeing Beyond His Own Time: the Sounds of Jerry Goldsmith," *Sounds of the Future: Essays on Music in Science Fiction Film*, ed. M.J. Bartkowiak (Jefferson, NC, 2010), 210–22
J. Halfyard: "Scoring Fantasy Girls: Music and Female Agency in *Indiana Jones* and *The Mummy* films," *The Music of Fantasy Cinema*, ed. J. Halfyard (London, 2012), 175–92
L. Barron: "Fantasy Meets Electronica: *Legend* and the Music of Tangerine Dream," *The Music of Fantasy Cinema*, ed. J. Halfyard (London, 2012), 79–94
G. Biancorosso: "Memory and Leitmotif in Cinema," *Representation in Western Music*, ed. J. Walden (Cambridge, 2013), 203–23
J. Fitzgerald and P. Hayward: "The Sound of an Upside-Down World: Jerry Goldsmith's Landmark Score for *Planet of the Apes* (1968)," *Music and the Moving Image* vi/ 2 (Summer, 2013), 32–43
M. Dupuis and C. Martini: *Jerry Goldsmith: Music Scoring for American Movies* (Middletown, DE, 2014)

MARTIN MARKS/R

Gottschalk, Louis F.

(*b* St. Louis, MO, 7 Oct 1869; *d* Los Angeles, 15 July 1934). American composer and conductor. Shortly after Gottschalk's birth, his father was elected governor of Missouri. After graduating from high school in St. Louis in 1885, he studied composition with Heinrich Urban and conducting with Gustav Kogel in Berlin. In 1891, based in Los Angeles, he wrote a comic opera, *Yorktown*. By 1896 he was musical director at the Los Angeles Theater, conducting *The Pirates of Penzance* and other comic operas. A recital of his music compositions took place in Los Angeles in 1897. Between 1899 and 1912 in New York he was music director for more than a dozen Broadway musical comedies, revues, and operettas, many by Victor Herbert. He was the music director for the American première of Franz Lehar's *The Merry Widow* in 1907. By 1913 he was back in Los Angeles for the première of *The Tik-Tok Man of Oz*, the first of his Oz-themed comic operas. The following year he became vice president and chief composer for the Oz Film Manufacturing Co., formed by L. Frank Baum, creator of the Oz books. Gottschalk composed incidental music for several films, including *The Patchwork Girl of Oz*. In 1916 producer Thomas H. Ince tapped him to prepare music for two productions. He spent one season in New York to conduct the musical revue, *The Century Girl*. Returning to Los Angeles in 1917 he was musical director for Julian Eltinge and at the Burbank Theater. Beginning in 1918 he supplied Paramount and *Moving Picture World* with music suggestions. Between 1918 and 1921 he worked on four films directed by D.W. Griffith and between 1921 and 1923 one with Douglas Fairbanks and two with Mary Pickford. He was music director at the Los Angeles Forum in 1927. With the advent of sound films, he served as a consultant in the scoring and syncing of music. Due to failing health he retired around 1931.

Works

(*selective list*)

Film scores

The Patchwork Girl of Oz (dir. J.F. MacDonald), 1914
Honor's Altar (dir. W. Edwards), 1916 (composed and selected music)
The Curse of Eve (dir. F. Beal), 1917 (original score)
Broken Blossoms (dir. D.W. Griffith), 1919 (composed, arranged, and adapted music)
The Fall of Babylon (dir. D.W. Griffith), 1919 (incidental music for New York presentation)
Little Lord Fauntleroy (dir. A.E. Green and J. Pickford), 1921 (arranged music for New York presentation)
Orphans of the Storm (dir. D.W. Griffith), 1921 (composed and arranged music with W. Peters)
The Three Musketeers (dir. F. Niblo), 1921 (compiled score)
The Girl I Loved (dir. J. De Grasse), 1923 (synchronized music for Los Angeles presentation)
Rosita (dir. E. Lubitsch and R. Walsh), 1923 (music score)
The Rainbow Man (dir. F.C. Newmeyer), 1929 (music supervisor, Los Angeles)
The Birth of a Nation (dir. D.W. Griffith), 1930, synchronized version of abridged 1915 film (adapted J.C. Breil's score)

Stage

(*as composer*)
Yorktown (F. Gaylord, libretto), 1891
The Liberty Belles (additional music), 1901–2
The Tik Tok Man of Oz (L. Baum), 1913

(*as music director; names of composers are given in parentheses, all New York productions*)
The Ameer (V. Herbert), 1899–1900
The Gingerbread Man (A. Sloane), 1905–6
Dream City (V. Herbert), 1906–7
The Merry Widow (F. Lehar), 1907–8
Old Dutch (V. Herbert), 1909–10
Gypsy Love (F. Lehar), 1911
The Century Girl (V. Herbert, I. Berlin), 1916–7

Writings

"The Importance of a Musical Synopsis," *Paramount Artcraft Progress-Advance*, iv/22 (25 April 1918), 434

Bibliography

"Our Home-Grown Music Composer," *Los Angeles Times* (9 March 1913)
Obituaries: *Los Angeles Times* (17 July 1934); *Variety* (17 July 1934)

WARREN M. SHERK

Grusin, Dave

(*b* Littleton, CO, 26 June 1934). American composer, pianist, arranger, and record producer. The son of classical musicians, he took up piano at an early age and later earned a degree in classical piano performance from the University of Colorado. But he became increasingly drawn toward jazz. After college he took a job as accompanist to Andy Williams, and later assumed the duties of arranging and directing for "The Andy Williams Show." In the 1960s he recorded with several jazz groups, and worked as an arranger for such artists as Peggy Lee and Sergio Mendes. His performance in Quincy Jones's score for *The Slender Thread* brought him to Hollywood, and introduced him to director Sydney Pollack, with whom he would collaborate on nine films. He began composing for television and in 1967 moved to film, contributing music for *The Graduate* and penning his first score for the film *Divorce, American Style*. Grusin became known for his versatility and tunefulness, writing memorable themes for the television shows "Baretta" and "St. Elsewhere," a country music score for *W.W. and the Dixie Dance Kings*, much-lauded jazz scores for *Three Days of the Condor* and the Grammy-winning *The Fabulous Baker Boys*, and a Caribbean-inflected score for *The Milagro Bean War*, which earned him an Academy Award. Grusin's prolificacy expanded even more in the 1980s and 90s, writing the infectious score and song "It Might Be You" from *Tootsie*, the lush romantic music for *On Golden Pond*, and the propulsive light action score for *The Goonies*. In addition to his film scores, Grusin has remained an active jazz musician, arranger, and producer. He also founded the record label GRP. He recorded Grammy award-winning tributes to George Gershwin and Duke Ellington as well as a big band version of Leonard Bernstein's *West Side Story*.

Works

Film scores

(*selective list*)
Divorce American Style (dir. B. Yorkin), 1967
The Heart is a Lonely Hunter (dir. R.E. Miller), 1968
Candy (dir. H.J. Leder), 1969
Winning (dir. J. Goldstone), 1969
The Gang That Couldn't Shoot Straight (dir. J. Goldstone), 1971
Fuzz (dir. R.A. Colla), 1972
The Great Northfield Minnesota Raid (dir. P. Kaufman), 1972
The Friends of Eddie Coyle (dir. P. Yates), 1974
The Yakuza (dir. S. Pollack), 1974
Three Days of the Condor (dir. S. Pollack), 1975
W.W. and the Dixie Dance Kings (dir. J.G. Avildsen), 1975
The Front (dir. M. Ritt), 1976

Heaven Can Wait (dir. W. Beatty and B. Henry), 1978
. . . And Justice For All (dir. N. Jewison), 1979
The Champ (dir. F. Zeffirelli), 1979
The Electric Horseman (dir. S. Pollack), 1979
My Bodyguard (dir. T. Bill), 1980
On Golden Pond (dir. M. Rydell), 1981
Author! Author! (dir. A. Hiller), 1982
Tootsie (dir. S. Pollack), 1982
The Little Drummer Girl (dir. G.R. Hill), 1984
The Pope of Greenwich Village (dir. S. Rosenberg), 1984
The Goonies (dir. R. Donner), 1985
Lucas (dir. D. Seltzer), 1986
Ishtar (dir. E. May), 1987
The Milagro Beanfield War (dir. R. Redford), 1988
Tequila Sunrise (dir. R. Towne), 1988
The Fabulous Baker Boys (dir. S. Kloves), 1989
The Bonfire of the Vanities (dir. B. De Palma), 1990
Havana (dir. S. Pollack), 1990
For the Boys (dir. M. Rydell), 1991
The Firm (dir. S. Pollack), 1993
Mulholland Falls (dir. L. Tamahori), 1996
Selena (dir. G. Nava), 1997
Hope Floats (dir. F. Whitaker), 1998

DAN BLIM

Hagen, Earle

(*b* Chicago, IL, 9 July 1919; *d* Rancho Mirage, CA, 26 May 2008). American composer for film and television, arranger, and trombonist. His family relocated to Los Angeles when he was still a boy; at Hollywood High School he picked up the trombone and baritone. He left home at sixteen to pursue a career as a trombonist in big bands, ultimately playing with Ray Noble, Benny Goodman, and Tommy Dorsey. While with Noble, he wrote the jazz standard "Harlem Nocturne" in 1939, which he would later use as the theme for "Mike Hammer" (1984–7). Largely self-taught as a composer, Hagen studied with Ernst Toch in 1944. During the war, he arranged for the orchestra of the Army Air Corps Radio Production Unit, subsequently arranging and orchestrating (under Alfred Newman) for Twentieth Century-Fox during the late 1940s into the 1950s. Hagen orchestrated such films as *Kiss of Death* (1947), *Gentlemen Prefer Blondes* (1953), *Carousel* (1956), and *Compulsion* (1959). In the meantime, he composed uncredited extra music for Fox releases (including *Love Me Tender*) and began to work in television, initially as composer (with Herbert Spencer) for the Danny Thomas series "Make Room for Daddy" (1953–60). Thomas and producer Sheldon Leonard consistently worked with Hagen on television shows beginning with "The Andy Griffith Show"

(1960–68), the memorable whistling theme of which established his career as television composer. Other important series themes included those for "The Dick Van Dyke Show" (1961–6), "Gomer Pyle U.S.M.C." (1964–9), "I Spy" (1965–8), "That Girl" (1966–71), "The Mod Squad" (1968–72), and "The Dukes of Hazzard" (1983–5). His autobiography suggests that he composed and conducted three thousand television episodes in all. He possessed the ability to create an appropriate and memorable theme through effective melodic writing, colorful scoring, and stylistic deftness, regardless of the show's genre. Hagen won an Emmy in 1968 for his compositional work on "I Spy." He retired from film and television composition in 1986. In his later years, he informally taught at UCLA and USC, and authored two textbooks about film scoring and an autobiography. His manuscript scores for television music are preserved at UCLA.

Works

Film scores

The Girl Rush (dir. R. Pirosh), 1955
Spring Reunion (dir. R. Pirosh), 1957
Let's Make Love (dir. G. Cukor), 1960 (uncredited)
The New Interns (dir. J. Rich), 1964

Television movies

The Monk (dir. G. McCowan), 1969
The Runaways (dir. H. Harris), 1975
Having Babies (dir. R. Day), 1976
Killer on Board (dir. P. Leacock), 1977
True Grit (dir. R.T. Heffron), 1978
Ebony, Ivory and Jade (dir. J.L. Moxey), 1979
Alex and the Doberman Gang (dir. B. Chudnow), 1980
The Hustler of Muscle Beach (dir. J. Kaplan), 1980
Farewell to the Planet of the Apes (dir. D. McDougall and J.M. Lucas), 1981
Stand by your Man (dir. J. Jameson), 1981
Muggable Mary, Street Cop (dir. S. Stern), 1982
I Take these Men (dir. L. Peerce), 1983
Murder Me, Murder You (dir. G. Nelson), 1983
More than Murder (dir. G. Nelson), 1984
North Beach and Rawhide (dir. H. Falk), 1985
Return to Mayberry (dir. B. Sweeney), 1986
The Return of Mickey Spillane's Mike Hammer (dir. R. Danton), 1986

Television series

Where's Raymond?, 1953
Make Room for Daddy, 1953–60

The Barbara Stanwyck Show, 1960–61
The Andy Griffith Show, 1960–68
The Dick Van Dyke Show, 1961–6
Gomer Pyle, U.S.M.C., 1964–9
I Spy, 1965–8
That Girl, 1966–71
Accidental Family, 1967
Rango, 1967
The Danny Thomas Hour, 1967–8
The Guns of Will Sonnett, 1967–9
The Mod Squad, 1968–72
Mayberry R.F.D., 1968–71
The new People, 1969
The new Andy Griffith Show, 1971
The Don Rickles Show, 1972
M*A*S*H, 1972–83
Planet of the Apes, 1974
Mary Hartman, Mary Hartman, 1976–7
Eight is Enough, 1977–81
The Dukes of Hazzard, 1983–5
Mickey Spillane's Mike Hammer, 1984–5

Stage

The Love Offering (musical), 1982
unperformed

Instrumental

Harlem Nocturne, 1939

Writings

Scoring for Films: A Complete Text (Los Angeles, 1971)
Advanced Techniques for Film Scoring: A complete Text (Los Angeles,1990)
Memoirs of a Famous Composer Nobody Ever Heard Of (Philadelphia, 2000)

Bibliography

J. Burlingame: *TV's Biggest Hits: the Story of Television Themes from "Dragnet" to "Friends"* (New York, 1996)
B. Babcock: "Memoirs of a Famous Film Composer: an Interview with Earle Hagen," *Score*, xviii/4 (2003), 12–17
E. Frankel: "A Eulogy for Earle Hagen," *The Cue Sheet*, xxiii/3 (2008), 22–31

JAMES DEAVILLE

Hajos, Karl T.

(*b* Budapest, Hungary, 28 Jan 1889; *d* Hollywood, CA, 1 Feb 1950). American composer and conductor of Hungarian birth. He emigrated to the United States in 1924 and was naturalized in 1930. He was educated at the Academy of Music in Budapest and studied piano with Emil Saur in Vienna. In 1921 and 1922, he composed operettas in Berlin, Germany, before emigrating to New York, where he continued writing operettas through 1928. Moving to Hollywood, he scored films at Paramount as a staff composer from 1928 to 1934. He spent a year at Universal in 1935, then two at Republic, where his music made its way into Westerns and serials. Seeking other work he became the conductor of the short-lived California Symphony Orchestra in 1937, provided commentary for California Opera radio broadcasts in 1938, and served as musical director for a Los Angeles Civic Light Opera production in 1942. Returning to film scoring in 1943, it took him two years before he landed at Producers Releasing Corp. (PRC). In 1945 he scored a half dozen PRC films before being named musical director for the company the following year. He was charged with supervising the composing, orchestrating, and recording for company productions and continued to provide his own original scores for a dozen films over the next two years. Around 1947 he founded Karl Hajos Music Service and scored films until his death in 1950.

Works

(*selective list*)

Film scores

Loves of an Actress (dir. R.V. Lee), 1928
Morocco (dir. J. von Sternberg), 1930
Dishonored (dir. J. von Sternberg), 1931
The Song of Songs (dir. R. Mamoulian), 1933
Four Frightened People (dir. C.B. DeMille), 1934
Hitler's Madman (dir. D. Sirk), 1943
Summer Storm (dir. D. Sirk), 1944
Kill or Be Killed (dir. M. Nosseck), 1950

Film songs

Sunbeams Bring Dreams of You, 1928 [from *Loves of an Actress*]
Adoration, 1928 [title song]
Beggars of Life, 1928 [title song]
Lonely Little Senorita, 1933 [from *Cradle Song*]
Manhattan Moon, 1935 [title song]
My Other Me, 1935 [from *Manhattan Moon*]
Waitin' for the Sun, 1937 [from *Rainbow on the River*]
Summer Storm, 1944 [title song]

Operettas

The Red Cat, Berlin, 1923
The Waltz King, New York, 1925
Her Majesty, New York, 1927

Stage musicals

White Lilacs, New York, 1928 [based on the life of Frederic Chopin]
America Sings, New York, 1934 [based on the life of Stephen Foster]

Orchestral

Two symphonic poems for orchestra
Phantasy for Piano and Orchestra
Numerous works published in Berlin, Budapest, and Vienna in the 1920s

MSS in USC Department of Special Collections

WARREN M. SHERK

Hamlisch, Marvin (Frederick)

(*b* New York, 2 June 1944; *d* Los Angeles, 6 Aug 2012). American composer. After demonstrating precocious talent, he became the youngest student to attend the Juilliard School of Music, where he studied piano reluctantly from 1951 to 1965; while still there, he worked as a rehearsal pianist for *Funny Girl* (1964). In 1965 he attained early success as a popular songwriter when two songs he composed with a high school friend, Howard Liebling, "Sunshine, Lollipops, and Rainbows" and "California Nights," were recorded by Lesley Gore; one other song he composed as a teenager, "Travelin' Life," was recorded years later by Liza Minnelli, another high school friend, on her first album. Concurrently with his studies in music at Queens College, from which he graduated in 1967, Hamlisch was employed for two seasons as a vocal arranger and rehearsal pianist for a wide variety of acclaimed performers on "The Bell Telephone Hour." An engagement as a pianist at a private party for the producer Sam Spiegel led to *The Swimmer* (1968), the first of more than three dozen film scores over the next thirty years. A prominent early film success was an Academy Award nomination for "Life is what you make it" (lyrics by Johnny Mercer) from *Kotch* (1971). Three years later Hamlisch gained national celebrity when he became the first film composer to win three Oscars in one year, for both the score and title tune from *The Way We Were*, and for the adaptation of Scott Joplin's music in *The Sting* (the year's Best Picture). Among Hamlisch's later film scores, several received nominations for Best Song. These included two songs with the lyricist Carol Bayer Sager, "Nobody does it better" from *The Spy Who Loved Me* (1977) and

"Through the Eyes of Love" from *Ice Castles* (1978); two songs with Alan and Marilyn Bergman, "The Last Time I Felt Like This" from *Same Time, Next Year* (1978) and "The Girl Who Used to Be Me" from *Shirley Valentine* (1989); and "Surprise, Surprise" with the lyricist Edward Kleban, newly composed for the 1985 film version of *A Chorus Line*. He also received another Best Score nomination for *Sophie's Choice* (1982).

Hamlisch's first Broadway musical, *A Chorus Line* (1975), a show about the inner lives, dreams, and fears of seventeen dancers desperately auditioning for eight spots on a chorus line, was a triumph for the director and choreographer Michael Bennett and a major hit, running for over six thousand performances. In addition to winning the Tony and New York Drama Critics' Circle Awards for best musical and Tony Awards for Hamlisch's music and Kleban's lyrics, *A Chorus Line* was also the first musical in fifteen years to be awarded a Pulitzer Prize for Drama. A second international success followed four years later: *They're Playing Our Song*, with a book by Neil Simon and a pervasive disco score. The show, which featured only two stars, each however frequently backed by a trio of alter egos, was loosely based on a real-life romance between Hamlisch and Sager. Future musicals achieved neither commercial nor, with isolated exceptions, critical success. *Jean Seberg* (1983), which depicted the stormy and politically sensitive life of the actress, quickly opened and closed in London. The next musical, *Smile* (1986), an adaptation of a cult movie about a teenage beauty pageant, with the lyricist Howard Ashman also serving as both the librettist and the director, was quickly deemed a failure and closed after forty-eight Broadway performances, although it was later praised as "perhaps the most underappreciated musical of the eighties" by Mandelbaum (1991). Hamlisch's second collaboration with Neil Simon, an adaptation of Simon's successful film *The Goodbye Girl* (1977), also closed after a short Broadway run in 1993 and, after extensive revisions and new lyrics by Don Black, fared even less well in London. Hamlisch's later Broadway work includes the scores to two shows that opened for short runs in 2002, *Sweet Smell of Success: the Musical*, a musical version of the dark 1957 film classic with lyrics by Craig Carnelia and a book by John Guare, and Nora Ephron's *Imaginary Friends*, a play with music, also with lyrics by Carnelia. His death occurred during a tryout at the Tennessee Performing Arts Center in Nashville of a musical directed by Jerry Lewis based on the 1963 film *The Nutty Professor*.

In a style with pronounced, albeit generally scaled-down, rock features, Hamlisch produced both memorable lyrical ballads ("The Way We Were," "What I Did for Love") as well as rhythmically driving numbers ("I hope I get it," "They're playing our song"). *Chorus Line* in particular demonstrates Hamlisch's ability to evoke a wide variety of dance styles ranging from soft shoe ("I can do that") to the waltz ("At the Ballet"), with musical numbers that present formally complex musical biographical stories and dramas in a varied mixture of song, recitative, speech, and intricate ensembles.

Works

Stage

(unless otherwise stated, dates are those of first New York performances; librettists and lyricists are listed in that order in parentheses)

A Chorus Line (J. Kirkwood and N. Dante, E. Kleban), orchd B. Byers, H. Kay, and J. Tunick, Public Theatre, 15 April 1975 [incl. One, What I Did for Love]; film, 1985

They're Playing Our Song (N. Simon, C. Bayer Sager), orchd R. Burns, R. Hazard, and G. Page, Imperial, 11 Feb 1979 [incl. Fallin', They're playing our song]

Jean Seberg (J. Barry, C. Adler), London, National, 15 Nov 1983

Smile (H. Ashman), orchd S. Ramin, Byers, Hazard, and T. Zito, Lunt-Fontanne, 24 Nov 1986 [after film, 1975; incl. Smile, In Our Hands]

The Goodbye Girl (N. Simon, D. Zippel), orchd Byers and Zito, Marquis, 4 March 1993 [after film, 1977; incl. No More]; rev. London, Albery, 1997

Film scores

(selective list)

The Swimmer (dir. F. Perry and S. Pollack), 1968

The April Fools (dir. S. Rosenberg), 1969

Take the Money and Run (dir. W. Allen), 1969

Flap (dir. C. Reed), 1970

Move (dir. S. Rosenberg), 1970

Bananas (dir. W. Allen), 1971

Kotch (dir. J. Lemmon), 1971

Something Big (dir. A.V. McLaglen), 1971

Fat City (dir. J. Huston), 1972

The War between Men and Women (dir. M. Shavelson), 1972

Save the Tiger (dir. J.G. Avildsen), 1973

The Sting (dir. G.R. Hill), 1973

The Way We Were (dir. S. Pollack), 1973

The Prisoner of Second Avenue (dir. M. Frank), 1975

The Spy Who Loved Me (dir. L. Gilbert), 1977

Same Time, Next Year (dir. R. Mulligan), 1978

The Champ (dir. F. Zeffirelli), 1979

Chapter Two (dir. R. Moore), 1979

Starting Over (dir. A.J. Pakula), 1979

Ordinary People (dir. R. Redford), 1980

Seems Like Old Times (dir. J. Sandrich), 1980

The Fan (dir. E. Bianchi), 1981

Pennies from Heaven (dir. H. Ross), 1981

I Ought to Be in Pictures (dir. H. Ross), 1982

Sophie's Choice (dir. A.J. Pakula), 1982

Romantic Comedy (dir. A. Hiller), 1983

A Chorus Line (dir. R. Attenborough), 1985

Three Men and a Baby (dir. L. Nimoy), 1987

Little Nikita (dir. R. Benjamin), 1988
The Experts (dir. D. Thomas), 1989
The January Man (dir. P. O'Connor), 1989
Shirley Valentine (dir. L. Gilbert), 1989
Frankie and Johnny (dir. G. Marshall), 1991
Missing Pieces (dir. L. Stern), 1992
The Mirror Has Two Faces (dir. B. Streisand), 1996
The Informant! (dir. S. Soderbergh), 2009

Orchestral

Individual songs, incl. Sunshine, Lollipops, and Rainbows, 1965
Break It to Me Gently, 1977
Anatomy of Peace, 1991
One Song, 1992 [for Olympics, Barcelona]
Good Morning, America [theme song]

Bibliography

A. Kasha and J. Hirschhorn: *Notes on Broadway: Conversations with the Great Songwriters* (Chicago, 1985)
D.M. Flinn: *What They Did for Love: the Untold Story behind the Making of "A Chorus Line"* (New York, 1989)
K. Mandelbaum: *"A Chorus Line" and the Musicals of Michael Bennett* (New York, 1989)
K. Kelly: *One Singular Sensation: the Michael Bennett Story* (New York, 1990)
J.P. Swain: *The Broadway Musical: a Critical and Musical Survey* (New York, 1990)
K. Mandelbaum: *Not since Carrie: 40 Years of Broadway Musical Flops* (New York, 1991)
M. Hamlisch (with G. Gardner): *The Way I Was* (New York, 1992) [autobiography]
G. Stevens: *The Longest Line: Broadway's Most Singular Sensation* (New York, 1995)
R. Viagas: *On the Line: the Creation of "A Chorus Line," with the Entire Original Cast* (Pompton Plains, NJ, 2006)

GEOFFREY BLOCK/R

Hancock, Herbie [Herbert Jeffrey]

(*b* Chicago, 12 April 1940). American jazz pianist, keyboard player, and composer. He was born into a musical family and began studying piano at the age of seven. Four years later he performed the first movement of Mozart's Piano Concerto no.5 with the Chicago SO in a young people's concert. He formed his own jazz band while attending Hyde Park High School; his early influences were from Oscar Peterson, Bill Evans, and the harmonies of Clare Fischer, Gil Evans, and Ravel. Hancock began studies at Grinnell College with a double major in music and engineering, the latter an early interest that later was manifested in his groundbreaking synthesizer work. He switched to composition in his junior year, and by the time he left Grinnell in 1960 he was already working in jazz clubs in Chicago with Coleman Hawkins. The trumpeter Donald Byrd invited him to join his quintet and move to New York, where during Hancock's first recording session with the group, Blue Note was sufficiently impressed to offer him his first date as a leader, in May 1962. The resulting album, *Takin' Off*, drew considerable public attention through an original tune, "Watermelon Man," which had a strong gospel influence and charted on jazz and R&B radio. Hancock also worked briefly in Eric Dolphy's group and recorded with Hank Mobley, Jimmy Heath, Oliver Nelson, and Kenny Dorham.

In May 1963 Hancock joined Miles Davis's group, which became known as the trumpeter's second great quintet. Hancock's piano style had by this time evolved into a highly personal blend of blues and bop with sophisticated harmony and exquisite tone. With Davis's sidemen Ron Carter and Tony Williams, Hancock helped revolutionize traditional jazz concepts of the rhythm section and its relation to the soloists, and established a musical rapport with an extraordinary degree of freedom and interaction. During his five years with the quintet Hancock also led his own groups, recording several albums for Blue Note including *Maiden Voyage* (1965), *Speak Like a Child* (1968), and *The Prisoner* (1969). These featured compositions that have since become jazz standards: "Maiden Voyage," "Dolphin Dance," "Cantaloupe Island," and "Speak Like a Child." Hancock also composed the score for Michelangelo Antonioni's film *Blow-Up* (1966) and worked as a sideman with Blue Mitchell, Lee Morgan, Bob Brookmeyer, Sonny Rollins, Jackie McLean, Sam Rivers, and Woody Shaw, as well as with his fellow sidemen in Davis's band Williams and Wayne Shorter. Although he officially left Davis's group in 1968, Hancock continued to record with him until 1970 and played electric piano and organ on many of Davis's important jazz-rock albums including *In a Silent Way*, *Bitches Brew* (both 1969, Col.), and *A Tribute to Jack Johnson* (1970, Col.).

From 1970 to 1973 Hancock led a sextet that combined elements of jazz, rock, and African and Indian music with electronic devices and instruments. He also used the name Mwandishi during this period. Influenced by Davis's fusion recordings the sextet, which included Joe Henderson, Johnny Coles, and Billy Hart, was notable for its colorful doubling of instruments, tasteful blend of acoustic and electronic sounds, and mastery of compound meters (*Mwandishi*, 1970, WB, and *Sextant*, 1972, Col.). Thereafter Hancock began to use electric and electronic instruments more extensively, including the Fender-Rhodes piano which he played through a variety of signal processors such as wah-wah and fuzz pedals. Later he turned to the Mellotron and the Hohner Clavinet and finally to various synthesizers, sequencers, and electronic percussion units. Hancock's album *Head Hunters* (1973, Col.) with his ensemble of the same name, was the first by a jazz artist to go platinum and marked the beginning of a commitment to more commercial types of music, particularly rock, funk, and disco, and contained the Sly Stone–influenced hit single "Chameleon." Although Hancock returned occasionally to jazz projects in the late 1970s, particularly with his Davis-alumni band V.S.O.P and his piano duos with Chick Corea, his focus during this period was on crossover music that achieved considerable commercial success. In 1983 the single "Rockit" reached the top of the pop charts, and its promotional video received widespread critical acclaim; it demonstrated Hancock's ability to use the most complex innovations in electronic technology to produce fascinating music.

After this success Hancock turned his attention almost exclusively to jazz for the next two years. He acted and played in the film *Round Midnight* (1986) and won an Oscar for his score. From 1987 he recorded and toured internationally with all-star groups that included Carter, Williams, Gil Scott-Heron, Michael Brecker, Jack DeJohnette, Dave Holland, Pat Metheny, Vernon Reid (of Living Colour), and Shorter. Hancock's album *Dis is da Drum* (1994, Verve) included material in a hip hop style, and on *The New Standard* (1996, Verve) he recorded versions of pop songs by the Beatles, Prince, Simon and Garfunkel, and Steely Dan, among others. During the late 1990s Hancock worked with a reunited Headhunters band and recorded an album of works by Gershwin (*Gershwin's World*, 1998, Verve) which won multiple Grammy awards. Hancock's music also began to reappear on the charts through the sampling of his earlier material, notably the use of "Cantaloupe Island" by the British hip hop group Us3 on "Cantaloop (Flip Fantasia)" (BN, 1993). Since then his projects have continued to explore crossover influences and collaborators. His recording *River: the Joni Letters* (2007, Verve) featured compositions by Joni Mitchell and became only the second jazz album to win the Grammy Award for Album of the Year, and his tribute to John Lennon, *The Imagine Project* (2010, Hancock), included such varied artists as John Legend, Dave Matthews, and The Chieftains.

Works

(*selective list*)

Film scores

Blow-Up (dir. M. Antonioni, 1966)
Death Wish (dir. M. Winner, 1974)
A Soldier's Story (dir. N. Jewison, 1984)
Round Midnight (dir. B. Tavernier, 1985)
Colors (dir. D. Hopper, 1988)
Harlem Nights (dir. E. Murphy, 1989)
Livin' Large! (dir. Michael Schultz, 1991)
On the Shoulders of Giants (dir. Deborah Morales, 2011)
Occupy Los Angeles (dir. Joseph G. Quinn, 2012)

Instrumental

Driftin', Watermelon Man (from Takin' Off; 1962, BN)
Cantaloupe Island, One Finger Snap (from Empyrean Isles; 1964, BN)
Dolphin Dance, Little One, Maiden Voyage (from Maiden Voyage; 1965, BN)
Riot, Speak Like a Child, The Sorcerer (from Speak Like a Child; 1968, BN)
Chameleon, Watermelon Man (from Head Hunters; 1973, Col.)
I Thought it was You (from Sunlight; 1978, Col.)
Rockit (from Future Shock; 1983, Col.)

Bibliography

B. Johnson: "Herbie Hancock: into his own Thing," *DB*, xxxviii/2 (1971), 14 only
R. Townley: "Hancock Plugs In," *DB*, xli/17 (1974), 13
D. Milano and others: "Herbie Hancock," *Contemporary Keyboard*, iii/11 (1977), 26
C. Silvert: "Herbie Hancock: Revamping the Past, Creating the Future," *DB*, xliv/15 (1977), 16
D.N. Baker, L.M. Belt, and H.C. Hudson, eds.: "Herbie Hancock," *The Black Composer Speaks* (Metuchen, NJ, 1978), 108–38 [incl. list of compositions]
B. Primack: "Herbie Hancock: Chameleon in his Disco Phase," *DB*, xlvi/10 (1979), 12
J. Balleras: "Herbie Hancock's Current Choice," *DB*, xlix/9 (1982), 15–17
L. Lyons: "Herbie Hancock," *The Great Jazz Pianists: Speaking of their Lives and Music* (New York, 1983/*R*), 269–84
H. Mandel: "Herbie Hancock: of Films, Fairlights, Funk . . . and all that other Jazz," *DB*, liii/7 (1986), 16–19 [incl. discography]
N. Suzuki: *Herbie Hancock: 1961–1969* (Shizuoka, Japan, 1988) [discography]
J. Tamarkin: "Herbie Hancock: Energy in the Environment," *JT* (Sept 2010), also available at http://jazztimes.com/articles/26370-herbie-hancock-energy-in-the-environment
Oral history material in *Neij*

BILL DOBBINS/BARRY LONG/R

Harline, Leigh

(*b* Salt Lake City, 26 March 1907; *d* Long Beach, CA, 10 Dec 1969). American composer and conductor. He studied music at the University of Utah and took private piano and organ lessons with the conductor of the Mormon Tabernacle Choir, J. Spencer Cornwall. After working for radio stations in his native city, he moved to California (1928), where he arranged music and conducted for radio stations in Los Angeles and San Francisco. From 1932 to 1941 he worked for Walt Disney, writing for the Silly Symphony series and many other short films. He also composed for Disney's first two animated feature films: *Snow White and the Seven Dwarfs* and *Pinocchio*; for the latter he won Academy Awards for best original score and best song ("When you Wish upon a Star"). After leaving Disney he worked at various studios (mainly RKO and Twentieth Century-Fox), composing, conducting, and arranging for more than 120 feature films and several television programs. Although sometimes typecast as a scorer of comedies, Harline was a skillful, imaginative, and often original craftsman, whose best work reveals a genuine dramatic flair. Two of his Disney scores, *The Pied Piper* (1933), a miniature operetta, and *The Old Mill* (1937), in its lyrical expression, musical unity, use of "symphonic" scoring, and textless female chorus, must be considered among his most agreeable and imaginative works.

Works

(*selective list*)

Film scores

Silly Symphonies (dir. W. Jackson), 1932–9 [incl. The Pied Piper, 1933, Music Land, 1935, The Country Cousin, 1936]
The Old Mill (dir. W. Jackson), 1937
Snow White and the Seven Dwarfs (dir. W. Cottrell, D. Hand, W. Jackson, L. Morey, P. Pearce, and B. Sharpsteen), 1937, collab. P.J. Smith, F. Churchill
Pinocchio (dir. N. Ferguson, T. Hee, W. Jackson, J. Kinney, H. Luske, B. Roberts, and B. Sharpsteen), 1940
Mr. Bug Goes to Town (dir. D. Fleischer and S. Culhane), 1941
The Pride of the Yankees (dir. S. Wood), 1942
Tender Comrade (dir. E. Dmytryk), 1943
China Sky (dir. R. Enright), 1945
Isle of the Dead (dir. M. Robson), 1945
Johnny Angel (dir. E.L. Marin), 1945
Man Alive (dir. R. Enright), 1945
The Farmer's Daughter (dir. H.C. Potter), 1947
A Likely Story (dir. H.C. Potter), 1947
The Boy with Green Hair (dir. J. Losey), 1948
They Live by Night (dir. N. Ray), 1949
The Happy Years (dir. W.A. Wellman), 1950
Perfect Strangers (dir. B. Windust), 1950
Broken Lance (dir. E. Dmytryk), 1954
Good Morning, Miss Dove (dir. H. Koster), 1955
The Enemy Below (dir. D. Powell), 1957
The Wayward Bus (dir. V. Vicas), 1957
Ten North Frederick (dir. P. Dunne), 1958
The Wonderful World of the Brothers Grimm (dir. H. Levin and G. Pal), 1962
7 Faces of Dr. Lao (dir. G. Pal), 1964

Orchestral

Civic Center Suite, 1941
Centennial Suite, 1947

Bibliography

R.V. Steele: "Fairyland Goes Hollywood," *Pacific Coast Musician*, xxvi/22 (1937), 10 only [interview]

R. Care: "The Film Music of Leigh Harline," *Film Music Notebook*, iii/2 (1977), 32–48 [incl. complete list of film scores]; repr. in *Film Music Notebook: a Complete Collection of the Quarterly Journal, 1974–1978*, ed. E. Bernstein (Sherman Oaks, CA, 2004), 406–22

FRED STEINER/R

Hayman, Richard (Warren)

(*b* Cambridge, MA, 27 March 1920; *d* New York, 5 Feb 2014). American conductor, arranger, harmonica player, and composer. He began his professional career in 1938 as a performer and arranger with the Borrah Minevitch Harmonica Rascals. His arrangements for this ensemble brought him to the attention of commercial musicians, and within a few years he was working as an orchestrator for Metro-Goldwyn-Mayer studios on musical films that included *Girl Crazy, Meet me in St. Louis*, and *As Thousands Cheer*. After returning to Boston, where he was music director of the Vaughn Monroe Orchestra in the late 1940s, Hayman was named principal arranger for the Boston Pops Orchestra in 1950. In the decades that followed he served as music director for numerous leading entertainers, including Bob Hope, Johnny Cash, Red Skelton, Johnny Carson, Andy Williams, Pat Boone, Olivia Newton-John, and Bobby Vinton. His tune "Ruby" (from the soundtrack for the film *Ruby Gentry* [1953], featuring Hayman's own solo harmonica playing) was a best-selling recording, as was his disco arrangement of themes from Beethoven's Fifth Symphony ("A Fifth of Beethoven") in the late 1970s. Hayman expanded his activities in the early 1970s to include appearances as guest conductor for "pops" concerts presented by symphony orchestras, eventually obtaining the title of principal pops conductor with the orchestras in Detroit and St. Louis. Something of a showman, Hayman had a flamboyant style on the podium that was augmented by his extravagant costumes and quick-witted banter.

JAMES WIERZBICKI/R

Hayton, Lennie [Leonard] (George)

(*b* New York, 13 Feb 1908; *d* Los Angeles, 24 April 1971). American musical director, conductor, and arranger. He began his career as a pianist, playing and arranging for jazz artists, in particular for the Paul Whiteman Orchestra in the late 1920s. His arrangements of classic songs for Whiteman, such as "Nobody's Sweetheart," are considered among the finest of their era, blending jazz instruments with those of the traditional orchestra. His later arrangement of "Star

Dust" provided a hit in the early 1940s for clarinetist Artie Shaw. In 1940 he became musical director for Metro Goldwyn Mayer studios before moving to Twentieth Century-Fox in 1953. He was involved in arranging scores for a number of films and musicals, including *The Harvey Girls* (1945) and *The Pirate* (1948); the arrangements reflect the complexity achieved in his work for Whiteman, although film music had only recently incorporated jazz into its idioms. He was nominated for Academy Awards for his work on several notable musicals, including *Singin' in the Rain* (1952) and *Hello Dolly!* (1969). He received the Oscar in 1949 for his musical direction, with Roger Edens, of *On the Town*, based on Leonard Bernstein's ballet *Fancy Free*. His connection with jazz was sustained alongside his film music career through his marriage to jazz vocalist Lena Horne. She credited Hayton with helping her to develop her voice, and he managed her professional singing career.

Bibliography

SchullerEJ
SchullerSE
L. Horne and R. Schickel: *Lena* (New York, 1965)

KATE DAUBNEY

Heindorf, Ray

(*b* Haverstraw, NY, 25 Aug 1908; *d* Los Angeles, 3 Feb 1980). American musical director, orchestrator, and conductor. His association with cinema music began as a young man with employment as a pianist and organist for a silent movie theater in Mechanicsville, New York. He became a protégé of Leo Forbstein, the first musical director at Warner Bros. studios, after helping with the scoring of *The Jazz Singer* (1927). He effectively served his apprenticeship with Warner Bros., rising through the music department as a performer and orchestrator-arranger. During this period he orchestrated for Max Steiner on *Daughters Courageous* (1939). When Forbstein retired in 1947, Heindorf succeeded him, remaining as head of the department until 1959, although he continued to conduct and arrange scores. He was nominated for eighteen Academy Awards between 1942 and 1968 and received three: for the musical direction on *Yankee Doodle Dandy* (1942) and *This is the Army* (1943, which was based on the songs of Irving Berlin) and for the adaptation to film of the Broadway musical *The Music Man* (1962). Despite the traditional pedigree of the Warners department, Heindorf was supportive of developments in film scoring style, most notably in his conducting of Alex North's original jazz score for *A Streetcar Named Desire* (1951). Among the few scores for which he was principal composer are *Hollywood*

Canteen (1944), *Young Man with a Horn* (1950), a biography of Bix Beiderbecke, and *Pete Kelly's Blues* (1955), which achieved minor cult status largely due to its score.

Bibliography

W. Darby and J. Du Bois: *American Film Music: Major Composers, Techniques, Trends, 1915–1990* (Jefferson, NC, 1991)

KATE DAUBNEY

Herrmann, Bernard

(*b* New York, 29 June 1911; *d* Los Angeles, 24 Dec 1975). Composer and conductor. In 1929, while still a student at DeWitt Clinton High School, he enrolled for classes in composition and conducting at New York University. The subsequent year he followed his conducting teacher Albert Stoessel to the Juilliard School of Music, where he was taught composition by the Dutch émigré Bernard Wagenaar. He left the Juilliard School after less than two years, apparently because he found the institution too conservative, and returned informally to New York University during the academic year 1932–3 to attend a course in composition and orchestration given by Percy Grainger. Grainger's eclectic approach revealed to Herrmann the range and diversity of the musical materials available to the contemporary composer. Early in 1933 he formed the New Chamber Orchestra from a group of unemployed musicians as a vehicle for his talents as both conductor and composer. The orchestra's repertory brought together contemporary compositions (including those of Charles Ives, with whom Herrmann formed a lasting friendship) and works by English composers such as Henry Purcell and Edward Elgar, symptomatic of his anglophile tendencies.

In 1934 Herrmann was appointed assistant to Johnny Green, a conductor and composer at CBS, and from 1936 to 1940 composed a considerable quantity of incidental music for the radio series "The Columbia Workshop" (1936–7, at least seventy-five shows), "The Mercury Theater on the Air" (1938, twenty-two shows directed by Orson Welles), and "The Campbell Playhouse" (1938–40, fifty-six shows, also directed by Welles). During his apprenticeship in radio theater he developed a musical style that was immediate and economical, both in terms of the instrumental resources employed and melodic and harmonic language. The partnership he forged with Welles resulted in his first film score, *Citizen Kane*, composed in 1940 and released by RKO in 1941. In 1942 he scored a second film for Welles, *The Magnificent Ambersons*, but refused to let his name appear in the credits after the savage cutting of his music following poor audience response to the preview.

In the subsequent twelve years, Herrmann composed a number of scores for Fox studios, but it was his partnership with Alfred Hitchcock at Paramount and MGM (1955–64) that cemented his reputation. *Vertigo* (1958), *North by Northwest* (1959), and *Psycho* (1960) are generally held to represent the summit of his film scoring achievement; the infamous shower scene of *Psycho*, which Hitchcock initially intended to be unscored, is one of the most frequently referenced and influential cues in cinematic history. Throughout this period he composed cues and stock scores for CBS TV series such as "Rawhide," "The Twilight Zone," and "The Alfred Hitchcock Half Hour." In 1966 Herrmann felt unable and unwilling to acquiesce to Hitchcock's demand for a more overtly popular score for *Torn Curtain*, and composed no further music for him thereafter. During the final ten years of his career, he worked with the directors François Truffaut (*Fahrenheit 451*, 1966, and *La mariée était en noir*, 1967), Brian de Palma (*Sisters*, 1973, and *Obsession*, 1976), and ultimately Martin Scorsese on *Taxi Driver* (1976).

For Herrmann, orchestration was a composer's musical thumbprint. Unlike most other Hollywood composers of his generation, he orchestrated his own music rather than passing a short score to a team of orchestrators. His instrumentation was often unusual: *The Day the Earth Stood Still* (1951) uses two theremins (an electronic instrument previously used by Miklós Rózsa in his 1945 scores for *The Lost Weekend* and *Spellbound*), electronic violin, bass, and guitar, four harps, four pianos, percussion, and brass; *Psycho* is scored for string orchestra; *Journey to the Center of the Earth* (1959) requires five organs; *On Dangerous Ground* (1951) has a solo part for viola d'amore. Herrmann generally avoided the "leitmotif" system adopted by many film composers, finding that short phrases were less limiting to the composer than the closed forms of eight- and sixteen-bar melodies. Ostinato figures built around one- or two-bar units feature prominently in his later scores, often being associated with obsessive behavior. Although his musical language is fundamentally tonal, he makes sustained use of dissonance and chromatic embellishment, and employs complex harmonic units such as the superimposed E♭ minor and D major triads near the beginning of *Vertigo*.

Despite his wide acclaim as a film composer, Herrmann's concert works and operas have not had the same level of public success. His opera *Wuthering Heights* (1943–51) is perhaps his finest and most sustained achievement in this field. A complex and enigmatic figure who could be egotistical and irascible, refined and sentimental by turns, who hustled at the center of the American culture industry, yet yearned for the English pastoral, he remains one of the central figures of film-music composition.

Works

Film scores

All that Money can Buy (dir. W. Dieterle), 1941
Citizen Kane (dir. O. Welles), 1941

The Magnificent Ambersons (dir. O. Welles, F. Fleck, R. Wise), 1942
Jane Eyre (dir. R. Stevenson), 1943
Hangover Square (dir. J. Brahm), 1945
Anna and the King of Siam (dir. J. Cromwell), 1946
The Ghost and Mrs. Muir (dir. J.L. Mankiewicz), 1947
The Day the Earth Stood Still (dir. R. Wise), 1951
On Dangerous Ground (dir. N. Ray and I. Lupino), 1951
5 Fingers (dir. J.L. Mankiewicz), 1952
The Snows of Kilimanjaro (dir. H. King and R.W. Baker), 1952
Beneath the Twelve Mile Reef (dir. R.D. Webb), 1953
King of the Khyber Rifles (dir. H. King), 1953
White Witch Doctor (dir. H. Hathaway), 1953
The Egyptian (dir. M. Curtiz), 1954, collab. A. Newman
Garden of Evil (dir. H. Hathaway), 1954
The Kentuckian (dir. B. Lancaster), 1955
Prince of Players (dir. P. Dunne), 1955
The Trouble with Harry (dir. A. Hitchcock), 1955
The Man in the Gray Flannel Suit (dir. N. Johnson), 1956
The Man who Knew Too Much (dir. A. Hitchcock), 1956
Williamsburg: the Story of a Patriot (dir. G. Seaton), 1956
The Wrong Man (dir. A. Hitchcock), 1956
A Hatful of Rain (dir. F. Zinnemann), 1957
The Naked and the Dead (dir. R. Walsh), 1958
The Seventh Voyage of Sinbad (dir. K. Zeman), 1958
Vertigo (dir. A. Hitchcock), 1958
Blue Denim (dir. P. Dunne), 1959
Journey to the Center of the Earth (dir. H. Levin), 1959
North by Northwest (dir. A. Hitchcock), 1959
The 3 Worlds of Gulliver (dir. J. Sher), 1960
Psycho (dir. A. Hitchcock), 1960
Cape Fear (dir. J.L. Thompson), 1961
Mysterious Island (dir. C. Endfield), 1961
Tender is the Night (dir. H. King), 1961
The Birds (dir. A. Hitchcock), 1963, as sound consultant
Jason and the Argonauts (dir. D. Chaffey), 1963
Marnie (dir. A. Hitchcock), 1964
Joy in the Morning (dir. A. Segal), 1965
Fahrenheit 451 (dir. F. Truffaut), 1966
Torn Curtain (dir. A. Hitchcock), 1966, rejected score
La mariée était en noir [The bride wore black] (dir. F. Truffaut), 1967
Twisted Nerve (dir. R. Boulting), 1968
The Battle of Neretva (dir. V. Bulajic), 1969
Endless Night (dir. S. Gilliat), 1971
The Road Builder [The Night Digger] (dir. A. Reid), 1971
Sisters (dir. B. De Palma), 1973

It's Alive (dir. L. Cohen), 1974
Obsession (dir. B. De Palma), 1976
Taxi Driver (dir. M. Scorsese), 1976

Television and radio

Television music

(all series or compilations partly scored by Herrmann)
The Alfred Hitchcock Half Hour
Alfred Hitchcock Presents
The Americans
Collector's Item
Convoy
Ethan Allan
Forecast
Gunsmoke
Have Gun Will Travel
House on "K" Street
Impact
The Kraft Suspense Theatre
Landmark
Pursuit
Rawhide
Studio One
The Twilight Zone
The Virginian

Radio

The Campbell Playhouse
Columbia Presents Corwin
The Columbia Workshop
Crime Classics
Mercury Summer Theatre
The Mercury Theater on the Air
Orson Welles Show
Suspense
others

Vocal

Operas

Wuthering Heights (op, L. Fletcher, after E. Brontë), 1943–51
A Christmas Carol (TV op, M. Anderson, after C. Dickens), 1954
A Child is Born (TV op, after S.V. Benét), 1955

Musicals

The King of Schnorrers (D. Lampert and S. Wencelberg after I. Zangwill), 1968

Cantatas

Moby Dick (W.C. Harrington, after H. Melville), solo vv, male chorus, orch, 1937–8
Johnny Appleseed, solo vv, chorus, orch, 1940, inc.

Other works

The Fantasticks (N. Breton), song cycle, S, A, T, B, chorus, orch, 1942

Instrumental

Orchestral

Variations on Deep River and Water Boy, 1933
Currier and Ives, suite, 1935
Nocturne and Scherzo, 1936
Sym., 1939–41
For the Fallen, 1943
Welles Raises Kane, suite, 1943

Chamber

Aria, fl, hp, 1932
Marche Militaire, chbr orch, 1932
Aubade, 14 insts, 1933, rev. as Silent Noon, 1975
Prelude to Anathema, 15 insts, 1933
Sinfonietta, strs, 1935
Echoes, str qt, 1965
Souvenirs de voyage, cl, str qt, 1967

Principal publisher: Novello

Bibliography

E. Johnson: *Bernard Herrmann: Hollywood's Music Dramatist* (Rickmansworth, UK, 1977)
G. Bruce: *Bernard Herrmann: Film Music and Narrative* (Ann Arbor, 1985)
L.T. Zador and G. Rose: "A Conversation with Bernard Herrmann," *Film Music 1*, ed. C. McCarty (Los Angeles, 1989, 2/1998), 209–254
C. Palmer: *The Composer in Hollywood* (London and New York, 1990)
S.C. Smith: *A Heart at Fire's Center: the Life and Music of Bernard Herrmann* (Berkeley and Los Angeles, 1991)
R.S. Brown: *Overtones and Undertones: Reading Film Music* (Berkeley and Los Angeles, 1994)
H.S. Wright: "Bernard Herrmann: a Selected Secondary Bibliography," *Music Reference Services Quarterly*, iv/1 (1995), 49–68

F. Thomas: "Musical Keys to *Kane*," *Perspectives on Citizen Kane*, ed. R. Gothesman (New York, 1996), 172–96
D. Neumeyer: "Tonal Design and Narrative in Film Music: Bernard Herrmann's *A Portrait of Hitch* and *The Trouble with Harry*," *Indiana Theory Review*, xix/1–2 (1998), 87–123
D. Cooper: *Bernard Herrmann's "Vertigo": a Film Score Handbook* (Westport, CT, 2001)
The Journal of Film Music, i/2–3 (2003) [issue devoted to Herrmann]
D. Cooper: *Bernard Herrmann's "The Ghost and Mrs. Muir": a Film Score Guide* (Latham, MD, 2005)
L. Whitesell: "Concerto Macabre," *MQ*, lxxxviii/2 (2005), 167–203
J. Sullivan: *Hitchcock's Music* (New Haven, CT, 2007)
J. Wierzbicki: "Shrieks, Flutters, and Vocal Curtains: Electronic Sound/Electronic Music in Hitchcock's *The Birds*," *Music and the Moving Image* i/2 (2008), 27–53
J. Wierzbicki: "*Psycho*-analysis: Form and Function in Bernard Herrmann's Music for Hitchcock's Masterpiece," *Terror Tracks: Music, Sound, and Horror Cinema*, ed. P. Hayward (London, 2009), 14–46
W. Wrobel: "The Deleted Music and Scenes from *Journey to the Center of the Earth*," *Popular Music History* v/1 (2010), 35–54
J. Waxman: "Lessons from Ives: Elements of Charles Ives's Musical Language in the Film Scores and Symphonic Works of Bernard Herrmann," *Popular Music History* v/1 (2010), 21–33
S. Deutsch: "*Psycho* and the Orchestration of Anxiety," *The Soundtrack* iii/1 (2010), 53–66
S. Husarik: "Suspended Motion in the Title Scene from *The Day the Earth Stood Still*," *Sounds of the Future, Essays on Music in Science Fiction Film*, ed. M. Bartkowiak (Jefferson, NC, 2010), 164–76
T. Schneller: "Unconscious Anchors: Bernard Herrmann's Music for *Marnie*," *Popular Music History* v/1 (2010), 55–104
R. Fenimore: "Voices that Lie Within: The Heard and Unheard in *Psycho*," *Music in the Horror Film: Listening to Fear*, ed. N. Learner (New York, 2010), 80–97
D. Blim: "Musical and Dramatic Design in Bernard Herrmann's Prelude to *Vertigo* (1958)" *Music and the Moving Image*, vi/2 (2013), 21–31

DAVID COOPER/R

Holdridge, Lee [Elwood]

(*b* Port-Au-Prince, Haiti, 3 March 1944). American composer and arranger of Haitian birth. Born to an American father and a Puerto Rican mother and raised in Costa Rica, where he studied the violin with Hugo Mariani, he arrived in the United States in 1958. After studying composition and conducting in high school with Henry Lasker in Boston, he attended the Manhattan School of Music under the tutelage of Nicolas Flagello and Ludmila Ulehla. In New York he specialized in writing dance arrangements for musical productions beginning in 1966. By 1970 he was composing for the contemporary instrumental group The Seventh Century. That same year, for "Summerland," from the Joffrey Ballet's *Trinity*, he combined a rock band with an orchestra. Work as Neil Diamond's music director and arranger led him to adapt the singer's music for the 1973 film *Jonathan Livingston Seagull*. Holdridge went on to score *Mr. Mom, The Old Gringo*, and others. His themes for television series include "Eight Is Enough," "Moonlighting," and "Beauty and the Beast." With more than one hundred television features, such as *Do You Know the Muffin Man?* and *The Mists of Avalon*, he is one of the most prolific composers in the genre. High-profile miniseries include *East of Eden* and *Tuskegee Airmen*. In addition to composing for the major television and cable networks, he has provided music for Steve Krantz Productions, Wolf Film Productions, and numerous others. His compositional output for the concert hall has been eclectic, encompassing ballet, one-act operas, and symphonic works. He has provided arrangements for recording artists ranging from John Denver to Placido Domingo. Holdridge has scored six documentaries for Moriah Films, based at the Simon Wiesenthal Center, from *The Long Way Home* to *I Have Never Forgotten You*. Blending contemporary pop and traditional music, Holdridge is equally adept at symphonic, rock, and electronic scoring. His music tends to be lyrical, thematic, and story-driven.

Works

(*selective list*)

Film scores

Jonathan Livingston Seagull (dir. H. Bartlett), 1973, arranger for N. Diamond
The Other Side of the Mountain Part 2 (dir. L. Peerce), 1978
The Beastmaster (dir. D. Coscarelli), 1982
Mr. Mom (dir. S. Dragoti), 1983
Micki & Maude (dir. B. Edwards), 1984
Splash (dir. R. Howard), 1984
Big Business (dir. J. Abrahams), 1988
Old Gringo (dir. L. Puenzo), 1989
Unlikely Heroes (dir. R. Trank), 2003
Against the Tide (dir. Trank), 2009
Brothers at War (dir. J. Rademacher), 2009
Winston Churchill: Walking with Destiny (dir. Trank), 2010
Hell and Mr. Fudge (dir. J. Wood), 2012
It is No Dream (dir. Trank), 2012
Great Voices Sing John Denver (dir. K. Shapiro (as K.R. Shapiro)), 2013
The Prime Ministers: the Pioneers (dir. Trank), 2013
Dulce Rosa, 2015
The Prime Ministers: Soldiers and Peacemakers, 2015

Television music

East of Eden (ABC miniseries), 1981
Moonlighting (ABC series theme), 1985
Beauty and the Beast (CBS series theme), 1989

Do You Know the Muffin Man? (CBS movie), 1990
Call of the Wild (CBS movie), 1993
Buffalo Girls (CBS movie), 1995
Tuskegee Airmen (HBO miniseries), 1996
Mutiny (NBC movie), 1999
The Mists of Avalon (TNT movie), 2002
Saving Milly (CBS movie), 2005
The Shunning (movie), 2011
Liz & Dick (movie), 2012
The Confession (movie), 2013
When Calls the Heart (series), 2013

Concert music

"Summerland," from the ballet Trinity (2d mvt), for orch, choir, rock ens, 1970
Scenes of Summer, sym. suite, 1973
Serenade, ob, str, 1973
Conc., vn, str orch, 1975
Conc., va, chbr orch, 1977
Conc. no.2, vn, orch, 1981
Ode to Orion, Fantasy, solo hn, orch, 2005

Opera

Lazarus and his Beloved (1, K. Gibran) 1977, sym. suite, 1981
Journey to Cordoba (1, R. Sparks) 1995
Concierto para Mendez (1, R. Sparks), 2006
Tanis in America (1, R. Sparks), 2009

Bibliography

M. Humphrey: "Lee Holdridge: Matching the Music to the Moment," *Hollywood Reporter* (22 Jan 1988)
L. Barth: "Lee Holdridge: a Man of Many Styles," *The Score* xix/3 (2004), 13, 20, 22

WARREN M. SHERK/R

Hopkins, Kenyon

(*b* Coffeyville, KS, 15 Jan 1912; *d* Princeton, NJ, 7 April 1983). American composer, arranger, recording artist, and conductor. He studied theory and composition at Oberlin College and Temple University, where he graduated in 1933. In New York he arranged for Andre Kostelanetz and Paul Whiteman, and for radio and theater. Hopkins joined the Coast Guard during World War II, and returned to a variety of musical activities. During the 1950s he was primary composer and arranger for Radio City Music Hall.

In spite of working mostly in New York, Hopkins was part of the new wave of Hollywood composers in the 1950s who eschewed the heavy sound of classic symphonic scoring and introduced a less-is-more, often jazz-influenced sound into the Hollywood of the post-studio era. His total score for *Twelve Angry Men* (1957) is only eight minutes in length.

Hopkins's first feature score, for Elia Kazan's controversial production of Tennessee Williams's *Baby Doll* (1956), fuses naive lyricism and sensual jazz with a touch of rock-and-roll. Previously he had produced an effective jazz score for Rossen's *The Hustler* (1961). For Sydney Lumet's *The Fugitive Kind* (1960), Hopkins created an intimately minimalist score that both plays against and accentuates the darker Tennessee Williams mythos. He introduced twelve-tone techniques into *The Strange One* (1957). Most of his films from this period produced soundtrack LPs.

Hopkins recorded for Cadence, ABC Paramount Capitol, MGM, and Verve records. His albums include *Shock!*, *Panic!*, *Son of Shock*, and other classic examples of what is now called Space Age Pop. Due to contractual issues some of these albums were credited to the Creed Taylor Orchestra. Hopkins was music director for CBS (1963–4) and Paramount Pictures television (1970–73), and served as music supervisor for television films during this period.

Works

Film scores

Baby Doll (dir. E. Kazan), 1956
The Strange One (dir. J. Garfein), 1957
12 Angry Men (dir. S. Lumet), 1957
The Fugitive Kind (dir. S. Lumet), 1960
Wild River (dir. E. Kazan), 1960
The Hustler (dir. R. Rossen), 1961
Wild in the Country (dir. P. Dunne), 1961
The Yellow Canary (dir. B. Kulik), 1963
The Cara Williams Show (dir. K. Brasselle), 1964
Lilith (dir. R. Rossen), 1964
Mister Buddwing (dir. D. Mann), 1966
This Property Is Condemned (dir. S. Pollack), 1966
Doctor, You've Got to Be Kidding! (dir. P. Tewksbury), 1967
A Lovely Way to Die (dir. D. Rich), 1968
Downhill Racer (dir. M. Ritchie), 1969
The Tree (dir. M. Ritchie), 1969

Television music

Once Upon a Christmas Tree (dir. K. Browning), 1959
East Side/West Side (dir. R. Winston), 1963

To Tell the Truth, 1963
What's My Line?, 1963
20th Century, 1963
The Reporter (dir. J. Weidman), 1964
Hawk (dir. A. Sloane), 1966
The Secret of Michelangelo (dir. M. Fruchtman), 1968
Barefoot in the Park (dir. C. Rondeau), 1970
Love, American Style (dir. Rondeau), 1970
The Undersea World of Jacques Cousteau (dir. J. Thompson), 1970
The Young Lawyers (dir. M. Zagor), 1970
Mannix (dir. R. Levinson and W. Link), 1970–71
Mission: Impossible (dir. B. Geller), 1970–72
Funny Face (dir. C. Kleinschmitt), 1971
The Brady Bunch (dir. S. Schwartz), 1971–3
The New Healers (dir. Kowalski), 1972
Women in Chains (dir. B. Kowalski), 1972
The Devil's Daughter (dir. J. Szwarc), 1973
The World Turned Upside Down (dir. R. Guenette), 1973
Lincoln: Trial by Fire (dir. E. Spiegel), 1974

Orchestral

Sym. in 2 Movts
Town and Country Dances, chbr orch

Bibliography

G. Bachmann: "Composing for Films: Kenyon Hopkins Interviewed," *Film and TV Music*, xvi/5 (1957), 15–16

K. Hopkins: "Notes on Three Scores: The Strange One, Twelve Angry Men, Baby Doll," *Film and TV Music*, xvi/5 (1957), 12–15

ROSS CARE

Horner, James (Roy)

(*b* Los Angeles, 14 Aug 1953; *d* Santa Barbara, CA, 22 June 2015). American film composer and conductor. The son of the Bohemian American production designer Harry Horner, James Horner studied at the RCM, where his teachers included György Ligeti. He moved to California in the early 1970s and attended the University of the Pacific and then USC. He then earned the master's degree in composition and music theory at UCLA, where he also taught music theory and worked on a doctorate; his professors included Paul Chihara. In 1978

Horner scored a series of films for the American Film Institute (including *The Watcher*), and in 1979 he began scoring feature-length films, including work for B-movie producer Roger Corman.

Horner often incorporated electronic elements, choral or solo vocal music (including wordless female voices), and Celtic and other "world music" elements. He scored a large number of science fiction and action films, and also many dramas and children's films. Horner also wrote TV scores ("Amazing Stories," etc.) and themes ("The CBS Evening News," 2006–), music for short films (including Epcot Center's *Captain EO*), studio and THX logo themes, and several concert works. Some of his movie themes (such as for *Aliens* and *Glory*) have become familiar through recycling in trailers for other movies.

Horner won Grammys for "Somewhere Out There" (from *An American Tail*), "Glory," and the Celine Dion song "My Heart Will Go On" (from *Titanic*); he also won two Oscars and two Golden Globes for *Titanic* (for score and song). The soundtrack album for that film sold twenty-four million copies worldwide, making Horner a multimillionaire.

Works

Film and television scores

(film scores unless otherwise noted)
Battle beyond the Stars (dir. J.T. Murakami), 1980
Humanoids from the Deep (dir. B. Peeters), 1980
48 Hrs. (dir. W. Hill), 1982
Star Trek II: the Wrath of Khan (dir. N. Meyer), 1982
The Dresser (dir. P. Yates), 1983
Gorky Park (dir. M. Apted), 1983
Krull (dir. Yates), 1983
Star Trek III: the Search for Spock (dir. L. Nimoy), 1984
Alamo Jobe (TV, episode of "Amazing Stories"), 1985
Cocoon (dir. R. Howard), 1985
Commando (dir. M.L. Lester), 1985
The Pied Piper of Hamelin (TV, episode of "Faerie Tale Theatre"), 1985
Aliens (dir. J. Cameron), 1986
An American Tail (dir. D. Bluth), 1986
The Name of the Rose (dir. J.-J. Annaud), 1986
Willow (dir. Howard), 1988
Field of Dreams (dir. P.A. Robinson), 1989
Glory (dir. E. Zwick), 1989
Honey, I Shrunk the Kids (dir. J. Johnston), 1989
Cutting Cards (TV, episode of "Tales from the Crypt"), 1990
An American Tail: Fievel Goes West (dir. P. Nibbelink and S. Wells), 1991

Crossroads (theme), 1992
Fish Police (TV, theme), 1992
Patriot Games (dir. P. Noyce), 1992
Swing Kids (dir. T. Carter), 1993
Legends of the Fall (dir. E. Zwick), 1994
Apollo 13 (dir. Howard), 1995
Braveheart (dir. M. Gibson), 1995
Titanic (dir. Cameron), 1997
Deep Impact (dir. M. Leder), 1998
The Mask of Zorro (dir. M. Campbell), 1998
Mighty Joe Young (dir. R. Underwood), 1998
Bicentennial Man (dir. C. Columbus), 1999
How the Grinch Stole Christmas (dir. Howard), 2000
The Perfect Storm (dir. W. Petersen), 2000
A Beautiful Mind (dir. Howard), 2001
Enemy at the Gates (dir. Annaud), 2001
House of Sand and Fog (dir. V. Perelman), 2003
Troy (dir. Petersen), 2004
The Legend of Zorro (dir. Campbell), 2005
The CBS Evening News (TV, theme), 2006
The Boy in the Striped Pajamas (dir. M. Herman), 2008
The Spiderwick Chronicles (dir. M. Waters), 2008
Avatar (dir. Cameron), 2009
The Karate Kid (dir. H. Zwart), 2010
Day of the Falcon (dir. Annaud), 2011
The Amazing Spider-Man (dir. M. Webb), 2012
First in Flight (short, dir. B. Hess), 2012
For Greater Glory: the True Story of Cristiada (dir. D. Wright), 2012
The Lost Berserker (short, dir. C. Coleman and J.F. Sullivan), 2012
Reflections on Titanic (dir. E. W. Marsh), 2012
Starship Valiant: Legacy (short, dir. B. Foster), 2014, with others
The 33 (dir. P. Riggen), 2015
Living in the Age of Airplanes (dir. B.J. Terwilliger), 2015
One Day in Auschwitz (dir. S. Purcell), 2015
Southpaw (dir. A. Fuqua), 2015
Wolf Totem (dir. Annaud), 2015
The Magnificent Seven (dir. Fuqua), 2016, with S. Franglen

Concert music

Conversations, 1976
Spectral Shimmers, 1977
A Forest Passage, 2000
Pas de Deux, 2014

Bibliography

L. Kendall and J. Bond: "Letters about James Horner's *Titanic*," *Film Score Monthly* iii/3 (1997)

A. Ross: "Oscar Scores," *The New Yorker* (9 March 1998)

DURRELL BOWMAN/R

Howard, James Newton

(*b* Los Angeles, 9 June 1951). American composer. Starting the piano at the age of four, he undertook classical studies at the Music Academy of the West (Santa Barbara, California) and the University of Southern California (Los Angeles), but left formal education in favor of work as a studio musician (although he later studied orchestration with the West Coast jazz arranger Marty Paich). He toured with Elton John in 1975 and 1976, and at that time began arranging and conducting for the rock star. During the late 1970s and early 1980s he continued to perform, arrange, and produce through collaborations with Bob Seger, Rod Stewart, Olivia Newton-John, Randy Newman, Cher, Chaka Khan, and others.

Howard found his niche when he was commissioned to compose for a film (*Head Office*) in 1985. By the 1990s he was scoring dramas (*Grand Canyon*, *The Prince of Tides*), action films (*The Fugitive*), romantic comedies (*My Best Friend's Wedding*), and Westerns (*Wyatt Earp*). By the early 2000s he was considered one of Hollywood's most talented and versatile composers, adding thrillers (especially those of director M. Night Shyamalan, including *The Sixth Sense*, *Signs*, and *The Village*), animated films (*Dinosaur*), and big-budget fantasy epics (*King Kong*) to his resumé. His understanding of both the traditional orchestra and more contemporary pop idioms kept him in demand. In addition, he has employed non-Western music in his compositions as appropriate (African sounds in *Blood Diamond*, choir and Japanese shakuhachi in *Snow Falling on Cedars*).

He enjoyed a long-running television hit with the theme for "ER," and partnered with another popular composer, Hans Zimmer, on *Batman Begins* (2005) and the even more successful *The Dark Knight* (2008). In 2009 his first concert commission, a twenty-minute orchestral work titled *I Will Plant a Tree*, had its début by the Pacific Symphony in Costa Mesa, California.

Works

(*selective list*)

Film scores

Flatliners (dir. J. Schumacher), 1990
Pretty Woman (dir. G. Marshall), 1990

Grand Canyon (dir. L. Kasdan), 1991
The Man in the Moon (dir. R. Mulligan), 1991
The Prince of Tides (dir. B. Streisand), 1991
Glengarry Glen Ross (dir. J. Foley), 1992
Alive (dir. F. Marshall), 1993
Dave (dir. I. Reitman), 1993
The Fugitive (dir. A. Davis), 1993
Wyatt Earp (dir. L. Kasdan), 1994
Outbreak (dir. W. Petersen), 1995
Restoration (dir. M. Hoffman), 1995
Waterworld (dir. K. Reynolds), 1995
Space Jam (dir. J. Pytka), 1996
The Devil's Advocate (dir. T. Hackford), 1997
My Best Friend's Wedding (dir. P.J. Hogan), 1997
Runaway Bride (dir. G. Marshall), 1999
The Sixth Sense (dir. M.N. Shyamalan), 1999
Snow Falling on Cedars (dir. S. Hicks), 1999
Dinosaur (dir. E. Leighton and R. Zondag), 2000
Unbreakable (dir. Shyamalan), 2000
Atlantis: the Lost Empire (dir. G. Trousdale and K. Wise), 2001
Signs (dir. Shyamalan), 2002
Peter Pan (dir. Hogan), 2003
Collateral (dir. M. Mann), 2004
Hidalgo (dir. J. Johnston), 2004
The Village (dir. Shyamalan), 2004
Batman Begins (dir. C. Nolan), 2005, with H. Zimmer
The Interpreter (dir. S. Pollack), 2005
King Kong (dir. P. Jackson), 2005
Blood Diamond (dir. E. Zwick), 2006
Lady in the Water (dir. Shyamalan), 2006
I Am Legend (dir. F. Lawrence), 2007
Michael Clayton (dir. T. Gilroy), 2007
The Dark Knight (dir. Nolan), 2008, with Zimmer
Defiance (dir. Zwick), 2008
Duplicity (dir. T. Gilroy), 2009
Inhale (dir. B. Kormákur), 2010
The Last Airbender (dir. Shyamalan), 2010
Love & Other Drugs (dir. Zwick), 2010
Nanny McPhee Returns (dir. S. White), 2010
Salt (dir. P. Noyce), 2010
The Tourist (dir. F.H. von Donnersmarck), 2010
Gnomeo & Juliet (dir. K. Asbury), 2011, with C. Bacon and E. John
The Green Hornet (dir. M. Gondry), 2011
Green Lantern (dir. M. Campbell), 2011
Larry Crowne (dir. T. Hanks), 2011
Water for Elephants (dir. F. Lawrence), 2011
The Bourne Legacy (dir. T. Gilroy), 2012

Darling Companion (dir. L. Kasdan), 2012
The Hunger Games (dir. G. Ross), 2012
Snow White and the Huntsman (dir. R. Sanders), 2012
After Earth (dir. Shyamalan), 2013
The Hunger Games: Catching Fire (dir. Lawrence), 2013
Parkland (dir. P. Landesman), 2013
Cut Bank (dir. M. Shakman), 2014
The Hunger Games: Mockingjay Part 1 (dir. Lawrence), 2014
Maleficent (dir. R. Stromberg), 2014
Nightcrawler (dir. D. Gilroy), 2014
Pawn Sacrifice (dir. Zwick), 2014
Concussion (dir. P. Landesman), 2015
The Hunger Games: Mockingjay Part 2 (dir. Lawrence), 2015
Fantastic Beasts and Where to Find Them (dir. D. Yates), 2016
The Huntsman: Winter's War (dir. C. Nicolas-Troyan), 2016
Detroit (dir. K. Bigelow), 2017
The Lotto (dir. G. Noffsinger), 2017
Roman J. Israel, Esq. (dir. D. Gilroy), 2017
Red Sparrow (dir. Lawrence), 2018
Saved (dir. C.R. Notarile), 2018

Television music

Go Toward the Light (TV movie), 1988
Descending Angel (TV movie), 1990
The Image (TV movie), 1990
Revealing Evidence: Stalking the Honolulu Strangler, 1990
Somebody Has to Shoot the Picture (TV movie), 1990
2000 Malibu Road (theme), 1992
A Private Matter (TV movie), 1992
ER (theme), 1994
The Sentinel (theme), 1996
From the Earth to the Moon (one episode), 1998
Gideon's Crossing (theme), 2000
What Lives Inside (one episode), 2015
All the Way (TV movie), 2016
Mario and Luigi's Almost Not-so Near Death Experience (TV movie), 2017
A Series of Unfortunate Events (five episodes), 2017

Bibliography

M. Schelle: *The Score: Interviews with Film Composers* (Los Angeles, 1999) 175–96

J. Burlingame: "He Scores, They Shoot: the Unusual Twist of 'Unbreakable'," *Los Angeles Times* (25 Nov 2000)

J. Burlingame and S. Knolle: "Billion Dollar Composer: James Newton Howard," *Daily Variety* (17 July 2006)

E. Heine: *James Newton Howard's Signs: a Film Score Guide* (Lanham, MD, 2016)
V. Hexel: *Hans Zimmer and James Newton Howard's "The Dark Knight": a Film Score Guide* (Lanham, MD, 2016)
A. Gadzinski: *James Newton Howard's Soundtrack zu "Michael Clayton" (2007): Filmmusik auf der Höhe ihrer Zeit* (diss., U. of Vienna, 2017)

JON BURLINGAME/R

Isham, Mark

(*b* New York, 7 Sept 1951). American composer and trumpeter. Born into a musical family, he learned the piano and violin at an early age before taking up the trumpet. He left high school and moved to San Francisco, where he played classical trumpet. Once there, he quickly took an interest in jazz and rock, especially the music of Miles Davis, Wayne Shorter, Chick Corea, Carlos Santana, and Cold Blood. He also became involved with the electronic music scene in San Francisco. Isham has released several solo jazz albums and has collaborated with such artists as the Rolling Stones, Willie Nelson, Joni Mitchell, and Bruce Springsteen. Isham has also been a prolific film composer, although he did not initially intend to pursue film music as a career. In 1982 an electronic piece for Chinese instruments and synthesizers made its way into the director Carroll Ballard's hands, and he was asked to compose the score for the film *Never Cry Wolf.* Since 1990 Isham has been a notably prolific and versatile composer, working closely with directors Alan Rudolph and Paul Haggis. Many of his film scores, particularly early ones including *Reversal of Fortune* and *Point Break,* combine Isham's interest in electronic music with orchestral instruments. Other scores reflect his background in jazz, such as *Short Cuts, The Cooler, Bad Lieutenant: Port of Call New Orleans,* and the period films *Mrs. Parker and the Vicious Circle* and *Quiz Show.* Director Brian De Palma admired Isham's mournful trumpet work and specifically sought him out to score his *The Black Dahlia.* His warm, lush score for *A River Runs Through It,* a departure from his sparer style, earned him an Academy Award nomination.

Works

(*selective list*)

Film and television scores

(*film scores unless otherwise noted*)
Never Cry Wolf (dir. C. Ballard), 1983
Mrs. Soffel (dir. G. Armstrong), 1984

The Times of Harvey Milk (dir. R. Epstein), 1984
Trouble in Mind (dir. A. Rudolph), 1985
The Hitcher (dir. R. Harmon), 1986
Made in Heaven (dir. Rudolph), 1987
The Moderns (dir. Rudolph), 1988
Love at Large (dir. Rudolph), 1990
Reversal of Fortune (dir. B. Schroeder), 1990
Billy Bathgate (dir. R. Benton), 1991
Crooked Hearts (dir. M. Bortman), 1991
Little Man Tate (dir. J. Foster), 1991
Mortal Thoughts (dir. Rudolph), 1991
Point Break (dir. K. Bigelow), 1991
Cool World (dir. R. Bakshi), 1992
Of Mice and Men (dir. G. Sinise), 1992
A River Runs Through It (dir. R. Redford), 1992
Made in America (dir. R. Benjamin), 1993
Nowhere to Run (dir. Harmon), 1993
Short Cuts (dir. R. Altman), 1993
The Getaway (dir. R. Donaldson), 1994
Mrs. Parker and the Vicious Circle (dir. Rudolph), 1994
Nell (dir. M. Apted), 1994
Quiz Show (dir. Redford), 1994
Timecop (dir. P. Hyams), 1994
Home for the Holidays (dir. Foster), 1995
Losing Isaiah (dir. S. Gyllenhaal), 1995
Miami Rhapsody (dir. D. Frankel), 1995
The Net (dir. I. Winkler), 1995
Fly Away Home (dir. Ballard), 1996
Last Dance (dir. B. Beresford), 1996
Night Falls on Manhattan (dir. S. Lumet), 1996
Kiss the Girls (dir. G. Fleder), 1997
Blade (dir. S. Norrington), 1998
The Gingerbread Man (dir. Altman), 1998
At First Sight (dir. Winkler), 1999
October Sky (dir. J. Johnston), 1999
Varsity Blues (dir. B. Robbins), 1999
Rules of Engagement (dir. W. Friedkin), 2000
Life as a House (dir. Winkler), 2001
The Majestic (dir. F. Darabont), 2001
Save the Last Dance (dir. T. Carter), 2001
Moonlight Mile (dir. B. Silberling), 2002
The Cooler (dir. W. Kramer), 2003
Crash (dir. P. Haggis), 2004
Miracle (dir. G. O'Connor), 2004
Spartan (dir. D. Mamet), 2004

Kicking and Screaming (dir. J. Dylan), 2005
Racing Stripes (dir. F. Du Chau), 2005
The Black Dahlia (dir. B. De Palma), 2006
Eight Below (dir. F. Marshall), 2006
Invincible (dir. E. Core), 2006
Running Scared (dir. W. Kramer), 2006
Freedom Writers (dir. R. LaGravenese), 2007, with Will.i.am
Next (dir. L. Tamahori), 2007
Reservation Road (dir. T. George), 2007
The Express (dir. G. Fleder), 2008
Pride and Glory (dir. O'Connor), 2008
The Secret Life of Bees (dir. G. Prince-Bythewood), 2008
Bad Lieutenant: Port of Call New Orleans (dir. W. Herzog), 2009
Crossing Over (dir. W. Kramer), 2009
Fame (dir. K. Tancharoen), 2009
My One and Only (dir. R. Loncraine), 2009
The Crazies (dir. B. Eisner), 2010
Dolphin Tale (dir. C.M. Smith), 2011
The Mechanic (dir. S. West), 2011
Warrior (dir. O'Connor), 2011
Once Upon a Time (TV series), 2011–18
The Factory (dir. M. O'Neill), 2012
The Lucky One (dir. S. Hicks), 2012
Stolen (dir. West), 2012
42 (dir. B. Helgeland), 2013
Homefront (dir. G. Fleder), 2013
The Inevitable Defeat of Mister & Pete (dir. G. Tillman jr), 2013, with A. Keys
Mob City (TV series), 2013
Beyond the Lights (dir. Prince-Bythewood), 2014
Blood & Oil (TV series), 2015
The Great Gilly Hopkins (dir. S. Herek), 2015
The Longest Ride (dir. G. Tillman jr), 2015
Papa: Hemmingway in Cuba (dir. B. Yari), 2015
Septembers of Shiraz (dir. W. Blair), 2015
American Crime (TV series), 2015–16
The Accountant (dir. O'Connor), 2016
Fallen (dir. S. Hicks), 2016
A Family Man (dir. M. Williams), 2016
Mechanic: Resurrection (dir. D. Gansel), 2016
Mr. Church (dir. Beresford), 2016
Once Upon a Time: Evil Reigns Once More, 2016
Instrument of War (dir. A.T. Anderegg), 2017
Let It Fall: Los Angeles 1892–1992 (dir. J. Ridley), 2017
Megan Leavey (dir. G. Cowperthwaite), 2017
Once Upon a Time: the Final Battle Begins (TV movie), 2017

Sun Dogs (dir. J. Morrison), 2017
Cloak & Dagger (TV series), 2018
Duck Duck Goose (dir. C. Jenkins), 2018

Bibliography

R. Hershon and D. Kraft: "Mark Isham," *Film Music Around the World*, ed. R. Larson (San Bernadino, CA, 1987), 71–4

D. Morgan: "Carnival of the Animals: Mark Isham on *Never Cry Wolf* and *Fly Away Home*," *Knowing the Score: Film Composers Talk About the Art, Craft, Blood, Sweat, and Tears of Writing Music for Cinema*, ed. D. Morgan (New York, 2000), 185–94

J. Woodard: "Mark Isham: Bumping into Film, Longing for Jazz," *Jazz Times* xxxvii/2 (2007), 32–6

DAN BLIM/R

Jackson, Howard (Manucy)

(*b* St. Augustine, FL, 8 Feb 1898; *d* St. Augustine, 4 Aug 1966). American composer, conductor, arranger, music director, and pianist. He learned to play the piano from his mother who was a pianist. As a teenager, Jackson played piano for vaudeville shows and at movie theaters. He studied harmony and counterpoint with Rubin Goldmark, a student of Dvořák. He served as conductor and music arranger for Fanchon and Marco, the vaudeville dance troupe that performed elaborate live stage shows before feature films in the mid-1920s. For the Broadway stage he composed music for Earl Carroll's Vanities, George White's Scandals, and Ziegfeld Follies. By 1928 he was in California, where he arranged music for two stage productions at the Hollywood Playhouse. He found success with his arrangements of Negro spirituals for *Hearts in Dixie* (1929) and for other early sound musicals. After a stint at Columbia in the mid-1930s, where his music became associated with a handful of Three Stooges short films, he settled in at Warner Bros. where he worked almost exclusively from 1936 to 1964. In addition to his work on close to two hundred feature films, he was a prolific composer of music for documentaries, short films, travelogues, trailers, and industrial films, as well as U.S. Army orientation films during World War II. Drawing on his experience with live-action shorts at Columbia and Universal, he found a niche in the genre at Warner Bros., where for nearly three decades he composed music for hundreds of the studio's shorts. These topical films covered a potpourri of subjects, such as animal antics, comedies, musicals, and educational and sports films. For ten years, beginning in 1948, he supplied music to shorts produced by Dudley, including lavishly filmed VistaVision travelogues released by Paramount. In addition to composing music for industrial films for Trans World Airlines, Union Pacific, and others, he arranged music for radio programs sponsored by Chrysler and Goodyear.

Works

(selective list)

Film scores

(as music director and/or arranger)
Broadway (dir. P. Fejos), 1929
Hearts in Dixie (dir. P. Sloane), 1929
Sunny Side Up (dir. D. Butler), 1929
The Great Gabbo (dir. J. Cruze), 1930
And So They Were Married (dir. E. Nugent), 1936

(as composer)
Sing Sinner Sing (dir. H. Christy), 1933
This Day and Age (dir. C. DeMille), 1933
Beloved (dir. V. Schertzinger), 1934
Glamour (dir. W. Wyler), 1934
It Happened One Night (dir. F. Capra), 1934, uncredited
Dizzy Dames (dir. W. Nigh), 1935
Counterfeit (dir. E. Kenton), 1936
The King Steps Out (dir. J. von Sternberg), 1936
Mr. Deeds Goes to Town (dir. F. Capra), 1936
Torchy Runs for Mayor (dir. R. McCarey), 1939
River's End (dir. R. Enright), 1940
Law of the Tropics (dir. R. Enright), 1941
Singapore Woman (dir. J. Negulesco), 1941
You're in the Army Now (dir. L. Seiler), 1941
Wild Bill Hickok Rides (dir. R. Enright), 1942
Club Havana (dir. E. Ulmer), 1945
Lullaby of Broadway (dir. D. Butler), 1951
Appointment in Honduras (dir. J. Tourneur), 1953
Run for Cover (dir. N. Ray), 1955
Cry Terror! (dir. A. Stone), 1958
Yellowstone Kelly (dir. G. Douglas), 1959
The Lost World (dir. I. Allen), 1960, with others
Sergeant Rutledge (dir. J. Ford), 1960
Merrill's Marauders (dir. S. Fuller), 1962

(title songs)
Hearts in Dixie (dir. P. Sloane), 1929
Run for Cover (dir. N. Ray), 1955

Stage

Tattle Tales, music revue, New York, 1933 [collab. with others]

Orchestral

Lazy Rhapsody, 1929 [sym. jazz]

WARREN M. SHERK

Jarre, Maurice

(*b* Lyons, France, 13 Sept 1924; *d* Malibu, CA, 28 March 2009). French composer. He studied engineering at the University of Lyons and at the Sorbonne, then attended the Paris Conservatoire, studying percussion with Passerone and composition with Honegger and Joseph Martenot, inventor of the ondes martenot. He served in the army during World War II, and in the late 1940s played percussion in the navy band, with the Orchestre Radio-Symphonique, and with the Compagnie Renaud-Barrault, where he became friends with Boulez and Delerue. When Jean Vilar became director of the Théâtre National Populaire, he made Jarre his musical director, resident composer, and conductor. In 1952 Georges Franju asked him to write the score for *Hôtel des invalides*. The film went on to become a minor classic, and Jarre turned henceforth almost exclusively to film music, writing scores for many French directors, including Jacques Demy, Alain Resnais, and Jean-Paul Rappeneau. His score for *Cybéle* (1961) brought him to the attention of American producer Sam Spiegel, which led to Jarre's first Hollywood scores: *The Crack in the Mirror* (1960), *The Big Gamble* (1961), and *The Longest Day* (1962). In 1962, David Lean commissioned the score for *Lawrence of Arabia*, originally to be co-written by Jarre, Khachaturian, and Britten. After the latter two dropped out, Richard Rogers was briefly considered, before the entire score was given to Jarre. Thus began a collaboration that would produce four films and three Academy Awards for the composer, for *Lawrence of Arabia, Doctor Zhivago* (1965), and *A Passage to India* (1984). After the immense success of *Lawrence of Arabia*, Jarre moved permanently to the United States, where he worked with some of the biggest directors in Hollywood, notably John Frankenheimer, Joseph Hardy, John Huston, Paul Mazursky, Alfred Hitchcock, and Peter Weir. But he never abandoned his European roots, scoring films for such luminaries as Luchino Visconti, Franco Zeffirelli, and Volker Schlöndorff. Jarre became, along with Delerue, France's most prominent and sought-after film composer of the second half of the twentieth century. In addition to his three Academy Awards, he received Oscar nominations for his contributions to *Cybèle* (1961), *The Life and Times of Judge Roy Bean* (1972), *Witness* (1985), *Gorillas in the Mist* (1988), and *Ghost* (1989). He received British Academy Awards for *Witness* and *Dead Poets Society* (1989), and a special César Award in 1985. He was the father of the composer Jean-Michel Jarre.

Jarre wrote more than 180 scores for film and television, as well as ballets, orchestral works, incidental music, and operas. His early concert music reflected his interest in twelve-note composition, in contrast to the more popular style of his theater works, of which the ballet *Notre Dame de Paris*, written in 1964 for the Paris Opéra, was the most successful. Jarre's earlier film scores use sparse, chamber music scoring, for example in *Cybèle*, written for double bass, zither, and flute. His eight scores for the poignant films of Franju were subtle but evocative. Once in Hollywood, however, he preferred a richer, more symphonic style, using full orchestral forces. A ceaseless experimenter, he took advantage of the exotic locations and subjects of Lean's films: the sweeping score for *Lawrence of Arabia* made extensive use of chromatic modes and wide interval leaps to evoke immense panoramas, and included in its scoring the ondes martenot, an instrument not used before in an American film. *Doctor Zhivago's* melancholy score suggests the influence of composers such as Borodin, and makes use of the balalaika, as well as Russian folksongs and modes. For the score of *Ryan's Daughter* (1970), however, Jarre and director Lean decided against the evocation of traditional Irish music. His scores for Luchino Visconti's *La caduta degli dei* (1969) and Volker Schlöndorff's *Die Blechtrommel* (1979) both use an orchestra made up entirely of cellos and double basses, augmented only by human whistling and the fujara, a Slovakian folk instrument. In the 1980s Jarre became interested in blending electronic sounds with those of traditional orchestral and occasionally non-Western instruments, often by means of digital sampling techniques. His most successful film scores involving electronics are *Witness* (1985), which required only five performers to evoke the early American feel of the Amish community; and *The Year of Living Dangerously* (1982), a subdued, evocative score that makes use of traditional Javanese gamelan. In *Jacob's Ladder* (1990), he again attempted a score that was "atmospheric rather than thematic," making use, alongside electronics, of Indian instruments and a Bulgarian women's chorus.

Works

Film scores

(English-language films only)

The Big Gamble (dir. R. Fleischer and E. Williams), 1961
Lawrence of Arabia (dir. D. Lean), 1962
The Longest Day (dir. K. Annakin, A. Marton, and B. Wicki), 1962
Behold a Pale Horse (dir. F. Zinneman), 1964

The Train (dir. J. Frankenheimer), 1964
The Collector (dir. W. Wyler), 1965
Doctor Zhivago (dir. D. Lean), 1965
Gambit (dir. R. Neame), 1966
Grand Prix (dir. J. Frankenheimer), 1966
The Night of the Generals (dir. A. Litvak), 1966
The Professionals (dir. R. Brooks), 1966
Barbarella (dir. R. Vadim), 1967
The Extraordinary Seaman (dir. J. Frankenheimer), 1968
Five Card Stud (dir. H. Hathaway), 1968
The Fixer (dir. J. Frankenheimer), 1968
Isadora (dir. K. Reisz), 1968
Villa Rides (dir. B. Kulik), 1968
The Only Game in Town (dir. G. Stevens), 1969
Topaz (dir. A. Hitchcock), 1969
Plaza Suite (dir. A. Hiller), 1970
Ryan's Daughter (dir. D. Lean), 1970
The Effect of Gamma Rays on Man-in-the-Moon Marigolds (dir. P. Newman), 1972
The Life and Times of Judge Roy Bean (dir. J. Huston), 1972
Pope Joan (dir. M. Anderson), 1972
Ash Wednesday (dir. L. Peerce), 1973
The Island at the Top of the World (dir. R. Stevenson), 1973
The Mackintosh Man (dir. J. Huston), 1973
Mrs. Uschyck (dir. G. Quinn), 1973
Mr. Sycamore (dir. P. Kohner), 1974
Great Expectations (dir. J. Hardy), 1975
Mandingo (dir. R. Fleischer), 1975
The Man Who Would Be King (dir. J. Huston), 1975
Posse (dir. K. Douglas), 1975
The Silence (dir. J. Hardy), 1975
The Last Tycoon (dir. E. Kazan), 1976
Shout at the Devil (dir. P. Hunt), 1976
March or Die (dir. D. Richards), 1977
The Prince and the Pauper (dir. D. Fleischer), 1977
Ishi, the Last of His Tribe (dir. R. Miller), 1978
Mourning Becomes Electra (dir. N. Havinga), 1978
One of a Kind (dir. H. Winer), 1978
Two Solitudes (dir. L. Chetwynd), 1978
The Users (dir. J. Hardy), 1978
The American Success Company (dir. W. Richert), 1979
The Black Marble (dir. H. Becker), 1979
Magician of Lublin (dir. M. Golan), 1979
Winter Kills (dir. W. Richert), 1979
Enola Gay: the Men, the Mission, the Atomic Bomb (dir. D. Rich), 1980
The Last Flight of Noah's Ark (dir. C. Jarrott), 1980
Lion of the Desert (dir. M. Akkad), 1980
Resurrection (dir. D. Petrie), 1980

Chu Chu and the Philly Flash (dir. D. Rich), 1981
Shogun (dir. J. London), 1981
Taps (dir. H. Becker), 1981
Coming Out of the Ice (dir. W. Hussein), 1982
Don't Cry, It's Only Thunder (dir. P. Werner), 1982
Firefox (dir. C. Eastwood), 1982
The Year of Living Dangerously (dir. P. Weir), 1982
Young Doctors in Love (dir. G. Marshall), 1982
Samson and Delilah (dir. L. Philips), 1983
Top Secret! (dir. J. Abrahams, D. Zucker, and J. Zucker), 1983
Dreamscape (dir. J. Ruben), 1984
A Passage to India (dir. D. Lean), 1984
The Sky's No Limit (dir. D. Rich), 1984
The Bride (dir. F. Roddam), 1985
Enemy Mine (dir. W. Peterson), 1985
Mad Max: Beyond Thunderdome (dir. G. Miller and G. Ogilvie), 1985
The Mosquito Coast (dir. P. Weir), 1985
Witness (dir. P. Weir), 1985
Apology (dir. R. Bierman), 1986
Solarbabies (dir. A. Johnson), 1986
Tai-Pan (dir. D. Duke), 1986
Fatal Attraction (dir. A. Lyne), 1987
Gaby: a True Story (dir. L. Mandoki), 1987
Julia and Julia (dir. P. Del Monte), 1987
No Way Out (dir. R. Donaldson), 1987
Buster (dir. D. Green), 1988
Distant Thunder (dir. R. Rosenthal), 1988
Gorillas in the Mist (dir. M. Apted), 1988
Moon Over Parador (dir. P. Mazursky), 1988
The Murder of Mary Phagan (dir. W. Hale), 1988
Wildfire (dir. Z. King), 1988
Chances Are (dir. E. Ardolino), 1989
Dead Poets Society (dir. P. Weir), 1989
Enemies, A Love Story (dir. P. Mazursky), 1989
Prancer (dir. J. Hancock), 1989
After Dark, My Sweet (dir. J. Foley), 1990
Almost An Angel (dir. J. Cornell), 1990
Ghost (dir. J. Zucker), 1990
Jacob's Ladder (dir. A. Lyne), 1990
Solar Crisis (dir. R. Sarafian), 1990
Fires Within (dir. G. Armstrong), 1991
Only The Lonely (dir. C. Columbus), 1991
School Ties (dir. R. Mandel), 1992
Shadow of the Wolf (dir. J. Dorfmann and P. Magny), 1992
Fearless (dir. P. Weir), 1993
Mr. Jones (dir. M. Figgis), 1993
A Walk In The Clouds (dir. A. Arau), 1995

The Mirror Has Two Faces (dir. B. Streisand), 1996
The Sunchaser (dir. M. Cimino), 1996
Sunshine (dir. I. Szabó), 1999
I Dreamed of Africa (dir. H. Hudson), 2000
Uprising (dir. J. Avnet), 2001

Bibliography

J. Burlingame: "Maurice Jarre," *The Cue Sheet*, xiii/3 (July 1997), 21–6
J. Westby: "Film scores of Maurice Jarre," *The Cue Sheet*, xiii/3 (July 1997), 27–34

MARK BRILL

Jones, Quincy (Delight) [Q]

(*b* Chicago, IL, 14 March 1933). American producer, composer, arranger, and musician. Epitomizing a fusion of record production excellence and astute artistic sensibility, he is best known for his success with Michael Jackson. However, he also has remarkable credentials for his creative and commercial consistency with other artists, for his work as a record label executive, and for his own composing and performing career. Few producers have been as well regarded within the music industry or have had such recognition beyond it, and his solo releases have incorporated every major aspect of the African American popular music experience, including hip-hop. By the early 2010s he had won the greatest number of Grammy Awards for a non-classical artist. He has worked with key creative figures spanning generations in the music business.

Jones grew up in Seattle, where he played with the young Ray Charles as a teenager before taking up a scholarship at Boston's Schillinger House (now the Berklee School of Music) in 1950; he earned money for his education by playing strip-joint gigs at night. With an appetite for jazz fueled by work with Count Basie, Jones played trumpet with Lionel Hampton, touring internationally for several years from 1951, and later became an arranger in Dizzy Gillespie's band; he has described Gillespie and Miles Davis as his creative essence. Having spent much of the 1950s on the road, toward the end of the decade he opted to remain in Paris, where he studied composition with the renowned pedagogue Nadia Boulanger and arranged music for the French record label Barclay.

A disastrous experience managing an eighteen-piece big band based in Europe between 1959 and 1960 saddled Jones with debt for several years after the event. His efforts to combine composing with band management resulted in the sale of his publishing companies, but heightened his awareness of the industry's business aspects. After returning to the United States, he became the first black A&R executive at Mercury Records and served as its vice president from 1961 to

1968. Lesley Gore's "It's my party" was an early success and other hits followed while he remained creatively active in freelance production and arranging, notably with Charles and Frank Sinatra.

After paying off his European debts, Jones freed himself from the restrictive record executive role. Instead, he followed his artistic temperament: he began a career in film and television soundtrack composition with Sidney Lumet's *The Pawnbroker* (1964) and raised his profile with other cinema hits such as *In the Heat of the Night* (1967) and the TV drama "Ironside." By 1969 he was a solo artist with A&M Records, generating albums, such as *Walking in Space* (A&M, 1969), that combined orchestral, jazz-oriented arrangements and funky, groove-driven rhythms; *Walking in Space* was recorded in three days and won a Grammy Award for Best Instrumental Jazz Performance. Jones's dramatic music for the television series "Roots" (1977) garnered acclaim and his second gold album after *Body Heat* (A&M, 1974).

A simultaneous spell in pop production began inauspiciously, with the chart failure of Aretha Franklin's album *Hey Now Hey (The Other Side of the Sky)* (Atlantic, 1973). However, there were major commercial results in the second half of the decade with the Brothers Johnson, Rufus & Chaka Khan, and Jackson, whose album *Off the Wall* (Epic, 1979) foreshadowed future success. Despite his developing strong pop and R&B credentials, Jones was perceived as an unusual choice for Jackson because of his extensive jazz credentials. However, *Off the Wall* revealed that Jones's creative instincts were as sharp as ever.

Jones achieved greater solo success with *The Dude* (A&M, 1981). It is worth noting that he never sang on his own records; instead he hired vocalists and concentrated on playing to his production and arranging strengths. These found full form on Jackson's album *Thriller* (Epic, 1982), which had become the best-selling album of all time by 1984, though its sales have since been surpassed. In 1980, Jones had also established his own record label imprint, Qwest, and gained major hits including George Benson's platinum album *Give Me the Night* (Warner Bros.,1980) and Patti Austin and James Ingram's duet "Baby, Come to Me" (Qwest, 1982).

In a decade of major successes in the 1980s, Jones produced the multi-million-selling humanitarian single "We are the World," for which he steered the superstar talents of several eras and consolidated his impeccable industry status. After scoring the soundtrack and serving as co-producer for the hit movie *The Color Purple* (1986), producing Jackson's follow-up to *Thriller, Bad* (Epic, 1987), and his own platinum Grammy Award-winning album *Back on the Block* (Qwest, 1989), Jones was less visibly active in the pop world. However, with his platinum release *Q's Jook Joint* (Qwest, 1995), Jones continued extending the scope of his creative activities. In the early twenty-first century he became known as the consummate artistic mentor, philosopher, humanitarian, and entrepreneur, in which roles he shared the benefits of his experiences and ambitions.

Bibliography

M. Clifford, ed.: *The Illustrated Encyclopedia of Black Music* (New York, 1982)
R. Horricks and T. Middleton: *Quincy Jones* (New York, 1985)
C.S. Ross: *Listen Up: the Lives of Quincy Jones* (New York, 1990)
D. Seay: "Quincy Jones, Record-Making Executive," *Billboard*, 16 Dec. 1995: 36.
E. Olsen, P. Verna, C. Wolff, eds.: *The Encyclopedia of Record Producers* (New York, 1999)
Q. Jones: *Q: the Autobiography of Quincy Jones* (New York, 2001)

MIKE ALLEYNE

Kamen, Michael

(*b* New York, 15 April 1948; *d* London, 18 Nov 2003). American film composer, orchestral arranger, conductor, oboist, horn player, and keyboardist. The son of a dentist and a teacher, Kamen attended the High School of Music & Art with classmates the singer-songwriter Janis Ian and fellow future film composer Mark Snow (*b* Martin Fulterman). He then attended the Juilliard School alongside Leonard Slatkin and played the oboe under Jean Morel. With Fulterman and the cellist-composer Dorian Rudnytsky he formed the rock/classical fusion band the New York Roll & Roll Ensemble, which performed in 1967 as Janis Ian's backing ensemble, played in 1969 in Leonard Bernstein's Young People's Concerts with the New York PO at Lincoln Center, and made a series of albums from 1968 to 1972.

Kamen's early combination of orchestral music with rock firmly established the direction of his career. He composed orchestral works, including several dozen film and TV scores, ballets (beginning with *Rodin mis en vie* for the Harkness Ballet, 1973), saxophone (1990) and guitar concertos, and the symphonic poem *The New Moon in the Old Moon's Arms* (2000). His work in popular music continued during the 1970s with contributions on the horn, oboe, and synthesizer to the soundtrack for *Godspell* and to albums by Jim Croce, Tim Curry, and others; he also served as music director and performer on David Bowie's tour for *Diamond Dogs* (1974). He contributed orchestral arrangements for such British artists as Pink Floyd (especially *The Wall*, 1979, but also including solo projects by David Gilmour and Roger Waters), Eurythmics, Queen, the Who, and Kate Bush. In addition, he worked with the Irish band the Cranberries, Canadian artists Liona Boyd, Bryan Adams, and Rush (*Counterparts*, 1993), and such US artists as Indigo Girls, Queensrÿche, and Metallica (*S&M*, 1999).

Kamen's earliest film scores were for little-known shorts and TV and feature films from 1976 onward. His reputation brought him more prominent scoring assignments in the early 1980s, and he became particularly associated with action-adventure films, working at least twice with the directors Terry Gilliam, Richard Donner, and John McTiernan.

In 1996 Kamen created the Mr. Holland's Opus Foundation (named for the popular 1995 film about a music teacher) in order to support music education; he arranged and conducted *Diana, Princess of Wales: Tribute* (1997), and he similarly arranged and conducted the string orchestra for the 2002 memorial "Concert for George [Harrison]". The music for *Edge of Darkness* won a British Academy of Film and Television Arts Award for best original television music; *Robin Hood: Prince of Thieves* won a Grammy for best pop instrumental performance, and its theme song, "(Everything I Do) I Do It for You," likewise won a Grammy; *An American Symphony* from *Mr. Holland's Opus* won a Grammy for Best Instrumental Arrangement; and the *S&M* version of Metallica's *The Call of Ktulu* won the 2000 Grammy for Best Rock Instrumental Performance. Kamen was diagnosed with multiple sclerosis in 1997 and died of a heart attack in 2003.

Works

Film and television scores

(film scores unless otherwise noted)
The Next Man (dir. R.C. Sarafian), 1976
Polyester (dir. J. Waters), 1981
The Dead Zone (dir. D. Cronenberg), 1983
Brazil (dir. T. Gilliam), 1985
Edge of Darkness (TV mini-series), 1985
Amazing Stories (TV), 1986
Highlander (dir. R. Mulcahy), 1986
Mona Lisa (dir. N. Jordan), 1986
Shoot for the Sun (TV, dir. I. Knox), 1986
Adventures in Babysitting (dir. C. Columbus), 1987
Lethal Weapon (dir. R. Donner), 1987, with E. Clapton
Someone to Watch Over Me (dir. R. Scott), 1987
Suspect (dir. P. Yates), 1987
The Adventures of Baron Munchausen (dir. Gilliam), 1988
Crusoe (dir. C. Deschanel), 1988
Die Hard (dir. J. McTiernan), 1988
Lethal Weapon 2 (dir. Donner), 1989, with E. Clapton and D. Sanborn
Licence to Kill (dir. J. Glen), 1989
Road House (dir. R. Herrington), 1989
Die Hard 2 (dir. R. Harlin), 1990
The Krays (dir. P. Medak), 1990
Hudson Hawk (dir. M. Lehmann), 1991, with R. Kraft
The Last Boy Scout (dir. T. Scott), 1991
Robin Hood: Prince of Thieves (dir. K. Reynolds), 1991
Lethal Weapon 3 (dir. Donner), 1992, with Clapton and Sanborn
Tales from the Crypt, 1992–3

Last Action Hero (dir. McTiernan), 1993
Splitting Heirs (dir. R. Young), 1993
The Three Musketeers (dir. S. Herek), 1993
Don Juan DeMarco (dir. J. Leven), 1994, with R.J. Lange
Die Hard: With a Vengeance (dir. McTiernan), 1995
Mr. Holland's Opus (dir. Herek), 1995
101 Dalmatians (dir. Herek), 1996
Event Horizon (dir. P.W.S. Anderson (as P. Anderson)), 1997, with Orbital
The Winter Guest (dir. A. Rickman) 1997
From the Earth to the Moon (TV mini-series), 1998
Jerry Seinfeld: "I'm Telling You for the Last Time" (dir. M. Callner), 1998
Lethal Weapon 4 (dir. Donner), 1998, with Clapton and Sanborn
The Iron Giant (dir. B. Bird), 1999
X-Men (dir. B. Singer), 2000
Band of Brothers (TV mini-series), 2001
Mr. Dreyfuss Goes to Washington (dir. R. Lyon (as R.V. Lyon)), 2001
Open Range (dir. K. Costner), 2003

Orchestral

Rodin mis en vie ballet, 1973
Sax Conc., 1990
The New Moon in the Old Moon's Arms, 2000

Writings

"Rock: Can the Atomic Oboe be Far Behind?" *New York Times* (2 Jan 1972)

Bibliography

D. Morgan: "Adaptation," *Knowing the Score: Film Composers Talk About the Art, Craft, Blood, Sweat, and Tears of Writing Music for Cinema*, ed. D. Morgan (New York, 2000), 202–3

F. Groult: "Mr. Kamen's Opus," *Underscores: le magazine de la musique de film* (3 July 2008) [in French, interview made in 2001]

DURRELL BOWMAN/R

Kanno, Yōko

(*b* Miyagi, Japan, 19 March 1964). Japanese pianist, arranger, and composer. Since 1988 she has composed and arranged select studio tracks for a wide range of mostly female Japanese pop artists. Her longest musical relationship has been with the singer Maaya Sakamoto, with whom she collaborated on eight albums between 1997 and 2009. Her initial forays into film music were for Japanese video games. Combining her pop studio work and game scoring, she developed a typically Japanese approach to film scoring based on polyglot styles, studio ensemble production, and embellished orchestral arrangements. Her first distinctive work accompanied a range of anime (Japanese animation) titles, mostly based on shojo manga (girls' comics), which included theme music for *Please Save my Earth* (1994) and *The Vision of Escaflowne* (1996). Their floral vocal harmonies and swirling mix of real and synthesized instrumentation aptly interpret the baroque richness of shojo manga. Kanno's break-out score was for the television series "Cowboy BeBop" (1998), which employed a range of jazz idioms to color the series' characters with an emotional complexity unexpected for anime at the time. Successive anime series established her creative power in moulding character through musical portraiture: "Earth Girl Arjuna" (1998), "Brain Powerd" (1998), "Ghost in the Shell: Stand Alone Complex" (2002–5), and "Darker than Black" (2007). Her feature film scores for live action titles, most of which have been screened at international film festivals, evidence her most delicate orchestrations and arrangements: *Woman of Water* (2002), *Tokyo. Sora* (2002), *Kamikaze Girls* (2004), *Ashura* (2005), *Su-ki-da* (2005), and *Honey and Clover* (2006).

Works

Film scores

(selective list)
Please Save my Earth, 1994
Takeru Yamato (dir. T. Okawara), 1994
Boku wa benkyo ga dekinai (dir. Y. Yamamoto), 1996
Natsu jikan no otonatachi (dir. T. Nakashima), 1997
Beautiful Sunday (dir. Nakashima), 1998
Escaflowne: the Movie (dir. K. Akane and Y. Takei), 2000, with H. Mizoguchi and I. Zur
Cowboy Bebop: the Movie (dir. S. Watanabe, with T. Okamura, Y. Takei, and H. Okiura), 2001
Tokyo.Sora (dir. H. Ishikawa), 2002
Woman of Water (dir. H. Sugimori), 2002
Kamikaze Girls (dir. Nakashima), 2004
Ashura-jô no hitomi (dir. Y. Takita), 2005
Su-ki-da (dir. H. Ishikawa), 2005
Hachimitsu to Clover (dir. M. Takada), 2006
The Show Must Go On (dir. J.-R. Han), 2007
Surely Someday (dir. S. Oguri), 2010
Petaru dansu (dir. H. Ishikawa), 2013
Our Little Sister (dir. H. Koreeda), 2015

Television music

Macross Plus, 1994
Escaflowne, 1996
Brain Powerd, 1998
Cowboy Bebop, 1998
Turn-A Gundam, 1999–2000
Arjuna, 2001
Ghost in the Sheel: Stand Alone Complex, 2002–5
Wolf's Rain, 2003–4
Darker Than Black, 2007
Macross Frontier, 2008
Aquarion EVOL, 2012
Gochisôsan, 2013–14
Terror in Resonance, 2014
Onna jōushu Naotora, 2017

Video-game music

Romance of the Three Kingdoms, 1985
Nobunaga's Ambition: Zenkokuban, 1986
Genghis Khan, 1987
Nobunaga's Ambition: Sengoku Gunyūden, 1988
Ishin No Arashi, 1989
Nobunaga's Ambition: Bushō Fuunroku, 1990
Uncharted Waters, 1990
Nobunaga's Ambition: Haōden, 1992
Uncharted Waters 2: New Horizons, 1993
Nobunaga's Ambition: Tenshōki, 1994
Napple Tale: Arsia in Daydream, 2000
Cowboy Bebop, 2001
Cowboy Bebop: Tsuitou no yakyoku, 2005
Ragnarok Online 2, 2007
Continent of the Ninth, 2011
Ragnarok Online 2: Legend of the Second, 2012

Bibliography

R. Bridges and N. Manabe: *Yoko Kanno's "Cowboy Bebop" Soundtrack* (New York, 2017)

PHILIP BROPHY/R

Kaper, Bronislaw

(*b* Warsaw, Poland, 5 Feb 1902; *d* Los Angeles, 26 April 1983). American composer of Polish birth. He was educated at the Warsaw Conservatory and was active as a composer and pianist in Warsaw, Berlin, Vienna, London, and Paris before settling in Hollywood and joining the staff of MGM in 1940. He was one of a number of versatile musicians of European origin and orientation who helped to create Hollywood music. He composed a number of popular songs besides his articulate and closely knit film scores. His best work dates from the 1960s: *Mutiny on the Bounty* (1962) and *Lord Jim* (1965) reveal a pronounced flair for musical depiction of the sea and tropical landscapes. Kaper's theme from *Green Dolphin Street* (1947) became popularized when recorded in a jazz idiom by Miles Davis; his theme for *Invitation* (1952) was also widely recorded. Kaper's dramatic score for the science fiction film *Them!* (1954) is largely regarded as one of the classics of horror movie music of the period; regrettably, a "Fugue for Ants" that Kaper wrote for the film was ultimately deleted from the final soundtrack. After twenty-eight years and more than one hundred scores for MGM, Kaper, like many Hollywood composers in the mid-1960s, found film work declining as pop music became more prevalent. As a result he turned to composing for television.

Kaper's style, which was securely rooted in late European Romanticism, has fluency, melodic charm, and fine, elegant craftsmanship; like many Hollywood composers he established a useful rapport between popular and symphonic music (e.g., from his Oscar-winning score, the song "Hi-lili, Hi-lo" in *Lili*, 1953, and the use of extended ballet in *The Glass Slipper*, 1955). While his music is warm, colorful, and melodically appealing, it is rarely meretricious and, within the confines of its idiom, achieves a certain individuality of voice. Other notable scores of his include *Gaslight* (1944), *The Naked Spur* (1952), "The FBI" (television theme, 1965), *Tobruk* (1967), and *The Way West* (1967).

Bibliography

T. Thomas: *Music for the Movies* (Los Angeles, 1973, expanded and updated 2/1997), 103–13

W.F. Krasnoborski: "A Conversation with B. Kaper," *Soundtrack Collector's Newsletter*, no.2 (1975), 13; no.3 (1976), 3; repr. in *Motion Picture Music*, ed. L. Van de Ven (Mechelen, Belgium, 1980), 122

E. Bernstein: "Interview with Bronislau Kaper," *Film Music Notebook*, iv/2 (1978), 12–28

T. Thomas: *Film Score: the View from the Podium* (South Brunswick, NJ, and New York, 1979), 115–25

V.J. Francillon, ed.: *Film Composers Guide* (Los Angeles, 1990, 3/1996), 223–4

CHRISTOPHER PALMER/RANDALL D. LARSON

Karlin, Fred(erick James)

(*b* Chicago, 16 June 1936; *d* Culver City, CA, 26 March 2004). American composer and arranger. As a teenager in Chicago he began playing trumpet. After graduating from Amherst College in 1956, he returned to Chicago and played at the Jazz Limited Club. After moving to New York, he wrote stage band arrangements, conducted recordings, and assisted Rayburn Wright at Eastman

School's summer Arrangers' Laboratory-Institute and at Radio City Music Hall. In addition to Wright, he studied privately with William Russo and Tibor Serly. His first feature film score was for *Up the Down Staircase* (1967). After writing "Come Saturday Morning" his career took a new direction with his Academy Award for "For All we Know" from *Lovers and Other Strangers* (1970). On other film songs he collaborated with his wife, Meg Welles Karlin, sometimes credited as Tylwyth Kymry, her adopted Welsh name. The couple, who met in New York when he became music director for her jazz quintet, relocated to Los Angeles in 1969. He collected American music in all forms, and his own music reflected his knowledge and interest in folk, jazz, Dixieland, and Civil War and minstrel songs. After the success of his music for *The Autobiography of Miss Jane Pittman* in 1974, he went on to score nearly one hundred television movies. He founded and led the Fred Karlin Film Scoring Workshop at ASCAP from 1988 to 1996. In the 1990s he concentrated on writing and teaching, produced a documentary on Jerry Goldsmith, and made jazz arrangements of film themes for recordings. *On the Track*, cowritten with Wright, became the authoritative manual on contemporary film scoring.

Works

(selective list)

Film scores

The Last Man, 1965
Up the Down Staircase (dir. R. Mulligan), 1967
Yours, Mine, and Ours (dir. M. Shavelson), 1968
The Sterile Cuckoo (dir. A. Pakula), 1969
The Baby Maker (dir. J. Bridges), 1970
Lovers and Other Strangers (dir. C. Howard), 1970
The Little Ark (dir. J. Clark), 1972
Westworld (dir. M. Crichton), 1973
Futureworld (dir. R. Heffron), 1976
Leadbelly (dir. G. Parks), 1976
Greased Lightning (dir. M. Schultz), 1977
Loving Couples (dir. J, Smight), 1980
Strawberry Road (dir. K. Kurahara), 1991

Film songs

(names of lyricists are given in parentheses)
"Come Saturday Morning" (D. Previn) from The Sterile Cuckoo (dir. A. Pakula), 1969
song score, including "People Come, People Go" (T. Kymry) from The Baby Maker (dir. J. Bridges), 1970
"For All we Know" (R. Royer, J. Griffin) from Lovers and Other Strangers (dir. C. Howard), 1970
"Come Follow, Follow Me" (M. Karlin) from The Little Ark (dir. J. Clark), 1972

Television music

The Autobiography of Miss Jane Pittman, 1974
Minstrel Man, 1977
Jacqueline Susann's Valley of the Dolls, 1981
Dream West, 1985
Robert Kennedy and his Times, 1985

Concert music

Reflections, 1993
The Peace Seeker (C. Hai), orch, folk-rock band, vocalists, boys choir, 3 actors, 1998

MSS in American Heritage Center, University of Wyoming

Writings

On the Track: a Guide to Contemporary Film Scoring (New York, 1990, rev. 2004)
Listening to Movies: the Film Lover's Guide to Film Music (New York, 1994)

Bibliography

ASCAP Biographical Dictionary (New York, 4/1980), 261
D. Mangodt: "Music Is my Life: an Interview with Fred Karlin," *Soundtrack!* xiii/52 (Dec 1994), 19–21
Obituaries: *Los Angeles Times*, 4 May 2004; *Variety*, weekly ed., 10 May 2004

WARREN M. SHERK

Karpman, Laura

(*b* La Jolla, CA, 1 March 1959). American composer for film, television, and the concert stage. She began composing at the age of seven, later studying with Nadia Boulanger and completing the PhD in composition at the Juilliard School under Milton Babbitt. After moving to Los Angeles in 1989, she established herself as a film and television composer. She scored twenty-one episodes of the documentary series "The Living Edens" (1997–2002), for which she received four Emmys. She then composed the music for Steven Spielberg's miniseries *Taken* (2002), and worked on other series, including *Odyssey 5*, *In Justice*, *Masters of Science Fiction*, and *Craft in America*. Since 2004 she has also composed extensively for video games, producing a symphonic score for *EverQuest II*, among others. Her multimedia opera *Ask your Mama*, based on a text by Langston Hughes and created in collaboration with Jessye Norman, received its première on 16 March 2009 in Carnegie Hall, and her concert music has been performed at Lincoln Center and the Tanglewood Music Festival. She has received the Ives Fellowship from the American Academy of Arts and Letters and two ASCAP

Foundation grants, and has participated in residencies at Tanglewood, the MacDowell Colony, and the Sundance Institute.

Works

Film scores

(*selective list*)
Lover's Knot (dir. P. Shaner), 1995
Break Up (dir. P. Marcus), 1998
Restless (dir. J. Gilfillan), 1998
The Annihilation of Fish (dir. C. Burnett), 1999
Climb Against the Odds (dir. K. Carlson and S. Michelson), 1999
Fish Don't Blink (dir. C. DeBus), 2002
Girl Play (dir. L. Friedlander), 2004
The Last Run (dir. J. Segal), 2004
A Monkey's Tale (dir. E. Goldberg), 2006
Man in the Chair (dir. M. Schroeder), 2007
Out at the Wedding (dir. Friedlander), 2007
Center Stage: Turn It Up (dir. S. Jacobson), 2008
The Butch Factor (dir. C. Hines), 2009
The Tournament (dir. S. Mann), 2009
Whiz Kids (dir. T. Shepard), 2009
Nothing Special (dir. A.G. Combs), 2010
Something Ventured (dir. D. Geller and D. Goldfine), 2011
Black Nativity (dir. K. Lemmons), 2013, with R. Saadiq
The Galapagos Affair: Satan Came to Eden (dir. Geller and Goldfine), 2013
Regarding Susan Sontag (dir. N.D. Kates), 2014, with N. Kroll-Rosenbaum
States of Grace (dir. H. Cohen and M. Lipman), 2014
CODE: Debugging the Gender Gap (dir. R. Hauser (as R. Hauser Reynolds)), 2015, with N. Kroll-Rosenbaum
The Making of a Mensch (dir. T. Shlain), 2015
The State of Marriage (dir. J. Kaufman), 2015, with Kroll-Rosenbaum
The Cinema Travellers (dir. S. Abraham and A. Madheshiya), 2016
Paris Can Wait (dir. E. Coppola), 2016
Phil's Camino (dir. A. O'Neil and J. Lewis), 2016
The Beguiled (dir. S. Coppola), 2017
The Reagan Show (dir. S. Pettengill and P. Velez), 2017
Step (dir. A. Lipitz), 2017, with Saadiq
93Queen (dir. P. Eiselt), 2018
Every Act of Life (dir. Kaufman), 2018, with Kroll-Rosenbaum
Inventing Tomorrow (dir. L. Nix), 2018
Set It Up (dir. C. Scanlon), 2018
Step Sisters (dir. C. Stone III), 2018, with Saadiq

Television music

My Brother's Wife, 1989
Rita Hayworth: Dancing Into the Dream, 1990
The Broken Cord, 1992
A Child Lost Forever: the Jerry Sherwood Story, 1992
Doing Time on Maple Drive, 1992
A Mother's Revenge, 1993
World of Discovery, 1993–4
A Century of Women, 1994
Moment of Truth 1994
If Someone Had Known, 1995
A Woman of Independent Means, 1995
Blue Rodeo, 1996
A Promise to Carolyn, 1996
Sex, Censorship, and the Silver Screen, 1996
The Living Edens, 1997
Labor of Love, 1998
Dash and Lillly, 1999
Run the Wild Fields, 2000
Egypt beyond the Pyramids, 2001
Carrie, 2002
Odyssey 5, 2002
Taken, 2002
Reversible Errors, 2004
Masters of Science Fiction, 2007
Craft in America, 2007–17
Sins of the Mother, 2010
Makers: Women Who Make America, 2014
A Christmas Melody, 2015
Toni Braxton: Unbreak my Heart, 2016
Underground, 2016–17
Love by the 10th Date, 2017

Video-game music

EverQuest II, 2004
EverQuest II: the Spitpaw Saga, 2005
EverQuest II: the Fallen Dynasty, 2006
EverQuest II: Kingdom of Sky, 2006
EverQuest: Prophesy of Ro, 2006
Field Commander, 2006
Untold Legends: Dark Kingdom, 2006
EverQuest: the Buried Sea, 2007
Kinect Disneyland Adventures, 2011
Kung Fu Panda 2, 2011
Guardians of Middle-Earth, 2012

Project Spark, 2014
Mission ISS, 2017

Opera

Escape, 1997
110 Project, 2009
Ask your Mama, 2009
Balls, 2016
Wilde Tales, 2016

Large ensemble

Duets, Trios, Quintets, 1986
Six of One, Half Dozen of Another, 1987
Switching Stations, 1990
Butter my Tongue, 2000
Plum Sugar, 2000
Scat, 2005
The Transitive Property of Equality, 2005
Heebie Jeebies, 2006
Plucky, 2009
Out of Bounds, 2011
The Hidden World of Girls, 2012
Siren Songs, 2015

Chamber works

Matisse and Jazz, 1987
String Quartet, 1987
Invariably Paganini, 1988
Greetings from L.A., 1989
Portrait of Jaco, 1989
Song Pictures, 1989
Caprices for String Trio, 1990
Love is Not All, 1999
Rounds, 2000
About Joshua, 2003
Conversations for Piano Four Hands, 2004
Melting Pot, 2005
Take 4, 2008
Now All Set, 2011
Waxing Nostalgic, 2011
Different Lanes, 2012

Solo works

Saxmaniac, 1987
Untitled, 1998

Common Tone, 2004
Stick Trick, 2015

Bibliography

L. Hunter: "Exploring the Concert Saxophone Repertoire: Laura Karpman's 'Matisse and Jazz'," *Saxophone Journal*, viii (1989), 32–7

J. Bond: "'Taken' with her Music (Interview with Laura Karpman)," *Film Score Monthly*, viii/6 (2003), 30–31

M. Carlsson: "Women in Film Music, or How Hollywood Learned to Hire Female Composers for (at Least) Some of their Movies," *IAWM Journal*, xi/2 (2005), 16–9

J. Kelly: *In Her Own Words: Conversations with Composers in the United States* (Urbana, IL, 2013)

JAMES DEAVILLE/R

Kaun, Bernhard Theodor Ludwig

(*b* Milwaukee, WI, 5 April 1899; *d* Baden-Baden, Germany, 3 Jan 1980). German composer of American birth, son of Hugo Kaun. Largely self-taught as a composer, he was tutored by his father, and studied violin and piano while attending Gymnasium in Berlin. During World War I he served in the German army, playing clarinet in a military band. After the war he arranged and conducted for RCA Victor in Berlin for several years. In 1924 he moved to the United States, where he worked as a music copyist in New York, conducted at the Alhambra Theater in Milwaukee (1924), and taught at the Eastman School of Music (1925–8). Recognized particularly for his orchestrations, he arranged music from Richard Wagner's music dramas for the New York release of Fritz Lang's film *Siegfried* and orchestrated Howard Hanson's *Legend of Beowulf* and Organ Concerto.

In 1930 Kaun was invited to Hollywood by Heinz Roemheld, music director of Universal Studios. Over the following decade he worked for both Warner Bros. and Paramount, composing music for over 170 films; his first assignments included the first full-length score for a sound film (*Heaven on Earth*, 1931) and music for *Frankenstein* (1931). Highly sought after as an orchestrator, he orchestrated now classic film scores for Max Steiner (*King Kong*, 1933; *Gone with the Wind*, 1939), Erich Wolfgang Korngold, Ernst Toch (*Peter Ibbetson*, 1935), Dimitri Tiomkin (*Lost Horizon*, 1937), and Charlie Chaplin, as well as orchestrating his own scores. His eclectic, coloristic style, influenced by the music of Richard Strauss, Jean Sibelius, Maurice Ravel, and early Arnold Schoenberg, was praised by Igor Stravinsky. In 1941 Kaun left Hollywood for New York, where he devoted himself to composing concert music. He returned to Germany in 1953, where he conducted the Graunke Orchestra (Munich) until 1963.

Works

(selective list)

Film and television scores

(film score unless otherwise noted)

Frankenstein (dir. J. Whale), 1931
Heaven on Earth (dir. R. Mack), 1931
Doctor X (dir. M. Curtiz), 1932
I am a Fugitive from a Chain Gang (dir. M. LeRoy), 1932
The Mystery of the Wax Museum (dir. M. Curtiz), 1932
20,000 Years at Sing Sing (dir. M. Curtiz), 1932
A Farewell to Arms (dir. F. Borzage), 1933, collab. W.F. Harling and others
Luxury Liner (dir. L. Mendes), 1933
Death Takes a Holiday (dir. M. Leisen), 1934, collab. M. Roder and others
The Firebird (dir. W. Dieterle), 1934 [after Stravinsky]
The Scarlet Empress (dir. J. von Sternberg), 1934, collab. J. Leipold and others
Oil for the Lamps of China (dir. M. LeRoy), 1935, collab. H. Roemheld
She (dir. L. C. Holden and I. Pichel), 1935, collab. M. Steiner
The Black Legion (dir. A. Mayo), 1936
The Petrified Forest (dir. A. Mayo), 1936
Story of Louis Pasteur (dir. W. Dieterle), 1936, collab. Roemheld
The Walking Dead (dir. M. Curtiz), 1936
The Patient in Room 18 (dir. B. Connolly and C. Wilbur), 1937
The Return of Doctor X (dir. V. Sherman), 1939
Forest Murmurs (dir. J. Hoffman and S. Vorkapich), 1947
Special Delivery (dir. J. Brahm), 1955
Alle Wege führen heim (dir. H. Deppe), 1957
Lassie (TV series), 1958–9

Other works

Entice Italienne; Zeitstimmung, female vv
Sketches, suite, orch, 1927
Nederländisches Volkslied, 1v, pf, 1929–30
Romantic Sym., C, 1930s, rev. 1960s
Qnt, ob, str, 1940
Sinfonia concertante, hn, orch, 1940
The Vagabond, suite, orch, 1956 [based on film and TV scores]
20 pf pieces

Bibliography

W.H. Rosar: "Music for the Monsters: Universal Pictures' Horror Film Scores of the Thirties," *Quarterly Journal of the Library of Congress*, xl (1983), 390–421

C. McCarty: *Film Composers in America: a Filmography 1911–1970* (Oxford, 2000)

WILLIAM ROSAR

Korngold, Erich Wolfgang

(*b* Brno, Moravia [now Czech Republic], 29 May 1897; *d* Hollywood, CA, 29 Nov 1957). Austrian composer. The second son of the eminent music critic Julius Korngold (1860–1945), he was a remarkable child prodigy composer. In 1906 he played his cantata *Gold* to Gustav Mahler, who pronounced him a genius and recommended that he be sent to Zemlinsky for tuition. At age eleven he composed the ballet *Der Schneemann*, a sensation when it was first performed at the Vienna Court Opera (1910); he followed this with a Piano Trio and a Piano Sonata in E that so impressed Artur Schnabel that he championed the work all over Europe. Richard Strauss remarked: "One's first reaction that these compositions are by a child are those of awe and concern that so precocious a genius should follow its normal development. . . . This assurance of style, this mastery of form, this characteristic expressiveness, this bold harmony, are truly astonishing!" Giacomo Puccini, Jean Sibelius, Bruno Walter, Arthur Nikisch, Engelbert Humperdinck, Karl Goldmark, and many others were similarly impressed.

Korngold was fourteen when he wrote his first orchestral work, the *Schauspiel Ouvertüre*; his *Sinfonietta* appeared the following year. His first operas, *Der Ring des Polykrates* and *Violanta*, were completed in 1914. With the appearance of the opera *Die tote Stadt*, completed when he was twenty-three and acclaimed internationally after its dual première in Hamburg and Cologne (1920), his early fame reached its height, and he briefly outstripped Richard Strauss as the most performed composer from German-speaking countries. After completing the first Left Hand Piano Concerto, commissioned by Wittgenstein in 1923, he began his fourth and arguably greatest opera, *Das Wunder der Heliane* (1927), and started arranging and conducting classic operettas by Johann Strauss and others. He also began teaching opera and composition at the Vienna Staatsakademie and was awarded the title Professor *honoris causa* by the president of Austria.

Max Reinhardt, with whom Korngold had collaborated on versions of *Die Fledermaus* and *La belle Hélène*, invited him to Hollywood in 1934 to work on his celebrated film of Shakespeare's *A Midsummer Night's Dream*. Over the next four years, Korngold pioneered a new art form, the symphonic film score, in such classics as *Captain Blood, The Prince and the Pauper*, and *Anthony Adverse* (for which he won the first of two Academy Awards). The Anschluss prevented him from staging his fifth opera, *Die Kathrin*, and he remained in Hollywood composing some of the finest music written for the cinema. *The Adventures of Robin Hood* (1938, winner of his second Academy Award), *The Sea Hawk* (1940), and *Kings Row* (1941) are his greatest works in the genre. Treating each film as an "opera without singing" (each character has his or her own leitmotif), he created intensely romantic, richly melodic, and contrapuntally intricate scores, the best of which are a cinematic paradigm for the tone poems of Richard Strauss and Franz Liszt. He intended that, when divorced from the moving image, these scores could stand alone in the concert hall. His style exerted a profound influence on modern film music.

After the war Korngold returned to absolute music, composing, among other works, a Violin Concerto (1937, rev. 1945) first performed by Heifetz, a Cello Concerto (1946), a Symphonic Serenade for String Orchestra (1947) given its première by Furtwängler, and the Symphony in F♯ (1947–52). His late-Romantic style, however, was completely out of step with the postwar era and when he died at the age of sixty, he believed himself forgotten. After decades of neglect, a gradual reawakening of interest in his music occurred. At the time of his centenary (1997) his works were becoming increasingly popular, appearing on major recordings and concert programs around the world. By 2010, his Violin Concerto and the opera *Die tote Stadt* had become repertoire works again, and all of his works had been recorded.

Eric Wolfgang Korngold conducting, 1936
Photofest

Works

(selective list)

Film scores

A Midsummer Night's Dream (dir. M. Reinhardt), 1934 [arr. of Mendelssohn]
Captain Blood (dir. M. Curtiz), 1935
Anthony Adverse (dir. M. Le Roy), 1936
Give Us This Night (dir. A. Hall), 1936
The Green Pastures (dir. W. Keighley), 1936 [orch sequences]
Rose of the Rancho, 1936 [one song]
Another Dawn (dir. W. Dieterle), 1937
The Prince and the Pauper (dir. Keighley), 1937
The Adventures of Robin Hood (dir. Curtiz and Keighley), 1938
Juarez (dir. Dieterle), 1939
The Private Lives of Elizabeth and Essex (dir. Curtiz), 1939
The Sea Hawk (dir. Curtiz), 1940
Kings Row (dir. S. Wood), 1941
The Sea Wolf (dir. Curtiz), 1941
The Constant Nymph (dir. E. Goulding), 1942
Between Two Worlds (dir. E.A. Blatt), 1944
Of Human Bondage (dir. Goulding), 1944
Deception (dir. I. Rapper), 1946
Devotion (dir. C. Bernhardt), 1946
Escape Me Never (dir. P. Godfrey), 1946
Magic Fire (dir. Dieterle), 1954 [arr. of Wagner]

Operas

Der Ring des Polykrates (1, J. Korngold and L. Feld, after H. Teweles), op.7, 1913, Munich, 28 March 1916
Violanta (1, H. Müller), op.8, 1914, Munich, 28 March 1916
Die tote Stadt (3, P. Schott [E.W. and J. Korngold], after G. Rodenbach: *Bruges la morte*), op.12, 1916–20, Hamburg and Cologne, 4 Dec 1920
Das Wunder der Heliane (3, Müller, after H. Kalneker), op.20, 1921–7, Hamburg, 7 Oct 1927
Die Kathrin (3, E. Decsey), op.28, 1932–7, Stockholm, 7 Oct 1939

Other stage music

Gold (cant.), solo vv, pf, 1906, lost
Der Schneemann (ballet pantomime, E.W. Korngold), 1908–9, Vienna, 4 Oct 1910 [orchd Zemlinsky, rev. Korngold 1913]
Much Ado about Nothing (incid music, W. Shakespeare), op.11, 1918–19, 6 May 1920
The Silent Serenade (stage comedy, E.W. Korngold, B. Reisfeld, and W. Okie), op.36, 1946, Vienna, 26 March 1951

Orchestral

Schauspiel Ouvertüre, op.4, 1911
Sinfonietta, op.5, 1912
Sursum corda, sym. ov., op.13, 1919
Pf Conc., C♯, op.17, pf left hand, orch, 1923
Baby Serenade, op.24, small orch, 1928–9
Vn Conc., D, op.35, 1937, rev. 1945
Tomorrow, sym. poem, op.33, Mez, chorus, orch, 1942
Vc Conc., C, op.37, 1946
Sym. Serenade, B♭, str, op.39, 1947
Sym., F♯, op.40, 1947–52
Theme and Variations, op.42, school orch, 1953

Chamber and keyboard

Don Quixote, pf, pieces, 1907–8
Pf Sonata no.1, d, 1908
Pf Trio, D, op.1, 1909
Pf Sonata no.2, E, op.2, 1910
Märchenbilder, 7 pf pieces, op.3, 1910
Sonata, D, op.6, vn, pf, 1912
Str Sextet, D, op.10, 1914–16
Pf Qnt, E, op.15, 1921
Str Qt no.1, A, op.16, 1920–23
4 Little Caricatures, op.19, pf, 1926
Tales of Strauss, op.21, pf, 1927
Suite, op.23, pf left hand, str, 1928–30
Pf Sonata no.3, C, op.25, 1931
Str Qt no.2, E♭, op.26, 1933
Str Qt no.3, D, op.34, 1944–5
Romance impromptu, vc, pf, op. posth., 1946

Songs

6 einfache Lieder (J.F. von Eichendorff, E. Honold, H. Kipper, S. Trebitsch), op.9, 1911–13
[4] Abschiedslieder (C. Rosetti, A. Kerr, E. Ronsperger, E. Lothar), op.14, A, pf/orch, 1920–21
3 Lieder (H. Kaltneker), op.18, 1924
3 Lieder (K. Kobald, E. van der Straten), op.22, 1928–9
The Eternal (E. van der Straten), song cycle, op.27, 1933
4 Lieder (Shakespeare: *Othello, As You Like It*), op.31, 1937
Songs of the Clown (W. Shakespeare: *Twelfth Night*), op.29, 1937
5 Lieder (R. Dehmel, Eichendorff, H. Koch, Shakespeare), op.38, medium v, pf, 1948
Sonett für Wien (Kaltneker), op.41, Mez, pf, 1953

MSS in *US-Wc*

Principal publisher: Schott

Bibliography

KdG (S. Rode-Breymann)

E. Newman: "The Problem of Erich Korngold," *The Nation* (24 Aug 1912)

R.S. Hoffmann: *Erich Wolfgang Korngold* (Vienna, 1922)

E.W. Korngold: "Some Experiences in Film Music," *Music and Dance in California*, ed. J. Rodríguez (Hollywood, 1940), 137–9

R. Behlmer: "Erich Wolfgang Korngold: Established Some of the Film Music Basics Film Composers Now Ignore," *Films in Review*, no.182 (1967), 86–100

L. Korngold: *Erich Wolfgang Korngold* (Vienna, 1967)

J. Korngold: *Die Korngolds in Wien* (Zürich, 1991)

S. Blickensdorfer: *Erich Wolfgang Korngold: Opern und Filmmusik* (diss., U. of Vienna, 1993)

R. van der Lek, trans. M. Swithinbank: "Concert Music as Reused Film Music," *AcM*, lxvi (1994), 8–112

B.G. Carroll: *The Last Prodigy* (Portland, OR, 1997)

B. Winters: *Erich Wolfgang Korngold's "The Adventures of Robin Hood": a Film Score Guide* (Lanham, MD, 2007)

G. Wagner: *Korngold "Musik ist Musik"* (Berlin, 2008)

A. Stollberg, ed: *Erich Wolfgang Korngold: Wunderkind der Moderne oder Letzter Romantiker* (Munich, 2009)

N. Platte: "Dream Analysis: Korngold, Mendelssohn, and Musical Adaptations in Warner Bros.' *A Midsummer Night's Dream* (1935)," *19th-Century Music* xxxiv/3 (Spring, 2011), 211–36

B. Winters: "The Composer and the Studio: Korngold and Warner Bros.," *The Cambridge Companion to Film Music*, ed. M. Cooke and F. Ford (Cambridge, 2016), 51–66.

BRENDAN G. CARROLL/R

Lange, Arthur

(*b* Philadelphia, 16, April 1889; *d* Washington, DC, 7 Dec 1956). American composer, arranger, conductor, author, and pianist. He studied piano with his mother from age five. He later studied piano and violin with several teachers in Philadelphia, but was otherwise self-taught. His music career began in 1907 as a pianist and burgeoning arranger. In 1917 he joined Fred Fisher as an arranger and for the next decade wrote and arranged dance band instrumentals, notably *Dardanella*, for New York's Tin Pan Alley publishers from Leo Feist to Shapiro-Bernstein. In 1929, at the height of Lange's popularity, producer Irving Thalberg asked him to relocate to Hollywood to supervise music at Metro-Goldwyn-Mayer studios. For the next two years, Lange served as music director at MGM, where he organized the first permanent studio orchestra and helped pioneer techniques for prerecording music for playback during filming. In 1931 he became the general music director for RKO Pathé, then served in that capacity at Fox from 1932 to 1938, notably for films starring Shirley Temple. Throughout the 1930s he specialized in musical comedies, drawing on his experience with popular music and paraphrasing light classics. In 1939 he cofounded Co-Art Records, which specialized in unrecorded works by American composers, such as Charles Wakefield Cadman. A brief stint as music director for International Pictures in 1944 was followed by a decade of freelance work. After World War II, he concentrated on writing concert works as an American Romanticist, served as music director and conductor of the Santa Monica Civic Symphony, taught privately and at the Los Angeles Conservatory, and served as president of the American Society of Music Arrangers.

Works

(*selective list*)

Film scores

(*as music director*)

The Hollywood Revue (dir. C. Reisner), 1929
Devotion (dir. R. Milton), 1931
The Little Colonel (dir. D. Butler), 1935
Rebecca of Sunnybrook Farm (dir. A. Dwan), 1938

Film scores

(*as composer*)

Dynamite (dir. C.B. DeMille), 1929, with W. Axt
Cavalcade (dir. F. Lloyd), 1933, with L. De Francesco
The Great Ziegfeld (dir. R.Z. Leonard), 1936
The Great Victor Herbert (dir. A.L. Stone), 1939
Lady of Burlesque (dir. W.A. Wellman), 1943
Belle of the Yukon (dir. W.A. Seiter), 1945
Casanova Brown (dir. S. Wood), 1945
The Woman in the Window (dir. F. Lang), 1945, with H. Friedhofer
Rancho Notorious (dir. F. Lang), 1952, with H. Friedhofer

Orchestral

Water Whispers, sym. suite, 1928
A Gosling in Gotham, sym. narrative in 1 movt, 1937
The Fisherman and His Soul, sym. suite (based on O. Wilde), narr. orch, 1939, “The Witches Dance,” perf. 1941
California Suite [also known as American Pastorale], 1946–50: Antelope Valley, 1946, cond. F. Black, 20 July 1947; Big Trees, 1947, cond. A. Lange, Santa Monica, July 1948; Mount Whitney, 1950
Sym. no. 1 (Lyric-American), 1948
Arabesque, hp, orch, 1953, cond. A. Lange, Santa Monica, 3 May 1953

MSS in Arthur Lange Collection at *US-NYp*

Writings

Arranging for the Modern Dance Orchestra (New York, 1926)
Spectrotone: System of Orchestration (Beverly Hills, 1943)
"The Epigrammatic Nature of Motion Picture Music," *The Score*, iv/2 (1950), 8–9
A New and Practical Approach to Harmony (Los Angeles, 1954)

Bibliography

L. Bowling: "Arthur Lange: a Biographical Sketch," *The Cue Sheet* vii/4 (1990), 128–39 [entire issue devoted to Lange]

WARREN M. SHERK

Lava, William [Bill]

(*b* St. Paul, MN, 18 March 1911; *d* Los Angeles, 20 Feb 1971). American composer and arranger. Lava was a prolific composer of scores for animated shorts as well as theme and incidental music for numerous television series; his output also extended to feature films as well as documentary features and short subjects. After receiving education at Northwestern University, Lava studied conducting under Albert Coates in Los Angeles. Upon arriving in Hollywood in 1936, Lava began arranging music for numerous musical radio programs and scored several feature films, including a number of low-budget Westerns. During the 1940s, Lava scored numerous documentaries, many of them on World War II–based topics. In the mid-1950s, he was hired by Walt Disney Productions to compose music for several shows including "The Mickey Mouse Club" (1955–9) and *Zorro* (1957–60). Lava's extensive television credits continued his association with the Western genre with the theme and incidental music for "Cheyenne" (1955–63) and the comedy "F Troop" (1965–7). Besides television, Lava's most notable contributions were scores for dozens of animated shorts. Beginning in 1962, Lava scored cartoons for Warner Bros., taking over from the recently deceased Milt Franklyn. After Warner closed its animation studio, Lava continued to provide music for cartoons produced by DePatie-Freleng Enterprises. Lava's cartoon music differed markedly from the work of Carl Stalling and Franklyn in its increased reliance on dissonance and atonality; percussion is also more prominent in his scores. Because of the lower budgets given to these cartoons, Lava worked with smaller ensembles than Stalling and Franklyn, which further contributed to the "mechanical" quality of Lava's work for animation. Perhaps his greatest success in animation came with his scores for the *Pink Panther* cartoon series, the first of which being the Academy Award-winning *The Pink Phink* (1964); these scores extensively adapted Henry Mancini's original *Pink Panther* theme. His final cartoon score was for *Injun Trouble* (1969). Lava continued to compose for film and television in the years immediately preceding his death.

Works

Film scores

Hawk of the Wilderness (dir. J. English and W. Witney), 1938
Red River Range (dir. G. Sherman), 1938
Three Texas Steers (dir. G. Sherman), 1939
The Courageous Dr. Christian (dir. B. Vorhaus), 1940
The Nurse's Secret (dir. N.M. Smith), 1941
Shady Lady (dir. G. Waggner), 1945
Moonrise (dir. F. Borzage), 1948
Flaxy Martin (dir. R.L. Bare), 1949
Homicide (dir. F. Jacoves), 1949
Barricade (dir. P. Godfrey), 1950
Colt. 45 (dir. E.L. Marin), 1950
Highway 301 (dir. A.L. Stone), 1950
Cattle Town (dir. N.M. Smith), 1952
Retreat, Hell! (dir. J.H. Lewis), 1952
Hell Bent for Leather (dir. G. Sherman), 1960
Wall of Noise (dir. R. Wilson), 1963
Chamber of Horrors (dir. H. Averback), 1966
Chubasco (dir. A.H. Miner), 1967
Dracula vs. Frankenstein (dir. A. Adamson), 1971

Television music

The Mickey Mouse Club (1955–9)
Cheyenne (1955–63)
Disneyland (1955–63)
Zorro (1957–60)
Have Gun—Will Travel (1960–62)
Bonanza (1960–65)
Gunsmoke (1961)
The Twilight Zone (1961)
The Dakotas (1963)
F Troop (1965–7)
O'Hara, U.S. Treasury (1971–2)

Animated shorts

Good Noose, 1962
The Jet Cage; 1962
Now Hear This, 1962
Shishkabugs, 1962
Banty Raids, 1963
Devil's Feud Cake, 1963
Hare-Breadth Hurry, 1963

Mexican Cat Dance, 1963
The Million Hare, 1963
To Beep or Not to Beep, 1963
Transylvania 6–5000, 1963
The Unmentionables, 1963
Dr. Devil and Mr. Hare, 1964
A Message to Gracias, 1964
The Pink Phink, 1964
War and Pieces, 1964
Active Duck, 1965
Dial "P" for Pink, 1965
The Great De Gaulle Stone Operation, 1965
Moby Duck, 1965
An Ounce of Pink, 1965
Pickled Pink, 1965
Pinkfinger, 1965
We Give Pink Stamps, 1965
A-Haunting We Will Go, 1966
Cock a Doodle Deux-Deux, 1966
The Pink Blueprint, 1966
Go Away Stowaway, 1967
Hocus Pocus Powwow, 1968
See Ya Later Gladiator, 1968
Fistic Mystic, 1969
The Great Carrot-Train Robbery, 1969
Injun Trouble, 1969

Bibliography

The ASCAP Biographical Dictionary of Composers, Authors, and Publishers, ed. D.I. McNamara (New York, 1948, 4/1980)

W. Lava:, "Music By the Yard," *Music and Dance in California and the West*, ed. R.D. Sauners (Pasadena, 1948), 76–7, 128

B. Cotter: *The Wonderful World of Disney Television: a Complete History* (New York, 1997)

K. Whitehead: "Carl Stalling, Improviser & Bill Lava, Acme Minimalist," *The Cartoon Music Book*, ed. D. Goldmark and Y. Taylor (Chicago, 2002), 141–50

G. Webb: *The Animated Film Encyclopedia: a Complete Guide to American Shorts, Features, and Sequences, 1900–1979* (Jefferson, NC, 2006)

C.P. Lehman: *American Animated Cartoons of the Vietnam Era: a Study of Social Commentary* (Jefferson, NC, 2007)

DANIEL SHERIDAN

Legrand, Michel

(*b* Paris, France, 24 Feb 1932; *d* Paris, 26 Jan 2019). French composer, pianist, and arranger, son of the composer Raymond Legrand (*b* 1908) and brother of the singer Christiane Legrand (*b* 1930). A musical prodigy, he enrolled at the Paris Conservatoire at the age of eleven. He attended from 1943 to 1950, studied conducting with Nadia Boulanger and harmony with Henri Chaland, and graduated as a first-prize winner in composition. A Dizzy Gillespie concert in Paris in 1947 awakened his passion for jazz. In the 1950s he became a popular bandleader, singer, and songwriter, and wrote and conducted ballets for Roland Petit. In 1954 he became the bandleader and conductor for Maurice Chevalier and traveled with him to New York. That same year he recorded the album *I Love Paris*. In the late 1950s his arrangements for the album *Legrand Jazz* (1958, Col.) featured the playing of Miles Davis, Ben Webster, Art Farmer, Hank Jones, Bill Evans, and John Coltrane.

In the 1950s he also began writing film music. His first important collaborations were with some of the masters of French cinema, notably Marcel Carné, but he is indelibly linked with the emergence of the French New Wave, writing scores for directors such as Jean-Luc Godard (seven films), Agnès Varda (six films), and Jacques Demy (ten films). He appeared and performed in Varda's *Cléo de 5 à 7* (1962). He achieved his greatest success with Demy's *Les parapluies de Cherbourg* (1964), which brought worldwide recognition to both the director and the composer, including the Palme d'Or at the 1964 Cannes Film Festival. Hollywood took notice, and Legrand began working for American directors; he made four films for Joseph Losey, whose *The Go-Between* won the Palme d'Or in 1971. In 1968 he had his biggest American success with the score for Norman Jewison's *The Thomas Crown Affair*, which included the hit song "The Windmills of your Mind." Thereafter Legrand had a number of successes including *Summer of '42* (1971), and his jazz score for *Lady Sings the Blues* (1972), the biographical film about Billie Holiday. In the late 1960s Legrand moved to the United States and for the next three decades divided his efforts equally between France and Hollywood, not always with the same measure of success.

Legrand's career alternated between contemporary subjects and period pieces, and he used many different styles in his scores. From an early age Legrand's style leaned towards light popular music and jazz, and he often emphasized thematic unity, although many scores are overshadowed by a central popular theme. *Les parapluies de Cherbourg* met with considerable critical acclaim. The director's vision was to make a musical film in a completely different vein from the Hollywood musical tradition, a "mixture of poetry, color, and music." The film is entirely sung, in free verse; the lyrics were written by Demy. The direction was regulated by the music, and all aspects of the productions were subordinate to the musical rhythm. The score contains a wide range of styles, from haunting ballads such as "I will wait for you," to jazz, tangos, mambos, and several light popular melodies.

In recent years Legrand struggled to adapt his craft to contemporary musical styles. His popular idiom, well received in the 1960s and 70s, subsequently lost some of its appeal and was often modified to reflect evolving aesthetics. Subsequent achievements include the Barbra Streisand film *Yentl* (1983), the jazz score for *Dingo* (1992), co-written with Miles Davis, and the sweeping, dark music of *Les Misérables* (1996). In 1997, at age sixty-five, Legrand scored his first musical, *Le passe muraille*, which then became the Broadway show *Amour* in 2002, for which Legrand won a Tony Award nomination. This was followed by the musical *Marguerite* which premièred in London in 2008.

Legrand composed more than 220 film and television scores and recorded more than one hundred jazz, classical, and popular music albums. His jazz highlights include the album *Paris Jazz Piano* (1959) with Guy Pedersen and Gus Wallez, followed by *At Shelly's Manne-Hole* (1968, Verve) with Shelly Manne and Ray Brown; *Jazz le grand* (1979) and *After the Rain* (1982, Pablo), both with Phil Woods and Zoot Sims; *Grappelli & Legrand* (1993) with Stephane Grappelli; and *Michel Plays Legrand* (2002). He was nominated for Academy Awards for his contributions to *Les parapluies de Cherbourg, Les demoiselles de Rochefort, The Happy Ending, Pieces of Dreams, Best Friends, The Thomas Crown Affair, Summer of '42,* and *Yentl*, winning Oscars for the last three.

Works

(selective list)

Film and television scores

(film score unless otherwise noted)

Love is a Ball (dir. D. Swift), 1963
Les parapluies de Cherbourg (dir. J. Demy), 1964
The Plastic Dome of Norma Jean (dir. J. Compton), 1965
Les demoiselles de Rochefort (dir. J. Demy), 1967
Pretty Polly (dir. G. Green), 1967
How to Save a Marriage and Ruin your Life (dir. F. Cook), 1968
Ice Station Zebra (dir. J. Sturges), 1968
Sweet November (dir. R. Miller), 1968
The Thomas Crown Affair (dir. N. Jewison), 1968
Castle Keep (dir. S. Pollack), 1969
The Happy Ending (dir. R. Brooks), 1969
The Picasso Summer (dir. R. Sallin and S. Bourguignon), 1969
Play Dirty (dir. A. de Toth), 1969
A World in Music (Champion), 1969
The Go-between (dir. J. Losey), 1970
The Lady in the Car with Glasses and a Gun (dir. A. Litvak), 1970
The Magic Garden of Stanley Sweetheart (dir. L. Horn), 1970
Pieces of Dreams (dir. D. Haller), 1970
To Catch a Pebble (dir. J. Collier), 1970

Wuthering Heights (dir. R. Fuest), 1970
Brian's Song (TV movie, dir. B. Kulik), 1971
Le Mans (dir. L. Katzin), 1971
Summer of '42 (dir. R. Mulligan), 1971
Lady Sings the Blues (dir. S. Furie), 1972
One is a Lonely Number (dir. M. Stuart), 1972
Portnoy's Complaint (dir. E. Lehman), 1972
A Time for Loving (dir. C. Miles), 1972
The Adventures of Don Quixote (dir. A. Rakoff), 1973
A Bequest to the Nation (dir. J. Jones), 1973
Breezy (dir. C. Eastwood), 1973
Cops and Robbers (dir. A. Avakian), 1973
A Doll's House (dir. J. Losey), 1973
F for Fake (dir. O. Welles), 1973
40 Carats (dir. M. Katselas), 1973
Impossible Object (dir. J. Frankenheimer), 1973
The Nelson Affair (dir. J. C. Jones), 1973
The Three Musketeers (dir. R. Lester), 1973
It's Good to be Alive (dir. M. Landon), 1974
Cage without a Key (TV movie, dir. B. Kulik), 1975
Our Time (dir. P. Hyams), 1975
Sheila Levine is Dead and Living in New York (dir. S. J. Furie), 1975
Blind Sunday (TV episode, dir. L. Elikann), 1976
Gable and Lombard (dir. S. J. Furie), 1976
Gulliver's Travels (dir. P. Hunt), 1976
Jalousie (dir. N. Trintignant), 1976
Ode to Billy Joe (dir. M. Baer), 1976
The Other Side of Midnight (dir. C. Jarrott), 1977
Michel's Mixed up Musical Bird (TV episode, dir. M. Legrand), 1978
Blind Love (Legrand), 1979
Lady Oscar (dir. J. Demy), 1979
Les fabuleuses aventures du légendaire Baron de Munchausen (dir. J. Image), 1979
Falling in Love Again (dir. S. Paul), 1980
The Hunter (dir. B. Kulik), 1980
Melvin and Howard (dir. J. Demme), 1980
The Mountain Men (dir. R. Lang), 1980
Atlantic City (dir. L. Malle), 1981
Your Ticket is no Longer Valid (dir. G. Kaczender), 1981
Best Friends (dir. N. Jewison), 1982
Friends of the Family (dir. Y. Abolafia), 1982
A Woman Called Golda (dir. A. Gibson), 1982
Never Say Never Again (dir. I. Kershner), 1983
Yentl (dir. B. Streisand), 1983
The Jesse Owens Story (dir. R. Irving), 1984
Slapstick of Another Kind (dir. S. Paul), 1984
Micki & Maude (dir. B. Edwards), 1985

Promises to Keep (dir. N. Black), 1985 [television film]
Secret Places (dir. Z. Barron), 1985
As Summers Die (dir. J.-C. Tramont), 1986
Crossings (TV series, dir. K. Arthur), 1986
Casanova (TV movie, dir. S. Langton), 1987
Children and the White Whale (dir. J. Kerchbron), 1987
The Jeweller's Shop (dir. M. Anderson), 1988
Switching Channels (dir. T. Kotcheff), 1988
Eternity (dir. S. Paul), 1989
Grand Piano (Coulson), 1989
Fate (dir. S. Paul), 1990
Inspiration (dir. O. Rojas), 1990
The Jeweller's Shop (dir. M. Anderson), 1990
Mirage (dir. M. Wyn), 1990
Not a Penny More, Not a Penny Less (dir. C. Donner), 1990
The Return (Dayan), 1990
Sunday Pursuit (Zetterling), 1990
Tropical Gamble (dir. M. Wyn), 1990
Dingo (dir. R. de Heer), 1991
Mountain of Diamonds (TV movie, dir. J. Szwarc), 1991
The Pickle (dir. P. Mazursky), 1993
Prêt-à-Porter (dir. R. Altman), 1994
The Ring (TV movie, dir. A. Mastroianni), 1996
Madeline (dir. D. von Scherler Mayer), 1998
Doggy Bag (dir. F. Comtet), 1999
Cavalcade (dir. S. Suissa), 2005
The Legend of Simon Conjurer (dir. S. Paul), 2006
Disco (dir. F. Onteniente), 2008
Oscar and the Lady in Pink (dir. E. Schmitt), 2009
The Price of Fame (dir. X. Beauvois), 2014
The Guardians (dir. X. Beauvois), 2017
The Other Side of the Wind (dir. O. Welles), 2018

Bibliography

F. Porcile: "Collaborateurs de création du jeune cinéma français," *Cinéma 64*, no.89 (1964), 50–66

P. Cook: "The Sound Track," *Films in Review*, xvi (1965), 170–72; see also xx (1969), 308–10; xxii (1971), 225–8; xxii (1971), 425–8; xxvii (1976), 308–10; xxxv (1984), 48–50

L. Lyons: "Profile: Michel Legrand," *DB*, xliii/3 (1976), 34

R.S. Brown: "Music and 'Vivre sa Vie'," *US Quarterly Review of Film Studies*, v/3 (1980), 319–33

D. Rabourdin: "Entretien avec Michel Legrand," *Cinéma 81*, nos.271–2 (1981), 68–71

P. Sweeney: "The Man Who Always Knew the Score," *The Independent*, (27 Sept 1999)

R. Hill: "Donkey Skin (Peau d'âne)," *Film Quarterly*, lix/2 (2005–6), 40–44

M. Bennett: "Does the Song Really Remain the Same? *The Windmills of Your Mind* as Narrational Vehicle in *The Thomas Crown Affair* (1968 and 1999)," *The Soundtrack* vii/2 (2014): 79–88

MARK BRILL/R

Leipold, John

(*b* Hunter, NY, 26 Feb 1888; *d* Dallas, 8 March 1970). American composer, arranger, and conductor. He was largely self-taught as a musician, although he later studied composition with Ernst Toch in Los Angeles. In New York, he conducted vaudeville and light opera from 1912 to 1922, before spending four years as musical director for the Al G. Fields Minstrels, a touring theatrical group. After a stint as an arranger for Remick Music Co. from 1927 to 1928, he moved to Hollywood, finding work as a staff composer and arranger at Paramount Pictures. Starting as a music librarian under music department head Nat W. Finston, Leipold would select stock music to accompany films, often adding his own original compositions. During the 1930s and 1940s he often went uncredited when supplying additional music or arrangements for films scored by Frederick Hollander, Victor Young, and others. His work on two films with the Marx Brothers went uncredited. He was one of four composers to receive an Academy Award for Music Scoring for *Stagecoach* (1939), a film with a score based almost entirely on American folk songs. During the next two years he scored nearly a dozen Westerns for Harry Sherman Productions. Freelancing from 1942 to 1944, Leipold wrote music for numerous Columbia productions, including two films featuring the Three Stooges. By the mid-1940s his work graced three hundred films; however, after World War II his output dwindled to two dozen films, partly due to responsibilities composing and conducting for the Columbia Broadcasting System (CBS) from 1943 to 1948, notably for *Romance of the Ranchos* (1948). Beginning in 1948, Leipold independently taught composition, arranging, and counterpoint based on his self-published textbooks. From 1949 to 1952 his music accompanied a handful of films starring Gene Autry and he arranged classical music for *The Happy Time* (1952). His music appeared in films, such as *Gunfight at the O.K. Corral* (1957), as late as 1957.

Works

(*selective list*)

Film scores

(*not all scores wholly by Leipold*)

The Wild Party (dir. D. Arzner), 1929, uncredited
The Love Parade (dir. E. Lubitsch), 1930, uncredited
A Farewell to Arms (dir. F. Borzage), 1932, uncredited
Horse Feathers (dir. N.Z. McLeod), 1932, uncredited
Love Me Tonight (dir. R. Mamoulian), 1932, uncredited

Duck Soup (dir. L. McCarey), 1933, uncredited
Four Frightened People (dir. C.B. DeMille), 1934, uncredited
The Scarlet Empress (dir. J. von Sternberg), 1934, uncredited
The Big Broadcast of 1936 (dir. N. Taurog), 1935, uncredited
Rhythm on the Range (dir. N. Taurog), 1936, uncredited
Souls at Sea (dir. H. Hathaway), 1937, uncredited
Scandal Street (dir. J.P. Hogan), 1938, uncredited
Disputed Passage (dir. F. Borzage), 1939
Stagecoach (dir. J. Ford), 1939
Union Pacific (dir. C.B. DeMille), 1939
The Fargo Kid (dir. E. Killy), 1940
The Parson of Panamint (dir. W.C. McGann), 1941
Riders of the Timberline (dir. L. Selander), 1941
Sweetheart of the Fleet (dir. C. Barton), 1942, uncredited
The Desperadoes (dir. C. Vidor), 1943
Good Luck, Mr. Yates (dir. R. Enright), 1943
The Heat's On (dir. G. Ratoff), 1943
Henry Aldrich's Little Secret (dir. H. Bennett), 1944, uncredited
Hey, Rookie (dir. C. Barton), 1944, uncredited
Bulldog Drummond at Bay (dir. S. Salkow), 1947, uncredited
Riders in the Sky (dir. J. English), 1949, uncredited
Gene Autry and the Mounties (dir. J. English), 1951, uncredited
Whirlwind, (dir. J. English), 1951, uncredited

WARREN M. SHERK

Lipstone, Louis

(*b* Chicago, 5 June 1892; *d* Beverly Hills, CA, 18 March 1954). American music executive, music director, conductor, and violinist. He had a lengthy career in Chicago from 1917 to 1939. While considering a career as a physician, he played violin in restaurants and theaters. He studied violin with Harry Diamond at the Metropolitan Conservatory. Beginning in 1917, for Barney Balaban and Sam Katz, he served as orchestral leader at the Central Park Theater for six years, with stints at the Roosevelt, Riviera, and Uptown. In 1925 he became the general music director for the Balaban & Katz theater chain, which merged with Paramount theaters to become Publix Theaters Corporation. By 1930 he headed the production department for Paramount Publix where his duties included supervising area theaters and contracting musicians. His appointment as general music director for Paramount Pictures in 1939 prompted a move to Hollywood and he worked for the studio until his death. In addition to administrative duties, he supervised film scoring and hired composers, arrangers, and songwriters.

WARREN M. SHERK

Luz, Ernst J.

(*b* Allentown, PA, 15 Feb 1878; *d* New York, 2 Oct 1937). American composer, conductor, and film music journalist. In 1892 he moved to New York and quickly found work as a trumpet player at Niblo's Garden. Years later in 1909, Luz became pianist at Loew's Broadway Theater and, by March 1913, became its general music director. Marcus Loew appointed him general music director of the Loew's Circuit in late 1913; Luz served this position for eighteen years until 18 June 1931 when the advent of sound film displaced the majority of live theater musicians and rendered his job obsolete. In August 1912 he became musical editor of *Moving Picture News* (later *Motion Picture News*) and from 12 October 1912 to 2 December 1916 edited its "Music and the Picture" column (alternatively titled "The Musician and the Picture" and "Picture Music"). Through this column, Luz helped develop the standard practices of early film music by giving accompanists practical advice and offering musical suggestions for the latest pictures in the form of early cue sheets. After ending his contract with *MPN* on 1 December 1916, his musical suggestions continued to appear both in that paper and in *Moving Picture World* well into 1919. During his tenure at Loew's, Luz simultaneously managed the Photo Play Music Co., which published numerous volumes of silent film photoplay music—many bearing his name. For his own series, including most notably *A.B.C. Dramatic Set*, Luz composed and arranged hundreds of tunes, most of which were simple arrangements of classical repertory.

Works

(*selective list*)

Cue sheets

Across to Singapore
The Adventurer
All at Sea
The Awakening
The Baby Cyclone
The Barrier
Beau Broadway
Beyond the Sierras
Brotherly Love
Buttons
China Bound
Circus Rookies
College
Cordelia the Magnificent
The Cossacks
The Crowd
The Devil Dancer
Devil-May-Care

The Dove
Dream of Love
Excess Baggage
Fire Brigade
The Flying Fleet
For Her: Romance
Foreign Devils
Four Horsemen of the Apocalypse
The Gaucho
Honeymoon
In Old Kentucky
A Lady of Chance
The Latest from Paris
The Law of the Range
The Lovelorn
Loves of Casanova
Mademoiselle from Armentieres
Money Talks
Over There
Peg o' My Heart
The Prisoner of Zenda
Quality Street
Quincy Adams Sawyer
Revenge
Riders of the Dark
Rose Marie
Shadows of the Night
Show People
A Single Man
Smoldering Embers
Spoilers of the West
Tarnished Reputation
Tea for Three
Telling the World
Trifling Women
Two Arabian Knights
Way Down East
Where the Pavement Ends
White Shadows in the South Sea
Wickedness Preferred
Untamed

Film scores

Prudence, the Pirate (dir. W. Parke), 1916
The Four Horsemen of the Apocalypse (dir. R. Ingram), 1921
Hearts Aflame (dir. R. Barker), 1922
Peg o' My Heart (dir. K. Vidor), 1922

The Prisoner of Zenda (dir. R. Ingram), 1922
Quincy Adams Sawyer (dir. C.G. Badger), 1922
Trifling Women (dir. R. Ingram), 1922
The Toll of the Sea (dir. C.M. Franklin), 1923
Where the Pavement Ends (dir. R. Ingram), 1923
The Temptress (dir. F. Niblo), 1926
Love (dir. E. Goulding), 1927
Submarine (dir. F. Capra), 1928

Photoplay music

A.B.C. Dramatic Set (New York, 1915–20)
A.B.C. Feature Photoplay Edition (New York, 1917)
A.B.C. Photo Play Concert Edition (New York, 1917–8)
Luz Feature Photo Play Edition (New York, 1919–20)
Incidental Symphonies (New York, 1922)

Writings

Motion Picture Synchrony: For Motion Picture Exhibitors Organists and Orchestras (New York, 1925)

Bibliography

"Luz, Loew Director, Joins 'News' Music Staff," *Motion Picture News* xi/26 (1915), 130
Obituary, *Variety* cxxviii/5 (1937), 62
G. Anderson: *Music for Silent Films 1894–1929: a Guide* (Washington, DC, 1988)
C. McCarty: *Film Composers in America: a Filmography 1911–1970* (New York, 2000), 195
R. Altman: *Silent Film Sound* (New York, 2004)

PETER GRAFF

Malotte, Albert Hay

(*b* Philadelphia, PA, 19 May 1895; *d* Hollywood, CA, 16 Nov 1964). American composer, lyricist, and organist. The son of a choirmaster, he was a boy soprano and studied piano and organ at an early age, the latter with William S. Stansfield. He continued his training in Europe, working as a theater organist for motion-picture houses including the Plaza Theatre in London, and studied in Paris with Georges Jacob and Eugene Sizes. After returning to the United States he moved to Hollywood, where he opened a school in 1927 to train theater organists. However, the introduction of sound into films forced him to close his school the following year. Before turning to composing full time, Malotte was an amateur prizefighter (supposedly once facing Jack Dempsey) and worked as a cowboy on a cattle ranch in Wyoming.

In the summer of 1934 Malotte's scores for two ballets, *Carnival in Venice* and *Little Red Riding Hood,* were performed during two separate concerts at the Hollywood Bowl. This work brought him to the attention of Walt Disney; he joined Disney's studio in April 1935. Malotte worked at Disney for four years, providing music for numerous shorts. During this time he also wrote his most famous work, a setting of "The Lord's Prayer." After leaving Disney he continued scoring films, including work at Paramount and for independent companies. His manuscript scores are held at the Library of Congress and his papers at the Enoch Pratt Free Library, Baltimore.

Works

(selective list)

Short films

Broken Toys (dir. B. Sharpsteen), 1935, uncredited
Three Blind Mouseketeers (dir. D. Hand), 1936
Little Hiawatha (dir. D. Hand), 1937
Ferdinand the Bull (dir. D. Rickard), 1938
Moth and the Flame (dir. B. Gillett), 1938
The Ugly Duckling (dir. J. Cutting and C. Geronimi), 1939

Feature films

The Enchanted Forest (dir. L. Landers), 1945
The Big Fisherman (dir. F. Borzage), 1959

Stage

Carnival in Venice, Hollywood Bowl, 20 July 1934, cond. Raymond Paige
Little Red Riding Hood, Hollywood Bowl, 31 Aug 1934, cond. R.A. Shepherd
The Voice of the Prophet, Hollywood High School, 14 June 1946, cond. Albert Hay Malotte

Songs

Bring Back that Old-Fashioned Waltz (1923)
The Lord's Prayer (1935)
Song of the Open Road (1935)
The Twenty-Third Psalm (1937)
The Beatitudes (1938)
Ferdinand the Bull (Morey) (1938)
For My Mother (Sutherland) (1939)

Principal publisher: G. Schirmer

PAUL C. ECHOLS/DANIEL GOLDMARK

Mancini, Henry

(*b* Cleveland, OH, 16 April 1924; *d* Beverly Hills, CA, 14 June 1994). American arranger, composer, conductor, and pianist. Raised in West Aliquippa near Pittsburgh, he learned the flute and piano as a child. In his early teens he developed an interest in jazz, especially music of the big bands; he began to teach himself arranging, then had lessons with the theater conductor and arranger Max Adkins in Pittsburgh. In 1942 he enrolled at the Juilliard School, but was in the Air Force after less than a year and served until 1946, mostly as a member of military bands. He then became a pianist and arranger for the Glenn Miller-Tex Beneke Orchestra, in whose employ he met the vocalist Virginia O'Connor, whom he married in 1947 after moving to Los Angeles. For the next five years Mancini worked freelance, mostly as an arranger for dance-bands and night-club acts, also composing music for radio programs. He studied composition privately with Mario Castelnuovo-Tedesco, Ernst Krenek, and Alfred Sendrey.

In 1952 Mancini joined the staff of Universal, under Joseph Gershenson (the studio's music director), and alongside such experienced men as Hans Salter, Frank Skinner, Herman Stein, and David Tamkin. He was employed as both an arranger and a composer, and worked on films of many types, including musicals (notably *The Glenn Miller Story*) and many routine comedies, mysteries, B Westerns, and monster pictures. Gradually he was given increased responsibility, and in 1958 he worked with Orson Welles on *Touch of Evil*, for which he composed an effective and innovative score. In the same year, however, Universal let most of its music staff go. Now on his own, Mancini was quickly hired by Blake Edwards (another budding talent at the studio) as the composer for a new television series, "Peter Gunn." A recording of Mancini's theme music for the show became a hit, as did his music for Edwards' next series, "Mr. Lucky." Thereafter, from the early 1960s until the late 1980s, Mancini composed an average of three or four film scores per year, including more than two dozen that were written, produced and/or directed by Edwards.

Simultaneously Mancini developed a successful career as a recording and concert artist, and he reworked many of his film scores into best-selling commercial albums, most of them issued by RCA. However, these albums normally contained commercial arrangements of the main themes and consequently are not reliable indicators of his gifts as a dramatic composer. Often he gave fifty or more concerts each year as a guest pianist and/or conductor of bands and "pops" orchestras. Some of his later albums (including recordings with James Galway and Luciano Pavarotti) were milestones of the popular/classical "crossover" approach. He received four Academy Awards (two for best score, two for best song), twenty Grammy Awards, and several career achievement awards. In 1989 he cowrote an engaging and informative memoir.

Mancini's greatest influence as a Hollywood composer was felt from 1958 to about 1965, the period when he pioneered fundamentally new styles. He made imaginative use of jazz and popular idioms, which he applied not only to detective stories and *film noir* (building upon convention) but also to sophisticated romantic comedy, slapstick, and other genres. He became known for well-crafted and dramatically apt theme songs—notably those for *Breakfast at Tiffany's* ("Moon River"), *The Days of Wine and Roses*, *Charade*, and *Darling Lili* ("Whistling Away the Dark")—and for witty instrumental pieces, as for *Hatari!*, *The Pink Panther*, and *The Great Race*. In general he favored subtlety and restraint, and liked to score somewhat "against" the scene. For example in *Breakfast at Tiffany's* the first kiss between the romantic leads (Audrey Hepburn and George Peppard) is underplayed, with a soft, shimmering *tremolo* that evaporates into silence; and the "Baby Elephant Walk" in *Hatari!* matches an unexpected variant of a boogie-woogie to the animal's movements. Repeatedly Mancini came up with novel instrumental effects (one trademark being his fondness for alto and/or bass flutes), and he was equally skilled in writing for orchestra, jazz band, and small ensembles. In 1962 he wrote and published a guide to orchestration which was widely used by arrangers for years.

After 1965, notwithstanding his celebrity as a "pop" artist, Mancini continued to compose dramatic music for many serious films that either failed at the box office or enjoyed only moderate success. Some fine examples are *Two for the Road*, *The Molly Maguires*, *The White Dawn*, *That's Life!*, and *The Glass Menagerie* (and also Hitchcock's *Frenzy*, for which in 1968 he drafted a score that was rejected as being too serious). His scores for two of the later Edwards films, *10* and *Victor/Victoria*, again brought him popular acclaim. The songs for the latter film (lyrics by Leslie Bricusse) included Mancini's most familiar trademarks: a poignantly lyric waltz, "Crazy World," and a lively band number, "Le Jazz Hot." The film's gender-bending ambiguities (a favorite theme of Edwards throughout his career) has made it enduringly topical, and led to its adaptation as a stage musical which opened on Broadway in 1995. Mancini, suffering from cancer, died while the work was still in development; several other musicians thus had a hand in the revised score, but his songs, including several new ones, constitute the heart of the production.

Works

Collection

Henry Mancini Songbook, ed. M. Okun (Greenwich, CT, 1981)

Film scores

(as co-composer and/or arranger)

Has Anybody Seen my Gal (dir. D. Sirk), 1952

Horizons West (dir. B. Boetticher), 1952

Lost in Alaska (dir. J. Yarbrough), 1952

The Raiders (dir. L. Selander), 1952

(Willie and Joe) Back at the Front (dir. G. Sherman), 1952
Abbott and Costello Go to Mars (dir. C. Lamont), 1953
All I Desire (dir. D. Sirk), 1953
City Beneath the Sea (dir. B. Boetticher), 1953
Girls in the Night (dir. J. Arnold), 1953
It Came from Outer Space (dir. J. Arnold), 1953
It Happens Every Thursday (dir. J. Pevney), 1953
Law and Order (dir. N. Juran), 1953
The Lone Hand (dir. G. Sherman), 1953
Walking My Baby Back Home (dir. L. Bacon), 1953
Creature from the Black Lagoon (dir. J. Arnold), 1954
The Far Country (dir. A. Mann), 1954
Four Guns to the Border (dir. R. Carlson), 1954
The Glenn Miller Story (dir. A. Mann), 1954
Johnny Dark (dir. G. Sherman), 1954
Ma and Pa Kettle at Home (dir. C. Lamont), 1954
Tanganyika (dir. A. De Toth), 1954
Abbott and Costello Meet the Keystone Kops (dir. C. Lamont), 1955
Abbott and Costello Meet the Mummy (dir. C. Lamont), 1955
Ain't Misbehavin' (dir. E. Buzzell), 1955
The Private War of Major Benson (dir. J. Hopper), 1955
So This Is Paris (dir. R. Quine), 1955
The Spoilers (dir. J. Hibbs), 1955
Tarantula (dir. J. Arnold), 1955
This Island Earth (dir. J.M. Newman), 1955
To Hell and Back (dir. J. Hibbs), 1955
Behind the High Wall (dir. A. Biberman), 1956
The Benny Goodman Story (dir. V. Davies), 1956
A Day of Fury (dir. H. Jones), 1956
Francis in the Haunted House (dir. C. Lamont), 1956
The Great Man (dir. J. Ferrer), 1956
Rock, Pretty Baby! (dir. R. Bartlett), 1956
Man Afraid (dir. H. Keller), 1957
Mister Cory (dir. B. Edwards), 1957
Flood Tide (dir. A. Biberman), 1958
This Happy Feeling (dir. B. Edwards), 1958
Operation Petticoat (dir. B. Edwards), 1959
others

(as principal or sole composer)
Touch of Evil (dir. O. Welles), 1958
Voice in the Mirror (dir. H. Keller), 1958
Never Steal Anything Small (dir. C. Lederer), 1959
High Time (dir. B. Edwards), 1960
Bachelor in Paradise (dir. J. Arnold), 1961, incl. title song (lyrics, M. David)
Breakfast at Tiffany's (dir. B. Edwards), 1961, incl. Moon River (lyrics, J. Mercer)

The Great Impostor (dir. R. Mulligan), 1961
Days of Wine and Roses (dir. B. Edwards), 1962, incl. title song (lyrics, Mercer)
Experiment in Terror (dir. B. Edwards), 1962
Hatari! (dir. H. Hawks), 1962, incl. Baby Elephant Walk
Mr. Hobbs Takes a Vacation (dir. H. Koster), 1962
Charade (dir. S. Donen), 1963, incl. title song (lyrics, Mercer)
The Pink Panther (dir. B. Edwards), 1963
Soldier in the Rain (dir. R. Nelson), 1963
Dear Heart (dir. D. Mann), 1964, incl. title song (lyrics, J. Livingston and R. Evans)
Man's Favorite Sport? (dir. H. Hawks), 1964
A Shot in the Dark (dir. B. Edwards), 1964
The Great Race (dir. B. Edwards), 1965, incl. The Sweetheart Tree (lyrics, Mercer)
Arabesque (dir. S. Donen), 1966
Moment to Moment (dir. M. LeRoy), 1966
What Did You Do in the War, Daddy? (dir. B. Edwards), 1966
Gunn (dir. B. Edwards), 1967
Two for the Road (dir. S. Donen), 1967
Wait Until Dark (dir. T. Young), 1967
The Party (dir. B. Edwards), 1968
Gaily, Gaily (dir. N. Jewison), 1969
Me, Natalie (dir. F. Coe), 1969
Darling Lili (dir. B. Edwards), 1970, incl. Whistling Away the Dark (lyrics, Mercer)
The Hawaiians (dir. T. Gries), 1970
The Molly Maguires (dir. M. Ritt), 1970
Sometimes a Great Notion (dir. P. Newman), 1970, incl. All His Children (lyrics, A. and M. Bergman)
Sunflower (dir. V. De Sica), 1970
The Night Visitor (dir. L. Benedek), 1971
Oklahoma Crude (dir. S. Kramer), 1973
The Thief Who Came to Dinner (dir. B. Yorkin), 1973
The Girl from Petrovka (dir. R.E. Miller), 1974
The White Dawn (dir. P. Kaufman), 1974
The Great Waldo Pepper (dir. G.R. Hill), 1975
The Return of the Pink Panther (dir. B. Edwards), 1975
Alex and the Gypsy (dir. J. Korty), 1976
The Pink Panther Strikes Again (dir. B. Edwards), 1976, incl. Come to me (lyrics, D. Black)
Silver Streak (dir. A. Hiller), 1976
W.C. Fields and Me (dir. A. Hiller), 1976
House Calls (dir. H. Zieff), 1978
Revenge of the Pink Panther (dir. B. Edwards), 1978
Who is Killing the Great Chefs of Europe? (dir. T. Kotcheff), 1978
10 (dir. B. Edwards), 1979, incl. It's easy to say (lyrics, C.B. Sager)
A Change of Seasons (dir. R. Lang), 1980
Little Miss Marker (dir. W. Bernstein), 1980
The Shadow Box (dir. P. Newman), 1980

Mommie Dearest (dir. F. Perry), 1981
S.O.B. (dir. B. Edwards), 1981
Trail of the Pink Panther (dir. B. Edwards), 1982
Victor Victoria (dir. B. Edwards), 1982, lyrics, L. Bricusse, rev. for stage, 1995
The Man Who Loved Women (dir. B. Edwards), 1983
Harry and Son (dir. P. Newman), 1984
Lifeforce (dir. T. Hooper), 1985
Santa Claus (dir. J. Szwarc), 1985
A Fine Mess (dir. B. Edwards), 1986
The Great Mouse Detective (dir. R. Clements, B. Mattinson, D. Michener, and J. Musker), 1986
That's Life! (dir. B. Edwards), 1986, incl. Life in a Looking Glass (lyrics, Bricusse)
Blind Date (dir. B. Edwards), 1987
The Glass Menagerie (dir. P. Newman), 1987
Sunset (dir. B. Edwards), 1988
Without a Clue (dir. T. Eberhardt), 1988
Peter Gunn (dir. B. Edwards), 1989
Skin Deep (dir. B. Edwards), 1989
Welcome Home (dir. F.J. Schaffner), 1989
Fear (dir. R.S. O'Bannon), 1990
Ghost Dad (dir. S. Poitier), 1990
Never Forget (dir. J. Sargent), 1991
Switch (dir. B. Edwards), 1991
Son of the Pink Panther (dir. B. Edwards), 1993

Television music

TV series, mini-series, and films incl. Peter Gunn, 1958
Mr. Lucky, 1959
NBC Mystery Movie, 1971
Remington Steele, 1982
The Thorn Birds, 1983

Film shorts for Universal

The World's Most Beautiful Girls, 1952
4 others

Orchestral

Beaver Valley '37 Suite, ?1970

Some MSS, notes and sketches in *US-LAuc*

Bibliography

GroveA (M. Marks) [incl. further bibliography]
H. Mancini: *Sounds and Scores: a Practical Guide to Professional Orchestration* (Northridge, CA, 1963, 2/1973)

H. Mancini and G. Lees: *Did They Mention the Music?* (Chicago, 1989)
W. Darby and J. Du Bois: "Henry Mancini," *American Film Music: Major Composers, Techniques, and Trends, 1915–1990* (Jefferson, NC, 1990)
S. Elhaïk and D. Mangodt: "A Filmography/Discography of Henry Mancini," *Soundtrack!* [Belgium], ix/34 (1990), 12–15; 9/35 (1990), 37–43
S. Fry: "The Film and Television Music of Henry Mancini: a Selective Annotated Bibliography of the Literature," *The Cue Sheet* [Los Angeles], ix/2 (1992), 27–33
R.S. Brown: *Overtones and Undertones: Reading Film Music* (Berkeley, 1994)
J. Burlingame: *TV's Biggest Hits: the Story of Television Themes from "Dragnet" to "Friends"* (New York, 1996)
T.E. Scheurer: "Henry Mancini: an Appreciation and Appraisal," *Journal of Popular Film and Television*, xxiv/1 (1996), 34–43
T. Thomas: *Music for the Movies* (Los Angeles, 1973, 2/1997)
J. Smith: *The Sounds of Commerce: Marketing Popular Film Music* (New York, 1998)
J. Burlingame: *Sound and Vision: Sixty Years of Motion Picture Soundtracks* (New York, 2000)
C. McCarty: *Film Composers in America: a Filmography, 1911–1970* New York, 2/2000)
J. Smith: "That Money-Making 'Moon River' Sound: Thematic Organization and Orchestration in the Film Music of Henry Mancini," *Music and Cinema*, ed. J. Buhler, C. Flinn, and D. Neumeyer (Hanover, NH, 2000), 247–71
J. Leeper: "Crossing Musical Borders: the Soundtrack for *Touch of Evil*," *Soundtrack Available: Essays on Film and Popular Music*, ed. P.R. Wojcik and A. Knight (Durham, NC, 2001), 226–43
H. Mancini and R. Phillipe, ed.: *Case History of a Film Score: "The Thorn Birds"* (Miami, 2004)
J. Sullivan: *Hitchcock's Music* (New Haven, CT, 2006)
G. Lees: *Arranging the Score: Portraits of the Great Arrangers* (London, 2000), 193–221
G. Hubai: "'Murder Can Be Fun': the Lost Music of *Frenzy*," *Hitchcock Annual*, xvii (2011), 169–94
J. Caps: *Henry Mancini: Reinventing Film Music* (Urbana, IL, 2012)

MARTIN MARKS

Marquardt, Paul A(lfred)

(*b* Rudolstadt, Germany, 13 Jan 1889; *d* Los Angeles, 30 Oct 1960). Composer, arranger, and orchestrator of German birth, naturalized American. Often credited as P.A. Marquardt, he graduated from the Dresden Conservatory of Music, where he studied violin with Henri Petri, harmony and composition with Felix Draeseke, and conducting with Hermann Ludwig Kutzschbach. After playing first violin with the Gewerbehaus Symphony in Dresden, he conducted European theater orchestras and grand opera and led an orchestra for Anna Pavlova for two years. He emigrated to the United States in 1925 and was naturalized in 1931. Between approximately 1926 and 1929 Marquardt conducted at the Roof Theatre in New York and composed and arranged dramatic music to accompany silent film. This generic music included arrangements of dozens of classical pieces as well as original compositions for the Symphonic Incidentals and Symphonic Color Classics series published by Music Buyers Corp. Used widely in theaters, the mood music also found its way into thematic cue sheets for United Artists films, including *The Son of the Sheik* and *The Black Pirate* (both 1926) and accompanied synchronized sound films, such as *The Battle of the Sexes* (1928). Marquardt befriended Capitol Theater music director William Axt, and when Axt moved to Los Angeles to work at Metro-Goldwyn-Mayer, Marquardt followed in 1929, working at the studio until 1954, when he decided to freelance. Having already cocomposed the score for *The Bellamy Trial* (1929) with Axt, Marquardt went on to orchestrate for Axt throughout the 1930s, collaborating on at least 50 features and a dozen short films. He also provided arrangements for Daniele Amfitheatrof and for musical pictures scored by Herbert Stothart, including *Maytime* (1937) and *The Wizard of Oz* (1939). During World War II he orchestrated Army Signal Corps documentaries for Dimitri Tiomkin. After the war, he joined Tiomkin's scoring team providing orchestrations for a number of films, including *It's a Wonderful Life* (1946) and *High Noon* (1952).

Works

(*selective list*)

Film scores

Incidental mood music

Symphonic Color Classics No.6, A Sex Drama, 1926
A Desert Dance, 1927
The Hermit's Dream, 1928
Symphonic Incidentals, 1928

As composer

A Farewell to Arms (dir. F. Borzage), 1932, with W. Franke Harling and others

As orchestrator, scores by William Axt

Romance (dir. C. Brown), 1930
Lazy River (dir. G.B. Seitz), 1934
Manhattan Melodrama (dir. W.S. Van Dyke), 1934
Untamed (dir. G. Archainbaud), 1940

As orchestrator, scores by Herbert Stothart

Naughty Marietta (dir. R.Z. Leonard and W.S. Van Dyke), 1935
Maytime (dir. R.Z. Leonard), 1937
The Girl of the Golden West (dir. R.Z. Leonard), 1938
Sweethearts (dir. W.S. Van Dyke), 1938
The Wizard of Oz (dir. V. Fleming), 1939

As orchestrator, scores by Dimitri Tiomkin

Dillinger (dir. M. Nosseck), 1945
War Comes to America (dir. F. Capra and A. Litvak), 1945
It's a Wonderful Life (dir. F. Capra), 1947
Red River (dir. H. Hawks and A. Rosson), 1948
The Men (dir. F. Zinnemann), 1950
High Noon (dir. F. Zinnemann), 1952
Friendly Persuasion (dir. W. Wyler), 1956
Search for Paradise (dir. O. Lang), 1957

As orchestrator, scores by others

A Day at the Races (comp. F. Waxman, dir. S. Wood), 1937
Lassie Come Home (comp. D. Amfitheatrof, dir. F. M. Wilcox), 1943

Concert music

American Patrol, orchestrated for J. Iturbi, 1943
The Valiants of Wisconsin, band arrangement, *c*1946

MSS in Performing Arts Special Collections, UCLA

Bibliography

J. Rodriguez, ed.: "Marquardt, Paul A.," *Music and Dance in California* (Hollywood, CA, 1940), 393–4

WARREN M. SHERK

McBride, Robert (Guyn)

(*b* Tucson, AZ, 20 Feb 1911; *d* Tuscon, 1 July 2007). American composer and instrumentalist. At an early age he learned, mostly by himself, to play clarinet, oboe, saxophone, and piano and performed locally in jazz bands and school music groups. He studied composition with Otto Luening at the University of Arizona (BM 1933, MM 1935), where he later taught (1957–76). He also taught at Bennington College (1935–46) and in various summer music programs. He appeared as an oboe and clarinet soloist both live and on New Music Quarterly Recordings. In 1941 he toured South America as a member of the League of Composers Woodwind Quintet. During the years 1945–7 he was a composer and arranger for Triumph Films in New York, producing scores for *Farewell to Yesterday, The Man with my Face*, and a number of short subjects. In 1952, on commission by F. Campbell-Watson, he reorchestrated George

Gershwin's *Second Rhapsody*. He returned to Tuscon in 1957. Among the honors he received are a Guggenheim Fellowship, commissions from the League of Composers and the New York City Ballet, and awards from the American Academy of Arts and Letters, the Composers Press, and the University of Arizona. He performed widely at colleges and with various orchestras. The titles, character, and musical idioms of his works in opera, dance, chamber music, and orchestral music reflect his interest and involvement in jazz and theatrical music.

Works

(*selective list*)

Film Music

Farewell to Yesterday (documentary), 1950
The Man with my Face (dir. E. Montagne), 1951
Garden of Eden (dir. M. Nosseck), 1954

Ballets

Show Piece (E. Hawkins), 1937
Punch and Judy (M. Graham), 1941
Furlough Music, pf, 1945
Jazz Sym., 1954
Brooms of Mexico (A. Gordon), 1970

Orchestral

Fugato on a Well Known Theme, 1935
Mexican Rhapsody, 1935
Prelude to a Tragedy, 1935
Workout, chbr orch, 1936
Swing Stuff, cl, orch, 1940
Stuff in G, 1942
Strawberry Jam (Homemade), 1943
Sherlock Holmes Suite, band, 1945–6
Conc. for Doubles, cl, b cl, a sax, orch, 1947
Variety Day, vn conc., 1948
Hollywood Suite, band, *c*1950
Panorama of Mexico, 1960
Hill-country Sym., wind orch, 1962
Country Music Fantasy, wind orch, 1963
Sym. Melody, 1968
Folksong Fantasy, 1973
Light Fantastic, 1976–7
Sportmusic, band, 1976–7

Chamber

Depression Sonata, vn, pf, 1934
Workout, ob, pf, 1936
Qnt, pf, str, 1937
Pumpkin-Eater's Little Fugue, str orch, 1955
5 Winds Blowing, wind qnt, 1957
Str Foursome, str qt, 1957
Variations on Various Popularisms, eng hn, cl, bn, 1965
1776 Ov., pf 4 hands, 1975
other short inst and kbd pieces

Vocal

Sir Patrick Spence (anon.), male vv, 1932
Hot Stuff (We Hope) (R. McBride), TTBB, cl, pf, 1938
The Golden Sequence (11th-century, anon.), SATB, org, 1974
Improvisation (McBride), TrTrAA, 1976
songs

MSS in ACA, New York

Principal publishers: Associated, C. Fischer, Gornston (Sam Fox), Peters

Bibliography

EwenD
N. McKelvey: "Practical Music Maker: Robert McBride," *ACAB*, viii/1 (1958), 7–13

STEVEN E. GILBERT/R

McCarthy, Dennis

(*b* Burbank, CA, 3 July 1945). American composer for television. With early training in the piano and some experience playing in rock bands, he accepted a job working as a session guitarist with country singer Glen Campbell before graduating from college. As that position grew to include conducting and arranging, McCarthy became the musical coordinator for "The Glen Campbell Goodtime Hour," a televised variety show that began in 1969. McCarthy became interested in orchestrating and arranging and started to assist the well-established composer Alex North with such films as *Wise Blood* (dir. John Huston, 1979). His first opportunity to score a serial television show came in 1981 with "Enos," a short-lived spin-off from "The Dukes of Hazzard." A successful last-minute orchestral score that McCarthy wrote for the television miniseries "V: The Final Battle" led to his working on the series "V," which in turn led to composing work on several other series, including "Dynasty" and "MacGyver." In 1987 he began his extended involvement with the Star Trek franchise, scoring the pilot episode of "Star Trek: the Next Generation" and twelve of the first season's twenty-five episodes. McCarthy, Ron Jones, and Jay Chattaway were the main composers during the series' seven-season run, and McCarthy continued as the franchise expanded to include "Star Trek: Deep Space Nine," "Star Trek: Voyager," and "Star Trek: Enterprise." Executives insisted that, in contrast to the original "Star Trek" series of the 1960s, which regularly featured melodramatic, occasionally orientalist scores, the music in "Star Trek: the Next Generation" be quite subdued and unobtrusive, leading McCarthy to quip that he "treated everything in the show as the second movement of a symphony, even the battle scenes" (Burlingame, 119). His versatility in the series was eventually rewarded with the assignment to score the feature film *Star Trek: Generations*. McCarthy's theme music for "Deep Space Nine" received the Primetime Emmy Award for Outstanding Main Title Theme Music; his scoring of various episodes across the Star Trek franchise was recognized with eight nominations (five for episodes of "Star Trek: the Next Generation," two for episodes of "Star Trek: Voyager," and one for an episode of "Star Trek: Enterprise").

Works

Film scores

(*selective list*)

Last Plane Out (dir. D. Nelson), 1983
Off the Wall (dir. R. Friedberg), 1983
Star Trek: Generations (dir. D. Carson), 1994
The Utilizer (dir. C. Barron), 1996
McHale's Navy (dir. B. Spicer), 1997
Letters from a Killer (dir. Carson), 1998
In Your Face (dir. T. Tommasino), 2002
Die, Mommie, Die! (dir. M. Rucker), 2003
Landers (dir. S. Findley), 2004
Death of a Nation (dir. D. D'Souza and B. Schooley), 2018

Television music

The Glen Campbell Goodtime Hour (musical director), 1969
Enos, 1981
V: The Final Battle (miniseries), 1984
V, 1984–5
The Colbys, 1985–7
Dynasty, 1985–9
MacGyver, 1985–91
Trapper John, M.D., 1986

The Twilight Zone, 1986–7
Houston Knights, 1987–8
Star Trek: the Next Generation, 1987–94
Parker Lewis, 1990–93
Star Trek: Deep Space Nine, 1993–9
Star Trek: Generations, 1994
Star Trek: Voyager, 1995–2001
Breast Men, 1997
McHale's Navy, 1997
Letters from a Killer, 1998
Project Greenlight, 2001–2
Star Trek: Enterprise, 2001–5
Die, Mommie, Die!, 2003
Related, 2005
Prayer Hour, 2011
Starship Antyllus, 2014–15

Bibliography

P. Kelly: "Dennis McCarthy: Scoring '*Star Trek: Generations*'," *Film Score Monthly*, liii–liv (1995), 19–21
J. Burlingame: *TV's Biggest Hits: the Story of Television Themes from "Dragnet" to "Friends"* (New York, 1996)
R. Koppl: "Dennis McCarthy: Hot Rods to Hell," *Film Music Magazine*, i (Sept 1998), 12–16
J. Bond: *The Music of "Star Trek": Profiles in Style* (Los Angeles, 1999)

NEIL LERNER/R

Mendoza, David

(*b* New York, 13 March 1894; *d* New York, 23 May 1975). American composer, conductor, and violinist. Mendoza began his music training on violin at the age of seven with Franz Kreisel. He continued his studies at the Institute of Musical Art with Rubin Goldmark and Percy Goetschius. As a violinist, Mendoza was concertmaster of the Russian Symphony Orchestra (New York), the New York Symphony Orchestra, and later the Victor Talking Machine Orchestra. Mendoza entered the film industry in 1917 as second concertmaster at the Rialto Theater and the following year he became concertmaster at the Rivoli. By 1920 he transitioned to the podium, where he began his nine-year tenure as music director at New York's Capitol Theater, where William Axt and Erno Rapee were also on the staff. While at the Capitol, Mendoza and Axt penned the score to *Don Juan* (1926), the first movie with synchronized music and sound effects. Both men worked for

Metro-Goldwyn-Mayer starting around 1925 and later worked on sound films, primarily for Warner Bros. In addition to film, Mendoza also worked in radio, conducting the Paramount Radio Orchestra in 1929 and directing orchestras for the "Eastman Kodak Hour," "Maxwell House Melodies," "Paul Ash's Stage Show," and others throughout the 1930s. Around 1932, Mendoza's work in film focused primarily on film shorts and by 1940 he had stepped away from the medium to work almost exclusively in radio and with various live dance and theatre ensembles.

Works

(selective list)

Film scores

(Collaboration with William Axt)
Madame DuBarry (Passion) (dir. E. Lubitsch), 1919, United States release 1920
The Sea Hawk (dir. F. Lloyd), 1924
Ben-Hur (dir. F. Niblo), 1925
The Big Parade (dir. K. Vidor and G.W. Hill), 1925
La Bohème (dir. K. Vidor), 1925
The Merry Widow (dir. E. von Stroheim), 1925
Annie Laurie (dir. J.S. Robertson), 1926
Camille (dir. F. Niblo), 1926
Don Juan (dir. A. Crosland), 1926
The Fire Brigade (dir. W. Nigh), 1926
Mare Nostrum (dir. R. Ingram), 1926
The Scarlet Letter (dir. V. Sjöström), 1926
Slide, Kelly, Slide (dir. E. Sedgwick), 1926
The Garden of Allah (dir. R. Ingram), 1927
Our Dancing Daughters (dir. H. Beaumont), 1928
The Student Prince in Old Heidelberg (dir. E. Lubitsch and J.M. Stahl), 1928
The Trail of '98 (dir. C. Brown), 1928
White Shadows in the South Seas (dir. W.S. Van Dyke and R.J. Flaherty), 1928
A Woman of Affairs (dir. C. Brown), 1928
The Kiss (dir. J. Feyder), 1929
The Single Standard (dir. J.S. Robertson), 1929

Film scores

(without Axt)
Glorious Betsy (dir. A. Crosland), 1928
The Careless Age (dir. J.G. Wray), 1929, collab. L. Leonardi
Disraeli (dir. A.E. Green), 1929
Gold Diggers of Broadway (dir. R. Del Ruth), 1929, collab. A. Reiser
Captain Thunder (dir. A. Crosland), 1930, collab. X. Cugat and L. Rosebrook
The Girl of the Golden West (dir. J.F. Dillon), 1930 (love theme)
The Lash (dir. F. Lloyd), 1930, collab. X. Cugat and L. Rosebrook

Little Caesar (dir. M. LeRoy), 1930 (main title, stock)
Mother's Cry (dir. H. Henley), 1930
Oh Sailor Behave (dir. A. Mayo), 1930, collab. L. Leonardi
Song of the Flame (dir. A. Crosland), 1930
Sweet Kitty Bellairs (dir. A.E. Green), 1930, collab. R. Dunn and L. Leonardi
Young Man of Manhattan (dir. M. Bell), 1930 (main title)
Alexander Hamilton (dir. J.G. Adolfi), 1931
The Bargain (dir. R. Milton), 1931
Chances (dir. A. Dwan), 1931 (main title)
Children of Dreams (dir. A. Crosland), 1931
Compromised (dir. J.G. Adolfi), 1931
Father's Son (dir. W. Beaudine), 1931, collab. C. Copping and L. Rosebrook
Gold Dust Gertie (dir. L. Bacon), 1931, collab. C. Copping
God's Gift to Women (dir. M. Curtiz), 1931
Honor of the Family (dir. L. Bacon), 1931 (main title, end title, stock)
I Like Your Nerve (dir. W. C. McGann), 1931
Kiss Me Again (dir. W.A. Seiter), 1931
Local Boy Makes Good (dir. M. LeRoy), 1931 (main theme, stock)
The Mad Genius (dir. M. Curtiz), 1931
Men of the Sky (dir. A.E. Green), 1931
My Past (dir. R. Del Ruth), 1931
Penrod and Sam (dir. W. Beaudine), 1931 (main title, stock)
The Public Enemy (dir. W.A. Wellman), 1931 (main theme)
The Reckless Hour (dir. J.F. Dillon), 1931
The Ruling Voice (dir. R.V. Lee), 1931 (main title, end title, stock)
Smart Money (dir. A.E. Green), 1931 (main title)
Svengali (dir. A. Mayo), 1931

Short films

Detectuvs (dir. A.J. Goulding), 1932
Dixieland (documentary, dir. J.B. Kennedy), 1934
Hail Columbia (documentary, dir. J.B. Kennedy), 1934
Remember the Alamo (dir. I. Genet), 1934
The Blue and the Gray (documentary, dir. J.B. Kennedy and V. Kilian), 1935
Attic of Terror (dir. J. Henabery), 1937
Roping 'em Alive! (dir. I. Genet), 1937
Dear Old Dad (dir. J. Henabery), 1938

Songs

(Collaboration with William Axt)
Love's Symphony (H. Hoexter), 1922
Chimes of Seville (R. Klages), 1927
Flaming Ruth (A. Bryan and E. Lyn), 1927
Cross Roads (R. Klages), 1928
Flower of Love (D. Dreyer and H. Ruby), 1928

I Found Gold When I Found You (H. Mooney and E. Lyn), 1928
I Loved You Then As I Love You Now (B. MacDonald), 1928
In a Little Hideaway (H. Dietz), 1928
In Romany (M. Harris), 1928
Live and Love (R. Klages), 1928
Love Brought the Sunshine (D. Dreyer and H. Ruby), 1928
Love's first Kiss (R. Klages), 1929
You're the Only One for Me (R. Klages), 1929
At the Sign of the Green and White (R. Simon), 1930

Bibliography

Obituary, *Variety*, cclxxix/ 4 (1975), 79
The ASCAP Biographical Dictionary, 4th ed. (New York, 1980), 342
C. McCarty: *Film Composers in America: a Filmography 1911–1970* (New York, 2000), 206
A. Slide: "An Interview with David Mendoza," *Silent Topics: Essays on Undocumented Areas of Silent Film* (Lanham, MD, 2005), 69–76
T. Hischak: *The Encyclopedia of Film Composers* (Lanham, MD, 2015), 448–9

PETER GRAFF

Millar, Cynthia

(*b* England, 5 June 1956). British ondes martenot player and film and television music composer. She is well known for her international appearances with orchestras performing on the ondes martenot and for her recordings on film scores. Millar studied the ondes martenot with John Morton and Jeanne Loriod, and piano with Philip Fowke. As a performer of ondes martenot she can be heard in over one hundred film and television scores, including *The Black Calderon* (1985), *The Good Son* (1993), *My Left Foot: the Story of Christy Brown* (1989), *The Good Mother* (1988), *Amazing Grace and Chuck* (1987), *Legal Eagles* (1986), and *Ed Wood* (1994), for composers including Elmer Bernstein, Richard Rodney Bennett, Maurice Jarre, Henry Mancini, and Miklós Rózsa. She composed her first score in 1992 for *Crazy in Love* directed by Martha Coolidge.

Works

Film scores

The Run of the Country (dir. P. Yates), 1995
Three Wishes (dir. M. Coolidge), 1995
Little Ghost (dir. L. Shayne), 1997
Brown's Requiem (dir. J. Freeland), 1998
Digging to China (dir. T. Hutton), 1998

Television music

Crazy in Love (dir. M. Coolidge), 1992
Foreign Affairs (dir. J. O'Brien), 1993
The Portrait (dir. A. Penn), 1993
Voices from Within (dir. E. Till), 1994
Beyond Reason (dir. J. O'Brien), 1995
Tourist Trap (dir. R. Benjamin), 1998
A Storm in Summer (dir. R. Wise), 2000
Confessions of an Ugly Stepsister (dir. G. Miller), 2002
Stephen Hawking's Universe (documentary series for BBC/WNET)

JEANNIE GAYLE POOL

Mizzy, Vic(tor)

(*b* New York, 9 Jan 1915; *d* Los Angeles, 17 Oct 2009). American composer of popular songs and of music for film and television. His first instrument was the accordion, and he took piano lessons to the age of thirteen. At fourteen he met his future lyricist and long-term collaborator Irving Taylor, with whom he wrote a series of hit songs during the 1940s, while they served together in the navy. Mizzy entered New York University in 1931; at the same time he started composing for variety shows. He taught himself both composition and orchestration, skills that were fostered by his activities as a studio pianist for a Brooklyn radio station and as a member of various local bands. Among other songs, he wrote the hits "My dreams are getting better all the time," "Three Little Sisters," "Pretty Kitty Blue Eyes," and "The whole world is singing my song." After the war Mizzy married radio singer Mary Small, who performed the début of a number of his songs. Mizzy's songs appeared in films of the 1940s, but he began to compose for screen media through work for television. David Levy, head of programming for NBC, convinced him to relocate to Los Angeles, so that Mizzy could score "The Shirley Temple Storybook" (1960–61) and other short-lived television series. His break came in 1964 when Levy invited Mizzy to score a new television series, "The Addams Family." The theme became iconic for its finger snapping and use of harpsichord—the composer himself played the instrument and performed the vocals. The light, comical style of his work for "The Addams Family" typecast Mizzy as composer for sitcoms, prompting CBS to engage him to score "Green Acres" (1965–71), which featured an equally memorable theme song. Mizzy continued working for television through the late 1970s, with music for (among others) "The Don Rickles Show" (1972) and "Quincy M.E." (1978) as well as a number of television movies. At the same time, he composed the music for all five of the Universal Studios Don Knotts comedies from the late 1960s and early 1970s, and scored several other feature films of the 1960s. Mizzy was a practitioner of the Schillinger System and taught it at NYU for a short period in the 1950s.

Works

Film scores

In Society (dir. J. Yarbrough), 1944
The Night Walker (dir. W. Castle), 1964
A Very Special Favor (dir. M. Gordon), 1965
The Ghost and Mr. Chicken (dir. A. Rafkin), 1966
The Busy Body (dir. W. Castle), 1967
The Caper of the Golden Bulls (dir. R. Rouse), 1967
Don't Make Waves (dir. A. Mackendrick), 1967
The Perils of Pauline (dir. H.B. Leonard and J. Shelley), 1967
The Reluctant Astronaut (dir. E. Montagne), 1967
The Spirit Is Willing (dir. W. Castle), 1967
The Shakiest Gun in the West (dir. A. Rafkin), 1968
The Love God? (dir. N. Hiken), 1969
How to Frame a Figg (dir. A. Rafkin), 1971

Television movies

The Deadly Hunt, 1971
A Very Missing Person, 1972
Terror on the 40th Floor, 1974
The Million Dollar Rip-Off, 1976
Halloween with The New Addams Family, 1977
The Munsters' Revenge, 1981

Television series

Shirley Temple's Storybook, 1960–61
The Richard Boone Show, 1963–4
Kentucky Jones, 1964–5
The Addams Family, 1964–6
Green Acres, 1965–71
The Double Life of Henry Phyfe, 1966
Captain Nice, 1967
The Pruitts of Southampton, 1967
Pioneer Spirit, 1969
The Don Rickles Show, 1972
The Snoop Sisters, 1972–4
Temperature's Rising, 1972–4
Shakespeare Loves Rembrandt, 1974
Quincy M.E., 1978

Songs

All Out for Uncle Sam, 1942
Three Little Sisters, 1942
I had a little talk with the Lord, 1943

Take It Easy, 1943
Pretty Kitty Blue Eyes, 1944
My dreams are getting better all the time, 1945
The Whole World Is Singing My Song, 1946
With a Hey and a Hi and a Ho-Ho-Ho, 1947
Choo'n Gum, 1950
A Beautiful Waste of Time, 1952
Bluebird With a Broken Wing, 1954
The Jones Boy, 1954
All I have is a love song, 1956
many others

Bibliography

R.D. Larson: "*The Addams Family*: the Man Behind the Music," *Cinefantastique*, xxii (1991), 42
J. Burlingame: *TV's Biggest Hits: the Story of Television Themes from "Dragnet" to "Friends"* (New York, 1996)
W.W. Vaché: *The Unsung Songwriters: American's Masters of Melody* (Lanham, MD, 2000)

JAMES DEAVILLE

Moross, Jerome

(*b* Brooklyn, NY, 1 Aug 1913; *d* Miami, 25 July 1983). American composer. He held a Juilliard Fellowship (1931–2) and graduated from New York University in 1932. Initially he supported himself by writing ballets and music for the theatre, although his first complete show, the revue *Parade* (1935), was not a great success. George Gershwin engaged him as assistant conductor and pianist for a West Coast production of *Porgy and Bess*, and Moross began training the principals during the summer following Gershwin's death in July 1937. During this period he went to Chicago for a production of his ballet *American Pattern* and began work on one of his most successful scores, the ballet *Frankie and Johnny*. Other works which established Moross's early reputation include the orchestral pieces *Biguine*, *Paeans*, *A Tall Story*, and *Those Everlasting Blues*. When he went to Hollywood in 1940, however, he found that this very reputation effectively prevented him from finding work; his American vernacular idiom was not understood by Hollywood producers, who preferred the romanticized Americana epitomized by such works as Grofé's *Grand Canyon Suite*. So for nearly ten years Moross earned a living as an orchestrator of film scores, collaborating with Copland (*Our Town*), Waxman, Adolph Deutsch, Frederick Hollander, and Friedhofer (*The Best Years of our Lives*).

During this period Moross produced a substantial number of works, notably the First Symphony (which received its première in Seattle under Sir Thomas

Beecham in 1943) and *Ballet Ballads*, a series of four one-act ballet-operas. Much of Moross's most interesting theatre music was cast in hybrid or experimental forms, such as ballet-opera, or for the semipopular musical stage; he was especially concerned to reconcile elements derived from popular and art genres. The two-act opera *The Golden Apple* (including the song "Lazy Afternoon") and *Gentlemen, Be Seated!*, a portrait of the Civil War in the form of a minstrel show, belong to this category.

In 1948 Moross composed his first original film score (*Close-Up*), and after the success of *When I Grow Up* (1950) he found himself able to give up commercial orchestration more or less permanently. Other effective scores include *The Proud Rebel*, *The Adventures of Huckleberry Finn*, *The Cardinal*, *The War Lord*, and *The Big Country*; the last-named is one of the finest scores written for a Western, and was nominated for an Academy Award. Moross assembled the highlights of his film career from 1952 to 1965 in the suite *Music for the Flicks*. He composed less music in other genres during this period, but his ballet *The Last Judgement* (1953) must be ranked among his best works.

Among his last compositions, the Concerto for flute and string quartet and the Sonata for piano duet and string quartet epitomize Moross's facility for writing music which has both spontaneous popular appeal and strength of musical purpose. American folk and popular idioms form the basis of his style, which is plain and vigorous, diatonically simple, and full of lyrical warmth and expressiveness. Reminiscences of rags, blues, and stomps abound (e.g. in *Frankie and Johnny*), but these are informed both with formal discipline and individuality. Unfailingly positive in tone, the aggressive, spotlit scoring of his music features instruments at the upper extremes of their ranges (as when a D trumpet crowns the climax of the First Symphony's fugal finale), and his contrapuntal writing is clean and sharp.

Works

(*selective list*)

Stage

Parade (revue), 1935
American Pattern (ballet), 1936
Frankie and Johnny (ballet), 1937–8, arr. as orch suite
Ballet Ballads (4 ballet-ops, each 1, J. Latouche): Susanna and the Elders, 1940–41
The Eccentricities of Davy Crockett, 1945
Willie the Weeper, 1945
Riding Hood Revisited, 1946
The Golden Apple (op, 2, Latouche), 1948–50
The Last Judgement (ballet), 1953, arr. as orch suite
Gentlemen, Be Seated! (op, E. Eager), 1955–6
Sorry, Wrong Number! (op, after L. Fletcher), 1977

Film scores

Close-up (dir. J. Donohue), 1948
When I Grow Up (dir. M. Kanin), 1950
Captive City (dir. R. Wise), 1952
Hans Christian Andersen (dir. C. Vidor), 1952 [incl. The Little Mermaid (ballet), based on themes by F. Liszt]
The Sharkfighters (dir. J. Hopper), 1952
The Seven Wonders of the World (dir. T. Garnett), 1955 [only part by Moross]
The Proud Rebel (dir. M. Curtiz), 1957
The Big Country (dir. W. Wyler), 1958, arr. as orch suite
The Adventures of Huckleberry Finn (dir. Curtiz), 1959
The Jayhawkers (dir. M. Frank), 1959
The Mountain Road (dir. D. Mann), 1960
Five Finger Exercise (dir. Mann), 1961
The Cardinal (dir. O. Preminger), 1963
The War Lord (dir. J. Farrow), 1965
Rachel, Rachel (dir. P. Newman), 1967
The Valley of Gwangi (dir. J. O'Connolly), 1968
Hail, Hero (dir. D. Miller), 1969

Television music

Lancer
Wagon Train

Other works

Orchestral

Paeans, 1931
Those Everlasting Blues (A. Kreymborg), 1v, small orch, 1932
Biguine, 1934
A Tall Story, 1938
Sym. no.1, 1941–2
Variations on a Waltz, 1946–66
Music for the Flicks, suite, 1965 [based on film scores, 1952–65]

Chamber

Recitative and Aria, vn, pf, 1944
[4] Sonatinas for Divers Instruments: cl choir, 1966; db, pf, 1966; brass qnt, 1969; ww qnt, 1970
Sonata, pf 4 hands, str qt, 1975
Conc., fl, str qt/str orch, 1978

Bibliography

D. Ewen: *American Composers: a Biographical Dictionary*
A. Copland: "Our Younger Generation: Ten Years Later," *Modern Music* xiii/4 (1936), 3–11

J. Caps: "An Interview with Jerome Moross," *Cue Sheet* v/3-4 (1998), 73–80, 99–108
C. Palmer: "From the Big Country with Big Style," *Gramophone*, lxxi (October 1993), 18
C. Turner: "Jerome Moross: an Introduction and Annotated Worklist," *Notes* lxi/3 (2005), 657–727
M. Whitmer: *Jerome Moross's "The Big Country": a Film Score Guide* (Lanham, MD, 2012)

CHRISTOPHER PALMER/MICHAEL MECKNA/R

Morricone, Ennio

(*b* Rome, Italy, 10 Nov 1928). Italian composer. A favorite pupil of the distinguished Italian composer Goffredo Petrassi, he also substituted discreetly for his trumpeter father in a light music orchestra. He thus developed two distinct sides to his musical personality: one of these led him to embrace serialism (e.g., in *Distanze* and *Musica per 11 violini*, 1958) and the experimental work of the improvisation group Nuova Consonanza (from 1965); the other gained him a leading role, principally as an arranger, in all types of popular music, including songs for radio, radio and television plays, and the first successful television variety shows. In the early days of the record industry his innovative contribution played a decisive part in the success of the first Italian singer-songwriters ("cantautori").

After many minor cinematic collaborations, Morricone achieved wider recognition with Sergio Leone's series of four Westerns, beginning with *Per un pugno di dollari* (released in the United States as *A Fistful of Dollars*, 1964). He subsequently collaborated with directors such as Bernardo Bertolucci (from 1964), Pier Paolo Pasolini (from 1966), and Elio Petri (from 1968), and had particularly successful films with Paolo and Vittorio Taviani (*Allonsanfàn*, 1974; *Il prato*, 1979), Valerio Zurlini (*Il deserto dei tartari*, 1976), Roland Joffè (*The Mission*, 1986), and Brian De Palma (*Casualties of War*, 1989). Despite inevitable self-repetitions over a total of more than four hundred film scores, his work provides many examples of a highly original fusion of classical and popular idioms. This is noticeable, albeit in somewhat crude form, in Leone's series of Westerns, where the music for the opening titles juxtaposes three distinct types of music: a synthetic folk idiom, using the jaw harp, acoustic guitar, and harmonica to accompany human whistling; a contemporary, urban rock sound, featuring the electric guitar; and an unabashedly sentimental choral-orchestral style. With *Giù la testa* (1971) Morricone entered an experimental phase in which he developed a technique based on melodic, rhythmic, or harmonic "modules" (usually of four, eight, or sixteen beats in length), each differently characterized and often featuring a particular instrument. These are juxtaposed and combined to create very different stylistic atmospheres. The most impressive application of the modular technique is found in *The Mission*, where the single modules, more extended and clearly defined than before, interact dialectically, assuming very clear symbolic functions.

Morricone's non-film works form a large and increasingly widely performed part of his output. Many of them use his technique of "micro-cells," a pseudo-serial approach often incorporating modal and tonal allusions, which, with its extreme reduction of compositional materials, has much in common with his film-music techniques. His most fruitful season of concert-music composition began with the Second Concerto for flute, cello, and orchestra (1985, from which the *Cadenza* for flute and tape of 1988 is derived) and continued with *Riflessi* (1989–90), three pieces for cello which represent perhaps the highpoint of his chamber music output, attaining a high degree of lyrical tension.

Morricone is an Officier de l'Ordre des Arts et des Lettres, Commendatore dell'Ordine "Al Merito della Repubblica Italiana," and Knight in the Order of Légion d'honneur. He is a member of Accademia Nazionale di Santa Cecilia (1996). Among other honors, he has received one Academy Award for Best Achievement in Music (2016) and an Honorary Academy Award (2007), a Grammy Award, a Leone d'oro "Alla carriera," and an Award from the Society for Preservation of Film Music (1994). In 2000 he was awarded the Laurea Honoris Causa by the University of Cagliari (2000) and in 2002 "Tor Vergata" by the University of Rome. Between 1991 and 1996 he taught film music (sharing a post with Sergio Miceli) at the Accademia Musicale Chigiana, Siena.

Ennio Morricone, 2016
(Michal Krumphanzl/CTK via AP) SLOVAKIA OUT, EDITORIAL USE ONLY (CTK via AP Images).

Works

(*selective list*)

Film scores

Per un pugno di dollari (dir. S. Leone), 1964
La battaglia di Algeri (dir. G. Pontecorvo), 1965
Il buono il brutto il cattivo (dir. S. Leone), 1966
C'era una volta il West (dir. S. Leone), 1968
Teorema (dir. P. P. Pasolini), 1968
Il decamerone (dir. P. P. Pasolini), 1970
Indagine su un cittadino al di sopra di ogni sospetto (dir. E. Petri), 1970
Two Mules for Sister Sara (dir. D. Siegel), 1970
Giù la testa (dir. S. Leone), 1971
Allonsanfàn (dir. P. Taviani and V. Taviani), 1974
Il deserto dei tartari (dir. V. Zurlini), 1976
L'eredità Ferramonti (dir. M. Bolognini), 1976
Novecento (dir. B. Bertolucci), 1977
Days of Heaven (dir. T. Malick), 1978
La cage aux folles (dir. E. Molinaro), 1978
Il prato (dir. P. Taviani and V. Taviani), 1979
Once upon a Time in America (dir. S. Leone), 1984
The Mission (dir. R. Joffé), 1986
The Untouchables (dir. B. De Palma), 1987
Cinema Paradiso (dir. G. Tornatore), 1988
Frantic (dir. R. Polanski), 1988
Casualties of War (dir. B. De Palma), 1989
Atame! [Tie me up! Tie me down!] (dir. P. Almodóvar), 1990
Hamlet (dir. F. Zeffirelli), 1990
Bugsy (dir. B. Levinson), 1991
Wolf (dir. M. Nichols), 1994
Lolita (dir. A. Lyne), 1997
Bulworth (dir. W. Beatty), 1998
The Legend of 1990 (dir. G. Tornatore), 1998
Canone inverso – Making Love (dir. R. Tognazzi), 2000
Malèna (dir. G. Tornatore), 2000
Mission to Mars (dir. B. De Palma), 2000
Vatel (dir. R. Joffé), 2000
Aida of the Trees (dir. G. Manuli), 2001
The Sleeping Wife (dir. S. Agosti), 2001
Black Angel (dir. T. Brass), 2002
Ripley's Game (dir. L. Cavani), 2002
The End of a Mystery (dir. M. Hermoso), 2003
72 Meters (dir. V. Khotinenko), 2004
Fateless (dir. L. Koltai), 2005
The Unknown Woman (dir. G. Tornatore), 2006

The Demons of St. Petersburg (dir. G Montaldo), 2008
Baarìa (dir. G. Tornatore), 2009
Love Story (dir. F. Habicht), 2011
The Best Offer (dir. G. Tornatore), 2013
The Hateful Eight (dir. Q. Tarantino), 2015
The Sun is Dark (dir. G. Papasso), 2015
Correspondence (dir. G. Tornatore), 2016

Opera

Partenope (1, G. Barbieri and S. Cappelletto), 1996

Vocal

Caput Coctu Show (P.P. Pasolini), Bar, orch, 1970
Bambini del mondo, chorus, 1979
Gestazione (cant., E. Giovannini), female v, va, clav, pf, tam-tam, db, orch, tape, 1980
Frammenti di Eros (cant., S. Miceli), S, pf, orch, 1985
Cantata per l'Europa, 2 spkrs, S, mixed chorus, orch, 1988
3 scioperi (Pasolini), children's chorus, b drum, 1988
4 anamorfosi latine (Miceli), S, Mez, T, Bar, orch, 1990
Una via crucis (Miceli), solo vv, chorus, orch, 1991
Epitaffi sparsi (Miceli), S, pf/S, pf, str, vv, orch, 1993
Vida aquam, S, small orch, 1993
Il silenzio, il gioco, la memoria (Miceli), children's chorus, 1994
Flash, 2nd vers. (E. Sanguineti, S. Benni, Miceli), double chorus, str qt, 2000

Instrumental

Orchestral

Conc. for Orch, 1957
Conc. no.2, fl, vc, orch, 1985
Conc. no.3, gui, mar, str, 1991
UT, tpt, perc, str, 1991
Conc. no.4, org, 2 tpt, 2 trbn, orch, 1993

Chamber and solo instrumental

4 pezzi, gui, 1957
Distanze, vn, vc, pf, 1958
Musica per 11 violini, 1958
Suoni per Dino, va, 2 tape recorders, 1969
Rag in frantumi, pf, 1986
Cadenza, fl, tape, 1988
Fluidi, 10 insts, 1988
4 studi, pf, 1989

Specchi, cl, ob, bn, hn, pf, 1989
Riflessi, vc, 1989–90
Esercizi, 10 str, 1993

Principal publishers: BMG, Edi-Pan, Salabert, Suvini Zerboni

Bibliography

A. Lhassa and J. Lhassa: *Ennio Morricone: biographie* (Lausanne, 1989)
H.J. de Boer and M. van Wouw: *The Ennio Morricone Musicography* (Amsterdam, 1990)
S. Miceli: *Morricone: la musica, il cinema* (Milan, 1994/R)
S. Miceli: "Forme visive e forme sonore: le musiche di Ennio Morricone per *The Life and Death of Richard III* (1912)," *Musica/Realtà* (1997), 54
E. Morricone and S. Miceli: *Comporre per il cinema: teoria e prassi della musica nel film* (Rome, 2001)
C. Leinberger: *Ennio Morricone's "The Good, the Bad, and the Ugly": a Film Score Guide* (Oxford, 2004)
G. Lucci, ed.: *Morricone: cinema e oltre* (Milan, 2007)
S. Miceli: *Musica per film: storia, estetica-analisi, tipologie* (Milan, 2009)
C. Leinberger: "The *Dollars* Trilogy: 'There are Two Kinds of Western Heroes, My Friend!'" in *Music in the Western: Notes from the Frontier*, ed. K. Kalinak (New York, 2012), 131–47
G. Heldt, T. Krohn, P. Moormann, and W. Strank: *Ennio Morricone* (München, 2013)
F. Fabbri and G. Plastino: "Provisionally Popular: a Conversation with Ennio Morricone," *Made in Italy: Studies in Popular Music*, ed. F. Fabbri and G. Plastino (New York, 2014), 223–33
S. Miceli: "Leone, Morricone and the Italian way to Revisionist Westerns," *The Cambridge Companion to Film Music* (Cambridge, 2016): 265–93
A. De Rosa, ed. *Ennio Morricone: In His Own Words* (Oxford, 2019)

SERGIO MICELI/R

Morros, Boris

(*b* Minsk, Russia, 1 Jan 1891; *d* New York, 8 Jan 1963). American music executive, music director, and cellist, born in Russia, emigrated to the United States in 1922, and naturalized in 1929. Born into a family with longstanding musical ties to Russian royalty, he was educated at the Imperial Conservatory in St. Petersburg, where he studied with Alexander Glazunov and Rimsky-Korsakov. Leaving Russia after World War I, he eventually made his way via Constantinople to the United States as music director of a touring French musical revue. Conducting for the Publix Theater circuit resulted in his appointment as associate to the general director of music, Nat W. Finston. In 1928, Morros succeeded Finston when the latter was transferred to Paramount's studio in Hollywood. With Publix through 1933, Morros became the managing director of New York's Paramount Theater in 1934. When Finston left Paramount for MGM in 1935, Morros succeeded him as general music director. Between 1936 and 1939 he supervised scoring on nearly 150 films for Walter Wanger Productions and Paramount, assigning films to contemporary composers such as George Antheil, Werner Janssen, and Kurt Weill. Forming Boris Morros Productions in 1939, he went on to a career as an independent producer, notably for *Carnegie Hall* (1947). In 1957 he was exposed as a Soviet counterspy. His autobiography was turned into the biographical picture, *Man on a String* (1960), starring Ernest Borgnine.

Works

(*selective list*)

Film scores

(*as music director*)
The General Died at Dawn, 1936 (score by W. Janssen)
Rhythm on the Range, 1936 (score by J. Leipold)
Angel, 1937 (score by F. Hollander)
High, Wide and Handsome, 1937 (score by R.R. Bennett)
The Plainsman, 1937 (score by G. Antheil)
Blockade, 1938 (score by W. Janssen)
Tropic Holiday, 1938 (score by G. Jenkins)
You and Me, 1938 (score by K. Weill)
Zaza, 1939 (score by Hollander)

Stage

(*as composer*)
King Saul, New York, 1925

Bibliography

"Boris Morros, Musician by Heritage," *Publix Opinion* iii/22 (1930), 7 only
B. Morros and C. Samuels: *My Ten Years As a Counterspy* (New York, 1959)

WARREN M. SHERK

Muskett, Jennie

(*b* Johannesburg, South Africa, 6 Jan 1955). South African film and television composer, active in Great Britain and the USA. Trained at the Royal College of Music in London, she began her career as a cellist, performing with UK orchestras, and is self-taught in composition. Since 1982, she has composed more than eighty projects for Miramax, Paramount, Disney, Discovery, National Geographic, IMAX, and the BBC, including three feature films with American director Martha Coolidge. Passionate about environmental concerns, Muskett's documentary scores incorporate a wide variety of world music elements. Muskett has won two Emmy awards (including one for Best Outstanding Original score for her score for Discovery Channel's *Spirits of the Forest* and another for *Jewels of the Caribbean*) and five Emmy nominations. She won a Peabody Award for *People of the Forest* (National Geographic). Credited with the theme for the popular British television series *Spooks*, she also writes the underscoring. Her music is heartfelt and eloquent, reflecting a wide range of emotion. Muskett has also written incidental music for two Royal Shakespeare Company productions: *After Easter* (M. Attenborough) and *The Honest Whore* (J. Shepherd). Recordings of her music are available on Nicabella Records, Cube Records, IMAX, and Hollywood Records.

Works

Film scores

Daniel Defoe's Robinson Crusoe (dir. R. Hardy and G. Miller), 1997
B. Monkey (dir. M. Radford), 1998
Mr. In-Between (dir. P. Sarossy), 2001
Boxed (dir. M. Comer), 2002
Material Girls (dir. M. Coolidge), 2006
The Prince & Me (dir. M. Coolidge), 2004
An American Girl: Chrissa Stands Strong (dir. M. Coolidge), 2009

Television documentaries and shorts

Baka: The People of the Rainforest (dir. P. Agland), 1987
People of the Forest: Chimps of Gombe (dir. H. Van Lawick), 1988
Great White Shark, Lonely Lord of the Sea, 1991
Secrets of Life on Earth, 1993
Spirits of the Rainforest, 1994
Great White Shark (dir. P. Atkins), 1995
Survival Island (dir. D. Douglas), 1996
Nature, 1996–2008
Nova: Night Creatures of the Kalahari, 1998

Other television

Cyclops (dir. B. Nalluri), 2001
Dead Gorgeous (dir. S. Harding), 2002
Spooks [MI-5], seasons 1–5, 2002–5
Butterfly World (dir. C. Röhl), 2003
Too Good to be True (dir. Harding), 2003
Twelve Days of Christmas Eve (dir. M. Coolidge), 2004

Pizza My Heart (dir. A. Wolk), 2005
Hello Sister, Goodbye Life (dir. S. Robman), 2006
The State Within (dir. M. Offer and D. Percival), 2006
Clever Monkeys (dir. M. Fletcher), 2008
Miss Austen Regrets (dir. J. Lovering), 2008
Compulsion (dir. Harding), 2009

JEANNIE GAYLE POOL

Newman, Alfred

(*b* New Haven, CT, 17 March 1901; *d* Los Angeles, 17 Feb 1970). American composer and conductor. He was a piano prodigy, making his first public appearance at the age of eight. He studied in New York with Rubin Goldmark and George Wedge. In 1914 he was offered a piano scholarship by Sigismond Stojowski for a place at the von Ende School of Music, New York. Family poverty compelled him to abandon a concert career while still young; instead, he played in Broadway theaters and on vaudeville circuits. He studied conducting with William Daly and was the youngest conductor to date to appear on Broadway. As well as serving as music director for the *George White Scandals* (1920) and for the *Greenwich Village Follies* (1922–5), he conducted shows by George and Ira Gershwin, Otto Harbach, and Rodgers and Hart. In 1930 Newman went to Hollywood, where he was soon appointed music director at United Artists. He worked primarily in film musicals but gradually became more interested in traditional Hollywood scoring, especially after the success of his score for *Street Scene* (1931). From 1940 to 1960 he was head of the Twentieth Century-Fox music department and divided his time between composing and supervising and conducting film scores. He also supported the careers of such composers as Bernard Herrmann and Alex North, whose music was often regarded as unconventional. Newman worked on more than 230 films, winning nine Academy awards and forty-five nominations; his last score (for *Airport*) was completed just before his death. Other activities included recordings with the Hollywood Bowl orchestra and guest conducting appearances with various American orchestras. His brothers Emil and Lionel also composed and conducted film scores in Hollywood, as have his sons Thomas and David Newman, his daughter Maria Newman, and his nephew Randy Newman.

One of the key figures in the history of American film music, Newman was among the first screen composers to establish the romantic symphonic style of Hollywood film scores, prevalent from the early 1930s to the mid-1950s. In comparison to composers such as Erich Wolfgang Korngold and Max Steiner, he was essentially self-taught as a composer; the few private lessons he took with Arnold Schoenberg in Hollywood had no appreciable effect on his musical style. His musical talents

From left: Alfred Newman, Bernard Herrmann, and Murray Spivack, 1954
Twentieth Century-Fox Film Corporation ©Twentieth Century-Fox Film Corporation

and fine dramatic sensibility, however, enabled him to learn on the job. When he encountered his first truly challenging scores around 1935, he began to show a knack for developing motivic material and an appreciation for the sound track's potential to incorporate new and interesting musical effects. By 1939 his music had developed into the style with which his name is associated. Well wrought and full textured, his scores sometimes (especially in the string writing) attain a high degree of lyrical and dramatic expressiveness. The manner in which certain sequences follow overt or hidden implications of the dialogue resembles the leitmotivic procedures of Richard Wagner and Richard Strauss.

Newman's scores for *Wuthering Heights*, *The Prisoner of Zenda*, *The Hunchback of Notre Dame*, *Captain from Castile*, and *The Robe* represent Hollywood film music at its best. As a conductor he had a great flair for molding music to the texture and rhythm of a picture and for coordinating the elements involved in the preparation and recording of a film musical. In his capacity as studio music director he encouraged the improvement of recording technique; the so-called Newman System for music synchronization, created for him during his United Artists years by musician Charles Dunworth, was still in use in the early twenty-first century.

Works

(selective list of film scores)
Street Scene (dir. K. Vidor), 1931
We Live Again (dir. R. Mamoulian), 1934
The Dark Angel (dir. S. Franklin), 1935
Beloved Enemy (dir. H. C. Potter), 1936
The Prisoner of Zenda (dir. J. Cromwell), 1937
Beau Geste (dir. W. A. Wellman), 1939
Gunga Din (dir. G. Stevens), 1939
The Hunchback of Notre Dame (dir. W. Dieterle), 1939
Wuthering Heights (dir. W. Wyler), 1939
Young Mr. Lincoln (dir. J. Ford), 1939
Brigham Young (dir. H. Hathaway), 1940
How Green Was My Valley (dir. J. Ford), 1941
The Song of Bernadette (dir. H. King), 1943
Wilson (dir. H. King), 1944
Captain from Castile (dir. H. King), 1947
The Snake Pit (dir. A. Litvak), 1948
Prince of Foxes (dir. H. King), 1949
Twelve O'Clock High (dir. H. King), 1949
The Robe (dir. H. Koster), 1953
The Egyptian (dir. M. Curtiz), 1954, collab. B. Herrmann
A Man Called Peter (dir. H. Koster), 1955
Anastasia (dir. A. Litvak), 1956
The Counterfeit Traitor (dir. G. Seaton), 1962
How the West Was Won (dir. J. Ford, H. Hathaway, and G. Marshall), 1962
The Greatest Story Ever Told (dir. G. Stevens), 1965
Nevada Smith (dir. H. Hathaway), 1966
Camelot (dir. J. Logan), 1967
Airport (dir. G. Seaton), 1970

Bibliography

DAB (F. Steiner)
H. Brown: "The Robe," *Film Music*, xiii/2 (1953), 3–17
K. Darby: "Alfred Newman Biography and Filmography," *Film Music Notebook: a Complete Collection of the Quarterly Journal* (Sherman Oaks, CA, 1974–8), 219–27
F. Steiner: *The Making of an American Film Composer: a Study of Alfred Newman's Music in the First Decade of the Sound Era* (diss., U. of Southern California, 1981) [incl. complete list of film scores]
C. Palmer: *The Composer in Hollywood* (London and New York, 1990)
T. Thomas: *Film Score* (Burbank, CA, 1991)
K. Darby: *Hollywood Holyland: the Filming and Scoring of "The Greatest Story Ever Told"* (Metuchen, NJ, and London, 1992), 163ff
M. Cooke: *A History of Film Music* (New York, 2008)

M. Malsky: "Sounds of the City: Alfred Newman's *Street Scene* and Urban Modernty," *Lowering the Boom: Critical Studies in Film Sound*, ed. J. Beck and T. Grajeda (Urbana, IL, 2008), 105–22

CHRISTOPHER PALMER/FRED STEINER/JESSICA GETMAN/R

Newman, David (Louis)

(*b* Los Angeles, 11 March 1954). American composer, son of Alfred Newman, brother of Thomas Newman, and cousin of Randy Newman. He studied the violin and piano as a child and earned music degrees from the University of Southern California (bachelor's in violin, master's in conducting). He worked regularly as a violinist in the Hollywood studios from 1977 to 1982, playing for such film composers as John Williams and Jerry Goldsmith.

Newman wrote his first film score in 1986 and was immediately embraced by the Hollywood community. He subsequently produced an average of five or six scores per year for his first few years in the business. Although a fine composer for dramas (*Hoffa, Brokedown Palace*), he became more sought-after for big-budget comedies (*The War of the Roses, The Nutty Professor, Galaxy Quest*) and animated films (*The Brave Little Toaster, Anastasia, Ice Age*). He received an Oscar nomination for his *Anastasia* score, forty-one years after his father's Oscar nomination for a live-action version of the same story.

Unlike most of his colleagues, Newman has demonstrated a passion for unearthing and preserving American film music, wherever possible making it available for concert performance. In 1987 he launched a film-music preservation program at Robert Redford's Sundance Institute, which resulted in several high-profile classic film-music concerts that he conducted. He has continued to conduct such programs at the Hollywood Bowl and elsewhere. He championed the work of Goldsmith, commissioning several new concert suites, during a three-year American Youth Symphony program that ended in 2010.

Newman has also written several concert works, including an unusual Los Angeles Philharmonic video-and-music collaboration (*1001 Nights*, 1998) and a six-movement woodwind concerto in which each of the first five movements is devoted to a single soloist and the final movement to all (2007).

Works

(*selective list of film scores*)

Critters (dir. S. Herek), 1986
Vendetta (dir. B. Logan), 1986
The Brave Little Toaster (dir. J. Rees), 1987
The Kindred (dir. S. Carpenter, and J. Obrow), 1987

Malone (dir. H. Cokeliss (as H. Cokliss)), 1987
Throw Momma from the Train (dir. D. DeVito), 1987
Bill & Ted's Excellent Adventure (dir. Herek), 1989
Heathers (dir. M. Lehmann), 1989
The War of the Roses (dir. DeVito), 1989
DuckTales: the Movie (dir. B. Hathcock), 1990
The Freshman (dir. A. Bergman), 1990
Bill & Ted's Bogus Journey (dir. P. Hewitt), 1991
Hoffa (dir. DeVito), 1992
Honeymoon in Vegas (dir. Bergman), 1992
The Mighty Ducks (dir. Herek), 1992
The Sandlot (dir. D.M. Evans), 1993
The Flintstones (dir. B. Levant), 1994
Boys on the Side (dir. H. Ross), 1995
Jingle All the Way (dir. Levant), 1996
Matilda (dir. DeVito), 1996
The Nutty Professor (dir. T. Shadyac), 1996
The Phantom (dir. S. Wincer), 1996
Anastasia (dir. D. Bluth and G. Goldman), 1997
Bowfinger (dir. F. Oz), 1999
Brokedown Palace (dir. J. Kaplan), 1999
Galaxy Quest (dir. D. Parisot), 1999
Never been Kissed (dir. R. Gosnell), 1999
102 Dalmations (dir. K. Lima), 2000
Nutty Professor II: the Klumps (dir. P. Segal), 2000
The Affair of the Necklace (dir. C. Shyer), 2001
Dr. Dolittle 2 (dir. S. Carr), 2001
Ice Age (dir. C. Wedge and C. Saldanha), 2002
Scooby-Doo (dir. R. Gosnell), 2002
The Cat in the Hat (dir. B. Welch), 2003
Daddy Day Care (dir. Carr), 2003
How to Lose a Guy in 10 Days (dir. D. Petrie), 2003
Scooby-Doo 2: Monsters Unleashed (dir. Gosnell), 2004
Monster-in-Law (dir. R. Luketic), 2005, with Rosey
Serenity (dir. J. Whedon), 2005
Norbit (dir. B. Robbins), 2007
The Spirit (dir. F. Miller), 2008
Alvin and the Chipmunks: the Squeakquel (dir. B. Thomas), 2009
Animals United (dir. R. Klooss and H. Tappe), 2010
Crazy on the Outside (dir. T. Allen), 2010
The Spy Next Door (dir. B. Levant), 2010
Big Mommas: Like Father, Like Son (dir. J. Whitesell), 2011
Tarzan (dir. R. Klooss), 2013
5 Flights Up (dir. R. Loncraine), 2014
Behaving Badly (dir. T. Garrick), 2014
Some Kind of Beautiful (dir. T. Vaughan), 2014, with S. Endelman

Army of One (dir. L. Charles), 2016
Girls Trip (dir. M.D. Lee), 2017
Naked (dir. M. Tiddes), 2017

Bibliography

J. Burlingame: "L.A. Music's First Family: Range, Verstility David's Hallmark," *Daily Variety* (15 July 1997)

R. Koppl: "David Newman: the Calm before the Storm," *Film Music* (Oct 1998) 11–14

T. Greiving: "Prince David," *Film Score Monthly Online*, xiv/6 (2009) and xiv/7 (2009)

T. Hoover: "Keeping Score with David Newman," *Keeping Score: Interviews with Today's Top Film, Television, and Game Music Composers*, ed. T. Hoover (Boston, 2010), 21–8

D. Mermelstein: "In Hollywood, Discord on What Makes Music," *The Routledge Film Music Sourcebook*, ed. J. Wierzbicki, N. Platte, and C. Roust (New York, 2012), 278–81

JON BURLINGAME/R

Newman, Lionel

(*b* New Haven, CT, 4 Jan 1916; *d* Los Angeles, 3 Feb 1989). American composer and conductor. The youngest of ten born to immigrant Russian-Jewish parents, his oldest sibling was Alfred Newman, who would become one of the pioneers of American film music. The younger Newman studied composition with Joseph Schillinger in New York and, later in Los Angeles, with Joseph Achron and Mario Castelnuovo-Tedesco.

Like his older brother, Lionel Newman left school early to pursue a career as a musician. At the age of fifteen he conducted for theater producer Earl Carroll in Florida (eventually conducting Carroll's *Vanities* show on Broadway in 1940), and in the 1930s he conducted touring shows for Tom Mix and Mae West. He followed his older brother to Hollywood and achieved early success as a songwriter (including a 1938 Oscar nomination for his title song for *The Cowboy and the Lady*).

Newman began stints as songwriter and rehearsal pianist at Twentieth Century-Fox in late 1939, soon after his brother Alfred became music director for the studio. All ten of his subsequent Oscar nominations were for Fox films, either as songwriter or musical director. He won the 1969 adaptation-score Oscar for *Hello, Dolly!* (with Lennie Hayton). Among his film songs were "As if I didn't have enough on my mind" (with Harry James, from *Do You Love Me?*) and "Never" (from *Golden Girl*), but his biggest hit was "Again" (sung by Ida Lupino in *Road House*), which spent nineteen weeks on radio's *Hit Parade* in 1949 and generated six top-ten hits for performers including Doris Day, Mel Tormé, and Vic Damone.

Marilyn Monroe insisted on Newman as her personal musical director on Fox films including *Gentlemen Prefer Blondes*, *River of No Return*, *There's No Business Like Show Business*, and *Let's Make Love*. He was promoted to director of television music at Fox in 1959 and wrote some of the studio's best-known TV themes, including "Adventures in Paradise," "The Many Loves of Dobie Gillis," "Hong Kong," and "Daniel Boone." He also wrote several dramatic scores including *The Proud Ones*, *Love Me Tender*, *Compulsion*, *North to Alaska*, and *The Boston Strangler*. But his first love was conducting, and he conducted many Fox scores by Jerry Goldsmith, Alex North, and other composers during the 1950s, 1960s, and 1970s.

He succeeded Alfred as general music director for the studio in 1963, overseeing all feature and television music; he became vice president in 1977 and senior vice president in 1982, retiring in 1985. He briefly returned to the business as head of music for MGM-UA in 1988.

Works

Film scores

The Kid from Left Field (dir. H. Jones), 1953
The Gambler from Natchez (dir. H. Levin), 1954
The Killer Is Loose (dir. B. Boetticher), 1956
A Kiss Before Dying (dir. G. Oswald), 1956
The Last Wagon (dir. D. Daves), 1956
Love Me Tender (dir. R.D. Webb), 1956
The Proud Ones (dir. R.D. Webb), 1956
Bernardine (dir. H. Levin), 1957
The Way to the Gold (dir. R.D. Webb), 1957
Sing Boy Sing (dir. H. Ephron), 1958
Compulsion (dir. R. Fleischer), 1959
North to Alaska (dir. H. Hathaway), 1960
Move Over, Darling (dir. M. Gordon), 1963
Do Not Disturb (dir. R. Levy), 1965
The Boston Strangler (dir. R. Fleischer), 1968

As music director

Road House, 1948
You Were Meant for Me, 1948
Golden Girl, 1951
Gentlemen Prefer Blondes, 1953
Niagara, 1953
River of No Return, 1954
There's No Business Like Show Business, 1954
The Girl Can't Help It, 1956
Mardi Gras, 1958

Say One for Me, 1959
Let's Make Love, 1960
The Pleasure Seekers, 1964
Doctor Dolittle, 1967
Hello, Dolly!, 1969
At Long Last Love, 1975

Bibliography

J. Tynan: "Lionel Newman," *BMI News* (Oct 1963), 30–33
"Lionel Newman," *BMI: The Many Worlds of Music*, (1974)
Obituary: *Los Angeles Times* (7 Feb 1989)

JON BURLINGAME

Newman, Randy [Randall] (Stuart)

(*b* Los Angeles, 28 Nov 1943). American popular singer, songwriter, and pianist. He was born into a musical family: three of his uncles, Alfred, Lionel, and Emil, composed and conducted film scores in Hollywood. His family lived in various Southern cities, then, when Newman was seven, they settled in Los Angeles where he began to take piano lessons. He had begun writing songs by the age of fifteen and while still in high school he was hired by Metric Music in California as a staff songwriter for a salary of $50 a week. Newman attended UCLA, where he studied music composition but left before completing his degree.

While at Metric, Newman wrote songs that were performed by many artists including the Fleetwoods, Gene McDaniels, and the O'Jays. One of his first songs to be widely recognized is "I think it's going to rain today," recorded by Judy Collins in 1966. Other artists have continued to record and perform his material over the years: Three Dog Night sang a truncated version of "Mama told me not to come" (1970), and Bonnie Raitt (1997) and Neil Diamond (2010) have both covered "Feels Like Home" from his musical *Faust*.

Newman began to record his own songs in 1968. He wrote and arranged all of the material on *Randy Newman Creates Something New under the Sun*, often using a full orchestra. It was this setting that allowed Newman's vocal delivery—drawling, untrained—to stand out, thus heightening the irony of his lyrics and the stories present in his songs. His concise songs—many of the early ones are less than two minutes long—generally narrate stories and often incorporate a device Newman refers to as the untrustworthy narrator. In "Davy the Fat Boy," for instance, the narrator presents himself as Davy's best friend, promising to take care of him when Davy's parents' die, yet he turns Davy into a carnival attraction sideshow. Newman has returned frequently to this device in various guises throughout his songwriting career. He is a slow songwriter and established an early pattern of completing enough songs to fill an album every two to three years, recording the album, and then making a tour. The songs range from the standard pop structure of verse and chorus to through-composed pieces. His work varies from a traditional rock style to jazz, blues, show tunes, and classical sources. Early songs that attracted attention include "Short People" (1977) and "I love L.A." (1983).

In 1970 Newman began his foray into the world of film scores with his work on *Cold Turkey* with Norman Lear; that year he also conducted the music for *Performance*, which starred Mick Jagger. However, Newman dismissed this effort later, crediting his orchestrator Arthur Morton, instead. Newman did not compose for film again until 1981, when he wrote for Miloš Forman's *Ragtime*, which earned him an Academy Award nomination for the song "One More Hour." In 1984 he earned his second Academy Award nomination and a Grammy Award for Best Instrumental for his work on *The Natural*. Newman has subsequently continued to write film scores and has been nominated for and won several Academy Awards. He has had frequent pairings with the Walt Disney animation division, on such films as the *Toy Story* trilogy (1995, 1999, 2010), *Cars* (2006), *Cars 3* (2017), and *The Princess and the Frog* (2009).

Despite his work in film, Newman has continued to write and produce albums of his own songs for release. *Harps and Angels* (Nonesuch, 2008) displays the same characteristics as his earlier albums. Newman is widely respected in both the rock and film score communities and continues to tour venues around the world.

Selected recordings

Randy Newman Creates Something New under the Sun (Reprise, 1968)
12 Songs (Reprise, 1970)
Sail Away (Reprise, 1972)
Good Old Boys (Warner Bros. and Rhino, 1974)
Little Criminals (Warner Bros., 1977)
Born Again (Warner Bros., 1979)
Trouble in Paradise (Warner Bros., 1983)
Land of Dreams (Reprise, 1988)
Faust (Reprise, 1995)
Bad Love (Dreamworks, 1999)
Harps and Angels (Nonesuch, 2008)
Black Matter (Nonesuch, 2017)

Works

Film scores

Cold Turkey (dir. N. Lear), 1971
Herbstkatzen (dir. R. Klaholz), 1981

Ragtime (dir. M. Forman), 1981
The Natural (dir. B. Levinson), 1984
Gotcha! (dir. J. Kanew), 1985
Huey Long (dir. K. Burns), 1985
¡Three Amigos! (dir. J. Landis), 1986
Avalon (dir. B. Levinson), 1990
Awakenings (dir. P. Marshall), 1990
Maverick (dir. R. Donner), 1994
The Paper (dir. R. Howard), 1994
Toy Story (dir. J. Lasseter), 1995
James and the Giant Peach (dir. H. Selick), 1996
Michael (dir. N. Ephron), 1996
Cats Don't Dance (dir. M. Dindal), 1997
A Bug's Life (dir. J. Lasseter and A. Stanton), 1998
Pleasantville (dir. G. Ross), 1998
Toy Story 2 (dir. J. Lasseter and A. Brannon), 1999
Meet the Parents (dir. J. Roach), 2000
Monsters, Inc. (dir. P. Docter, D. Silverman, and L. Unkrich), 2000
Mike's New Car (dir. P. Docter and R. Gould), 2001
The Making of "Seabiscuit" (dir. L. Bouzereau), 2003
Meet the Fockers (dir. J. Roach), 2003
Seabiscuit (dir. G. Ross), 2003
Cars (dir. J. Lasseter and J. Ranft), 2006
The Road to Cars (TV movie, dir. T. James), 2006
Leatherheads (dir. G. Clooney), 2008
The Princess and the Frog (dir. R. Clements and J. Musker), 2009
Toy Story 3 (dir. L. Unkrich), 2010
Monsters University (dir. D. Scanlon), 2013
Cars 3 (dir. B. Fee), 2017
The Meyerowitz Stories (New and Selected) (dir. N. Baumbach), 2017

Bibliography

K. Courrier: *Randy Newman's American Dreams* (Toronto, 2005)

A. Murphy: "Randy Newman: Shaping a Complicated Musical Landscape," *Sound and Music in Film and Visual Media*, ed. G. Harper, R. Doughty, and J. Eisentraut (New York, 2009), 472–79

D. Stafford and C. Stafford: *Maybe I'm Doing it Wrong: The Life & Music of Randy Newman* (London, 2016)

JON PARELES/JENNIFER MATTHEWS/R

Newman, Thomas

(*b* Los Angeles, 20 Oct 1955). American film composer. The youngest son of Alfred Newman, one of the central figures of Hollywood film music within the studio system of the mid-twentieth century, Thomas Newman has been a prolific, innovative, and influential composer of film scores in the late twentieth and early twenty-first century. Newman was taught the piano and violin as a child, then studied composition privately with George Tremblay and with Frederick Lesemann and David Raksin during Newman's two years at the University of Southern California. After transferring to Yale University (BA 1977), Newman continued his compositional studies with Robert Moore, Bruce MacCombie, and Jacob Raphael Druckman, completing the master's degree in composition in 1978. Newman formed an important early connection with Broadway composer Stephen Sondheim, who helped Newman hone his interest in combining music and drama during the time when Newman wrote a musical theatre piece, *Three Mean Fairy Tales*, which received a workshop performance. An opportunity to orchestrate a cue from John William's score for *Star Wars VI: Return of the Jedi* fuelled Newman's growing interest in writing for film, and after working as a musical assistant on the 1984 film *Reckless*, Newman began to receive his own solo composing assignments. Consciously claiming the influence of composers such as Charles Ives, Igor Stravinsky, and Bernard Herrmann,

Thomas Newman, left, and Alexandre Desplat, 2014
(Photo by John Shearer/Invision/AP)

Newman possesses a similarly pioneering spirit, and his imaginative approach to timbre has given his music a rare distinctiveness in a Hollywood landscape that often demands stylistic conformity. By the mid-1990s, Newman was recognized as one of the most original and influential composers working in Hollywood, as evidenced in part by his dual nominations for a Best Score Oscar for two 1994 scores, *Little Women* and *The Shawshank Redemption*. His music frequently blends digitally processed sounds together with acoustic instruments, and his strategic use of pedal points and drones highlights timbral qualities over harmonic progression and thereby lends his music an occasionally non-teleological quality. Newman has also created stirring symphonic scores in the tradition of his father's generation. Several of his scores show a fondness for pitched percussion, and compositions like his Oscar-nominated score for *American Beauty* quickly became a stock sound for television commercials and derivative film scores. In addition to his dramatic works, Newman has received several commissions for concert works, including *Reach Forth Our Hands* for the 1996 Cleveland Bicentennial; a concerto for double bass and orchestra titled *At Ward's Ferry, Length 180 Ft.*, commissioned in 2001 by the Pittsburgh Symphony; and *It Got Dark*, initially commissioned by the Kronos Quartet in 2009 with a subsequent commission from the Los Angeles Philharmonic for a version for solo string quartet and orchestra.

Works

Film scores

Grandview, U.S.A. (dir. R. Kleiser), 1984
Reckless (dir. J. Foley), 1984
Revenge of the Nerds (dir. J. Kanew), 1984
Desperately Seeking Susan (dir. S. Seidelman), 1985
The Man with One Red Shoe (dir. S. Dragoti), 1985
Real Genius (dir. M. Coolidge), 1985
Jumpin' Jack Flash (dir. P. Marshall), 1986
Less Than Zero (dir. M. Kanievska), 1987
Light of Day (dir. P. Schrader), 1987
The Lost Boys (dir. J. Schumacher), 1987
The Great Outdoors (dir. H. Deutch), 1988
Welcome Home, Roxy Carmichael (dir. J. Abrahams), 1990, with M. Etheridge
Career Opportunities (dir. B. Gordon), 1991
Fried Green Tomatoes (dir. J. Avnet), 1991
The Linguini Incident (dir. R. Shepard), 1991
The Rapture (dir. M. Tolkin), 1991
The Player (dir. R. Altman), 1992
Scent of a Woman (dir. M. Brest), 1992
Flesh and Bone (dir. S. Kloves), 1993
Josh and S.A.M. (dir. B. Weber), 1993
Little Women (dir. G. Armstrong), 1994

The Shawshank Redemption (dir. F. Darabont), 1994
Threesome (dir. A. Fleming), 1994
The War (dir. Avnet), 1994
How to Make an American Quilt (dir. J. Moorhouse), 1995
Unstrung Heroes (dir. D. Keaton), 1995
American Buffalo (dir. M. Corrente), 1996
The People vs. Larry Flynt (dir. M. Forman), 1996
Phenomenon (dir. J. Turteltaub), 1996
Up Close & Personal (dir. Avnet), 1996
Mad City (dir. Costa-Gavras), 1997
Oscar and Lucinda (dir. G. Armstrong), 1997
Red Corner (dir. Avnet), 1997
The Horse Whisperer (dir. R. Redford), 1998, with G. Owen
Meet Joe Black (dir. Brest), 1998
American Beauty (dir. S. Mendes), 1999
The Green Mile (dir. Darabont), 1999
Boston Public (TV, theme), 2000
Erin Brockovich (dir. S. Soderbergh), 2000
Pay It Forward (dir. M. Leder), 2000
In the Bedroom (dir. T. Field), 2001
Six Feet Under (TV miniseries, theme), 2001
Road to Perdition (dir. Mendes), 2002
The Salton Sea (dir. D.J. Caruso), 2002
White Oleander (dir. P. Kosminsky), 2002
Angels in America (TV miniseries), 2003
Finding Nemo (dir. A. Stanton and L. Unkrich), 2003
Lemony Snicket's A Series of Unfortunate Events (dir. B. Silberling), 2004
Cinderella Man (dir. R. Howard), 2005
Jarhead (dir. Mendes), 2005
The Good German (dir. Soderbergh), 2006
Little Children (dir. T. Field), 2006
Towelhead (dir. A. Ball), 2007
Revolutionary Road (dir. Mendes), 2008
WALL-E (dir. A. Stanton), 2008
Brothers (dir. J. Sheridan), 2009
The Debt (dir. J. Madden), 2010
The Adjustment Bureau (dir. G. Nolfi), 2011
The Best Exotic Marigold Hotel (dir. Madden), 2011
The Help (dir. T. Taylor), 2011
The Iron Lady (dir. P. Lloyd), 2011
Skyfall (dir. Mendes), 2012
Saving Mr. Banks (dir. J.L. Hancock), 2013
Side Effects (dir. Soderbergh), 2013
Get on Up (dir. Taylor), 2014
The Judge (dir. D. Dobkin), 2014
Bridge of Spies (dir. S. Spielberg), 2015
He Named Me Malala (dir. D. Guggenheim), 2015

The Second Best Exotic Marigold Hotel (dir. Madden), 2015
Spectre (dir. Mendes), 2015
Finding Dory (dir. A. Stanton and A. MacLane), 2016
Passengers (dir. M. Tyldum), 2016
Thank You for Your Service (dir. J. Hall), 2017
Victoria and Abdul (dir. S. Frears), 2017
Unsane (dir. Soderbergh (as D.W. Savage)), 2018

Bibliography

D. Schweiger: "Thomas Newman: Scoring *The Shawshank Redemption*," *Film Score Monthly*, li (Nov 1994), 8–9 [interview]

D. Adams: "Unstrung Newman: Thomas Newman Continues to be Interesting and Good," *Film Score Monthly*, lxv–lxvii (Jan–Feb–March 1996), 10–13 [interview]

L. Danly: "An Interview with Thomas Newman," *The Cue Sheet*, xii/3 (1996), 8–16

M. Schelle: "Thomas Newman," *The Score: Interviews with Film Composers* (Los Angeles, 1999), 267–92

R. Care: "Thomas Newman," *International Dictionary of Film and Filmmakers*, ed. S. Pendergast and T. Pendergast (Detroit, MI, 2000), 635–7

D. Adams: "Finding Newman," *Film Score Monthly*, ix/1 (Jan 2004), 14–17

S. Link: "Nor the Eye Filled with Seeing: the Sound of Vision in Film," *American Music* xxii/1 (Spring 2004), 76–90

A. Bushard: "The Very Essence of Tragic Reality: Aaron Copland and Thomas Newman's Suburban Scoring," *Anxiety Muted: American Film Music in a Suburban Age*, ed. S. Pelkey and A. Bushard (New York, 2015), 260–85

NEIL LERNER/R

North, Alex

(*b* Chester, PA, 4 Dec 1910; *d* Los Angeles, 8 Sept 1991). American composer and conductor. After attending the Curtis Institute, where he studied the piano with George Frederick Boyle, he won a scholarship (1929) to the Juilliard School. He also studied on scholarship at the Moscow Conservatory (from 1933) and went on to serve as music director of the German Theatre Group and the Latvian State Theatre. He was the only American member of the Union of Soviet Composers, from which he received commissions for two choruses and a set of piano variations. In 1935 he returned to the United States and taught music for dance at Finch, Briarcliff, Sarah Lawrence, and Bennington colleges. In New York he studied composition with Aaron Copland and Ernst Toch and composed ballet scores for Martha Graham, Hanya Holm, and Agnes De Mille. In 1939 he went to Mexico as music director for Anna Sokolow's dance troupe, and while there he studied with Silvestre Revueltas and conducted concerts at the Palace of Fine Arts in Mexico City.

During World War II North served as a captain in the US Army; he organized therapeutic programs for veterans and scored more than eighty documentaries for the Office of War Information. In 1946 his *Revue* for clarinet and orchestra was performed by Benny Goodman with the City Symphony of New York under Leonard Bernstein. He continued to compose for the theater, particularly ballet scores, and after the success of his music for Elia Kazan's production of Arthur Miller's *Death of a Salesman*, Kazan invited him to write for the film version of Tennessee Williams's *A Streetcar Named Desire*. This, the first jazz-based symphonic score to be written for a film, brought North wide acclaim, and in the 1950s he became a leading Hollywood composer.

North made no stylistic distinction between his film music and his works in other genres; his entire output is grounded in the traditions of symphonic and chamber music. Fundamentally dramatic in conception, although often not emotionally demonstrative, his works include moments of light and dark, violent dissonance, and gentle lyricism or resignation. Although he used large symphonic forces to excellent effect (notably in the film scores for *Spartacus* and *Cleopatra*), he often wrote for smaller ensembles (as in *The Bachelor Party* and *Who's Afraid of Virginia Woolf?*). He was adept at integrating jazz elements (as in *A Streetcar Named Desire*, *The Long, Hot Summer*, and *The Rose Tattoo*) and like Bernard Herrmann preferred to exploit timbre, affect, and understated stylistic references, rather than referential themes and leitmotivic networks.

From left: Alex North, Leonard Bernstein, and Benny Goodman, 1946
Photofest

Works

Film scores

(**-documentaries*)
*China Strikes Back (dir. H. Dunham and I. Lerner), 1936
*Heart of Spain (dir. H. Kline and C. Korvin), 1937
*People of the Cumberland (dir. E. Kazan, J. Leyda, S. Meyers, and B. Watts), 1937
*Mount Vernon, 1940
*A Better Tomorrow (dir. A. Hammid), 1944
*Library of Congress (dir. A. Hammid), 1945
*Venezuela, 1945
*City Pastorale, 1946
*Recreation, 1946
*Rural Nurse, 1946
*Coney Island USA, 1950
Death of a Salesman (dir. L. Benedek), 1951
The 13th Letter (dir. O. Preminger), 1951
A Streetcar Named Desire (dir. E. Kazan), 1951
Les Misérables (dir. L. Milestone), 1952
Pony Soldier (dir. J. M. Newman), 1952
Viva Zapata! (dir. E. Kazan), 1952
*The American Road (dir. G. C. Stoney), 1953
*Decision for Chemistry, 1953
The Member of the Wedding (dir. F. Zinnemann), 1953
Desirée (dir. H. Koster), 1954
Go, Man, Go! (dir. J. W. Howe), 1954
Man with the Gun (dir. R. Wilson), 1955
The Racers (dir. H. Hathaway), 1955
The Rose Tattoo (dir. D. Mann), 1955
Unchained (dir. H. Bartlett), 1955
The Bad Seed (dir. M. LeRoy), 1956
I'll Cry Tomorrow (dir. D. Mann), 1956
The King and Four Queens (dir. R. Walsh), 1956
The Rainmaker (dir. J. Anthony), 1956
The Bachelor Party (dir. D. Mann), 1957
Hot Spell (dir. D. Mann), 1958
The Long, Hot Summer (dir. M. Ritt), 1958
South Seas Adventure (dir. C. Dudley, R. Goldstone, F. D. Lyon, W. Thompson, and B. Wrangell), 1958
Stage Struck (dir. S. Lumet), 1958
The Sound and the Fury (dir. M. Ritt), 1959
The Wonderful Country (dir. R. Parrish), 1959
Spartacus (dir. S. Kubrick), 1960
The Children's Hour (dir. W. Wyler), 1961
The Misfits (dir. J. Huston), 1961
Sanctuary (dir. T. Richardson), 1961
All Fall Down (dir. J. Frankenheimer), 1962

Cleopatra (dir. J. L. Mankiewics), 1963
The Outrage (dir. M. Ritt), 1964
The Agony and the Ecstasy (dir. C. Reed), 1965
Cheyenne Autumn (dir. J. Ford), 1965
Who's Afraid of Virginia Woolf? (dir. M. Nichols), 1966
2001: a Space Odyssey (dir. S. Kubrick), 1967 [not used]
The Devil's Brigade (dir. A. V. McLaglen), 1968
The Shoes of the Fisherman (dir. M. Anderson), 1968
A Dream of Kings (dir. D. Mann), 1969
Hard Contract (dir. S. L. Pogostin), 1969
Willard (dir. D. Mann), 1971
Pocket Money (dir. S. Rosenberg), 1972
The Rebel Jesus (dir. L. Buchanan), 1972
Once upon a Scoundrel (dir. G. Schaefer), 1973
Lost in the Stars (dir. D. Mann), 1974 [adaptation of work by Weill, 1949]
Shanks (dir. W. Castle), 1974
Bite the Bullet (dir. R. Brooks), 1975
Journey into Fear (dir. D. Mann), 1975
The Passover Plot (dir. M. Campus), 1976
Somebody Killed her Husband (dir. L. Johnson), 1978
Carny (dir. R. Kaylor), 1980
Wise Blood (dir. J. Huston), 1980
Dragonslayer (dir. M. Robbins), 1981 [after 2001: a Space Odyssey]
Under the Volcano (dir. J. Huston), 1984
Prizzi's Honor (dir. J. Huston), 1985
The Dead (dir. J. Huston), 1987
Good Morning, Vietnam (dir. B. Levinson), 1987
The Penitent (dir. C. Osmond), 1988
The Last Butterfly (dir. K. Kachyna), 1991
other documentaries

Other works

Stage

Hither and Thither of Danny Dither (children's op, J. Gury), 1941
ballets and dance scores, TV scores, incid music and musical revues, other children's works

Instrumental

Quest, chbr orch, 1938
Suite, fl, cl, bn, 1938
Rhapsody, pf, orch, 1939
Suite, str qt, 1939
Trio, ww, 1939
Wind Qnt, 1942
Window Cleaner, cl, 2 pf, 1945
Revue, cl, orch, 1946
Sym. no.1, 1947

Dance Preludes, pf, 1948
Holiday Set, orch, 1948
Death of a Salesman, suite, orch, 1951 [based on film score]
A Streetcar Named Desire, suite, orch, 1951 [based on film score]
Viva Zapata!, suite, orch, 1952 [based on film score]
Rhapsody, tpt, pf, orch, 1956 [for film Four Girls in Town]
Sym. no.2, 1968 [based on TV score Africa]

Vocal

Negro Mother (cant., L. Hughes), A, chorus, orch, 1940
Ballad of Valley Forge (A. Kreymborg), Bar, chorus, orch, 1941
Rhapsody, USA (A. Hayes), S, A, T, B, chorus, orch, 1942
Morning Star (cant., M. Lampell), chorus, orch, 1946
many songs

Recorded interviews in *US-NHoh*; *MSS* in *US-LAum*

Principal publishers: Marks, Mills, North, Northern

Bibliography

GroveA (C. Palmer/C. McCarty) [incl. further bibliography]
D. Kraft: "A Conversation with Alex North," *Soundtrack!*, iv/13 (1985), 3–8
W. Darby and J. Du Bois: *American Film Music: Major Composers, Techniques, Trends, 1915–1990* (Jefferson, NC, 1990), 398–424
T. Thomas: *Film Score: the Art and Craft of Movie Music* (Burbank, CA, 1991), 182–94
G. Burt: *The Art of Film Music* (Boston, 1994), 59ff
S.S. Henderson: *Alex North, Film Composer: a Biography, with Musical Analyses of "A Streetcar Named Desire," "Spartacus," "The Misfits," "Under the Volcano," and "Prizzi's Honor"* (Jefferson, NC, 2003)
P.A. Merkley: "'Stanley Hates This but I Like It!': North vs. Kubrick on the Music for *2001: a Space Odyssey*," *Journal of Film Music*, ii/1 (2007), 1–33
A. Davison: *Alex North's "A Streetcar Named Desire": a Film Score Guide* (Lanham, MD, 2009)

CLIFFORD MCCARTY/DAVID NEUMEYER

Portman, Rachel (Mary Berkeley)

(*b* Haslemere, England, 11 Dec 1960). English composer. She studied music at Worcester College, Oxford, and composition with Roger Steptoe; she also composed for productions at the Oxford Playhouse and scored a student film, *Privileged*, which was sold to the BBC. Her first professional film scoring commission came from David Puttnam in 1982 with *Experience Preferred . . . But Not Essential*. Her early television scores included "The Storyteller" (1986–8 and 1990), a series by Jim Henson, for which she was awarded the British Film Institute's Young Composer of the Year Award in 1988. In 1991 she composed for Mike Leigh's *Life is Sweet* (1990), her first feature film score. Since 1992 she has been in demand for Hollywood productions, and remains one of the few female composers to have achieved significant success at this level. With *Emma* (1996) she became the first female composer to receive an Academy Award.

Her film scores embrace a variety of styles, although she is best known for composing clear, string-dominated textures, often shaded with lyrical woodwind lines. She orchestrates much of her own music, but also works closely with orchestrator Jeff Atmajian. Although Portman gained renown as a composer for romantic comedies, her versatility is reflected in the many genres she has explored since the late 1990s, which range from serious drama to psychological thriller. In particular, she has collaborated with Lasse Hallström on *Cider House Rules* (1999) and *Chocolat* (2000), the scores of which were nominated for Academy Awards. Her scores for director Jonathan Demme's *Beloved* (1998) and *Manchurian Candidate* (2004) are especially striking; both scores depart from her more familiar orchestral sound. In particular, *Beloved* features solo voice, chorus, and African instruments instead of full orchestra. In 2003 her opera *The Little Prince* had its première at the Houston Grand Opera and has since been performed throughout the United States and recorded under the auspices of the BBC. Based on Antoine de Saint-Exupéry's novel of the same name, Portman's *The Little Prince* is one of relatively few operas intended for both children and adults. Characterized by cleanly etched vocal lines for boy soprano and lively children's choruses, the opera represents the composer's most ambitious work.

Works

Television music

The Storyteller, 1986–8, 1990
Oranges Are Not the Only Fruit, 1990
Antonia and Jane, 1991
Friends, 1993

Film scores

Experience Preferred . . . But Not Essential (dir. P. Duffell), 1982
Privileged (dir. M. Hoffman), 1982
Life is Sweet (dir. M. Leigh), 1990
Where Angels Fear to Tread (dir. C. Sturridge), 1991
Used People (dir. B. Kidron), 1992
Benny and Joon (dir. J.S. Chechik), 1993
Ethan Frome (dir. J. Madden), 1993
The Joy Luck Club (dir. W. Wang), 1993
Only You (dir. N. Jewison), 1994
Sirens (dir. J. Duigan), 1994
War of the Buttons (dir. J. Roberts), 1994
A Pyromaniac's Love Story (dir. J. Brand), 1995

Smoke (dir. W. Wang), 1995
To Wong Foo, Thanks for Everything! Julie Newmar (dir. B. Kidron), 1995
The Adventures of Pinocchio (dir. S. Barron), 1996
Emma (dir. D. McGrath), 1996
Marvin's Room (dir. J. Zaks), 1996
Addicted to Love (dir. G. Dunne), 1997
Beloved (dir. J. Demme), 1998
The Cider House Rules (dir. L. Hallström), 1999
The Other Sister (dir. G. Marshall), 1999
Ratcatcher (dir. L. Ramsay), 1999
Chocolat (dir. L. Hallström), 2000
The Legend of Bagger Vance (dir. R. Redford), 2000
The Emperor's New Clothes (dir. A. Taylor), 2001
Hart's War (dir. G. Hoblit), 2002
The Truth about Charlie (dir. J. Demme), 2002
The Human Stain (dir. R. Benton), 2003
Mona Lisa Smile (dir. M. Newell), 2003
Lard (dir. O. Spenceley), 2004
The Manchurian Candidate (dir. J. Demme), 2004
Because of Winn-Dixie (dir. W. Wang), 2005
Oliver Twist (dir. R. Polanski), 2005
Infamous (dir. D. McGrath), 2006
The Lake House (dir. A. Agresti), 2006
The Duchess (dir. S. Dibb), 2008
Grey Gardens (dir. M. Sucsy), 2009
Never Let Me Go (dir. M. Romanek), 2010
One Day (dir. L. Scherfig), 2011
Snow Flower and the Secret Fan (dir. W. Wang), 2011
Bel Ami (dir. D. Donnellan and N. Ormerod), 2012
Private Peaceful (dir. P. O'Connor), 2012
The Vow (dir. M. Sucsy), 2012
Belle (dir. A. Asante), 2013
Paradise (dir. D. Cody), 2013
The Right Kind of Wrong (dir. J.S. Chechik), 2013
Still Life (dir. U. Pasolini), 2013
Dolphin Tale 2 (dir. C.M. Smith), 2014
Bessie (dir. D. Rees), 2015
Despite the Falling Snow (dir. S. Sarif), 2016
Race (dir. S. Hopkins), 2016
Remembering Christmas (dir. J. Scanlan), 2016
Their Finest (dir. L. Scherfig), 2016
A Dog's Purpose (dir. L. Hallström), 2017

Opera and musicals

The Little Prince (N. Wright), Houston, Houston Grand Opera, 31 May 2003
Little House on the Prairie (R. Sheinkin), Minneapolis, Guthrie Theater, 26 July 2008

Bibliography

H. Lumme: *Great Women of Film* (New York, 2002), 100–103

S. Kennedy: "A Night at the Opera: Rachel Portman Takes on Her First Concert Work, Saint-Exupéry's *The Little Prince*," *Film Score Monthly*, viii/6 (2003), 14–16

L.M. Timm: *The Soul of Cinema: an Appreciation of Film Music* (Upper Saddle River, NJ, 2003)

F. Karlin and R. Wright: *On the Track: a Guide to Contemporary Film Scoring* (New York, 1990, 2/2004)

C. DesJardins: *Inside Film Music: Composers Speak* (Los Angeles, 2006), 196–204

DAVID KERSHAW/NATHAN PLATTE/R

Post, Mike [Postil, Leland M.]

(*b* Los Angeles, 29 Sept 1944). American composer. He grew up in the San Fernando Valley and, after high school, became a session musician for popular artists (he played guitar on Sonny and Cher's 1965 hit "I got you Babe"). In his early twenties he became an arranger and producer of pop material, including *The First Edition* (the band which catapulted Kenny Rogers to fame) and Mason Williams's *Classical Gas* (which earned Post a 1968 Grammy award).

In 1969 Post became musical director on "The Andy Williams Show," the youngest person to hold such a post in the history of television variety shows. The year before he had befriended the trombonist and arranger Pete Carpenter, then in his mid-fifties, who possessed years of experience composing and orchestrating for television. The two launched a partnership writing dramatic underscores; their first series was "Toma" in 1973, one of several collaborations with the producer Stephen J. Cannell over the next two decades.

"Music by Mike Post and Pete Carpenter" became a familiar television credit in the 1970s and 80s. They brought more contemporary sounds, including electric guitar, synthesizers, and backbeat, to the otherwise staid, traditional orchestral approach for most TV series. Their themes were also radio-friendly, generating pop hits for shows including "The Rockford Files," "The Greatest American Hero," and "Magnum, P.I." Carpenter—with whom Post also scored "The White Shadow," "The A-Team," and "Hunter"—died in 1987, after scoring an estimated 1800 hours of television with Post.

On his own, Post enjoyed continued success with several Steven Bochco–produced series from the 1980s and 90s including "Hill Street Blues," "Doogie Howser M.D.," "L.A. Law," "NYPD Blue," and "Murder One" (the last of which won Post an Emmy). He also scored all of the "Law & Order" series beginning in 1990, creating a familiar transitional device often referred to as the "chung-chung," a musical sound effect similar to a jail cell slamming shut.

Works

(selective list)

Film scores

Rabbit Test (dir. J. Rivers), 1978, with Carpenter
Deep in the Heart (dir. T. Garnett), 1984
The River Rat (dir. T. Rickman), 1984
Hadley's Rebellion (dir. F. Walton), 1987
Dead above Ground (dir. C. Bowman), 2002, with A. Örvarsson
Home is Where you Find It (dir. A. Soares), 2009
Rust (dir. C. Bernsen), 2010, with B. McCormick
New York Says Thank You (dir. S. Rettberg), 2011, with M.J. Leslie and M.Q. Rankin
Behind the Gate (dir. J. Lucarelli and M. Giardino), 2013

Television series music (with Pete Carpenter)

Toma, 1973
The Rockford Files, 1974
Baa Baa Black Sheep (later Black Sheep Squadron), 1976
Richie Brockelman, Private Eye, 1978
The White Shadow, 1978
The Duke, 1979
Magnum, P.I., 1980
Tenspeed and Brown Shoe, 1980
The Greatest American Hero, 1981
Tales of the Gold Monkey, 1982
The A-Team, 1983
Hardcastle & McCormick, 1983
Hunter, 1984
Riptide, 1984
Stingray, 1986

Television themes (with the lyricist Stephen Geyer)

Richie Brockelman, 1981
The Greatest American Hero, 1981
Hardcastle & McCormick, 1983
Blossom, 1990

Television movie music (with Carpenter)

Two on a Bench, 1971
Gidget Gets Married, 1972
The Morning After, 1974
The Invasion of Johnson County, 1976
Coach of the Year, 1980
Will: G. Gordon Liddy, 1982

Hard Knox, 1984
The Gin Game, 2003

Television series music (Post alone)

Hill Street Blues, 1981–7
Bay City Blues, 1983
L.A. Law, 1986–94
Hooperman, 1987–9
Wiseguy, 1987–90
B.L. Stryker, 1989
Unsub, 1989
Quantum Leap, 1989–90
Doogie Howser, M.D., 1989–93
Law & Order, 1990–2010
The Commish, 1991
Silk Stalkings, 1991
NYPD Blue, 1993–2004
Murder One, 1995–7
Brooklyn South, 1997–8
Law & Order: Special Victims Unit, 1999–2018
Law & Order: Criminal Intent, 2001–11
L.A. Dragnet, 2003–4
Blind Justice, 2005
Law & Order: Trial by Jury, 2005–6
Inside the FBI: New York, 2017

Television movie music (Post alone)

Adam, 1983
Heart of a Champion: the Ray Mancini Story, 1985
Nashville Beat, 1989
The Ryan White Story, 1989
Unspeakable Acts, 1990
Without Her Consent, 1990
The Gin Game, 2003

Bibliography

J. Burlingame: "Mike Post: He Makes TV Sound the Way It Sounds," *Washington Post* (TV Week, 24 July 1994)

J. Burlingame: *TV's Biggest Hits: the Story of Television Themes from "Dragnet" to "Friends"* (New York, 1996)

E. Fink: "Episodic's Music Man: Mike Post," *Journal of Popular Film and Television*, xxv/4 (1998), 155–60

JON BURLINGAME/R

Powell, Edward (B.)

(*b* Savanna, IL, 5 Dec 1909; *d* Los Angeles, 29 Feb 1984). American orchestrator, arranger, composer, and conductor. As a teenager, he played the alto saxophone in a St. Louis high school orchestra. His dissatisfaction with published dance band arrangements led him to write his own and eventually brought him to the attention of Fletcher Henderson in New York. Once there, Powell worked as a staff arranger at the music publisher Harms from 1930 to 1934, orchestrating Broadway musical comedies, notably George and Ira Gershwin's *Let 'em Eat Cake*. Largely self-taught, he studied harmony and counterpoint with Mortimer Wilson and Joseph Schillinger, later taking up musical analysis with Arnold Schoenberg in Los Angeles. His petition for bankruptcy in 1933 may have prompted his relocation to Hollywood the following year. His long association with Alfred Newman began at Samuel Goldwyn Productions, where Powell was under contract from 1934 to 1939. At Goldwyn, drawing on his Broadway experience, Powell excelled at arranging for musical pictures. He followed Newman to Twentieth Century-Fox, working as a staff arranger and orchestrator from 1940 to 1960. Powell also regularly orchestrated for Hugo Friedhofer, Cyril Mockridge, Alex North, and Franz Waxman. Freelancing in the 1960s, he worked on a handful of Alex North scores before retiring in the late 1960s. He did not always receive credit on the hundreds of films he orchestrated; contributions of original music to films scored by others also often went uncredited. Highly regarded and admired by his peers, he is widely considered to be one of the finest orchestrators ever to work in film.

Works

(*selective list*)

Film scores

(*as orchestrator and/or arranger*)

The Goldwyn Follies (dir. G. Marshall and H.C. Potte (uncredited), comp. A. Newman), 1938
The Song of Bernadette (dir. H. King, comp. Newman), 1943
My Darling Clementine (dir. J. Ford, comp. D. Buttolph), 1946
Captain from Castile (dir. King, comp. Newman), 1947
All About Eve (dir. J.L. Mankiewicz, comp. F. Waxman), 1950
Broken Arrow (dir. D. Daves, comp. H. Friedhofer), 1950
The Robe (dir. H. Koster, comp. Newman), 1953
Prince Valiant (dir. H. Hathaway, comp. Waxman), 1954
There's No Business Like Show Business (dir. W. Lang, comp. Newman), 1954
The King and I (dir. Lang, comp. Newman), 1956
Peyton Place (dir. M. Robson, comp. Waxman), 1957

South Pacific (dir. J. Logan, comp. Newman), 1958
The Sound and the Fury (dir. M. Ritt, comp. A. North), 1959
From the Terrace (dir. Robson, comp. E. Bernstein), 1960
Hang 'em High (dir. T. Post, comp. D. Frontiere), 1968

Film scores

(as composer)
Topper Takes a Trip (dir. N.Z. McLeod), 1939, with H. Friedhofer
State Fair (dir. W. Lang), 1945, with A. Newman and others

Stage

(as orchestrator, all New York)
Garrick Gaieties, 1930
Earl Carroll's Vanities, 1932
Murder at the Vanities, 1933

MSS in *US-LAum*

Bibliography

J. Rodriguez, ed.: *Music and Dance in California* (Hollywood, CA, 1940)
L. Maury: "Edward Powell," *The Score* vol.iv/2 (1950), 5
R. Jackson: "The Vision Scenes in *Bernadette*: Newman's and Powell's Contributions," *Journal of Film Music* vol.iii/2 (2010), 111–25

WARREN M. SHERK/R

Raksin, David

(*b* Philadelphia, 4 Aug 1912; *d* Los Angeles, 9 Aug 2004). American composer, arranger, conductor, and author. He first learned about music from his father, who conducted an orchestra for silent films. While at school he studied several instruments and played professionally in dance bands; at the University of Pennsylvania he studied composition with Harl McDonald and developed a strong interest in jazz. He went to New York (1934), studied privately with Isadore Freed, and continued to play and arrange for bands; his arrangement of "I got rhythm" impressed Gershwin and won him a position as an arranger at Harms/Chappell.

In 1935 Raksin went to Hollywood to work with Charlie Chaplin on the music for *Modern Times*. This collaboration yielded one of the most effective original scores ever written for a silent film. He also met Alfred Newman, who nurtured his career as a film composer. Raksin settled permanently in Los Angeles in 1937, working in the Hollywood studios as a composer, arranger, and orchestrator and studying privately with Arnold Schoenberg. Raksin's unusually complex textures and harmonies typecast him as a specialist in horror films and mysteries, but he was adept in other genres, including Westerns and comedies.

In the early 1940s Raksin was employed at Fox, for which he wrote the score to *Laura* (1944), one of his most original and enduring works. The film's reputation as a classic owes much to the haunting score; at its heart is Raksin's elusive melody for the title character, which, remarkably, is never completed. The theme was a great popular success as a song (lyrics by Johnny Mercer), became a jazz standard, and is one of the most widely performed and recorded of all film themes. The score also includes distinctive jazz-influenced harmonies, innovative orchestrations, evocative distortion effects, and highly skillful variation and contrapuntal elaboration of the principal melody. Many film music books (especially Burt and Brown) offer analyses of its key sequences.

Laura (1944)
20th Century-Fox/Photofest ©20th Century-Fox Film Corporation

Raksin worked regularly as a film composer until the early 1970s; his body of about one hundred scores includes perhaps twenty works that rank among Hollywood's best, although of the later films, only *The Bad and the Beautiful* (1952) approaches the success of *Laura*. His finest film scores, such as those for *Force of Evil* (1949), *Al Capone* (1959), *The Redeemer* (1966), and the cartoon *The Unicorn in the Garden* (1953), demonstrate a highly original, versatile, and emotionally committed musical mind combined with a flair for unusual technical feats.

Highly regarded as a teacher, administrator, author, and raconteur, he did much to promote the understanding of film music. From 1956 he was an adjunct professor of music at the University of Southern California and served as president of the Composers and Lyricists Guild of America (1962–70). He arranged many of his film scores for concert performance, notably *Laura*, *Forever Amber*, and *The Bad and the Beautiful*. Raksin was the first member of his profession to have received a Coolidge Commission from the Library of Congress (having previously been the first invited to establish a collection of his manuscripts there). He conducted the première of the resulting *Oedipus Memneitai* in 1986. A book of his songs, most not previously published, was issued in 1997.

Works

(selective list)

Film scores

The Undying Monster (dir. J. Brahm), 1942
Laura (dir. O. Preminger), 1944
Fallen Angel (dir. Preminger), 1945
Smoky (dir. L. King), 1946
Forever Amber (dir. Preminger, J.M.Stahl (uncredited)), 1947
The Secret Life of Walter Mitty (dir. N.Z. McLeod), 1947
Force of Evil (dir. A. Polonsky), 1949
Whirlpool (dir. Preminger), 1949
Giddyap (cartoon, dir. A Babbitt), 1950
The Magnificent Yankee (dir. J. Sturges), 1950
Across the Wide Missouri (dir. W.A. Wellman), 1951
The Man with a Cloak (dir. F. Markle), 1951
The Bad and the Beautiful (dir. V. Minnelli), 1952
Carrie (dir. W. Wyler), 1952
Madeline (cartoon, dir. R. Cannon), 1952
Pat and Mike (dir. G. Cukor), 1952
The Unicorn in the Garden (cartoon, W.T. Hurtz), 1953
Apache (dir. R. Aldrich), 1954
Suddenly (dir. L. Allen), 1954
The Big Combo (dir. J.H. Lewis), 1955
Bigger than Life (dir. N. Ray), 1956
Hilda Crane (dir. P. Dunne), 1956
Jubal (dir. D. Daves), 1956

Separate Tables (dir. D. Mann), 1958
Al Capone (dir. R. Wilson), 1959
Too Late Blues (dir. J. Cassavetes), 1961
Two Weeks in Another Town (dir. Minnelli), 1962
Sylvia (dir. G. Douglas), 1965
A Big Hand for the Little Lady (dir. F. Cook), 1966
The Redeemer (dir. J. Breen and F. Palacios), 1966
Will Penny (dir. T. Gries), 1968
What's the Matter with Helen? (dir. C. Harrington), 1971

Arrangements and partial film scores

Modern Times (dir. C. Chaplin), 1936
Marked Woman (dir. L. Bacon), 1937
Mr. Moto's Last Warning (dir. N. Foster), 1939
Dead Men Tell (dir. H. Lachman), 1941

Scores for American television series

The Olympics, a History of the Golden Games (1976) [pilot]
Ben Casey
Breaking Point
Wagon Train

Other works

Oedipus Memneitai (Raksin), B-Bar, nar/soloist, 6vv, chbr ens, 1986
Stage works, incl. musicals, ballets, and incid. music; radio music; songs
Arrs. of film music for orch (film in parentheses): Theme (Laura); Suite (Forever Amber); Scenarios (The Bad and the Beautiful); Nocturne and Finale (Force of Evil); Grande Polonaise (The Best of the Bolshoi)
Arrs. of film music for chbr ens. (film in parentheses): Hoofloose, Fancy Free (Giddyap); Serenade (The Unicorn in the Garden); A Song after Sundown (Too Late Blues)
Other arrs., incl. Circus Polka (Stravinsky), band

MSS in *US-Wc*; recorded interviews in *US-NHoh*

Principal publishers: Warner Chappell Music, EMI Music, ASCAP, EKAY Music, RCA/BMG Recordings

Writings

"Humor in Music," *Writer's Congress: Los Angeles 1943* (Los Angeles, 1944), 251–5
"Talking Back: a Hollywood Composer States the Case for his Craft," *New York Times* (20 Feb 1949)
"Whatever Became of Movie Music?" *Film Music Notebook*, i/1 (1974), 22–6
with C. Palmer: *Laura—Scenarios from The Bad and the Beautiful—Forever Amber*, RCA Red Seal ARL 1–1490 (1976); reissued on CD as *David Raksin Conducts his Great Film Scores*, RCA Victor 1490–2-RG (1989) [liner notes]

"Life with Charlie," *Quarterly Journal for the Library of Congress*, xl/3 (1983), 234–53; repr. in *Wonderful Inventions*, ed. I. Newsom (Washington, DC, 1985), 158–71
"Holding a Nineteenth-Century Pedal at Twentieth Century-Fox," *Film Music 1*, ed. C. McCarty (New York, 1989), 167–81
Hollywood Composers: David Raksin Remembers his Colleagues (Los Altos, CA, 1995) [pamphlet]
"David Raksin Remembers *The Bad and the Beautiful,*" *The Bad and the Beautiful*, Rhino Movie Music, R272400 (1996) [liner notes]

Bibliography

E. Bernstein: "A Conversation with David Raksin," *Film Music Notebook*, ii (1976), no.2, 14–21; no.3, 9–18
R. Prendergast: *Film Music: a Neglected Art* (New York, 1977, 2/1992)
T. Thomas: "David Raksin," *Film Score: the View from the Podium* (South Brunswick, NJ, 1979, 2/1991 as *Film Score: the Art and Craft of Movie Music*), 195–206
J. Newsom: "'A Sound Idea': Music for Animated Films"; " David Raksin: a Composer in Hollywood," *Wonderful Inventions*, ed. I. Newsom (Washington, DC, 1985), 58–79, 116–58
K. Kalinak: *Settling the Score: Music and the Classical Hollywood Film* (Madison, WI, 1992)
R.S. Brown: *Overtones and Undertones: Reading Film Music* (Berkeley, CA, 1994), 294–304
G. Burt: *The Art of Film Music* (Boston, 1994)
P. Zollo: *Hollywood Remembered: an Oral History of its Golden Age* (New York, 2002)
J. Hubbert: "'Whatever Happened to Great Movie Music?': Cinéma Vérité and Hollywood Film Music of the Early 1970s," *AM*, xxi/2 (2003), 180–213
J. Burlingame: "Obituary: David Raksin Dead at 92," *The Cue Sheet*, xix/4 (2004), 23–7
M. Cooke: *A History of Film Music* (Cambridge, 2008)
R.R. Ness: "A Lotta Night Music: the Sound of Film Noir," *Cinema Journal*, xv/2 (2008), 52–73

MARTIN MARKS/R

Rapee, Erno

(*b* Budapest, Hungary, 4 June 1891; *d* New York, 26 June 1945). American conductor, arranger, composer, and pianist of Hungarian birth. He studied the piano and later conducting at the National Conservatory in Budapest and graduated in 1909. He then worked as a conductor at the Dresden Opera, Germany, and at the Kattowitz Opera House, Poland. After touring Mexico and South America performing as a pianist, Rapee became the director of the Hungarian Opera Company in New York (1912). In 1917 he was appointed conductor at the Rialto Theater (the first New York film theatre with a symphony orchestra) and later at the Rivoli (1918) and Capitol theaters (1920) in New York and at the Fox Theater in Philadelphia (1923). Determined to introduce good music to the audiences of silent films, Rapee made popular arrangements of the classics, including his famous arrangement of Liszt's Hungarian Rhapsody no.13, which he wrote while at the Capitol Theater.

From 1924 to 1926 Rapee conducted in Europe; he led the Universum Film AG (UFA) Orchestra in Berlin and was also a guest conductor of the Berlin PO and the Budapest PO, among others. After many European successes, he returned to New York in 1926 and in March 1927 became the music director of the new Roxy Theater, conducting an orchestra of 110 musicians.

Although he continued to arrange orchestral music for silent films, Rapee also wrote his own scores; notable examples are *If Winter Comes* (1923), *What Price Glory?* (1926, for which he composed the song "Charmaine" with Lew Pollack), and *7th Heaven* (1927, which includes another collaboration with Pollack, "Diane"). Rapee also initiated a series of weekly symphonic radio broadcasts from the Roxy Theater, which aired on Sunday afternoons and which introduced millions of listeners to classical music.

In 1930 Rapee went to California as the general music director for Warner Bros. and First National Pictures, but he soon returned to New York and was appointed the general music director for NBC the following year. He was also a guest conductor of the Philadelphia Orchestra for two summer seasons (1932 and 1933). With the opening of Radio City Music Hall in New York in December 1932, he was appointed the music director, a position he held until his death.

Rapee continued to conduct weekly radio broadcasts, now titled "The Music Hall of the Air," a program that lasted until 1942. On 12 April 1942 he was awarded the Mahler Medal of Honor by the Bruckner Society of America for the first radio presentation of Gustav Mahler's Eighth Symphony, which was played at the five hundredth "Music Hall" broadcast.

During his career, he was also responsible for many condensed stage versions of operas, such as Giuseppe Verdi's *Aida* and Giacomo Puccini's *Madama Butterfly*, and he continually provided arrangements of works by other composers such as Ludwig van Beethoven, Franz Liszt, Piotr Il'yich Tchaikovsky, Mahler, and Richard Strauss. Rapee's most important contributions, however, were his silent film scores. He was a true innovator in film music, serving as a writer, arranger, and compiler of *Motion Picture Moods for Pianists and Organists* (1924) and *Erno Rapee's Encyclopedia of Music for Pictures* (1925), both of which reflect his musical principles. They remain important sources of silent film accompaniment practice.

Works

Film scores

(Music for silent films published by Robbins-Engel Music as part of the Capitol Photoplay Series (1923), many with William Axt)

Over the Hill to the Poorhouse (dir. H.F. Millarde (as H. Millarde)), 1920
A Connecticut Yankee in King Arthur's Court (dir. E.J. Flynn), 1921
The Queen of Sheba (dir. J.G. Edwards), 1921
Nero (dir. Edwards), 1922
If Winter Comes (dir. Millarde), 1923
The Last Man on Earth (dir. J.G. Blystone), 1924
The Man without a Country (dir. R.V. Lee), 1925
Varieté (dir. E.A. Dupont), 1925, with S. Horne
Ein Walzertraum (dir. L. Berger), 1925, with O. Straus
Die Brüder Schellenberg (dir. K. Grune), 1926, with W.R. Heymann
Faust (dir. F.W. Murnau), 1926, with others
Manon Lescaut (dir. A. Robison), 1926
Monte Carlo (dir. C. Cabanne), 1926
Der Prinz und die Tänzerin (dir. R. Eichberg), 1926
Wehe, wenn sie losgelassen (dir. C. Froelich), 1926
What Price Glory? (dir. R. Walsh), 1926
7th Heaven (dir. F. Borzage), 1927
The Missing Link (dir. C. Reisner), 1927
Sunrise (dir. F.W. Murnau), 1927
Uncle Tom's Cabin (dir. H.A. Pollard), 1927
Fazil (dir. H. Hawks), 1928
The Man Who Laughs (dir. P. Leni), 1928
Mother Knows Best (dir. J.G. Blystone), 1928
Mother Machree (dir. J. Ford (uncredited)), 1928
The Red Dance (dir. R. Walsh), 1928
Street Angel (dir. F. Borzage), 1928
Making the Grade (dir. A.E. Green), 1929
Whispering Winds (dir. J. Flood), 1929
Der Tanz geht weiter (dir. W. Dieterle), 1930
Men of the Sky (dir. A.E. Green), 1931
Chloe, Love is Calling You (dir. M. Neilan), 1934
The Dead March (dir. B. Pollard), 1937
Invasion (dir. Pollard), 1941
Conquer by the Clock (dir. F. Ullman jr and S. Vorkapich), 1942

Writings

Motion Picture Moods for Pianists and Organists (New York, 1924; repr. New York, 1974)

Erno Rapee's Encyclopedia of Music for Pictures (New York, 1925; repr. New York, 1974)

Bibliography

P. Murray: "Erno Rapee: Music Educator," *Musical Courier*, xcviii (3 Jan 1929), 39

D. Ewen: *The Man with the Baton: the Story of Conductors and their Orchestras* (New York, 1936), 336

J.H. Walker: "Erno Rapee, Director of Music at the Music Hall, Speaks Thus," *New York Herald Tribune* (29 May 1938)

N. Benchley: "A Pioneer of Incidental Music," *New York Herald Tribune* (24 Sept 1939)

H.W. Levinger: "Finding the Link between Symphony, Film and Radio," *Musical Courier*, cxxxi (15 Jan 1945), 22

Obituaries: *New York Herald Tribune* (27 June 1945); *New York Times* (27 June 1945)

R. Sauer: "Photoplay Music: a Reusable Repertory for Silent Film Scoring, 1914–1929," *American Music Research Center Journal*, viii–ix (1998–9), 55

P. Graff: "Deconstructing the 'Brutal Savage' in John Ford's *The Iron Horse*," *The Sounds of Silent Films: New Perspectives on History, Theory, and Practice*, ed. C. Tieber and A. Windisch (Basingstoke, 2014), 141–55

R. Melnick: *American Showman: Samuel "Roxy" Rothafel and the Birth of the Entertainment Industry, 1908–1935* (New York, 2014)

MARY A. WISCHUSEN/R

Riesenfeld, Hugo

(*b* Vienna, Austria, 26 Jan 1879; *d* Los Angeles, 10 Sept 1939). American composer, music director, and conductor of Austrian birth; naturalized American in 1912. He was educated at the Vienna Conservatory and University of Vienna, studying violin with Jakob Grün and Arnold Rosé and composition with Robert Fuchs. After playing violin with the Vienna Court Opera, he emigrated to the United States in 1907. He was the concertmaster at the Manhattan Opera house until 1911, then conducted Klaw & Erlanger productions for three years and the Century Opera Company for one. As music director of three Broadway film theaters from 1916 to 1925 under Samuel L. Rothafel, then Paramount, he oversaw a large staff of composers, arrangers, copyists, and librarians to produce elaborate music presentations for films that earned the distinction, "photoplays deluxe." He became the music director of the Rialto in 1916, the Rivoli in 1917, and the Criterion in 1920. He raised the standards for exhibition and music, arranged popular melodies, and popularized classics. Drawing from an extensive library, he assembled compiled scores supplemented by original and arranged music. After 1925 his music accompanied films at several theaters before he became music director at the Colony in 1927. In Hollywood from 1928 to 1930 he headed music and scoring for United Artists. He returned to New York in 1932 and 1933 to the Roxy, then Rivoli. Back in Hollywood in 1934 he was at the Filmarte Theatre, where Abe Meyer was his associate. Shortly before his death Riesenfeld handled the Meyer Synchronizing Service. He was often referred to as Dr. Hugo Riesenfeld.

Works

(selective list)

Film scores

(not all films wholly scored by Riesenfeld)

Carmen (dir. C.B. DeMille), 1915
The Aryan (dir. R. Barker, W.S. Hart, and C. Smith), 1916
Woman (dir. M. Tourneur), 1918
Deception, New York presentation, 1921
The Covered Wagon (dir. J. Cruze), 1923
Monsieur Beaucaire (dir. S. Olcott), 1924
Les Misérables, New York presentation (dir. H. Fescourt), 1925
The Vanishing American (dir. G.B. Seitz), 1925
Beau Geste (dir. H. Brenon), 1926
Old Ironsides (dir. J. Cruze), 1926
The King of Kings (dir. C.B. DeMille), 1927
Ramona (dir. E. Carewe), 1928
Two Lovers (dir. F. Niblo), 1928
The Woman Disputed (dir. H. King and S. Taylor), 1928
Alibi (dir. R. West), 1929
Condemned! (dir. W. Ruggles), 1929
Eternal Love (dir. E. Lubitsch), 1929
The Iron Mask (dir. A. Dwan), 1929
Lady of the Pavements (dir. D.W. Griffith), 1929
Lucky Boy (dir. N. Taurog and C.C. Wilson), 1929
Hell's Angels (dir. H. Hughes), 1930
One Romantic Night (dir. P.L. Stein), 1930
Tabu (dir. F.W. Murnau), 1931
Thunder over Mexico (dir. S.M. Eisenstein), 1933
The President Vanishes (dir. W.A. Wellman), 1935
Tarzan's Revenge (dir. D.R. Lederman), 1938
Also, Schirmer's Photoplay Series, 5 vols. (New York, 1916–23), includes music by Riesenfeld

Concert music

Overture in Romantic Style, orch, New York Philharmonic, première, 1920
Symphonic Epos, orch, Los Angeles SO, première, 1920

MSS in Museum of Modern Art Silent Film Music Collection, Music Division, Library of Congress

Principal publishers: Schirmer; Fischer

Writings

"Music and Motion Pictures," *The Annals*, cxxviii/217 (Nov 1926), 58–62
"Synchronization of Music for Motion Picture," *Who Is Who in Music*, ed. S. Spaeth (Chicago, 1929), 30–31

Bibliography

J. Van Broekhoven: "Hugo Riesenfeld, Concertmaster, Composer, and Director of the Rivoli, Rialto and Criterion Theatres," *Musical Observer*, xix/5 (May 1920), 18, 28
J. Vila: "Hugo Riesenfeld Tells How He Scores a Film," *Musical Courier*, xciv/7 (17 Feb 1927), 48–9
Obituary, *New York Times* (11 Sept 1939)
T. Ramsaye: "Hugo Riesenfeld Dies," *Motion Picture Herald* (16 Sept 1939)

WARREN M. SHERK

Ritmanis [Ritmanix], Lolita

(*b* Portland, OR, 1 Nov 1962). American television, film, and concert composer, and orchestrator. Ritmanis studied composition in both traditional concert genres and film music in Los Angeles at the Dick Grove School of Music. While working at Warner Bros. and Walt Disney, she began a successful career as an orchestrator, working throughout the 1990s on dozens of feature films and television series. While working on "The Flash" (1990), Ritmanis met composer Shirley Walker, a relationship that led to her hiring for Walker's "Batman" series (1992–4). Here she met Michael McCuistion and Kristopher Carter, with whom she formed Dynamic Music Partners (DMP), the trio with which she now primarily composes. They have focussed over the last fifteen years on scoring DC animated superhero series, occasionally scoring unrelated feature films, also under the DMP moniker. Although DMP operates as a group, each partner usually scores television episodes individually, so they are able to maintain thematic continuity. Ritmanis also maintains a successful career as a concert composer. During her teenage years, she toured as a performer in the Latvian popular group Dzintars, and continues to have her works performed by Latvian ensembles around the world. She has been nominated for ten Emmy awards, and won an Emmy for the animated series "Batman Beyond" (2001).

Works

Television music

(*alone and with DMP*)
Batman, 1992–4
Superman: the Last Son of Krypton, 1996
Superman, 1996–9

The New Batman Adventures, 1998
Batman Beyond, 1999–2000
The Zeta Project, 2001–2
Justice League, 2001–6
Teen Titans, 2003–6
Legion of Super Heroes, 2006–8
The Spectacular Spiderman, 2008–9
Ben 10: Alien Force, 2008–10
Batman: the Brave and the Bold, 2008–11
Tower Prep, 2010
Ben 10: Ultimate Alien, 2010–12
Young Justice, 2010–18
New Teen Titans, 2011–12
Kaijudo: Rise of the Duel Masters, 2012–13
Marvel's Avengers Assemble, 2013–18
DC Super Friends, 2015
Flip the Script, 2017
Wacky Races, 2017
Marvel Rising: Secret Warriors, 2018

Film scores

(*with DMP*)
Broke Sky (dir. T.L. Callaway), 2007
Dangerous Calling (dir. J. Daws and J. Daws), 2008
An Act of Love (dir. S. Sheppard), 2015
Give Til It Hurts (dir. Callaway), 2015
Batman: the Killing Joke (dir. S. Liu), 2016
Batman: Return of the Caped Crusaders (dir. R. Morales), 2016
Batman and Harley Quinn (dir. Liu), 2017
Scooby-Doo & Batman: the Brave and the Bold (dir. J. Castorena), 2018

Orchestrator

Arthur 2: On the Rocks (dir. B. Yorkin), 1988
Robin Hood: Prince of Thieves (dir. K. Reynolds) 1991
Lethal Weapon 3 (dir. R. Donner), 1992
Demolition Man (dir. M. Brambilla), 1993
Last Action Hero (dir. J. McTiernan), 1993
The Three Musketeers (dir. S. Herek), 1993
On Deadly Ground (dir. S. Seagal), 1994
Free Willy 2: the Adventure Home (dir. D.H. Little), 1995
Centennial Olympic Games: Opening Ceremonies (dir. D. Mischer), 1996
Escape from L.A. (dir. J. Carpenter), 1996
Lethal Weapon 4 (dir. Donner), 1998
Final Destination (dir. J. Wong), 2000
Swimfan (dir. J. Polson), 2002
Jeepers Creepers II (dir. V. Salva), 2003
Peaceful Warrior (dir. Salva), 2006

Concert works

Farewell to Riga, 1982
A New Day, 1986
Tas Vakars Piektdiena [Same Time Next Friday], 1989
Skudra Un Sienazis [The Ant and the Grasshopper], 1999
Turp Un Atpakal, 1999
Rudentins Pie Durvim Klauve, 2003
Eslingena, 2005

Bibliography

M. Carlsson: "Women in Film Music, or How Hollywood Learned to Hire Female Composers for (at least) Some of their Movies," *IAWM Journal*, xi/2 (2005), 16–19
"The Dynamic Trio," *Film Score Monthly*, xii (2007), no.1, p.13; no.2, p.9

LOUIS NIEBUR/R

Robbins, Richard (Stephen)

(*b* South Weymouth, MA, 4 Dec 1940; *d* Rhinebeck, NY, 7 Nov 2012). American composer. He attended the New England Conservatory of Music (1962–8) and studied the piano with Howard Goding. He then studied in Vienna with Hilda Langer-Rühl (1972–4), later becoming the director of the Music School at Rivers (Weston, MA, 1980–84). While there, he met the film producer Ismail Merchant and the director James Ivory, who helped him to make a documentary about MannesÁs musically gifted children, *Sweet Sounds* (1976). Two years later he was asked to score the Merchant–Ivory adaptation of Henry JamesÁs *The Europeans* (1979). He scored more than a dozen films directed by Ivory, and worked on other independent films and related projects.

Robbins achieved particular distinction in his music for the three Merchant–Ivory films taken from E.M. Forster novels (*A Room with A View*, 1986; *Maurice*, 1987; and *Howards End*, 1992), as well as in *Remains of the Day* (1993) and *Surviving Picasso* (1996). These reveal a consistent style, in which plaintive melodic fragments are superimposed upon recurring rhythmic and harmonic patterns, often in a neo-Baroque, Impressionist, or Minimalist vein. The music rarely mimics particular screen actions or ties itself thematically to individual characters, but provides moody and shimmering atmosphere (often enhanced by synthesizer tracks). He has also incorporated appropriate music by other composers into Merchant–Ivory films, such as W.A. Mozart in *Jane Austen in Manhattan*, Giacomo Puccini in *A Room with a View*, and Arcangelo Corelli and Antonio Sacchini in *Jefferson in Paris*. Other projects by Robbins include the documentary film, *Street Musicians in Bombay* (1993), and *Via Crucis*, an installation-piece composed for an exhibition by visual artist Michael Schell (1994).

Works

(selective list)
The Europeans (dir. J. Ivory), 1979
Jane Austen in Manhattan (dir. J. Ivory), 1980
Quartet (dir. J. Ivory), 1981
Heat and Dust (dir. J. Ivory), 1983
The Bostonians (dir. J. Ivory), 1984
My Little Girl (dir. C. Kaiserman), 1986
A Room with a View (dir. J. Ivory), 1986
Maurice (dir. J. Ivory), 1987
Sweet Lorraine (dir. S. Gomer), 1987
Slaves of New York (dir. J. Ivory), 1989
Bail Jumper (dir. C. Faber), 1990
Mr. and Mrs. Bridge (dir. J. Ivory), 1990
The Ballad of the Sad Cafe (dir. S. Callow), 1991
Howards End (dir. J. Ivory), 1992
The Remains of the Day (dir. J. Ivory), 1993
Jefferson in Paris (dir. J. Ivory), 1995
The Proprietor (dir. I. Merchant), 1996
Surviving Picasso (dir. J. Ivory), 1996
A Soldier's Daughter Never Cries (dir. J. Ivory), 1998
The Golden Bowl (dir. J. Ivory), 2000
The Mystic Masseur (dir. I. Merchant), 2001
Le Divorce (dir. J. Ivory), 2003
The White Countess (dir. J. Ivory), 2005

Publishers: Angel Records, Epic, Point Records, Sony Publishing

Bibliography

R.E. Long: *The Films of Merchant Ivory* (New York, 1991, 2/1997)
R.S. Brown: "A Major Film/Music Collaboration: Richard Robbins and Merchant/Ivory," *Fanfare*, xv/6 (1992), 69–81
H. Alford: "Taking a Page from their Book" *New York Times Magazine* (15 Sept 1996), 46 [interview with I. Merchant and J. Ivory]
The Music of Merchant Ivory (Medford, OR, 1998) [Peter Britt Festivals: program]

MARTIN MARKS/R

Roemheld, Heinz

(*b* Milwaukee, WI, 1 May 1901; *d* Huntington Beach, CA, 11 Feb 1985). American composer. After graduating from the Wisconsin College of Music (1918) he studied in Germany with Hugo Kaun, Rudolf Breithaupt, and Egon Petri. He made his concert début as a pianist with the Berlin PO in 1922. From 1923 to 1929 he was musical director for Carl Laemmle theaters in Milwaukee (the Alhambra, 1923–6), Washington, DC (the Rialto, 1927–8), and Berlin (1928–9). In 1929 Laemmle brought him to Universal Studios in Hollywood, where he succeeded David Broekman as general music director in 1930. Sometimes writing under the pseudonym Rox Rommell, he was the most prolific composer in Hollywood; he composed music for over three hundred films, working for every major motion picture studio, as well as for many independent producers. He wrote music for more Warner Bros. films than any of his colleagues. In 1942 he and Ray Heindorf shared an Academy Award for *Yankee Doodle Dandy* (1942). In 1945 he was appointed chief of the film, theater, and music section of the Information Control Division for US Forces in Europe. His song "Ruby," featured in the film *Ruby Gentry* (1952), became a standard. After retiring from film composing in 1960, he devoted his compositional energies to concert music.

Stylistically conservative, Roemheld's film music reflects the influence of his teacher Kaun and the eclectic late Romantic-Impressionist-Gershwinesque style prevalent in Hollywood throughout the 1930s and 40s. Despite these influences, his scores are rarely lush and given to excess. The musical language of his concert music is more progressive than that of his film scores; written in a neoclassical vein, these works show him to be a master of short forms.

Works

(selective list)

Film scores

White Hell of Pitz Palu (dir. A. Fanck and G.W. Pabst), 1929
All Quiet on the Western Front (dir. L. Milestone), 1930
Captain of the Guard (dir. J.S. Robertson), 1930
The Invisible Man (dir. J. Whale), 1933
The Black Cat (dir. E. G. Ulmer), 1934
Bombay Mail (dir. E. L. Marin), 1934
Imitation of Life (dir. J. M. Stahl), 1934
Oil for the Lamps of China (dir. M. LeRoy), 1935, collab. B. Kaun
Private Worlds (dir. G. La Cava), 1935
Ruggles of Red Gap (dir. L. McCarey), 1935
Dracula's Daughter (dir. L. Hillyer), 1936
The Story of Louis Pasteur (dir. W. Dieterle), 1936, collab. B. Kaun
The White Angel (dir. W. Dieterle), 1936
It's Love I'm After (dir. A Mayo), 1937
San Quentin (dir. L. Bacon), 1937, collab. C. Maxwell and D. Raksin
Brother Rat (dir. W. Keighley), 1938
Invisible Stripes (dir. L. Bacon), 1939
Brother Orchid (dir. L. Bacon), 1940
Knute Rockne, All American (dir. L. Bacon), 1940
The Strawberry Blonde (dir. R. Walsh), 1941

Gentleman Jim (dir. R. Walsh), 1942
Yankee Doodle Dandy (dir. M. Curtiz), 1942
The Hard Way (dir. V. Sherman), 1943
The Desert Song (dir. R. Florey), 1944
Janie (dir. M. Curtiz), 1944
Wonder Man (dir. H.B. Humberstone), 1945
Christmas Eve (dir. E.L. Marin), 1947
The Lady from Shanghai (dir. O. Welles), 1948
My Dear Secretary (dir. C. Martin), 1948
The Good Humour Man (dir. L. Bacon), 1950
Valentino (dir. L. Allen), 1951
The Big Trees (dir. F.E. Feist), 1952
Jack and the Beanstalk (dir. J. Yarbrough), 1952
Ruby Gentry (dir. K. Vidor), 1952
The 5000 Fingers of Dr. T (dir. R. Rowland), 1953, collab. F. Holländer and H.J. Salter
The Moonlighter (dir. R. Rowland), 1953
Female on the Beach (dir. J. Pevney), 1955
The Monster that Challenged the World (dir. A. Laven), 1958
Ride Lonesome (dir. B. Boetticher), 1959
Lad, a Dog (dir. A. Avakian and L.H. Martinson), 1961

Other works

Instrumental

Str Trio, 1941
2 Old Shanties, va, pf, 1952
Str Qt, 1952
Sinfonia breve, orch, 1953
Ruby and Six Variations, orch, 1964
Concert Piece, vc, orch, 1970
Serenade (to a Ballerina), orch
Introduction and Fantasia, orch
4 Frags., va, pf
For Kathy, vc, pf

Piano solo

Sonatina no.1, 1966
Sonatina no.2, 1968
Suite, 1969
4 Short Pieces, 1970, orchd
3 Pieces, 1971
Sonatina no.3, 1972
7 Preludes, 1973, orchd
Sonatina no.4, 1973

Songs (1v, pf)

3 Songs (R. Herrick), 1939
Ballad
5 Lieder, 1956, arr. 1v, orch

Bibliography

W.H. Rosar: "Music for the Monsters: Universal Pictures' Horror Film Scores of the Thirties," *Quarterly Journal of the Library of Congress*, xl (1983), 390–421

C. McCarty: *Film Composers in America: a Filmography 1911–1970* (New York, 2000)

WILLIAM ROSAR

Rose, David

(*b* London, 15 June 1910; *d* Burbank, 23 Aug 1990). American composer, arranger, and conductor. His family emigrated from England when he was four, and he grew up in Chicago, absorbing the vibrant sounds of the emerging jazz scene. During the 1930s he worked with Benny Goodman and other dance bands, eventually moving to Hollywood to work in the film and recording industries. A long association with MGM resulted in many film scores and, after the introduction of LPs, regular record albums. In 1941 he became Judy Garland's first husband, and his radio show "California Melodies" grew into something of an American institution, providing the showcase for his new compositions. In 1943 Rose startled the Light Music establishment with his *Holiday for Strings*, in turn inspiring a whole generation of composers including Leroy Anderson, Trevor Duncan, and Robert Farnon. Following war service in the US Army Air Force, Rose gained his first Oscar nomination for his score for the 1944 film *The Princess and the Pirate*, and subsequent high-profile movies included *Jupiter's Darling* (1955), *Operation Petticoat* (1959), and *Please Don't Eat the Daisies* (1960). Later he tended to concentrate more on television and is remembered for the "Red Skelton Show" and "specials" featuring Jack Benny, Bob Hope, and Fred Astaire. Popular series that he scored include "Sea Hunt," "Little House on the Prairie," "Father Murphy," and "Bonanza." Today his music still crops up in many new film productions.

Rose was a frequent visitor to the recording studios, initially for RCA, then MGM (which released the vast majority of his considerable output), followed by Kapp and Capitol. His many albums (over fifty in total) usually featured a distinctive string sound that was instantly recognizable to his admirers, and his own inventive compositions were always in demand. Rose received six gold discs, twenty-two Grammys, four Emmys, and two Oscar nominations. In 1962, just when his composing career was waning, his most enduring composition, "The Stripper," was released as the B side to a single; he was always associated with it thereafter.

Works

(selective list)

Film scores

The Princess and the Pirate (dir. D. Butler), 1944
Just This Once (dir. D. Weis), 1952
The Clown (dir. R.Z. Leonard), 1953
Bright Road (dir. G. Mayer), 1953
Jupiter's Darling (dir. G. Sidney), 1955
Operation Petticoat (dir. B. Edwards), 1959
Please Don't Eat the Daisies (dir. C. Walters), 1960
Hombre (dir. M. Ritt), 1967

Television scores

Bonanza, 1959–73
Little House on the Prairie, 1974–83
Father Murphy, 1981–83

Orchestral

Holiday for Strings, 1943
Our Waltz, 1943
Gay Spirits, 1946
Manhattan Square Dance, 1947
American Hoe Down, 1950
Stringopation, 1951
Fiesta in Seville, 1953
Parade of the Clowns, 1953
Satan and the Polar Bear, 1953
Holiday for Trombones, 1962
The Stripper, 1962
The Tiny Ballerina, 1967

DAVID ADES

Rosenman, Leonard

(*b* Brooklyn, NY, 7 Sept 1924; *d* Woodland Hills, CA, 4 March 2008). American composer. Originally trained as a painter, he began musical studies at the age of fifteen. After war service, he studied composition with Arnold Schoenberg, Roger Sessions, and Luigi Dallapiccola, and the piano with Bernard Abramowitsch. In 1953 he served as composer-in-residence at the Berkshire Music Center and received a Koussevitzky Foundation commission for an opera; however this was never completed. From 1962 to 1966 he lived in Rome where he scored television programs and gained experience as a conductor. He taught at the universities of Southern California and New York, was a member of the board of directors of the

California branch of ISCM, and served as musical director of the New Muse, a chamber orchestra specializing in performances of avant-garde music.

An important figure in the history of American film music, his score for *The Cobweb* is said to be the first in Hollywood to employ twelve-note procedures. In *Fantastic Voyage* he experimented with *Klangfarben*, while portions of his *Chamber Music I* found their way into his score for *The Savage Eye*. In his scores for the James Dean films *East of Eden* and *Rebel Without a Cause* he effected a successful synthesis of the traditional and modern. At other times he showed himself both willing and able to compose music in a more traditional romantic style; his score for *Cross Creek*, for example, is influenced by American folk music.

Works

(*selective list*)

Film scores

The Cobweb (dir. V. Minnelli), 1955
East of Eden (dir. E. Kazan), 1955
Rebel Without a Cause (dir. N. Ray), 1955
Edge of the City (dir. M. Ritt), 1957
The Young Stranger (dir. J. Frankenheimer), 1957
Pork Chop Hill (dir. L. Milestone), 1959
The Savage Eye (dir. B. Meddow, S. Meyers, and J. Strick), 1959
The Crowded Sky (dir. J. Pevney), 1960
The Plunderers (dir. J. Pevney), 1960
Hell Is for Heroes (dir. D. Siegel), 1961
The Outsider (dir. D. Mann), 1961
The Chapman Report (dir. G. Cukor), 1962
Convicts 4 (dir. M. Kaufman), 1962
A Covenant With Death (dir. L. Johnson), 1966
Fantastic Voyage (dir. R. Fleischer), 1966
Countdown (dir. R. Altman), 1968
Beneath the Planet of the Apes (dir. T. Post), 1969
A Man Called Horse (dir. E. Silverstein), 1969
Battle for the Planet of the Apes (dir. J.L. Thompson), 1973
Race with the Devil (dir. J. Starrett), 1975
Birch Interval (dir. D. Mann), 1976
Bound for Glory (dir. H. Ashby), 1976
The Car (dir. E. Silverstein), 1977
September 30, 1955 (dir. J. Bridges), 1977
An Enemy of the People (dir. G. Schaefer), 1978
The Lord of the Rings (dir. R. Bakshi), 1978
Promises in the Dark (dir. J. Hellman), 1979
Prophecy (dir. J. Frankenheimer), 1979
Hide in Plain Sight (dir. J. Caan), 1980

Making Love (dir. A. Hiller), 1982
Cross Creek (dir. M. Ritt), 1983
Sylvia (dir. M. Firth), 1985
Star Trek IV: The Voyage Home (dir. L. Nimoy), 1986
The Color of Evening (dir. S. Stafford), 1990
Robocop II (dir. I. Kershner), 1990
Ambition (dir. S. Goldstein), 1991
Mrs. Munck (dir. D. Ladd), 1995
Levitation (dir. S.D. Goldstein), 1997
Jurij (dir. S. Gabrini), 2001

Stage

A Short History of Civilization (theater work with film), 1972

Other

Orchestral

Vn Conc., 1951
Threnody on a Song of K.R., jazz ens, orch, 1971
Foci, orch, tape, 1972
Chbr Music III–VI (Alto ego), vn, va, chbr orch, cptr, 1976
Foci I, 1981, rev. 1983
Vn Conc. no.2, 1991
Sym. no.1 of Dinosaurs, 1997
Double Conc., ob, cl, 1998
Walk in New York, 1999

Vocal

Time Travel, S, orch, 1996 [based on H. Wolf songs]
6 Songs (F. García Lorca), Mez, pf, 1952–4
Chbr Music II, S, 10 players, tape, 1968
Looking Back at Faded Chandeliers (A. Giraud), S, 5 players, 1990
Prelude and 4 Scenes (García Lorca), S, 11 players, 1992

Chamber and solo instrumental

Concertino, pf, ww, 1948
Sonata, pf, 1949
Theme and Elaborations, pf, 1951
Duo, cl, pf, 1960
Chbr Music I, 16 players, 1961
Duo, vn, pf, 1970
Fanfare, 8 tpt, 1970
Two Grand Pianos, 2 amp pf
Chbr Music IV, db, 4 str qt, 1976

Chbr Music V, pf, 6 players, 1979
Str Qt, 1996
Str Qt, 1999

Principal publisher: Peer-Southern

Writings

"Notes on the Score to East of Eden," *Film Music*, xiv/5 (1955), 3–12
"Notes from a Sub-Culture," *PNM*, vii/1 (1968–9), 122–35

Bibliography

I. Bazelon: "Interview with Leonard Rosenman," *Knowing the Score: Notes on Film Music* (New York, 1975), 181–7

J. McBride, ed.: "The Composer: Leonard Rosenman," *Filmmakers and Filmmaking* (Los Angeles, 1983), 111–24

G. Burt: *The Art of Film Music* (Boston, 1994), 184ff

J. Bond: "Rosenman and the Fantastic," *The Cue Sheet* xxiii/1–2 (January-April, 2008), 24–30

J. Burlingame: "Leonard Rosenman: an Appreciation," *The Cue Sheet* xxiii/1–2 (January-April, 2008), 2–5

D. Schwartz: "An Intreview with Leonard Rosenman," *The Cue Sheet* xxiii/1–2 (January-April, 2008), 46–57

S. Feisst: "Serving Two Masters: Leonard Rosenman's Music for Films and the Concert Hall," *The Cue Sheet* xxiii/1–2 (January-April, 2008), 31–45

G. Redner: "The Division of 'One': Leonard Rosenman and the Score for *East of Eden*," *Sound and Music in Film Visual Media*, ed. G. Harper, R. Doughty, and J. Eisentraut (New York, 2009), 692–724

CHRISTOPHER PALMER/FRED STEINER/R

Rosenthal, Laurence

(*b* Detroit, MI, 4 Nov 1926). American composer. He began piano studies with his mother at the age of three, and appeared as a soloist with the Detroit Symphony while still in high school. He studied piano with Sandor Vas and composition with Howard Hanson and Bernard Rogers at the Eastman School of Music (BM 1947, MM 1951), then traveled to Paris for two years of further study with Nadia Boulanger. During the Korean War, Rosenthal enlisted in the Air Force and was assigned to the Documentary Film Squadron, where he composed scores for historical and informational films including a documentary on the history of Russia. After service, he found work on Broadway, composing incidental music for plays (*Rashomon, Becket*), ballet pieces for musicals (*The Music Man*), and musicals of his own (*Sherry!*, based on *The Man Who Came to Dinner*).

He also began scoring feature films. Several of his early 1960s films are now considered classics: *A Raisin in the Sun, The Miracle Worker, Requiem for a Heavyweight,* and *Becket* (the last, bringing him his first Academy Award nomination for its Gregorian chant-based score). More than two dozen films followed over the next four decades, including *The Return of a Man Called Horse* (incorporating Lakota tribal chants) and *Clash of the Titans* (a Ray Harryhausen-effects fantasy based on Greek myths).

Rosenthal quickly earned a reputation as a composer of integrity whose music accurately reflected period, location, and emotional tone. He found regular employment in television, garnering rave reviews and multiple Emmy Awards for such lavish miniseries scores as *George Washington, Mussolini: The Untold Story, Peter the Great, Anastasia: The Mystery of Anna,* and *The Bourne Identity.* Among his finest work were seventeen scores for George Lucas's TV production "The Young Indiana Jones Chronicles" (1992–7).

His concert works include a concerto for violin, percussion, and orchestra; a song cycle based on poems by the thirteenth-century mystic Rumi; and a piece for chorus and orchestra based on a poem by Henry Wadsworth Longfellow.

Works

Film scores

This Is Russia, 1955
Yellowneck (dir. R.J. Hugh), 1957
Naked in the Sun (dir. R.J. Hugh), 1960
Dark Odyssey (dir. W. Kyriakis and R. Metzger), 1961
A Raisin in the Sun (dir. D. Patrie), 1961
The Miracle Worker (dir. A. Penn), 1962
Requiem for a Heavyweight (dir. R. Nelson), 1962
Becket (dir. P. Glenville), 1964
Hotel Paradiso (dir. P. Glenville), 1966
The Comedians (dir. P. Glenville), 1967
Three (dir. J. Salter), 1969
The African Elephant (dir. S. Trevor), 1971
A Gunfight (dir. L. Johnson), 1971
Man of La Mancha (dir. A. Hiller), 1972
Rooster Cogburn (dir. S. Millar), 1975
The Wild Party (dir. J. Ivory), 1975
The Return of a Man Called Horse (dir. I. Kershner), 1976
The Island of Dr. Moreau (dir. D. Taylor), 1977
Portrait of a Hitman (dir. A.A. Buckhantz), 1977
Brass Target (dir. J. Hough), 1978
Who'll Stop the Rain (dir. K. Reisz), 1978
Meetings With Remarkable Men (dir. P. Brook), 1979
Meteor (dir. R. Neame), 1979
Clash of the Titans (dir. D. Davis), 1981

Easy Money (dir. J. Signorelli), 1983
Heart Like a Wheel (dir. J. Kaplan), 1983
A Time for Dancing (dir. P. Gilbert), 2002

Television series music

(selective list)
The Twentieth Century, 1960
Coronet Blue, 1967
Fantasy Island, 1977
Logan's Run, 1977
The Young Indiana Jones Chronicles, 1992

Television films and miniseries music

(selective list)
The Power and the Glory, 1961
Michelangelo: the Last Giant, 1965
How Awful About Allan, 1970
Sweet, Sweet Rachel, 1971
Portrait: a Man Whose Name Was John, 1973
Pueblo, 1973
The Missiles of October, 1974
21 Hours at Munich, 1976
The Story of David, 1976
Young Pioneers, 1976
The Amazing Howard Hughes, 1977
Orphan Train, 1979
The Day Christ Died, 1980
FDR: The Last Year, 1980
The Patricia Neal Story, 1981
The Letter, 1982
Who Will Love My Children?, 1983
George Washington, 1984
The Lost Honor of Kathryn Beck, 1984
Evergreen, 1985
The Hearst and Davies Affair, 1985
Mussolini: The Untold Story, 1985
Anastasia: The Mystery of Anna, 1986
On Wings of Eagles, 1986
Peter the Great, 1986
Proud Men, 1987
The Bourne Identity, 1988
To Heal a Nation, 1988
Gore Vidal's "Billy the Kid," 1989
My Name Is Bill W., 1989
Blind Faith, 1990

Mark Twain and Me, 1991
The Strauss Dynasty, 1991
Catherine the Great, 1995
The Member of the Wedding, 1997
Inherit the Wind, 1999

Concert works

Orchestral

Overture in C, 1947
Horas, 1948
Ode (the Exequy), 1956
The Miracle Worker (from film score), 2002
Becket (film suite), 2003
Prophetic Voices, vn, perc, orch, 2004
Vienna: Sweet & Sour, str orch, hp, 2005

Chamber and solo instrumental

Little Suite ob, pf, 1946
Sonatina, pf, 4 hands, 1948
Partita, vn, pf, 1950
Prayer, pf, 4 hands, 1953
Four Orphic Tableaux, vn, pf, 1965
The Piper at the Gates of Dawn, fl, 1972
Petit Bouquet, pf, 1978
Heptad, vn, vc, pf, 2010

Vocal

O When I Take My Love Out Walking, mixed chorus, pf, 1952
Songs to the Beloved (Mystical Poems of Rumi), Mez, fl, hp, str qt, 1996
The Tide Rises, the Tide Falls, chorus, orch, 2006
numerous other song settings

Bibliography

C. Dudley: "Interview With Laurence Rosenthal," 12 Feb 1994, http://www.conversations.org/story.php?sid=16

J. Burlingame: *TV's Biggest Hits: The Story of Television Themes From "Dragnet" to "Friends"* (New York, 1996)

J. Burlingame: "An Interview With Laurence Rosenthal," *The Cue Sheet*, xxi/2 (April 2006)

JON BURLINGAME

Rota, Nino

(*b* Milan, Italy, 3 Dec 1911; *d* Rome, Italy, 10 April 1979). Italian composer. A child prodigy, he was composing at the age of eight. He attended the Milan Conservatory (from 1923), then moved to Rome (1926), where he took his diploma at the St. Cecilia Conservatory (1929). On the advice of Toscanini he studied at the Curtis Institute in Philadelphia (1931–2) with Rosario Scalero (composition) and Fritz Reiner (conducting). He formed a friendship with Aaron Copland and discovered American popular song, cinema, and the music of George Gershwin: all these elements were grafted onto his passion for Italian popular song and operetta. Rota's idiom was exceptionally and uninhibitedly responsive to a wide variety of influences and was supported by a masterly technique, an elegant manner, and a capacity for stylistic assimilation.

After World War II Rota established himself as a film composer, despite the low standing it held within the contemporary music scene. In film music he used his eclectic inclinations and treated the boundaries of the film medium as a challenge, so producing some of the finest music of the genre. In 1942 he began his long collaboration with the company Lux Film. He created the music for around sixty films in ten years by such directors as Renato Castellani, Mario Soldati, Alberto Lattuada, and Eduardo De Filippo. In 1952, with *Lo sceicco bianco*, he began an association with Federico Fellini which lasted until the composer's death. Of their sixteen films, some achieve an extraordinary marriage of music and image, such as *I vitelloni*, *La strada*, *La dolce vita*, *8½*, *Amarcord*, and *Il Casanova di Federico Fellini*. Although it is generally thought that the director dominated the composer, the situation was more subtle and problematic as the music was required to fulfill a narrative and psychological role, and was frequently featured at the expense of the text itself. Rota's film career, amounting to more than 150 titles, included collaborations with Luchino Visconti and such directors as René Clément, Franco Zeffirelli, King Vidor, and Sergei Bondarchuk, as well as on the first two parts of Francis Ford Coppola's *The Godfather* trilogy. As a whole Rota's work often features a dense web of quotation, using continual, multiple references where—in line with the composer's declared intention—film music and art music are allowed equal dignity.

Works

(*selective list*)

Film scores

Treno popolare (dir. R. Matarazzo), 1933
Zazà (dir. R. Castellani), 1944
Le miserie del signor Travet (dir. M. Soldati), 1946
Mio figlio professore (dir. R. Castellani), 1946
Daniele Cortis (dir. M. Soldati), 1947

L'eroe della strada (dir. C. Borghesio), 1948
Senza pietà (dir. A. Lattuada), 1948
Totò al Giro d'Italia (dir. M. Mattoli), 1948
The Glass Mountain (dir. H. Cass), 1950
Napoli milionaria (dir. E. De Filippo), 1950
Vita da cani (dir. M. Monicelli and Steno), 1950
Filumena Marturano (dir. E. De Filippo), 1951
Anna (dir. A. Lattuada), 1952
Lo sceicco bianco (dir. F. Fellini), 1952
I vitelloni (dir. F. Fellini), 1953
Appassionatamente (dir. G. Gentilomo), 1954
Senso (dir. L. Visconti), 1954
La strada (dir. F. Fellini), 1954
Amici per la pelle (dir. F. Rossi), 1955
Il bidone (dir. F. Fellini), 1955
War and Peace (dir. K. Vidor), 1956
Le notti di Cabiria (dir. F. Fellini), 1957
La dolce vita (dir. F. Fellini), 1960
Le tentazioni del dottor Antonio (dir. F. Fellini), 1962
8½ (dir. F. Fellini), 1963
Giulietta degli spiriti (dir. F. Fellini), 1965
The Taming of the Shrew (dir. F. Zeffirelli), 1967
Romeo and Juliet (dir. F. Zeffirelli), 1968
Toby Dammit (dir. F. Fellini), 1968
Fellini's Satyricon (dir. F. Fellini), 1969
I clowns (dir. F. Fellini), 1970
Waterloo (dir. S. Bondarchuk), 1970
The Godfather (dir. F.F. Coppola), 1972
Roma (dir. F. Fellini), 1972
Amarcord (dir. F. Fellini), 1973
Film d'amore e d'anarchia (dir. L. Wertmüller), 1973
The Godfather: Part II (dir. F.F. Coppola), 1974
Il Casanova di Federico Fellini (dir. F. Fellini), 1976
Death on the Nile (dir. J. Guillermin), 1978
Prova d'orchestra (dir. F. Fellini), 1979

Bibliography

P.M. De Santi: *La musica di Nino Rota* (Bari, 1983)
F. Borin, ed.: *La Filmografia di Nino Rota* (Florence, 1999)
R. Dyer: *Nino Rota: Music, Film and Feeling* (New York, 2010)
F. Sciannameo: *Nino Rota's "The Godfather" Trilogy: a Film Score Guide* (Lanham, MD, 2010)

GIORDANO MONTECCHI/R

Rózsa, Miklós

(*b* Budapest, Hungary, 18 April 1907; *d* Los Angeles, 27 July 1995). American composer of Hungarian birth. Raised in Budapest and on his father's rural estate in nearby Tomasi, he was exposed to Hungarian peasant music and folk traditions from an early age. He studied the piano with his mother, a classmate of Béla Bartók at the Budapest Academy, and the violin and viola with his uncle, Lajos Berkovits, a musician with the Royal Hungarian Opera. By the age of seven, Rózsa was composing his own works. Later, as a student at the Realgymnasium, he championed the work of Bartók and Zoltán Kodály, keeping his own notebook of collected folktunes.

In 1926 Rózsa left Budapest to enroll at the Leipzig Conservatory, where he studied composition with Hermann Grabner and musicology with Theodor Kroyer. By 1929 his chamber works, published by Breitkopf & Härtel, were being promoted and performed throughout Europe. In 1931 he moved to Paris where he completed his *Theme, Variations and Finale* (1933, rev. 1943 and 1966), a work that soon gained international recognition. (It was on the program the night Leonard Bernstein made his conducting début with the New York PO in 1943.) In recognition of his musical achievements, Rózsa was awarded the Franz Joseph Prize from the municipality of Budapest in 1937 and 1938.

Rózsa was introduced to the genre of film music through his friend Arthur Honegger. From 1935 to 1939 he frequently shuttled between Paris and London, where he composed for London Films under the Hungarian-born producer Alexander Korda. In 1940 he accompanied Korda to Hollywood to complete the score of *The Thief of Baghdad*, and was soon in great demand as a freelance film composer and conductor. As a staff member at MGM (1948–62), he became one of the most highly regarded composers in the industry, writing music for over one hundred films. From 1945 to 1965 he also taught film music at the University of Southern California.

Most of Rózsa's film scores employ leitmotifs that accompany and represent specific characters or events on the screen. His angular melodies and contrapuntal textures helped to define the 1940s genre of *film noir*. Scores for epic and period films in the 1950s distinguished themselves by the accuracy of their well-researched historical detail. Rózsa won Academy Awards for the soundtracks of *Spellbound* (1945), *A Double Life* (1948), and *Ben-Hur* (1959), and a César award for the score for *Providence* (1977).

The essence of Rózsa's musical style springs from his early experiences with Magyar peasants; his harmonic and melodic constructions characteristically derive from the pentatonic and modal qualities of Hungarian folk music. His works are also infused with the vitality of Hungarian dance rhythms and the sentimental lyricism of the gypsy tradition. Rózsa does not quote folk melodies in his compositions, however. Instead, in works such as *North Hungarian Peasant*

Miklós Rózsa, 1959

Songs and Dances (1929), *Three Hungarian Sketches* (1958), and *Notturno ungherese* (1964), he invents his own folklike material. His skill at manipulating traditional forms is particularly evident in the Concerto for Strings (1943, rev. 1957) and the Piano Sonata (1948). Also noteworthy are his virtuosic concertos for the violin (1953), piano (1966), cello (1968), and viola (1979).

Works

Film scores

The Divorce of Lady X (dir. T. Whelan), 1937
Four Dark Hours (Race Gang, or The Green Cockatoo) (dir. W.C. Menzies), 1937
Knight without Armour (dir. J. Feyder), 1937
The Squeaker (Murder on Diamond Row) (dir. W.K. Howard), 1937
Thunder in the City (dir. M. Gering), 1937
The Four Feathers (dir. Z. Korda), 1939
On the Night of the Fire (The Fugitive) (dir. B.D. Hurst), 1939
The Spy in Black (U-Boat 29) (dir. M. Powell), 1939
Ten Days in Paris (Missing Ten Days, or Spy in the Pantry) (dir. T. Whelan), 1939
The Thief of Baghdad (dir. L. Berger and M. Powell), 1940
Lydia (dir. J. Duvivier), 1941
Sundown (dir. H. Hathaway), 1941

That Hamilton Woman (Lady Hamilton) (dir. Z. Korda), 1941
Jacaré (dir. C.E. Ford), 1942
The Jungle Book (dir. Z. Korda), 1942
Five Graves to Cairo (dir. B. Wilder), 1943
Sahara (dir. Z. Korda), 1943
So Proudly We Hail (dir. M. Sandrich), 1943
The Woman of the Town (sir. G. Archainbaud), 1943
Dark Waters (dir. A. DeToth), 1944
Double Indemnity (dir. B. Wilder), 1944
The Hour before the Dawn (dir. F. Tuttle), 1944
The Man in Half Moon Street (dir. R. Murphy), 1944
Blood on the Sun (dir. F. Lloyd), 1945
Lady on a Train (dir. C. David), 1945
The Lost Weekend (dir. B. Wilder), 1945
A Song to Remember (Chopin) (dir. C. Vidor), 1945
Spellbound (dir. A. Hitchcock), 1945
Because of Him (dir. R. Wallace), 1946
The Killers (Time for Action) (dir. R. Siodmak), 1946
The Strange Love of Martha Ivers (dir. L. Milestone), 1946
Brute Force (dir. J. Dassin), 1947
Desert Fury (dir. L. Allen), 1947
The Other Love (dir. A. DeToth), 1947
The Red House (dir. D. Daves), 1947
Song of Scheherazade (Rimsky-Korsakov) (dir. W. Reisch), 1947
Criss Cross (dir. R. Siodmak), 1948
A Double Life (dir. G. Cukor), 1948
Kiss the Blood off My Hands (Blood on My Hands) (dir. N. Foster), 1948
The Naked City (dir. J. Dassin), 1948, collab. F. Skinner
The Secret Beyond the Door (dir. F. Lang), 1948
A Woman's Vengeance (The Gioconda Smile) (dir. Z. Korda), 1948
Adam's Rib (dir. G. Cukor), 1949
The Bribe (dir. R.Z. Leonard), 1949
Command Decision (dir. S. Wood), 1949
East Side, West Side (dir. M. LeRoy), 1949
Madame Bovary (dir. V. Minnelli), 1949
The Red Danube (dir. G. Sidney), 1949
The Asphalt Jungle (dir. J. Huston), 1950
Crisis (dir. C. Grant), 1950
The Miniver Story (dir. H.C. Potter), 1950, collab. H. Stothart
Ivanhoe (dir. R. Thorpe), 1951
The Light Touch (dir. R. Brooks), 1951
Quo vadis? (dir. M. LeRoy), 1951
Plymouth Adventure (dir. C. Brown), 1952
All the Brothers were Valiant (dir. R. Thorpe), 1953
Julius Caesar (dir. J.L. Mankiewicz), 1953
Knights of the Round Table (dir. R. Thorpe), 1953
The Story of Three Loves (dir. V. Minnelli and G. Reinhardt), 1953

Young Bess (dir. G. Sidney), 1953
Green Fire (dir. A. Marton), 1954
Men of the Fighting Lady (Panther Squadron) (dir. A. Marton), 1954
Seagulls over Sorrento (Crest of the Wave) (dir. W. Douglas), 1954
Valley of the Kings (dir. R. Pirosh), 1954
Diane (dir. D. Miller), 1955
The King's Thief (dir. R.Z. Leonard), 1955
Moonfleet (dir. F. Lang), 1955
Bhowani Junction (dir. G. Cukor), 1956
Lust for Life (dir. V. Minnelli), 1956
Tribute to a Badman (dir. R. Wise), 1956
The Seventh Sin (dir. R. Neame), 1957
Something of Value (dir. R. Brooks), 1957
Tip on a Dead Jockey (Time for Action) (dir. R. Thorpe), 1957
A Time to Love and a Time to Die (dir. D. Sirk), 1958
Ben-Hur (dir. W. Wyler), 1959
The World, the Flesh, and the Devil (dir. R. MacDougall), 1959
El Cid (dir. A. Mann), 1961
King of Kings (dir. N. Ray), 1961
Sodom and Gomorrah (dir. R. Aldrich), 1962
The V.I.P.s (dir. A. Asquith), 1963
The Green Berets (dir. R. Kellogg and J. Wayne), 1968
The Power (dir. B. Haskin), 1968
The Private Life of Sherlock Holmes (dir. B. Wilder), 1970 [based on Vn Conc.]
The Golden Voyage of Sinbad (dir. G. Hessler), 1973
Providence (dir. A. Resnais), 1977
Fedora (dir. B. Wilder), 1978
The Private Files of J. Edgar Hoover (dir. L. Cohen), 1978
The Last Embrace (dir. J. Demme), 1979
Time after Time (dir. N. Meyer), 1979
Eye of the Needle (dir. R. Marquand), 1980
Dead Men Don't Wear Plaid (dir. C. Reiner), 1981

Instrumental

Orchestral

North Hungarian Peasant Songs and Dances, op.5, vn, orch/pf, 1929
Rhapsody, op.3, vc, orch/pf, 1929
Variations on a Hungarian Peasant Song, op.4, vn, orch/pf, 1929
3 Pieces, orch, 1930
Scherzo, op.11, 1930
Sym, op.6, 1930, rev. 1993
Serenade, op.10, small orch, 1932, rev. 1946 as Hungarian Serenade, op.25
Theme, Variations and Finale, op.13, 1933, rev. 1943, 1966
Hungaria (ballet), 1935
Capriccio, pastorale e danza, op.14, 1938, rev. 1958 as 3 Hungarian Sketches, op.14*a*
Conc., op.17, str orch, 1943, rev. 1957

Spellbound Conc., pf, orch, 1946 [based on film score]
Vn Conc., op.24, 1953
Ov. to a Sym. Concert, op.26, 1957, rev. 1963
Notturno ungherese, op.28, 1964
Pf Conc., op.31, 1966
Sinfonia concertante, op.29, vn, vc, orch, 1966, rev. 1978
Vc Conc., op.32, 1968
Tripartita, op.33, 1972
Festive Flourish, brass, perc, 1975
Va Conc., op.37, 1979
suites from film scores

Chamber

Trio-Serenade, op.1, str trio, 1927, rev. 1974
Qnt, f, op.2, str qt, pf, 1928
Duo, op.7, vn, pf, 1931
2 Pieces, vc, pf, 1931
Str Qt, 1931
2 Hungarian Dances, vn, pf, 1933
Sonata, op.15, 2 vn, 1933, rev. 1973
Str Qt no.1, op.22, 1950
Str Qt no.2, op.38, 1981

Solo instrumental

Bagatellen, op.12, pf, 1932, arr. str qt
Variations, op.9, pf, 1932
Kaleidoscope, op.19, pf, 1945, orchd, 1946
Pf Sonata, op.20, 1948
The Vintner's Daughter, op.23, pf, 1952, orchd 1956
Sonatina, op.27, cl, 1957
Toccata capricciosa, op.36, vc, 1977
Sonata, op.39, fl, 1983
Sonata, op.40, vn, 1985
Sonata, op.41, cl, 1986
Sonata, op.42, gui, 1986
Sonata, ondes martenot, 1987
Sonata, op.43, ob, 1987
Introduction and Allegro, op.44, va, 1988

Vocal

Choral

Lullaby (R. Kipling), SATB, 1942 [from Jungle Book Suite]
To Everything There is a Season (Bible: *Ecclesiastes* iii.1–8), motet, op.21, SSAATTBB, org ad lib, 1943
Lullaby and Madrigal of Spring (M.T. Krone), op.18a–b, SSAA, 1944

12 Short Choruses from Ben-Hur, SATB, 1961
The Vanities of Life (Bible: *Ecclesiastes* i.1–18), motet, op.30, SATB, org ad lib, 1964
Ps xxiii, op.34, SATB, org ad lib, 1972
3 Chinese Poems (trans. A. Waley), op.35, SATB, 1975

Solo

2 Songs (Lord Vansittart), op.16, C, pf, 1940
High Flight (J. Magee), T, pf, 1942
Nostalgia (M. Gyarmathy), 2 songs, S, T, pf, 1972

MSS, sketches, documents, photographs, recordings in *US-SY*

Principal publishers: Breitkopf & Härtel, Broude Bros., Eulenberg, Schott, Edition Kunzelmann

Bibliography

EwenD
C. Palmer: *Miklós Rózsa* (London, 1975)
M. Rózsa: *Double Life* (London, 1982, 2/1989) [autobiography]
R. Bohn: "The Film Music of Miklós Rózsa: a Checklist," *Pro Musica Sana*, xlv/fall (1986), 8–23; xlvi/sum. (1987), 8–28 [incl. discography]
S. Wescott: "Miklós Rózsa's 'Ben-Hur': the Musical-Dramatic Function of the Hollywood Leitmotiv," *Film Music I*, ed. C. McCarty (New York, 1989), 183–207
S. Wescott: *Miklós Rózsa: a Portrait of the Composer as Seen through an Analysis of his Early Works for Feature Films and the Concert Stage* (diss., U. of Minnesota, 1990)
E. Rieger: *Alfred Hitchcock und die Musik: Eine Untersuchung zum Verhältnis von Film, Musik, und Geschlecht* (Bielefeld, 1996)
J. Dane: *A Composer's Notes: Remembering Miklós Rózsa* (Lincoln, NE, 2006)
J. Sullivan: *Hitchcock's Music* (New Haven, CT, 2007)
R. Hickman: *Miklós Rózsa's "Ben-Hur": a Film Score Guide* (Lanham, MD, 2011)
N. Platte: "Music for *Spellbound* (1945): a Contested Collaboration," *JM*, xxviii/4 (2011), 418–63
K. Barnett: "The Selznick Studio, *Spellbound*, and the Marketing of Film Music," *Music and Patronage*, ed. P. Merkley (Burlington, VT, 2012), 483–504
L. Schubert: "Anxieties of Accuracy: Miklós Rózsa's Score for *Quo vadis* (1951)," *Anxiety Muted: American Film Music in a Suburban Age*, ed. S. Pelkey and A. Bushard (New York, 2015), 69–86
S. Meyer: "The Politics of Authenticity in Miklós Rózsa's Score to *El Cid*," *Music in Epic Film: Listening to Spectacle* (New York, 2017): 86–101

STEVEN D. WESCOTT/R

Salinger, Conrad

(*b* Brookline, MA, 1901; *d* BelAir, CA, ?17 June 1962). American orchestrator and composer. Part of lyricist Arthur Freed's production unit at MGM, Salinger orchestrated some of the greatest film musicals released during the 1940s and 50s. The unit's first project was *Meet Me in St. Louis* (1944) directed by Vincente Minnelli, with songs by Hugh Martin and Ralph Blane. Salinger orchestrated the score with a musical adaptation by Roger Edens and musical direction by George Stoll and Lennie Hayton. The musical featured songs that were integrated into the narrative fabric, rather than following the show-stopping Broadway tradition: Salinger shared producer Freed's desire to blend the timbre of the songs with that of the soundtrack as a whole. He used about thirty-six musicians instead of the hundred-strong orchestra usually employed for film musicals. He also worked on other classic film musicals such as *The Wizard of Oz* (1939), *Easter Parade* (1948), *Seven Brides for Seven Brothers* (1954), and *Gigi* (1958), and he received an Academy Award nomination, with Adolph Deutsch, for his musical direction of *Show Boat* (1951). Salinger was also involved in the 1952 remake of David Selznick's 1937 film *The Prisoner of Zenda*. He used the principal themes from Alfred Newman's original score, but critics have described his reorchestration and placement of the melodies as more dramatically effective than the original.

Works

(*selective list*)

Composer

(*film scores unless otherwise noted*)
The Unknown Man (dir. R. Thorpe), 1951
Washington Story (dir. R. Pirosh), 1952
Dream Wife (dir. S. Sheldon), 1953
The Last Time I Saw Paris (dir. R. Brooks), 1954
Tennessee Champ (dir. F.M. Wilcox), 1954
The Scarlet Coat (dir. J. Sturges), 1955
Bachelor Father (TV series), 1957

Orchestrator

(*all film scores*)
Le Lieutenant Souriant (dir. E. Lubitsch), 1931
Carefree (dir. M. Sandrich), 1938
The Wizard of Oz (dir. V. Fleming), 1939
Lady Be Good (dir. N.Z. McLeod), 1941
For Me and My Gal (dir. B. Berkeley), 1942
Meet Me in St Louis (dir. V. Minnelli), 1944
Yolanda and the Thief (dir. V. Minnelli), 1945
Centennial Summer (dir. O. Preminger), 1946
Till the Clouds Roll By (dir. R. Whorf), 1946
Easter Parade (dir. C. Walters), 1948
The Kissing Bandit (dir. L. Benedek), 1948

Summer Holiday (dir. R. Mamoulian), 1948
The Barkleys of Broadway (dir. C. Walters), 1949
In the Good Old Summertime (dir. R.Z. Leonard), 1949
On the Town (dir. S. Donen and G. Kelly), 1949
Three Little Words (dir. R. Thorpe), 1950
An American in Paris (dir. V. Minnelli), 1951
Royal Wedding (dir. S. Donen), 1951
Show Boat (dir. G. Sidney), 1951
The Belle of New York (dir. C. Walters), 1952
The Prisoner of Zenda (dir. R. Thorpe), 1952
Singin' in the Rain (dir. S. Donen and G. Kelly), 1952
The Band Wagon (dir. V. Minnelli), 1953
Brigadoon (dir. V. Minnelli), 1954
Seven Brides for Seven Brothers (dir. S. Donen), 1954
High Society (dir. C. Walters), 1956
Funny Face (dir. S. Donen), 1957
Gigi (dir. V. Minnelli), 1958

Bibliography

W. Darby and J. Du Bois: *American Film Music: Major Composers, Techniques, Trends, 1915–1990* (Jefferson, NC, 1991)

P. Hay: *MGM: When the Lion Roars* (Atlanta, GA, 1991)

H. Fordin: *MGM's Greatest Musicals: the Arthur Freed Unit* (New York, 1996)

G. Marmorstein: *Hollywood Rhapsody: Movie Music and its Makers, 1900 to 1975* (New York, 1997), 155ff

KATE DAUBNEY

Salter, Hans

(*b* Vienna, Austria, 14 Jan 1896; *d* Studio, City, CA, 23 July 1994). American composer and conductor of Austrian birth. He studied at the University of Vienna with Guido Adler, Egon Wellesz, and Hans Gál, and at the Vienna Music Academy with Franz Schreker. Later, while working as an assistant conductor in Viennese theaters, he studied conducting with Felix Weingartner and composition with Alban Berg. From 1930 to 1933 he composed musicals and drama scores for UFA Studios in Neubabelsberg. He emigrated to Hollywood in 1937.

Originally hired as an orchestrator for Universal Studios, Salter was soon promoted to the rank of composer. With Frank Skinner he wrote music for serials, Westerns, dramas, Deanna Durbin musicals, and Abbott and Costello comedies. Although he received six Academy Award nominations for his musical comedy and drama scores, he is remembered today chiefly for his contribution to horror films such as *The Wolf Man* (1941), *Frankenstein Meets the Wolf Man* (1943), and *House of Frankenstein* (1944). When he retired in 1967, he had completed scores for over two hundred films. He was honored with lifetime achievement awards from the Society of Horror, Science Fiction, and Fantasy Films, and the Society for the Preservation of Film Music. He received an additional tribute at the Viennale Film Festival in 1993.

Works

(*selective list*)

Film scores

It Started with Eve (dir. H. Koster), 1941
The Wolf Man (dir. G. Waggner), 1941, collab. F. Skinner, C. Previn
The Amazing Mrs. Holliday (dir. B. Manning), 1943, collab. F. Skinner
Frankenstein Meets the Wolf Man (dir. R.W. Neill), 1943
Can't Help Singing (dir. F. Ryan), 1944
Christmas Holiday (dir. R. Siodmak), 1944
House of Frankenstein (dir. E.C. Kenton), 1944, collab. P. Dessau
The Merry Monahans (dir. C. Lamont), 1944
Scarlet Street (dir. F. Lang), 1945
This Love of Ours (dir. W. Dieterle), 1945
Magnificent Doll (dir. F. Borzage), 1946
Bend of the River (dir. A. Mann), 1952

Bibliography

P.N. Jones: "The Ghost of Hans J. Salter," *Cinefantastique*, vii/2 (1978)
J. Marcello: "The Music of the Wolf Man," *The Wolf Man*, ed. P. Riley (Absecon, NY, 1993)

PRESTON NEAL JONES

Sawtell, Paul [Sawatzki]

(*b* Gilve, Poland, 3 Feb 1906; *d* Los Angeles, 1 Aug 1971). Composer, arranger, conductor, and violinist of Polish birth, naturalized American. He took up the violin at age six in Germany where his family had relocated from Poland, and later studied in Essen and Munich. At age eighteen he emigrated to the United States after Balaban and Katz recruited him for their Chicago Theatre. From 1926 to 1928 he conducted at the Biograph Theatre and for the Lubliner and Trintz circuit in Chicago. While trying to make a living as a violinist from 1928 to 1933, he worked in real estate and for several investment security firms.

When he obtained US citizenship in 1930 the court ordered his surname be changed from Sawatzki. Moving on to Cleveland, Ohio, in 1934, he found work with WTAM radio, an NBC affiliate, as a violinist and arranger, and contributed to the Cleveland Symphony's Standard Oil Program. At the same time he operated a violin and piano studio; and in Canton he directed and appeared with the Walberg Brown Viennese ensemble while supplying the latter with special material. He accompanied Ben Bernie and All the Lads in a cross-country tour ending in Los Angeles in 1935. Sawtell settled in the area and began to study harmony and composition with composer and orchestrator Max Reese. He found odd jobs arranging for orchestras led by David Broekman, Andre Kostelanetz, and Victor Young and conducted some Jack Benny radio shows. His film music career commenced in 1939 at RKO Radio Pictures when he was engaged as a musical director. From 1943 to 1955 he scored a number of Tarzan films. From 1955 to 1970 he collaborated with composer Bert Shefter. During a particularly prolific five-year period beginning in 1957, the pair composed music for more than three dozen films and they also helped establish the television music department at Warner Bros. From 1958 to 1961 Sawtell and Shefter provided music supervision and library cues for Warner's episodic television through Sawtell's Music Scores, Inc. Sawtell and Shefter shared equal credit and, in 1961, with the formation of Bert Shefter Productions, they contractually formalized their relationship. Sawtell's music for Westerns and scores for Irwin Allen films are notable.

Works

(selective list)

Film scores

Bullet Code (dir. D. Howard), 1940
Along the Rio Grande (dir. E. Killy), 1941
Jungle Woman (dir. R. LeBorg), 1944
The Fighting Guardsman (dir. H. Levin), 1945
Tarzan and the Amazons (dir. K. Neumann), 1945
Born to Kill (dir. R. Wise), 1947
Desperate (dir. A. Mann), 1947
Trail Street (dir. R. Enright), 1947
Walk a Crooked Mile (dir. G. Douglas), 1948
Black Magic (dir. G. Ratoff), 1949
Tarzan and the Slave Girl (dir. L. Sholem), 1950
Arrowhead (dir. C.M. Warren), 1953
Inferno (dir. R.W. Baker), 1953
A Lawless Street (dir. J.H. Lewis), 1955
Tall Man Riding (dir. L. Selander), 1955
Texas Lady (dir. T. Whelan), 1955
Kronos (dir. K. Neumann), 1957

Last of the Badmen (dir. P. Landres), 1957
The Story of Mankind (dir. I. Allen), 1957
The Fly (dir. K. Neumann), 1958
The Hunters (dir. D. Powell), 1958
It! The Terror from Beyond Space (dir. E.L. Cahn), 1958
The Big Circus (dir. J.M. Newman), 1959
The Lost World (dir. I. Allen), 1960
Voyage to the Bottom of the Sea (dir. I. Allen), 1961
Five Weeks in a Balloon (dir. I. Allen), 1962
Faster, Pussycat! Kill! Kill! (dir. R. Meyer), 1965

Film and television songs

Texas Lady (lyric by J. Mann), 1955
Broken Arrow (lyric by N. Washington), television series, 1957

Concert works

Dance Morocco, orch, 1938
Fatal Mood, from Another Man's Poison, pf solo, 1952

MSS in UCLA Library, Performing Arts Special Collections

Bibliography

R. Saunders, ed.: "Sawtell, Paul," *Music and Dance in California and the West* (Hollywood, CA, 1948), 248

ASCAP Biographical Dictionary (New York, 4/1980), 443

J. Redford: "The Paul Sawtell Collection: a Preliminary Inventory," *The Cue Sheet*, xvii/1 (2001), 33–9

WARREN M. SHERK

Scharf, Walter

(*b* Brooklyn, NY, 1 Aug 1910; *d* Brentwood, CA, 24 Feb 2003). American arranger, composer, musical director, and pianist. He began his career at an early age playing the piano for silent films and serving as Helen Morgan's accompanist. At the age of seventeen he orchestrated George Gershwin's Broadway musical *Girl Crazy*. Later he worked as a session pianist with bands such as Glenn Miller and the Dorsey Brothers, jobs that earned him enough income to study at New York University and in Berlin.

His lengthy and prolific Hollywood career as a musical director, arranger, and composer began in the early 1930s. This included much composition of uncredited stock music cues for B pictures. At Paramount he orchestrated the original version of Irving Berlin's "White Christmas" for *Holiday Inn* (1942) and later scored many of the Jerry Lewis comedies and several Elvis Presley vehicles.

In the 1960s he created new scores for some Harold Lloyd silent film compilations. With the lyricist Don Black he composed the theme song for the horror film *Ben* (1972). The Motown recording of this song by Michael Jackson became a top-ten pop hit in America and Britain and won a Golden Globe award.

Scharf was also active in radio and television during the 1960s. He scored episodes (but not the main themes) of "Ben Casey," "The Man from U.N.C.L.E.," and "Mission: Impossible." Some of his best-known TV music is for the "National Geographic" and "Undersea World of Jacques Cousteau" documentaries, scored between 1965 and 1976; the music for the Cousteau series garnered an Emmy Award.

Scharf worked most prolifically in films and received ten Academy Award nominations for musical direction on such pictures as the Danny Kaye–Frank Loesser *Hans Christian Andersen* (1952), *Funny Girl* (1968), and *Willy Wonka and the Chocolate Factory* (1971). For his entire career Scharf received the Golden Score Award from the American Society of Music Arrangers and Composers in 1997.

Works

Film scores

Doughboys (dir. E. Sedgwick), 1930
The Adventures of Sherlock Holmes (dir. A.L. Werker (as A. Werker)), 1939
Return of the Cisco Kid (dir. H.I. Leeds), 1939
Susannah of the Mounties (dir. W.A. Seiter and W. Lang (uncredited)), 1939
The Three Musketeers (dir. A. Dwan), 1939
Mercy Island (dir. W. Morgan), 1941
The Glass Key (dir. S. Heisler), 1942
The Lady and the Monster (dir. G. Sherman), 1944
Storm over Lisbon (dir. Sherman), 1944
Earl Carroll Vanities (dir. J. Santley), 1945
City across the River (dir. M. Shane), 1949
Yes Sir That's my Baby (dir. Sherman), 1949
Buccaneer's Girl (dir. F. De Cordova), 1950
Two Tickets to Broadway (dir. J.V. Kern), 1951
Hans Christian Andersen (dir. C. Vidor), 1952
3 Ring Circus (dir. J. Pevney), 1954
The Court Jester (dir. M. Frank and N. Panama), 1955
Three Violent People (dir. R. Maté), 1956
The Joker is Wild (dir. Vidor), 1957
Loving You (dir. H. Kanter), 1957
The Geisha Boy (dir. F. Tashlin), 1958
King Creole (dir. M. Curtiz), 1958
Don't Give Up the Ship (dir. N. Taurog), 1959
The Bellboy (dir. J. Lewis), 1960

Cinderfella (dir. F. Tashlin), 1960
The Nutty Professor (dir. Lewis), 1963
Where Love Has Gone (dir. E. Dmytryk), 1964
Funny Girl (dir. W. Wyler), 1968
If It's Tuesday, This Must Be Belgium (dir. M. Stuart), 1969
Pendulum (dir. G. Schaefer), 1969
Willy Wonka and the Chocolate Factory (dir. Stuart), 1971
Ben (dir. P. Karlson), 1972
Walking Tall (dir. Karlson), 1973
Final Chapter: Walking Tall (dir. J. Starrett), 1977

Television music

The Jerry Lewis Show, 1958
Shirley Temple's Storybook, 1960–61
National Geographic Specials, 1965–76
Mission: Impossible, 1966–7
The Undersea World of Jacques Cousteau, 1968–73
From Here to Eternity, 1980

Orchestral

The Palestine Suite, 1945
The Tree Still Stands: a Symphonic Portrait of the Stages of a Hebraic Man, 1989
Israeli Suite, 1993

Writings

Composed and Conducted by Walter Scharf (Totowa, NJ, 1988)

Bibliography

J. Murrells: *Million-Selling Records from the 1900s to the 1980s* (New York, 1985), 348
W. Scharf and M. Freedland: *Composed and Conducted* (London, 1988)
"Walter Scharf, 92, Film Score Composer," *New York Times* (1 March 2003) [obituary]
J. Burlingame: "Walter Scharf, 1910–2003," *The Cue Sheet*, xxi/1 (2006)
M. Isaacson: "Walter Scharf," *The Cue Sheet*, xxi/1 (2006)

ROSS CARE/R

Schumann, Walter

(*b* New York, 8 Oct 1913; *d* Minneapolis, 21 Aug 1958). American composer for film and television, arranger, and conductor. His only early musical training was a three-year period of piano lessons. He initially pursued law at USC, but left to perform full-time in a dance band he created. After studying arranging and conducting, he worked for Eddie Cantor on radio in the late 1930s. During the war years, Schumann served as musical director of the Armed Forces Radio Service and conducted the orchestra for the touring production of Irving Berlin's *This Is the Army*. After the war he settled in Los Angeles, where he worked first for RKO-Radio Pictures, but primarily for Universal, providing scores and stock music for Abbott and Costello and Ma and Pa Kettle films, among others. Jack Webb tapped Schumann in 1949 to compose a theme for his radio program "Dragnet," which has since become one of the most recognized musical ideas from television. The theme made the transition to the televised version of the program in 1951, was featured on a 1953 Capitol recording by Ray Anthony, was used in the 1954 feature film *Dragnet* (underscore by Schumann), and served in eponymous television reincarnations of the series (1967–70 and 2003–4). However, he was accused by film composer Miklós Rózsa of plagiarizing the "Dragnet" theme from Rózsa's score for the 1946 Universal film *The Killers*—Schumann had been working at the studio at that time. Rósza's publisher won the lawsuit, which resulted in copyright ownership for the company and composing credit (and royalties) for Rózsa. Most of Schumann's remaining activity centered on composing and conducting the music for the "Dragnet series," for which he won an Emmy in 1955. He also scored Charles Laughton's *The Night of the Hunter* (1955) and composed music for the television series "Steve Canyon" (1958–9). His film/television style was varied, ranging from the comical (his Abbott and Costello scores) to the dramatic. Schumann also wrote and made arrangements of popular songs, composed the opera *John Brown's Body* (premièred in Los Angeles in 1953), and formed a twenty-strong choir "The Voices of Walter Schumann," which recorded "easy listening" music. A persistent heart ailment led to his premature death at the age of forty-four. His papers are housed at the University of Wyoming.

Works

Film scores

Escape to Paradise (dir. E.C. Kenton), 1939 (vocal arranger; as "Walter Schuman")
Buck Privates Come Home (dir. C. Barton), 1947
I'll Be Yours (dir. W.A. Seiter), 1947 (musical director)
The Wistful Widow of Wagon Gap (dir. C. Barton), 1947
The Noose Hangs High (dir. C. Barton), 1948
Africa Screams (dir. C. Barton), 1949
Dragnet (dir. J. Webb), 1954
The Night of the Hunter (dir. C. Laughton), 1955

Television music

Dragnet (1951–9)
Dateline Disneyland (1955, musical director)
Steve Canyon (1958–9)

Stage

John Brown's Body (musical), 1953, Los Angeles, 21 Sept 1953

Bibliography

E.J. Lewis: "The Archive Collections of Film Music at the University of Wyoming," *The Cue Sheet, Journal of the Film Music Society*, vi (1989), 143–61

J. Burlingame: *TV's Biggest Hits: the Story of Television Themes from "Dragnet" to "Friends"* (New York, 1996)

E. Studwell: "The Obscure Popular Songwriters' Hall of Fame, Part 2: M–Z," *Music Reference Services Quarterly*, iv (1996), 1–16

M. Forman: "'One Night on TV Is Worth Weeks at the Paramount': Musicians and Opportunity in Early Television, 1948–55," *Popular Music*, xxi (2002), 249–76

M. Hayde: *My Name's Friday: The Unauthorized but True Story of "Dragnet" and the Films of Jack Webb* (Nashville, TN, 2001)

R. Rodman: *Tuning in: American Narrative Television Music* (Oxford, 2009)

JAMES DEAVILLE

Shaiman, Marc

(*b* Scotch Plains, NJ, 22 Oct 1959). American composer, arranger, lyricist, and performer. Before embarking on a professional musical career that embraces Broadway, film, television, and popular music, Shaiman trained in community theater productions around Newark, New Jersey, as a pianist and music director. Throughout the 1980s and early 1990s he worked with Bette Midler as an arranger and co-producer. His collaborations with Midler included recording "Wind beneath my Wings" for the film *Beaches* (1988) and preparing material for her performance on the penultimate episode of Johnny Carson's "Tonight Show" in 1992. From 1984 through 1987 Shaiman contributed to "Saturday Night Live" skits; this work showcased Shaiman's skills as a musical humorist and led to additional engagements with the "Saturday Night Live" cast member Billy Crystal. Through Crystal, Shaiman met the actor and filmmaker Rob Reiner, who hired Shaiman as an arranger for *When Harry Met Sally . . .* (1989). For Reiner's next film, the psychological thriller *Misery* (1990), Shaiman composed his first original film score. Shaiman's ability to engage with radically different material prompted Reiner to hire Shaiman for subsequent films ranging from *A Few Good Men* (1992) to *And So It Goes* (2014). Shaiman's nuanced and wistful melodies support films like *The American President* (1995) and *The Bucket List* (2008), while gleeful parodies—often based upon earlier film scoring styles—dominate *City Slickers* (1991), *South Park: Bigger, Longer & Uncut* (1999), and *Down with Love* (2003).

Shaiman has also contributed songs, background music, and arrangements for Broadway shows and revues since 1979. He and his partner Scott Wittman received a Tony Award for their music in *Hairspray* (2002; film version, 2007). More recently Shaiman and Wittman have collaborated on *Martin Short: Fame Becomes Me* (2006) and the Broadway adaptations of *Catch me if you Can* (2011) and *Charlie and the Chocolate Factory* (2017). Amid Hollywood and Broadway projects, Shaiman has continued to serve as music director and composer for television specials and awards shows, including the Academy Awards and Tony Awards. In 2007 Shaiman received ASCAP's Henry Mancini Award for Lifetime Achievement.

Works

(*selective list*)

Stage

Hairspray (S. Wittman), Neil Simon Theatre, New York, 15 Aug 2002
Martin Short: Fame Becomes Me (Wittman), Bernard B. Jacobs Theatre, New York, 17 Aug 2006
Catch me if you Can (Wittman), Neil Simon Theatre, New York, 10 March 2011
Charlie and the Chocolate Factory (Wittman), Lunt-Fontanne Theatre, New York, 23 April 2017

Film and television music

(*film score unless otherwise noted*)
Billy Crystal: Don't Get me Started (dir. B. Crystal and P. Flaherty), 1986
Misery (dir. R. Reiner), 1990
The Addams Family (dir. B. Sonnenfeld), 1991
City Slickers (dir. R. Underwood), 1991
A Few Good Men (dir. Reiner), 1992
Mr. Saturday Night (dir. Crystal), 1992
Sister Act (dir. E. Ardolino), 1992
Sleepless in Seattle (dir. N. Ephron), 1993
The American President (dir. Reiner), 1995
Ghosts of Mississippi (dir. Reiner), 1996
George of the Jungle (dir. S. Weisman), 1997
Simon Birch (dir. M.S. Johnson), 1998
South Park: Bigger, Longer & Uncut (dir. T. Parker), 1999
61* (dir. Crystal), 2001
Down with Love (dir. P. Reed), 2003
The Bucket List (dir. Reiner), 2007
Prop 8: the Musical (dir. A. Shankman), 2008
Flipped (dir. Reiner), 2010
The Magic of Belle Isle (dir. Reiner), 2012

Parental Guidance (dir. A. Fickman), 2012
Smash (TV series), 2012
And So It Goes (dir. Reiner), 2014
LBJ (dir. Reiner), 2016

Bibliography

M. Schelle: "Marc Shaiman," *The Score: Interviews with Film Composers* (Los Angeles, 1999), 293–318

C. DesJardins: "Marc Shaiman," *Inside Film Music: Composers Speak* (Los Angeles, 2006), 232–40

R. Davis: *Complete Guide to Film Scoring* (Boston, 2/2010), 356–65

NATHAN PLATTE/R

Sherman, Richard M.

(*b* New York, 12 June 1928). American popular songwriter. He is known for his collaborations with his brother Robert B. Sherman (*b* New York, 19 Dec 1925; *d* London, 5 March 2012). Their father was the songwriter Al Sherman. In the 1950s they wrote the hit song "You're sixteen" for Johnny Burnette and songs for Annette Funicello, which gained them the attention of Walt Disney, for whom they subsequently wrote the songs for the film *The Parent Trap* (1961). From the early 1960s, as staff writers for Disney, they contributed songs to films including *The Sword in the Stone* (1963), which began a long-term association with the feature-length animated film. In the same year they wrote "It's a small world" for the 1964 World's Fair, a song which has subsequently become identified worldwide with Disneyland. They went on to contribute the now classic score to *Mary Poppins* (1964), with such numbers as "Supercalifragilisticexpialidocious," "Feed the birds," and "A Spoonful of Sugar." Their later Disney scores to wholly animated films include *The Jungle Book* (1967; "I wanna be like you"), *The Aristocats* (1970; "Everybody wants to be a cat"), and *Bedknobs and Broomsticks* (1971; "The Beautiful Briny"). Their song score for *Chitty Chitty Bang Bang* (1968) illustrates their consistent ability to provide contrasting memorable songs encompassing the rousing theme ("Chitty Chitty Bang Bang"), the sentimental ballad ("Hushabye Mountain"), the vigorous dance number ("Me Old Bamboo"), and the swaggering march ("P.O.S.H."). Other film scores include *Charlotte's Web* (1973) and the Cinderella remake, *The Slipper and the Rose* (1976). They also have written for the stage with *Over Here* (1974), a World War II tribute show that included the remaining two Andrews Sisters (Maxene and Patty), and the unsuccessful musical *Stage Door Charley* (1995). Their music has been honored with two Academy Awards and many additional nominations. They have also received a Grammy Award, a Laurel Award, induction into the National

Songwriters Hall of Fame, the 2008 National Medal of Arts, and a star on the Hollywood Walk of Fame. Their catchy songs can be heard on countless films and also in Disney theme parks around the world.

Bibliography

G. Marmorstein: *Hollywood Rhapsody: Movie Music and its Makers 1900 to 1975* (New York, 1997), 348–50

R.B. Sherman and R.M. Sherman: *Walt's Time: from Before to Beyond* (Santa Clarita, CA, 1998)

Shire, David (Lee)

(*b* Buffalo, NY, 3 July 1937). American composer and lyricist. He learned piano and played in his father's dance band in Buffalo, then studied music at Yale (BA 1959) and Brandeis University. He collaborated with the lyricist and fellow Yale student Richard Maltby, Jr. (*b* Ripon, WI, 6 Oct 1937) on songs for the Broadway musical *The Sap of Life* (1961). He played the piano in the orchestra for *Funny Girl* on Broadway, beginning an association with Barbra Streisand who recorded Maltby and Shire's "Autumn" and "No More Songs for Me"; Shire became an assistant arranger and conductor and an accompanist to Streisand. After some successful television work he moved to Hollywood (1969) and has written or contributed to many film scores, winning an Academy Award for the song "It goes like it goes" (lyrics by N. Gimbel) from the film *Norma Rae* (1979); he also adapted music for the hugely successful *Saturday Night Fever* (1977). Further music for television includes the score for the miniseries *The Kennedys of Massachusetts*, which was nominated for an Emmy Award (1990).

Shire has a malleable style that can encapsulate simply a defining mood and so is well suited to the demands of film and television scoring. This is shown in his musical theater work through the creation of individually satisfying musical numbers, drawing mainly on light pop and jazz idioms, that underpin the strong, self-contained narratives of the lyrics by his regular partner, Richard Maltby, Jr. Consequently their greatest successes have been in shows that use a revue format, particularly *Baby* (1983) and *Closer than Ever* (1989). Shire's eclectic style and ability to write concise and memorable tunes is shown in the former through the infectious funk of "Fatherhood Blues," and in the latter through the sophisticated jazz inflections of "Miss Byrd," the rock influence of "What am I doin'?," and the lyricism of the poignant ballad "Life Story." A revue, *The Story Goes On: the Music of Maltby and Shire*, was presented in New York (1998).

Works

(selective list)

Stage

(dates of first New York performance unless otherwise stated; lyrics by Richard Maltby, Jr.)

The Sap of Life (musl), Sheridan Square, 2 Oct 1961
Graham Crackers (revue), Upstairs and Downstairs, 1965
The Unknown Soldier and his Wife, Vivian Beaumont, 1967
How Do You Do, I Love You, 1968
Love Match (musl), Los Angeles, Almanson, 1970
Starting Here, Starting Now (revue), Barbarann, 7 March 1977
Baby (musl, 2, S. Pearson), Ethel Barrymore, 4 Dec 1983
Closer than Ever (revue, 1), Eighty-Eights, Jan 1989, rev. (2), Cherry Lane, 6 Nov 1989
Big (musl, J. Weidman, after G. Ross and A. Spielberg), Schubert, 28 April 1996, rev. Wilmington, DE, Playhouse, 26 Sept 1997 [after film]
incid music for plays

Film scores

(whole or part scores)

c40 scores for television films and mini series
One More Train to Rob (dir. A.V. McLaglen), 1971
Skin Game (dir. P. Bogart), 1971
Summertree (dir. A. Newley), 1971
Drive, He Said (dir. J. Nicholson), 1972
To Find a Man (dir. B. Kulik), 1972
Class of '44 (dir. P. Bogart), 1973
Showdown (dir. G. Seaton), 1973
Two People (dir. R. Wise), 1973
The Conversation (dir. F.F. Coppola), 1974
The Taking of Pelham 1-2-3 (dir. J. Sargent), 1974
Farewell, My Lovely (dir. D. Richards), 1975
The Hindenburg (dir. R. Wise), 1975
All the President's Men (dir. A.J. Pakula), 1976
The Big Bus (dir. J. Frawley), 1976
Harry and Walter Go to New York (dir. M. Rydell), 1976
Saturday Night Fever (dir. J. Badham), 1977
Straight Time (dir. U. Grosbard), 1978
Fast Break (dir. J. Smight), 1979
Norma Rae (dir. M. Ritt), 1979 [incl. It goes like it goes; lyrics, N. Gimbel]
Old Boyfriends (dir. J. Tewkesbury), 1979
The Promise (dir. G. Cates), 1979 [incl. I'll never say goodbye; lyrics A. and M. Bergman]
The Earthling (dir. P. Collinson), 1981 [song only; Halfway Home]
The Night the Lights Went Out in Georgia (dir. R.F. Maxwell), 1981
Only When I Laugh (dir. G. Jordan), 1981 [incl. title song]

Paternity (dir. D. Steinberg), 1981
Max Dugan Returns (dir. H. Ross), 1982
The World According to Garp (dir. G.R. Hill), 1982
Oh God, You Devil (dir. P. Bogart), 1984
2010: The Year We Make Contact (dir. P. Hyams), 1984
Return to Oz (dir. W. Murch), 1985
'night Mother (dir. T. Moore), 1986
Short Circuit (dir. J. Badham), 1986
Backfire (dir. G. Cates), 1988
Monkey Shines (dir. G.A. Romero), 1988
Vice Versa (dir. B. Gilbert), 1988
Paris Trout (dir. S. Gyllenhaal), 1991
Bed and Breakfast, 1992 (dir. R.E. Miller)
The Journey Inside (dir. B. Jackson), 1994
One Night Stand (dir. M. Figgis), 1995
Ash Wednesday (dir. E. Burns), 2002
The Tollbooth (dir. D. Kirschner), 2004
Zodiac (dir. D. Fincher), 2007
Beyond a Reasonable Doubt (dir. P. Hyams), 2009
Quitters (dir. N. Pritzker), 2015
Walk On By (dir. N. Woltersdorf), 2015
The American Side (dir. J. Ricker), 2016
Love After Love (dir. R. Harbaugh), 2017

Bibliography

W. Darby and J. Du Bois: *American Film Music: Major Composers, Techniques and Trends, 1915–1990* (Jefferson, NC, 1990), 494–5

B. Rosenfield: *Closer than Ever*, RCA-Victor 60399-2-RG (1990) [liner notes]

I. Isenberg: *Making it Big: the Diary of a Broadway Musical* (New York, 1996)

D. Morgan: *Knowing the Score: Film Composers Talk about the Art, Craft, Blood, Sweat, and Tears of Writing Music for Cinema* (New York, 2000), 18–24

S.B. Armstrong: "High Above the Ground: a Conversation with David Shire," *Film Score Monthly*, ix/4 (2004), 14–17

J. Smith: "The Sound of Intensified Continuity," *The Oxford Handbook of New Audiovisual Aesthetics*, ed. J. Richardson, C. Gorbman, and C. Vernallis (New York, 2013), 331–56

C. Juan: *David Shire's "The Conversation": a Film Score Guide* (Lanham, MD, 2015)

JOHN SNELSON/R

Shore, Howard

(*b* Toronto, 18 Oct 1946). Canadian composer, orchestrator, and conductor. Shore attended Boston's Berklee College of Music, where he studied with John Bavicchi, John LaPorta, William Maloof, and Charlie Mariano. He returned to Toronto as an alto saxophone player, songwriter, and arranger (1969–72) in the

Canadian jazz-rock band Lighthouse. He served as the musical director of the 1970–71 Canadian television variety show "The Hart and Lorne Terrific Hour" and wrote music for the 1974 show *Spellbound*. From 1975 to 1980, Shore worked as the first musical director of "Saturday Night Live," in which he also appeared in many music-related comedy sketches.

Shore's first film score was for the Canadian horror film *I Miss You, Hugs and Kisses* (1978). Subsequently, from 1979 to 2014, he composed the music for all but one of the Canadian director David Cronenberg's psychological thrillers. Shore's music for Cronenberg appropriately often features a brooding, repressive aesthetic. The score for *The Fly* (1986) was reworked as an opera (it received its première at Le Théâtre du Chalet in Paris in 2008), with music by Shore, a libretto by David Henry Hwang, directed by Cronenberg, and conducted by Plácido Domingo.

Shore's early film scoring work for American and international film directors included Martin Scorsese's comedy *After Hours* (1985); he later scored the same director's historical dramas *Gangs of New York* (2002), *The Aviator* (2004), *The Departed* (2006), and *Hugo* (2011). Shore's other collaborations include films for Jonathan Demme and David Fincher. Shore also scored the online video-game *Soul of the Ultimate Nation* (2007), and a number of television episodes, made-for-television movies, and short films.

Shore is best known for his music for Peter Jackson's film trilogy of J.R.R. Tolkien's adventure-fantasy novels *The Lord of the Rings*: *The Fellowship of the Ring* (2001), *The Two Towers* (2002), and *The Return of the King* (2003). The scores include full orchestra and choral elements—such as a boys' chorus to represent the Hobbits along with various soloists (including Renée Fleming, Enya, and Annie Lennox, among others)—as well as complex instances of combining music and sound effects. Among many honors, Shore won Academy Awards for the scores of the first and third of these films, as well as a co-writer Oscar for the third film's song "Into the West." Shore completed his *The Lord of the Rings Symphony* in 2004; he has also conducted live performances of his music synchronized to the films. His *Fanfare* for organ and brass received its première in 2008 by Peter Richard Conte on the Wanamaker organ at Macy's in Philadelphia. Shore received honorary doctorates from Toronto's York University (2007) and from Boston's Berklee College of Music (2008).

Works

Film scores

I Miss You, Hugs and Kisses (dir. M. Markowitz), 1978
The Brood (dir. D. Cronenberg), 1979
Scanners (dir. Cronenberg), 1981

Videodrome (dir. Cronenberg), 1983
After Hours (dir. M. Scorsese), 1985
The Fly (dir. Cronenberg), 1986
Big (dir. P. Marshall), 1988
Dead Ringers (dir. Cronenberg), 1988
Naked Lunch (dir. Cronenberg), 1991
The Silence of the Lambs (dir. J. Demme), 1991
Single White Female (dir. B. Schroeder), 1992
M. Butterfly (dir. Cronenberg), 1993
Mrs. Doubtfire (dir. D. Columbus), 1993
Philadelphia (dir. Demme), 1993
The Client (dir. J. Schumacher), 1994
Ed Wood (dir. T. Burton), 1994
Se7en (dir. D. Fincher), 1995
Crash (dir. Cronenberg), 1996
That Thing You Do! (dir. T. Hanks), 1996
The Game (dir. Fincher), 1997
Analyze This (dir. H. Ramis), 1999
Dogma (dir. K. Smith), 1999
eXistenZ (dir. Cronenberg), 1999
The Cell (dir. T. Singh), 2000
High Fidelity (dir. S. Frears), 2000
The Lord of the Rings: the Fellowship of the Ring (dir. P. Jackson), 2001
Gangs of New York (dir. Scorsese), 2002
The Lord of the Rings: the Two Towers (dir. P. Jackson), 2002
Panic Room (dir. Fincher), 2002
Spider (dir. Cronenberg), 2002
The Lord of the Rings: the Return of the King (dir. P. Jackson), 2003
The Aviator (dir. Scorsese), 2004
A History of Violence (dir. Cronenberg), 2005
The Departed (dir. Scorsese), 2006
Eastern Promises (dir. Cronenberg), 2007
The Last Mimzy (dir. R. Shaye), 2007
Doubt (dir. J. Patrick Shanley), 2008
Edge of Darkness (dir. M. Campbell), 2010
The Twilight Saga: Eclipse (dir. D. Slade), 2010
A Dangerous Method (dir. Cronenberg), 2011
Hugo (dir. Scorsese), 2011
Cosmopolis (dir. Cronenberg), 2012
The Hobbit: an Unexpected Journey (dir. P. Jackson), 2012
The Hobbit: the Desolation of Smaug (dir. P. Jackson), 2013
Jimmy P. (dir. A. Desplechin), 2013
The Hobbit: the Battle of the Five Armies (dir. P. Jackson), 2014
Maps to the Stars (dir. Cronenberg), 2014
Rosewater (dir. J. Stewart), 2014

Spotlight (dir. T. McCarthy), 2015
Denial (dir. M. Jackson), 2016
The Catcher Was a Spy (dir. B. Lewin), 2018

Other works

The Lord of the Rings Symphony, chorus, orch, 2004
Soul of the Ultimate Nation (video game score), 2007
Fanfare, org, brass, 2008
The Fly (op), 2008
Ruin and Memory, conc., pf, orch, 2010
Mythic Gardens, conc., vc, orch, 2012
A Palace Upon the Ruins, song cycle, 2014

Bibliography

K. Rugg: "In the Service of Two Masters: Singing the Praises of Williams and Shore," *Film Score Monthly*, ix (2004), 19–21, 48

D. Bowman: "Dark Mirrors and Dead Ringers: Music for Suspense Films about Twins," *Intersections: Canadian Journal of Music*, xxvii (2006), 54–74

"A New Buzz in the Opera World," *Gramophone*, May 2007, 12 only

D. Adams, *The Music of the Lord of the Rings Films* (Van Nuys, CA, 2010)

DURRELL BOWMAN/R

Silvers, Louis

(*b* New York, 6 Sept 1889; *d* Los Angeles, 26 March 1954). American composer and songwriter, music director, conductor, and pianist. Educated in Brooklyn public schools, he played piano as a youth and performed his own songs in cafes. After a stint as a vaudeville theater pianist he got involved in Broadway musicals. Throughout the 1910s he served as musical director for Gus Edwards's musical revues and became the general music director of The Song Review Co. By 1916 he was writing music with Jean Havez for musicals at the Palace Theatre and Harlem Opera House. He left Edwards to work on George M. Cohan revues. He was in charge of music for the Friars Club and musical director for the Hasty Pudding Club productions at Harvard University for ten years. In the 1920s he supplied music scores for four films by D.W. Griffith, starting with *Way Down East* (1920). Silvers became one of the first salaried film composers on the production side through his association with the Griffith organization. In lieu of playing to general settings with mood music, he gave attention to individual onscreen actions and emotions and developed techniques for character-driven music. He specialized in compiled scores that incorporated original incidental music. He wrote the song "April Showers," recorded and popularized by singer Al Jolson for *Bombo* in 1921. He went on to score a trio of films starring Jolson, including *The Jazz Singer* (1927). He was the general music director for Vitaphone, then Warner Bros. (1927–31), Metro-Goldwyn-Mayer (1933), Columbia Pictures (1934–5), and Fox (1936–40), where he contributed to the Shirley Temple films. Silvers had a talent for selecting popular songs and folk music to use as a basis for dramatic underscore and to establish time and place. As musical director for Lux Radio Theatre from 1936 to 1950, he provided incidental music for the hour-long radio adaptations of popular films.

Works

(*selective list*)

Film scores

(*as composer*)
Way Down East (dir. D.W. Griffith), 1920
Dream Street (dir. D.W. Griffith), 1921
The Singing Fool (dir. L. Bacon), 1928
Sonny Boy (dir. A. Mayo), 1929
Weary River (dir. F. Llyod), 1929
One Night of Love (dir. V. Schertzinger), 1934
Stanley and Livingstone (dir. H. King and O. Brower), 1939, with others
The Powers Girl (dir. N.Z. McLeod), 1943

(*as music director or supervisor*)
The Jazz Singer (dir. A. Crosland), 1927
Gold Diggers of Broadway (dir. R. DelRuth), 1929
It Happened One Night (dir. F. Capra), 1934
Crime and Punishment (dir. J. von Sternberg), 1935
The Country Doctor (dir. H. King), 1936
Poor Little Rich Girl (dir. I. Cummings), 1936
The Prisoner of Shark Island (dir. J. Ford), 1936
The Road to Glory (dir. H. Hawks), 1936
Seventh Heaven (dir. H. King), 1937
Little Miss Broadway (dir. I. Cummings), 1938

Film songs

(*names of lyricists are given in parentheses*)
Chatter-Box (J. Havez), from Way Down East, 1920
April Showers (B.G. DeSylva), 1921

Fascination (A. Francis, S. Greene), 1922
Weary River (G. Clarke), 1929

Musical revues and comedies

(*as composer*)
A Nightmare Revue (with J. Havez), 1916
An Operatic Courtship (with J. Havez), 1916
The Girl from Kelly's (with G. Kahn), 1924

Bibliography

F. Van Vranken: "With Music By—," *Photoplay*, xx/4 (Oct 1921), 54, 105
"Silvers, Louis," *Motion Picture News Blue Book* (New York, 1930), 244
Obituary, *Los Angeles Times* (28 March 1954)

WARREN M. SHERK

Silvestri, Alan

(*b* New York, 26 March 1950). American film and television composer. Deciding upon a music career as a teenager, he spent two years studying as a guitar and composition major at the Berklee School of Music (as it was called at that time) before moving to the West Coast to tour with Wayne Cochran and the C.C. Riders. While he initially wanted to be a bebop guitarist, he was somewhat serendipitously given the opportunity to score the low-budget feature *The Doberman Gang*. After a few more films, Silvestri began to compose for episodes of the television series "CHiPs," relying on his background as a rhythm guitarist to provide rhythmically driving scores. Silvestri made the uncommon transition from television composer to film composer by generating, on short notice, a sample cue for a chase scene for the 1984 film *Romancing the Stone*; his audition cue impressed the film's director, Robert Zemeckis, and Silvestri's score for this film began what would become an extended and successful collaboration. Silvestri began to compose for larger symphonic forces in his scores for *Fandango* and *Back to the Future*, the latter being one of several later projects with Zemeckis that also include *Who Framed Roger Rabbit*, *Forrest Gump*, *Contact*, *What Lies Beneath*, and *Cast Away*. Silvestri possesses an unusually large palette of compositional styles, allowing him to write scores ranging from the more aggressive affects of films like *Predator*, *The Abyss*, and *Shattered* to the noir and cartoon nostalgia in *Who Framed Roger Rabbit*, and even to delicate, intimate scores like his music for *Forrest Gump*. Several of his film scores have been recognized with

Alan Silvestri, 2014
(Photo by Richard Shotwell/Invision/AP)

Grammy Awards and he has twice been nominated for Oscars, first for *Forrest Gump* and second for his song "Believe" from *Polar Express*.

Works

Film and television scores

(film score unless otherwise noted)
The Doberman Gang (dir. B. Chudnow (as B.R. Chudnow)), 1972, with B. Craig
The Amazing Dobermans (dir. Chudnow), 1976
The Fifth Floor (dir. H. Avedis), 1978
CHiPs (TV series), 1978–83
Starsky and Hutch (TV series), 1979
Manimal (TV series), 1983
Romancing the Stone (dir. R. Zemeckis), 1984

Back to the Future (dir. Zemeckis), 1985
Cat's Eye (dir. Teague), 1985
Fandango (dir. K. Reynolds), 1985
Summer Rental (dir. C. Reiner), 1985
Amazing Stories (TV series), 1986
American Anthem (dir. A. Magnoli), 1986
The Clan of the Cave Bear (dir. M. Chapman), 1986
The Delta Force (dir. M. Golan), 1986
Flight of the Navigator (dir. R. Kleiser), 1986
No Mercy (dir. R. Pearce), 1986
Predator (dir. J. McTiernan), 1987
My Stepmother is an Alien (dir. R. Benjamin), 1988
Who Framed Roger Rabbit (dir. Zemeckis), 1988
The Abyss (dir. J. Cameron), 1989
Back to the Future Part II (dir. Zemeckis), 1989
Tales from the Crypt (TV series), 1989–95
Back to the Future Part III (dir. Zemeckis), 1990
Predator 2 (dir. S. Hopkins), 1990
Young Guns II (dir. G. Murphy), 1990
Dutch (dir. P. Faiman), 1991
Father of the Bride (dir. C. Shyer), 1991
Ricochet (dir. R. Mulcahy), 1991
Shattered (dir. W. Petersen), 1991
The Bodyguard (dir. M. Jackson), 1992
Death Becomes Her (dir. Zemeckis), 1992
FernGully: the Last Rainforest (dir. B. Kroyer), 1992
Grumpy Old Men (dir. D. Petrie), 1993
Super Mario Bros. (dir. A. Jankel and R. Morton), 1993
Forrest Gump (dir. Zemeckis), 1994
Richie Rich (dir. Petrie), 1994
Father of the Bride Part II, (dir. Shyer) 1995
Grumpier Old Men (dir. H. Deutch), 1995
Judge Dredd (dir. D. Cannon), 1995
The Perez Family (dir. M. Nair), 1995
The Quick and the Dead (dir. S. Raimi), 1995
Eraser (dir. C. Russell), 1996
The Long Kiss Goodnight (dir. R. Harlin), 1996
Sgt. Bilko (dir. J. Lynn), 1996
Contact (dir. Zemeckis), 1997
Fools Rush In (dir. A. Tennant), 1997
Mouse Hunt (dir. G. Verbinski), 1997
Volcano (dir. Jackson), 1997
Holy Man (dir. S. Herek), 1998
The Odd Couple II (dir. H. Deutch), 1998
The Parent Trap (dir. N. Meyers), 1998

Practical Magic (dir. G. Dunne), 1998
Stuart Little, (dir. R. Minkoff) 1999
Cast Away (dir. Zemeckis), 2000
Reindeer Games (dir. J. Frankenheimer), 2000
What Lies Beneath (dir. Zemeckis), 2000
What Women Want (dir. Meyers), 2000
The Mexican (dir. G. Verbinski), 2001
The Mummy Returns (dir. S. Sommers), 2001
Serendipity (dir. P. Chelsom), 2001
Lilo & Stitch (dir. D. DeBlois and C. Sanders), 2002
Maid in Manhattan (dir. W. Wang), 2002
Showtime (dir. T. Dey), 2002
Stuart Little 2 (dir. Minkoff), 2002
Identity (dir. J. Mangold), 2003
Lara Croft Tomb Raider: the Cradle of Life (dir. J. de Bont), 2003
The Polar Express (dir. Zemeckis), 2004
Van Helsing (dir. Sommers), 2004
Night at the Museum (dir. S. Levy), 2006
Beowulf (dir. Zemeckis), 2007
A Christmas Carol (dir. Zemeckis), 2009
G.I. Joe: the Rise of Cobra (dir. Sommers), 2009
Night at the Museum: Battle of the Smithsonian (dir. Levy), 2009
The A-Team (dir. J. Carnahan), 2010
Captain America: the First Avenger (dir. J. Johnston), 2011
The Avengers (dir. J. Whedon), 2012
Flight (dir. Zemeckis), 2012
The Croods (dir. K. DeMicco and C. Sanders), 2013
RED 2 (dir. D. Parisot), 2013
Cosmos: a Spacetime Odyssey (TV series), 2014
Night at the Museum: Secret of the Tomb (dir. Levy), 2014
The Walk (dir. Zemeckis), 2015
Allied (dir. Zemeckis), 2016
Avengers: Infinity Wars (dir. A. and J. Russo), 2018
Ready Player One (dir. S. Spielberg), 2018

Bibliography

A. Dursin: "The Alan Silvestri Interview," *Film Score Monthly*, l (Oct 1994), 12–15

D. Schweiger: "Alan Silvestri: Scoring *The Quick and The Dead*," *Film Score Monthly*, lx–lxi (March–April 1995), 12 [interview]

C. DesJardins: "Alan Silvestri," *Inside Film Music: Composers Speak* (Los Angeles, 2006), 251–61

C.L. Gengaro: "Music in Flux: Musical Transformation and Time Travel in *Back to the Future*," *The Worlds of "Back to the Future": Critical Essays on the Films*, ed. S.N. Fhlainn (Jefferson, NC, 2010), 112–32

N. Lerner: "'Things are Never Black as They are Painted': Minstrelsy and Musical Framing in *Who Framed Roger Rabbit?*," *Drawn to Sound: Animation Film Music and Sonicity*, ed. R. Coyle (London and Oakville, CT, 2010), 104–19

NEIL LERNER/R

Simon, Walter Cleveland

(*b* Cincinnati, 27 Oct 1884; *d* New York, 5 March 1958). American Composer, pianist, and organist. He was educated at the Pittsburgh College of Music and the New England Conservatory. He spent a year as pianist with exhibitor Lyman Howe's traveling film theater. Leaving Pittsburgh for New York, in 1911 he self-published the *Progress Course of Music*, drawing on his experience playing for moving pictures and vaudeville. When he began supplying "Special Music," original incidental music cued to a specific film, for the Kalem Company in 1911, he became one of the first film composers in America. Around this time he was accompanying films on pipe organ in a Bronx theater. He continued writing for Kalem short films through 1913. The music was for piano or a combination of four instruments, often characterized by short sections repeated as needed to fit the onscreen action. Kalem published and sold the scores. By the mid-teens he had scored two Kalem features. In 1912 and 1916 he supplied musical suggestions to *Moving Picture News* and *Moving Picture World*, respectively. The latter published his "Phototune," original sixteen-bar mood music compositions oriented vertically to allow pianists to jump from number to number. In 1916 he accompanied feature photoplays at F.F. Proctor's 23rd Street Theatre. He was recorded performing on a Wurlitzer organ in New Jersey in 1928 for Edison disc recordings that went unreleased. In 1930–31 he could be heard playing piano on WGBS radio broadcasts in New York. In later years he performed nostalgic programs with descriptive numbers, such as the piano recital he gave in Le Mars, Iowa, in 1944.

Works

(*selective list*)

Film scores

(*as composer or compiler*)

Short films

Arrah-Na-Pogue (dir. S. Olcott), 1911
An Arabian Tragedy (dir. S. Olcott), 1912

Captured by Bedouins (dir. S. Olcott), 1912
The Drummer Girl of Vicksburg (dir. K. Buel), 1912
The Fighting Dervishes of the Desert (dir. S. Olcott), 1912
The Siege of Petersburg (dir. K. Buel), 1912
The Soldier Brothers of Susanna (dir. K. Buel), 1912
The Spanish Revolt of 1836 (dir. G. Melford), 1912
A Spartan Mother (dir. K. Buel), 1912
Tragedy of the Desert (dir. S. Olcott), 1912
Under a Flag of Truce (dir. K. Buel), 1912
The Tragedy of Big Eagle Mine, 1913

Feature films

Midnight at Maxim's (dir. G.L. Sargent), 1915
The Black Crook (dir. R.G. Vignola), 1916
The Echo of Youth (dir. I. Abramson), 1919
large catalog of motion picture mood music. Berg's Incidental Series (New York, 1916–17), includes music by Simon

Popular music

Favorite Melodies for Solovox and Piano, 1941

Principal publisher: Kalem

Bibliography

ASCAP Biographical Dictionary (New York, 1948), 339–40
H. Reynolds: "Music for Kalem Films: the Special Scores, with Notes on Walter C. Simon," *The Sounds of Early Cinema*, ed. R. Abel and R. Altman (Bloomington, IN, 2001), 241–51

WARREN M. SHERK

Skinner, Frank (Chester)

(*b* Meredosia, IL, 31 Dec 1897; *d* Los, Angeles, 9 Oct 1968). American composer and arranger. A graduate of the Chicago Musical College, he found early employment in vaudeville and went on to perform and arrange for dance bands. This work brought him to New York, where from 1925 to 1935 he arranged about two thousand popular songs for Robbins Publishing. By the time he left Manhattan for Hollywood, he had written two books on arranging for dance bands.

After a short period at MGM, working on musical settings for *The Great Ziegfeld* (1936), Skinner was hired by Universal Studios. Over the course of his thirty years there, he composed music for more than two hundred films. Although he continued to work on musicals, he quickly mastered the art of dramatic scores, eventually earning five Academy Award nominations (1938–43). His distinctive approach to scoring horror films, such as *Son of Frankenstein* (1939) and *The Wolf Man* (1941), has been characterized as a "passion for chromatic lines . . . mirrored contours . . . [and] restrained, yet ominously Mythical orchestrations" (Marcello). He gained new recognition in the 1950s for his lush romantic scores, including *Magnificent Obsession* (1954) and *Written on the Wind* (1956). Despite many changes in the film industry, his book *Underscore* (1950) has survived as an excellent introduction to film music composition.

Works

(*selective list*)

Film scores

scores for the Bonzo and Francis series
Mad About Music (dir. N. Taurog), 1938, collab. C. Previn
Destry Rides Again (dir. G. Marshall), 1939
Son of Frankenstein (dir. R.V. Lee), 1939
The House of the Seven Gables (dir. J. May), 1940
Back Street (dir. R. Stevenson), 1941
The Wolf Man (dir. G. Waggner), 1941, collab. H.J. Salter, Previn
Arabian Nights (dir. J. Rawlins), 1942
The Amazing Mrs. Holliday (dir. B. Manning), 1943, collab. Salter
Harvey (dir. H. Koster), 1950
Magnificent Obsession (dir. D. Sirk), 1954
Written on the Wind (dir. D. Sirk), 1956

Writings

Frank Skinner's Simplified Method for Modern Arranging (New York, 1928/*R*)
Frank Skinner's New Method for Orchestra Scoring (New York, 1935)
Underscore (Hollywood, CA, 1950)

Bibliography

"Recording Sound Tracks for Musical Movies," *Metronome*, i/8 (1934)
B. Feigenblatt: "Frank Skinner: an Unsung Film Composer," *Movie Music* (Aug 1991), 11–12

PRESTON NEAL JONES

Snow, Mark [Fulterman, Martin]

(*b* New York, 26 Aug 1946). American composer. He studied the oboe and composition at the Juilliard School of Music. In 1967 Snow co-founded the New

York Rock and Roll Ensemble with Juilliard roommate Michael Kamen, whose future career also included composing for film. The rock fusion group performed on rock and classical instruments (Snow played oboe and drums) and recorded five albums before breaking up in the early 1970s.

Snow then moved to Southern California to pursue a career in television music. His first major assignment included contributing music to the final season of the crime drama, "The Rookies" (1975–6). The initial engagement proved prescient; Snow's prolific output for television movies and series has since frequently accompanied the adventures of detectives or superheroes facing criminals and, in later years, supernatural phenomena.

Snow's musical style has shifted along with television production practices. His score for the television movie *The Boy in the Plastic Bubble* (1976) features a chamber-sized orchestra in which piano solos and delicate woodwind chorales unfold within glassy string textures. Beginning in 1986, Snow began composing and rendering his scores for synclavier, a fiscally expedient approach that helped prompt a heightened demand among producers for synthesized sounds in television scores. In the 1990s digital samples of acoustic instruments allowed Snow to merge starkly electronic timbres with acoustically based sounds, an approach developed extensively in his much celebrated music for "The X-Files" (1993–2002, 2016–18). Over the course of the series, Snow's often ambient music dissolved distinctions between sound design and musical score. His work on "The X-Files" led to further collaborations with series creator Chris Carter, including "Millennium" (1996–9), "Harsh Realm" (1999–2000), and "The Lone Gunmen" (2001). In addition to writing extensively for television, Snow has composed music for feature films (*White Irish Drinkers*, 2010) and video games (*Syphon Filter: the Omega Strain*, 2004; *Syphon Filter: Dark Mirror*, 2006).

Works

Film and television scores

The Rookies (TV series), 1975–6
The Boy in the Plastic Bubble (TV movie, dir. R. Kleiser), 1976
Skateboard (film, dir. G. Gage), 1978
Starsky and Hutch (TV series, theme music only), 1978–9
Hart to Hart (TV series), 1979–84
T.J. Hooker (TV series), 1982–6
Falcon Crest (TV series), 1986–8
The X-Files (TV series), 1993–2002, 2016–18
Nowhere Man (TV series), 1995–6
Millennium (TV series), 1996–9
20,000 Leagues Under the Sea (TV series), 1997
The X-Files (film, dir. R. Bowman), 1998
Harsh Realm (TV series), 1999–2000
The Lone Gunmen (TV series), 2001

Smallville (TV series), 2001–7
Ghost Whisperer (TV series), 2005–10
White Irish Drinkers (film, dir. J. Gray), 2010, with The Shillaly Brothers
Blue Bloods (TV series), 2010–18
The Hunters (film, dir. C. Briant), 2011
Ringer (TV series), 2011–12
You Ain't Seen Nothin' Yet (film, dir. A. Resnais), 2012
Life of Riley (film, dir. Resnais), 2014
Monster of the Week (TV series), 2015
43:45 – The Makings of a Struggle (film, dir. J. Ng), 2016
Season X (film, dir. Ng), 2016

Bibliography

G. Rule: "A Day in the Life of the X-Files: Mark Snow," *Keyboard*, xxii/3 (1996), 24–8, 33–46

G. Rule: *Electro Shock! Groundbreakers of Synth Music* (San Francisco, 1999)

R. Davis: *Complete Guide to Film Scoring* (Boston, 1999, 2/2010), 372–6

R. Stilwell: "The Sound is Out There: Score, Sound Design, and Exoticism in *The X-Files*," *Analyzing Popular Music*, ed. A. Moore (Cambridge, MA, 2003), 60–79

J. Bond: "Snow Season: Mark Snow Celebrates 30 Years in the Biz," *Film Score Monthly*, x/3 (2005), 14–16

NATHAN PLATTE/R

Spencer, Herbert

(*b* Santiago, Chile, 7 April 1905; *d* Los Angeles, 18 Sep 1992). American orchestrator, arranger, and composer born in Chile. He graduated from a boarding school in New Jersey where he played clarinet and saxophone in the band. At the University of Pennsylvania he dropped out of engineering school to study music. There he discovered jazz, arranged for a dance band, and met fellow student David Raksin. Moving to New York, he studied harmony, counterpoint, and theory with Pietro Floridia. As a saxophonist in the Vincent Lopez Orchestra in 1928 and 1929, he contributed some arrangements. He began studying with Joseph Schillinger, and would later study with Ernst Toch in Los Angeles. Spencer worked as an arranger for CBS for four years. Shortly after signing on as an arranger for music publisher Harms in 1934, he was assigned to Bobby Dolan who had a radio show in Los Angeles with George Burns and Gracie Allen who happened to be making a film. In Los Angeles, Spencer's friend Edward Powell introduced him to Alfred Newman. When Newman joined Twentieth Century-Fox, Spencer was offered a contract as an arranger. He stayed until 1953. At Fox, he specialized in arranging musical numbers for Shirley Temple and others. Leaving Fox, he partnered with Earle Hagen to form Music Service

Inc. to write and package music for television. The pair supplied music to comedy and variety shows until their partnership fell apart in 1963. After working on *Scrooge* (1970) in London he stayed there for two years, before moving to Spain. Returning to the United States in 1976, he orchestrated primarily for John Williams until his death.

Works

(*selective list*)

Film scores

(*as orchestrator*)
On the Avenue (dir. R. Del Ruth, comp. C. Mockridge), 1937
That Night in Rio (dir. I. Cummings, comp. A. Newman), 1941
Irish Eyes Are Smiling (dir. G. Ratoff, comp. Newman), 1944
Centennial Summer (dir. O. Preminger, comp. Newman), 1946
Forever Amber (dir. Preminger, J.M. Stahl (uncredited), comp. D. Raskin), 1947
There's No Business Like Show Business (dir. W. Lang, comp. Newman), 1954
Guys and Dolls (dir. J.L. Mankiewicz, comp. Mockridge), 1955
Carousel (dir. H. King, comp. Newman), 1956
The Best of Everything (dir. J. Negulesco, comp. Newman), 1959
Valley of the Dolls (dir. M. Robson, comp. J. Williams), 1967
Funny Girl (dir. W. Wyler, comp. W. Scharf), 1968
Hello, Dolly! (dir. G. Kelly, comp. L. Hayton), 1969
M*A*S*H (dir. R. Altman, comp. J. Mandel), 1970
Jesus Christ Superstar (dir. N. Jewison, comp. A. Lloyd Webber), 1973
The Way We Were (dir. S. Pollack, comp. M. Hamlisch), 1973
Star Wars (dir. G. Lucas, comp. Williams), 1977
Raiders of the Lost Ark (dir. S. Spielberg, comp. Williams), 1981
E.T.: The Extra-Terrestrial (dir. Spielberg, comp. Williams), 1982
Cocoon (dir. R. Howard, comp. J. Horner), 1985
Home Alone (dir. C. Columbus, comp. Williams), 1990

WARREN M. SHERK

Stalling, Carl

(*b* Lexington, MO, 10 Nov 1891; *d* Los Angeles, 29 Nov 1972). American film composer. He began playing the piano for films by the early 1900s and worked professionally by about 1910. He was a theater musician around the Kansas City area (with an unspecified time spent in Chicago) through the 1910s and 1920s. While directing the orchestra at the Isis Theatre, he first met the young animator Walt Disney, who was then working for Kansas City Film Ad. When Disney decided to add sound to a series of animated shorts featuring a new character,

Mickey Mouse, he asked Stalling in the autumn of 1928 to create musical scores for two of them, *Plane Crazy* and *Gallopin' Gaucho*. Stalling loaned Disney money when the latter was struggling, just before the worldwide success of Mickey Mouse.

Stalling suggested that Disney pursue a series of cartoons in which the musical score would guide the story, unlike the character-driven Mickey Mouse cartoons. The resulting series, the Silly Symphonies, began with *The Skeleton Dance* (1929). Stalling left the Disney studio in January 1930 and went to work first for the Van Beuren studio in New York, and then became the musical director for Ub Iwerks studio in Los Angeles. During this time he continued to provide the orchestration for several dozen Disney shorts, including *Three Little Pigs* (W. Jackson, 1933), for which he also played the piano on the soundtrack.

In 1936 Stalling became musical director for the Warner Bros. animation division; his first score for the studio was *Porky's Poultry Plant*. From that year until his retirement in 1958 he was the animation studio's musical director, working closely with his longtime orchestrator, Milt Franklyn. His last score for the studio was *To Itch his Own* (1958), at which point he was succeeded at the studio by Franklyn. After his retirement from Warner Bros., Stalling continued composing independently. In spite of the ubiquity of the Warner Bros. shorts in theatres and then on syndicated television in the United States, Stalling's name was not widely known until excerpts of soundtracks for the Warner Bros. shorts were released on two successive recordings, *The Carl Stalling Project*, volumes one (1988) and two (1990).

Stalling's manuscripts and memorabilia are held in the American Heritage Center, University of Wyoming, Laramie, and Cinematic Arts Library, University of Southern California.

Carl Stalling, Kansas City, 1920s. Courtesy of Michael Barrier.

Works

(selective list; all scores for short films)

For Walt Disney

The Barn Dance (dir. W. Disney) 1928
Gallopin' Gaucho (dir. U. Iwerks), 1928
Plane Crazy (dir. Disney and Iwerks), 1928
The Barnyard Battle (dir. Iwerks), 1929
The Haunted House (dir. Disney), 1929
Hell's Bells (dir. Iwerks), 1929
The Jazz Fool (dir. Disney and Iwerks), 1929
Jungle Rhythm (dir. Disney), 1929
The Karnival Kid (dir. Disney and Iwerks), 1929
The Merry Dwarfs (dir. Disney), 1929
Mickey's Choo-choo (dir. Iwerks), 1929
Mickey's Follies (dir. Iwerks and W. Jackson), 1929
The Opry House (dir. Iwerks and Disney), 1929
The Plow Boy (dir. Disney), 1929
The Skeleton Dance (dir. Disney), 1929
Springtime (dir. Disney), 1929
El Terrible Toreador (dir. Disney), 1929
When the Cat's Away (dir. Disney), 1929
Wild Waves (dir. B. Gillett), 1929

For Ub Iwerks

(directed by Iwerks unless shown otherwise)
Cuckoo Murder Case, 1931
Fiddlesticks, 1931
The Village Barber, 1931
The Village Smitty, 1931
Don Quixote, 1934
The Headless Horesman, 1934
The Little Red Hen, 1934, with S. Culhane and A. Eugster
Puss in Boots, 1934, with Culhane and Eugster
Rasslin' Round, 1934
Robin Hood, Jr., 1934
Viva Willie, 1934
Balloonland, 1935
The Bremen Town Musicians, 1935
Humpty Dumpty, 1935
Old Mother Hubbard, 1935
Simple Simon, 1935
Sinbad the Sailor, 1935
Ali Baba, 1936
Dick Whittington's Cat, 1936

Happy Days, 1936
Little Boy Blue, 1936
Tom Thumb, 1936

For Warner Bros.

Coo-Coo Nut Grove (dir. F. Freleng (as I. Freleng)), 1936
Milk and Money (dir. T. Avery (as F. Avery)), 1936
Porky's Poultry Plant (dir. F. Tashlin (as F. Tash)), 1936
The Case of the Stuttering Pig (dir. F. Tashlin), 1937
Clean Pastures (dir. Freleng), 1937
The Fella With the Fiddle (dir. Freleng), 1937
He Was Her Man (dir. Freleng), 1937
I Only Have Eyes for You (dir. Avery), 1937
Pigs Is Pigs (dir. Freleng), 1937
Porky's Duck Hunt (dir. Avery), 1937
Porky's Hero Agency (dir. R. Clampett), 1937
Rover's Rival (dir. Clampett), 1937
September in the Rain (dir. Freleng), 1937
She Was an Acrobat's Daughter (dir. Freleng), 1937
Speaking of the Weather (dir. Tashlin), 1937
Cinderella Meets Fella (dir. Avery), 1938
Cracked Ice (dir. Tashlin), 1938
The Daffy Doc (dir. Clampett), 1938
Daffy Duck and Egghead (dir. Avery), 1938
Daffy Duck in Hollywood (dir. Avery), 1938
Have You Got Any Castles? (dir. Tashlin and Freleng (uncredited)), 1938
Injun Trouble (dir. Clampett), 1938
The Isle of Pingo Pongo (dir. Avery), 1938
Katnip Kollege (dir. C. Dalton and C. Howard), 1938
My Little Buckeroo (dir. Freleng), 1938
The Night Watchman (dir. C. Jones), 1938
Porky and Daffy (dir. Clampett), 1938
Porky at the Crocadero (dir. Tashlin), 1938
Porky in Wackyland (dir. Clampett), 1938
Porky's Hare Hunt (dir. B. Hardaway and C. Dalton (uncredited)), 1938
Wholly Smoke (dir. Tashlin), 1938
You're an Education (dir. Tashlin), 1938
Daffy Duck and the Dinosaur (dir. Jones), 1939
A Day at the Zoo (dir. Avery), 1939
Detouring America (dir. Avery), 1939
Dog Gone Modern (dir. Jones), 1939
The Good Egg (dir. Jones), 1939
Hamateur Night (dir. Avery), 1939
Hare-um Scare-um (dir. C. Dalton and B. Hardaway), 1939
Jeepers Creepers (dir. Clampett), 1939
The Lone Stranger and Porky (dir. Clampett), 1939
Old Glory (dir. Jones), 1939

Porky and Teabiscuit (dir. Dalton and Hardaway), 1939
Robin Hood Makes Good (dir. Jones), 1939
Sioux Me (dir. Dalton and Hardaway), 1939
Sniffles and the Bookworm (dir. Jones), 1939
The Bear's Tale (dir. Avery), 1940
Calling Dr. Porky (dir. Freleng), 1940
The Chewin' Bruin (dir. Clampett), 1940
Cross Country Detours (dir. Avery), 1940
Little Blabbermouse (dir. Freleng), 1940
Prehistoric Porky (dir. Clampett), 1940
The Timid Toreador (dir. Clampett and N. McCabe), 1940
A Wild Hare (dir. Avery), 1940
You Ought to be in Pictures (dir. Freleng), 1940
All This and Rabbit Stew (dir. Avery), 1941
A Coy Decoy (dir. Clampett), 1941
Elmer's Pet Rabbit (dir. Jones), 1941
Goofy Groceries (dir. Clampett), 1941
The Heckling Hare (dir. Avery), 1941
The Henpecked Duck (dir. Clampett), 1941
Hiawatha's Rabbit Hunt (dir. Freleng), 1941
Hollywood Steps Out (dir. Avery), 1941
Inki and the Lion (dir. Jones), 1941
Notes to You (dir. Freleng), 1941
Porky's Preview (dir. Avery), 1941
Rhapsody in Rivets (dir. Freleng), 1941
Sniffles Bells the Cat (dir. Jones), 1941
Wabbit Twouble (dir. R. Clampett (as W. Cwampett)), 1941
Bugs Bunny Gets the Boid (dir. Clampett), 1942
Case of the Missing Hare (dir. Jones), 1942
Coal Black and de Sebben Dwarfs (dir. Clampett), 1942, with E. Beale
Conrad the Sailor (dir. Jones (as C.M. Jones)), 1942
Ding Dog Daddy (dir. Freleng), 1942
The Dover Boys (dir. Jones), 1942
Fresh Hare (dir. Freleng), 1942
The Hep Cat (dir. Clampett), 1942
Horton Hatches the Egg (dir. Clampett), 1942
The Impatient Patient (dir. N. McCabe), 1942
My Favorite Duck (dir. Jones), 1942
A Tale of Two Kitties (dir. Clampett), 1942
The Wabbit Who Came to Supper (dir. Freleng), 1942
The Wacky Wabbit (dir. Clampett), 1942
The Aristo Cat (dir. Jones), 1943
A Corny Concerto (dir. Clampett), 1943
Daffy the Commando (dir. Freleng), 1943
Greetings Bait (dir. Freleng), 1943
Little Red Riding Rabbit (dir. Freleng), 1943
Pigs in a Polka (dir. Freleng), 1943

Super-Rabbit (dir. Freleng), 1943
Tin Pan Alley Cats (dir. Clampett), 1943
To Duck or Not to Duck (dir. Jones), 1943
Tortoise Wins by a Hair (dir. Clampett), 1943
The Wise Quacking Duck (dir. Clampett), 1943
Yankee Doodle Daffy (dir. Freleng), 1943
Buckaroo Bugs (dir. Clampett), 1944
Bugs Bunny and the Three Bears (dir. Jones), 1944
Bugs Bunny Nips the Nips (dir. Freleng), 1944
Goldilocks and the Jivin' Bears (dir. Freleng), 1944
I Got Plenty of Mutton (dir. Tashlin), 1944
The Old Grey Hare (dir. Clampett), 1944
Plane Daffy (dir. Tashlin), 1944
The Stupid Cupid (dir. Tashlin), 1944
The Swooner Crooner (dir. Tashlin), 1944
What's Cookin', Doc? (dir. Clampett and Freleng (uncredited)), 1944
The Bashful Buzzard (dir. Clampett), 1945
Draftee Daffy (dir. Clampett), 1945
A Gruesome Twosome (dir. Clampett), 1945
Hare Tonic (dir. Clampett), 1945
Herr Meets Hare (dir. Freleng), 1945
Life with Feathers (dir. Freleng), 1945
Bacall to Arms (dir. R. Clampett (uncredited) and A. Davis (uncredited)), 1946
The Big Snooze (dir. Clampett), 1946
Book Revue (dir. Clampett), 1946
The Great Piggy Bank Robbery (dir. Clampett and M. Sasanoff (uncredited)), 1946
Hair Raising Hare (dir. Jones), 1946
Holiday for Shoestrings (dir. Freleng), 1946
Rhapsody Rabbit (dir. Freleng), 1946
Walky Talky Hawky (dir. R. McKimson), 1946
Easter Yeggs (dir. McKimson), 1947, with M. Franklyn
A Hare Grows in Manhattan (dir. Freleng), 1947
Rabbit Transit (dir. Freleng), 1947
Tweetie Pie (dir. Freleng), 1947
Back Alley Oproar (dir. Freleng), 1948
Bugs Bunny Rides Again (dir. Freleng), 1948
Dough Ray Me-ow (dir. A. Davis), 1948
The Foghorn Leghorn (dir. McKimson), 1948
Gorilla My Dreams (dir. McKimson), 1948
Hot Cross Bunny (dir. McKimson), 1948
Mississippi Hare (dir. Jones), 1948
The Pest That Came to Dinner (dir. Davis), 1948
Rabbit Punch (dir. Jones), 1948
Scaredy Cat (dir. Jones), 1948, with M. Franklyn
Awful Orphan (dir. Jones), 1949
The Bee-Deviled Bruin (dir. Jones), 1949
Bye, Bye Bluebeard (dir. Davis), 1949

Curtain Razor (dir. Freleng), 1949
Dough for the Do-Do (dir. Clampett (uncredited) and Freleng (uncredited)), 1949
Fast and Furry-ous (dir. Jones), 1949
For Scent-imental Reasons (dir. Jones), 1949
High Diving Hare (dir. Freleng), 1949
Long-Haired Hare (dir. Jones), 1949
Mouse Mazurka (dir. Freleng), 1949
Mouse Wreckers (dir. Jones), 1949
Rabbit Hood (dir. Jones), 1949
The Ducksters (dir. Jones), 1950
Hillbilly Hare (dir. McKimson), 1950
Homeless Hare (dir. Jones), 1950
Hurdy Gurdy Hare (dir. McKimson), 1950
The Hypo-chondri-cat (dir. Jones), 1950
The Leghorn Blows at Midnight (dir. McKimson), 1950
Rabbit of Seville (dir. McKimson), 1950
The Scarlet Pumpernickel (dir. Jones), 1950
What's Up, Doc? (dir. McKimson), 1950
Chow Hound (dir. Jones), 1951
Rabbit Fire (dir. Jones), 1951
Scent-imental Romeo (dir. Jones), 1951
Feed the Kitty (dir. Jones), 1952
Mouse Warming (dir. Jones), 1952
Operation: Rabbit (dir. Jones), 1952
Rabbit Seasoning (dir. Jones), 1952
Water, Water, Every Hare (dir. Jones), 1952
Don't Give Up the Sheep (dir. Jones), 1953
Duck Amuck (dir. Jones), 1953
Duck Dodgers in the 24½th Century (dir. Jones), 1953
Duck, Rabbit, Duck (dir. Jones), 1953
Punch Trunk (dir. Jones), 1953
Robot Rabbit (dir. Freleng), 1953
From A to Z-Z-Z-Z (dir. Jones), 1954
Lumber Jack Rabbit (dir. Jones), 1954
Birds Anonymous (dir. Freleng), 1957
Zoom and Bored (dir. Jones), 1957, with M. Franklyn
To Itch his Own (dir. Jones), 1958

Bibliography

M. Barrier, M. Gray, and B. Spicer: "An Interview with Carl Stalling," *Funnyworld*, no.13 (1971), 21–9

D. Goldmark: *Tunes for 'Toons: Music and the Hollywood Cartoon* (Berkeley, 2005)

DANIEL GOLDMARK

Steiner, Fred

(*b* New York, 24 Feb 1923; *d* Ajijic, Jalisco, Mexico, 23 June 2011). American composer, arranger, orchestrator, and conductor. Son of George Steiner, a Hungarian-born violinist and composer for short films and cartoons in New York. At age six Fred studied piano, before taking up the cello as a teenager. At Oberlin Conservatory he studied composition with Normand Lockwood. After graduating he found work as a composer and arranger on more than a dozen network radio programs between 1943 and 1954, first in New York, then in Hollywood beginning in 1947. For CBS television he composed, arranged, and conducted music for live programming from 1950 to 1955. At the same time he composed music for a handful of CBS and Desilu filmed television shows featuring Ray Bolger, Amos and Andy, and others. From 1958 to 1960 he lived in Mexico, working for a recording company. Returning to Los Angeles, he provided music for more than two-dozen television series during the 1960s and 1970s, notably for "Star Trek" and "Twilight Zone," and the series theme for "Perry Mason." Although his screen credits as sole composer are limited to a handful of films, he wrote and orchestrated music for films scored by others. In the 1970s, while pursuing a PhD in Musicology at the University of Southern California, where David Raksin served on his dissertation committee, he developed into a film music historian, lecturer, writer of articles, and conductor of film music recordings. During this time Steiner became a driving force behind the formation of the Film Music Society. He remained active after retiring to Santa Fe, New Mexico, in 1990.

Works

(*selective list*)

Film scores

(*as composer*)
Run for the Sun (dir. R. Boulting), 1956
United Productions of America (U.P.A.) animated films, 1956
Time Limit (dir. K. Malden), 1957
The St. Valentine's Day Massacre (dir. R. Corman), 1967
The Sea Gypsies (dir. S. Raffill), 1978

Film scores

(*as composer of additional music*)
The Greatest Story Ever Told (comp. A. Newman, dir. G. Stevens), 1965
The Color Purple (comp. Q. Jones, dir. S. Spielberg), 1985
Gremlins 2: The New Batch (comp. J. Goldsmith, dir. J. Dante), 1990, animated sequences
Mrs. Doubtfire (comp. H. Shore, dir. C. Columbus), 1993, animated sequences

Film scores

(as orchestrator)
The Man with the Golden Arm (comp. E. Bernstein, dir. O. Preminger), 1955
Seven Cities of Gold (comp. H. Friedofer, dir. R.D. Webb), 1955
Prizzi's Honor (comp. A. North, dir. J. Huston), 1985

Television music

The Ed Wynn Show, 1950
The Burns and Allen Show, 1952
The Red Skelton Show, 1954
The Ray Bolger Show, 1955
Perry Mason (theme), 1957
Rawhide, 1959–64
The Bullwinkle Show, 1961–2
Twilight Zone, 1961–3
The Andy Griffith Show, 1964–8
Star Trek, 1966–9
The Virginian, 1969–70
Mannix, 1969–71
Hawaii Five-0, 1978–9
Amazing Stories, 1986
Tiny Toon Adventures, 1990–91

Radio music

This Is Your FBI, 1945–53

Concert music

Navy Log March, sym. band, based on Steiner's music for the television series, 1955
5 Pieces, str trio, 1958
Vc Sonata, 1958
Tower Music, brass, perc
Pezzo Italiano, vc, pf
Indian Music, va, pf
Act Without Words, suite, perc ens

MSS in Special Collections and University Archives, University of Oregon Libraries, Eugene, Oregon

Writings

"Herrmann's 'Black and White' Music for Hitchcock's *Psycho*," *Film Music Notebook*, i (1974–5), no.1, 28–36; no.2, 26–46
The Making of an American Film Composer: a Study of Alfred Newman's Music in the First Decade of the Sound Era (diss., U. of Southern California, 1981)
with M. Marks: "Film Music," *AGrove*

Bibliography

J. Tynan: "Fred Steiner," *BMI Bulletin* (Feb 1964), 36–9

T. Thomas: "Fred Steiner," *Film Score: the View from the Podium* (South Brunswick, NJ, 1979), 175–86

International Who's Who: Popular Music (London, 2002)

WARREN M. SHERK

Steiner, Max(imilian Raoul Walter)

(*b* Vienna, Austria, 10 May 1888; *d* Beverly, Hills, CA, 28 Dec 1971). American composer and conductor of Austrian birth. His father was a theatrical producer and his grandfather managed the Theater an der Wien when the operettas of Jacques Offenbach and Johann Strauss were produced there. Steiner showed exceptional musical talent at an early age, publishing his first song in 1897 and composing a one-act operetta, *Die schöne Griechin*, in 1903. He received academic training at the Vienna Conservatory, and a practical apprenticeship conducting and composing small works in the theaters of his father and of other contemporary Viennese impresarios. From 1904 to 1914 he worked throughout Europe, most frequently in London, Ireland, and Paris, acting as the musical director and conductor for a range of theatrical shows. He composed ballets for the Tiller Girls dance troupe, and he worked on shows for George Dance and Ned Wayburn. At the outbreak of World War I he moved to New York, where he worked as a copyist and later as an arranger, orchestrator, and conductor of musicals and revue shows, on and off Broadway. These shows included the George Gershwin's *Lady Be Good!* (1924), Jerome Kern's *Sitting Pretty* (1924), and Vincent Youmans's *Rainbow* (1928). His only Broadway show, *Peaches*, was composed during this period. He also worked extensively with Victor Herbert, arranging many of the composer's dance numbers and acting as the musical director for a touring production of *Oui Madame* (1920). Herbert's influence can be seen in the attention to orchestration that characterizes Steiner's film scores. For musical theater he learned to combine small numbers of instruments to create the impression of a fuller orchestral sound, a skill that was to prove useful in the underfunded music departments of Hollywood.

Steiner's introduction to Hollywood came in 1929 when RKO Radio Pictures bought the rights to the musical *Rio Rita*. Harry Tierney, for whom Steiner had orchestrated and conducted the stage version, insisted that he be hired by the studio. He worked for RKO from 1929 to 1936, composing music for more than 130 films, during a period when Hollywood was still judging the value of music in film. His first original score, *Cimarron* (1930), is striking in two ways. It was the first sound film to include non-diegetic music, the placement of which foreshadows the later widely used Hollywood technique of emphasizing emotional, unspoken elements of the narrative. Also, Steiner reuses material from the title sequence in the body of the film, establishing from the outset his thematic approach to the structuring of film scores. In his film score for *King Kong* (1933), he provided the first of the full-length Hollywood film scores, and its rich orchestration and use of repeated motifs and themes show how quickly Steiner had established his technique of scoring. These features of his approach owe as much to his experience of musical theater as they do to more conventional interpretations of symphonic and Wagnerian influences. Recording techniques and versatile orchestration created a symphonic illusion from the small studio ensembles, and the development of tunes and themes voiced characterization as clearly as song numbers. This latter feature is apparent throughout his scores across a wide range of genres: Philip Carey's physical and metaphorical limp in *Of Human Bondage* (1934), Gypo Nolan's traitorous deceit in the Academy Award–winning score for *The Informer* (1935), antebellum Southern pride in the title theme "Tara" for *Gone with the Wind* (1939), Charlotte Vale's emotional insecurity in his Academy Award–winning score for *Now Voyager* (1942), and General Custer's military single-mindedness in *They Died with their Boots on* (1941).

In 1936 Steiner joined Warner Bros. from RKO, after a brief spell at Selznick International. His output of scores in the late 1930s topped ten per year as principal composer, with involvement in many more as an assistant composer, and he continued to create scores at a high rate into the 1950s when he became freelance. This rate of output was made possible by his exceptional relationship with his orchestrators, particularly Hugo Friedhofer, who later became a successful film composer in his own right. Steiner's careful and detailed construction and annotation of the four-stave short scores made the translation to full orchestral score closer to a copyist's task than a full instrumental arrangement. Among Steiner's other notable scores are *Since you Went Away* (1944), for which he won his third and last Academy Award, *Saratoga Trunk* (1946), *The Fountainhead* (1949), and *A Summer Place* (1959), the main theme of which became a popular song in the 1960s. His last score was *Two on a Guillotine* in 1965.

Steiner's score for *Now Voyager* is a fine example of the approach to narrative interpretation that typified his and Hollywood's film music of the period, and that has come to be regarded as a classical model for film scoring. There are five central themes, expressing each of the main characters, differentiated and connected by the use of diatonic and chromatic melodies and harmonies. There are also a further seven melodies that are used to capture less prominent features of the narrative and a number of quotations from current popular songs. This reference to music outside cinema was typical of Steiner's idiomatic anchorage of his score to contemporary popular taste, and though it has been criticized for its lack of subtlety, it reflects the Hollywood goal of making all aspects of a film

Max Steiner
Photofest

accessible to the audience. The score also employs the technique of "mickey-mousing," the catching of physical movements on the screen in the movement of musical language in the score. Such a feature seems unsophisticated to modern audiences, but it is a further example of Steiner's belief in the power of music to emphasize and support all elements of the dramatic film narrative. A substantial collection of Steiner's film score manuscripts and other personal documentation is available in the Steiner Collection in the Harold B. Lee Library at Brigham Young University.

Works

(*selective list*)

Film scores

Cimarron (dir. W. Ruggles), 1930
Bird of Paradise (dir. K. Vidor), 1932
The Most Dangerous Game (dir. I. Pichel and E.B. Schoedsack), 1932
Symphony of Six Million (dir. G. LaCava), 1932
King Kong (dir. M.C. Cooper and E.B. Schoedsack), 1933
Little Women (dir. G. Cukor), 1933
The Lost Patrol (dir. J. Ford), 1934
Of Human Bondage (dir. J. Cromwell), 1934
The Informer (dir. J. Ford), 1935
The Three Musketeers (dir. R.V. Lee), 1935

The Charge of the Light Brigade (dir. M. Curtiz), 1936
The Garden of Allah (dir. R. Boleslawski), 1936
Little Lord Fauntleroy (dir. J. Cromwell), 1936
The Life of Emile Zola (dir. W. Dieterle), 1937
A Star is Born (dir. W.A. Wellman), 1937
Jezebel (dir. W. Wyler), 1938
Dark Victory (dir. E. Goulding), 1939
Dodge City (dir. M. Curtiz), 1939
Gone with the Wind (dir. V. Fleming), 1939
All This, and Heaven Too (dir. A. Litvak), 1940
The Letter (dir. W. Wyler), 1940
They Died with Their Boots On (dir. R. Walsh), 1941
In This Our Life (dir. J. Huston), 1942
Now, Voyager (dir. I. Rapper), 1942
Casablanca (dir. M. Curtiz), 1943
The Adventures of Mark Twain (dir. I. Rapper), 1944
Arsenic and Old Lace (dir. F. Capra), 1944
The Conspirators (dir. J. Negulesco), 1944
Passage to Marseilles (dir. M. Curtiz), 1944
Since You Went Away (dir. J. Cromwell), 1944
The Corn Is Green (dir. I. Rapper), 1945
Mildred Pierce (dir. M. Curtiz), 1945
The Big Sleep (dir. H. Hawks), 1946
Saratoga Trunk (dir. S. Wood), 1946
Life with Father (dir. M. Curtiz), 1947
Johnny Belinda (J. Negulesco), 1948
Key Largo (dir. J. Huston), 1948
The Treasure of the Sierra Madre (dir. J. Huston), 1948
Adventures of Don Juan (dir. V. Sherman), 1949
The Fountainhead (dir. K. Vidor), 1949
The Glass Menagerie (dir. I. Rapper), 1950
Operation Pacific (dir. G. Waggner), 1951
The Jazz Singer (dir. M. Curtiz), 1953
This is Cinerama (dir. M.C. Cooper), 1953
The Caine Mutiny (dir. E. Dmytryk), 1954
King Richard and the Crusaders (dir. D. Butler), 1954
Come Next Spring (dir. R.G. Springsteen), 1955
Helen of Troy (dir. R. Wise), 1956
The Searchers (dir. J. Ford), 1956
The FBI Story (dir. M. LeRoy), 1959
John Paul Jones (dir. J. Farrow), 1959
A Summer Place (dir. D. Daves), 1959
The Dark at the Top of the Stairs (dir. D. Mann), 1960
The Sins of Rachel Cade (dir. G. Douglas), 1961
Rome Adventure (dir. D. Daves), 1962

Spencer's Mountain (dir. D. Daves), 1963
Youngblood Hawke (dir. D. Daves), 1964
Two on a Guillotine (dir. W. Conrad), 1965

MSS in *US-PRV*

Principal publishers: Remick, Witmarck, Berlin, Fox

Writings

Notes to You, unpubd. [autobiography; MS in *US-PRV*]
"Scoring the Film," *We Make the Movies*, ed. N. Naumberg (New York, 1937), 216–38
"The Music Director," *The Real Tinsel*, ed. B. Rosenberg and H. Silverstein (New York, 1970), 387–98

Bibliography

T. Thomas, ed.: *Film Score* (South Brunswick, NJ, 1979)

C. Gorbman: "Classical Hollywood Practice: The Model of Max Steiner," *Unheard Melodies* (London and Bloomingon, IN, 1987), 70–98

K. Kalinak: "Max Steiner and the Classical Hollywood Film Score," *Film Music 1*, ed. C. McCarty (New York, 1989), 123–42

C. Palmer: *The Composer in Hollywood* (London, 1990)

W. Darby and J. Du Bois: *American Film Music: Major Composers, Techniques, Trends, 1915–1990* (Jefferson, NC, 1990)

G. Maas: "King Kongs musikalischer Kammerdiener: Max Steiners Musik zu King Kong (1933) im Blickwinkel der Kritik Hanns Eislers," *Film- und Fernsehwissenschaftliches Kolloquium: Berlin 1989* (Münster, 1990), 153–66

K. Kalinak: *Settling the Score: Music and the Classical Hollywood Film* (Madison, WI, 1992)

J.V. D'Arc and J.N. Gillespie, eds.: *The Max Steiner Collection* (Provo, UT, 1996)

K. Daubney: *The View from the Piano: a Critical Examination and Contextualisation of the Film Scores of Max Steiner, 1939–1945* (diss. U. of Leeds, 1996)

K. Daubney: *Max Steiner's "Now, Voyager": a Film Score Guide* (Westport, CT, 2000)

M. Marks: "Music, Drama, Warner Brothers: the Cases of *Casablanca* and *The Maltese Falcon*," *Music and Cinema*, ed. J. Buhler, C. Flinn, and D. Neumeyer (Hanover, NH, 2000), 161–86

P. Franklin: "*King Kong* and Film on Music: Out of the Fog," *Film Music: Critical Approaches*, ed. K.J. Donnelly (New York, 2001), 88–102

P. Berthomieu: "Max Steiner à Hollywood : valse viennoise et slow californien," *Vienne et Berlin à Hollywood: Nouvelles approches*, ed. M. Cerisuelo (Paris, 2006), 163–99

N. Lerner: "The Horrors of One-Handed Pianism: Music and Disability in *The Beast with Five Fingers*," *Sounding Off: Theorizing Disability in Music*, ed. N. Lerner and J.N. Straus (New York, 2006), 75–89

M. Slobin: "The Steiner Superculture," *Global Soundtracks: Worlds of Film Music*, ed. M. Slobin (Middletown, CT, 2008), 3–35

P. Wegele and W. Thiel: *Max Steiner: Composing, "Casablanca," and the Golden Age of Film Music* (Lanham, MD, 2014)

N. Platte: "A Star is Born: Max Steiner in the Studios, 1929–1939," *The Routledge Companion to Screen Music and Sound* (New York, 2017), 257–69
N. Platte: *Making Music in Selznick's Hollywood* (New York, 2018)

KATE DAUBNEY (WITH JANET B. BRADFORD)/R

Stoloff, Morris

(*b* ?1898; *d* Los Angeles, April 1980). American musical director, orchestrator, and conductor. He studied the violin with Leopold Auer from the age of sixteen, and during his early twenties became a first violinist with the Los Angeles PO, under Walter Henry Rothwell. In 1928, he became concertmaster of the Paramount studio orchestra, and in 1936 he moved to Columbia studios as principal music director. He received eighteen Academy Award nominations for musical direction. As department head at Columbia he received a nomination for Dmitri Tiomkin's score for *Lost Horizon* (1937), but he was nominated for his own work on films such as *The Talk of the Town* (1942) and *A Song to Remember* (1945), the latter of which renewed commercial interest in the music of its subject, Chopin. Stoloff was also the principal composer of the scores to *You'll Never Get Rich* (1941) and *Fanny* (1961). He received Academy Awards for *Cover Girl* (1944), *The Jolson Story* (1946), and *Song Without End* (1960). He remarked that *The Jolson Story* provided the greatest challenge of all his scores, because it required detailed research into the musical style of productions from the years of Jolson's career on Broadway. (See W. Darby and J. Du Bois: *American Film Music: Major Composers, Techniques, Trends, 1915–1990*, Jefferson, NC, 1991)

KATE DAUBNEY

Stothart, Herbert (Pope)

(*b* Milwaukee, WI, 11 Sept 1885; *d* Los, Angeles, 1 Feb 1949). American composer and conductor. He was educated in Milwaukee and then became involved in conducting and composing for theatrical productions at the University of Wisconsin. He began working as a conductor on Broadway in 1920, writing songs with the lyricists Oscar Hammerstein II and Otto Harbach, and collaborating with the composers Rudolf Friml, George Gershwin, and Vincent Youmans. In 1929 he moved to Hollywood to work for MGM, where he remained until his death, conducting and composing for more than one hundred films. As a music director he was associated mainly with film musicals, notably *The Wizard of Oz*, for which he won an Academy Award, and those starring

Jeanette MacDonald and Nelson Eddy. As a composer he worked on almost all of MGM's prestige productions of the 1930s and 40s. His idiom incorporates thematic quotation from other composers, including Chopin (*A Tale of Two Cities*, 1935, *The Picture of Dorian Gray* 1945), Delius (*The Yearling*, 1947), and Tchaikovsky (*Conquest* and *Romeo and Juliet*, both 1937). This was partly a response to an emphasis at MGM on broadening the experience of its audience through the inclusion of "classical music" in film. His scoring technique also reflects his interest in Wagner's operas and the leitmotif: this traditional conception of film music also reflects his experience as a songwriter for music theater, and his career on Broadway gave him an understanding of how music might be integrated with dramatic action. His scoring was versatile and he wrote music for films from a range of genres, including *Mutiny on the Bounty* (1935), *David Copperfield* (1935), *The Good Earth* (1937), and *Mrs. Miniver* (1942). He was nominated for twelve Academy Awards, for scoring both dramatic and musical pictures, and his songs, including "I wanna be loved by you," appeared in over fifty films.

Works

(*selective list*)

Stage

(all are musicals and, unless otherwise stated, have librettos and lyrics by O. Hammerstein II and O. Harbach; dates are those of first New York performance)

Wildflower, collab. V. Youmans, 7 Feb 1923
Rose-Marie, collab. R. Friml, 2 Sept 1924
Song of the Flame, collab. G. Gershwin, 30 Dec 1925
Golden Dawn, collab. E. Kálmán, 30 Nov 1927
Good Boy (libretto by Hammerstein and Harbach; lyrics by B. Kalmar), collab. H. Ruby, 5 Sept 1928

Film scores

The Squaw Man (dir. C.B. DeMille), 1931
Night Flight (dir. C. Brown), 1933
Treasure Island (dir. V. Fleming), 1934
Anna Karenina (dir. C. Brown), 1935
David Copperfield (dir. G. Cukor), 1935
Mutiny on the Bounty (dir. F. Lloyd), 1935
A Tale of Two Cities (dir. J. Conway), 1935
Camille (dir. G. Cukor), 1937
Conquest (dir. C. Brown), 1937
The Good Earth (dir. S. Franklin), 1937

Romeo and Juliet (dir. G. Cukor), 1937
Marie Antoinette (dir. W.S. Van Dyke), 1938
Northwest Passage (dir. K. Vidor), 1940
Waterloo Bridge (dir. M. LeRoy), 1940
Mrs. Miniver (dir. W. Wyler), 1942
The Human Comedy (dir. C. Brown), 1943
Random Harvest (dir. M. LeRoy), 1943
Dragon Seed (dir. H.S. Bucquet), 1944
Madame Curie (dir. M. LeRoy), 1944
The White Cliffs of Dover (dir. C. Brown), 1944
National Velvet (dir. C. Brown), 1945
The Picture of Dorian Gray (dir. A. Lewin), 1945
The Yearling (dir. C. Brown), 1947

Choral

China: a Sym. Narrative (H. Kronman), pageant, spkrs, chorus, orch, 1943
Voices of Liberation (Stothart), male vv, orch/pf, 1947

Bibliography

M.N. Fisher: "'Milwaukeean' New Victor Herbert," *Milwaukee Journal* (1 April 1934), 4, 11

H. Stothart: "Il problema della musica nel film storico," *Cinema*, no.17 (Rome, 1937), 178

H. Stothart: "Film Music," *Behind the Screen: How Films are Made*, ed. S. Watts (London, 1938), 139–44

H. Stothart, Jr: "Herbert Stothart," *Films in Review*, xxi (1970), 622–30 [incl. list of film scores]

W. Rosar: "Herbert Stothart: a Biographical Sketch," *Cue Sheet*, i/1 (1984), 3–5

C. Palmer: *The Composer in Hollywood* (London, 1990)

W. Darby and J. Du Bois: *American Film Music: Major Composers, Techniques, Trends, 1915–1990* (Jefferson, NC, 1991)

R. Rodman: "'There's No Place Like Home': Tonal Closure and Design in *The Wizard of Oz*," *Indiana Theory Review* xix/1–2 (Spring–Fall, 1998), 125–43

R. Rodman: "Tonal Design and the Aesthetic of Pastiche in Herbert Stothart's *Maytime*," *Music and Cinema*, ed. J. Buhler, C. Flinn, and D. Neumeyer (Hanover, NH, 2000), 187–206

N. Platte: "Nostalgia, the Silent Cinema, and the Art of Quotation in Herbert Stothart's Score for *The Wizard of Oz* (1939)," *The Journal of Film Music* iv/1 (2011), 45–64

R. Rodman: "The Operatic Stothart: Leitmotifs and Tonal Organization in Two Versions of *Rose-Marie*," *The Journal of Film Music* iv/1 (2011), 5–19

KATE DAUBNEY (WITH WILLIAM ROSAR)/R

Tiomkin, Dmitri

(*b* Kremenchuk, Ukraine, 10 May 1894; *d* London, England, 11 Nov 1979). American composer and pianist of Ukrainian birth. He studied at the St. Petersburg Conservatory under Blumenfeld and Alexander Glazunov and later in Berlin under Egon Petri, Michael Zadora, and Ferruccio Busoni. He made his début as a concert pianist in Berlin after World War I and gave the European première of George Gershwin's Concerto in F at the Paris Opéra in 1928. In 1929 he accompanied his first wife (the choreographer Albertina Rasch) to Hollywood, where the success of his music for *Lost Horizon* led to a busy career as a film composer. During World War II he worked mainly on war documentaries, but in 1952 won great renown with his song-based score for *High Noon*. When he left Hollywood (1968) to settle in London he had worked on approximately 140 films and been nominated twenty-three times for Academy Awards for both original scoring and songs: he won the award for Best Score for *The High and Mighty* (1954), *The Old Man and the Sea* (1958), and *High Noon*, for which he also won Best Song. His last major project was *Tchaikovsky*, for which he acted as both general musical director and executive producer.

Tiomkin took up composition late in life: he was over forty when his film career began in earnest, and he was nearing sixty when his mature style crystallized. His scoring style reflects the spirit and color of nineteenth- and twentieth-century Russian and French concert hall music. It also sustains the common emphasis in 1940s film scoring on melodic writing but incorporates a more rhythmic, energetic, and compact style during the 1950s. Similarly, his orchestration evolves from string-dominated textures to a more colorful and varied orchestral palette, including use of solo voice and wordless chorus. He scored films from a range of genres, particularly the Western (*Duel in the Sun*, 1946, *Giant*, 1956, *The Alamo*, 1960), the thriller (Hitchcock's *Strangers on a Train*, 1951, *I Confess*, 1953, and *Dial M for Murder*, 1954), adventure (*The Guns of Navarone*, 1961, *55 Days at Peking*, 1963), fantasy (*Lost Horizon*, 1937), and science fiction (*The Thing*, 1951). He also wrote a number of songs for films that reflected his aptitude for using song as a narrative device, including "Do not forsake me, oh my darlin'" from *High Noon* and "The Green Leaves of Summer" from *The Alamo*.

Tiomkin's approach favored instinctive emotional engagement with the drama, rather than intellectual interpretation of the narrative. For example, the use of the ballad theme song for *Gunfight at the OK Corral* (1957) evokes the chorus in Greek tragedy, responding to the highly charged atmosphere of the film. He preferred to become involved in the production process from the earliest stage possible, but he was also aware of the influence of the musical expectations of the audience, shown by his use of common musical and instrumental codes in scores such as *Red River* (1948).

Dimitri Tiomkin
Photofest

Works

(*selective list*)

Film scores

Lost Horizon (dir. F. Capra), 1937
The Great Waltz (dir. J. Duvivier), 1938 [after J. Strauss II]
Spawn of the North (dir. H. Hathaway), 1938
Mr. Smith Goes to Washington (dir. F. Capra), 1939
The Moon and Sixpence (dir. A. Lewin), 1942
Shadow of a Doubt (dir. A. Hitchcock), 1942
Dillinger (dir. M. Nosseck), 1945
Duel in the Sun (dir. K. Vidor), 1946
It's a Wonderful Life (dir. F. Capra), 1947
The Long Night (dir. A. Litvak), 1947 [after Beethoven]
Red River (dir. H. Hawks), 1948
Champion (dir. M. Robson), 1949
Portrait of Jennie (dir. W. Dieterle), 1949 [after Debussy]
D.O.A. (dir. R. Maté), 1950
The Men (dir. F. Zinnemann), 1950
Strangers on a Train (dir. A. Hitchcock), 1951
The Thing from Another World! (dir. H. Hawks), 1951
The Well (dir. L.C. Popkin), 1951
The Big Sky (dir. H. Hawks), 1952
The Four Poster (dir. I. Reis), 1952
High Noon (dir. F. Zinnemann), 1952
The Steel Trap (dir. A.L. Stone), 1952

I Confess (dir. A. Hitchcock), 1953
Jeopardy (dir. J. Sturges), 1953
Return to Paradise (dir. M. Robson), 1953
Dial M for Murder (dir. A. Hitchcock), 1954
The High and the Mighty (dir. W.A. Wellman), 1954
Land of the Pharaohs (dir. H. Hawks), 1955
Friendly Persuasion (dir. W. Wyler), 1956
Giant (dir. G. Stevens), 1956
Tension at Table Rock (dir. G.M. Warren), 1956
Gunfight at the OK Corral (dir. J. Sturges), 1957
Night Passage (dir. J. Neilson), 1957
Search for Paradise (dir. O. Lang), 1957
The Young Land (dir. T. Tetzlaff), 1957
The Old Man and the Sea (dir. J. Sturges), 1958
Wild Is the Wind (dir. G. Cuckor), 1958
Last Train from Gun Hill (dir. J. Sturges), 1959
Rhapsody of Steel (dir. C. Urbano), 1959 [cartoon]
The Alamo (dir. J. Wayne), 1960
The Unforgiven (dir. J. Huston), 1960
The Guns of Navarone (dir. J.L. Thompson), 1961
Town Without Pity (dir. G. Reinhardt), 1961
55 Days at Peking (dir. N. Ray), 1963
Circus World (dir. H. Hathaway), 1964
The Fall of the Roman Empire (dir. A. Mann), 1964
36 Hours (dir. G. Seaton), 1965
Tchaikovsky (dir. K. Russell), 1971

Bibliography

D. Tiomkin and P. Buranelli: *Please Don't Hate Me* (New York, 1959) [autobiography]

T. Thomas: *Music for the Movies* (South Brunswick, NJ, 1973)

W. Rosar: "Lost Horizon: an Account of the Composition of the Score," *Film Music Notebook*, iv/2 (1978), 40–52

C. Palmer: *Dmitri Tiomkin: a Portrait* (London, 1984)

C. Palmer: *The Composer in Hollywood* (London, 1990)

W. Darby and J. Du Bois: *American film Music: Major Composers, Techniques, Trends, 1915–1990* (Jefferson, NC, 1991)

T. Thomas: *Film Score: The Art and Craft of movie Music* (Burbank, CA, 1991)

E. Rieger: *Alfred Hitchcock und die Musik: Eine Untersuchung zum Verhältnis von Film, Musik, und Geschlecht* (Bielefeld, 1996)

N. Lerner: "'Look at that big Hand Move Along': Clocks, Containment, and Music in High Noon," *South Atlantic Quarterly*, civ/1 (2005), 151–73

J. Sullivan: *Hitchcock's Music* (New Haven, 2007)

B. Winters: "Silencing the Truth: Music and Identity in *The Unforgiven*," *Music in the Western: Notes from the Frontier*, ed. K. Kalinak (New York, 2012), 77–93

A. Bushard: "Who's Who in Hadleyville? The Civic Voice in *High Noon* (1952)," *Anxiety Muted: American Film Music in a Suburban Age*, ed. A. Bushard and S. Pelkey (New York, 2015), 49–68
N. Platte: *Making Music in Selznick's Hollywood* (New York, 2018)

KATE DAUBNEY (WITH WILLIAM ROSAR)/R

Walden, W(illiam) G(arrett) [Snuffy]

(*b* Baton Rouge, LA, 13 Feb 1950). American television composer and guitarist. After early experience playing guitar in rock bands, Walden was a member of the blues-based rock trio Stray Dog, with whom he recorded two albums on Emerson, Lake, and Palmer's Manticore label. After moving to Hollywood in 1974, Walden pursued session recording work with major figures such as Stevie Wonder, Rita Coolidge, Donna Summer, Eric Burdon, Greg Lake, Carl Palmer, and Chaka Khan. While Walden lacked notational skills and experience scoring for television, the producers of the 1980s television series "thirtysomething" were intrigued by the name "Snuffy," a curiosity that led to an audition and ultimately his assignment to compose for the series (along with fellow composers Jay Gruska and Stewart Levin). The success of "thirtysomething" led to a steady stream of further work in television. He has long been associated with the serial dramas made by the Bedford Falls Company, whose work besides "thirtysomething" includes "My So-Called Life," "Relativity," and "Once and Again," all of which were scored by Walden, usually with a combination of bluesy acoustic guitar riffs and consonant synthesizer pads. Walden's versatile talents for underscoring character-driven dramas were recognized in his work for the series "The West Wing," whose opening music received an Emmy Award for Outstanding Main Title Theme. Walden abandoned his guitar-based sound in "The West Wing" for an orchestral palette whose stylistic roots can be traced back, via scores like Jerry Goldsmith's for *Air Force One*, to Aaron Copland's well-known populist works that have become standard musical codes for the American pastoral vision.

Works

Television music

thirtysomething, 1987–90
The Wonder Years, 1988, 1993
Sisters, 1991
I'll Fly Away, 1991–3
Roseanne, 1993–7
The Stand, miniseries, 1994
My So-Called Life, 1994–5

Ellen, 1994–8
Relativity, 1996–7
Sports Night, 1998–2000
Felicity, 1998–2002
The Drew Carey Show, 1998–2003
Providence, 1999–2001
Once and Again, 1999–2002
The West Wing, 1999–2006
Huff, 2004–6
The War at Home, 2005–7
Kidnapped, 2006–7
Studio 60 on the Sunset Strip, 2006–7
Friday Night Lights, 2006–11
Lipstick Jungle, 2008–9
The Beast, 2009
Huge, 2010
Serving Life, 2011
A Gifted Man, 2011–12
Under the Dome, 2013–15
Nashville, 2013–18
Coming Back with Wes Moore, 2014
Swallow Your Bliss, 2014
Aquarius, 2015
Guilt by Association, 2015
SEAL Team, 2017
Ten Days in the Valley, 2017
Tenure, 2017
Reverie, 2018

Bibliography

J. Sievert: "Prime-time Acoustic: Snuffy Walden of *thirtysomething* and *The Wonder Years*," *Guitar Player*, xxiv (1990), 42–8

P. Kaye: "Writing Music for Quality TV: an Interview with W.G. 'Snuffy' Walden," *Quality TV: Contemporary American Television and Beyond*, ed. J. McCabe and K. Akass (London and New York, 2007), 221–7

J. Rodgers: "Behind the Scenes," *Acoustic Guitar* xviii/8 (2008): 18

NEIL LERNER/R

Walker, Shirley

(*b* Napa, CA, 10 April 1945; *d* Reno, NV, 30 Nov 2006). American film and television composer, orchestrator, arranger, pianist, and conductor. She began composing at an early age and appeared as a pianist with the San Francisco and

Oakland symphonies. Walker attended San Francisco State University, studying with Roger Nixon (composition) and Harold Logan (piano).

After a decade of writing jingles and music for industrial films, she began her career in film in 1979 playing synthesizer on Carmine Coppola's score for *Apocalypse Now* and writing additional music for *The Black Stallion*. After writing music for two "Lou Grant" television episodes, she began orchestrating feature films, often conducting the scoring sessions, including scores for Danny Elfman, Hans Zimmer, and others.

Walker earned her first Hollywood composition credit for John Carpenter's *Memoirs of an Invisible Man* (1992), followed by numerous other films, television shows, and documentaries, particularly in Action-Adventure and Animation. Serving as supervisory composer for several television series, she also composed themes for "The New Batman Adventures," "Growing Pains," and "Superman: the Last Son of Krypton" (1996), among others. In 1996 she won a Daytime Emmy Award as music director on "The Adventures of Batman & Robin"; she won a Daytime Emmy Award in music composition for "Batman Beyond" in 2001. Her bold, innovative, and dramatic music was deeply rooted in classical

Shirley Walker. The Film Music Society.

symphonic traditions. She was commissioned to compose *Oncogenic Quietude* for the UC Santa Barbara Symphony in 2005.

Active in the Society of Composers and Lyricists and the Executive Music Branch of the Academy of Motion Picture Arts & Sciences, Walker was a staunch advocate for composers. Her memorial service was held at the Warner Bros. Eastwood Scoring Stage where a plaque hangs in her honor.

Works

(*selective list*)

Film scores

End of August (dir. B. Graham), 1982
Touched (dir. J. Flynn), 1983
Violated (dir. R. Cannistraro), 1984
The Dungeonmaster (dir. D. Allen and others), 1985, with R. Band
Ghoulies (dir. L. Bercovici), 1985, with R. Band
Chicago Joe and the Showgirl (dir. B. Rose), 1990, with H. Zimmer
Strike It Rich (dir. J. Scott), 1990
Born to Ride (dir. G. Baker), 1991
Memoirs of an Invisible Man (dir. J. Carpenter), 1992
Batman: Mask of the Phantasm (dir. E. Radomski and others), 1993
Escape from L.A. (dir. Carpenter), 1996, with J. Carpenter
Turbulence (dir. R. Butler), 1997
Final Destination (dir. J. Wong), 2000, with A. Hamilton
Final Destination 2 (dir. D.R. Ellis), 2003
Willard (dir. G. Morgan), 2003
Black Christmas (dir. Morgan), 2006
Final Destination 3 (dir. Wong), 2006

Television music

Falcon Crest, 1985–9
Cagney and Lacey, 1986
China Beach, 1989–90
Batman, 1992
Flash III: Deadly Nightshade, 1992
Majority Rule, 1992
Haunting of Seacliff Inn, 1994
Adventures of Captain Zoom in Outer Space, 1995
Space: Above and Beyond, 1995–6
Crying Child, 1996
It Came from Outer Space II, 1996
Asteroid, 1997
Love Bug, 1997

Spawn, 1997
New Batman Adventures, 1997–8
Baby Monitor: Sound of Fear, 1998
Batman Beyond, 1999–2001
Ritual, 2001
Zeta Project, 2001–3
Disappearance, 2002

Bibliography

M. Schelle: "Shirley Walker," *The Score: Interviews with Film Composers* (Los Angeles, CA, 1999), 359–80

J. Burlingame: "Composer Walker Dies," *Variety* (4 Dec 2006)

J. Doyle: "Shirley Walker: Film Score Composer," *The San Francisco Chronicle* (10 Dec 2006) [obituary]

V.J. Nelson: "Shirley Walker, 62, Won Emmys for Film Scores," *Los Angeles Times* (26 Dec 2006) [obituary]

"Shirley Walker Remembered," *The Cue Sheet*, xxii/3 (2007) [Shirley Walker issue]

JEANNIE GAYLE POOL/R

Wallace, Oliver

(*b* London, England, 6 Aug 1887; *d* Los Angeles, 16 Sept 1963). American composer, arranger, pianist, and organist of English birth. He studied music privately in England before moving to North America in 1904. In Canada, Wallace played piano for vaudeville and early silent films. On moving to America he was the first musician to use a pipe organ for film accompaniment, at the Dream Theatre in Seattle in 1908. In his early career he developed a reputation as a creative and highly respected organist for silent films and was noted for his skill in improvisation. He also published songs, including the standard "Hindustan," written with Harold Weeks.

In the early 1930s Wallace moved to Hollywood, composing mostly uncredited stock music cues for the lesser studios. At Universal he played the pipe organ part for Franz Waxman's *Bride of Frankenstein* score (1935).

He joined the Disney studio in the late 1930s, remaining there until his death. He first scored character shorts, and evolved into the major composer for the Donald Duck cartoon series through the 1950s, including *Duck Pimples* (1945), his score a sharp parody of "suspense" thriller radio music, and the droll *Tea for Two Hundred* (1948). For the short feature *Dumbo* (1941) his contributions included two songs, an instrumental "Dumbo" theme, and circus band cues. One of his songs, "Pink Elephants on Parade," was the basis for one of the studio's most surreal animation sequences. Its orchestration includes Wallace playing the Novachord, a Hammond organ-like electronic keyboard that he also used in several of his short cartoon scores (*The Little Whirlwind*, 1941). Wallace was nominated for an Academy Award five times, and for *Dumbo* he shared the Oscar for best score with Frank Churchill. Wallace scored a number of Disney's World War II propaganda films. His title song for *Der Fuehrer's Face* (1943), for which he also wrote lyrics, became a substantial hit for Spike Jones and his City Slickers.

For later features Wallace served as both music director and composer-arranger; his original music was mostly limited to background underscoring. But for *Alice in Wonderland* (1951) and *Peter Pan* (1953) he also contributed secondary songs. He composed the orchestral Headless Horseman chase music for *Ichabod and Mister Toad* (1949). Wallace also worked in Disney's live-action films. He scored the first True Life Adventure documentary short, *Seal Island* (1948), as well as several People and Places travel shorts. He also scored several features, notably the charming Irish fantasy *Darby O'Gill and the Little People* (1959).

Works

Film scores

Sixteen Fathoms Deep (dir. A. Schaefer), 1933
Girl in the Case (dir. E. Frenke), 1934
Alias Mary Dow (dir. K. Neumann), 1935
Bulldog Courage (dir. S. Newfield), 1935
Frisco Waterfront (dir. A. Lubin and J. Santley), 1935
It Happened in New York (dir. A. Crosland), 1935
Life Returns (dir. E. Frenke and J.P. Hogan), 1935
Murder by Television (dir. C. Sanforth), 1935
Tailspin Tommy in The Great Air Mystery (dir. R. Taylor), 1935
Early to Bed (dir. N.Z. McLeod), 1936
Sinners in Paradise (dir. J. Whale), 1938
Dumbo (dir. S. Armstrong), 1941, collab. F. Churchill
Victory Through Air Power (dir. J. Algar), 1943, collab. P. Smith, E. Plumb
Make Mine Music (dir. R. Cormack), 1946
Fun & Fancy Free, 1947
The Adventures of Ichabod and Mr. Toad (dir. J. Algar), 1949
Cinderella (dir. C. Geronimi, W. Jackson, and H. Luske), 1950, collab. P. Smith
Alice in Wonderland (dir. C. Geronimi, W. Jackson, and H. Luske), 1951
Peter Pan (dir. C. Geronimi, W. Jackson, and H. Luske), 1953
Lady and the Tramp (dir. C. Geronimi, W. Jackson, and H. Luske), 1955
Old Yeller (dir. R. Stevenson), 1957
Tonka (dir. L.R. Foster), 1958
White Wilderness (dir. J. Algar), 1958

Darby O'Gill and the Little People (dir. R. Stevenson), 1959
Jungle Cat (dir. J. Algar), 1959
Ten Who Dared (dir. W. Beaudine), 1960
Nikki, Wild Dog of the North (dir. J. Couffer and D. Haldane), 1961
Big Red (dir. N. Tokar), 1962
The Legend of Lobo, 1962
The Incredible Journey (dir. F. Markle), 1963
Savage Sam (dir. Tokar), 1963

Short films

Clock Cleaners (dir. B. Sharpsteen), 1937
Mickey's Amateurs (dir. P. Colvig, E. Penner, and W. Pfeiffer), 1937
Mr. Mouse Takes a Trip (dir. C. Geronimi), 1940
The Little Whirlwind (dir. R. Thomson), 1941
The New Spirit (dir. W. Jackson and B. Sharpsteen), 1942
Der Fuehrer's Face (dir. J. Kinney), 1943
Education for Death (dir. C. Geronimi), 1943
Duck Pimples (dir. J. Kinney), 1945
Chip an' Dale (dir. J. Hannah), 1947
Pluto's Blue Note (dir. C.A. Nichols), 1947
Donald's Dream Voice (dir. J. King), 1948
Seal Island (dir. J. Algar), 1948
Tea for Two Hundred (dir. J. Hannah), 1948
Crazy over Daisy (dir. J. Hannah), 1950
Ben and Me (dir. H. Luske), 1953
Working for Peanuts (dir. J. Hannah), 1953
Casey Bats Again (dir. J. Kinney), 1954
Grand Canyonscope (dir. C.A. Nichols), 1954
Pigs Is Pigs (dir. J. Kinney), 1954
Siam (dir. R. Wright), 1954
Bearly Asleep (dir. J. Hannah), 1955
Beezy Bear (dir. J. Hannah), 1955
Switzerland (dir. B. Sharpsteen), 1955
How to Have an Accident at Work (dir. C.A. Nichols), 1959

Bibliography

D.E. Tietyen: *The Illustrated Disney Song Book* (New York, 1979), 26–9
R. Care: "Make Walt's Music: Music for Disney Animation, 1928–1967," *The Cartoon Music Book*, ed. D. Goldmark and Y. Taylor (Chicago, 2002), 30–31
R. Care: "Oliver Wallace," *The Cue Sheet*, xviii/3–4 (2002), 28–33

ROSS CARE

Waxman [Wachsmann], Franz

(*b* Königshütte, Germany, 24 Dec 1906; *d* Los Angeles, 24 Feb 1967). American composer of German birth. After pursuing a career in banking for two years, he completed his musical studies in Dresden and Berlin. While a student, he supported himself by playing the piano in nightclubs, especially with the Weintraub Syncopators. It was this employment that led him, in 1929, to UFA, Germany's leading film studio, where he was hired to arrange and conduct Frederick Holländer's score for *The Blue Angel*. The success of that film produced additional film work, ultimately leading to his emigration to Los Angeles in 1934.

Waxman's arrival in Hollywood was timely; film music was just developing into a major art form and his fluent, highly Romantic style, coupled with a gift for melodic writing, was ideally suited to the medium. He quickly took his place as one of the most important composers of Hollywood's golden age. His first original film score, *The Bride of Frankenstein* (1935), re-used many times in other horror films of the period, set the style of scores for that genre. He went on to compose for some of Hollywood's classic films, including *Captains Courageous* (1937), *The Philadelphia Story* (1940), *Rebecca* (1940), *Dr. Jekyll and Mr. Hyde* (1941), *Prince Valiant* (1954), *The Nun's Story* (1959), and *Taras Bulba* (1962). In all, he worked on 144 films and received twelve Academy Award nominations, winning twice in consecutive years for *Sunset Boulevard* (1950) and *A Place in the Sun* (1951). His music for the cinema appears on many recordings.

Of Waxman's concert works, the most important are the oratorio *Joshua* (1959) and the dramatic song cycle *The Song of Terezin* (1965), his last composition. Perhaps his most famous work, however, is the *Carmen Fantasie*, a brilliant showpiece for violin and orchestra based on themes from Bizet's opera, originally composed for the film *Humoresque* in 1947. Also a gifted conductor, Waxman founded the Los Angeles International Music Festival in 1948 and for the next twenty years presented important premières of works by Stravinsky, Dmitry Shostakovich, Ralph Vaughan Williams, William Walton, Schoenberg, and many others. A frequent guest conductor in the United States, Europe, and Israel, in 1962 he was the first American to conduct major orchestras in the Soviet Union.

Works

(*selective list*)

Film scores

The Bride of Frankenstein (dir. J. Whale), 1935
Diamond Jim (dir. A.E. Sutherland), 1935
Fury (dir. F. Lang), 1936

Love on the Run (dir. W.S. Van Dyke), 1936
Magnificent Obsession (dir. J.M. Stahl), 1936
The Bride Wore Red (dir. D. Arzner), 1937
Captains Courageous (dir. V. Fleming), 1937
A Christmas Carol (dir. E.L. Marin), 1938
The Adventures of Huckleberry Finn (dir. R. Thorpe), 1939
Boom Town (dir. J. Conway), 1940
The Philadelphia Story (dir. G. Cukor), 1940
Rebecca (dir. A. Hitchcock), 1940
Strange Cargo (dir. F. Borzage), 1940
Dr. Jekyll and Mr. Hyde (dir. V. Fleming), 1941
Suspicion (dir. A. Hitchcock), 1941
Woman of the Year (dir. G. Stevens), 1942
Edge of Darkness (dir. L. Milestone), 1943
Old Acquaintance (dir. V. Sherman), 1943
Objective, Burma (dir. R. Walsh), 1944
Confidential Agent (dir. H. Shumlin), 1945
God Is My Co-Pilot (dir. R. Florey), 1945
Cry Wolf (dir. P. Godfrey), 1947
Dark Passage (dir. D. Daves), 1947
Humoresque (dir. J. Negulesco), 1947
The Paradine Case (dir. A Hitchcock), 1947
Possessed (dir. C. Bernhardt), 1947
The Unsuspected (dir. M. Curtiz), 1947
Sorry, Wrong Number (dir. A. Litvak), 1948
Johnny Holiday (dir. W. Goldbeck), 1949
Dark City (dir. W. Dieterle), 1950
Sunset Boulevard (dir. B. Wilder), 1950
The Blue Veil (dir. C. Bernhardt), 1951
A Place in the Sun (dir. G. Stevens), 1951
Red Mountain (dir. W. Dieterle), 1951
My Cousin Rachel (dir. H. Kosters), 1952
I, the Jury (dir. H. Essex), 1953
Man on a Tightrop (dir. E. Kazan), 1953
Demetrius and the Gladiators (dir. D. Daves), 1954
Prince Valiant (dir. H. Hathaway), 1954
Rear Window (dir. A. Hitchcock), 1954
Mister Roberts (dir. J. Ford and M. LeRoy), 1955
The Silver Chalice (dir. V. Saville), 1955
Back from Eternity (dir. J Farrow), 1956
Crime in the Streets (dir. D. Siegel), 1956
Miracle in the Rain (dir. R. Maté), 1956
Peyton Place (dir. M. Robson), 1957
Sayonara (dir. J. Logan), 1957
The Spirit of St. Louis (dir. B. Wilder), 1957
Run Silent Run Deep (dir. R. Wise), 1958

Beloved Infidel (dir. H. King), 1959
The Nun's Story (dir. F. Zinnemann), 1959
Cimarron (dir. A. Mann), 1960
The Story of Ruth (dir. H. Koster), 1960
Return to Peyton Place (dir. J. Ferrer), 1961
My Geisha (dir. J. Cardiff), 1962
Taras Bulba (dir. J.L. Thompson), 1962
Lost Command (dir. M. Robson), 1966

Orchestral

Scherzetto (Theme and Variations), chbr orch, 1936
Athaneal, ov., tpt, orch, 1946
Carmen Fantasie, vn, orch, 1947 [based on Bizet, from film score Humoresque]
Tristan und Isolde, fantasia, vn, pf, orch, 1947
Passacaglia, 1948
The Charm Bracelet, chbr orch, 1949
Sinfonietta, str, timp, 1955
Goyana, 4 Sketches, pf, str, perc, 1960
Ruth, sym. suite, 1960
Taras Bulba, sym. suite, 1962

Vocal

Joshua (orat, J. Forsyth), nar, chorus, orch, 1959
The Song of Terezin (concentration camp children), song cycle, Mez, mixed chorus, children's chorus, orch, 1965

MSS, papers and recordings in *US-SY*

Principal publisher: Fidelio

Bibliography

P. Cook: "Franz Waxman was One of the Composers Who Thought Film Music Could Be an Art," *Films in Review* (1968), Aug–Sept, 415–30
T. Thomas: *Music for the Movies* (London, 1973/*R*)
T. Thomas, ed.: *Film Score: the View from the Podium* (New York 1979)
W. Darby and J. Du Bois: *American Film Music* (Jefferson, NC, 1990), 116ff
C. Palmer: *The Composer in Hollywood* (London, 1990)
F. Karlin: *Listening to Movies: the Film Lover's Guide to Film Music* (New York, 1994)
R.S. Brown: *Overtones & Undertones: Reading Film Music* (Los Angeles, 1994)
M. Cleslinsk: *Franz Waxman: the Winner of Oscars from Konigshutte* (Chorzow, Poland, 2007)
R. Segal: *Franz Waxman: Composer as Auteur in Golden Era Hollywood* (diss., U. of Newcastle, 2010)
D. Neumeyer and N. Platte: *Franz Waxman's "Rebecca": a Film Score Guide* (Lanham, MD, 2012)

C. Gier: "Music and Mimicry in *Sunset Boulevard* (1950)," *Anxiety Muted: American Film Music in a Suburban Age*, ed. A. Bushard and S. Pelkey (New York, 2015), 31–48
N. Platte: *Making Music in Selznick's Hollywood* (New York, 2018)

BRENDAN G. CARROLL/R

Williams, John (Towner)

(*b* New York, 8 Feb 1932). American composer, arranger, conductor, and pianist. He learned the piano from the age of eight and after moving to Los Angeles with his family in 1948 studied with the pianist and arranger Bobby Van Eps. He served in the US Air Force (1951–4), orchestrating for and conducting service bands, then moved back to New York, where he studied for a year with Rosina Lhévinne at the Juilliard School and played in jazz clubs and recording studios. After returning to the West Coast he enrolled at UCLA and took up private composition studies with Arthur Olaf Andersen and Mario Castelnuovo-Tedesco, among others. From 1956 Williams was a studio pianist in Hollywood and two years later began arranging and composing music for television, contributing the main title to "Checkmate" (1960; see Thomas and Burlingame). Through the mid-1960s he composed for several series and worked for Columbia Records as a pianist, arranger, and conductor; he also made a number of albums with André Previn. During this period Williams began scoring feature films, with many of his earliest scores for comedies, such as *John Goldfarb, Please Come Home* (1964), and *How to Steal a Million* (1966). He also worked on more serious projects with major directors, including Robert Altman (*Images*, 1972, and *The Long Goodbye*, 1973). Williams briefly became typecast as a disaster-film specialist, owing to his successful score for *The Poseidon Adventure* (1972); it contained one of his few popular song hits, "The Morning After," with lyrics by Marilyn and Alan Bergman. Indicative of his talent at this time are the Americana of *The Reivers* (1969), the heartfelt English lyricism of *Jane Eyre* (1971) and the rousing Western style of *The Cowboys* (1972). Williams later arranged music from each of these three films into popular concert works.

The long and close association of Williams with the director Steven Spielberg began with *The Sugarland Express* (1974) and *Jaws* (1975). In 1977 he scored Spielberg's masterly *Close Encounters of the Third Kind*, released only a few months after *Star Wars*, the film that began his similarly close association with director George Lucas. These and following films marked Williams's ascent to a pre-eminent position in Hollywood, as well as the re-emergence and critical approbation of the symphonic film score, dormant for nearly a decade. Within the next six years came music of comparable power for *The Fury* (1978), *Superman* (1978), *Dracula* (1979), *The Empire Strikes Back* (1980), *Return of the Jedi* (1983), *Raiders of the Lost Ark* (1981), and *E.T.: the Extra Terrestrial* (1982). Since then, Williams has remained a uniquely famous and popular film composer; he has generally scored two films each year, including every Spielberg film except *The Color Purple* (scored by Quincy Jones). No less notable are his recent scores for the director Oliver Stone (*Born on the Fourth of July*, 1989, *JFK*, 1991, and *Nixon*, 1995), as well as lighter, more lyrical, and witty projects such as *The Accidental Tourist* (1988), *Stanley and Iris* (1990), *Home Alone* (1990), and *Sabrina* (1995). He has also composed several signature tunes for NBC and a series of popular Olympic fanfares; by 2018 he had received five Academy Awards from fifty-one nominations and more than thirty Grammy awards and nominations.

Williams freely acknowledges his stylistic debt to various twentieth-century concert composers—among them Elgar, whom he greatly admires—and perpetuates the traditions of film-scoring developed by such composers as Erich Wolfgang Korngold, Alfred Newman, Miklós Rózsa, as well as arrangers such as Conrad Salinger. His own skill as an arranger, for example in *Goodbye, Mr. Chips* (1969), *Fiddler on the Roof* (1971), and *Tom Sawyer* (1973), owes much to Salinger, as does the poetic feeling for the beauty of sound manifest in all his orchestral work. In the 1980s, in films such as *Indiana Jones and the Temple of Doom* (1984) and *Empire of the Sun* (1987), Williams steadily expanded his stylistic range, partly by incorporating choral textures (sometimes with text). His unerring dramatic instinct and musical inventiveness are well shown in Spielberg's contrasting projects, *Jurassic Park* and *Schindler's List* (both 1993). Moreover, his score for the latter, along with those for *Born on the Fourth of July*, *JFK*, and *Saving Private Ryan* (1998), display his acute response to tragedy and sense of the epic.

Williams is fundamentally a romantic traditionalist, but often blends traditional musical syntax and expression with avant-garde techniques and elements of popular music. More than any of his contemporaries he has developed the ability to express the dramatic essence of a film in memorable musical ideas; likewise, he is able to shape each score to build climaxes that mirror a particular narrative structure. The score to *Close Encounters*, for example, is built upon a small range of related motivic fragments: a 5-note "aliens" theme, the first four notes of the Dies irae, an ascending tritone, and a related, disguised kernel from the Disney standard, "When You Wish upon a Star." These fragments, relevant to the narrative, are interwoven to shape a score with dramatic, emotional, and musical logic, and which moves from a harmonically clouded beginning to a lush and expansive diatonic climax.

Williams has always maintained a steady flow of concert works, mostly written in an advanced but still tonal and intelligibly expressive idiom. Among the early works, his Essay for strings (1966) has been widely played and his Symphony (1966) received an important London performance in 1972 under Previn. He has composed several concertos, beginning with dissonant ones for flute (1969) and violin (begun in 1974, following the death of his first wife, and completed in 1976). More recent concertos are written in simpler idioms, and the bassoon concerto (The Five Sacred Trees, 1995), inspired by the writings of the British poet and mythologist Robert Graves, is personal and reflective. In 1980 Williams

John Williams, 1980
(AP Photo)

succeeded Arthur Fiedler as conductor of the Boston Pops Orchestra, a position which enabled him to compose many occasional pieces, as well as to conduct numerous best-selling recordings of works in the classical and film repertories. Although he retired from this position in 1993, he has continued to make frequent guest appearances in Boston and at Tanglewood, as well as with numerous other major orchestras, ranking high among America's most eloquent and representative composers. He was a recipient in 2004 of the Kennedy Center Honors.

Works

(*selective list*)

Film scores

Diamond Head (dir. G. Green), 1963
John Goldfarb, Please Come Home (dir. J.L. Thompson), 1964
How to Steal a Million (dir. W. Wyler), 1966
Fitzwilly (dir. D. Mann), 1967
Valley of the Dolls (dir. M. Robson), 1967
Heidi (TV movie), 1968
The Reivers (dir. M. Rydell), 1969
Goodbye, Mr. Chips (dir. H. Ross), 1969 [adaption of score by L. Bricusse]
Fiddler on the Roof (dir. N. Jewison), 1971 [adaption of score by J. Bock]
Jane Eyre (TV movie, dir. D. Mann), 1971

The Cowboys (dir. M. Rydell), 1972
Images (dir. R. Altman), 1972
The Poseidon Adventure (dir. R. Neame), 1972
The Long Goodbye (dir. R. Altman), 1973
The Paper Chase (dir. J. Bridges), 1973
Tom Sawyer (dir. D. Taylor), 1973
Cinderella Liberty (dir. M. Rydell), 1974
Conrack (dir. M. Ritt), 1974
Earthquake (dir. M. Robson), 1974
The Towering Inferno (dir. J. Guillermin), 1974
The Sugarland Express (dir. S. Spielberg), 1974
Jaws (dir. S. Spielberg), 1975
Family Plot (dir. A. Hitchcock), 1976
The Missouri Breaks (dir. A. Penn), 1976
Close Encounters of the Third Kind (dir. S. Spielberg), 1977
Star Wars (dir. G. Lucas), 1977
The Fury (dir. B. DePalma), 1978
Superman (dir. R. Donner), 1978
Dracula (dir. J. Badham), 1979
1941 (dir. S. Spielberg), 1979
The Empire Strikes Back (dir. I. Kershner), 1980
Raiders of the Lost Ark (dir. S. Spielberg), 1981
E.T.: the Extra Terrestrial (dir. S. Spielberg), 1982
Monsignor (dir. F. Perry), 1982
Return of the Jedi (dir. R. Marquand), 1983
Indiana Jones and the Temple of Doom (dir. S. Spielberg), 1984
The River (dir. M. Rydell), 1984
Empire of the Sun (dir. S. Spielberg), 1987
The Witches of Eastwick (dir. G. Miller), 1987
The Accidental Tourist (dir. L. Kasdan), 1988
Always (dir. S. Spielberg), 1989
Born on the Fourth of July (dir. O. Stone), 1989
Indiana Jones and the Last Crusade (dir. S. Spielberg), 1989
Home Alone (dir. C. Columbus), 1990
Presumed Innocent (dir. A.J. Pakula), 1990
Stanley and Iris (dir. M. Ritt), 1990
Hook (dir. S. Spielberg), 1991
JFK (dir. O. Stone), 1991
Far and Away (dir. R. Howard), 1992
Jurassic Park (dir. S. Spielberg), 1993
Schindler's List (dir. S. Spielberg), 1993
Nixon (dir. O. Stone), 1995
Sabrina (dir. S. Pollack), 1995
Sleepers (dir. B. Levinson), 1996
Amistad (dir. S. Spielberg), 1997
The Lost World: Jurassic Park (dir. S. Spielberg), 1997
Rosewood (dir. J. Singleton), 1997

Seven Years in Tibet (dir. J.-J. Annaud), 1997
Saving Private Ryan (dir. S. Spielberg), 1998
Stepmom (dir. C. Columbus), 1998
Angela's Ashes (dir. A. Parker), 1999
Star Wars: Episode I, the Phantom Menace (dir. G. Lucas), 1999
The Patriot (dir. R. Emmerich), 2000
A.I. Artificial Intelligence (dir. S. Spielberg), 2001
Harry Potter and the Sorcerer's Stone (dir. C. Columbus), 2001
Catch Me If You Can (dir. S. Spielberg), 2002
Harry Potter and the Chamber of Secrets (dir. C. Columbus), 2002
Minority Report (dir. S. Spielberg), 2002
Star Wars: Episode II, Attack of the Clones (dir. G. Lucas), 2002
Harry Potter and the Prisoner of Azkaban (dir. A. Cuarón), 2004
The Terminal (dir. S. Spielberg), 2004
Memoirs of a Geisha (dir. R. Marshall), 2005
Munich (dir. S. Spielberg), 2005
Star Wars: Episode III, Revenge of the Sith (dir. G. Lucas), 2005
War of the Worlds (dir. S. Spielberg), 2005
Indiana Jones and the Kingdom of the Crystal Skull (dir. S. Spielberg), 2008
A Timeless Call (dir. S. Spielberg), 2008
The Adventures of Tintin (dir. S. Spielberg), 2011
War Horse (dir. S. Spielberg), 2011
Lincoln (dir. S. Spielberg), 2012
The Book Thief (dir. B. Percival), 2013
Star Wars: The Force Awakens (dir. J.J. Abrams), 2015
The BFG (dir. S. Spielberg), 2016
Rogue One: A Star Wars Story (dir. G. Edwards), 2016
Dear Basketball (dir. G. Keane), 2017
The Post (dir. S. Spielberg), 2017
Star Wars: The Last Jedi (dir. R. Johnson), 2017

Television music

1958–60: Episodes of Bachelor Father; Checkmate [also title theme]; General Electric Theater; Gilligan's Island; Tales of Wells Fargo; Wagon Train; Wide Country
1961–3: Alcoa Premiere
1963–5: Kraft Suspense Theater
1965–8: Lost in Space, The Time Tunnel, Land of the Giants
1985: The Mission Theme and others, NBC News
1988: The Olympic Spirit, NBC Sports

Other works

Orchestral and choral

Essay, str, 1966
Sym., 1966, rev. 1972
Jubilee 350 Fanfare, 1980

America . . . the Dream Goes On (A. and M. Bergman), male v, chor, orch, 1981
Fanfare for a Festive Occasion, 1981
Pops on the March, 1981
Esplanade Ov., 1982
Olympic Fanfare and Theme, 1984
Celebration Fanfare, 1986
Liberty Fanfare, 1986
A Hymn to New England, 1987
We're lookin' good (A. and M. Bergman), 1987
Fanfare for Michael Dukakis, 1988
To Lenny! To Lenny!, 1988
Fanfare for Ten-Year-Olds, 1989
Winter Games Fanfare, 1989
Celebrate Discovery!, 1990
Fanfare for Prince Philip, 1992
Sound the Bells!, 1993
Satellite Celebration, 1995
Variations on "Happy Birthday," 1995
Summon the Heroes, 1996
Seven for Luck (R. Dove), song cycle, s, orch, 1998
Air and Simple Gifts, vn, vc, pf, cl [composed for President Barack Obama inauguration]

Concertos

Fl Conc., 1969
Vn Conc., 1976
Tuba Conc., 1985
Cl Conc., 1991
Cel Conc., 1994
Bn Conc. "The Five Sacred Trees," 1995
Tpt Conc., 1996
Hn Conc., 2003
Conc. for Vn and Va, 2009
Hp Conc., 2009
Ob Conc., 2011

Other instrumental

Pf Sonata, 1951
Prelude and Fugue, wind ens, perc, 1968
A Nostalgic Jazz Odyssey, 1971
many suites adapted from film music

Principal publishers: Colgems, Fox Fanfares, H. Leonard, MCA Music, Warner Bros.

Bibliography

CBY 1980

I. Bazelon: *Knowing the Score: Notes on Film Music* (New York, 1975), 193–206

D. Elley: "The Film Composer: John Williams," *Films and Filming*, xxiv (1977–8), no.10, 20–24; no.11, 30–33

T. Thomas: "John Williams," *Film Score: the View from the Podium* (South Brunswick, NJ, 1979, 2/1991 as *Film Score: the Art and Craft of Movie Music*), 324–40

F. Karlin and R. Wright: *On the Track: a Guide to Contemporary Film Scoring* (New York, 1990, 2/2004)

The Cue Sheet, viii/1 (1991) [John Williams issue]

K. Kalinak: *Settling the Score: Music and the Classical Hollywood Film* (Madison, WI, 1992), 184–202

J. Burlingame: *TV's Biggest Hits: the Story of Television Themes from "Dragnet" to "Friends"* (New York, 1996)

Film Score Monthly, ii/1 (1997) [*Star Wars* issue]

T. Scheurer: "John Williams and Film Music Since 1971," *Popular Music and Society*, xxi/1 (1997), 59–72

D. Adams: "The Sounds of the Empire: Analyzing the Themes of the *Star Wars* Trilogy," *Film Score Monthly*, iv/5 (1999), 22–5

R. Dyer: "Making *Star Wars* Sing Again," *Boston Globe* (28 March 1999); repr. in *Film Score Monthly*, iv/5 (1999), 18–21

J. Buhler: "*Star Wars*, Music, and Myth," *Music and Cinema*, ed. J. Buhler, C. Flinn, and D. Neumeyer (Hanover, NH, 2000), 33–57

N. Lerner: "Nostalgia, Masculinist Discourse, and Authoritarianism in John Williams' Scores for *Star Wars* and *Close Encounters with the Third Kind*," *Off the Planet: Music, Sound and Science Fiction Cinema*, ed. P. Hayward (London, 2004), 96–108

M. Cooke: *A History of Film Music* (New York, 2008), 456–66

P. Moormann: *Spielberg-Variationen: die Filmmusik von John Williams* (Baden-Baden, 2010)

J. Williams: "Star Wars," *The Hollywood Film Music Reader*, ed. M. Cooke (New York, 2010), 233–44

R. Rodman: "John William's Music to Lost in Space: the Monumental, the Profound, and the Hyperbolic," *Music in Science Fiction Television: Tuned to the Future*, ed. K. Donnelly and P. Hayward (New York, 2013), 34–51

E. Audissino: *John William's Film Music: "Jaws," "Star Wars," "Raiders of the Lost Ark," and the Return of Classical Hollywood Music Style* (Madison, WI, 2014)

T. Schneller: "Sweet Fulfillment: Allusion and Teleological Genesis in John William's *Close Encounters of the Third Kind*," *MQ*, xcvii/1 (2014), 98–131

F. Lehman: "Scoring the President: Myth and Politics in John Williams's *JFK* and *Nixon*," *JSAM*, ix/4 (2015): 409–44

CHRISTOPHER PALMER/MARTIN MARKS/R

Williams, Patrick M(oody)

(*b* Bonne Terre, MO, 23 April 1939; *d* Santa Monica, CA, 25 July 2018). American composer. He graduated from Duke University in 1961, then pursued graduate studies at Columbia University through 1963. During the mid-1960s, Williams worked as an arranger-producer-composer in New York and, from 1968, as a composer for films and television in Los Angeles. Both his classical training and his contemporary jazz background proved useful in Hollywood. During the 1970s and 80s Williams scored hundreds of episodes of popular TV series including "The Mary Tyler Moore Show," "The Bob Newhart Show," "The Streets of San Francisco," "Lou Grant," "The Days and Nights of Molly Dodd," "Columbo," and others, variously lending a warm, comic, jazzy, or dramatic sound as needed. His scores for more than one hundred television films and miniseries (mostly in the 1980s and 90s) included such diverse material as *Geronimo*, *Kingfish: a Story of Huey P. Long*, *Jesus*, and *Blonde*. He received four Emmys for his music for television. He also scored dozens of feature films, including *Casey's Shadow*, *Swing Shift*, and *All of Me*, and earned a 1979 Oscar nomination for his use of Italian opera in the bicycle-racing movie *Breaking Away*.

Throughout this period he continued to write and record pieces of his own, striving (both in his jazz albums and in his concert commissions) to combine jazz and classical elements in a smoother, more organic way than had been previously achieved. He received a Pulitzer Prize nomination for his *An American Concerto* (1976) for jazz quartet and symphony orchestra. His contemporary big-band albums include *Threshold* (1973), *Dreams & Themes* (1983), *10th Avenue* (1986), *Sinatraland* (1998), and *Aurora* (2010). He also arranged and conducted Frank Sinatra's final studio recordings (*Duets*, *Duets II*) and wrote a piece for narrator and symphony orchestra based on *Gulliver's Travels* (1986).

Williams was also active in music education, lecturing around the country and serving for five years (2002–6) as artistic director for the Henry Mancini Institute, training young musicians for careers in music. Several of his later orchestral works (*Adagio for Orchestra*, *Memento Mei*, *August*) received their débuts during the institute's annual summer seasons in Los Angeles.

Works

(*selective list*)

Film scores

How Sweet it Is (dir. J. Paris), 1968
Don't Drink the Water (dir. H. Morris), 1969
Macho Callahan (dir. B.L. Kowalski (as B. Kowalski)), 1970
Evel Knievel (dir. M.J. Chomsky (as M. Chomsky)), 1971
Casey's Shadow (dir. M. Ritt), 1978
The Cheap Detective (dir. R. Moore), 1978
The One and Only (dir. C. Reiner), 1978

Breaking Away (dir. P. Yates), 1979
Butch and Sundance: the Early Days (dir. R. Lester), 1979
Cuba (dir. Lester), 1979
Hero at Large (dir. M. Davidson), 1980
How to Beat the High Co$t of Living (dir. R. Scheerer), 1980
It's My Turn (dir. C. Weill), 1980
Used Cars (dir. R. Zemeckis), 1980
The Toy (dir. R. Donner), 1982
Marvin & Tige (dir. E. Weston), 1983
All of Me (dir. Reiner), 1984
Best Defense (dir. W. Huyck), 1984
The Buddy System (dir. G. Jordan), 1984
Swing Shift (dir. J. Demme), 1984
The Slugger's Wife (dir. H. Ashby), 1985
Just Between Friends (dir. A. Burns), 1986
Fresh Horses (dir. D. Anspaugh), 1988, with D. Foster
The Cutting Edge (dir. P.M. Glaser), 1992
The Grass Harp (dir. C. Matthau), 1995
Julian Po (dir. A. Wade), 1997
That Old Feeling (dir. Reiner), 1997

Television music

The Music Scene, 1969
The Mary Tyler Moore Show, 1970–77
The Streets of San Francisco, 1972–6
The Bob Newhart Show, 1972–7
The Magician, 1973–4
Friends and Lovers, 1974
The Tony Randall Show, 1976–7
Lou Grant, 1977–80
Columbo, 1977–92
A Man Called Sloane, 1979
The Devlin Connection, 1982
Mr. Smith, 1983
AfterMASH, 1983–4
The Slap Maxwell Story, 1987
The Days and Nights of Molly Dodd, 1987–91
FM, 1989
Black Tie Affair, 1993
Cutters, 1993
Extreme, 1995

Television movie and miniseries music

San Francisco International, 1970
Incident in San Francisco, 1971
Mrs. Sundance, 1974

The Lives of Jenny Dolan, 1975
The Princess and the Cabbie, 1981
Laguna Heat, 1987
Decoration Day, 1990
In Broad Daylight, 1991
Danielle Steel's Jewels, 1992
Geronimo, 1993
Murder in the Heartland, 1993
Zelda, 1993
The Corpse had a Familiar Face, 1994
Kingfish: a Story of Huey P. Long, 1995
The West Side Waltz, 1995
The Siege at Ruby Ridge, 1996
Solomon, 1997
Jesus, 1999
Passion's Way, 1999
A Song from the Heart, 1999
Blonde, 2001
Hercules, 2005

Concert works

(*selective list*)
An American Conc., jazz qt, orch, 1976
The Prayer of St. Francis, fl, str, 1981
Romances, jazz sax, orch, 1982
Gulliver (J. Swift: *Gulliver's Travels*), nar, orch, 1986
Spring Wings, jazz sax, pf, orch, 1986
La Fuerza, jazz trbn, orch, 1987
An Ov. to a Time, Afro-Cuban perc, orch, 1991
Appalachian Morning, 1992
Theme for Earth Day, 1992
Memento Mei, S, orch, 2001
Some Notes for Hank, 2001
A Bird from Missouri, 5 sax, orch, 2002
Cascades, 2 jazz pf, orch, 2003
Adagio for Orch, 2005
A Conc. in Swing, cl, jazz band, 2005
August, 2006

Bibliography

L. Feather: "From Pen to Screen: Pat Williams," *International Musician* (Feb 1971)
J. Burlingame: "Scoring Big," *Emmy*, xiii/4 (July–Aug 1991), 28, 30, 32
J. Burlingame: "Profile: Patrick Williams," *BMI Music World* (Fall 1997)

JON BURLINGAME

Wilson, Mortimer

(*b* Chariton, IA, 6 Aug 1876; *d* New York, 27 Jan 1932). American composer, conductor, and teacher. At the Chicago Conservatory he studied with the composer Frederick G(rant) Gleason, the organist Wilhelm Middelschulte, and the violinist S.E. Jacobson. He spent three years, beginning in 1899, at the Culver Military Academy in Indiana. At the University School of Music in Lincoln, Nebraska, in 1901 he became the leader of the cadet band and violin department. By the time he left in 1908 he was head of the composition department. He spent the next three years teaching privately in Vienna and Leipzig, where he studied with composers Max Reger and Hans Sitt. Back in the United States, he lived in Georgia from 1912 to 1916, directing the Atlanta Philharmonic, conducting light opera, and teaching at Brenau College in Gainesville. After moving to New York, he taught at the Malkin School of Music and contributed music to a National Academy of Music university course. He spent 1919 in Great Britain and France, conducting vaudeville shows in Paris. After he settled in New York in 1920, his composition "New Orleans" received a prize in a competition sponsored by Hugo Riesenfeld. Wilson's "1849" overture to *The Covered Wagon* (1923), scored by Riesenfeld, brought him to the attention of Douglas Fairbanks. Fairbanks invited Wilson to Hollywood for *The Thief of Bagdad* and two successive films all featuring original continuous orchestral scores written during production. For films his music synchronizes broadly and is generally diatonic, melodious, contrapuntal, and harmonically rich and colorful. Concertizing in New York from 1927 to 1929, Wilson organized and conducted the String Sinfonietta. His pedagogical writings on harmony and orchestration found wide use in eastern universities. Robert Emmett Dolan, Joseph Littau, and John Tasker Howard were among his students.

Works

(*selective list*)

Film scores

The Covered Wagon (dir. J. Cruze), 1923, ov. only
The Thief of Bagdad (dir. R. Walsh), 1924
Don Q, Son of Zorro (dir. D. Crisp), 1925
The Black Pirate (dir. A. Parker), 1926
The Good-Bye Kiss (dir. M. Sennett), 1928, collab. E. Bierman
The Night Watch (dir. A. Korda), 1928, collab. Bierman

Concert music

(*date is year of first publication unless otherwise indicated*)

Echoes from Childhood, 1v, pf, 1912
Sonata, vn, pf, op.16, 1914

From my Youth, suite, orch, op.5, *c*1918
Silhouettes from the Screen, pf, op.55, 1919
New Orleans, ov., orch, 1920
Bagatelles, pf, op.12, 1920
From the Hickery and the Cotton, 17 American tunes for org, 1920
Sonata, C, org, 1920
Trio, g, vn, vc, pf, 1920
Tubulariana: Adaptations for Brass Sextette, 2 tpt, 2 hn, 2 trbn, 1921
Ov. "1849," orch, 1923
The Thief of Bagdad: a Fantasy of the Arabian Nights, pf/orch, 1924
Lyric Suite, pf, vc, op.81, first perf. 1927
My Country: a Scenic Fantasy, orch, op.70, first perf. 1927

Principal publishers: Boston, Composer's Music Corporation, J. Fischer & Bro.

MSS in Performing Arts Special Collections, UCLA

Writings

Harmonic and Melodic Technical Studies (Lincoln, NE, 1907)
The Rhetoric of Music (Lincoln, NE, 1907)
The University Course of Music Study, prepared by the editorial staff of the National Academy of Music (New York, 1920)
Orchestral Training (New York, 1921)
Tonal, Harmonic and Modulatory Relationships (New York, 1921)
"Moving Pictures, Audiences, and Other Things," *Billboard* (13 Dec 1923)

Bibliography

Obituary, *New York Times* (28 Jan 1932)
ASCAP Biographical Dictionary (New York, 4/1980)
G.B. Anderson: "A Consummation and a Harbinger of the Future: Mortimer Wilson's Accompaniments for Douglas Fairbanks," *Film International*, iii/13 (2005), 32–9

WARREN M. SHERK

Young, Christopher [Chris]

(*b* Red Bank, NJ, 28 April 1957). American film, television, and video-game composer. Young graduated from Hampshire College, Massachusetts, with the bachelor's degree in music, followed by graduate work at North Texas State University. In 1980 he moved to Los Angeles and attended the UCLA Department of Motion Pictures, Television, and Radio, where he studied film scoring under David Raksin. Here he scored his first film, *The Dorm that Dripped Blood* (1982), a student film that was picked up for distribution during the slasher-movie craze of the early 1980s. After this success, he built his early reputation on horror and science fiction, with scores for such successful films as *Hellraiser* (1987) and *Species* (1995). Young showed his range during these early years with comedies (*The Man who Knew too Little*, 1997) and drama (*Bat*21*, 1988). His television work, although not prolific, has been acclaimed, and includes two Emmy-nominated projects, *Last Flight Out* (1990) and *Norma Jean and Marilyn* (1996). Young's style in recent years, particularly in his numerous action films, has been defined by their traditional orchestral forces combined with driving electronic rhythms, such as his collaboration with the DJ Paul Oakenfold for the score for *Swordfish* (2001). Young received a Golden Globe nomination for *The Shipping News* (2001) and has been nominated six times for a Saturn Award, given by the Academy of Science Fiction, Fantasy & Horror Films. In 2008 Young received the Richard Kirk Career Achievement Award from BMI.

Works

Film scores

The Dorm that Dripped Blood (dir. S. Carpenter and J. Obrow), 1982
Avenging Angel (dir. R.V. O'Neill), 1985
Barbarian Queen (dir. H. Olivera), 1985, with J. Horner
Def-Con 4 (dir. P. Donovan and others), 1985
A Nightmare on Elm Street Part 2: Freddy's Revenge (dir. J. Sholder), 1985
Invaders from Mars (dir. T. Hooper), 1986
Flowers in the Attic (dir. J. Bloom), 1987
Hellraiser (dir. C. Barker), 1987
Bat*21 (dir. P. Markle), 1988
Hellbound: Hellraiser II (dir. T. Randel), 1988
The Fly II (dir. C. Walas), 1989
Jennifer Eight (dir. B. Robinson), 1992
The Vagrant (dir. Walas), 1992
The Dark Half (dir. G.A. Romero), 1993
Judicial Consent (dir. W. Bindley), 1994
Copycat (dir. J. Amiel), 1995
Species (dir. R. Donaldson), 1995
Tales from the Hood (dir. R. Cundieff), 1995
Virtuosity (dir. B. Leonard), 1995
Set it Off (dir. F.G. Gray), 1996
Unforgettable (dir. J. Dahl), 1996
The Man who Knew too Little (dir. J. Amiel), 1997
Murder at 1600 (dir. D.H. Little (as D. Little)), 1997
Hard Rain (dir. M. Salomon), 1998
Hush (dir. J. Darby), 1998
Rounders (dir. J. Dahl), 1998
Urban Legend (dir. J. Blanks), 1998
Entrapment (dir. Amiel), 1999
The Hurricane (dir. N. Jewison), 1999, with J. Sweet

In too Deep (dir. M. Rymer), 1999
Bless the Child (dir. C. Russell), 2000
The Gift (dir. S. Raimi), 2000
Wonder Boys (dir. C. Hanson), 2000
Bandits (dir. B. Levinson), 2001
The Glass House (dir. D. Sackheim), 2001
The Shipping News (dir. L. Hallström), 2001
Swordfish (dir. D. Sena), 2001, with P. Oakenfold
The Tower (dir. E.G. Webb (as G. Webb), and J. Elliot), 2002
The Core (dir. Amiel), 2003
Runaway Jury (dir. G. Fleder), 2003
The Grudge (dir. T. Shimizu), 2004
Beauty Shop (dir. B. Woodruff), 2005
Ghost Rider (dir. M.S. Johnson), 2007
Lucky You (dir. C. Hanson), 2007
Spider-Man 3 (dir. S. Raimi), 2007
The Informers (dir. G. Jordan), 2008
Sleepwalking (dir. B. Maher (as W. Maher)), 2008
Untraceable (dir. G. Hoblit), 2008
Creation (dir. Amiel), 2009
Drag me to Hell (dir. Raimi), 2009
Love Happens (dir. B. Camp), 2009, with A. Spence
The Uninvited (dir. C. and T Guard (as The Guard Brothers)), 2009
The Black Tulip (dir. S.N. Cole), 2010
Gone with the Pope (dir. D. Mitchell), 2010, with others
When in Rome (dir. M.S. Johnson), 2010, with T. Karlsson
Priest (dir. S. Stewart), 2011, with A. Spence
The Rum Diary (dir. B. Robinson), 2011
The Baytown Outlaws (dir. B. Battles), 2012, with K. Christides
Scary or Die (dir. B. Badway, M. Emanuel, and I. Meglic), 2012, with others
Sinister (dir. S. Derrickson), 2012
Gods Behaving Badly (dir. M. Turtletaub), 2013
Killing Season (dir. M.S. Johnson), 2013
Tyler Perry's A Madea Christmas (dir. T. Perry), 2013
Deliver Us from Evil (dir. S. Derrickson), 2014
The Monkey King (dir. S. Cheang (as P.-S. Cheang)), 2014
The Single Moms Club (dir. Perry), 2014
The Monkey King 2 (dir. Cheang), 2016
A Symphony of Hope (dir. B. Weidling), 2017
7Seconds (dir. J. Obrow), 2018

Television music

Last Flight Out, 1990
Max and Helen, 1990
Norma Jean & Marilyn, 1996
The Warden, 2001
Dominion, 2014

Video-game music

Wilson's Heart, 2017

Bibliography

M. Schelle: *The Score: Interviews with Film Composers* (Los Angeles, 1999)
J. Fichera: *Scored to Death: Conversations with Some of Horror's Greatest Composers* (Los Angeles, 2016)

LOUIS NIEBUR/R

Young, Victor

(*b* Chicago, 8 Aug 1900; *d* Palm Springs, CA, 10 Nov 1956). American composer, conductor, and violinist. He began to play the violin at the age of six and four years later went to live with his grandfather in Warsaw, where he studied at the conservatory. He made his début as a soloist with the Warsaw PO in 1917. In 1920 he returned to the United States and the following year made his American début at Orchestra Hall in Chicago. Between 1922 and 1929 he was a leader in movie theaters, a musical supervisor of vaudeville productions, a violinist and arranger for Ted Fiorito's orchestra, and the assistant musical director of the Balaban and Katz theater chain.

He first worked for radio in 1929 and in 1931 became music director for Brunswick Records, where in 1932 he arranged and conducted several selections from *Show Boat* with soloists, chorus, and orchestra; released on four discs, it was the first American album made from the score of a Broadway musical. In 1935 he moved to Hollywood, where he formed his own orchestra and joined the staff of Paramount Pictures.

During the next twenty years Young composed and conducted music for many television and radio shows and record albums, and wrote scores (some with collaborators) for more than 225 films. He also composed instrumental pieces (some of which originated in film scores), two Broadway shows, and a number of popular songs. He had a gift for writing pleasing melodies but his music for the most part is conventional. His film scores are often overwrought and incorporate excessively sentimental string writing, but they are dramatically adequate and occasionally even eloquent. He won an Academy Award (posthumously) for his score to *Around the World in 80 Days*.

Works

(*selective list*)

Film scores

Ebb Tide (dir. J. Hogan), 1937
Maid of Salem (dir. F. Lloyd), 1937

Golden Boy (dir. R. Mamoulian), 1939
Gulliver's Travels (dir. D. Fleischer), 1939
The Light that Failed (dir. W.A. Wellman), 1940
North West Mounted Police (dir. C.B. DeMille), 1940
Hold Back the Dawn (dir. M. Leisen), 1941
I Wanted Wings (dir. M. Leisen), 1941
Reap the Wild Wind (dir. C.B. DeMille), 1942
The Palm Beach Story (dir. P. Sturges), 1942
For Whom the Bell Tolls (dir. S. Wood), 1943
Frenchman's Creek (dir. M. Leisen), 1944
Kitty (dir. M. Leisen), 1945
The Blue Dahlia (dir. G. Marshall), 1946
To Each His Own (dir. M. Leisen), 1946
Unconquered (dir. C.B. DeMille), 1947
The Big Clock (dir. J. Farrow), 1948
The Night Has a Thousand Eyes (dir. J. Farrow), 1948
Samson and Delilah (dir. C.B. DeMille), 1949
Sands of Iwo Jima (dir. A. Dwan), 1949
Rio Grande (dir. J. Ford), 1950
Payment on Demand (dir. C. Bernhardt), 1951
The Quiet Man (dir. J. Ford), 1952
Scaramouche (dir. G. Sidney), 1952
Shane (dir. G. Stevens), 1953
The Country Girl (dir. G. Seaton), 1954
Three Coins in the Fountain (dir. J. Negulesco), 1954
The Left Hand of God (dir. E. Dmytryk), 1955
Around the World in 80 Days (dir. M. Anderson), 1956

Stage

Pardon our French (revue, E. Heyman), New York, 5 Oct 1950
Seventh Heaven (musical, V. Wolfson, S. Unger; lyrics, Unger), New York, 26 May 1955

Songs

Sweet Sue (W.J. Harris), 1928
9 songs, incl. A Hundred Years from Today, in Blackbirds of 1933 (revue)
Sweet Madness, in Murder at the Vanities (musical play), 1933
Stella by Starlight (N. Washington; from the film: The Uninvited, 1944)
Love Letters (E. Heyman; from the film, 1945)
The Searching Wind (Heyman; from the film, 1946)
Golden Earrings (J. Livingston and R. Evans; from the film, 1947)
My Foolish Heart (Washington; from the film, 1949)
Our Very Own (J. Elliot; from the film, 1949)
Alone at Last (B. Hilliard; from the film: Something to Live For, 1952)
When I Fall in Love (Heyman; from the film: One Minute to Zero, 1952)
Wintertime of Love (Heyman; from the film: Thunderbirds, 1952)

Bon Soir (Heyman; from the film: A Perilous Journey, 1953)
Call of the Faraway Hills (M. David; from the film: Shane, 1953)
Change of Heart (Heyman; from the film: Forever Female, 1953)
The world is mine (S. Adams; from the film: Strategic Air Command, 1955)
Around the World in 80 Days (H. Adamson; from the film, 1956)
I only live to love you (M. Gordon; from the film: The Proud and Profane, 1956)
Written on the Wind (S. Cahn; from the film, 1956)

Instrumental

(for orchestra unless otherwise indicated—most composed 1935–52)
Arizona Sketches
Columbia Square
Elegy to F.D.R.
For whom the Bell Tolls
Hollywood Panorama
In a November Garden
Leaves of Grass (after W. Whitman)
Manhattan Conc., pf, orch [based on the film scores]
Overnight
Pearls on Velvet, pf, orch
Stella by Starlight, pf, orch [based on the film score The Uninvited]
Stephen Foster, str qt
Travelin' Light

Principal publishers: Famous, Joy, Northern, Paramount

Bibliography

V. Young: "Confessions of a Film Composer," *Music Journal*, xiv/7 (1956), 16, 38
C. McCarty: "Victor Young," *Film and TV Music*, xvi/5 (1957), 21
T. Thomas: *Music for the Movies* (South Brunswick, NJ, 1973), 43–8

CLIFFORD MCCARTY

Zamecnik, John Stephan

(*b* Cleveland, 14 May 1872; *d* Los Angeles, 13 June 1953). American composer. Born to parents of Czech descent, he studied in the late 1890s with Antonín Dvořák at the Prague Conservatory, where he was a classmate of Jan Kubelik. Zamecnik returned to the United States, played second violin in the Pittsburgh Symphony under Victor Herbert, and was a member of numerous ensembles in Cleveland, including the Cleveland SO, which performed his *Slavonic Fancies* in 1900.

In 1907 Zamecnik began work as the musical director and composer for the Cleveland Hippodrome, a 3548-seat theater that opened on 30 December 1907. Zamecnik provided music for two shows, *Coaching Days* and *Cloud Burst*, in the opening production. He wrote music for several other productions, working with established revue composers William J. Wilson and R.H. Burnside. Around this time Zamecnik also joined Cleveland's Hermit Club, a local performing arts fraternity, writing music for five of the group's annual revues, one of which was produced as a musical, *The Girl I Love* (1911), in Chicago at the La Salle Opera House.

In 1908 Zamecnik published his first work, "College Yell," with Cleveland-based Sam Fox. He quickly became the company's primary composer and arranger; a 1919 article describes him as having been "musical editor on the staff of the Sam Fox Company since 1914...." The dual role of composer and editor explains the hundreds of publications, mostly instrumentals, that bore his name, as well as those that carried one of more than a dozen pseudonyms he used, including Jules Reynard, Dorothy Lee, and Lionel Baxter.

Zamecnik is best known for his work in music for early films, primarily in two areas: photoplay music and theme songs. Sam Fox was one of the first publishers to produce original photoplay music; Zamecnik composed four volumes of music for piano, *Sam Fox Moving Picture Music*, five volumes of the *Sam Fox Photoplay*

John Zamecnik, 1915. USC Libraries Special Collections

Edition (for mixed ensembles), and countless other collections for various forces. Zamecnik wrote his first movie theme song in 1923 for *La Rosita*; others included "Neapolitan Nights" (which had been originally published as an instrumental in 1923) for *Fazil*, "Your Love is All" for *Old Ironsides*, "Paradise" for *The Wedding March*, "Rosemary" for *Abie's Irish Rose*, "Redskin" for *Redskin*, and the title song for *Wings* (1927), which won the first Academy Award for Best Picture, Production. Zamecnik also wrote some of the earliest film scores for synchronized sound, although these scores were essentially ordered sets of photoplay music, tailored to specific films.

Zamecnik moved to California in 1924, ostensibly to be closer to the movie industry to which he dedicated most of his efforts. He remained on staff with Sam Fox, although his output lessened considerably. One of his late works was well known in the sound era: the World Events March became the theme for Fox Movietone newsreels beginning in the 1930s.

Works

(selective list)

Film scores

Photoplay music

Sam Fox Moving Picture Music, Volume 1 (1913)
Sam Fox Moving Picture Music, Volume 2 (1913)
Sam Fox Moving Picture Music, Volume 3 (1914)
Sam Fox Photoplay Edition, Volume 1 (1920)
Sam Fox Motion Picture Themes Series (1921)
Sam Fox Photoplay Edition, Volume 2 (1922)
Sam Fox Moving Picture Music, Volume 4: New 1923–1924 Edition (1923)
Sam Fox Photoplay Edition, Volume 3 (1925)
Sam Fox Photoplay Edition, Volume 4 (1927)
Sam Fox Photoplay Edition, Volume 5 (1929)

Published music for films

Old Ironsides (dir. J. Cruze), 1927, with Riesenfeld
Wings (dir. W.A. Wellman and H. d'Abbadie d'Arrast (uncredited)), 1927
Abie's Irish Rose (dir. V. Fleming), 1928
Betrayal (dir. L. Milestone), 1929
Redskin (dir. V. Schertzinger), 1929

Songs

Love Eyes, 1905
Napoleon March and Two Step, 1905
Cleveland News March and Two-Step, 1906

Daisies (Wilson), 1907
College Yell, 1908
Fishing (Bell), 1908
Wonderland (Bell), 1908
A Trip to the North Pole, 1909
Amazon March, 1911
Mandy's Ragtime Waltz, 1912
Movie Rag, 1913
Co-ed, 1914
World Peace, 1914
California (Humphrey), 1915
All America, 1916
For the Freedom of the World, 1917
Spirit of America, 1917
Jealous Moon (Kerr), 1918
My Paradise (Kerr), 1918
On the Fields of France (Mayo), 1918
Neapolitan Nights, 1923
Indian Dawn (Roos), 1924
Wings (MacDonald), 1927
Paradise (Kerr), 1928
Redskin (Kerr), 1929

MSS and memorabilia located at *US-LAusc*

Principal publisher: Sam Fox

Bibliography

"Do your Best," *Jacobs' Orchestra Monthly* (Oct 1919), 26–8
G. Whyte: "J.S. Zamecnik," *The Metronome* (1 Sept 1927)
W.H. Thomas: *The Pit, the Footlights, and the Wings: the Dramatic Record of the Hermit Club, 1904–1954* (Cleveland, OH, 1954)
R. Sauer: "Photoplay Music: a Reusable Repertory for Silent Film Scoring, 1914–1929," *American Music Research Center Journal*, viii–ix (1998–9), 55–76

DANIEL GOLDMARK

Zimmer, Hans Florian

(*b* Frankfurt, 12 Sept 1957). German film composer, keyboardist, and producer. He moved to London in his teens and later wrote jingles there for commercials. He briefly played synthesizers with the British New Wave rock band the Buggles (appearing in the video for *Video Killed the Radio Star* in 1979), the Italian electronic-pop group Krisma (playing synthesizer on its 1980 album *Cathode Mamma*), and New Zealand singer Zaine Griff. He also co-formed the band Helden (1980–83, known for two singles and a bootleg album) and worked with the Spanish synth-pop band Mecano (1983–5). While apprenticing from 1982 to 1985 with the British film composer Stanley Myers, Zimmer combined his "synthetic" work as a popular music synthesizer player and songwriter with more traditional, orchestral film sounds. Zimmer's collaborations with Myers included *Moonlighting* (1982), *Insignificance* (1985), and *My Beautiful Laundrette* (1985); he then moved to the United States.

Zimmer's "pseudo-orchestral" (or other hybrid) approach, largely through the use of synthesizers and sampling, has characterized his career in film scoring. In addition to electronic and orchestral sounds, he has included steel drums, slide guitar, Japanese instruments, and African drumming and choirs. Zimmer has also composed music for TV, has executive-produced numerous film scores by other composers, and has helped launch the careers of many other film composers. He won an Oscar and a Golden Globe for *The Lion King* (both 1994), a Grammy for *Crimson Tide* (1995), a BMI Richard Kirk Award for Lifetime Achievement (1996), a Golden Globe for *Gladiator* (2001), a National Board of Review Career Achievement Award (2003), a Frederick Loewe Award at the Palm Springs International Film Festival (2003), an ASCAP Henry Mancini Award for Lifetime Achievement (2003), and a Grammy for *The Dark Knight*

Hans Zimmer, 2001
(AP Photo/Rene Macura)

(with James Newton Howard, 2008). He performed live with a one-hundred-piece orchestra and a one-hundred-voice choir at the twenty-seventh Annual Flanders International Film Festival (2000). Zimmer and his family live in Los Angeles.

Works

Film and television music

(excludes most co-composed scores; flim scores unless otherwise noted)
Moonlighting (dir. J. Skolimowski), 1982, with S. Myers, credited for electronic music
Success is the Best Revenge (dir. Skolimowski), 1984, with Myers
Insignificance (dir. N. Roeg), 1985, with Myers, credited for additional music
My Beautiful Laundrette (dir. S. Frears), 1985, with Myers, credited as music producer
Going for Gold (TV, themes), 1987
Terminal Exposure (dir. N. Mastorakis), 1987, with Myers
First Born (TV), 1988
Rain Main (dir. B. Levinson), 1988
A World Apart (dir. C. Menges), 1988
Black Rain (dir. R. Scott), 1989
Driving Miss Daisy (dir. B. Beresford), 1989
Days of Thunder (dir. T. Scott), 1990
Green Card (dir. P. Weir), 1990
Backdraft (dir. R. Howard), 1991
Thelma & Louise (dir. R. Scott), 1991
A League of their Own (dir. P. Marshall), 1992
The Power of One (dir. J.G. Avildsen), 1992
True Romance (dir. T. Scott), 1993
The Lion King (dir. R. Allers and R. Minkoff), 1994
Crimson Tide (dir. T. Scott), 1995
The Preacher's Wife (dir. P. Marshall), 1996
As Good as it Gets (dir. J.L. Brooks), 1997
The Prince of Egypt (dir. B. Chapman, S. Hickner, and S. Wells), 1998
The Thin Red Line (dir. T. Malick), 1998
Gladiator (dir. R. Scott), 2000, with L. Gerrard
Mission: Impossible II (dir. J. Woo), 2000
Black Hawk Down (dir. R. Scott), 2001
Hannibal (dir. R. Scott), 2001
Pearl Harbor (dir. M. Bay), 2001
The Ring (dir. G. Verbinski), 2002
Spirit: Stallion of the Cimarron (dir. K. Asbury and L. Cook), 2002
The Last Samurai (dir. E. Zwick), 2003
Shark Tale (dir. B. Bergeron, V. Jenson, and R. Letterman), 2004, with J.L. Gosselin
Spanglish (dir. J.L. Brooks), 2004
Batman Begins (dir. C. Nolan), 2005, with J.N. Howard

The Da Vinci Code (dir. R. Howard), 2006
Pirates of the Caribbean: Dead Man's Chest (dir. G. Verbinski), 2006
Pirates of the Caribbean: At World's End (dir. Verbinski), 2007
The Simpsons Movie (dir. D. Silverman), 2007
The Dark Knight (dir. Nolan), 2008, with J.N. Howard
Frost/Nixon (dir. Howard), 2008
Angels and Demons (dir. Howard), 2009
How do you Know (dir. J.L. Brooks), 2010
Inception (dir. Nolan), 2010
Megamind (dir. T. McGrath), 2010, with L. Balfe
The Dilemma (dir. Howard), 2011, with L. Balfe
Jealous of the Birds (dir. J. Bahat), 2011, with A. Igudesman
Kung Fu Panda 2 (dir. J.Y. Nelson), 2011, with J. Powell
Pirates of the Caribbean: On Stranger Tides (dir. R. Marshall), 2011
Rango (dir. Verbinski), 2011
Sherlock Holmes: a Game of Shadows (dir. G. Ritchie), 2011, with L. Balfe
Through the Wormhole (TV series), 2011–16
The Dark Knight Rises (dir. Nolan), 2012
Madagascar 3: Europe's Most Wanted (dir. E. Darnell, T. McGrath, and C. Vernon), 2012
12 Years a Slave (dir. S. McQueen), 2013
Last Love (dir. S. Nettelbeck), 2013
The Lone Ranger (dir. Verbinski), 2013
Man of Steel (dir. Z. Snyder), 2013
Rush (dir. Howard), 2013
The Amazing Spider-Man 2 (dir. M. Webb), 2014, and others
Interstellar (dir. Nolan), 2014
Son of God (dir. C. Spencer), 2014, with L. Balfe
Winter's Tale (dir. A. Goldsman), 2014, with R. Gregson-Williams
Chappie (dir. N. Blomkamp), 2015
Freeheld (dir. P. Sollett), 2015, with J. Marr
The Little Prince (dir. M. Osborne), 2015, with R. Harvey
Sons of Liberty (TV mini-series), 2015
Woman in Gold (dir. S. Curtis), 2015, with M. Phipps
Batman v Superman: Dawn of Justice (dir. Z. Snyder), 2016, with Junkie XL
Hidden Figures (dir. T. Melfi), 2016, with P. Williams and B. Wallfisch
Inferno (dir. Howard), 2016
Kung Fu Panda 3 (dir. A. Carloni and J.Y. Nelson), 2016
The Last Face (dir. S. Penn), 2016
Planet Earth II (TV mini-series), 2016
Blade Runner 2049 (dir. D. Villeneuve), 2017, collab, B. Wallfisch
The Boss Baby (dir. T. McGrath), 2017, collab S. Mazzaro
Dunkirk (dir. Nolan), 2017
The Road of Love (dir. D. Hajibarat), 2017
Believer (dir. D. Argott), 2018

Bibliography

T. Conniff: "Q&A: Hans Zimmer," *Billboard* cxviii/21 (2006), 21

M. Hurwitz: "Sound for Pictures: Hans Zimmer's Scoring Collective – Composer Collaboration at Remote Control Productions (2007)," *The Routledge Film Music Sourcebook*, ed. J. Wierzbicki, N. Platte, and C. Roust (New York, 2012), 254–7

B. Wright: "Music and the Moving Image: a Case Study of Hans Zimmer," *The Routledge Reader on the Sociology of Music*, ed. J. Shepherd and K. Devine (New York, 2015), 319–27

V. Hexel, *Hans Zimmer and James Newton Howard's 'The Dark Knight': a Film Score Guide* (Lanham, MD, 2016)

F. Lehman: "Manufacturing the Epic Score: Hans Zimmer and the Sounds of Significance," *Music in Epic Film: Listening to Spectacle*, ed. S.C. Meyer (New York, 2017), 27–55

J. Tillman: "*Topoi* and Intertextuality: Narrative Function in Hans Zimmer's and Lisa Gerrado's Music to *Gladiator*," *Music in Epic Film: Listening to Spectacle*, ed. S.C. Meyer (New York, 2017), 55–85

DURRELL BOWMAN

Index